SPEAK·TRUTH·TO·POWER

COMMANDER
STEVEN HAINES
ROYAL NAVY

SAVING THE OCEANS THROUGH LAW

Saving the Oceans Through Law

*The International Legal Framework for
the Protection of the Marine Environment*

JAMES HARRISON

OXFORD
UNIVERSITY PRESS

OXFORD

UNIVERSITY PRESS

Great Clarendon Street, Oxford, OX2 6DP,
United Kingdom

Oxford University Press is a department of the University of Oxford.
It furthers the University's objective of excellence in research, scholarship,
and education by publishing worldwide. Oxford is a registered trade mark of
Oxford University Press in the UK and in certain other countries

© James Harrison 2017

The moral rights of the author have been asserted

First Edition published in 2017

Impression: 1

Published in the United States of America by Oxford University Press
198 Madison Avenue, New York, NY 10016, United States of America

British Library Cataloguing in Publication Data

Data available

Library of Congress Control Number: 2017947311

ISBN 978–0–19–870732–5

Printed and bound by
CPI Group (UK) Ltd, Croydon, CR0 4YY

Acknowledgements

I am incredibly grateful to several individuals who have supported me in the writing of this book. First and foremost, I am indebted to my colleague Alan Boyle, for his insights and observations on international law of the sea and international environmental law. I have been lucky enough to have had the opportunity to discuss these topics with him on many occasions, both before and during the process of writing this book, and I have been influenced by his own work on international law-making. I have also benefited from generous and constructive comments and suggestions on my work and ideas, inter alia, from Erik Molenaar, Yara Saab, Henrik Ringbom, Elisa Morgera, Naporn Popattanachai, Dan Carr, and Rosemary Rayfuse. Finally, I would like to thank Chloe Wenman and Silke Mooldijk, who provided research assistance at various stages of this project. Comments from the anonymous reviewer also greatly assisted in refining the text prior to publication. Naturally, I take full responsibility for the final text, including any omissions or errors.

Table of Contents

Table of Cases

List of Abbreviations

ACCOBAMS	Agreement on the Conservation of Cetaceans of the Black Sea and Mediterranean
AFS	Anti-fouling system
APEI	Area of Particular Environmental Interest
APM	Associated protective measure
ASCOBANS	Agreement on the Conservation of Small Cetaceans of the Baltic, North East Atlantic, Irish and North Seas
ASMA	Antarctic Specially Managed Area
ASPA	Antarctic Specially Protected Area
ATCM	Antarctic Treaty Consultative Meeting
BAT	Best available technology
BEP	Best environmental practices
BLG	Biodiversity Liaison Group
BSPA	Baltic Sea Protected Area
BWM	Ballast water management
CBD	Convention on Biological Diversity
CCAMLR	Commission for the Conservation of Antarctic Marine Living Resources
CCS	Carbon capture and storage
CITES	Convention on International Trade in Endangered Species of Wild Fauna and Flora
CMS	Convention on Migratory Species
COP	Conference of the Parties
DOALOS	Division for Ocean Affairs and the Law of the Sea
EBSA	Ecologically or Biologically Significant Marine Areas
EEDI	Energy Efficiency Design Index
EEZ	Exclusive economic zone
EIA	Environmental impact assessment
EIF	Entry into force
EMP	Environmental management plan
ETS	Emissions trading scheme
EU	European Union
FAO	Food and Agriculture Organization of the United Nations
FRA	Fisheries Restricted Area
GEP	Global Environment Facility
GESAMP	Group of Experts on the Scientific Aspects of Marine Environmental Protection
GFCM	General Fisheries Commission for the Mediterranean
GPOA	Global Programme of Action
ICES	International Council for the Exploration of the Sea
ICJ	International Court of Justice
ICP	United Nations Open-ended Informal Consultative Process on Oceans and the Law of the Sea
ICRW	International Convention for the Regulation of Whaling

ICCAT	International Commission for the Conservation of Atlantic Tunas
ILC	International Law Commission
ILO	International Labour Organization
IMO	International Maritime Organization
IOTC	Indian Ocean Tuna Commission
IPCC	Intergovernmental Panel on Climate Change
IPOA	International Plan of Action
IRZ	Impact Reference Zone
ISM	International Safety Management
ITLOS	International Tribunal for the Law of the Sea
IUU	Illegal, unregulated, and unreported
IWC	International Whaling Commission
JWGSS	Joint Working Group on Ship Scrapping
LDC	London Dumping Convention
LDP	London Dumping Protocol
MAP	Mediterranean Action Plan
MEPC	Marine Environment Protection Committee
MOU	Memorandum of Understanding
MPA	Marine protected area
MSAS	Member State Audit Scheme
MSC	Maritime Safety Committee
MSY	Maximum sustainable yield
NAFO	North West Atlantic Fisheries Organization
NASCO	North Atlantic Salmon Conservation Organization
NEAFC	North East Atlantic Fisheries Commission
NGO	Non-governmental organization
NPFC	North Pacific Fisheries Commission
OPPRC	Oil Pollution Preparedness, Response and Co-operation
POP	Persistent organic pollutant
PRZ	Preservation Reference Zone
PSSA	Particularly Sensitive Sea Area
RFMO	Regional Fisheries Management Organization
RO-RO	Roll on-Roll off
SBSTTA	Subsidiary Body on Scientific, Technical and Technological Advice
SEAFO	South East Atlantic Fisheries Organization
SEEMP	Ship Energy Efficiency Management Plan
SPAMI	Specially Protected Areas of Marine Importance
SPRFMO	South Pacific Regional Fisheries Management Organization
STS	Ship-to-ship
TAC	Total allocable catch
TBT	Tributyl tin
UN	United Nations
UNCLOS	United Nations Convention on the Law of the Sea
UNEP	United Nations Environment Programme
UNESCO	United Nations Education, Scientific and Cultural Organization
UNFCCC	United Nations Framework Convention on Climate Change
UNFSA	United Nations Fish Stocks Agreement
UNGA	United Nations General Assembly
VCLT	Vienna Convention on the Law of Treaties

VME	Vulnerable Marine Ecosystem
WCED	World Commission on Environment and Development
WCN	World Charter for Nature
WCPFC	Western and Central Pacific Fisheries Commission
WTO	World Trade Organization

1

Introduction

1.1 Major Threats to the Marine Environment

Humankind has been using the oceans for centuries, as a source of food and natural resources, as a medium for transport, and as a place to dispose of waste and other unwanted substances. Yet, as the twentieth century progressed, the rapid industrialization of the oceans has meant that any lingering belief that the seas were 'inexhaustible' gave way to a growing sense of crisis.[1] This trend has continued to the extent that, today, there are warning signs that the oceans are at a tipping point, owing to the impacts of pollution and other environmental stresses caused by anthropogenic activity.[2] According to a report issued by the Joint Group of Experts on the Scientific Aspects of Marine Environmental Protection (GESAMP) at the turn of the twenty-first century, 'the state of world's seas and oceans is deteriorating' and 'most of the problems identified decades ago have not been resolved, and many are worsening'.[3] Moreover, the effects of human activities are spreading ever further into the open ocean.[4] One recent study concludes that '... no area [of the marine environment] is unaffected by human influence and ... a large fraction is strongly affected by multiple drivers'.[5]

The causes of this decline are varied and complex. Research suggests that the most serious pressures on the marine environment today stem from:[6]

- The destruction and alteration of habitats;
- Over-fishing and the effects of fishing on the marine environment;
- The harmful effects of chemicals and other noxious substances;

---

[1] See e.g. C Ray, 'Ecology, Law and the "Marine Revolution"' (1970) 3 *BC* 7–17.
[2] C Roberts, *Ocean of Life* (Penguin 2012) 4; JBC Jackson, 'Ecological Extinction and Evolution in the Brave New Ocean' (2008) 105 *PNAS* 11458–65.
[3] GESAMP, *A Sea of Troubles*, GESAMP Report and Studies No 70 (2001) 1.
[4] GESAMP, *Pollution in the Open Oceans: A Review of Assessments and Related Studies*, GESAMP Report and Studies No 79 (2009); see also World Commission on Environment and Development (WCED), *Our Common Future* (CUP 1987) 264.
[5] BS Halpern et al, 'A Global Map of Human Impact on Marine Ecosystems' (2008) 319 *Science* 948.
[6] GESAMP (n3) 1. This conclusion is confirmed by the more recent World Ocean Assessment; see P Bernal et al, 'Chapter 54: Overall Assessment of Human Impact on the Oceans', in L Inniss et al, *Global Oceans Assessment* (UN 2016).

- Eutrophication, caused mainly by nutrients from sewage and riverine inputs from agriculture and aquaculture;
- Changes in hydrology and the flow of sediments;
- Climate change and ocean acidification.

To make matter worse, these impacts do not operate in isolation. As noted by one eminent group of marine scientists, 'the cumulative result of our actions is a serial decline in the ocean's health and resilience.'[7] More worryingly, some studies suggest that the presence of multiple stressors can cause impacts to accumulate synergistically, meaning that the total impact is greater than the sum of its parts.[8] The only solution is action to tackle the sources of damage by regulating responsible activities.

1.2 The Protection of the Marine Environment as a *Common Concern of Humankind*

In light of the mounting scientific evidence of serious harm to the oceans, the need for action to tackle the problems of marine environmental degradation is now incontestable. Yet, the interconnected nature of the seas means that individual action by States is not sufficient to address the protection of the marine environment. The World Commission on Environment and Development explained in its seminal report in 1987 that 'the underlying unity of the oceans requires effective global management regimes'.[9] Nor is it only those marine areas that are considered global commons open to all States that demand cooperative management.[10] The transboundary movement of pollution accelerated by oceanic currents and the migratory nature of many marine species means that the impacts of many activities carried out by one State within its own jurisdiction can have implications for many other States. For example, serious pollution from land-based activities may spread beyond the limits of the State of origin and affect marine resources located in other States. This is particularly the case in enclosed or semi-enclosed seas, such as the Baltic Sea, Black Sea, or Red Sea. Another example is seabed drilling or dredging on the continental shelf of one coastal State that causes significant damage to the spawning grounds of a highly migratory species that is ordinarily fished by other States in their exclusive economic zone or on the high seas. These two examples illustrate the interconnectedness of the oceans and the interest that all States have in the management of marine activities, wherever they take place. The need for collective action is even more

---

[7] International Programme on the State of the Ocean, *Implementing the Global State of the Oceans Report* (2013) 3.

[8] MM Foley et al, 'Improving Ocean Management through the Use of Ecological Principles and Integrated Ecosystem Assessments' (2013) 63 *BioScience* 619, 621.

[9] WCED (n4) 264.

[10] On the challenges of managing the commons, see G Hardin, 'The Tragedy of the Commons' (1968) 162 *Science* 1243, and, more recently, T Dietz et al, 'The Struggle to Govern the Commons' (2003) 302 *Science* 1907. For a discussion of the distinction between maritime zones within and beyond national jurisdiction, see Chapter 2.

obvious in the case of controlling the effects of ships on the marine environment, as they are inherently mobile and regularly pass through the jurisdiction of multiple States in the course of a single voyage.

It is for these reasons that the protection of the marine environment should be considered a common concern of humankind, in common with other environmental issues such as the protection of the global atmosphere and the conservation of biological diversity.[11] The main purpose of applying this designation to the marine environment is to underline that all States have an interest in the way in which activities affecting the marine environment are carried out. The protection of marine areas both within and beyond national jurisdiction can be described as a common concern of humankind, as the concept does not affect the rights that States enjoy over marine resources or maritime areas, but rather it emphasizes that these rights 'are not unlimited or absolute, but must now be exercised within the confines of [their] global responsibilities'.[12] In other words, the concept of *common concern* is focused on the common challenge, not the underlying resources.[13]

Even though the concept of common concern does not require a specific course of action in each and every case,[14] there are several legal consequences of applying this designation. First, it means that States cannot seek refuge in sovereignty or exclusive domestic jurisdiction as a means to avoid the scrutiny of other States.[15] In the context of the marine environment, this principle extends not only to their actions at sea but also to land-based activities that affect the oceans.[16] Second, it acknowledges that States should seek to cooperate with a view to agreeing on common rules and principles to guide their actions to address the challenges that are of common concern.[17] Cooperation goes both ways, so that States may be required to take certain action in relation to an activity, but they may also expect support and assistance from other States to help them to achieve their common interests.[18] Furthermore, the establishment of

---

[11] See 1992 United Nations Framework Convention on Climate Change (UNFCCC) (EIF 21 March 1994), preamble; 1992 Convention on Biological Diversity (CBD) (EIF 29 December 1993), preamble. Some authors have already suggested the application of this concept to particular sources of pollution or specific aspects of the marine environment, e.g. coral reefs in EJ Goodwin, *International Environmental Law and the Conservation of Coral Reefs* (Routledge 2011) 31–3; marine plastics in E Hey, *An Advanced Introduction to International Environmental Law* (Edward Elgar 2016) 64.

[12] P Birnie, AE Boyle, and C Redgwell, *International Law and the Environment* (3rd edn: OUP 2009) 130.

[13] See J Brunnée, 'Commons Areas, Common Heritage and Common Concern', in D Bodansky et al (eds), *The Oxford Handbook of International Environmental Law* (OUP 2009) 564–5. In some respects, this concept could be considered as a reflection of an emergent international law for the Anthropocene, as it emphasizes that the actions of individual states can affect the entire planet. See D Vidas et al, 'International Law for the Anthropocene? Shifting Perspectives in the Regulation of the Oceans, Environment and Genetic Resources' (2015) 9 *Anthropocene* 1–13.

[14] Brunnée (n13) 566.

[15] See D Shelton, 'Common Concern of Humanity' (2009) 39 *EP&L* 83, 86.

[16] See Chapter 3.

[17] See e.g. D French, 'Common Concern, Common Heritage and other Global(-ising) Concepts: Rhetorical Devices, Legal Principles or a Fundamental Challenge?', in MJ Bowman et al (eds), *Research Handbook on Biodiversity and Law* (Edward Elgar 2015) 13.

[18] See e.g. Goodwin (n11) 34.

institutions has been identified as a key component of the common concern of humankind because 'it helps constitute the collectives, or "communities", that otherwise remain elusive, but that are crucial to the legal enterprise of addressing common environmental concerns'.[19] Such institutions can address both norm development and compliance. This process of institutionalization in the context of the protection of the marine environment is at the centre of the study in this book.

It is also sometimes suggested that the common concern of humankind can be considered to have other legal effects, which may be more controversial, yet nevertheless need to be mentioned. For example, it has been suggested that the common concern of humankind can be linked to the emergence of obligations *erga omnes*, meaning that the obligation is owed to the international community as a whole.[20] This argument remains contested, and detractors point to the lack of appropriate procedures in international law enabling actions to be brought on behalf of the international community.[21] Yet, in Chapter 2, it will be argued that such a proposition can be supported in the context of the legal framework for the protection of the marine environment, at least in relation to obligations *erga omnes partes* under the United Nations Convention on the Law of the Sea,[22] which contains its own procedures for compulsory dispute settlement. Moreover, many of the other individual treaty regimes studied in this book have developed their own *sui generis* compliance mechanisms, which can be considered as providing similar opportunities for collective enforcement action.

It has also been argued that the common concern of humankind designation implies recognition that non-State actors have an interest in the development of international law. For example, it has been suggested that the concept may create rights for individuals and future generations.[23] This interpretation of the concept is less easy to justify on the basis of current State practice,[24] although it has been recognized that non-State actors do have an increased involvement in international law-making, which suggests 'at least tentative developments towards a more inclusive approach to "global concerns of humanity as a whole".'[25] Indeed, as explained later in this chapter, public participation has emerged as a general principle of international environmental law and it is a factor that has influenced law-making in many maritime regimes. However, it will be argued that the requirement of public participation depends upon positive prescription of rules in individual treaty regimes, rather than as a result of the designation of the protection of the marine environment as the common concern of humankind.

---

[19] Brunnée (n13) 568.   [20] See Shelton (n15) 86.
[21] See e.g. the views of the ILC Special Rapporteur on the Protection of the Atmosphere in his Second Report, Document A/CN.4/681, 2 March 2015, para. 37.
[22] See 1982 United Nations Convention on the Law of the Sea (UNCLOS) (EIF 16 November 1994).
[23] Second Report of the ILC Special Rapporteur on the Protection of the Atmosphere (n21) para. 37.
[24] Ibid.
[25] Brunnée (n13) 570. On the role of non-state actors generally, see AE Boyle and C Chinkin, *The Making of International Law* (OUP 2007) 46–80.

1.3 International Law and the Protection of
the Marine Environment

Whilst there were sporadic and isolated attempts to address particular marine environmental challenges in the late nineteenth[26] and early twentieth centuries,[27] this topic began to gain more attention following the conclusion of the Second World War, when a number of treaties were concluded to deal with some of the more obvious damage to the marine environment caused by human activities: for example, the exploitation of marine species[28] and oil pollution from ships.[29] The question of legal protection for the marine environment was first systematically addressed at international level at the 1972 Stockholm Conference on the Human Environment, which is widely viewed as a seminal event in the development of international environmental law at the global level.[30] The Stockholm Conference was not concerned with prescribing detailed rules or standards for the protection of the environment, but rather it was charged with the task of articulating 'the legal, institutional and other requirements, at all levels of government, for the protection and conservation of the "biosphere", including ... the ocean environment'.[31] The recommendations for action adopted by the Stockholm Conference identified the need for the negotiation and adoption of a number of legal instruments to further these values.[32] Furthermore, the principles elaborated in the Stockholm Declaration on the Human Environment, as well as the General Principles for Assessment and Control of Marine Pollution which were also endorsed by States in Stockholm,[33] were designed to assist States in developing the legal framework, and they have had an important influence on many of the law-making activities considered throughout this book.[34]

The purpose of this book is to consider the nature of the legal framework that has emerged as a result of this process. In particular, the book will focus on the treaties

---

[26] See e.g. *Bering Fur Seals Arbitration* (1893) 263–76. Following this groundbreaking arbitration, several treaties for the protection of fur seals and sea otters were concluded; see Chapter 7 for more details.

[27] The League of Nations concluded a Convention on the Regulation of Whaling in 1931. It also attempted to conclude a treaty on oil pollution from ships, albeit unsuccessfully.

[28] Various treaties were concluded in the post-war period dealing with whales, seals, and fish stocks. See Chapter 7.

[29] The first major treaty on oil pollution was the 1954 International Convention for the Prevention of Pollution of the Sea by Oil (OILPOL Convention) (EIF 26 July 1956). See further, Chapter 6.

[30] DM Johnston, 'The Environmental Law of the Sea: Historical Development', in DM Johnston (ed.), *The Environmental Law of the Sea* (IUCN 1981) 39; J Brunnée, 'The Stockholm Declaration and the Structure and Processes of International Environmental Law', in MH Nordquist et al (eds), *The Stockholm Declaration and Law of the Marine Environment* (Martinus Nijhoff 2003) 67.

[31] Johnston (n30) 42; See also Brunnée (n30) 80; A Kiss, 'The Destiny of the Principles of the Stockholm Declaration', in MH Nordquist et al (eds), *The Stockholm Declaration and Law of the Marine Environment* (Martinus Nijhoff 2003) 53.

[32] Stockholm Action Plan (1972), Recommendations 86–94.

[33] Ibid., Recommendation 92(a); the principles can be found in the *Report of the United Nations Conference on the Human Environment*, UN Document A/Conf.48/14/Rev.1 (1972) 73.

[34] See, particularly, the discussion in Chapter 2, on the influence of the Stockholm Conference on the negotiation of UNCLOS.

and other international instruments relating to the regulation of activities that pose a potential threat to the marine environment and the obligations of States to prevent, reduce, and control ecological damage arising from those activities.[35] Before proceeding to a discussion of the nature of the international legal rules that have been adopted for the protection of the marine environment, it is first worth reflecting why States have chosen to order their relations through law in the first place. After all, States can cooperate in a variety of ways, many of which avoid any form of binding commitment.

The main advantage of pursuing cooperation through international law is that it provides greater stability for international relations, as it demands certain formalities to be completed before rights or obligations can be changed or denounced. It follows that the decision of States to enter into a legal relationship is significant because 'legal obligations represent a higher level of commitment by states than non-legal arrangements, with correspondingly higher reputational costs for violation [and they] therefore better reflect what states are, in fact, prepared to do'.[36] Furthermore, the establishment of a legally binding commitment provides a basis on which other States can demand compliance. It has thus been explained that entering into legal obligations means that '[States'] behavior thereunder is subject to scrutiny under the general rules, procedures, and discourses of international law, and often domestic law as well.'[37] This may involve a State being required to justify its behaviour to other States or even to defend its position before an international court or tribunal or some other independent adjudicatory or advisory body. A breach of international law leads to international responsibility, requiring a State to cease the unlawful act and, where appropriate, make reparation to the injured State or actor.[38] This 'compliance pull' of international law[39] makes it an important tool to address problems of an international character and it justifies the focus on international legal regulation found throughout this book. At the same time, it is important to understand that the lack of any legal obligations in some areas is not necessarily an indication that States are unwilling to take action through other means. Nevertheless, political cooperation and altruistic unilateralism fall outside the scope of the present study.

1.4 The Sources of International Law and the Protection of the Marine Environment

Given this book is concerned with the scope of protection for the marine environment offered by international law, it is necessary at the outset to explain the

---

[35] It will not address the question of compensation for damage caused by an activity.

[36] D Bodansky and E Deringer, *The Evolution of Multilateral Regimes: Implications for Climate Change* (Pew Center on Global Climate Change 2010) 7.

[37] KW Abbot et al, 'The Concept of Legalization' (2000) 54 *IO* 17–35, 17.

[38] International Law Commission, *Articles on State Responsibility* (UN 2001) Articles 30–1.

[39] L Henkin, *How Nations Behave* (Pall Mall Press 1968) 42. See, also, I Brownlie, 'The Reality and Efficiency of International Law' (1981) *BYIL* 1–8.

main sources of the international legal order. At its simplest, international law can be understood as a normative framework that governs relations between States or between States and other actors with international legal personality.[40] Given the lack of hierarchy between States, international law is by and large a decentralized system, based upon consent to relevant norms. In other words, 'the rules of law binding upon States ... emanate from their own free will',[41] although this consent can be expressed in several forms. For present purposes, the main sources of international law are custom, treaties, and general principles.[42]

1.4.1 Customary international law

Customary international law arises from widespread and consistent State practice, accompanied by a general belief that a course of conduct is mandatory.[43] An important feature of custom is its ability to generate rules for all States.[44] However, there is a high threshold for proving the existence of a rule of customary international law, with the burden of proof on those States asserting that a new custom has come into being.[45]

There are a number of important rules of customary international law in the field of environmental protection, particularly when it comes to the prevention of transboundary environmental harm.[46] Furthermore, as will be discussed in Chapter 2, the key provisions of United Nations Convention on the Law of the Sea (UNCLOS) are widely accepted as part of customary international law and they thus provide the basic framework for the development of subsequent legal treaties and other instruments in this area. Yet, customary international law tends to play a residual role in international environmental regulation by imposing basic duties where no more specific agreement has been forthcoming.[47] For this reason, custom will play a relatively minor role in this study, whose primary focus is on the active development of more detailed rules and standards relating to the protection of the marine environment.

[40] See e.g. V Lowe, *International Law* (OUP 2007) 5.   [41] See *The Lotus Case* (1927) 18.

[42] See 1945 Statute of the International Court of Justice (EIF 24 October 1945), Article 38(1).

[43] The second requirement is often called *opinio juris*. For more information on the formation of customary international law, see e.g. International Law Commission, *Identification of Customary International Law: Text of the Draft Conclusions Provisionally Adopted by the Drafting Committee*, Document A/CN.4/L.872 (2016).

[44] Birnie, Boyle, and Redgwell (n12) 22. Not all custom is universal, however, and it is possible for regional or even bilateral customs to emerge.

[45] As was observed by the Permanent Court of International Justice in one of its seminal cases, 'restrictions upon the independence of states cannot be presumed'; see *The Lotus Case* (1927) 18. See also *Asylum Case* (1950) 276.

[46] See e.g. *The Legality of the Threat or Use of Nuclear Weapons* (1996) para. 29; *Construction of a Road in Costa Rica along the San Juan River* (2015) para. 104.

[47] See e.g. D Bodansky, 'Customary (and Not So Customary) International Environmental Law' (1995) *IJGLS* 105, 118–19.

1.4.2 Treaties

Treaties are a much more important source of law for the protection of the marine environment. Treaties are written agreements containing obligations that are legally binding on those States or other actors that have agreed to them, a process known as becoming a 'contracting Party' or simply a 'Party'.[48] Treaties can be adopted by as few as two actors or they may be designed to govern relations between the entire international community. Thus, they are flexible devices which can be used in various circumstances. In general, treaties have the advantage of transparency, as they offer 'a clear and conclusive statement of the rights of the [Contracting Parties] to it in their relations with each other'.[49] This is one of the reasons why treaties are the main instruments through which legally binding relationships are established.[50]

It is important to recognize that treaties are often the product of compromise. Whilst all treaty rules are in theory legally binding and their breach leads in principle to some form of responsibility or liability, treaty rules and standards in practice exist along a spectrum of normativity, depending upon, inter alia, their content, language, and precision.[51] Some treaties in the field of marine environmental protection can be extremely detailed, setting out precise technical standards for a particular activity. This is the case, for example, with those treaties regulating pollution from ships, as will be explained in Chapter 6. Equally, treaty provisions may be more general in nature, and States may have a degree of discretion as to how they implement their treaty obligations. The language of a provision is crucial in this context. For example, there is a significant difference between an obligation to 'endeavour' to carry out an act, an obligation to carry out an act 'as far as possible and as appropriate', and an obligation simply to act. The form of a norm will ultimately depend upon the political choice of the drafters[52] and it reveals the degree to which the relevant States are willing to cooperate in achieving their common aims.

Treaties often do not exist in isolation. Many modern treaties establish institutions, which are granted a role in overseeing the implementation and development of the treaty. These institutions are often granted decision-making powers, and this trend has led to the emergence of what have been termed treaty regimes, comprising the treaty itself, as well as related institutional components and soft law instruments.[53]

---

[48] For a more detailed treatment of the rules relating to the conclusion and entry into force of a treaty, see M Fitzmaurice, 'The Practical Workings of Treaties', in MD Evans (ed.), *International Law* (4th edn: OUP 2014) 166–200.

[49] RR Churchill and AV Lowe, *The Law of the Sea* (3rd edn: MUP 1999) 6.

[50] AE Boyle and C Chinkin, *The Making of International Law* (OUP 2007) 233.

[51] RR Baxter, 'International Law in "Her Infinite Variety"' (1980) 29 *ICLQ* 549–66; L Rajamani, 'The 2015 Paris Agreement: Interplay between Hard, Soft and Non-Obligations' (2016) 28 *JEL* 337, 338.

[52] See e.g. KW Abbott and D Snidal, 'Hard and Soft Law in International Governance' (2000) 54 *IO* 421–56.

[53] See W Lang, 'Diplomacy and International Environmental Law-Making: Some Observations' (1992) 3 *YIEL* 108, 117–22.

Treaty regimes are a key phenomenon in the environmental field, in part, because of their flexibility to respond to changing circumstances relatively quickly.[54] The evolution of norms is of particular importance in the context of marine environmental protection given that there are significant gaps in the scientific evidence relating to the state of the oceans,[55] and, thus, the legal framework needs to adapt to new insights and emerging knowledge. Regular meetings of treaty bodies and the adoption of decisions on key issues relating to the treaty are an important means of achieving this objective. In this manner, treaty bodies are a source of a wealth of decisions, declarations, resolutions, and other international instruments relating to the actual treaty rules. Yet, the legal effect of these decisions varies, depending on their content and the circumstances of their adoption.[56] Occasionally, the enactments of treaty bodies are directly binding on the Parties to the treaty.[57] In other cases, treaty bodies can only adopt non-binding resolutions or recommendations, but even if they do not a priori possess legal force, such decisions can nevertheless influence the development of international law in important ways. For example, a decision of the Contracting Parties to a treaty can amount to an authoritative interpretation of the treaty itself, thereby specifying how the treaty must be implemented in practice.[58] Alternatively, such decisions may provide guidance that is more general or identify best practices, which are not necessarily the only way of implementing the treaty, but if observed, will provide evidence of compliance.[59] Non-binding decisions can also be used as a precursor to the negotiation of a new treaty or a means to fill a regulatory gap pending the entry into force of legally binding rules.[60] At the same time, the choice of a non-binding decision may simply indicate that States are not willing to constrain themselves by the adoption of legally binding obligations. Such instruments cannot necessarily be completely dismissed, as they may still generate political expectations, but they do not belong to the realm of law and they lack the consequences that attach to legally binding obligations.[61] It follows that this type of instrument must be analysed with some care before coming to a conclusion about its legal effects.[62]

International courts and tribunals can also play a role in developing the legal framework of a treaty. International law is a decentralized legal system, which means that no court or tribunal has compulsory jurisdiction to settle all legal disputes that

---

[54] P Birnie, A Boyle, and C Redgwell, (n12) 35.   [55] See e.g. Bernal et al (n6) 6.

[56] See e.g. *Legality of the Threat or Use of Nuclear Weapons* (1996) para. 70.

[57] One example is the role of the International Seabed Authority in developing regulations for seabed mining; see Chapter 8.

[58] See 1969 Vienna Convention on the Law of Treaties (VCLT) (EIF 27 January 1980) Article 31(3)(a). See, further, AE Boyle, 'Soft Law in International Law-Making', in MD Evans (ed.), *International Law* (4th edn: OUP 2014) 123.

[59] Ibid, 124.

[60] See J Harrison, 'Actors and Institutions for the Protection of the Marine Environment', in R Rayfuse (ed.), *Research Handbook on International Marine Environmental Law* (Edward Elgar 2015) 67.

[61] P Weil, 'Towards Relative Normativity in International Law?' (1983) 77 *AJIL* 413, 415. See also P-M Dupuy, 'Soft law and the International Law of the Environment' (1991) 12 *MJIL* 420–35.

[62] See e.g. J Brunnée, 'COPing with Consent: Law-making under Multilateral Environmental Agreements' (2002) 15 *LJIL* 1.

might arise, and jurisdiction ultimately rests upon the consent of the relevant States. Nevertheless, commentators have observed an increasing judicialization of international relations, evidenced by the rise in treaties providing for the compulsory settlement of disputes by international courts and tribunals.[63] Whilst this trend may be uneven,[64] it can certainly be observed in the law of the sea, where a number of treaties provide for the unilateral or consensual submission of a dispute to be submitted to a judicial forum.[65] One of the key tasks of international court and tribunals is to interpret the obligations at the centre of any dispute. Interpretation is a limited task, distinct from law-making and constrained by general rules. Thus, treaty interpretation is primarily concerned with identifying the ordinary meaning of the treaty, in light of its context and its object and purpose.[66] At the same time, the meaning of a treaty is not necessarily fixed at the time of its conclusion and its interpretation may be influenced by the subsequent practice of the Parties or the emergence of other relevant rules of international law.[67] In this respect, courts and tribunals play an important role in identifying the meaning to be attributed to a treaty at a particular point in time and they can, in this manner, contribute to the development of international law. It must be borne in mind that the decisions of courts and tribunals are formally only binding on the Parties to a dispute,[68] although they have a much greater influence in practice, by providing impartial and authoritative guidance on the scope and content of international obligations.[69] In this manner, where they are active, the decisions of courts and tribunals must be considered as an integral part of a treaty regime.

1.4.3 General principles

General principles are different in character to customary or treaty rules because they provide abstract guidance for States in relation to the objectives that they should pursue in their domestic and international affairs, whilst not prescribing in any detail what steps must be taken.[70] It follows that principles cannot

---

[63] For example, KJ Alter, 'The Multiplication of International Courts and Tribunals after the End of the Cold War', in C Romano et al (eds), *Oxford Handbook of International Adjudication* (OUP 2014) 63–89.

[64] See B Kingsbury, 'International Courts: Uneven Judicialization in Global Order', in J Crawford and M Koskenniemi (eds), *The Cambridge Companion to International Law* (CUP 2012) 203; C Romano, 'The Shadow Zones of International Adjudication', in C Romano et al (eds), *Oxford Handbook of International Adjudication* (OUP 2014) 90–110.

[65] For a discussion of compulsory dispute settlement under UNCLOS, see Chapter 2. The trend has earlier origins in this field, however. See e.g. OILPOL Convention, Article 13, providing for the unilateral submission of disputes to the International Court of Justice.

[66] VCLT, Article 31(1).   [67] Ibid, Article 31(3).

[68] See e.g. Statute of the International Court of Justice, Article 59; Statute of the International Tribunal for the Law of the Sea, Article 33(2).

[69] See, generally, H Lauterpacht, *The Development of International Law by the International Court* (Stevens & Sons 1958) 9–15.

[70] For a discussion of the distinction between principles and rules, see e.g. R Dworkin, *Taking Rights Seriously* (HUP 1977) 25. See also AE Boyle, 'Reflections on Treaties and Soft Law' (1999) 48 *ICLQ* 901, 907, noting that principles can also be used to guide international judicial bodies or political institutions.

be *breached* in the strict sense of the term. Yet, they are still important because of their ability to influence the interpretation, application and development of other rules of law, both by '[laying] down the parameters which affect the way courts decide cases [and] how an international institution exercises its discretionary powers'.[71] For this reason, it is still appropriate to talk about principles as having normative effect and 'they should not be confused with "non-binding" or emerging law'.[72]

Principles are sometimes expressly included in treaties, but the importance of general principles is that they can equally exercise an influence on a treaty regime, even if they have not been explicitly incorporated. Indeed, general principles of international environmental law have played a crucial role in promoting the evolution of existing treaty regimes. Important examples of general declarations of principles in the field of international environmental law are the 1972 Stockholm Declaration on the Human Environment, introduced above, and the 1992 Rio Declaration on Environment and Development.[73] This latter instrument was adopted by consensus at an unprecedented gathering of 172 governments and representatives of approximately 2,400 non-governmental organizations and it is considered to be 'the most universally endorsed statement of general rights and obligations of states affecting the environment'.[74] The Declaration is important because it signals a paradigm shift in environmental thinking by emphasizing that a wide range of environmental considerations must be integrated into all forms of decision-making, and it calls for greater precaution in environmental regulation. The Declaration may not be legally binding, but the international community has repeatedly endorsed the general principles of environmental protection that are contained therein,[75] and there is little doubt that it has had a significant influence on international environmental law-making.[76] This section will highlight some key principles that are relevant to the development of the international legal framework for the protection of the marine environment, as discussed later in the book.

The overarching concept in the Rio Declaration is sustainable development. Although the Declaration contains no definition of sustainable development,[77] the essence of the concept is captured by Principle 4, which proclaims that 'in order to achieve sustainable development, environmental protection shall constitute an integral part of the development process and cannot be considered in isolation from it'.

---

[71] Boyle (n58) 130. [72] Ibid.

[73] See 1992 Rio Declaration on Environment and Development (Rio Declaration).

[74] Birnie, Boyle, and Redgwell (n12) 112. It should be recognized that the Declaration is 'a synthesis of principles, including some that pre-existed its adoption'; JE Viñuales, 'The Rio Declaration on Environment and Development: A Preliminary Study', in JE Viñuales (ed.), *The Rio Declaration on Environment and Development: A Commentary* (OUP 2015) 21.

[75] See e.g. UNGA Resolution 66/288 (2012) Annex, para. 15.

[76] See Viñuales (n74) 20–1.

[77] However, see the Brundtland Commission Report, which referred to 'development that meets the needs of the present without compromising the ability of future generations to meet their own needs'; WCED (n4) 43.

This so-called integration principle has been identified as a major feature in modern international environmental law,[78] and Sands has argued that it is 'probably the most important long-term contribution' of the Rio Declaration to international affairs because it 'creates the possibility of moving environmental considerations and objectives from the periphery of international relations to the economic core'.[79]

The precise manner in which this balance must be made will depend in part on the States concerned. According to the principle of common but differentiated responsibilities, developed countries may be expected to undertake a greater burden in tackling common environmental problems than developing countries would, owing, in part, to their differing contribution to such problems, as well as their more advanced technical and financial capacity to respond.[80] Put another way, 'environmental standards, management objectives and priorities should reflect the environmental and development context to which they apply [and] standards applied by some countries may be inappropriate and of unwarranted economic and social cost to other countries, in particular developing countries'.[81] Common but differentiated responsibility is central to the package of principles adopted in the Rio Declaration and it is 'closely related to the concepts of sustainable development and of intragenerational equity'.[82] The different expressions of the principle found in the Rio Declaration can be understood as supporting the more general notion in Principle 6 of the Rio Declaration that 'the special situation and needs of developing countries, particularly the least developed and those most environmentally vulnerable, shall be given special priority'. It is important to understand that common but differentiated responsibility does not relieve developing countries of their obligation to protect the environment. Rather, it calls for obligations to be tailored to their circumstances. Yet, this principle does not dictate what degree of differentiation will be appropriate, which may depend on the nature of the problem and the types of resources that are required to tackle it. Indeed, as will be seen in the following chapters, whilst this principle has been explicitly incorporated into several treaties dealing with marine environmental degradation, normative differentiation is not ubiquitous in this field of law.

The requirements of sustainable development not only demand that environmental considerations are integrated into all forms of decision-making, but also that all potential forms of environmental harm are taken into account. In this respect, States have broadly endorsed a so-called ecosystem approach to oceans management. Although the ecosystems approach is not expressly mentioned in the Rio Declaration, it has emerged as a key principle in other international instruments[83]

---

[78] See e.g. CA Voigt, 'The Principle of Sustainable Development', in C Voigt (ed.), *Rule of Law for Nature: New Dimensions and Ideas in Environmental Law* (CUP 2013) 154; Birnie, Boyle, and Redgwell (n12) 116–17.

[79] P Sands, 'International Law in the Field of Sustainable Development' (1994) 65 *BYbIL* 324. The legal status of sustainable development is contested, however; see e.g. AV Lowe, 'Sustainable Development and Unsustainable Arguments', in AE Boyle and D Freestone (eds), *International Law and Sustainable Development* (OUP 1999) 19–37.

[80] Rio Declaration, Principle 7.   [81] Ibid, Principle 11.

[82] E Hey, 'Common but Differentiated Responsibilities', in *Max Planck Encyclopedia of Public International Law* (OUP 2011) para. 5.

[83] For example, CBD COP Decision V/6 (2000) section B; Johannesburg Programme for Further Implementation (2002) para. 30(d); UNGA Resolution 61/222 (2006) para. 119; UNGA Resolution

and it has been described as a 'landmark regulatory strategy' for the conservation of biological diversity,[84] which represents a significant shift in environmental policy.[85] There is no universally agreed definition of the ecosystem approach, but, at its core, it requires States to take measures to ensure the 'conservation of ecosystem structures and their functioning and key processes in order to maintain ecosystem goods and services'.[86] The ecosystems approach can be interpreted and applied in broad or narrow ways[87] but it generally requires a move away from ad hoc sectoral and zonal approaches to environmental protection, towards more holistic environmental strategies involving greater cooperation between States and international institutions.[88] Yet, States recognize that 'there is no single way to implement an ecosystem approach', and flexibility is important in order to take into account particular regional, subregional, national, or local circumstances.[89] Thus, the precise implications of taking an ecosystems approach will depend on the circumstances. How the ecosystems approach has been interpreted and applied in practice will be a key point of inquiry in the analysis of this book.

Another important development in environmental thinking evident in contemporary international environmental law is the need to take a precautionary approach to environmental protection. This concept emerged at the international level in the 1980s and the United Nations Environment Programme (UNEP) Governing Council expressly urged States to adopt what it called 'the principle of precautionary action' to efforts to combat marine pollution at its twelfth meeting in 1989.[90] The best-known formulation of the precautionary approach is found in Principle 15 of the Rio Declaration, which provides:

in order to protect the environment, the precautionary approach shall be widely applied by States according to their capabilities. Where there are threats of serious or irreversible damage, lack of full scientific certainty shall not be used as a reason for postponing cost-effective measures to prevent environmental degradation.

66/288 (2012) Annex, para. 158; Joint Ministerial Statement of the Helsinki and OSPAR Commissions on the Ecosystem Approach to the Management of Human Activities (2003).

[84] E Morgera, 'Ecosystem and Precautionary Approaches', in J Razzaque and E Morgera (eds), *Encyclopedia of Environmental Law: Biodiversity and Nature Protection* (Edward Elgar 2017) forthcoming.

[85] See V de Lucia, 'Competing Narratives and Complex Genealogies: The Ecosystem Approach in International Environmental Law' (2015) 27 *JEL* 91, 92.

[86] *Report of the Work of the United Nations Open-ended Informal Consultative Process on Oceans and Law of the Sea at Its Seventh Meeting*, Document A/61/156 (2006) para. 6(a). See also CBD COP Decision V/6 (2000) section B, principle 5.

[87] de Lucia (n85) 91–117, distinguishing between anthropocentric and ecocentric understandings of the ecosystem approach.

[88] See A Trouwborst, 'The Precautionary Principle and the Ecosystem Approach in International Law: Differences, Similarities and Linkages' (2009) 18 *RECIEL* 26, 26; Y Tanaka, 'Zonal and Integrated Management Approaches to Ocean Government: Reflections on a Dual Approach in International Law of the Sea' (2004) 19 *IJMCL* 483–514.

[89] *Report of the Work of the United Nations Open-ended Informal Consultative Process on Oceans and Law of the Sea at Its Seventh Meeting* (n86) para. 45. See also CBD COP Decision V/6 (2000) section A, para. 5.

[90] UNEP Governing Council Decision 15/27 (1989).

What is required by a precautionary approach is the subject of intense debate, how-ever, and there are contrasting views on the status of the precautionary approach in international law.[91] Perhaps the greatest significance of the concept is that it endorses action for the protection of the environment, even when there is no conclusive proof that environmental harm will occur. In other words, the precautionary approach signals a shift from a reactionary model of regulation to one that is proactive and anticipatory.[92] Beyond this central idea are many different ways of understanding what is required by a precautionary approach. Indeed, the wording of the precau-tionary approach found in Principle 15 does not specify precisely what States must do in order to protect the environment,[93] and the precautionary approach may be operationalized in a number of different forms in relation to marine environmen-tal protection.[94] In some cases, an activity may be allowed to proceed, albeit with a requirement to gather additional information on impacts and to review manage-ment strategies at a later stage. This approach has been captured by the concept of adaptive management, which requires that the effects of an activity are monitored and adjustments made to regulatory framework where potential adverse effects are identified.[95] Alternatively, where there are reasonable grounds for believing that an activity may cause significant and irreversible harm, a precautionary approach may call for an activity to be prohibited, at least until it can be shown than no such harm will occur. This stronger version of the precautionary approach thus has the effect of reversing the burden of proof for an activity.[96] Which version of the precautionary approach is appropriate for a particular activity will depend upon the States con-cerned and it will have to be negotiated on a case-by-case basis. Indeed, the formu-lation of Principle 15 expressly acknowledges that precautionary measures must be 'cost-effective' and that States can only apply a precautionary approach 'according to their capabilities'.[97] How this principle has been developed in relation to par-ticular sources of marine environmental degradation will be explored throughout this book.

Finally, modern international environmental law demands a more participatory approach to regulation. This requirement is captured by Principle 10 of the Rio Declaration, which provides that 'environmental issues are best handled with the participation of all concerned citizens, at the relevant level', and it further calls for access to environmental information, opportunities to participate in the decision-making process, and access to remedies.[98] There is obviously a wide range of policies

---

[91] For a summary of the debate, see M Schroeder, 'Precautionary Approach/Principle', in *Max Planck Encyclopaedia of Public International Law*, Online Edition (OUP 2009); Birnie, Boyle, and Redgwell (n12) 159–64; M Pyhala et al, 'The Precautionary Principle', in M Fitzmaurice et al (eds), *Research Handbook on International Environmental Law* (Edward Elgar 2010) 203–25.

[92] See Trouwborst (n88) 26.   [93] Birnie, Boyle, and Redgwell (n12) 161.

[94] See e.g. B Sage-Fuller, *The Precautionary Principle in Marine Environmental Law* (Routledge 2013).

[95] See Addis Ababa Guidelines on Sustainable Use (2004) Practical Principle 4; CBD COP Decision V/6 (2000) Section B, Principle 9.

[96] See e.g. C Foster, *Science and the Precautionary Principle* (CUP 2011) 240.

[97] Rio Declaration, Principle 15.

[98] See also the 2010 Bali Guidelines for the Development of National Legislation on Access to Information, Public Participation and Access to Justice in Environmental Matters.

and practices that can be introduced in order to pursue this policy, and international law would not appear to be prescriptive.[99] Indeed, the implementation of this principle in the context of the marine environment is challenging, given that the protection of the marine environment is a common concern of humankind, and it is often difficult to identify the range of 'relevant' stakeholders, particularly in areas beyond national jurisdiction. This is another issue that will have to be worked out on a case-by-case basis.

1.5 Outline of the Book

There is little doubt that international law has come to play an important role in the efforts made by States in order to tackle the common challenge associated with the deteriorating health of the oceans. States have adopted a number of treaties and other international instruments on this topic, which together form a complex legal framework for the protection of the marine environment. It is the progressive development of these treaties and instruments that is the principal subject of this book. The book inquires into how the key principles of international environmental law have been implemented in the different sectors of maritime regulation, what types of norms are used and the interrelationship between various levels of norms, as well as the institutional framework for the further development and enforcement of such norms.

Chapter 2 of the book starts by examining the way in which marine environmental protection is dealt with by UNCLOS, which is undoubtedly the most significant treaty concerning ocean activities. This central pillar of the international legal system both sets out the jurisdictional framework for the law of the sea and prescribes certain basic principles and rules relating to pollution of the marine environment and the sustainable use of marine living resources. Chapter 2 will analyse the nature of these provisions as an overarching framework for the subsequent development of more detailed regulation in relation to particular sectors or sources of marine environmental harm.

Chapter 3 considers another major trend in the modern law relating to the protection of the marine environment, namely the express recognition of the need to take steps to conserve marine biodiversity. Whilst UNCLOS only obliquely refers to the importance of protecting marine ecosystems, species, and habitats, this issue has come to play a much greater role in the modern law of the sea. The purpose of Chapter 3 is to provide an introduction to the emergence of biodiversity as a central organizing concept for modern regulation, by looking at the structure and content of the global and regional treaties that have introduced overarching and crosscutting obligations relating to the conservation and sustainable use of marine biodiversity.

---

[99] See J Ebbesson, 'Public Participation', in JE Viñuales (ed.), *The Rio Declaration on Environment and Development: A Commentary* (OUP 2015) 293, suggesting that 'the support for Principle 10 in environmental treaties differs also in the degree of details and ambitions, and in the scope of procedural issues'.

The book will then turn to the leading examples of sectoral regulation by looking at those treaties and other international instruments that give effect to the basic rules and principles in UNCLOS. Chapters 4 to 8 deal with the main threats to the marine environment on a sectoral basis, addressing, in turn, land-based activities, dumping of waste, shipping, fishing, and seabed activities. Each of these topics has seen the development of a number of international treaties and related instruments, containing rules and standards that seek to minimize or mitigate the harm caused by humankind to the oceans. These chapters will consider what types of norms have been developed by States in order to address the relevant threats to the marine environment and how the implementation of those rules and standards is overseen. Each chapter will also consider the relationship between these individual treaty regimes and the jurisdictional framework found in UNCLOS.

Chapter 9 addresses the impacts of climate change and ocean acidification and the extent to which international law has reacted to these emerging threats to the ecological integrity of the oceans. These issues differ from the sectoral regulation of maritime activities, because of their wide-ranging causes and effects. The chapter, therefore, considers both how the global legal regime relating to climate change has taken into account the oceans and how sectoral treaties dealing with specific maritime activities can themselves address climate change and ocean acidification within their normative framework.

Chapter 10 returns to an overarching perspective on marine environmental protection, recognizing that the world's oceans constitute a single, interconnected planetary system and, therefore, require a coordinated and integrated approach to regulation. The challenges in this regard cannot be overstated, given the decentralized nature of international law discussed above. The chapter will, therefore, assess the difficulties of developing a coherent and comprehensive legal framework for the protection of the marine environment, whilst also evaluating existing mechanisms for promoting coordination between sectoral treaties and assessing what further steps can be taken to strengthen the integrated protection of the oceans.

Finally, Chapter 11 will provide an overview of the current state of the overall legal framework for the protection of the marine environment, which attempts to draw general conclusions both about what legal strategies and approaches have been successfully employed to offer substantial protection to the oceans and what main challenges remain for the international community in tackling this important issue.

2

The United Nations Convention on the Law of the Sea and the Protection and Preservation of the Marine Environment

2.1 Introduction

The United Nations Convention on the Law of the Sea (UNCLOS), adopted on 10 December 1982, is, without doubt, the most important instrument in the modern law of the sea.[1] The Convention took over a decade to negotiate and just as long to enter into force. It finally did so on 16 November 1994. Today it is binding on 167 States from all over the world.[2] UNCLOS was adopted as a package deal so that States are bound to comply with all aspects of the legal regime and are not permitted to make reservations to any substantive rules in the Convention.[3] As a treaty instrument, the Convention is only binding on those entities that have become a Party to it.[4] Nevertheless, UNCLOS has a much wider importance. Many of its provisions are widely accepted as reflecting customary international law, at least insofar as the 'traditional uses of the oceans are concerned'.[5] Indeed, it has been suggested that some of the provisions were already influencing the development of customary international law, even prior to the conclusion of the Convention.[6] The widespread acceptance of UNCLOS and its place at the centre of the modern law of the sea mean that it is often described as 'the constitution for the oceans',[7] and it is generally

---

[1] See 1982 United Nations Convention on the Law of the Sea (UNCLOS) (EIF 16 November 1994).

[2] UN website, <http://www.un.org/depts/los/reference_files/chronological_lists_of_ratifications. htm#The%20United%20Nations%20Convention%20on%20the%20Law%20of%20the%20Sea>. The European Union is also a Party to the Convention.

[3] UNCLOS, Article 309.

[4] See 1969 Vienna Convention on the Law of Treaties (VCLT) (EIF 27 January 1980), Article 34.

[5] See 'United States Ocean Policy' (1983) 77 *AJIL* 619–23, in which the president of the United States confirmed that the United States would not become a signatory to the Convention, owing to its concerns over the Convention's deep-seabed mining provisions, but it would 'accept and act in accordance with the balance of interests relating to the traditional uses of the oceans—such as navigation and overflight'.

[6] See e.g. A de Mestrel, 'The Prevention of Pollution of the Marine Environment Arising from Offshore Mining and Drilling' (1979) 20 *HILJ* 469, 496.

[7] T Koh, 'A Constitution for the Oceans'; <http://www.un.org/depts/los/convention_agreements/ texts/koh_english.pdf>.

viewed as 'the legal framework within which all activities in the oceans and seas must be carried out'.[8]

By adopting UNCLOS, the international community set out to establish 'a legal order for the seas and oceans which will facilitate international communication, and will promote the peaceful uses of the seas and oceans, the equitable and efficient utilization of their resources, the conservation of their living resources, and the study, protection and preservation of the marine environment'.[9] It can be seen from this recital from the preamble to UNCLOS that the protection of the marine environment is explicitly listed as one of the objectives of the Convention. Indeed, UNCLOS was described at the time of its entry into force as 'the strongest comprehensive environmental treaty now in existence or likely to emerge for quite some time'.[10] It is in light of its central place in the modern law of the sea that it is vital to understand both the origins of UNCLOS and the manner in which it addresses the protection of the marine environment. This chapter will consider the negotiation of UNCLOS and its general structure and content. It will also consider the interrelationship between UNCLOS and other treaties and international instruments for the protection of the marine environment.

2.2 The Negotiation of UNCLOS

When the international community met in Stockholm in 1972 to consider what needed to be done to offer stronger protection to the world's environment,[11] discussions were already underway at the United Nations on reform of the international law of the sea more generally. By this time, there was widespread dissatisfaction with the existing treaties on the law of the sea that had been concluded in 1958.[12] These instruments had attracted varying degrees of support,[13] and many States, particularly those that had recently acquired independence, were concerned about the balance of rights and obligations contained in the treaties.[14] It was also clear that the 1958 treaties were deficient with regard to marine environmental protection. Their approach to the protection of the marine environment had been described as 'fragmentary',[15] and they were criticized as failing to address the wide-scale threats to the

---

[8] For example, UNGA Resolution 69/245 (2014) preamble. UNCLOS, preamble.
[10] J Stevenson and B Oxman, 'The Future of the United Nations Convention on the Law of the Sea' (1994) 88 *AJIL* 488, 496.
[11] See Chapter 1.
[12] The First United Nations Conference on the Law of the Sea adopted four substantive treaties: 1958 Convention on the High Seas (EIF 30 September 1962); 1958 Convention on the Territorial Sea and Contiguous Zone (EIF 10 September 1964); 1958 Convention on the Continental Shelf (EIF 10 June 1964); 1958 Convention on Conservation of Living Resources on the High Seas (EIF 20 March 1966).
[13] See RR Churchill and AV Lowe, *The Law of the Sea* (3rd edn: MUP 1997) Appendix 2, Table B.
[14] See J Harrison, *Making the Law of the Sea* (CUP 2011) 35–7.
[15] DM Johnston, 'The Environmental Law of the Sea: Historical Development', in DM Johnston (ed.), *The Environmental Law of the Sea* (IUCN, 1981) 49; see also A Yankov, 'The Significance of the 1982 Convention on the Law of the Sea for the Protection of the Marine Environment and the Promotion of Marine Science and Technology—Third Committee Issues', in BH Oxman and AW Koers (eds), *The 1982 Convention on the Law of the Sea* (Law of the Sea Institute 1984) 76.

oceans.[16] This may not be surprising given that environmental protection had not attracted as much attention at the international level at the time of their negotiation. By the 1970s, however, this was no longer the case, and, therefore, the decision of the United Nations General Assembly to negotiate a new comprehensive treaty on the law of the sea provided an opportunity to revisit the protection of the marine environment.

The 'preservation of the marine environment (including, inter alia, the prevention of pollution)' was identified as a key issue to be addressed when the Third United Nations Conference on the Law of the Sea was convened in 1973.[17] Indeed, before the negotiations had even commenced, States attending the Stockholm Conference on the Human Environment had urged full participation in the upcoming law of the sea negotiations 'with a view to bringing all significant sources of marine pollution within the marine environment ... under appropriate controls'.[18] Delegates at Stockholm were in agreement that:[19]

the capacity of the sea to assimilate wastes and render them harmless and its ability to regenerate natural resources are not unlimited. Proper management is required and measures to prevent and control marine pollution must be regarded as an essential element in this management of the oceans and seas and their natural resources.

This statement represents an important recognition of the shortcomings of previous attempts to regulate harmful activities and it has been heralded as a 'paradigm shift' in the approach to marine environmental protection. According to this view, 'pollution can no longer be regarded as an implicit freedom of the seas; rather its diligent control from all sources is a matter of comprehensive legal obligation affecting the marine environment as a whole....'[20]

In light of the increase in environmental consciousness, it is not surprising that the protection of the marine environment received a significant amount of attention in the work of the Third United Nations Conference on the Law of the Sea. Whilst the protection of the marine environment was expressly allocated to the third committee of the Conference,[21] in practice, the topic permeated the work of all three main negotiating committees set up to draft the substance of the new legal framework.[22] As a result, provisions on the protection of the marine environment can be found throughout the final text of UNCLOS. The centrality of this

---

[16] Few provisions dealt with environmental issues, but see 1958 Convention on the High Seas, Articles 24 (pollution by oil discharge from ships) and 25 (pollution from radioactive materials); 1958 Convention on the Continental Shelf, Article 5(7) (protection of living resources from harmful agents). The 1958 Convention on Fishing and Conservation of the Living Resources of the High Seas also required the formulation of 'conservation programmes', although its primary concern was the 'supply of food for human consumption'; Article 2.

[17] UNGA Resolution 2748(XXV)C (1970) para. 2.

[18] Stockholm Action Plan (1972) Recommendation 86(e).

[19] Ibid, Recommendation 92(a).

[20] P Birnie, AE Boyle, and C Redgwell, *International Law and the Environment* (3rd edn, OUP 2009) 383. See also de Mestrel (n6) 498.

[21] Yankov (n15) 72.

[22] CA Fleischer, 'Significance of the Convention: Second Committee Issues', in BH Oxman and AW Koers (eds), *The 1982 Convention on the Law of the Sea* (Law of the Sea Institute 1984) 54–5.

topic to the reformed law of the sea is, however, reflected in the fact that Part XII of the Convention, containing forty-six provisions, is dedicated to the protection and preservation of the marine environment.

Whilst the Convention sets an important benchmark for State action, it is important to understand the nature of the legal framework established by UNCLOS. The Convention does not purport to set out detailed rules and standards concerning the protection of the marine environment. Indeed, such a task would have been almost impossible if UNCLOS were to achieve its aim of addressing all sources of marine pollution; any rules and regulations would have quickly become outdated. Rather, UNCLOS has been described as an 'umbrella' convention,[23] meaning that it is 'assigned the role of a basic and coordinating international legal instrument in respect to all other agreements dealing with particular sources of marine pollution or applicable to specific areas of ocean space'.[24] It performs this function in a number of ways, which will be explored in the following sections.

2.3 The Nature of the UNCLOS Legal Framework

2.3.1 UNCLOS as a jurisdictional framework for maritime activities

First and foremost, UNCLOS establishes the jurisdictional framework that dictates which States have the power to adopt and enforce rules and standards for maritime activities in all ocean areas.[25] This jurisdictional framework includes powers to adopt and enforce legislation relating to the protection of the marine environment.

Who will be able to prescribe and enforce rules on marine environmental protection will depend upon the nature and location of a particular activity. Generally speaking, UNCLOS makes a basic distinction between areas within national jurisdiction and those beyond it. Whilst the precise functioning of the jurisdictional framework is a topic that will be addressed in detail throughout this book, the key features will be explained below.

Coastal States were among the strongest advocates for introducing new environmental provisions in UNCLOS.[26] As a result, the Convention confers important powers on coastal States to adopt and enforce environmental rules and regulations. It does so through the establishment of a system of maritime zones conferring particular competences on the coastal State.

[23] See M Nordquist et al (eds), *United Nations Convention on the Law of the Sea 1982: A Commentary—Vol. IV* (Martinus Nijhoff 1991) 21, 423. See further E Franckx, 'Regional Marine Environment Protection Regimes in the Context of UNCLOS' (1998) 13 *IJMCL* 307, 311; AE Boyle, 'Further Development of the Law of the Sea Convention: Mechanisms for Change' (2005) 54 *ICLQ* 563–84.

[24] Yankov (n15) 73.

[25] See, generally, P Allott, 'Power Sharing and the Law of the Sea' (1983) 77 *AJIL* 1.

[26] See Stockholm Action Plan (1972), Recommendation 92(a), noting 'the particular interest of coastal states in the marine environment'. Coastal States formed a special interest group at the Conference; see M Nordquist et al (eds), *United Nations Convention on the Law of the Sea 1982: A Commentary—Vol. I* (Martinus Nijhoff 1985) 70–2. However, between the coastal States, there were divisions about the importance to be attached to marine environmental protection; see Nordquist et al (n23) 12.

First, UNCLOS permits the coastal State to establish a territorial sea up to twelve nautical miles from baselines drawn around its coast.[27] The coastal State has sovereignty over the water column, seabed, and airspace within the territorial sea, with only some limitations on its powers.[28] The coastal State can, therefore, adopt and enforce legislation on a broad range of issues in this maritime zone, including the power to adopt measures for 'the conservation of the living resources of the sea' and 'the preservation of the environment of the coastal State and the prevention, reduction and control of pollution thereof'.[29] The powers of a coastal State are subject to some limitations when it comes to the regulation of ships in innocent passage through their territorial sea,[30] although it is notable that any ship causing 'willful and serious pollution' is deemed not to be in innocent passage and, thus, subject to the full jurisdiction of the coastal State.[31]

Second, UNCLOS permits the coastal State to establish an exclusive economic zone (EEZ) up to 200 nautical miles from its baselines.[32] Within this maritime zone, the coastal State has more limited powers to regulate certain activities relating to economic activity connected to the coastal State. Significantly, this includes, inter alia, powers relating to the conservation and management of living and non-living resources found in the water column and in or on the seabed.[33] The control of environmental effects of these activities would also fall within the jurisdiction of the coastal State. Yet, the coastal State also has a broader jurisdiction to regulate the protection and preservation of the marine environment.[34] This extension of coastal State competence recognizes that activities that take place beyond the territorial sea can have significant impacts on the environment of the coastal State, which has an interest in controlling such effects. Nevertheless, the exercise of powers by the coastal State in the EEZ is subject to a more complex set of limitations and safeguards in order to ensure that they do not exceed their authority and impede other legitimate uses of the seas.[35] In the context of marine environmental protection, this means that a balance must be struck between the interests of the coastal State and other States.

Third, the coastal State also has certain powers over activities taking place on the seabed on the continental shelf beyond 200 nautical miles, including drilling for oil and gas, mining for minerals, and fishing for sedentary species.[36] The coastal State may exercise exclusive control over such activities, including the environmental regulation thereof. This power does not affect activities taking place in the water column, however, which are subject to the legal regime of the high seas, discussed below.[37]

---

[27] UNCLOS, Article 3. On the drawing of baselines, see Ibid, Articles 5–14. See also the provisions on archipelagic States, which permit the drawing of baselines around the outer islands of an archipelago and to exercise sovereignty within the sea areas enclosed by the baselines, subject to certain safeguards; Ibid, Articles 46–54.

[28] Ibid, Article 2.   [29] Ibid, Article 21(1)(d) and (e).

[30] For a full discussion, see Chapter 6.   [31] UNCLOS, Article 19(2)(h).

[32] Ibid, Articles 55 and 57.   [33] Ibid, Article 56(a).   [34] Ibid, Articles 55 and 57.

[35] See, e.g. Ibid, Articles 58(1) and 68.   [36] Ibid, Article 77.   [37] Ibid, Article 78.

In areas beyond the jurisdiction of a coastal State, no single State has overall competence for the protection and preservation of the marine environment. Rather, these areas can be considered as 'the global commons'.[38] These areas pose particular governance and enforcement challenges because they are open to all States. Distinct regimes apply to the regulation of activities in the water column and activities on the seabed, encapsulating different approaches to management.

On the one hand, the regulation of activities on or in the water column is subject to the doctrine of freedom of the high seas,[39] which is underpinned by the principle of exclusive flag State jurisdiction.[40] It does not follow that States are free to pollute, or in the case of living resources, to over-exploit, but rather that each individual State must take action to regulate activities taking place under their control and no other State is allowed to interfere. It follows that coordinated action for the protection of the marine environment on the high seas is only possible if all States are able to agree upon common rules and standards. Furthermore, in principle, enforcement of international rules can only be carried out by the flag State of a vessel, unless States have agreed on cooperative enforcement mechanisms. This is a major challenge for developing effective international rules, in particular, relating to the regulation of shipping and fishing on the high seas, as will be discussed in Chapters 6 and 7.

On the other hand, the regulation of seabed activities beyond national jurisdiction is subject to a regime of the common heritage of mankind, which means that seabed activities in this area are managed by an international organization, authorized to act on behalf of the international community as a whole.[41] The Convention establishes the International Seabed Authority, which is granted the power to adopt regulations for all seabed activities, including the impact of such activities on the marine environment. This regime facilitates minimum standards that apply to all actors involved in seabed activities beyond national jurisdiction. The Authority is also given a power to enforce these regulations directly against these actors, whether they are States or private companies. This regime will be explained in more detail in Chapter 8.

There is some debate over the legal status of sedentary marine species living on the seabed beyond national jurisdiction. There is increasing interest in these species because of the opportunities to exploit their genetic material. Some States argue that these creatures are part of the common heritage of mankind, because of their location on the floor of the deep seabed.[42] Others argue that the deep-seabed regime was only intended to apply to the mining of non-living resources.[43] Both sides in this debate draw upon various provisions of UNCLOS to support their views, although in reality this question was not at the forefront of the drafters' minds. States have undertaken to conclude a new international agreement to address this ambiguity,[44]

---

[38] See Chapter 1.   [39] Ibid, Article 87.   [40] Ibid, Article 92(1).
[41] Ibid, Articles 136–7, 145.
[42] See e.g. Report of the Ad Hoc Open-ended Informal Working Group to Study Issues Relating to the Conservation and Sustainable Use of Marine Biological Diversity Beyond Areas of National Jurisdiction and Co-Chairs' Summary of Discussions, Document A/67/945 (2012) Annex, para. 15.
[43] Ibid.   [44] UNGA Resolution 69/292 (2015).

although negotiations to date suggest that deep divisions remain.[45] Whatever position is ultimately adopted, it is clear that any activity to harvest sedentary species on the seabed beyond national jurisdiction must be guided by the general principle to protect and preserve the marine environment.[46]

2.3.2 UNCLOS as a source of general principles relating to the protection of the marine environment

As well as conferring powers on States to regulate the environmental impacts of certain activities, UNCLOS also establishes general principles relevant to the protection of the marine environment, which guide States when exercising their jurisdiction within the jurisdictional framework described above.

Article 192, the opening provision of Part XII, provides that 'states have the obligation to protect and preserve the marine environment'.[47] According to one of the individuals involved in drafting the text, 'it is the first time that a legal rule of this kind has been incorporated in a multilateral treaty of a universal character'[48] and it 'should be considered as an important step in the codification and progressive development of the law of the sea'.[49] Article 192 is drafted in such a way that its status as a rule can be debated. Some tribunals have upheld the normative status of Article 192, suggesting that it imposes a distinct duty on States Parties.[50] However, it is difficult to see how a court or tribunal could give any substantive content to the highly ambiguous terms of Article 192 without overstepping its judicial role and straying into law-making. Indeed, those tribunals that have sought to interpret Article 192 as a provision with norm-creating character have gone on to say that 'the content of the general obligation in Article 192 is further detailed in the subsequent provisions of Part XII',[51] suggesting that Article 192 cannot be interpreted and applied in isolation. It is for this reason that Article 192 is perhaps better characterized as a statement of principle,[52] whose primary function is to determine the scope of Part XII as a whole. In this respect, several elements of Article 192 are significant in guiding the interpretation and application of the other provisions in Part XII.

First, Article 192 makes clear that Part XII applies to threats to the whole marine environment. There is no definition of the marine environment in UNCLOS, but there is little doubt that it includes the entire water column and the seabed, at least beyond the baselines from which States measure their maritime entitlements.[53]

---

[45] See issues requiring further discussions, in Chair's Overview of the Second Session of the Preparatory Committee (2016), Annex 1, Appendix 1.

[46] See also ibid, Appendix 5. To some extent, the debate is academic, as it is generally recognized that the environmental impacts of genetic sampling are minimal given the small sample sizes and the one-off nature of the activity. Impacts are only likely to increase if it were necessarily to harvest large amounts of a specimen because it was impossible to carry out laboratory culture. See the discussion in *Intersessional Workshops Aimed at Improving Understanding of the Issues and Clarifying Key Questions as an Input to the Work of the Working Group*, Document A/AC.276/6 (2013), para. 29.

[47] UNCLOS, Article 192.   [48] Yankov (n15) 75.   [49] Ibid, 76.

[50] *South China Sea Arbitration (Merits)* (2016) para. 940.   [51] Ibid, para. 942.

[52] Nordquist et al describe the reference to the protection and preservation as 'a long-term policy' (n23, 12).

[53] Estuaries also fall within the definition of the marine environment; see UNCLOS, Article 1(4).

Furthermore, the principle applies to areas within and beyond national jurisdiction[54] and it can even be applied to areas in which jurisdiction is contested.[55] There is less clarity about whether the duty to protect the marine environment extends to the air space above the water column. In this regard, several proposals advanced during the negotiating process included air space above the water column within the definition of the *marine environment*, although none of them were adopted. Nevertheless, even if one accepts that UNCLOS 'does not address directly the problem of pollution of the atmosphere itself',[56] it explicitly covers 'pollution of the marine environment from or through the atmosphere',[57] thereby recognizing the complex interactions between the atmosphere and the oceans.[58]

Second, Article 192 covers all types of harm to the marine environment. As will be shown below, many of the provisions in Part XII are focused on the prevention of pollution. However, this is only one type of impact that can cause harm to the marine environment. The principle in Article 192 is wide enough to cover other potential impacts, such as physical harm, destruction, or alteration of the marine environment and its components, whether or not it falls within the definition of pollution.[59] This has been confirmed by the International Tribunal for the Law of the Sea (ITLOS), which held that 'living resources and marine life are part of the marine environment'[60] and 'relevant conservation measures concerning living resources ... constitute an integral element in the protection and preservation of the marine environment'.[61] Another arbitral tribunal has similarly determined that the general obligation to protect and preserve the marine environment under Article 192 'may be broadly enough worded to include the obligation to protect and preserve marine biodiversity'.[62] It follows that the substantive provisions of Part XII should be interpreted broadly where possible.

Third, Article 192 refers to both protection and preservation of the marine environment. As interpreted by the Tribunal in the *South China Sea Arbitration*, the drafting of the provision calls on States to both protect the oceans from future threats, as well as to take positive action with a view to 'maintaining and improving its present condition'.[63]

Finally, the obligation described in Article 192 applies to and is owed to all States. Indeed, the obligation in Article 192 is arguably *erga omnes* in character, meaning

---

[54] *South China Sea Arbitration (Merits)* (2016) para. 940.
[55] *South China Sea Arbitration (Jurisdiction and Admissibility)* (2015) para. 408.
[56] Nordquist et al (n23) 212–13.
[57] UNCLOS, Articles 194(3)(a), 212, 222. For further discussion, see Chapter 8.
[58] See e.g. PS Liss and MT Johnson, *Ocean-Atmosphere Interactions of Gases and Particles* (Springer 2014).
[59] Molenaar is amongst several authors who have suggested that physical disturbance could be included within the definition of pollution; see EJ Molenaar, *Coastal State Jurisdiction over Vessel-Source Pollution* (Kluwer Law International 1998) 17.
[60] *Advisory Opinion in response to the Request submitted by the Sub-regional Fisheries Commission* (2015) para. 216.
[61] Ibid, para. 120.
[62] *South China Sea Arbitration (Jurisdiction and Admissibility)* (2015) para. 284.
[63] *South China Sea Arbitration (Merits)* (2016) para. 941.

that it is owed to the international community as a whole.[64] Such a reading of the principle would support the view that any State could invoke a violation of the provisions on the protection of the marine environment, even if they have not suffered individual harm.[65] This conclusion would appear to be supported implicitly by the recent *South China Sea Arbitration*, in which the Philippines brought claims relating to environmental harm caused by Chinese activities at various locations throughout the South China Sea. The Tribunal held that it had jurisdiction over these claims, even though the Philippines was not alleging that it had suffered harm within its own maritime zones. Indeed, the Tribunal emphasized that:

because the environmental obligations in Part XII apply to States irrespective of the where the alleged harmful activities took place, its jurisdiction is not dependent on the question of sovereignty over a particular feature, on a prior determination of the status of any maritime feature, on the existence of an entitlement by China or the Philippines to an exclusive economic zone in the area or on the prior delimitation of any overlapping entitlements.[66]

Thus, the Tribunal did not require the Philippines to demonstrate that it had been specially affected by the environmental harm.

Article 193 of UNCLOS can also be considered to establish a general principle, which is relevant to the interpretation of Part XII as a whole. It provides that 'states have the sovereign right to exploit their natural resources pursuant to their environmental policies and in accordance with their duty to protect and preserve the marine environment'. The importance of this principle is that it emphasizes that marine environmental protection is not an isolated policy goal, but rather that the protection of the marine environment must be pursued in tandem with the development of marine resources. In other words, UNCLOS calls for decisions on oceans management to take into account both economic and environmental considerations. From this perspective, this principle can be seen as a precursor to the emergence of sustainable development as an overarching policy goal in later international instruments. The need for such a balance is further reflected in the substantive rules in Part XII discussed in the following sections.

Of course, UNCLOS is not the sole source of principles that are relevant to the development of the law in this area. As discussed in Chapter 1, there are a number of other international instruments promoting important concepts and principles, many of which have emerged since the conclusion of UNCLOS itself, including common but differentiated responsibilities, the precautionary approach, the ecosystems approach, and the participatory approach. These concepts and principles are not only relevant for States when developing specific treaties and instruments for the protection of the marine environment; they can also be used to guide the

---

[64] On obligations *erga omnes*, see International Law Commission (ILC), Draft Articles on State Responsibility (UN 2001) Article 48; see also J Crawford (ed.), *The International Law Commission's Articles on State Responsibility: Introduction, Text and Commentaries* (CUP 2002) 278, using the example of 'an obligation aimed at protection of the marine environment in the collective interest' as an *erga omnes* obligation that could be invoked not only by a coastal State specially affected by a breach but also by any State as a member of the international community.

[65] Crawford (n64) 278. [66] *South China Sea Arbitration (Merits)* (2016) para. 927.

interpretation and application of UNCLOS itself. Indeed, the international community has explicitly called for the Convention to be implemented in a precautionary and anticipatory manner, taking into account integrated management and sustainable development.[67] The influence of these principles will, therefore, be considered when discussing the interpretation of the substantive and procedural rules for the protection of the marine environment found in UNCLOS.

2.3.3 UNCLOS as a source of substantive rules on the protection of the marine environment

UNCLOS contains a number of provisions that impose general rules of conduct on States to protect and preserve the marine environment, in furtherance of the general principles discussed above. Some of these rules relate to the protection of the marine environment generally, whereas other rules relate to specific activities.

Many of the provisions in Part XII are explicitly concerned with the prevention, reduction, and control of pollution of the marine environment. In this regard, Article 194(1) contains a general obligation, requiring that:

States shall take, individually or jointly as appropriate, all measures consistent with this Convention that are necessary to prevent, reduce and control pollution of the marine environment from any source, using for this purpose the best practicable means at their disposal and in accordance with their capabilities, and they shall endeavour to harmonize their policies in this connection.

Article 194(1) must be read in light of the definition of pollution of the marine environment used in the Convention, which was adopted from text originally developed by the Group of Experts on the Scientific Aspects of Marine Environmental Protection (GESAMP)[68] and which covers all threats posed by:

the introduction by man, directly or indirectly, of substances or energy into the marine environment, including estuaries, which results or is likely to result in such deleterious effects as harm to living resources and marine life, hazards to human health, hindrance to marine activities, including fishing and other legitimate uses of the sea, impairment of quality for use of sea water and reduction in amenities.[69]

It is clear that this provision is broad in scope and applicable to all sources of pollution. It covers what have been termed the classical contaminants,[70] such as sewage, heavy metals, persistent organic substances, petroleum hydrocarbons, and radionuclides, as well as more recently discovered threats to the marine environment such

---

[67] See e.g. Agenda 21 (1992) para. 17.1.

[68] General Principles for Assessment and Control of Marine Pollution, *Report of the United Nations Conference on the Human Environment*, UN Document A/Conf.48/14/Rev.1 (1972) 73. A similar definition of pollution is used in other instruments, such as the 1972 Convention for the Prevention of Marine Pollution by Dumping of Wastes and other Matter (EIF 30 August 1975), Article 1.

[69] UNCLOS, Article 1(4).

[70] GESAMP, *Protecting the Oceans from Land-based Activities*, GESAMP Reports and Studies No. 71 (2001) 9.

as heat[71] or noise.[72] Indeed, when drafting the forerunner of this text, GESAMP was explicit in seeking to ensure that 'the development and implementation of [pollution] control should be sufficiently flexible to ... take into account the fact that a number of new and hitherto unsuspected pollutants are bound to be brought to light'.[73] As a result, the definition is highly adaptable and it can be interpreted in a manner that allows UNCLOS to be applied to new threats to the oceans, such as climate change and ocean acidification[74] or alien invasive species.[75] This flexibility has meant that UNCLOS has been able to evolve to meet new challenges, and it has retained its place at the centre of the legal framework for the protection of the marine environment.

The obligation in Article 194(1) also has a broad geographical coverage and it applies wherever pollution takes place. UNCLOS expressly confirms the classical rule of international law that States shall take adequate measures to prevent significant harm to other States or to areas beyond national jurisdiction, encapsulated by the Latin maxim *sic utere tuo ut alienam non laedas*.[76] However, the obligation in Article 194(1) would appear to be broader and it would cover any pollution to the marine environment, whether or not it is transboundary in nature. Such a conclusion is also supported by the idea that the protection of the marine environment is the common concern of humankind.[77]

The general obligation in Article 194 is supplemented by rules that are more specific, requiring States to adopt national rules and standards to tackle specific sources of marine pollution, including pollution from land-based sources,[78] through the atmosphere,[79] from dumping,[80] from ships,[81] from seabed activities within national jurisdiction,[82] and from seabed mining in the Area.[83] These important provisions impose general obligations on States to adopt and enforce national legislation to regulate all of the principal sources of marine pollution. Each category of pollution is subject to slightly different requirements, which will be considered in more detail in the following chapters. The nature of the scheme contained in the Convention would seem to suggest that the categories of sources in the Convention are mutually exclusive. In other words, a particular activity can only fall within the scope of one of these provisions. In practice, this has led to some difficult boundary issues about

---

[71] Ibid, 20. See also Chapter 9.

[72] See HM Dotinga and AG Oude Elferink, 'Acoustic Pollution in the Oceans: The Search for Legal Standards' (2000) 31 *ODIL* 151, 158–9; K Scott, 'International Regulation of Undersea Noise' (2004) 53 *ICLQ* 287–324. See further Chapters 6 and 8.

[73] General Principles for Assessment and Control of Marine Pollution (n68) Principle 14.

[74] AE Boyle, 'Law of the Sea Perspectives on Climate Change' (2012) 27 *IJMCL* 831, 832. See also Report on the Work of the United Nations Open-Ended Informal Consultative Process on Oceans and the Law of the Sea at Its Fourteenth Meeting (2013) para. 9. See also the discussion in Chapter 9.

[75] Thus, Molenaar argues that 'the expression "substances" would also comprise the introduction of alien organisms into the marine environment' (n59, 17). For a more detailed discussion of alien invasive species from ships' ballast water, see Chapter 6.

[76] UNCLOS, Article 194(2).   [77] See Chapter 1.

[78] UNCLOS, Article 207; see Chapter 4.   [79] Ibid, Article 213; see Chapter 4.

[80] Ibid, Article 210; see Chapter 5.   [81] Ibid, Article 211; see Chapter 6.

[82] Ibid, Article 208; see Chapter 8.   [83] Ibid, Article 209; see Chapter 8.

how an activity is to be classified and, thus, what degree of regulation is required from a State.[84]

It is important to appreciate that none of these provisions can be understood as introducing a complete prohibition on all pollution of the marine environment. Rather, the relevant UNCLOS provisions tend to refer to the 'prevention, reduction and control' of pollution,[85] which leaves some flexibility as to the precise measures that States must take. This broad formulation is best understood as imposing a due diligence obligation, which means that States cannot be held responsible for harm if they have taken all reasonable measures to prevent foreseeable damage.[86] This reflects the character of many international environmental obligations[87] and it requires both 'the adoption of appropriate rules and measures but also a certain level of vigilance in their enforcement and the exercise of administrative control applicable to the public and private operators'.[88] The content of the due diligence obligations may vary depending on the circumstances of a particular case, taking into account a number of considerations.

The nature of the risk will be a primary factor in determining what action must be taken by States. As noted by the International Law Commission (ILC) in its discussion of due diligence, 'activities which may be considered ultra-hazardous require a much higher standard of care in designing policies and a much higher degree of vigour on the part of the state to enforce them'.[89] Yet, the standard will also depend to some extent on the evidence that is available about the risks of a particular activity. The precautionary approach offers a valuable contribution to the development of the law in this context because it lowers the threshold at which States are required to take action, although it does not dictate what action must be taken, and so States retain some discretion. According to the ILC, the precautionary approach 'implies the need for States to review their obligations of prevention in a continuous manner to keep abreast of the advances in scientific knowledge'.[90] Yet, it follows that the content of the due diligence standard is inherently evolutionary and it may 'change over time as measures considered sufficiently diligent at a certain moment may become not diligent enough in light, for instance, of new scientific or technological knowledge'.[91]

Another factor that may be relevant to determining the content of the due diligence obligation is the financial and technological capabilities of the State. The need to integrate socio-economic considerations into the regime for the protection of the environment had already been foreseen by the drafters of the Stockholm Declaration, who had agreed that 'the environmental policies of all States should enhance and not adversely affect the present or future development potential of

---

[84] See e.g. the discussion in Chapter 4.   [85] UNCLOS, Article 194(1).

[86] See *South China Sea Arbitration (Merits)* (2016) para. 944.

[87] See ILC, 'Draft Articles on the Prevention of Transboundary Harm from Hazardous Activities with Commentaries' (2001-II) *YbILC* 148, 154.

[88] *Pulp Mills on the River Uruguay* (2010) para. 197.   [89] ILC (n87) 154.

[90] Ibid, 163.

[91] *Responsibilities and Obligations of States Sponsoring Persons and Entities with Respect to Activities in the Area* (2011) para. 117.

developing countries',[92] and it has become even more central to modern international environmental law through the principle of common but differentiated responsibilities.[93] This principle was already implicit in UNCLOS, which identifies the means and capabilities of a State as a factor to be taken into account in determining the responsibility of that State to prevent, reduce, and control marine pollution. To this end, Article 194 says that States must use 'the best practicable means at their disposal and in accordance with their capabilities …',[94] and it follows that not all States will necessarily bear the same level of responsibility in preventing marine environmental harm.

Not all obligations relating to the protection of the marine environment will be subject to different levels of responsibility, however, because the application of the due diligence obligation depends not only upon relevant economic and social factors but also upon the nature of the activity. As will be seen in subsequent chapters, some areas of regulation require all States to adopt the same level of protection in order to avoid the circumvention of pollution standards by the relevant actor. This reasoning applies in particular in relation to pollution from ships and from seabed mining in the Area.[95]

Another way of addressing the different abilities of countries to tackle marine pollution is encapsulated in the UNCLOS provisions encouraging the development and promotion of 'programmes of scientific, educational, technical, and other assistance to developing countries for the protection and preservation of the marine environment and the prevention, reduction and control of marine pollution', including 'training of scientific and technical personnel' and supplying them with necessary equipment and facilities'.[96] The provisions in UNCLOS on this topic are highly abstract, and, in practice, this has become an important element of international negotiations concerning the protection of the environment, generally, and the protection of the marine environment, particularly, and it is reflected in many of the treaties and instruments that are considered throughout this book.

Whilst most provisions in Part XII are explicitly concerned with pollution, the Convention also covers other potential impacts of human activities on the marine environment. This issue has gained in prominence since the emergence of the ecosystems approach as a principle of international environmental law[97] and it has been explicitly addressed in a number of treaties that have emerged since the conclusion of UNCLOS.[98] Although the Convention does not explicitly refer to marine biodiversity, it has been argued that 'the convention's objects and purposes can readily be

---

[92] Stockholm Declaration on the Human Environment (1972) Principle 11.
[93] See Chapter 1.
[94] UNCLOS, Article 194(1). Emphasis added. To this end, the Tribunal in the Chagos Arbitration recognized that Article 194(1) 'is prospective and requires only the United Kingdom's best efforts'; *Chagos Marine Protected Area Arbitration* (2015) para. 539.
[95] See the discussion in Chapters 6 and 8.
[96] UNCLOS, Article 202. This furthers principles 12 and 20 of the Stockholm Declaration.
[97] See Chapter 1.   [98] See Chapter 3.

interpreted to include measures aimed at protecting marine biodiversity'.[99] Indeed, the need to take a comprehensive approach to marine environmental protection in applying Part XII of UNCLOS has received explicit recognition in recent decisions of courts and tribunals. Thus, the Tribunal in the *Chagos MPA Arbitration* held that 'Article 194 is ... not limited to measures aimed strictly at controlling pollution and extends to measures focused primarily on conservation and the preservation of ecosystems'[100] and it interpreted the obligation under Article 194(1) to harmonize policies in connection with the prevention, reduction, and control of pollution to include harmonization of policies related to marine protected areas. Such a broad understanding is also supported by the application of the principle in Article 192.

Article 194(5) is the provision in Part XII that is most explicit in its call for States to protect broader features of the marine environment. It requires States to take necessary measures to 'protect and preserve rare or fragile ecosystems, as well as the habitat of depleted, threatened or endangered species'.[101] The Convention does not define *ecosystem*, but it has been held that the 'internationally accepted definition' in Article 2 of the Convention of Biological Diversity should be applied,[102] namely 'a dynamic complex of plant, animal and micro-organism communities and their non-living environment interacting as a functional unit'.[103] The key point of this definition is that species and habitats are integrally interrelated and a threat to any single element of the ecosystem can have drastic effects on all other parts of the community.[104] It follows that an obligation to protect ecosystems entails an obligation to protect each and every living and non-living component thereof. Although like the obligation to prevent, reduce, and control pollution, the obligation to protect ecosystems is not absolute and it only applies to those ecosystems that are 'rare' or 'fragile'. Similarly, the obligation in Article 194(5) to protect habitats only applies to habitats of 'depleted, threatened, or endangered' species. These threshold requirements are inherently flexible and they must be understood by reference to scientific information concerning the State of the marine environment. The scope of this obligation may thus vary over time. One way of understanding these terms is to refer to other international treaties under which States have agreed that a particular species is depleted, threatened, or endangered. This was the approach taken by the Tribunal in the *South China Sea Arbitration* when it held that 'CITES forms part of the general corpus of international law that informs the content of Article 192 and 194(5) of the Convention.'[105] Other instruments may play a similar role by demonstrating

---

[99] AE Boyle, 'Relationship between International Environmental Law and Other Branches of International Law', in D Bodansky et al (eds), *Oxford Handbook of International Environmental Law* (OUP 2007) 139.

[100] *Chagos Marine Protected Area Arbitration* (2015) para. 538. See *South China Sea Arbitration (Jurisdiction and Admissibility)* (2015) para. 284.

[101] UNCLOS, Article 194(5).

[102] *South China Sea Arbitration (Merits)* (2016) para. 945.

[103] See 1992 Convention on Biological Diversity (CBD) (EIF 29 December 1993).

[104] Such effects can be diverse and unpredictable; for a classic example, see RG Anthony et al, 'Bald Eagles and Sea Eagles in the Aleutian Archipelago: Indirect Effects of Trophic Cascades' (2008) 89 *Ecology* 2725–35.

[105] *South China Sea Arbitration (Merits)* (2016) para. 956.

the agreement of States that a particular habitat is rare or fragile on the one hand[106] or a specific species is depleted, threatened, or endangered on the other hand.[107] Thus, UNCLOS can be informed by the evolution of international law relating to the conservation of marine biological diversity discussed in the following chapter. It is important to understand that the use of such instruments is only a means of identifying what ecosystems, species, or habitats may require protection; the question of what measures must be taken is a question in the first instance for the State concerned.[108] Nevertheless, States will have to display a minimum degree of diligence if they are to meet the requirements of UNCLOS. For example, in the *South China Sea Arbitration*, the Tribunal held that States were under 'a due diligence obligation to prevent the harvesting of species that are recognized internationally as being at risk of extinction',[109] and China was held to have violated this obligation by failing to control its nationals which had been harvesting corals and giant clams, which were listed on Appendix II of CITES, and collecting the eggs of sea turtles that were listed on Appendix I of CITES.[110] It follows that Article 194(5) can operate as a general rule that is capable of imposing specific obligations on States to protect and preserve the marine environment. Indeed, if Article 194(5) is interpreted in light of the broader principle to protect and *preserve* the marine environment in Article 192, it is possible to conclude that this provision should also require States to take steps to prevent ecosystems from becoming rare in the first place.

2.3.4 UNCLOS as a source of procedural rules on the protection of the marine environment

There are a number of other rules in the Convention reflecting procedural steps that must be taken by States in complying with their overarching duty to protect and preserve the marine environment. As noted by the Arbitral Tribunal in the *Chagos MPA Arbitration*, 'such procedural rules may, indeed, be of equal or even greater importance than the substantive standards existing in international law'.[111] This is particularly the case where there is a lack of detailed substantive rules or standards that may regulate the conduct of an activity.

Procedural obligations apply even before an activity commences. In the first place, Article 206 of UNCLOS establishes an obligation on States to assess the potential effects of planned activities on the marine environment.[112] This provision

---

[106] See the discussion of global and regional instruments in Chapter 3.

[107] For example, the 1979 Convention on Migratory Species (EIF 1 November 1983); see Chapter 3.

[108] For example, it has been explicitly stated that the process of identifying EBSAs is a scientific one and it does not dictate the adoption of particular management measures; see e.g. DC Dunn et al, 'The Convention on Biological Diversity's Ecologically or Biologically Significant Areas: Origins, Development and Current Status' (2014) 49 *MP* 137, 143.

[109] *South China Sea Arbitration (Merits)* (2016) para. 956.

[110] Ibid, paras 957–61. The Tribunal noted (para. 961) that part of this due diligence obligation was to 'adopt rules and measures to prevent such acts and to maintain a level of vigilance in enforcing those rules and measures'.

[111] *Chagos Marine Protected Area Arbitration* (2015) para. 322.

[112] UNCLOS, Article 206.

is generally understood as a requirement to carry out an environmental impact assessment (EIA), even though that term is not expressly used. EIA is central to modern international environmental law,[113] and, at least insofar as transboundary harm is concerned, the duty has become part of customary international law.[114] The obligation under UNCLOS would appear to be broader in that it applies to significant impacts to the marine environment, whether or not they have a transboundary element, reflecting the broad reach of the principle in Article 192. It also applies to all planned activities, whether they take place within or beyond national jurisdiction.[115]

The significance of Article 206 should not be underestimated, given that EIA was only pioneered as a policy of modern environmental law in the late 1960s[116] and many jurisdictions did not introduce a general requirement of EIA until much later.[117] Nevertheless, the generality of this provision creates some difficulties for its interpretation and application.

As with the substantive obligations discussed above, the scope of this procedural obligation should be broadly interpreted to cover all potential threats to the marine environment. The duty in Article 206 explicitly applies to 'planned activities' that 'may cause substantial pollution or significant and harmful changes to the marine environment', thus taking into account not only pollution but also physical impacts and other forms of environmental degradation. These obligations apply to all phases of a planned activity, including construction, operation, and decommissioning. Yet, the obligation would appear to be primarily directed at assessment of the environmental effects of individual projects, and it is less clear whether it would also require an element of strategic environmental assessment of plans or programmes relating to planned activities.[118]

A key challenge in implementing this obligation is that the threshold for conducting an environmental assessment is unclear. Not all activities will necessarily require a full assessment, and a State will have to conduct a screening exercise in order to determine whether an EIA is necessary. Craik has suggested that the use of two threshold criteria—'substantial pollution' or 'significant and harmful changes'—could lead to confusion, but he has argued that 'given that the two standards are disjunctive, the lower standard of "significant and harmful changes" will apply in any event'.[119] However, both of these thresholds are ambiguous and they will require

---

[113] EIA is reflected in Principle 17 of the Rio Declaration, as well as in several international treaties, including 1992 Convention on Biological Diversity, Article 14(a); 1991 Espoo Convention on Environmental Impact Assessment in a Transboundary Context (EIF 10 September 1997). See further N Craik, *The International Law of Environmental Impact Assessment* (CUP 2011) 167.

[114] *Pulp Mills on the River Uruguay* (2010) para. 204; *Construction of a Road in Costa Rica along the San Juan River* (2015) para. 101.

[115] See e.g. AG Oude Elferink, 'Environmental Impact Assessment in Areas beyond National Jurisdiction' (2012) 27 *IJMCL* 449, 455.

[116] See the US National Environment Policy Act 1969, which is considered as a template for developments in other countries.

[117] For example, the European Community only adopted its EIA Directive in 1985.

[118] So-called strategic environmental assessment has emerged as a tool under other treaties, e.g. the CBD; see Chapter 3.

[119] Craik (n113) 133.

interpretation on a case-by-case basis,[120] taking into account, inter alia, the size and ecological characteristics of the affected area and the magnitude, duration, and frequency of the activity. It would seem that the drafting of this provision gives the State proposing an activity a broad discretion to determine whether there are 'reasonable grounds' for believing that an activity meets the threshold.[121] Nevertheless, it has been argued that an interpretation of Article 206 taking into account the precautionary approach would lead to 'a low evidential threshold' for triggering the obligation of EIA.[122] Indeed, there is no doubt that Article 206 sets a minimum standard that must be met, and a State must, therefore, be able at least to adduce evidence that it has addressed this threshold question, taking into account all appropriate information.[123]

When it comes to the content of the EIA, the Convention is also vague and it does not specify the range of issues that must be addressed in the process, thus adding little to customary international law on this issue.[124] Precisely what is required will depend upon the 'nature and magnitude' of the proposed activity.[125] It follows that general rules can only suggest the broad parameters for an EIA. Further guidance may be gleaned from other international instruments dealing with EIA processes. Of particular relevance here may be the United Nations Environment Programme (UNEP) Goals and Principles on Environmental Impact Assessment, which the International Court of Justice (ICJ) held in the *Pulp Mills Case* were not formally binding, but should be taken into account by States when conducting an EIA.[126] The Goals and Principles explain the basic elements that should be included in an EIA, and this instrument thus offers a benchmark against which to assess a State's conduct. Of particular significance is their recognition of the need to address 'direct, indirect, cumulative, short-term and long-term effects' on the environment,[127] thus stressing the need to gather comprehensive information before a decision is made. The Goals and Principles also indicate the need to indicate 'gaps and knowledge and uncertainty',[128] a requirement that is also supported by application of the precautionary approach and confirmed in other relevant instruments identifying good practice in this field, such as the Revised Voluntary Guidelines for the Consideration of Biodiversity in EIAs and Strategic Environmental Assessments in Marine and Coastal Areas.[129]

---

[120] Ibid.

[121] See *South China Sea Arbitration (Merits)* (2016) para. 948; see also the discussion in L Kong, 'Environmental Impact Assessment under the United Nations Convention on the Law of the Sea' (2011) 10 *CJIL* 651, 659.

[122] AE Boyle, 'The Environmental Jurisprudence of the ITLOS' (2007) 22 *IJMCL* 369, 377.

[123] This is the case under customary international law; see *Construction of a Road in Costa Rica along the San Juan River* (2015) para. 154; *South China Sea Arbitration (Merits)* (2016) paras 987–90.

[124] See *Pulp Mills on the River Uruguay* (2010) para. 205, in which the ICJ noted that 'general international law [does not] specify the scope and content of an environmental impact assessment'.

[125] Ibid.   [126] Ibid.

[127] UNEP Goals and Principles on Environmental Impact Assessment (1987), Principle 4(d).

[128] Ibid, Principle 4(f).

[129] Revised Voluntary Guidelines for the Consideration of Biodiversity in Environmental Impact Assessments and Strategic Environmental Assessments in Marine and Coastal Areas: Note by the

Article 206 introduces further uncertainty by suggesting that an assessment shall be carried out 'as far as practicable'. This language recognizes that rigorous EIA depends upon the availability of relevant information to allow an appropriate assessment to be carried out. In practice, this is one of the greatest challenges of EIA in the marine context, particularly in areas beyond national jurisdiction.[130] Often baseline data simply do not exist, which makes even modelling of effects very difficult.[131] It follows that States may be restricted in their ability to carry out a comprehensive EIA in some circumstances and the language of this provision should be seen as introducing some flexibility as to the form and content of an EIA in this situation. Nevertheless, States should use their best efforts to ensure that they assess the effects of an activity using what information is available.

Where an EIA is carried out, UNCLOS requires that the results be published or distributed through a competent international organization. This is an important, albeit often neglected, procedural step, as it provides an opportunity for other States, and other actors, to comment on the content of the assessment and to determine whether the State concerned has complied with all relevant international rules or standards on the topic. Indeed, it has been stressed that this obligation is 'absolute'.[132]

Whilst the Convention does not explicitly say that States must take into account the results of an EIA in the final decision-making process, this obligation is arguably implicit in the due diligence standard that applies to the protection and preservation of the marine environment.[133] Indeed, without such an obligation, the whole EIA process is rendered futile.

There is little doubt that Article 206 is an important provision because of its broad scope of application. In practice, however, it can only provide a basic minimum standard[134] and it has been supplemented by rules and procedures that are more specific on EIA contained in treaties or other international instruments dealing with certain sources of marine pollution or environmental degradation, as discussed throughout this book. These specific rules also identify which institutions and actors may have to be consulted or would take part in the decision-making processes. One gap that has been highlighted is the application of environmental assessments in areas beyond national jurisdiction. The remote location of such activities increases the challenges for environmental assessment, not to mention the cost.[135] Moreover, identification of relevant 'stakeholders' in areas beyond national jurisdiction is complex, and various actors and institutions may claim to have a say in the evaluation of an activity.[136] It is for these reasons that States have agreed to include this topic within the scope of a new legally binding instrument for the conservation and sustainable use of marine biological diversity in areas beyond national jurisdiction.[137] Such an instrument could potentially provide a global framework

Executive Secretary (Voluntary EIA Guidelines for Marine and Coastal Areas), Document UNEP/CBD/COP/11/23 (2012) Annex.

[130] Ibid, para. 5(c).   [131] See e.g. J Holder, *Environmental Assessment* (OUP 2004) 40.
[132] *South China Sea Arbitration (Merits)* (2016) para. 948.   [133] C.f. Holder (n131) 54.
[134] D Freestone, 'Principles Applicable to Modern Oceans Governance' (2008) 23 *IJMCL* 385, 391.
[135] Voluntary EIA Guidelines for Marine and Coastal Areas, para. 5(c).
[136] Ibid, para. 8(c).   [137] UNGA Resolution 69/292 (2015) para. 2.

in order to coordinate efforts to carry out environmental assessments[138] in different sectors and regions, building upon the general provisions in UNCLOS. States have been clear that any new instrument should not undermine UNCLOS or any other relevant global, regional, or sectoral instrument and Article 206 is thus the 'departure point for the discussion'.[139] Nevertheless, a new instrument will provide the opportunity to specify the threshold for carrying out an environmental assessment, the precise content of such an assessment, the identification of stakeholders for the purposes of consultation, and how, if at all, assessments should be reviewed and published.

Once an activity is underway, UNCLOS also requires States to 'observe, measure, evaluate and analyse, by recognized scientific methods, the risks of effects of pollution of the marine environment'.[140] The scientific information gained from monitoring can then be used to determine appropriate action when carrying out their general obligation to protect and preserve the marine environment. In this manner, the procedural obligations can inform the substantive obligations in the Convention.[141] It is important to observe that the duty to monitor the impacts of activities on the marine environment is broad and it covers activities that may not have been subject to an environmental assessment under Article 206. At the same time, the text of Article 204 is limited to monitoring the risks or effects of pollution and it does not necessarily extend to wider impacts on marine biological diversity. One could argue that such an obligation was nevertheless implicit in other provisions, including the overarching principle in Article 192 and the obligation to protect rare and fragile ecosystems in Article 194(5). In practice, any lacuna is likely to have been filled by subsequent developments in international law relating to the conservation and sustainable use of biological diversity, discussed in the next chapter.

2.3.5 UNCLOS as a framework for future normative development

The principles and rules relating to the protection and preservation of the marine environment described above provide general guidance to States on what steps they must take to protect the marine environment. However, as has already been noted, many of these provisions are ambiguous and require further elaboration in order to provide more direction to States on what action they should take to protect the marine environment. It is for this reason that UNCLOS encourages further law-making activities in the field of marine environmental protection.

To this end, Article 197 contains a general duty for States to 'cooperate on a global basis and, as appropriate, on a regional basis, directly or through international

---

[138] It is possible that the new instruments will cover strategic environmental assessments, although this remains under discussion; see e.g. *Chair's Overview of the Second Session of the Preparatory Committee* (2016), Annex, Appendix 3.

[139] Ibid.

[140] UNCLOS, Article 204(1). Monitoring has also been held to be part of the due diligence standard; see *Pulp Mills on the River Uruguay* (2010) para. 197.

[141] The link between due diligence and EIA was made by the ICJ; ibid, para. 204.

organizations, in formulating and elaborating international rules, standards and recommended practices and procedures consistent with this Convention, for the protection and preservation of the marine environment...'.[142] This provision is central to the overarching framework established by UNCLOS and, as explained by ITLOS, 'the duty to cooperate is a fundamental principle in the prevention of pollution of the marine environment under Part XII of the Convention and general international law'.[143]

The drafters of UNCLOS refrained from establishing a single organization that was responsible for all aspects of oceans management. Rather, it was anticipated that various institutions would be involved in developing the legal framework for the protection of the marine environment. It is for this reason that those provisions in UNCLOS calling for cooperation in law-making tend to make a general reference to 'competent international organizations', indicating that States can turn to a range of bodies to address these issues.[144]

The work of many United Nations bodies and agencies has been particularly important in this field, including the International Maritime Organization,[145] the Food and Agriculture Organization,[146] UNEP,[147] and the United Nations General Assembly.[148] These global bodies have played an essential role because they are able to bring together all relevant actors within a single forum. Moreover, the specialized nature of some of these institutions means that particular expertise can be brought to bear on a problem.[149] Institutionalization of law-making in this manner has facilitated the emergence of global networks of experts in so-called epistemic communities, dedicated to tackling a particular problem or issue.[150] The role of these institutions in developing the international legal framework for the protection of the marine environment will be explored in detail throughout the subsequent chapters.

In addition, the Convention also explicitly recognizes a role for regional institutions in relation to some types of activities. Regional institutions can serve different functions, including promoting the implementation of global instruments at the regional level and developing specific regional rules that supplement global rules.[151] The advantage of regional institutions is their ability to reflect the political, legal, and ecological needs of a particular area, making cooperation easier to achieve compared with the global level, where 'a more diverse group of

---

[142] UNCLOS, Article 197.   [143] *MOX Plant Case* (2001) para. 82.

[144] See Nordquist et al (n23) 14. The one exception relates to pollution from ships, where the Convention refers to the competent international organization. For a discussion, see Chapter 6.

[145] See Chapters 6 and 9.   [146] See Chapter 7.   [147] See Chapters 4 and 8.

[148] See Chapters 7 and 10.

[149] See FL Kirgis, 'Specialized Law-Making' in CC Joyner (ed.), *The United Nations and International Law* (CUP 1997) 65–94.

[150] P Haas, 'Do Regimes Matter? Epistemic Communities and Mediterranean Pollution Control' (1989) 43 *IO* 377–403.

[151] See generally Y Tanaka, 'Four Models of Interaction between Global and Regional Legal Frameworks on Environmental Protection against Marine Pollution: The Case of the Marine Arctic' (2016) 30 *Ocean Yearbook* 345–76.

stakeholders with conflicting interests makes negotiations thornier'.[152] There is no single definition of what is meant by a 'region' in this context, but rather the question must be 'defined by the context in which the issue arises', influenced by ecology, geography, and politics.[153] Two particular types of regional bodies have emerged as key actors in the international legal framework for the protection of the marine environment. On the one hand, regional fisheries bodies are central to the development of rules relating to the conservation and management of marine living resources.[154] On the other hand, regional seas bodies play a vital role in developing policies, rules, and standards for the prevention, reduction, and control—and even elimination—of marine pollution, as well as the conservation of marine biological diversity.[155] Alongside autonomous regional seas bodies operating in the North-East Atlantic and the Baltic Sea, regional cooperation in relation to pollution control has been actively promoted through UNEP's Regional Seas Programme,[156] which covers fourteen regions: Black Sea, Wider Caribbean, Caspian Sea,[157] East Asian Seas, Eastern Africa, South Asian Seas, ROPME Sea Area (Persian Gulf), Mediterranean, North-East Pacific, North-West Pacific, Red Sea and Gulf of Aden, South-East Pacific, South Pacific, and Western Africa.[158] The activity of these bodies is relevant to several of the sources of marine environmental degradation that are considered in this book, and whilst the effectiveness of some of the regional institutions has been called into question,[159] it is clear that they are a key part of the institutional framework that is required to implement Part XII of UNCLOS.

UNCLOS not only codifies the duty to cooperate, but it also governs the relationship between any resulting agreement and the general legal framework. In the first place, UNCLOS provides that:

the provisions of [Part XII] are without prejudice to the specific obligations assumed by States under special conventions and agreements concluded previously which relate to the protection and preservation of the marine environment and to agreements which may be concluded in furtherance of the general principles set forth in this Convention.[160]

---

[152] J Rochette et al, 'The regional approach to the conservation and sustainable use of marine biodiversity in areas beyond national jurisdiction' (2014) 49 *MP* 109, 109.

[153] Birnie, Boyle, and Redgwell (n20) 391.   [154] See Chapter 6.

[155] See Chapter 3.

[156] See P Hulm, 'The Regional Seas Program: What Fate for UNEP's Crown Jewels?' (1983) 12 *Ambio* 2–13.

[157] The precise status of the Caspian Sea is contested; see EJ Molenaar, 'Port and Coastal States', in DR Rothwell et al (eds), *Oxford Handbook on the Law of the Sea* (OUP 2015) 281. It is however listed by UNEP as part of its regional seas programme and it follows the model of many other regional seas bodies.

[158] UNEP website: http://web.unep.org/regionalseas/who-we-are/overview.

[159] E Louka, *International Environmental Law: Fairness, Effectiveness and World Order* (CUP 2006) 153; N Oral, 'Forty Years of the UNEP Regional Seas Programme: from Past to Future', in R Rayfuse (ed.), *Research Handbook on International Marine Environmental Law* (Edward Elgar 2015) 348. See also UNEP, *Setting a Course for Regional Seas* (2014) 30; E Maruma Mrema, 'Regional Seas Programme: The Role played by UNEP in its Development and Governance', in DJ Attard et al (eds), *The IMLI Manual on International Maritime Law—Vol. III* (OUP 2016) 345–84.

[160] UNCLOS, Article 237.

The effect of this provision is, according to a leading commentary on UNCLOS, to 'accord priority ... to specific obligations assumed by States under existing or future conventions or agreements relating to the protection and preservation of the marine environment'.[161] This would appear to be the case, but UNCLOS also goes on to provide that 'specific obligations assumed by States under special conventions, with respect to the protection and preservation of the marine environment, should be carried out in a manner consistent with the general principles and obligations of this Convention'.[162] The use of the term *should* in this provision suggests that it does not set out a fundamental rule, which would invalidate future instruments incompatible with UNCLOS. Nevertheless, it provides strong encouragement to States to use the general principles and rules contained in UNCLOS as a normative framework for the development of subsequent international law in this area.

In some situations, UNCLOS goes even further by incorporating some international rules and standards into the general legal framework of the Convention through so-called rules of reference. As has been explained elsewhere, one of the functions of these rules of reference is to 'harmonise [UNCLOS] with existing instruments and replace the (generally unsatisfactory) lex generalis with explicit treaty rules (lex specialis) on the treaty relationship'.[163] Thus, the use of rules of reference 'creates a degree of dynamism as standards may change over time, without having to amend [UNCLOS]'.[164] This is, therefore, an important mechanism that ensures an appropriate response to contemporary threats to the marine environment through the interplay of UNCLOS with other sources of rules.

Rules of reference are used in different ways in relation to different categories of pollution, and not all rules of reference have the same effect.[165] On the one hand, some rules of reference directly incorporate international rules and standards in a way that establishes an international minimum standard with which all States must comply.[166] Such rules help to support effective regulatory regimes and deal with potential problems such as free-riding States that try to avoid regulations by staying outside of a particular treaty. On the other hand, some rules of reference merely require international rules or standards to be taken into account, indicating that States retain a significant degree of discretion when deciding upon an appropriate regulatory response.[167] The use of rules of reference in relation to different sources of pollution and how they have influenced the overall legal framework will be explored in subsequent chapters.

---

[161] Nordquist et al (n23) 425.   [162] UNCLOS, Article 237(2).

[163] C Redgwell, 'Mind the Gap in the GAIRS: The Role of Other Instruments in LOSC Regime Implementation in the Offshore Energy Sector' (2014) 29 *IJMCL* 600, 617.

[164] Harrison (n14) 171.

[165] See, generally, W Van Reenan, 'Rules of Reference in the New Convention on the Law of the Sea' (1981) *NYIL* 3.

[166] See Chapters 5, 6, and 8.   [167] See Chapters 4 and 7.

2.3.6 UNCLOS as a dispute settlement regime

Another important feature of UNCLOS is its compulsory dispute settlement system, which provides a means through which the obligations of the Convention can be upheld. States have some latitude concerning how to settle their disputes and UNCLOS prioritizes amicable settlement above all.[168] Nevertheless, disputes concerning most aspects of the interpretation and application of the Convention can ultimately be submitted to one of four procedures set out in Article 287, namely the ICJ, ITLOS, an ad hoc arbitral tribunal, or a specialist arbitral tribunal.

Dispute settlement under UNCLOS plays two important functions. First, it can be used to ensure compliance with the Convention's rules or standards. Given the erga omnes character of most rules in the Convention, a claim could be brought by any Party as a means of upholding the rights and obligations to protect and preserve the marine environment.[169] From this perspective, courts and tribunals can play a valuable role in securing international cooperation.[170] Second, as discussed in Chapter 1, courts and tribunals contribute to the development of the law through the interpretation of rules where they are ambiguous and there is a dispute over their meaning. In this sense, courts and tribunals can make an important contribution in their own right to developing the legal framework for the protection of the marine environment.

Most disputes relating to environmental harm will be subject to compulsory dispute settlement.[171] However, there are some exceptions, the most important of which for present purposes are the exclusion of disputes relating to coastal State rights and obligations over fisheries and marine scientific research within the EEZ.[172] In spite of these exclusions, courts and tribunals may be willing to settle the broader environmental aspects of a dispute, even if other parts of a dispute fall outside of their jurisdiction. This is demonstrated by the *Chagos MPA Arbitration*, where the Tribunal was willing to rule on the legality of the declaration of a marine protected area (MPA) around the Chagos Archipelago, even though the main protective measure taken within the MPA concerned a ban on fishing, and this particular issue was excluded from the jurisdiction of the Tribunal by virtue of the exception mentioned above. The Tribunal held that the question of its jurisdiction hinged 'on the characterization of the Parties' dispute and on the interpretation and application of Article 297.[173] It went on to reject the arguments of the United Kingdom that the MPA was solely a

---

[168] UNCLOS, Article 279.

[169] See e.g. RR Churchill, 'The Persisting Problem of Non-Compliance with the Law of the Sea Convention: Disorder in the Oceans' (2012) 27 *IJMCL* 813, 817. See the discussion of erga omnes obligations above.

[170] See Y Tanaka, 'Principles of International Marine Environmental Law', in R Rayfuse (ed.), *Research Handbook on International Marine Environmental Law* (Edward Elgar 2016) 54.

[171] See e.g. TA Mensah, 'The International Tribunal for the Law of the Sea and the Protection and Preservation of the Marine Environment' (1999) 8 *RECIEL* 1, 1.

[172] UNCLOS, Article 297. See also Article 298(1)(b) which allows States to opt out of compulsory settlement of disputes concerning law enforcement in relation to fisheries or marine scientific research. See further AE Boyle, 'Problems of Compulsory Jurisdiction and the Settlement of Disputes Relating to Straddling Fish Stocks' (1999) 14 *IJMCL* 1.

[173] *Chagos Marine Protected Area Arbitration* (2015) para. 283.

measure relating to fisheries, in part drawing upon the State's own characterization of the measure during the course of the legislative process and the court proceedings.[174] Whilst the Tribunal was not able to determine claims that related directly or indirectly[175] to decisions concerning rights to marine resources within the EEZ of the Chagos Archipelago, the fact that the MPA touched upon broader environmental issues and interests meant that the Tribunal could determine whether the United Kingdom had violated other rights that Mauritius had in relation to the Chagos Archipelago.[176]

UNCLOS also establishes a regime for the prescription of provisional measures, which explicitly allows States to apply to a court or tribunal to prescribe particular measures that must be taken pending the settlement of the dispute.[177] This facility can be extremely important in a dispute concerning the protection of the environment in order to prevent harm that might arise before a decision on the merits can be made by the court or tribunal. Indeed, the scope of available provisional measures under UNCLOS explicitly includes measures 'to prevent serious harm to the marine environment'.[178] This aspect of the power has been described as 'a significant legal innovation in enhancing opportunities for environmental protection in that such provisional measures can be requested not merely in respect of the traditional legal base of damage to the interests of the state concerned, but also in respect of potential or actual damage or harm to the marine environment'.[179]

Provisional measures may only be prescribed, however, if it can be demonstrated, inter alia, that the urgency of the situation so requires.[180] ITLOS has interpreted urgency to encompass the need to prevent any action likely to be taken which may cause serious harm to the marine environment.[181] Whilst there must be some evidence of imminent harm,[182] scientific uncertainty about a risk has not prevented courts and tribunals from prescribing provisional measures. Thus, in the *Southern Bluefin Tuna Cases*, ITLOS acknowledged that 'there is scientific uncertainty regarding measures to be taken to conserve the stock of southern bluefin tuna and … no agreement among the parties as to whether the conservation measures taken so far have led to the improvement in the stock'[183] and that it could not 'conclusively

---

[174] Ibid, paras 286–91.

[175] The Tribunal rejected the argument of Mauritius that the exception in Article 297(3)(a) only applied to disputes concerning sovereign rights of the coastal State but not to fishing rights of other States, by saying that 'In nearly any imaginable situation, a dispute will exist precisely because the coastal State's conception of its sovereign rights conflicts with the other party's understanding of its own rights. In short, the two are intertwined.' Ibid, para. 297.

[176] Ibid, paras 298 and 302.

[177] Where a dispute is submitted to an arbitral tribunal that is yet to be constituted, provisional measures may be prescribed by any court or tribunal agreed upon by the Parties or, failing such agreement within two weeks from the date of the request for provisional measures, ITLOS; see UNCLOS, Article 290.

[178] UNCLOS, Article 290(1). A similar innovation is found in Article 31(2) of the 1995 United Nations Fish Stocks Agreement (EIF 11 December 2001), which allows a court or tribunal to prescribe measures to 'prevent damage to the [fish stocks] in question'.

[179] D Ong, 'The 1982 UN Convention on the Law of the Sea', in M Fitzmaurice et al (eds), *Research Handbook on International Environmental Law* (Edward Elgar 2010) 579.

[180] UNCLOS, Article 290(5).   [181] *MOX Plant Case* (2001) para. 64.   [182] Ibid.

[183] *Southern Bluefin Tuna Cases (Provisional Measures)* (1999) para. 79.

assess the scientific evidence presented by the parties',[184] but nevertheless ordered the Parties to take measures 'to avert further deterioration of the southern bluefin tuna stock'.[185] Moreover, ITLOS has demonstrated that, even in the absence of evidence of actual harm, it can order the Parties to cooperate in exchanging information about environmental risks[186] and in taking measures to protect the marine environment.[187] Indeed, in practice, the Tribunal has played an important role in facilitating the settlement of environmental disputes by ordering and overseeing cooperation between litigants.[188]

Dispute settlement is a significant component of the international legal framework for the protection of the marine environment. In practice, however, States are not always willing to bring disputes over environmental matters to litigation. As noted by one author, 'few states have an environmental record so clean as to be able to throw the first stone'.[189] Moreover, litigation can be expensive and time-consuming. This means that the UNCLOS dispute settlement system is underused in practice, despite well-known cases of non-compliance,[190] and States have preferred to settle their disputes through other means, be it diplomatic forums or through alternative dispute settlement mechanisms, such as non-compliance procedures.[191] As will be seen in subsequent chapters, States have established a range of specialist dispute settlement systems under particular treaty regimes. Such procedural devices can take a number of forms, from simple reporting obligations to third-party review of behaviour. These procedures offer the advantage that they can be shaped to deal with a particular set of issues and specific remedies can be designed to offer incentives for States to bring themselves into compliance. Such procedures should ideally be designed to consider ongoing action taken by States to comply with their obligations in order to identify problems at an early stage and to recommend compensatory action. It is where such procedures do not exist or cannot effectively deal with a problem that UNCLOS provides an important remedy of last resort.[192]

---

[184] Ibid, para. 80.   [185] Ibid.

[186] *The MOX Plant Case* (2001) para. 64; *Dispute Concerning Delimitation of the Maritime Boundary between Ghana and Cote d'Ivoire in the Atlantic Ocean* (2015).

[187] *Land Reclamation in the Johor Straits (Provisional Measures)* (2003). See also *Southern Bluefin Tuna Cases* (1999).

[188] AE Boyle, 'The Environmental Jurisprudence of the ITLOS' (2007) 22 *IJMCL* 369, 379–80; B Mansfield, 'Compulsory Dispute Settlement after the Southern Bluefin Tuna Award', in AG Oude Elferink and DR Rothwell (eds), *Oceans Management in the 21st Century* (Martinus Nijhoff 2004) 255, 265; DR Rothwell, 'The Contributions of ITLOS to Oceans Governance through Marine Environmental Dispute Resolution', in TM Ndiaye and R Wolfrum (eds), *Law of the Sea, Environmental Law and the Settlement of Disputes: Liber Amicorum Judge Thomas A. Mensah* (Martinus Nijhoff 2007) 1007–24.

[189] C Romano, 'International Dispute Settlement', in D Bodansky et al (eds), *The Oxford Handbook of International Environmental Law* (OUP 2007) 1041. See also E Hey, *Advanced Introduction to International Environmental Law* (Routledge 2016) 122.

[190] Churchill (n168) 813–20.   [191] Birnie, Boyle, and Redgwell (n20) 238–9.

[192] The relationship between the UNCLOS dispute settlement system and other mechanisms is addressed in UNCLOS, Articles 280–2.

2.4 Conclusion

This chapter has explored the place of UNCLOS in the international legal frame-work for the protection of the marine environment. It has shown how UNCLOS constitutes a central pillar of the international legal system, prescribing a mixture of jurisdictional powers, general principles, substantive and procedural rules, and a dispute settlement regime. The importance of UNCLOS stems from its widespread acceptance by the international community, as the foundation of the modern law of the sea. However, as the analysis of the environmental provisions of UNCLOS has made clear, the Convention by itself is not sufficient to offer comprehensive and effective protection to the marine environment. Rather, its provisions require fur-ther elaboration, either through interpretation or through the negotiation of add-itional rules and standards. How this process works in practice will be explored in subsequent chapters, as we begin to look at the treaties and other instruments that have been negotiated by States at the international level in order to deal with specific sources of marine environmental degradation. Before we turn to this task, however, we will first consider how the general international legal framework for the protection of the marine environment in UNCLOS has been supplemented by the emergence of crosscutting rules that emphasize the importance of tackling threats to marine biological diversity.

3

Mainstreaming Marine Biological Diversity Conservation in the Law of the Sea

3.1 Introduction

According to the census for marine life, there are nearly 250,000 marine species found throughout the world's oceans, from the deep seas to shallow coastal waters.[1] Marine life varies from microorganisms that cannot be viewed by the naked eye to the world's largest living creature: the blue whale. The sheer diversity is staggering, and new species continue to be discovered, particularly in the deep seas.[2] Yet, many marine species are highly vulnerable to changes in their natural environment and, therefore, can be affected by a range of human activities. Direct exploitation of some marine species is obviously a threat, but marine life can be the victim of equally direct and indirect effects from other activities, including the release of toxic substances or habitat destruction. The protection of biological diversity is, therefore, a crosscutting issue which must be considered in the regulation of all activities that may affect the marine environment.

Concern for nature conservation emerged on the international agenda as part of the broader environmental movement, discussed in earlier chapters.[3] The 1972 Stockholm Declaration expressed the view that 'man has a special responsibility to safeguard and wisely manage the heritage of wildlife and its habitats which are now gravely imperiled by a combination of adverse factors'.[4] There followed the promulgation of a number of global and regional treaties aimed at protecting key species or habitats from human activities.

It was in the 1980s that the concept of *biodiversity* emerged as a new paradigm for the evolution of international rules relating to nature conservation. Early signs of this shift in philosophy are seen in the 1982 World Charter for Nature (WCN), adopted by the UN General Assembly as a set of 'principles of conservation by which

---

[1] Summary of the First Consensus of Marine Life 2010: <www.coml.org>.

[2] BBC News, 'New marine life found in deep sea vents': <http://www.bbc.co.uk/news/science-environment-38305989.

[3] Whilst there were sporadic attempts to regulate impacts on particular species in the early twentieth century, most authors agree that the development of more focused attention on these issues occurred at some point during the 1960s; see e.g. M Bowman et al (eds), *Lyster's International Wildlife Law* (2nd edn: CUP 2010) 11. See, further, Chapter 1.

[4] Stockholm Declaration on the Human Environment, Principle 4.

all human conduct is to be guided and judged'.[5] The WCN stresses the importance of ecosystem functioning[6] and it emphasizes that 'the genetic variability on the earth shall not be compromised, the population levels of all life forms, wild and domesticated, must be at least sufficient for their survival, and to this end necessary habitats shall be safeguarded'.[7] This declaration makes it clear that international law must extend its reach beyond those species that are the subject of direct exploitation and provide some level of protection for all species of fauna and flora. The WCN goes on to call for the regulation of any activity which may pose significant risks to nature.[8] Whilst the WCN is a non-binding instrument, it has, nevertheless, been described as 'one of the main foundation stones of international wildlife law'[9] and it set an important precedent for the subsequent development of other international treaties on this topic, including the 1992 Convention on Biological Diversity (CBD).[10] In this latter instrument, discussed in more detail below, the international community explicitly recognized the conservation of biological diversity as a common concern of humankind,[11] indicating that international cooperation is needed to address the key threats thereto.[12] States have also stressed that 'biodiversity underpins sustainable development', which cannot be achieved without promoting the conservation and sustainable use of biological resources.[13] To this end, the international community has recently adopted a target to 'sustainably manage and protect marine and coastal ecosystems to avoid significant adverse impacts, including strengthening their resilience, and take action for their restoration in order to achieve healthy and productive oceans' by 2020.[14] This means that those instruments aimed at the conservation of biological diversity in general will be relevant to the development of the international legal framework for the protection of the marine environment.

The international legal framework relating to nature conservation and biological diversity has a broad scope, but its application to marine species and habitats brings particular challenges, in part, owing to the greater scientific uncertainty surrounding many marine ecosystems, as well as the more complex jurisdictional regime that applies in this context. The purpose of the present chapter is to introduce the general legal framework relating to the conservation and sustainable use of biological diversity, in order to determine the manner in which it may influence and interact with the development of the other treaty regimes discussed in this book. First, the chapter will outline the global treaty regimes relating to the conservation and sustainable use of biological diversity, considering in particular how they apply to marine biological

---

[5] World Charter for Nature (WCN), preamble, contained in UNGA Resolution 37/7 (1982).

[6] Ibid, paras 3–4.   [7] Ibid, para. 2.

[8] Ibid, para. 11. The WCN calls for the implementation, inter alia, of environmental impact assessment, regulation of pollutants, and the utilization of best available technologies. It also contains an early call for disclosure of environmental information for the purposes of effective public consultation and participation; Ibid, para. 16.

[9] Bowman et al (n3) 17.

[10] Convention on Biological Diversity (CBD) (EIF 29 December 1993).

[11] Ibid, preamble.   [12] On the common concern of humankind, see Chapter 1.

[13] See the 2002 Hague Ministerial Declaration of the Conference of the Parties to the Convention on Biological Diversity, para. 5; CBD COP Decision X/2 (2010) Annex, para. 3.

[14] UNGA Resolution 70/1 (2015), Sustainable Development Goal 14.2.

diversity. It will focus on two treaties, namely the CBD and the Convention on Migratory Species (CMS). The chapter will then turn to the regional level, explaining how regional seas treaties have evolved to take into account the need to protect and preserve marine ecosystems. The analysis will identify the main obligations that have been agreed in this context and it will explain how these instruments interact with other relevant treaties relating to the protection of the marine environment.

3.2 The Convention on Biological Diversity

The mainstreaming of biological diversity in modern international environmental law owes a significant debt to the CBD, which is the leading global treaty for the conservation of biological diversity.[15] This treaty has been described as reflecting 'the realization of the interconnectedness of all life on Earth and the need to protect both genetic and species diversity to ensure continued human existence'.[16] The CBD was the first international treaty to address all aspects of biodiversity. The Convention is particularly important because of its large number of Parties; 195 States and the European Union are bound by it,[17] including all Parties to the United Nations Convention on the Law of the Sea (UNCLOS). In part, because of its quasi-universal acceptance, but also because of the nature of its provisions, discussed below, the CBD has a broad systematic influence on the development of international law in this area.

The Convention starts by defining *biological diversity* itself as 'the variability among living organisms from all sources including, inter alia, terrestrial, marine and other aquatic ecosystems and the ecological complexes of which they are part'.[18] This definition covers marine biological diversity both within and beyond national jurisdiction, although it will be seen below that the precise scope of application of the Convention depends upon the nature of the obligations concerned. The preamble to the Convention reflects a range of values associated with biodiversity, which includes not only economic, social, or cultural values but also the intrinsic value of biodiversity itself, including 'the importance of biological diversity for evolution and for maintaining life sustaining systems in the biosphere'. The Convention goes on to establish a general framework for the conservation of biological diversity and the sustainable use of its components. The CBD has three overarching objectives, namely the conservation of biodiversity, the sustainable use of its components, and the fair and equitable sharing of the benefits arising out of the utilization of genetic resources.[19] Whilst this last objective was central to the negotiation of the treaty[20] and it is currently an important issue in relation to genetic resources in areas beyond

[15] CBD (EIF 29 December 1993).
[16] R Rayfuse, 'Biological Resources', in D Bodansky et al (eds), *Oxford Handbook on International Environmental Law* (OUP 2007) 365.
[17] See the CBD website: <https://www.cbd.int/information/parties.shtml>.
[18] CBD, Article 2.   [19] Ibid, Article 1.
[20] P Birnie, AE Boyle, and C Redgwell, *International Law and the Environment* (3rd edn: OUP 2009) 630–1.

national jurisdiction,[21] the focus of the following sections will be on the obligations imposed by the CBD in relation to the conservation and sustainable use of marine biodiversity, as this aspect of the Convention is of most importance to the subject of this book.

Generally speaking, the CBD calls for the integration of biodiversity considerations into all relevant sectoral or cross-sectoral plans, programmes, and policies.[22] As part of this mandate, States should provide adequate financial resources to support its plans, policies, and programmes[23] and they must report to the other Contracting Parties on the measures they have taken.[24] Beyond this overarching obligation, the Convention specifies two broad types of substantive obligations relating to the *in situ* conservation and sustainable use of biological diversity.[25]

First, the Convention calls for the identification of processes and categories of activities, which have, or are likely to have, significant adverse impacts on biological diversity.[26] This includes an obligation to introduce appropriate procedures for environmental impact assessment (EIA) for individual projects. It has been pointed out that this obligation would appear to be procedural in nature,[27] and it thus falls short of an independent obligation to carry out an EIA of individual projects, as is found in UNCLOS. Yet, in other ways, the CBD would appear to go beyond UNCLOS, particularly when it calls for the introduction of 'appropriate arrangements to ensure that the environmental consequences of its programmes and policies that are likely to have significant adverse impacts on biological diversity are duly taken into account'.[28] In other words, the CBD expressly requires the introduction of some form of strategic environmental assessment.

Where a Party determines that an activity, programme, or policy is likely to have a significant adverse effect on biodiversity, it must 'regulate or manage the relevant processes and categories of activities'.[29] This obligation potentially has a broad scope, and the Parties have identified a range of activities which fall within its scope, including fishing, tourism, recreation, shipping, and land-based activities.[30] Indeed, it is important to note that the Convention applies to all activities and processes carried out under the jurisdiction or control of a Party, which includes activities or processes not only within national jurisdiction but also beyond national jurisdiction.[31] However, like the general duty to regulate certain activities in UNCLOS, this provision does not specify the particular measures that must be taken, but, rather, it would seem to be a due diligence obligation. The threshold of significant adverse

[21] See e.g. C Salpin, 'Marine Genetic Resources of Areas beyond National Jurisdiction: Soul Searching and the Art of Balance', in E Morgera and K Kulovesi (eds), *Research Handbook on International Law and Natural Resources* (Edward Elgar 2016) 411–31.

[22] CBD, Articles 6 and 10.

[23] Ibid, Article 20. See also Article 21 on the establishment of a financial mechanism to support developing countries in their efforts to implement the Convention.

[24] Ibid, Article 26.

[25] The Convention also contains important obligations relating to *ex situ* conservation in Article 9.

[26] CBD, Article 7.   [27] *Case Concerning Construction of a Road* (2015) para. 164.

[28] CBD, Article 14(b).   [29] Ibid, Article 8(l).

[30] CBD COP Decision II/10 and Annexes.   [31] CBD, Article 4(b).

effects also introduces some discretion for the Parties.[32] Moreover, in common with many of the obligations in the CBD, the duty to regulate applies 'as far as possible and as appropriate'. It has been observed that this language, which is pervasive in the text, weakens the normative force of the treaty,[33] and some commentators have suggested that the CBD should be understood as setting objectives, rather than concrete obligations.[34]

The second set of obligations found in the CBD relate to the identification of important components of biological diversity which may need special protection.[35] The Convention highlights the need for States, 'as far as possible and appropriate', to pay particular attention to, inter alia, highly diverse ecosystems and habitats, ecosystems and habitats that are unique or associated with key evolutionary or other biological processes, and threatened species or communities.[36] Unlike the obligations relating to processes and activities, this obligation only extends to marine areas under the jurisdiction of a Party, namely, the territorial sea and the exclusive economic zone (EEZ).[37] However, the Convention encourages Parties to cooperate in relation to areas beyond national jurisdiction.[38] The Convention identifies a range of measures that may be taken by States to protect important species, habitats, or ecosystems, including the implementation of legislation for the protection of threatened species and populations, the regulation of other important biological resources with a view to ensuring their sustainable use, the establishment of protected areas, and the rehabilitation or restoration of degraded ecosystems.[39] These provisions, therefore, emphasize the need for Parties to take measures proactively to protect habitats and ecosystems and the CBD would appear to go beyond the rather narrow requirements relating to the protection of rare and fragile ecosystems in UNCLOS. Nevertheless, the CBD leaves a large degree of discretion to Parties to determine which species, habitats, or ecosystems must be protected. Earlier provisions that would have listed specific areas or species in need of protection were removed from the text, leaving this issue to be determined by individual States.[40] Indeed, there is no definition of *threatened species* or *degraded ecosystem*, which leaves these key terms open to interpretation.

There is clearly a large overlap between these provisions in the CBD and the provisions of UNCLOS. Nevertheless, they can be read in a mutually supportive manner.[41] Indeed, the CBD itself stresses that it must be read in light of 'the rights and obligations of States under the law of the sea',[42] which is a veiled reference to the legal framework established by UNCLOS. The essence of both instruments is that

---

[32] L Glowka et al, *A Guide to the Convention on Biological Diversity* (IUCN 1994) 50.
[33] Birnie, Boyle, and Redgwell (n20) 617. [34] Glowka et al (n32) 1.
[35] CBD, Article 7(a). [36] Ibid, Annex. [37] Ibid, Article 4(a).
[38] Ibid, Article 5. [39] Ibid, Article 8. See also Article 9 on *ex situ* conservation measures.
[40] See Bowman et al (n3) 592.
[41] AE Boyle, 'Relationship between International Environmental Law and Other Branches of International Law', in D Bodansky et al (eds) *Oxford Handbook of International Environmental Law* (OUP 2007) 139.
[42] CBD, Article 22(2). See also *South China Sea Arbitration (Jurisdiction and Admissibility)* (2015) para. 288: 'Article 22(2) of the CBD recognises the substantial overlap between the two parallel conventions and therefore requires them to be implemented consistently.'

States must take further actions to regulate activities and processes, which may have a detrimental impact on the marine environment. Both treaties also leave it to States to determine, either individually or collectively, the precise measures which must be taken to fulfil these obligations. The CBD, therefore, requires further elaboration and it can thus be considered as an umbrella treaty, like UNCLOS itself.

Even though the provisions of the CBD may themselves be vague, subsequent practice of the Parties may provide guidance on what the Convention requires. The Conference of the Parties (COP) is the principal body charged with overseeing the implementation of the Convention[43] and it is rightly recognized as 'a prolific norm-creating body across all areas covered by the CBD and on issues that are directly or indirectly related to biodiversity'.[44] Whilst the COP has the power to adopt additional legally binding protocols to give more specific content to the general provisions of the Convention, it has used this power sparingly[45] and it has preferred to utilize non-binding decisions, actions plans, and targets adopted at its biennial meetings, in order to provide more specific advice to Parties on what steps they should take to fulfil their obligations.[46] Amongst its other activities, the COP has developed an ongoing work programme on coastal and marine biological diversity.[47] The initial work programme identified five themes for action, namely integrated marine and coastal area management, marine and coastal protected areas, sustainable use of marine and coastal living resources, mariculture, and alien species. These themes have allowed the COP to address a broad range of marine issues, but, in general, it has focused on identifying those activities it considers are not currently regulated fully or adequately by other international instruments. Thus, the CBD has played a key role in identifying gaps in addressing certain issues or activities, including ocean fertilization, ocean acidification, underwater noise, marine debris, and marine alien invasive species. Beyond its reiteration of the general duties of States to perform an environmental assessment and to take biodiversity into account when developing mitigation measures, however, the CBD has not itself performed a regulatory function, and it has tended to limit its activity to requesting or collecting further information on potential impacts[48] and supporting global cooperation through other appropriate bodies.[49] That is not to say that the CBD completely leaves the

---

[43] Ibid, Article 23(4).

[44] E Morgera and E Tsoumani, 'Yesterday, Today and Tomorrow: Looking Afresh at the Convention on Biological Diversity' (2010) 21 *YIEL* 3, 6–7.

[45] Two protocols have been adopted to date: 2000 Protocol on Biosafety (EIF 11 September 2003); 2010 Nagoya Protocol on Access to Genetic Resources (Ibid 12 October 2014).

[46] See SR Harrop and DJ Pritchard, 'A Hard Instrument Goes Soft: The Implications of the Convention on Biological Diversity's Current Trajectory' (2011) 21 *GEC* 474–80.

[47] For example, Draft Programme for Further Work on Marine and Coastal Biological Diversity, CBD COP Decision II/10 (1995) Annex II. This has been developed through further COP decisions; CBD COP Decision IV/5 (1998); CBD COP Decision VII/5 (2004); COP Decision X/29 (2010). For a discussion, see MM Goote, 'The Jakarta Mandate on Marine and Coastal Biological Diversity' (1997) 12 *IJMCL* 377–95.

[48] See e.g. CBD COP Decision IX/20 (2008) paras 3 (ocean fertilization) and 4 (ocean acidification); CBD COP Decision X/29 (2010) para. 12 (underwater noise); CBD COP Decision XI/18 (2012) para. 26.

[49] CBD COP Decision X/29 (2010) para. 12 (underwater noise); CBD COP Decision XII/23 (2014) para. 4 (underwater noise); CBD COP Decision XIII/10 (2016) paras 8–10 (marine debris).

issue to be regulated elsewhere, and the COP will often retain an oversight role with a view to ensuring the adoption of measures that are in line with the broad principles contained in the Convention. Clear examples of this interactive process are the development of ballast water management rules in the International Maritime Organization (IMO), to address alien invasive species, discussed in Chapter 6, and the emergence of rules on ocean fertilization in the context of the dumping regime, discussed in Chapter 9.

In other areas which are already highly regulated, the CBD has similarly played a role in encouraging further action to mainstream biodiversity considerations into the legal framework. In this context, the CBD COP has an ongoing role in encouraging further cooperation to address unsustainable fishing and the impacts of fishing on marine and coastal biodiversity.[50] Again, the CBD has not sought to regulate this matter directly and it has recognized the competence of the relevant sectoral bodies,[51] but it has collaborated with these organizations in order to promote an ecosystems approach to fisheries through the dissemination of information and the organization of expert workshops.[52]

Another key role played by the CBD COP has been the identification of priority habitats that require specific attention from States. The programme of work on marine and coastal biodiversity lists mangroves, tropical and cold-water coral reefs, seamounts, and seagrass communities as key ecosystems in need of protection.[53] In more recent years, the COP has developed priority actions to protect coral reefs[54] and a voluntary specific work plan on biodiversity in cold-water areas.[55] One of the more important developments in this context has been the emphasis placed on marine protected areas (MPAs), which can contribute to protecting biodiversity, promoting sustainable use of marine resources, and managing conflicts between different marine users.[56] At its seventh meeting in 2004, CBD Parties agreed that 'marine and coastal protected areas are one of the essential tools and approaches in the conservation and sustainable use of marine and coastal biodiversity',[57] and they set a goal of establishing and maintaining 'marine and coastal protected areas that are effectively managed, ecologically based and contribute to a global network'.[58] This goal was re-emphasized in the 2010 Strategic Plan for Biodiversity, which calls for '10% of coastal and marine areas, especially areas of particular importance for biodiversity and ecosystem services, to be conserved through effectively and equitably managed, ecologically representative and well connected systems of protected areas and other effective area-based conservation measures' by 2020.[59] States are urged to take individual action to designate appropriate MPAs within their jurisdiction[60] and to cooperate to establish MPAs in areas beyond national jurisdiction.[61] *Protected*

---

[50] CBD COP Decision X/29 (2010) paras 52–6.
[51] See CBD COP Decision XI/18 (2012) para. 2.   [52] See e.g. Ibid, para. 1.
[53] CBD COP Decision VII/5 (2004) Annex, operational objective 2.3.
[54] CBD COP Decision XII/23 (2014), Annex.
[55] CBD COP Decision XIII/11 (2016).
[56] CBD COP Decision VII/5 (2004), para. 12.   [57] Ibid, para. 16.
[58] Ibid, para. 18.   [59] CBD COP Decision X/2 (2010) Annex, Target 11.
[60] Ibid, para. 20.   [61] Ibid, para. 30.

areas are defined in the Convention as 'a geographically defined area which is designated or regulated and managed to achieve specific conservation objectives'.[62] This
broad definition clearly encompasses a range of different area-based measures and it
does not necessarily mean that all activities will be prohibited within an MPA, but
rather that threats must be managed.[63] Indeed, the CBD guidance emphasizes that
it is up to individual coastal States to decide on the appropriate balance between
MPAs where all activity is excluded or minimized to the greatest extent possible
and MPAs where activity is regulated or managed in line with general conservation
objectives.[64]

   In order to support States to meet this goal, the CBD COP has convened a series
of experts meetings and workshops with a view to developing criteria for identifying
ecologically or biologically significant marine areas (EBSAs) in need of protection.[65]
It has been stressed that the EBSA criteria are only intended to describe marine
areas worthy of protection, and they do not prejudge whether such an area would
be established as an MPA or what sort of management measures may be adopted
therein.[66] These criteria identify seven features which should be taken into account
by States in identifying areas in need of protection, namely importance for threatened, endangered, or declining species or habitats; vulnerability, fragility, sensitivity,
or slow recovery; uniqueness or rarity; special importance for the life-history stages
of species; biological diversity; naturalness; and biological productivity.[67] Whilst the
criteria were initially drafted with a view to identifying EBSAs in the open oceans,
States have also been encouraged to apply them within national jurisdiction.[68]
Alongside the EBSA criteria, the CBD COP also adopted scientific guidelines for
selecting areas to establish a representative network of marine protected areas.[69]

   As important as the criteria have been the process of coordinating regional workshops to discuss application of the criteria[70] and the establishment of a reposi-
tory of information on EBSAs.[71] Yet, this process does not remove the need for
States to go ahead and adopt measures in order to protect those areas which have
been identified as requiring protection. The CBD itself does not have the authority to regulate relevant activities directly and, therefore, it must work with other
international organizations in order to address relevant threats. To this end, the
CBD COP has emphasized that 'the identification of ... management measures is

   [62] CBD, Article 2.
   [63] See CBD COP Decision VII/5, para. 21, distinguishing between MPAs where threats are managed but extractive uses may be allowed and MPAs where extractive uses are excluded and other significant human pressures are removed or minimized. The COP Decision suggests that a network of MPAs
should include both types of protected area.
   [64] Ibid, para. 22.
   [65] See CBD COP Decision IX/20 (2008), Annex I. See DC Dunn et al, 'The Convention on
Biological Diversity's Ecologically or Biologically Significant Areas: Origins, Development, or Current
Status' (2014) 49 *Marine Policy* 137–45.
   [66] See CBD COP Decision IX/20 (2008), Annex III. See also CBD COP Decision X/29 (2010),
para. 26.
   [67] CBD COP Decision IX/20 (2008), Annex I.   [68] Ibid, para. 18.
   [69] See ibid, Annex II.
   [70] CBD COP Decision X/29 (2010), para. 36; CBD COP Decision XI/17 (2012), para. 12.
   [71] See CBD COP Decision XI/17 (2012), Annex; CBD COP Decision XII/17, Annex.

a matter for states and competent intergovernmental organizations, in accordance with international law including [UNCLOS]',[72] and it has 'encourage[d] parties and invite[d] other governments and intergovernmental organizations, within their respective jurisdictions and competencies, to take measures to ensure conservation and sustainable use by implementing relevant tools, ... including areas-based management tools, such as marine protected areas'.[73] Yet, there is little doubt that the CBD has played a crucial catalytic role in ensuring that this matter has been placed firmly on the agenda of relevant institutions, and examples of what international organizations have done in this respect will be considered throughout this work in relevant chapters.

3.3 Other Global Nature Conservation Treaties

The CBD deserves a significant amount of credit for mainstreaming biodiversity protection in modern international law, but it does not entirely overshadow other earlier treaties that were concerned with the protection of specific species, habitats, or other particular aspects of nature conservation.[74] These other treaties can all contribute towards the overarching goals of conserving biodiversity contained in the CBD, even if they do so in a 'piecemeal fashion'.[75] Indeed, the CBD COP itself has recognized the important role of these other treaties and the need to enhance synergies between the biodiversity-related conventions.[76]

One instrument that continues to play a central role in offering a broad range of protection to marine species is the CMS.[77] This treaty has the objective of promoting the favourable conservation status[78] of *migratory species*, defined as 'the entire population or any geographically separate part of the population of any species or lower taxon of wild animals, a significant proportion of whose members cyclically and predictably cross one or more national jurisdictional boundaries'.[79] Clearly, the protection of such species can only be achieved with the cooperation of all so-called range States.[80] The CMS explicitly applies to migratory marine species.[81] Moreover, it applies to migratory species wherever they are found, including beyond national jurisdiction.

Unlike the CBD, the CMS does provide targeted protection for identified species. The highest level of protection is offered to those migratory species which have been listed in Appendix I of the Convention, because the Parties agree they are endangered. Many marine species have been listed for the purposes of the Convention, including several species of whales, albatross, turtles, and sharks. The CMS specifies several measures that must be taken by range States of listed species. For this

---

[72] CBD COP Decision X/29 (2010), para. 26.
[73] CBD COP Decision XIII/12 (2016), para. 14.
[74] See e.g. V Koester, 'The Five Global Biodiversity-Related Conventions' (2001) 31 *EPL* 151–6.
[75] Bowman et al (n3) 594.   [76] See CBD COP Decision XIII/24 (2016).
[77] Convention on Migratory Species (CMS) (EIF 1 November 1983).
[78] See CMS, Article I(1)(c).   [79] Ibid, Article I(1)(a).   [80] Ibid, Article I(1)(h).
[81] See the definition of range in Ibid, Article I(1)(f).

purpose, a range State includes 'a State, flag vessels of which are engaged outside national jurisdictional limits in taking that migratory species'.[82]

First and foremost, range States must prohibit the taking of listed species.[83] This is an obligation of result and it imposes quite a clear duty on the Contracting Parties to take particular action. *Taking* is broadly defined to include not only the deliberate killing and capturing[84] of animals but also harassment.[85] This interpretation gives the Convention a potentially broad remit, which is recognized through subsequent decisions of the Parties, which have called for action to deal with disturbances caused by, inter alia, marine wildlife tourism[86] and marine renewable energy installations.[87] A limited range of exceptions applies, but Parties are encouraged to ensure that the exceptions are applied sparingly so that they do not operate to the disadvantage of the species.[88] Moreover, the invocation of an exception must be reported to the secretariat, and, therefore, their use can be monitored by the other Contracting Parties.

In addition to providing direct protection to the species, range States must also 'endeavour' to conserve and where appropriate, restore the habitats of the species, and prevent, reduce, or control other activities that may impede the migration of species or may contribute to the further endangerment of such species.[89] This obligation includes an obligation to protect Appendix I species against bycatch,[90] oil pollution,[91] and marine debris.[92] Yet, these obligations are weaker and they are softened by the inclusion of qualifiers of feasibility and appropriateness, which leads one author to conclude that range States are given 'considerable leeway in electing whether or not to undertake such measures'.[93]

The CMS also establishes a legal framework for further cooperation to protect migratory species with an unfavourable conservation status, identified in Appendix II.[94] The range States of Appendix II species are required to endeavour to enter into agreements for their conservation. Measures that may be included in agreements include exchange of information, coordinated conservation and management plans, maintenance of a network of suitable habitats relating to the migration routes of the species, and management of the taking of the species. Such agreements should cover the whole of the range of the listed species, including areas beyond national jurisdiction. A number of agreements have been concluded in this context which are relevant for the protection of migratory marine species, including the Agreement on the Conservation of Albatrosses and

---

[82] Ibid, Article I(1)(h).   [83] Ibid, Article III(5).

[84] See e.g. CMS COP Resolution 11.2 (2014) on Live Capture of Cetaceans from the Wild for Commercial Purposes.

[85] CMS, Article I(1)(i).

[86] CMS COP Resolution 11.29 (2014) on Sustainable Boat-Based Marine Wildlife Watching.

[87] CMS COP Resolution 11.27 (2014) on Renewable Energy and Migratory Species; see further Chapter 8.

[88] CMS, Article III(5).   [89] Ibid, Article III(4).

[90] CMS COP Resolution 6.2 (1999). See also Resolutions 7.2, 8.14, 8.16, and 9.18.

[91] CMS COP Resolution 7.3 (2002).

[92] CMS COP Resolution 11.30 (2014). See also Resolution 10.4.

[93] R Caddell, 'International Law and the Protection of Migratory Wildlife: An Appraisal of Twenty-Five Years of the Bonn Convention' (2005) 16 *CJIELP* 113, 117.

[94] CMS, Article IV.

Petrels;[95] the Agreement on the Conservation of Small Cetaceans of the Baltic, North East Atlantic, Irish and North Seas;[96] the Agreement on the Conservation of Cetaceans of the Black Sea, Mediterranean Sea, and Contiguous Atlantic Area;[97] and the Agreement on the Conservation of Wadden Sea Seals.[98] In addition, Parties have sometimes chosen to adopt measures for the protection of migratory species in the form of memoranda of understanding (MOU). These instruments are not legally binding but they are intended to guide States on how to implement the general obligations found in the CMS in relation to specific species. Relevant MOUs have been adopted in relation to Atlantic Turtles, Indian Ocean and South-East Asian Turtles, Sharks, and Pacific Island Cetaceans. A key feature of most of these instruments is the development of a conservation plan, which identifies a range of actions that should be undertaken by States, acting either individually or jointly.

The CMS and associated instruments are crosscutting in nature, which means that they can address a range of threats against a relevant species. Yet, it does not follow that these threats will be directly regulated under these instruments. Where a threat emanates from an activity in a sector that is already subject to regulation by a specialist institution, such as shipping or fishing, Parties to the CMS and related instruments will often have to cooperate with those institutions in order to achieve their objectives. Like the CBD, a key strategy of the CMS is, therefore, to foster linkages with relevant regional and international instruments to promote synergies and avoid duplication.[99]

3.4 Regional Seas Treaties and the Conservation and Sustainable Use of Marine Biological Diversity

Since the early 1970s, it has been recognized that regions had a key role to play in the protection of the marine environment. Through UNEP's regional seas programme, the scope of regional protection has increased so that many regions now have an institutional framework through which they can cooperate on key environmental challenges in that region.[100]

The early regional seas treaties were largely focused on pollution[101] and they had little to say on the subject of marine biological diversity. Yet, as this issue gained in

---

[95] See the 2001 Agreement on the Conservation of Albatrosses and Petrels (EIF 1 February 2004).

[96] See the 1991 Agreement on the Conservation of Small Cetaceans of the Baltic, North East Atlantic, Irish and North Seas (EIF 29 March 1994).

[97] See the 1996 Agreement on the Conservation of Cetaceans of the Black Sea, Mediterranean Sea and Contiguous Atlantic Area (EIF 1 June 2001).

[98] See the 1990 Agreement on the Conservation of Seals in the Wadden Sea (EIF 1 October 1991).

[99] See e.g. CMS COP Resolution 10.4 (2011), para. 9 (marine debris); CMS COP Resolution 10.14 (2011), para. 10 (bycatch in gillnet fisheries).

[100] See Chapter 2 and references therein.

[101] This is clear from the titles of the first regional treaties: 1972 Convention on the Prevention of Marine Pollution by Dumping from Ships and Aircraft (Oslo Convention) (EIF 7 April 1974); 1974 Convention for the Prevention of Marine Pollution from Land-based Sources (Paris Convention) (EIF

importance, the regional seas treaties were seen as an opportunity to further main-stream marine biological diversity into the legal framework for the protection of the marine environment. To this end, several regional seas bodies have adopted specific rules that deal with the conservation of biological diversity, either in the form of amendments to the framework treaty, the adoption of an annex, or the negotiation of a protocol. It follows that regional seas bodies have become key actors in this respect, to the extent that the global strategy for regional seas programmes has emphasized the important role that these institutions have to play in the conservation of biological diversity.[102]

The Mediterranean was one of the first regions to take concrete action towards the protection of marine ecosystems under the regional seas framework. The original text of the Barcelona Convention, whose title referred exclusively to the protection of the Mediterranean from pollution, did contain general language concerning the taking of appropriate measures 'to protect and enhance the marine environment'.[103] Building on this text, Parties to the Barcelona Convention convened a conference in Geneva in 1982 to adopt a Protocol Concerning Mediterranean Protected Areas. The 1982 Protocol established a basic obligation on the Parties to, 'to the extent possible, establish protected areas' in order to safeguard:

sites of biological or ecological value, the genetic diversity, as well as the satisfactory population levels, of species, and their breeding grounds and habitats, representative types of ecosystems and their ecological processes, and sites of particular importance because of their scientific, aesthetic, historical, archaeological, cultural or educational interest.[104]

It is clear that this is an obligation of due diligence, and it does not demand a particular outcome. Yet to aid implementation, the Parties also agreed to develop common guidelines on the selection, establishment, and management of MPAs, as well as on procedures for sharing information about these areas. Within designated MPAs, States were required to progressively take protective measures, including the regulation of any activity which might undermine the objectives of the MPA.[105] This obligation also allows a lot of flexibility as to how States manage activities within MPAs and it falls far short of requiring complete prohibition of all harmful activity. This understanding of protected areas is in line with the meaning later ascribed to protected areas under the CBD, discussed above. Yet, an interesting element of the Protocol is the encouragement to use buffer zones around MPAs, in which 'activities are less severely restricted whilst remaining compatible with the purposes of the protected area'.[106] It is also worth noting that the Protocol also encourages the Parties to

6 May 1968); 1976 Convention for the Prevention of Pollution of the Mediterranean Sea (Barcelona Convention) (EIF 12 February 1978).

[102] *Regional Seas Strategic Directions 2013-2016*, Document UNEP(DEPI) RS.15/WP.RS (2013) 3–4. See also N Oral, 'Forty Years of the UNEP Regional Seas Programme: From Past to Future', in R Rayfuse (ed.), *Research Handbook on International Marine Environmental Law* (Edward Elgar 2015) 352–6.

[103] Barcelona Convention, Article 4(1).

[104] See the1982 Protocol Concerning Mediterranean Specially Protected Areas (Geneva Protocol) (EIF 23 March 1986), Article 3.

[105] Ibid, Article 7.   [106] Ibid, Article 5.

'promote the participation of its public and its conservation organizations in measures that are necessary for the protection of the areas and species concerned'.[107] This is an early application of the participatory approach, later endorsed in Principle 10 of the Rio Declaration and it recognizes that local communities may be able to make important contributions to ensuring the effective management of protected areas.

Another important feature of the Protocol is the requirement for cooperation between Parties in achieving the goals of the instrument. Thus, if a state establishes a MPA under the Protocol, it must inform the other Parties, and it is anticipated that a directory of MPAs will be maintained for the Mediterranean region.[108] States shall also establish a cooperation programme to coordinate their activities under the Protocol.[109] In particular, if one Party intends to establish a protected area or buffer zone contiguous to a frontier, consultation with the neighbouring state shall take place with a view to examining the possibility of the other Party establishing a corresponding contiguous protected area, buffer zone, or other appropriate measure.[110] Such an arrangement is thus designed to ensure that MPAs are protected from transboundary threats.

The adoption of the Geneva Protocol was an important milestone, even though it does have serious limitations. First, the Protocol only applies to territorial waters, which meant that many types of marine ecosystems found beyond this limited area do not fall within the scheme of protection.[111] At the same time, the Protocol did recognize that States could include internal waters and land inside their baselines within MPAs, including wetlands and coastal areas. At least in this respect, States are encouraged to take an ecosystems approach to the designation of MPAs, and this is an early example of an emergent trend of integrated coastal zone management in the Mediterranean region.[112] The second drawback of the Protocol is that many of its obligations are couched in flexible terms, giving a large degree of discretion to the States concerned. Nevertheless, the Protocol envisages a meeting of the Parties to review measures taken under the agreement, thus providing some political oversight of the matter.

The Protocol is also important because of the influence it has had on other regions in developing instruments to address the protection of marine ecosystems. The 1983 Convention for the Protection and Development of the Marine Environment of the Wider Caribbean region is a good example of this trend.[113] Adopted only a year after the Geneva Protocol, the Convention already illustrates how important concepts can be transplanted and developed in the negotiation of regional treaties. Thus, in its preamble, the Convention recognizes the protection of the ecosystems of the marine environment of the wider Caribbean as one of its 'principal objectives' and the main body of the agreement included an obligation to take all appropriate measures

---

[107] Ibid, Article 11.   [108] Ibid, Article 8(2).   [109] Ibid, Article 12.
[110] Ibid, Article 6.   [111] Ibid, Article 2.
[112] Mediterranean States were later to adopt the 2008 Protocol on Integrated Coastal Zone Management in the Mediterranean.
[113] See the 1983 Convention for the Protection and Development of the Marine Environment of the Wider Caribbean (Cartagena Convention) (EIF 11 October 1986).

to protect and preserve rare or fragile ecosystems, as well as the habitat of depleted, threatened or endangered species in the Convention area.[114]

It can be seen that this language draws its inspiration from Article 194(5) of UNCLOS and the regional treaty can thus be seen as a means of implementing this obligation in a collaborative manner. The Convention goes on to specify that one of the key ways in which to satisfy this obligation is through the designation of protected areas.[115] Given that protected areas are not mentioned in UNCLOS, it is likely that this provision draws its inspiration from the Geneva Protocol adopted by the Mediterranean States a year earlier. The Convention does not give much more detail about what it meant by a 'protected area', simply providing that Parties should exchange information concerning the administration and management of such areas, which, in any case, will not affect the rights of other Parties or third States. This obligation would, therefore, appear to be very limited in scope. Nevertheless, the Parties have developed the legal regime in this respect through the negotiation of a Protocol Concerning Specially Protected Areas and Wildlife.[116]

In the first place, the Protocol elaborates the obligation on protected areas in Article 10 of the Cartagena Convention by dictating both substantive and procedural requirements relating to the establishment of MPAs, including the promulgation of criteria to be used by States when identifying MPAs.[117] The Protocol seeks to stabilize protection for MPAs by providing that 'changes in delimitation of legal status of an area or part thereof, ... may only take place for a significant reason' and it requires advance notification of such changes.[118] Whilst this falls short of a veto, it does mean that other States will have an opportunity to have their say before any changes can be made. This procedure suggests that the Protocol recognizes the interests of other States, even in relation to protected areas that fall wholly within the jurisdiction of another State.

The Protocol also extends the scope of the obligations under the Cartagena Convention by requiring Parties to take additional necessary measures to 'protect, preserve and manage in a sustainable way ... threatened or endangered species of flora and fauna'.[119] *Endangered species* is defined as a 'species or sub-species ... or their populations that are in danger of extinction throughout all or part of their range',[120] and *threatened species* is defined as species, subspecies, or populations 'that are likely to become endangered within the foreseeable future [or] that are rare because they are usually localized within restricted geographical areas or habitats or are thinly scattered over a more extensive range and which are potentially or actually subject to decline and possible endangerment or extinction'.[121] The Protocol not

[114] Ibid, Article 10.   [115] Ibid.

[116] See the 1990 Protocol Concerning Specially Protected Areas and Wildlife (Kingston Protocol) (EIF 18 June 2000).

[117] Ibid, Articles 4–9. The criteria include representative types of coastal and marine ecosystems; habitats and associated ecosystems critical to the survival and recovery of threatened or endangered species; productive ecosystems upon which the welfare of local inhabitants is dependent; and areas of special biological, ecological, educational, scientific, historical, cultural, recreational, archaeological, aesthetic, or economic value.

[118] Ibid, Article 15(1).   [119] Ibid, Article 3.   [120] Ibid, Article 1(f).

[121] Ibid, Article 1(g).

only demands that individual States identify and take steps to protect endangered or threatened species within their jurisdiction but also establishes a procedure for the establishment of a list of endangered species of flora and fauna, which shall receive protection across the region.[122] Once a species has been listed in the relevant Annex to the Protocol, States are under an obligation to 'ensure total protection and recovery' of such species.[123] For plant species this includes a prohibition on 'all forms of destruction or disturbance, including the picking, collecting, cutting, uprooting, or possession of, or commercial trade in such species'.[124] For animals, the Protocol requires a prohibition on the taking, possession, or killing of a species and a minimization on the disturbance of such species.[125] States must also evaluate the impact of planned activities within their jurisdiction on specially protected species.[126] More generally, the Parties are required to establish regional recovery programmes for listed species, with a view to halting and reversing declines in populations.[127]

Other regions have also followed this trend and they have included provisions on nature conservation in framework treaties[128] or they have adopted separate protocols on protected areas.[129] These developments were modelled upon the earlier treaties adopted in the Mediterranean and Caribbean. Nevertheless, it is clear that this trend was consolidated by the emergence of the CBD and, from 1992 onwards, most existing regional seas treaties that did not already include the objective of promoting marine ecosystems were amended to take into account, inter alia, the growing importance attached to the conservation of biological diversity at the international level. This led to what has been called the second generation of regional seas treaties,[130] reflecting to a much greater extent the emerging principles of environmental law endorsed in the 1992 Rio Declaration, and expressly incorporating biodiversity concerns.

The Baltic region was the first to amend the basic regional treaty in order to include an express reference to biodiversity. A new Convention was adopted in 1992, Article 15, of which provides that:

The Contracting Parties shall individually and jointly take all appropriate measures with respect to the Baltic Sea to conserve natural habitats and biological diversity and to protect ecological processes. Such measures shall also be taken to ensure the sustainable use of natural

---

[122] Ibid, Article 11(4)   [123] Ibid, Article 11(1).   [124] Ibid, Article 11(1)(a).
[125] Ibid, Article 11(1)(b).   [126] Ibid, Article 13.   [127] Ibid, Article 11(5).

[128] See e.g. 1985 Convention for the Protection, Management and Development of the Marine and Coastal Environment of the Eastern African Region (Nairobi Convention) (EIF 30 May 1996), Article 10. This has been replaced by the 2010 Amended Convention for the Protection, Management and Development of the Marine and Coastal Environment of the Western Indian Ocean.

[129] See e.g. 1985 Protocol Concerning Protected Areas and Wild Fauna and Flora in the Eastern African Region (Nairobi Protocol) (EIF 30 May 1996); 1989 Protocol for the Conservation and Management of Protected Marine and Coastal Areas of the South-East Pacific (Paipa Protocol) (EIF 24 January 1995). See also Annex V of the 1991 Protocol to the Antarctic Treaty on Environmental Protection, which provides, inter alia, for the designation of Antarctic Specially Protected Areas or Antarctic Specially Managed Areas in marine areas.

[130] See e.g. T Treves, 'Regional Approaches to the Protection of the Marine Environment', in MH Nordquist et al (eds), *The Stockholm Declaration and Law of the Marine Environment* (Martinus Nijhoff 2003) 143.

resources within the Baltic Sea Area. To this end, the Contracting Parties shall aim at adopting subsequent instruments containing appropriate guidelines and criteria.

It is clear that this provision only establishes a very basic obligation and its importance rather lies in the establishment of a legal basis for further cooperation. Indeed, this provision has been operationalized in the practice of the Parties, through a range of activities. First, States agreed to undertake a collaborative assessment of the ecosystem health of the Baltic Sea,[131] which provided baseline information for the promulgation of further measures. The Helsinki Commission, which is responsible for overseeing the Baltic Sea Convention, has also established a permanent working group on the state of the environment and nature conservation, whose tasks include exchanging information about threats to biodiversity across the region. Second, States integrated biodiversity targets into the Baltic Sea Action Plan, in which they committed to work towards achieving overall favourable conservation status for Baltic Sea biodiversity, with a specific emphasis on targets to provide protection to endangered or threatened species, such as seals, eels, and cod, as well as targets to restore lost biodiversity through measures such as the reintroduction of Baltic sturgeon and the restocking of salmon and sea trout.[132]

The Helsinki Commission has also used its powers under the Baltic Sea Convention to make recommendations to the Parties in order to promote further the conservation of marine biological diversity in the Baltic region. Two key sets of measures have been adopted in this context. First, the Commission has promoted the development of a network of MPAs throughout the Baltic region. In Recommendation 15/5, adopted in 1994 before the 1992 Convention had even entered into force, the Baltic States agreed to take all appropriate measures to establish a system of coastal and marine Baltic Sea Protected Areas (BSPAs). This Recommendation identified a number of areas to be protected in the Annex, but it also made it clear that the system of BSPAs should be 'gradually developed as new knowledge and information becomes available'.[133] States also agreed Guidelines for Designating Marine and Coastal BSPAs, which specify the factors to be taken into account when expanding the network, highlighting the need to protect important feeding areas; important migration routes; important reproduction areas; sensitive, threatened, or declining habitats; habitats of sensitive, threatened, declining, or keystone species; and areas with high biodiversity.[134] Once a BSPA has been designated, States are encouraged to develop monitoring programmes for biodiversity within the BSPA, institute management plans for the BSPAs, and ensure that any decisions that could lead to a reduction in protection or quality of the BSPA should be reported to the Commission. Whilst the Commission does not have the power to override the decision of the Contracting Party, this procedure allows some international scrutiny of

---

[131]   Helsinki Commission, Ecosystem Health of the Baltic Sea 2003–7 (2010). A second assessment is expected in June 2017; see http://www.helcom.fi/baltic-sea-trends/state-of-the-baltic-sea-2017/.
[132]   Baltic Sea Action Plan (2007) 19–21.
[133]   HELCOM Recommendation 15/5 (1994), para. (b).
[134]   See   <http://www.helcom.fi/action-areas/marine-protected-areas/Background%20of%20 HELCOM%20MPAs/selection-criteria/>.

management measures, and political pressure could be brought to bear on States in order to ensure that the conservation objectives of a BSPA are met.

These early developments in the Baltic Sea have since been consolidated as Parties to the Helsinki Convention have confirmed their commitment to the global target[135] of achieving by 2020 an ecologically coherent network of well-managed marine protected areas for the Baltic Sea[136] and they have revised Recommendation 15/5 in order to take into account these developments.[137] To date, Baltic States have identified 174 MPAs, covering an area of 53,642 km², although it has been observed that the majority of these sites are in coastal waters and there is a need to designate more sites in open waters. The Baltic Sea States have not yet engaged directly with the EBSA process initiated under the CBD, but this would be one way to increase the representativeness of its MPA network in an internationally recognized and transparent manner.[138] Another challenge for the Baltic Sea MPA network is that not all MPAs yet have management plans, and States have agreed that such plans should ideally be put in place within five years of designation.[139] Continued scrutiny by the Helsinki Commission will be important in ensuring that States follow these recommendations.

Alongside the identification of areas that need special protection, the Parties to the Helsinki Convention have also developed a Red List of species in the Baltic region that require special protection. Recommendation 37/2 calls for States to make an inventory of existing and planned conservation measures aimed at these species and then to identify additional activities that are needed in order to mitigate threats to these species.[140] For some species, the Parties have adopted specific recommendations aimed at ensuring their favourable conservation status, including Baltic Salmon and Sea Trout,[141] Seals,[142] and Harbour Porpoise.[143] Many of these instruments are crosscutting in nature and so they will be relevant when considering regulation of the range of activities that fall under the auspices of Helsinki Convention.

One sees a similar process of evolution under the OSPAR Convention, which was adopted in 1992, in order to replace two previous regional treaties relating to pollution by dumping and pollution from land-based activities. The new Convention included a general reference to the need to take measures to 'conserve marine ecosystems and, when practicable, restore marine areas'.[144] Further, it posed a general duty to 'take the necessary measures to protect the maritime area against adverse effects

---

[135] See above.

[136] See 2010 Moscow Ministerial Declaration, 10; 2013 Copenhagen Ministerial Declaration, para. 6(B).

[137] HELCOM Recommendation 35/1 (2014).

[138] However, see the decision at the 2016 Meeting of the Heads of Delegation, where states agreed to start planning a regional EBSA workshop; *Outcome of the 51st Meeting of the Heads of Delegation*, Document HOD 51-2016, para. 6.94.

[139] 2013 Copenhagen Ministerial Declaration, para. 8(B).

[140] HELCOM Recommendation 37/2 (2016).

[141] HELCOM Recommendation 32-33/11 (2011).

[142] HELCOM Recommendation 27-28/2 (2006).

[143] HELCOM Recommendation 17/2 (2013).

[144] OSPAR Convention, Article 2(1)(a).

of human activities',[145] and these provisions are arguably broad enough to cover the conservation of marine biodiversity. If there were any doubt about the mandate of the OSPAR Commission in this respect, it was removed as soon as the Convention entered into force, when a new annex on the protection and conservation of marine biological diversity was added.[146] This Annex expressly requires Parties, inter alia, to 'take, individually and jointly, the necessary measures to protect the maritime area against the adverse effects of human activities so as to safeguard human health and to conserve marine ecosystems'.[147] The Annex explicitly incorporates definitions of *biological diversity, ecosystem,* and *habitat* from the CBD, thereby ensuring a harmonized interpretation of the applicable legal framework.[148] Furthermore, the North-East Atlantic Environment Strategy reinforces the importance of the ecosystems approach and it calls for the adoption of further measures to promote ecosystem integrity.[149]

The OSPAR Commission is charged with drawing up plans and programmes for the purpose of achieving the objectives of Annex V. In furtherance of this provision, the Commission has adopted a biological diversity and ecosystems strategy, and the Parties have agreed on a list of threatened or declining species and habitats.[150] In addition, the Commission has adopted recommendations dealing with many individual species on this list. The recommendations are not binding, but Parties are nevertheless expected to report to the Commission on the measures that they have taken to comply. Moreover, the recommendations explicitly foresee that the OSPAR Commission will keep the recovery of species constantly under review and draw the question of strengthening the protection of a species to the attention of other competent international institutions. These recommendations are generally focused on collection of data and calling for States to regulate activities that may affect these species, without specifying any particular action. However, the OSPAR Contracting Parties have agreed that threatened species and habitats will be taken into account when undertaking assessments of environmental impacts of other human activities falling within the scope of the Convention.[151] Moreover, the recommendations also suggest that States should identify key habitats of threatened species which could be designated as marine protected areas.

As in the Baltic region, States in the North-East Atlantic have also agreed to promote the development of a representative network of MPAs in accordance with international targets.[152] OSPAR Recommendation 2003/3 thus calls for Parties to consider whether any areas within their national jurisdiction justify selection as MPAs under agreed criteria and to report to the OSPAR Commission the areas

---

[145] Ibid.
[146] See <http://www.ospar.org/site/assets/files/1169/pages_from_ospar_convention_a5.pdf>.
[147] OSPAR Convention, Annex V, Article 2.   [148] Ibid, Article 1.
[149] OSPAR Agreement 2010–13, para. 2. See also Joint Ministerial Statement of the Helsinki and OSPAR Commissions on the Ecosystem Approach to the Management of Human Activities (2003).
[150] OSPAR Agreement 2008/6.
[151] OSPAR Recommendation 2010/5, on assessments of environmental impact in relation to threatened and/or declining species and habitats.
[152] OSPAR Agreement 2010–13, Part II, para. 1.2(b).

that it has selected. For each area, the relevant Contracting Party should develop a management plan. A key difference in the establishment of a network of MPAs in the North-East Atlantic, compared with the Baltic Sea, is that the mandate of the OSPAR Commission extends to areas beyond national jurisdiction.[153] Thus, Parties are also encouraged to propose areas beyond national jurisdiction that should be selected by the OSPAR Commission as components of the OSPAR Network of MPAS.[154] Acting under this mandate, the OSPAR Ministerial Meeting decided in 2010 to establish six MPAs beyond national jurisdiction and it adopted accompanying recommendations on their initial management.[155] A further high seas site was added in 2012.[156] The recommendations set the general and specific management objectives for each MPA and they encourage States to identify activities and mitigating actions that promote the achievement of the conservation objectives. The recommendations also call on States to carry out EIAs and SEAs for activities that may conflict with the conservation objectives of the MPAs. These moves have not been without controversy, as the OSPAR Commission only includes States from the North-East Atlantic region in its membership, whereas any areas beyond national jurisdiction are clearly of interest to a much wider range of States. However, the measures recognize that they cannot affect the rights and interests of third parties. As a result, the OSPAR Convention itself will not be able to achieve fully its objectives in areas beyond national jurisdiction without wider cooperation and, therefore, it will be necessary for the Parties to raise awareness of the MPA network and to work with other States and relevant international organizations in order to further their management plans.[157] Given the fragmented nature of the international legal order highlighted in the following chapters on sectoral approaches to marine environmental protection, this is a significant challenge. It is an issue to which we will return in Chapter 10, when we consider the particular approaches to promoting coordination and cooperation adopted by the OSPAR Commission.

Other treaties have also been amended to reflect biodiversity considerations. A new version of the Barcelona Convention was adopted in 1995, with an express provision on biological diversity,[158] and a new Protocol Concerning Specially Protected Areas and Biological Diversity in the Mediterranean followed shortly thereafter to replace the 1982 Protocol. This new Protocol overcomes many of the shortcomings of the original instrument, including the ability to establish MPAs in zones partly or wholly on the high seas.[159] This is an important provision in the context of the Mediterranean, where many States have not yet claimed an EEZ, and, therefore,

---

[153] OSPAR Convention, Article 1.
[154] OSPAR Recommendation 2003/3, para. 3.1(d).
[155] Altair Seamount High Seas MPA (Decision 2010/3 and Recommendation 2010/14); Antialtair Seamount High Seas MPA (Decision 2010/4 and Recommendation 2010/15); Josephine Seamount High Seas MPA (Decision 2010/5 and Recommendation 2010/16); Mid-Atlantic Ridge North of the Azores High Seas MPA (Decision 2010/6 and Recommendation 2010/17).
[156] Charlie Gibbs North High Seas MPA (Decision 2012/1 and Recommendation 2012/1).
[157] See e.g. Recommendation 2012/1, para. 3.3.5(a).
[158] See the1995 Convention for the Protection of the Marine Environment and the Coastal Region of the Mediterranean (Revised Barcelona Convention), Article 10.
[159] SPAMI Protocol, Article 9(1)(b).

large parts of the marine area are beyond national jurisdiction.[160] Moreover, the new Protocol also extends protection to threatened and endangered species, and the Parties maintain lists of species for which they are required to take maximum possible protection and recovery measures.[161] The Parties to the Barcelona Convention have also adopted a Strategic Action Programme for the Conservation of Biological Diversity in the Mediterranean Region, which is further supplemented by a series of action plans, programmes of action, and guidelines relating to particular species, including turtles, cartilaginous fish, seabirds, monk seals, and cetaceans. Such instruments are not legally binding, but the meeting of the Contracting Parties has requested that States take measures to implement them.

Those regional seas treaties that have only emerged since the conclusion of the CBD have been drafted to cover the conservation of biological diversity from the outset,[162] and there has been a gradual increase in the number of protocols dealing with these issues, many of which follow the models promulgated in other regions.[163] However, as it is hoped, will be clear from the preceding analysis, the treaties themselves only establish a framework, and the real challenge for States is to collect the information concerning the precise nature of threats, and to adopt subsequent measures to address them. In doing so, States must ensure that they take into account the broader legal framework for the regulation of sectoral activities, both within a regional seas treaty regime and beyond.

3.5 Conclusion

There is little doubt that biodiversity protection today occupies a central place in the modern legal framework for the protection of the marine environment. This consideration has gradually emerged onto the international agenda since the early 1980s, but the conclusion of the CBD was critical in ensuring that this trend was consolidated, so that it is now a crosscutting concern in the regulation of all marine activities. One consequence of this development is that States must take into account the impact of their activities, not only on the marine species directly exploited as a resource, such as fish stocks, but on all aspects of marine life.

---

[160] See I Papanicolopulu, 'The Mediterranean Sea', in DR Rothwell et al (eds), *Oxford Handbook on the Law of the Sea* (OUP 2015) 611.

[161] See the 1995 Protocol Concerning Specially Protected Areas and Biological Diversity in the Mediterranean (SPAMI Protocol) (EIF 12 December 1999), Article 12.

[162] See e.g. 2002 Convention for Cooperation in the Protection and Sustainable Development of the Marine and Coastal Environment of the North-East Pacific (Antigua Convention) (not yet in force); 2003 Framework Convention for the Protection of the Marine Environment of the Caspian Sea (Tehran Convention) (EIF 12 August 2006).

[163] See the 2002 Black Sea Biodiversity and Landscape Protocol (EIF 20 June 2011); 2005 Protocol Concerning the Conservation of Biological Diversity and the Establishment of Networks of Marine Protected Areas in the Red Sea and Gulf of Aden; 2014 Protocol for the Conservation of Biological Diversity of the Caspian Sea (Ashgabet Protocol) (not yet in force). For further discussion of these instruments, see Oral (n102) 352–6.

The major global and regional treaties relating to nature conservation and bio-diversity have played an important role in identifying which species and habitats should be protected from undue human interference. These processes are ongoing, and States must periodically re-evaluate their efforts in order to ensure that sufficient action is being taken. Yet, beyond a basic duty to refrain from the direct taking or harm of protected species and habitats, the biodiversity treaties do not specify the precise measures that must be taken. Rather, their approach generally mirrors that of the marine environmental provisions of UNCLOS, in that they encourage the assessment and monitoring of activities that may have serious adverse effects on marine biodiversity and they encourage the development of additional mitigation measures in order to minimize such effects. It is generally left to States, individually or jointly, to decide what measures should be taken in this respect. At the same time, the meetings of the Parties to the biodiversity treaties have offered a forum in which to monitor these developments and to suggest priorities for action. In this way, the biodiversity treaties have provided an important catalyst for ensuring that subsequent measures are taken, either by individual States or through the competent international institutions. We will, therefore, return to the role of the biodiversity treaties when considering the evolution of specific sectoral regimes in the following chapters. Moreover, because they have a mandate to address the whole range of threats to biodiversity, the biodiversity treaties are able to push for coordination of measures in order to achieve an effective ecosystems approach,[164] an issue to which we will return in Chapter 10.

---

[164] See, further, E Franckx, 'The Protection of Biodiversity and Fisheries Management: Issues Raised by the Relationship between CITES and LOSC', in D Freestone et al (eds), *The Law of the Sea: Progress and Prospects* (OUP 2006) 634–5.

4

Land-Based Sources of Marine Pollution

4.1 Introduction

Land-based activities are among the most serious causes of marine environmental degradation and the most difficult to regulate. According to one estimate, land-based activities account for more than 80 per cent of marine pollution.[1] This category covers a range of processes and activities on land, including industrial, agricultural, and urban discharges. Pollutants may be released directly into the marine environment through outflows or pipelines, or they may reach the seas indirectly through rivers or the air. In either case, the cocktail of substances can have serious impacts once they enter the marine environment.

Some of the worst contaminants include toxic chemicals and radioactive materials, but more recent studies indicate that serious threats to the marine environment come not just from substances that kill or injure flora and fauna, but also from pollutants that have 'more subtle, but possibly even more damaging effects', such as 'changes in the structure and function of communities of marine life, through disrupting reproduction and altering behavior, and effects at the molecular level'.[2] For example, so-called endocrine-disrupting chemicals' discharged from land-based sources, both through water and air, have been discovered to disturb the development cycles of certain species.[3]

Another serious land-based source of marine pollution is the discharge of nutrients associated with agricultural run-off, transport by air, or sewage outfalls at sea.[4] The input of nutrients into the marine environment is not necessarily itself harmful, but it can provoke excessive growth of marine plant life, causing an increase in oxygen-consuming bacteria. So-called eutrophication can lead to 'hypoxic' or 'dead zones', in which most marine life suffocates and dies.[5] Eutrophication has been described as 'potentially one of the most damaging of the many harmful effects that humans have on the oceans, both in its scale and in its consequences',[6] and it

---

[1] See UNEP, *Protecting Coastal and Marine Environments from Land-based Activities: A Guide for National Action* (2006) 3.

[2] GESAMP, *Protecting the Ocean from Land-based Activities*, GESAMP Reports and Studies No. 71 (2001) 7.

[3] Ibid, 48.   [4] Ibid, 24.

[5] Dead zones have become a regular occurrence in some parts of the world, such as the Gulf of Mexico; see <http://oceanservice.noaa.gov/facts/deadzone.html>.

[6] GESAMP, *Sea of Troubles*, GESAMP Reports and Studies No. 70 (2001) 8.

is a phenomenon that has been reported to be increasing.[7] It is particularly a problem in enclosed or semi-enclosed seas where currents do not disperse discharges as effectively.

Litter from land-based sources is another growing threat to the marine environment,[8] which can both kill marine life through entanglement, but also lead to a number of other problems for marine species and habitats.[9] There is evidence that this problem is increasing in many parts of the world,[10] and marine litter has been identified by some observers as 'a global issue of pressing concern, given the long period of decay of plastics, their potential for long-distance transport and their tendency to disintegrate into extremely harmful micro-particles'.[11] For this reason, the international community has begun to highlight plastics and micro-plastics as an issue that requires priority attention.[12]

The challenge of tackling land-based sources of marine pollution has been on the international agenda for many years. In the early 1970s, the Stockholm Conference acknowledged that it was necessary to '[s]trengthen national controls over land-based sources of marine pollution, in particular in enclosed and semi enclosed seas'.[13] Given that pollution from multiple States can have cumulative effects on marine ecosystems, there is a need for States to coordinate their response to ensure that measures are effective in reducing overall pollution loads.

This chapter will seek to explain and evaluate the major international instruments that have been adopted to address land-based sources of marine pollution. It will start with the relevant provisions of the United Nations Convention on the Law of the Sea (UNCLOS), before turning to the other treaties and instruments that have been negotiated on this topic at the international and regional levels. In doing so, it will ask what types of legal tools and techniques are commonly used to combat land-based sources of marine pollution. It must be noted from the outset that the challenges of regulation in this area are significant given the range of activities that are implicated and the fact that many of these activities are 'closely bound up with crucial national programmes for economic, industrial and social development of those countries'.[14] In other words, it is 'a multiple-issue, multiple jurisdiction type problem at the interface of land and sea, where any preventative and remedial action

---

[7] UNEP Press Release, Further Rise in the Number of Marine 'Dead Zones', 19 October 2006.

[8] Litter from ships is also a problem; see Chapter 8.

[9] See JGB Derraik, 'The Pollution of the Marine Environment by Plastic Debris: A Review' (2002) 44 *MPB* 842.

[10] Perhaps the most infamous example is the Great Pacific Garbage Patch; see <http://marinedebris.noaa.gov/info/patch.html>.

[11] Proceedings of the United Nations Environment Assembly of the United Nations Environment Programme at its first session, Document UNEP/EA.1/10 (2014) para. 64.

[12] See UNGA Resolution 66/288 (2012) Annex, para. 163; UNEP Environmental Assembly, Resolution 1/6 (2014) para. 4; UNEP Environmental Assembly, Resolution 2/11 (2016) para. 1. Plastics, microplastics, and nanoplastics were the focus of the seventeenth meeting of the United Nations Informal Consultative Process, which took place in June 2016.

[13] Stockholm Action Plan (1972) Recommendation 86(e).

[14] Y Tanaka, 'Regulation of Land-based Marine Pollution in International Law: A Comparative Analysis between Global and Global and Regional Legal Frameworks' (2006) 66 *ZaöRV* 535, 548.

is likely to impinge upon a range of stakeholders and vested interests'.[15] Controlling land-based sources of marine pollution thus presents both a political and practical challenge, which is reflected in the multiple layers of regulation at the international level and the use of binding and non-binding instruments to address this problem.

4.2 UNCLOS and Land-Based Sources of Marine Pollution

Land-based activities are the first source of marine pollution to be addressed in Section 5 of Part XII of UNCLOS. Land-based sources are not explicitly defined in the Convention,[16] but it does refer to the regulation of pollution from 'rivers, estuaries, pipelines and outfall structures'.[17] This is, however, an illustrative list, and the obligation covers all potential land-based sources of marine pollution. Pollution of the marine environment from or through the atmosphere is addressed separately in Article 212 but in very similar terms.[18] The obligations under both provisions are addressed to 'States' generally, thereby including not only coastal States, but also landlocked States that may cause pollution that is transferred to the sea via rivers, aquifers, or through the air.[19] Thus, UNCLOS covers all major land-based inputs into the marine environment. The Convention contains both general procedural obligations and specific substantive rules that are applicable to land-based sources of marine pollution.

To the extent that land-based activities are likely to cause 'substantial pollution of or significant and harmful changes to the marine environment',[20] they will also be covered by the obligations to carry out an environmental impact assessment (EIA) under Article 206.[21] In the context of land-based sources of marine pollution, this obligation will have particular relevance to point source discharges, but it is more difficult to apply to diffuse sources of pollution, as individual activities will rarely have a substantial impact by themselves.

Where land-based activities are suspected of causing transboundary harm to neighbouring States, States may also be required to consult with affected States in relation to what action is necessary. In the *MOX Plant Case*, Ireland invoked, inter alia, Articles 123, 197, and 206 of UNCLOS to challenge the decision of the United Kingdom to authorize the construction of a nuclear facility on its coast.[22] Ireland alleged that the facility would cause serious and irreparable harm to the marine environment of the Irish Sea and it called for the United Kingdom to cease construction until it had carried out further consultations with Ireland on what remedial

---

[15] C Williams and B Davis, 'Land-based Activities: What Remains to Be Done' (1995) 29 *O&CM* 207, 208.

[16] See M Nordquist et al (eds), *1982 United Nations Convention on the Law of the Sea—A Commentary—Vol. IV* (Martinus Nijhoff 1991) 132.

[17] UNCLOS, Article 207(1).   [18] Ibid, Article 212.

[19] See also Montreal Guidelines for the Protection of the Marine Environment against Pollution from Land-based Sources (Montreal Guidelines) (1985) para. 5(b); Global Programme of Action for the Protection of the Marine Environment against Pollution from Land-based Activities (GPOA) (1995) para. 34.

[20] Ibid.   [21] See Chapter 2.   [22] *The MOX Plant Case* (2001) paras 55–121.

measures may be necessary. Although the International Tribunal for the Law of the Sea (ITLOS) refused to order the cessation of construction owing to a lack of evidence of imminent harm to the marine environment,[23] it nevertheless went on to say that 'prudence and caution require that Ireland and the United Kingdom cooperate in exchanging information concerning risks or effects of the operation of the MOX plant and in devising ways to deal with them, as appropriate'[24] and the Tribunal ordered the Parties to cooperate.[25] A similar result occurred in the *Case concerning Land Reclamation in the Johor Straits*, in which Malaysia had argued that the proposed land reclamation by Singapore would cause significant harm to the marine environment. ITLOS not only ordered the Parties to exchange information on the relevant activities and impacts, but also to cooperate in assessing the impacts of the activities by establishing a joint group of independent experts to conduct a study on the effects of Singapore's proposed land reclamation and to propose appropriate measures to deal with those effects.[26] The increased cooperation as a result of the order led the Parties to reach an amicable settlement.[27]

More generally, UNCLOS imposes a broad obligation on all States to 'keep under surveillance the effects of any activities that they permit or in which they engage in order to determine whether these activities are likely to pollute the marine environment'.[28] In essence, this requires a State to gather evidence relating to the state of the marine environment and identify any particular substances that may be causing harm. If such evidence is discovered, the obligation to exercise due diligence in the prevention, reduction and control of the sources of pollution will kick in, requiring States to investigate the sources of the harm and to take appropriate action. The monitoring obligation is particularly important for the identification of serious cases of pollution arising from diffuse sources, such as urban and agricultural run-off, and it will allow States to ascertain pollution hotspots that require special attention.

The obligation of due diligence in the context of land-based sources of marine pollution is found in Article 207, which requires States to adopt and enforce national laws and regulations[29] and to take 'other measures as may be necessary'[30] in order to protect the marine environment from land-based sources. Similar requirements apply to pollution from or through the atmosphere.[31] Given the nature of the activities that fall within the scope of these provisions and their connection with the economic development of a State, this is clearly an issue where the application of the common but differentiated responsibilities principle may lead to differential standards being applied to States, depending upon the financial and technical resources at their disposal and their overall developmental needs. Thus, the degree of prevention, reduction, or control that must be pursued by any single State could vary significantly. The Convention attempts to steer State policy to some extent by encouraging the adoption of national rules, standards, and recommended practices

---

[23] Ibid, para. 81.   [24] Ibid, para. 84.   [25] Ibid, dispositif.
[26] *Land Reclamation in the Johor Straits (Provisional Measures)* (2003) dispositif para. 1.
[27] *Land Reclamation in the Johor Straits (Settlement)* (2005).
[28] UNCLOS, Article 204(2).   [29] UNCLOS, Articles 207(1) and 213.
[30] Ibid, Article 207(2).   [31] Ibid, Articles 212(1), 212(2), and 222.

'designed to minimize, to the fullest extent possible, the release of toxic, harmful or noxious substances, especially those that are persistent, into the marine environment'.[32] The emphasis on this category of pollutants indicates a priority for action, but it does not exhaust the scope of measures to be adopted by States.

As well as requiring the adoption of national laws and regulations, UNCLOS also encourages international cooperation[33] on the prevention, reduction, and control of marine pollution from land-based sources. Such cooperation should be aimed at the adoption of 'global and regional rules, standards and recommended practices and procedures'.[34] The language of the provision suggests that the result of negotiations may include binding and non-binding instruments. As will be seen below, this is an area where both sorts of instruments have been employed in practice.

The results of such regional or global cooperation are to be taken into account by individual States when adopting national legislation,[35] but Articles 207 and 212 fall short of mandating compliance therewith. Rather, they reflect the wish of the drafters to 'preserve for themselves as much freedom of action as possible in balancing environmental protection measures against the needs of their own economies, where land-based pollution generated much of the most harmful pollution',[36] and unless States have individually consented to be bound by international agreements, UNCLOS leaves the discretion of States as to *how* they tackle pollution from land-based activities intact. Thus, in this context, UNCLOS only provides a basic framework that must be supplemented by additional rules or standards at the global or regional level.

4.3 The Global Framework for Addressing Land-Based Sources of Marine Pollution

4.3.1 The Montreal Guidelines for the protection of the marine environment against pollution from land-based sources

Given that the prevention and reduction of pollution of the marine environment from land-based sources does not clearly fall within the mandate of any specific UN specialized agency, the United Nations Environment Programme (UNEP) has taken the lead at the global level in implementing the provisions on land-based sources of marine pollution in UNCLOS,[37] in furtherance of its mandate to promote cooperation on environmental matters that were not covered by existing institutions and to coordinate the actions of the various institutions within the United Nations system.[38]

---

[32] Ibid, Article 207(5).   [33] Ibid, Articles 207(3), 207(4), and 212(3).

[34] Ibid, Articles 207(4) and 212(3).   [35] Ibid, Articles 207(1) and 212(1).

[36] P Birnie, A Boyle, and C Redgwell, *International Law and the Environment* (3rd edn: OUP 2009) 454.

[37] See B Vukas, 'Provisions of the Draft Convention on the Law of the Sea Relating to the Protection and Preservation of the Marine Environment and the UNEP's Involvement in Their Implementation', in B Vukas, *The Law of the Sea: Selected Writings* (Martinus Nijhoff 2004) 248.

[38] UNGA Resolution 2997(XXVII) (1972) para. 2.

Shortly after the conclusion of UNCLOS, the UNEP Governing Council established an ad hoc working group of experts to draft guidelines on the protection of the marine environment from land-based sources.[39] The resulting Montreal Guidelines for the Protection of the Marine Environment against Pollution from Land-based Sources were approved by UNEP in 1985.[40]

The Montreal Guidelines confirm the basic procedural obligations placed upon States by Article 207 of the UNCLOS[41] and they further encourage States to develop 'a comprehensive environmental management approach to the prevention, reduction and control of pollution from land-based sources'.[42] This recommendation seeks to promote an early form of coastal zone management.[43] An annex to the Guidelines suggests different measures that can be taken by States when managing land-based sources, including environmental quality objectives, discharge standards,[44] process standards, and economic measures. None of these measures is deemed mandatory, and the Guidelines explicitly recognize that 'flexibility will be an important consideration in the strategies or regulatory instruments implemented for various water bodies',[45] thus echoing the approach found in Article 207 of UNCLOS. In any case, the Guidelines make clear that they are 'recommendatory in nature',[46] and most of the provisions are expressed in hortatory language,[47] emphasizing their non-binding status. In sum, the Guidelines provide little more than 'a check-list of provisions suitable for inclusion in future regional agreements and national programmes'[48] and they certainly do not promulgate rules or standards that must be followed by States or other actors. Nevertheless, they offered a first attempt to guide States as to what action they should take in order to comply with their obligations under UNCLOS.

4.3.2 The Washington Declaration and the Global Programme of Action

At the 1992 United Nations Conference on Environment and Development, the international community decided to update and strengthen the Montreal Guidelines[49] and UNEP was invited to convene an intergovernmental meeting in order to take this work forward.[50] This led to the adoption in 1995 of the Washington Declaration and the Global Programme of Action for the Protection of the Marine Environment from Land-based Activities (GPOA), two non-binding instruments focused on the prevention, reduction, and control of marine pollution from land-based activities.

---

[39] See UNEP Governing Council Decision 10/24 (1982).
[40] The Montreal Guidelines were adopted by UNEP Governing Council Decision 13/18 (1985).
[41] Montreal Guidelines, paras 11–12.   [42] Ibid, para. 10.
[43] See ibid, Annex I, para. 1.3.2.1.
[44] See ibid, Annex II, which addresses classification of substances into black lists and grey lists.
[45] Ibid, Annex I, Introduction.   [46] See Introduction to the Montreal Guidelines.
[47] Evidenced by the repeated use of *should* throughout the document.
[48] AE Boyle, 'Land-based Sources of Marine Pollution: Current Legal Regime' (1992) 16 *MP* 20–35, 34. See also D Hassan, *Protecting the Marine Environment from Land-based Sources of Pollution* (Ashgate 2006) 91–2.
[49] Agenda 21 (1992) para. 17.25.(a).   [50] Ibid, para. 17.26.

The Washington Declaration is a general political statement on the need to protect and preserve the marine environment from pollution caused by land-based activities.[51] The GPOA is a more detailed document, which builds upon and expands the Montreal Guidelines. Whilst the GPOA provides more guidance to States on what action is necessary to tackle land-based sources of marine pollution, it is, like the 1985 Guidelines, a non-binding instrument and it does not purport to dictate what actions must be taken by States. To the contrary, the GPOA expressly recognizes that:

there are major differences among the different regions of the world [and] these variations will lead to different judgments on the appropriate priorities to be given to tackling the different problems [so that] each state will ... develop its own appropriate set of priorities for the tasks that it decides to undertake to protect the marine environment.[52]

To this end, the GPOA purports to offer 'a source of conceptual and practical guidance to be drawn upon by national and/or regional authorities in devising and implementing measures to prevent, reduce, control and/or eliminate marine degradation from land-based activities'.[53] Thus, the GPOA foresees implementing measures both at the national level, through national programmes of action, and at the regional level, through regional bodies or other frameworks for cooperation.

One notable development in the GPOA is the elaboration of the concept of integrated coastal area management, an idea that was only implicit in the Montreal Guidelines. The GPOA provides a structured framework for the development of national and regional regulatory strategies, with an emphasis on the following steps:

- Identification and assessment of problems;
- Establishment of priorities;
- Setting of management objectives;
- Identification, evaluation and selection of strategies and measures, including management approaches;
- Specification of criteria for evaluating the effectiveness of strategies and programmes;
- Implementation of programme support elements.

The GPOA also stresses the need to harmonize management of coastal areas with river basin management and land-use plans.[54] Institutional cooperation and integrated management is further highlighted in the 2001 Montreal Declaration on Land-based Sources of Marine Pollution as 'an important new element of international environmental governance'.[55] As part of this approach, States are encouraged to undertake cost-benefit analyses of options for action,[56] stakeholder consultation,[57]

---

[51] See 1995 Washington Declaration on Protection of the Marine Environment from Land-based Activities.
[52] GPOA, para. 53.   [53] Ibid, para. 14.   [54] Ibid, para. 19. See also para. 23(b).
[55] See 2001 Montreal Declaration on the Protection of the Marine Environment from Land-based Activities (Montreal Declaration), para. 9(d).
[56] GPOA, para. 22(b).   [57] Ibid, para. 23(a). See also para. 23(f) and 28(f).

and the adoption of a precautionary approach.[58] Thus, the GPOA has sought to explicitly incorporate modern principles of international environmental law into the legal framework for the control of land-based sources of marine pollution.

Compared with the Montreal Guidelines, the GPOA is more detailed concerning the actions that should be taken at the national, regional, and international level in relation to specific types of pollution and it highlights the need to take action on the following substances and activities: sewage, persistent organic pollutants, radioactive substances, heavy metals, oils, nutrients, sediments, litter, and physical alteration and destruction of habitats. In this respect, the GPOA has been praised by commentators as an important progression from the Montreal Guidelines.[59]

The other significant development in the GPOA is the emphasis on information sharing and capacity building. The GPOA stresses the need to cooperate to ensure that the most up-to-date information is available with respect to impacts on the marine environment from land-based activities.[60] In this regard, the GPOA calls for the establishment of a clearing-house mechanism to facilitate the exchange of relevant information and expertise.[61] It has been noted that such facilities are only worthwhile if countries have the expertise to use the information that is available.[62] To that end, the GPOA also highlights the need for capacity building within developing countries,[63] as well as the transfer of technology to developing countries to deal with these sources of pollution.[64] Both of these requirements, whilst expressed in hortatory language, nevertheless reflect general obligations in UNCLOS.[65] In practice, however, the establishment of a general clearing-house mechanism has been set back by a lack of resources,[66] emphasizing how legal rules of this type must be matched by political commitment and financial support.

Addressing the financial implications of tackling land-based sources of marine pollution is another way in which the GPOA fills a lacuna in the Montreal Guidelines. The GPOA recognizes that the mobilization of financial resources is an 'indispensible foundation' to address land-based sources of marine pollution.[67] In part, this stipulation is reflected in a call for States to prioritize this issue in their own national budgets.[68] At the same time, the drafters acknowledge the need for 'new and additional sources' of funding from international development assistance to help developing countries take action under the GPOA.[69] Annex B provides an illustrative list of external funding sources for countries in need of assistance and it calls upon international financial institutions and bilateral donors to give 'appropriate priority to assistance to projects aimed at the implementation of the

---

[58] Ibid, paras 23(i) and 24.   [59] Williams and Davis (n15) 217.
[60] GPOA, para. 41.
[61] Ibid, para. 40(b). See also UNGA Resolution 51/189 (1996) para. 8.
[62] Williams and Davis (n15) 216.
[63] GPOA, para. 40(a); see also 2006 Beijing Declaration on Furthering the Implementation of the Global Programme of Action, para. 18.
[64] Ibid.   [65] UNCLOS, Articles 200 and 202.
[66] UNEP, *Policy Guidance from Implementing the Global Programme of Action for the Protection of the Marine Environment from Land-based Activities over the Period 2012-2016*, Document UNEP/GPA/ IGR.3/3 (2011) para. 19.
[67] GPOA, para. 50.   [68] Ibid, para. 51.   [69] Ibid.

Programme'.[70] A particular emphasis is given to the potential role of the Global Environment Facility (GEF) in supporting the implementation of the GPOA.[71] The GEF was established in 1992 as an independent financial institution to support action to protect the environment.[72] Partly in response to the GPOA, the GEF has developed the International Waters Scheme, under which it provides financial assistance to projects relating, inter alia, to the reduction of pollution of coasts and large marine ecosystems.[73]

The elaboration of the GPOA was not intended to be an isolated act and States have established a process for overseeing its implementation through regular review meetings. The first intergovernmental review of the GPOA took place in 2001. At that time, States adopted the Montreal Declaration, in which they expressed concern about the lack of progress in implementing the GPOA and re-emphasized the need for 'new and additional financial resources to accelerate the implementation of the GPOA'.[74] Subsequent reviews took place in 2006[75] and 2012.[76] In the latest review, nutrient management,[77] marine litter,[78] and wastewater[79] have been highlighted as three issues requiring particular attention. In order to ensure ongoing attention to these topics, three global partnerships have been set up with a view to bringing together relevant international organizations, governments and non-governmental actors in order to develop practical actions to implement the GPOA.[80] As lead coordinator of the GPOA,[81] UNEP supports these initiatives, which seek to enhance further cooperation on key issues falling within the framework of the GPOA.

The quinquennial review is important, but those involved in the regime have urged the establishment of a bureau to maintain political commitment and oversight to the process between the global meetings.[82] Moreover, it has been noted that it is currently difficult to review implementation because governments are not

---

[70] GPOA, para. 62.   [71] Ibid, paras 69–71.

[72] See GEF, 'About Us': <https://www.thegef.org/about-us>.

[73] See GEF, 'International Waters Strategy': <https://www.thegef.org/topics/international-waters>. For examples of case studies, see GEF, *Catalysing Ocean Finance*, Vol. II (2012).

[74] Montreal Declaration, para. 7.

[75] See *Report of the Second Session of the Intergovernmental Review Meeting on the Implementation of the Global Programme of Action for the Protection of the Marine Environment from Land-based Activities*, Document UNEP/GPA/IGR.2/7 (2006).

[76] *Report of the Third Session of the Intergovernmental Review Meeting on the Implementation of the Global Programme of Action for the Protection of the Marine Environment from Land-based Activities*, Document UNEP/GPA/IGR.3/6 (2012). The next review is expected in early 2017.

[77] See 2012 Manila Declaration on Furthering Implementation of the Global Programme of Action for the Protection of the Marine Environment from Land-based Activities (Manila Declaration), para. 3(c)(i)–(ii).

[78] Ibid, para. 3(c)(iii); see also the Honolulu Strategy:t <http://wedocs.unep.org/bitstream/handle/20.500.11822/10670/Honolulu%20strategy.pdf?sequence=1&isAllowed=y>.

[79] Manila Declaration, para. 3(c)(iv)   [80] UNEP (n66) paras 32–4.

[81] GPOA, paras 74–6; See UNGA Resolution 51/189 (1996). UNEP coordinated the implementation of the international efforts on land-based sources through a UN-Oceans Task Force until 2007; see <http://www.unoceans.org/task-forces/en/>

[82] UNEP (n66), para. 35.

formally required to report on progress[83] and participation in the reviews has been patchy.[84]

It is clear that the GPOA is a significant step forward in comparison to the Montreal Guidelines, although there continue to be weaknesses. Nevertheless, when evaluating the GPOA, it is important to remember that it is not intended to provide the only means to address land-based sources of marine pollution at the international level. Rather, its role is to provide an overarching framework and to guide action at other levels. Thus, it must be viewed in light of other developments at the global and regional levels.

4.3.3 Additional global instruments on land-based sources of marine pollution

Although the GPOA itself does not seek to establish binding international obligations for the prevention of marine pollution from land-based activities, it does recognize 'the need for international rules, as well as recommended practices and procedures, to further the objectives of the Programme of Action'.[85] Two particular initiatives, both led by the UNEP, are worthy of mention in this context as they address substances that have been identified, inter alia, as posing serious threats to marine life and ecosystems owing to their toxicity and potential to accumulate in the tissues of organisms which are exposed to such substances. These initiatives relate to the regulation of Persistent Organic Pollutants (POPs) and Mercury.

Evidence of harm caused by POPs has been available for a number of years,[86] and many national governments have taken action to address the use of POPs within their territory. However, POPs were considered to require a coordinated solution because of their persistence in the environment and the fact that they could be carried for long distances, thus posing threats to the environment of all States. The Stockholm Convention on Persistent Organic Pollutants, adopted in 2001, establishes obligations to prohibit, restrict, or reduce the production and use of certain chemicals listed in annexes to the Convention.[87] The Convention requires Parties to eliminate well-known harmful pesticides such as Aldrin, Dieldrin, Chlordane, DDT, Heptachlor, Endrin, and Toxaphene. It also covers industrial pollutants, such as hexachlorbenzene and polychlorinated biphenyls (PCBs). The Convention provides for technical and financial support to assist developing countries complying with their obligations.[88] In fact, the POPs Convention has been incredibly

---

[83] DL VanderZwaag and A Powers, 'The Protection of the Marine Environment from Land-based Activities: Gauging the Tides of Global and Regional Governance' (2008) 23 *IJMCL* 423, 439.

[84] Ninety-eight countries attended the first review in Montreal in 2001. One-hundred and four countries attended the second review in Beijing in 2006. However, only sixty-four countries attended the third review in Manila in 2012.

[85] GPOA, para. 77(g).

[86] See in particular the seminal environmental work, R Carson, *Silent Spring* (Houghton Mifflin 1962). On the impact of this book, see CM Jameson, *Silent Spring Revisited* (Bloomsbury 2012).

[87] See 2001 Stockholm Convention on Persistent Organic Pollutants (POPs Convention) (EIF 17 May 2004).

[88] POPs Convention, Articles 12 and 13.

successful in terms of attracting the participation of States, currently having 179 Contracting Parties.

It is important to note that the Convention also allows for flexibility and Parties may make reservations (called exemptions) in relation to particular uses of individual POPs in accordance with a detailed scheme set out in the Annexes to the treaty. The permitted exceptions vary, depending on the chemical in question[89] and they are recorded in a register kept by the secretariat to the Convention. This flexibility is also limited as specific exemptions only last for five years, unless the Conference of the Parties (COP) agrees to an extension.[90] In practice, when the first set of exemptions came to be reviewed, no extensions were requested,[91] which suggests that this mechanism provides Parties additional time to comply with the Convention's requirements, rather than to justify a permanent opt-out. Another important role of the COP in overseeing and promoting implementation of the Convention has been to investigate and recommend alternative practices to make it easier to comply with the treaty prescriptions.

The scope of the POPs Convention has also been extended since its entry into force as new substances have been added to the annexes using the amendment procedures.[92] The Committee that is established to advise the COP on additions to the list is instructed to take a precautionary approach so that 'lack of full scientific certainty shall not prevent [a] proposal from proceeding',[93] and the COP itself should take decisions 'in a precautionary manner'.[94] However, despite this emphasis on precaution, additions to the annexes require a positive decision of the COP, and, therefore, decisions assume a political character. This aspect of the procedure has led some commentators to conclude that the POPs Convention is 'thin' on precaution.[95] Moreover, despite the fact that the treaty promotes the rapid entry into force of amendments through a default tacit acceptance procedure, many Parties have reserved the right to require positive acceptance of amendments to the annexes,[96] demonstrating a clear sensitivity concerning the regulation of these chemicals and a desire amongst States to retain maximum possible control over decisions as to their removal.

The 2013 Minamata Convention, when it enters into force, will follow a similar model with a view addressing another highly toxic substance: mercury. It is widely accepted that mercury poisoning can cause severe toxic effects to living organisms, and even death. The widespread poisoning of the local population in Minamata, Japan, caused by the release of methylmercury contained in industrial run-off is one

---

[89] PL Lallas, 'The Stockholm Convention on Persistent Organic Pollutants' (2001) 95 *AJIL* 692, 699.
[90] POPs Convention, Article 4(6). See also COP Decision SC-1/24 (2005); COP Decision SC-2/3 (2006); COP Decision SC-3/3 (2007).
[91] See Report of the Fourth Meeting of the Conference of the Parties to the Stockholm Convention, Document UNEP/POPS/COP.4/38 (2008) para. 33. See also COP Decision SC-4:3 (2008).
[92] Nine new POPs were added in 2009, an additional one in 2011, and a further one in 2013.
[93] POPs Convention, Article 8(7)(a).   [94] Ibid, Article 8(9).
[95] DL VanderZwaag, 'The Precautionary Approach and the International Control of Toxic Chemicals: Beacon of Hop, Sea of Confusion and Dilution' (2013) 33 *HJIL* 605, 618.
[96] POPs Convention, Article 25(4). See declarations of Argentina, Australia, Bahrain, Bangladesh, Botswana, Canada, China, Estonia, Guatemala, India, South Korea, Mauritius, Micronesia, Moldova, Russia, Slovenia, Spain, Vanuatu, and Venezuela.

of the most notorious incidents on record, and it is apt that the 2013 Convention bears the name of this city. The treaty seeks to control the production, trade, and use of mercury and mercury-added products and mercury compounds.[97] It does so by prescribing certain measures to be taken by Parties, as well as providing for a financial mechanism and technical assistance.[98] The Convention also allows Parties to make reservations, albeit for a more limited period than the POPs Convention.[99]

Both of these instruments deal with substances that can travel over long distances and thus pose a global threat. Most substances that enter the marine environment do not fall within this category and they are only harmful because of the large quantities that are emitted. They, therefore, require a different approach to regulation, and States have chosen to address them at a regional level.

4.4 Regional Cooperation on Land-Based Sources of Marine Pollution

4.4.1 Forms of regional cooperation

Given that the problems arising from land-based sources of marine pollution vary from place to place and the capacity of States to address such problems also differs, regional approaches to tackling this issue can ensure appropriate priorities are set to tackle the problems that are most pressing for a particular area, in accordance with the financial and technical resources available to those States. UNCLOS itself explicitly calls for the development of rules on land-based sources of marine pollution that take into account 'characteristic regional features'.[100] Similarly, the GPOA recognizes the importance of the regional approach and it calls for the improvement and strengthening of regional seas programmes because they 'serve as effective mechanisms for furthering the implementation of the [GPOA]...' itself.[101]

Regional cooperation on the regulation of land-based activities began in Europe in the mid-1970s. One of the first treaties on the subject was the Convention for the prevention of marine pollution from land-based sources, concluded by the North Sea States in Paris in 1974.[102] At about the same time, regional treaties were also adopted for the Baltic Sea[103] and the Mediterranean Sea,[104] both of which contained provisions on land-based sources of marine pollution. Such regional initiatives soon spread to other regions, largely as a result of UNEP's regional seas programme.[105]

---

[97] See 2013 Minamata Convention on Mercury (Minamata Convention) (not yet in force).
[98] Minamata Convention, Articles 13 and 14.
[99] Ibid, Article 6(6). See generally HH Eriksen and FX Perrez, 'The Minimata Convention: A Comprehensive Response to a Global Problem' (2014) 23 *RECIEL* 195, 206.
[100] UNCLOS, Article 207(4).   [101] Manila Declaration, para. 6.
[102] See 1974 Paris Convention for the Prevention of Marine Pollution from Land-based Sources (with annexes) (EIF 6 May 1978).
[103] See 1974 Helsinki Convention on the Protection of the Marine Environment of the Baltic Sea Area (with annexes and appendices) (1974 Helsinki Convention) (EIF 3 May 1980).
[104] See 1980 Protocol for the Protection of the Mediterranean Sea against Pollution from Land-based Sources (with annexes) (EIF 17 June 1983).
[105] See Chapter 2.

Given the significant impact of land-based sources of pollution on the marine environment, it is no surprise that this topic has been broadly addressed in most regional settings. All regional seas treaties contain a general provision on the prevention, reduction, or control of land-based sources of marine pollution. The Kuwait Convention is typical in this regard in its requirement that 'the Contracting States shall take all appropriate measures to prevent, abate and combat pollution caused by discharges from land reaching the Sea Area whether water-borne, air-borne, or directly from the coast including outfalls and pipelines'.[106] The precise language that is used in this context differs from region to region. Thus, the Helsinki Convention appears to be stricter in its reference to the need for measures to 'prevent and eliminate pollution of the Baltic Sea from land-based sources'.[107] This choice of language may indicate a more ambitious goal in the long-term, although it does not alter the fact that some pollution is still tolerated in the short-term. Overall, these general provisions in the regional treaties would appear to do little more than confirm the due diligence obligation contained in UNCLOS to take steps to tackle land-based sources of marine pollution.

These general treaty provisions are often accompanied by regional plans of action, which seek to identify actions that are more specific and strategies that should be taken to tackle pollution in the region. Such plans of action offer a basis for regional cooperation, but, as they are not binding and they are often drafted in very broad terms, they demonstrate only a minimal level of commitment. Nevertheless, the implementation of regional action plans is still overseen by regular meetings of concerned States and they, therefore, offer a means to scrutinize States' conduct in taking action to combat land-based sources of marine pollution.

Several regional seas arrangements have also adopted legally binding rules that are more specific, on the prevention, reduction, and control of land-based sources of marine pollution, either in the form of an annex or a protocol. At the time of writing, such instruments exist in the North-East Atlantic,[108] the Baltic,[109] the Mediterranean,[110] the Black Sea,[111] the Caribbean,[112] West African waters,[113] the

---

[106] See 1978 Kuwait Regional Convention for Cooperation on the Protection of the Marine Environment from Pollution (Kuwait Convention) (EIF 1 July 1979), Article VI.

[107] Helsinki Convention, Article 6(1). See also OSPAR Convention, Article 3.

[108] See 1992 Convention for the Protection of the Marine Environment in the North-East Atlantic (OSPAR Convention), (EIF 25 March 1998), Article III and Annex I.

[109] See 1992 Helsinki Convention on the Protection of the Marine Environment of the Baltic Sea Area (1992 Helsinki Convention) (EIF 17 January 2000), Articles 5–6 and Annexes I, II, and III.

[110] See 1980 Athens Protocol for the Protection of the Mediterranean Sea against Pollution from Land-Based Sources, as amended by 1996 Syracuse Protocol for the Protection of the Mediterranean Sea against Pollution from Land-Based Sources and Activities (Syracuse Protocol) (EIF 11 May 2008).

[111] See 2009 Protocol on the Protection of the Marine Environment of the Black Sea from Land-Based Sources and Activities (Black Sea Protocol) (not yet in force).

[112] See 1999 Protocol Concerning Pollution from Land-Based Sources and Activities to the Convention for the Protection and Development of the Marine Environment of the Wider Caribbean Region (Wider Caribbean Protocol) (EIF 13 August 2010).

[113] See 2012 Additional Protocol to the Abidjan Convention Concerning Cooperation in the Protection and Development of Marine and Coastal Environment from Land-Based Sources and Activities in the Western, Central and Southern African Region (Abidjan Protocol) (not yet in force).

Western Indian Ocean,[114] the Persian Gulf,[115] the South-East Pacific,[116] the Red Sea,[117] and the Caspian Sea.[118] These instruments demonstrate a stronger commitment to taking action and they provide an additional layer of regulation through the promulgation of more specific rules and standards relating to the prevention, reduction and control—and sometimes elimination—of marine pollution from land-based sources. The content of these rules and standards, however, differs across regions, and the different approaches and types of legal tools that are employed will be analysed in the following section.

4.4.2 Regional rules and standards on land-based sources of marine pollution

4.4.2.1 *Regulation of substances and authorization of discharges*

The basic approach taken in many regional instruments aimed at the regulation of land-based sources of marine pollution was to list specific substances, which, owing to their toxicity, persistence, or bioaccumulative characteristics, should be regulated. Both the 1974 Paris Convention and the 1974 Helsinki Convention listed substances whose input into the marine environment was to be progressively eliminated or limited by the Parties.[119] This approach has been retained in treaties that have replaced these early instruments[120] and it has since been followed by most other regional protocols.[121] For example, the Syracuse Protocol for the Protection of the Mediterranean Sea against Pollution from Land-Based Sources and Activities includes an obligation to 'eliminate pollution deriving from land-based sources and activities, in particular to phase out inputs of the substances that are toxic, persistent and liable to bioaccumulate listed in annex I'.[122] The precise substances that must be controlled vary from region to region, although the listing system means that additional substances can be added through amendment of the treaty.

Any discharges that do take place under these instruments are often subject to the issuance of a special permit by the relevant State, based upon criteria and guidelines

---

[114] See 2010 Nairobi Protocol for the Protection of the Marine and Coastal Environment of the Western Indian Ocean from Land-Based Sources and Activities (Nairobi Protocol) (not yet in force).

[115] See 1990 Kuwait Protocol for the Protection of the Marine Environment against Pollution from Land-based Sources (Kuwait Protocol) (EIF 1 February 1993).

[116] See 1983 Quito Protocol on the Protection of the South-East Pacific against Pollution Resulting from Land-based Sources (Quito Protocol) (EIF 23 September 1986).

[117] See 2005 Jeddah Protocol Concerning the Protection of the Marine Environment from Land-Based Activities in the Red Sea and Gulf of Aden (Jeddah Protocol) (not yet in force).

[118] See 2012 Moscow Protocol for the Protection of the Caspian Sea against Pollution from Land-based Sources and Activities (Moscow Protocol) (not yet in force).

[119] OSPAR Convention, Article 4; Helsinki Convention, Articles 5 and 6(2).

[120] See 1992 Helsinki Convention, Article 5 and Annex I; 1992 OSPAR Convention, Annex I, Article I and Appendix 2.

[121] For a discussion of developments in this respect, see M Pallemaerts, 'The North Sea and Baltic Sea Land-Based Sources Regimes: Reducing Toxics or Rehashing Rhetoric?' (1998) 13 *IJMCL* 421, 438–40.

[122] Syracuse Protocol, Article 5.

approved by the Parties.[123] Some of the treaties require States to develop specific environmental quality standards or objectives in relation to point sources and diffuse sources of pollution.[124] The approach taken by these instruments still allows some flexibility for States Parties in terms of which discharges should be permitted, but seeks to ensure that the overall harm to the marine environment is minimized. States may also be required to ensure compliance with regulations by establishing a system of inspections.[125] Such enforcement is obviously a vital component of any regulatory regime in order to ensure the rules are followed in practice.

Most regional seas treaties adopted since the Rio Conference also make explicit reference to the precautionary approach when addressing land-based sources of marine pollution. The Black Sea Protocol is typical in this regard in providing that:

the [C]ontracting [P]arties shall in particular apply the precautionary principle, by virtue of which where there are threats of serious or irreversible damage to the environment or to public health, lack of full scientific certainty shall not be used as a reason for postponing cost-effective measures to prevent such damage.[126]

Yet, the treaties do not further operationalize this principle for the purposes of preventing or controlling land-based sources of marine pollution, and it is left to States acting, either individually or collectively, to decide when precautionary action may be taken. This principle will be particularly relevant when considering whether to authorize a discharge of a controlled substance, but it falls short of requiring that an applicant must demonstrate that no harm will take place before authorization can be given. In this respect, it represents a softer form of the precautionary approach.

4.4.2.2 *Best available techniques and best environmental practices*

Some of the more modern treaties on land-based activities introduce an obligation for parties to use 'best available techniques' (BAT) and 'best environmental practices'[127] (BEP) when tackling land-based sources of marine pollution.[128] These standards would appear to be a step beyond the requirement to take 'appropriate' measures found in the original regional seas framework treaties. The OSPAR Convention defines BAT as 'the latest stage of development (state of the art) of processes, of facilities or of methods of operation which indicate the practical suitability of a particular measure for limiting discharges, emissions and waste',[129] whereas

---

[123] OSPAR Convention, Article 4(2); 1992 Helsinki Convention, Article 6(3); Syracuse Protocol, Article 6(1); Black Sea Protocol, Article 7(3).

[124] For example, Abidjan Protocol, Articles 7(3), 8(1), and Annex III.

[125] Syracuse Protocol, Article 6(2); Black Sea Protocol, Article 7(4). The latter instrument expressly provides that States may seek the assistance of the Black Sea Commission in establishing inspection or monitoring programmes, including special training for personnel.

[126] Black Sea Protocol, Article 4(2)(a). See also Nairobi Protocol, Article 4(2)(a); Abidjan Protocol, Article 5(2); Moscow Protocol, Article 4(2)(a).

[127] OSPAR Convention, Annex I, Article 1(1).

[128] See e.g. Moscow Protocol, Article 7 (pollution from point sources) and 8 (pollution from diffuse sources). Some regions had already made reference to these concepts in non-binding instruments; see e.g. 1988 Declaration on the Protection of the Marine Environment of the Baltic Sea Area.

[129] OSPAR Convention, Appendix I, para. 2.

BEP means 'the application of the most appropriate combination of environmental control measures and strategies'.[130] Similar definitions are found in other treaties.[131] Both of these concepts are dynamic, imposing requirements that will evolve over time as technology itself becomes more sophisticated and effective in combatting pollution.[132]

The obligation to 'ensure the application of' BAT and BEP has been held to be an obligation of result,[133] meaning that a State's failure to apply such rules to relevant operators can be enforced through legal proceedings. Courts and tribunals can also play an important role in determining what can be considered to be the best technique or practice in a particular context in the case of a dispute. For example, in the *Pulp Mills Case*, Argentina alleged that Uruguay had not complied with its obligation to meet the BAT standard by failing to introduce tertiary treatment of effluents prior to their discharge into the River Uruguay. The ICJ confirmed that the question of what constitutes BAT was an objective one that was subject to judicial interpretation. It subsequently determined the content of BAT by referring to industry standards and practices in the pulp and paper industry, ultimately finding that the technologies that were employed in the contested facility were built in accordance with these standards.[134] A failure to follow BEP was also alleged by Singapore in the *Johor Straits Case*,[135] although the dispute was settled before a decision could be made on the merits. Nevertheless, these cases both demonstrate that courts and tribunals can play a role in determining the content of BAT and BEP in practice.

References to BAT and BEP are not only found in treaties adopted by the developed countries, but have also been adopted in recent instruments negotiated by regions composed largely of developing countries. Both the 2010 land-based sources protocol adopted by the Parties to the Nairobi Convention and the 2012 land-based sources protocol adopted by the Parties to the Abidjan Convention make reference to BAT and BEP.[136] However, it is important to note that these instruments, which are applicable to some of the poorest countries on the planet, explicitly recognize that BAT and BEP are affected by economic and social factors.[137] It follows that the standards that may be expected from countries in these regions may be lower than are applied elsewhere. The Caribbean Protocol on Land-based Sources, adopted in 1999, avoids the language of BAT and BEP altogether, preferring a reference to the 'most appropriate technology', which is defined as 'the best of currently available techniques, practices or methods of operation to prevent, reduce or control pollution of the Convention area that are appropriate to the social, economic, technological, institutional, financial, cultural and environmental conditions of a

---

[130] Ibid, para. 6.
[131] See 1992 Helsinki Convention, Article 6(1); Syracuse Protocol, Article 5(4).
[132] OSPAR Convention, Appendix I, paras 3 and 8.
[133] *Dispute concerning Access to Information under Article 9 of the OSPAR Convention* (2003) para. 131.
[134] *Pulp Mills on the River Uruguay Case* (2010) para. 224.
[135] *Land Reclamation in the Johor Straits (Provisional Measures)* (2003) para. 89.
[136] Abidjan Protocol, Article 5; Nairobi Protocol, Articles 7(1), 8(2), and 11.
[137] For example, Abidjan Protocol, Annex I, paras A.2(c) and B.3.

Contracting Party or Parties'.[138] This definition would appear to give even more leeway to the Parties in deciding what measures to take, but it still sets a minimum standard that must be met.

4.4.2.3 Area-based measures

Another technique used by the regional treaties is to require area-based measures to prevent, reduce, and control land-based sources of marine pollution. Such measures are a way of targeting resources at tackling particularly serious problems, either because of the substantial pollution loads in an area or because of the sensitive features of an area.

Some regional regimes require parties to adopt a list of so-called pollution hot spots. This technique was pioneered by the Baltic States as part of the 1992 Baltic Sea Joint Comprehensive Environmental Action Programme and the Helsinki Commission reports that, as at December 2016, 118 out of the 162 hot spots on the regional list have been addressed.[139] This commitment has been placed on a legal footing in other regional regimes, with the Moscow Protocol providing a good example.[140] This instrument defines *hot spots* as 'a limited and definable land area, stretch of surface water or specific aquifer that is subject to excessive pollution and necessitates priority attention in order to prevent or reduce the actual or potential impacts on human health, ecosystems, or natural resources and amenities of economic importance'[141] and it requires parties to adopt and implement a national action plan, with timetables, for achieving substantial reductions of pollution loads in the hot spots that have been added to the regional list. States are also required to keep the list under review and to revise it every two years as appropriate.

Another type of area-based measure requires States to take steps to protect areas that may be particularly vulnerable to land-based activities. Article 9 of the Jeddah Protocol thus explicitly recognizes the threats posed by land-based activities to coastal habitats, including coral reefs and mangroves, and it duly places an obligation on parties to 'encourage conservation of environmentally sensitive marine areas'.[142] The Moscow Protocol also includes an innovative obligation to 'take special measures of protection against land-based pollution and activities potentially harmful for natural spawning grounds of sturgeon, Caspian salmon and other valuable species'.[143] The term *valuable* is ambiguous but it should arguably be interpreted in light of rules relating to the conservation of marine biological diversity, including the subsequently adopted 2014 Ashgabet Protocol for the Conservation

---

[138] Abidjan Protocol, Article I(e). See also Article III(1) which requires States to take appropriate measures, 'using for this purpose the best practicable means at its disposal and in accordance with its capabilities'.

[139] See HELCOM Hot Spots: < http://www.helcom.fi/action-areas/industrial-municipal-releases/helcom-hot-spots>.

[140] Moscow Protocol, Article 7(2). See also Abidjan Protocol, Article 7(4); Black Sea Protocol, Article 7(2); Nairobi Protocol, Article 4(2)(d).

[141] Moscow Protocol, Article 2(f).   [142] Jeddah Protocol, Article 9(3).

[143] Moscow Protocol, Article 2(f).

of Biological Diversity, whereby States have jointly compiled a list of species that require protection. Indeed, this latter instrument sets down an independent obligation to 'regulate activities having adverse effects on protected species and their habitats'.[144] Where an area has been designated as a specially protected area under the Protocol, States may be obliged to take even stronger measures, including a prohibition on the discharge of any substances, as well as the regulation or prohibition of any other activities that are likely directly or indirectly to impair the integrity or the natural or cultural characteristics of specially protected areas that have been designated under the Protocol.[145] This interrelationship between the protocol on land-based sources and the protocol on biodiversity conservation is just one example of the general need to interpret and apply regional rules on regulating land-based activities by reference to other environmental rules adopted in the region.[146] Overall, where a species or habitat has been designated as being in need of additional protection, it can be argued that a greater level of due diligence is required from the States concerned.

4.4.3 The progressive development of regional measures to combat land-based sources of marine pollution

Most regional treaties dealing with land-based sources of marine pollution envisage that the Parties will progressively agree upon joint programmes and measures to implement their treaty commitments.[147] The development of subsequent measures means that the regulatory framework under a regional instrument becomes dynamic and programmes of action can be strengthened over time, in response to changes in scientific knowledge and technological developments. The legal status of these measures will depend upon the powers that are conferred by the treaty. Most regional seas bodies only have the ability to adopt non-binding recommendations.[148] Even when regions have the possibility to adopt legally binding decisions,[149] States have nevertheless often chosen to adopt measures and programmes of action in the form of recommendations and other non-binding instruments.[150] This can be partly explained by the reluctance of States to give up control over activities that are central to their economy and the fact that States are keen to 'reserve to themselves as much freedom as possible in balancing environmental protection measures against the needs of their domestic economies, including industry and agriculture, whose activities generated much of the most harmful pollution'.[151] At the same time, it has been suggested that such recommendations, if secured by unanimity, can carry significant

---

[144] See 2014 Protocol for the Conservation of Biological Diversity to the Framework Convention for the Protection of the Marine Environment of the Caspian Sea (Ashgabet Protocol) (not yet in force), Article 6(b).
[145] Ashgabet Protocol, Articles 10(1)(a) and (g).   [146] See Chapter 3.
[147] OSPAR Convention, Article 4(2)–(3); 1992 Helsinki Convention, Article 6(2)–(5); Syracuse Protocol, Article 5(2) and 15; Nairobi Protocol, Article 11(2).
[148] See e.g. 1992 Helsinki Convention, Article 20(1)(b).
[149] OSPAR Convention, Article 13; Syracuse Protocol, Article 15.
[150] This is e.g. the case with the OSPAR Commission.   [151] Boyle (n48) 26.

political weight.[152] As they support the implementation of the treaty regime, 'they may be considered as articulating how [C]ontracting [P]arties should comply with such legally binding obligations'.[153] In other words, recommendations can provide an indication of what may be expected from States in carrying out their due diligence obligations, and, even if States are not bound to follow them, compliance with such recommendations would demonstrate appropriate implementation of the treaty. Moreover, even these non-binding instruments can be subject to scrutiny through regular meetings of the Contracting Parties.[154]

The regulation of nutrient inputs to the Baltic Sea provides an example of the role that joint programmes of action may play in addressing the reduction and control of particular pollutants from land-based activities. As an enclosed sea, the Baltic is particularly susceptible to eutrophication with nitrogen and phosphorus inputs from agriculture and industry being the main causes of this problem in the region.[155] The original 1974 Helsinki Convention called for measures to be taken to address nutrient inputs by treating municipal sewage and reducing the polluting load of industrial wastes.[156] However, these measures were described in the main body of the treaty as 'goals' and they gave a significant amount of leeway to States as to the action that must be taken.[157] In 1988, in the first Ministerial Declaration to be adopted by parties, States agreed on the urgency of reducing discharges of substances most harmful to the ecosystem of the Baltic, including nutrients, and they tentatively set a target of a 50 per cent reduction by 1995.[158] Whilst not binding, this Declaration nevertheless carried significant political weight and it has been described as 'the perfect way to initiate cooperation'.[159] At about this time, the Contracting Parties also began negotiations on the amendment of the Helsinki Convention, which lead to stricter requirements in the treaty text relating to municipal sewage and industrial wastes,[160] as well as the introduction of guidelines for minimizing inputs from agriculture.[161] Implementation of the 1988 Declaration was reviewed in 2001, leading to other important developments in the fight against eutrophication. In 2007, Baltic States adopted a provisional Nutrient Reduction Scheme, which is composed of maximum allowable levels of nutrient inputs across the region, as well as country-allocated reduction targets.[162] This scheme was confirmed by the 2013 Copenhagen Ministerial Declaration, which also revised the maximum allowable inputs and individual country targets on the basis of more up-to-date information. However, the

---

[152] M Fitzmaurice, 'Enhanced Marine Environmental Protection: A Case Study of the Baltic Sea', in J Barrett and R Barnes (eds), *Law of the Sea: UNCLOS as a Living Treaty* (BIICL 2016) 311.

[153] Ibid.

[154] See A Nollkaemper, 'The Distinction between Non-Legal and Legal Norms in International Affairs: An Analysis with Reference to International Policy for the Protection of the North Sea from Hazardous Substances' (1998) *13 IJMCL* 355, 361. See also the discussion below on compliance.

[155] See HELCOM, *Eutrophication in the Baltic Sea*, Baltic Sea Environmental Proceedings No. 115B (2009).

[156] See 1974 Helsinki Convention, Annex III.

[157] See 1974 Helsinki Convention, Article 6(6).

[158] See 1988 Declaration on the Protection of the Marine Environment of the Baltic Sea Area.

[159] Fitzmaurice (n152) 309.   [160] See 1992 Helsinki Convention, Annex III, Part I.

[161] Ibid, Part II.   [162] See Baltic Sea Action Plan.

2013 Declaration also recognized that it was not only coastal States in the region that were responsible for nitrogen and phosphorus inputs into the Baltic Sea and the Declaration thus also emphasized the need for efforts by non-parties acting through other international instruments dealing with long-range transport of pollutants by air[163] or through watercourses. This demonstrates the difficulties of following an ecosystems approach to marine environmental protection in a regional regime and the need to reach out to States outside the region.

The concepts of BEP and BAT may also be interpreted and developed through decisions of the Contracting Parties themselves, and many regional seas bodies have adopted a range of decisions in order to give further content to their legal commitments. For example, the OSPAR Commission has adopted dozens of programmes and measures related to land-based sources of marine pollution in the North-East Atlantic, either targeting particular substances,[164] or addressed to certain industries or activities,[165] all of which can be considered to give an indication of what practices and technology are expected to be implemented by the States concerned. Similarly, the Parties to the Helsinki Convention have identified general actions to be taken by Parties to achieve 'good environmental status' in the region, as well as additional recommendations on particular threats.[166] The Helsinki Commission has also adopted specific recommendations relating to the reduction in pollution from the glass industry,[167] the iron and steel industry,[168] the pulp and paper industry,[169] oil refineries,[170] hard coal cookeries,[171] the textiles industry,[172] and the chemicals industry,[173] as well as pollution from urban sources[174] and agriculture.[175] These decisions play a very important role in developing the legal framework that is applicable to land-based sources of marine pollution by providing practical guidance on the steps that should be taken by States in order to comply with their obligations.

---

[163] See the 1999 Gothenburg Protocol to Abate Acidification, Eutrophication and Ground-Level Ozone of the UNECE Convention on Long-range Transboundary Air Pollution (EIF 17 May 2005).

[164] For example, PARCOM Recommendation 91/4 on Radioactive Discharges (1991); PARCOM Decision 95/1 on the Phasing Out of Short-Chained Chlorinated Paraffins (1995).

[165] For example, PARCOM Recommendation 88/2 on the Reduction in Inputs of Nutrients to the Paris Convention Area (1988); PARCOM Recommendation 88/4 on Nuclear Reprocessing Plants (1988); PAROM Decision 90/3 on Reducing Atmospheric Emissions from Existing Chlor-Alkali Plants (1990); PARCOM Recommendation 94/6 on Best Environmental Practice (BEP) for the Reduction of Inputs of Potentially Toxic Chemicals from Aquaculture Use (1994); PARCOM Recommendation 93/2 on Further Restrictions on the Discharge of Mercury from Dentistry (1993); OSPAR Recommendation 2003/4 on Controlling Dispersal of Mercury from Crematoria (2003) (Amended by OSPAR Recommendation 2006/2 (2006)).

[166] See Baltic Sea Action Plan.   [167] HELCOM Recommendation 14/3 (1993).

[168] HELCOM Recommendation 24/4 (2003).

[169] HELCOM Recommendation 16/4 (1995); HELCOM Recommendation 17/8 (1996); HELCOM Recommendation 17/9 (1996).

[170] HELCOM Recommendation 23/8 (2002).

[171] HELCOM Recommendation 23/9 (2002).

[172] HELCOM Recommendation 23/12 (2002).

[173] HELCOM Recommendation 23/10 (2002); HELCOM Recommendation 23/11 (2002); HELCOM Recommendation 17/6 (1996); HELCOM Recommendation 20/2 (1999); HELCOM Recommendation 23/6 (2003).

[174] HELCOM Recommendation 13/2 (1992); HELCOM Recommendation 23/5 (2002).

[175] HELCOM Recommendation 24/3 (2003).

4.4.4 Access to information and public participation in the regulation of land-based sources of marine pollution

A significant development in the regional regimes relating to land-based sources of marine pollution has been the increasing emphasis on transparency in decision-making in furtherance of Principle 10 of the Rio Declaration.[176] Most regional treaties require information exchange between the Parties, either directly or through reports to the relevant treaty bodies.[177] Yet, it is also increasingly common to see provisions in the more modern regional seas treaties or protocols that demand that States provide information to the public about risks to the marine environment and measures that have been taken to combat such risks. This issue has a particular resonance in relation to land-based activities, given that this category of activities is more likely to cause pollution to in-shore areas with a greater chance of consequences for local residents who may be directly or indirectly affected.

The 1992 OSPAR Convention and the 1992 amended Helsinki Convention led the way in pushing for greater transparency in the regulation of activities likely to impact the marine environment through the inclusion of provisions on the publication of information relating to, inter alia, the state of the marine environment, activities that may detrimentally affect the marine environment, or measures taken to prevent or eliminate pollution of the marine environment.[178] In a rare arbitration under the OSPAR Convention, a tribunal held that the relevant provision in Article 9 of the Convention established an obligation of result, meaning that there was an enforceable obligation to provide the relevant information under the treaty, rather than an obligation 'merely to provide access to a domestic regime which is directed at obtaining the required result'.[179] At the same time, the arbitral tribunal also held that the right to information is not unrestricted. In that case, Ireland had challenged the United Kingdom for its failure to disclose certain information concerning the operation of a planned nuclear reprocessing plant on the coast of the Irish Sea. However, the arbitral tribunal held that the information requested by Ireland did not fall within the scope of the obligation, which was 'not a general freedom of information statute'[180] but only applied to information falling within the categories specified by the Convention. According to the tribunal, Ireland had failed to demonstrate that the requested information, which largely concerned the economics of the planned facility, was information on the state of the marine environment or information on an activity that was likely to affect the maritime area adversely.[181] This decision demonstrates the limited nature of this obligation. Indeed, even if information does fall within the scope of the duty, both the OSPAR Convention and the Helsinki Convention also contain exceptions, which allow information to

---

[176] See Chapter 1.
[177] For example, Antigua Convention, Article 11; Cartagena Convention, Article 22; Kuwait Convention, Article 23.
[178] Helsinki Convention, Article 17; OSPAR Convention, Article 9.
[179] *Dispute Concerning Access to Information under Article 9 of the OSPAR Convention* (2003) para. 137.
[180] Ibid, para 170.   [181] Ibid, para 179.

be withheld on the grounds, inter alia, of national security, commercial confidentiality, or the protection of personal data, thereby furthering narrowing the type of information that may be accessed under these provisions.

More recent regional treaties commonly make reference to access to information, although the nature of these obligations would appear to be weaker as States are merely required to 'give to the public appropriate access to information',[182] 'implement national legislation and regulations with the view to facilitating public access to the widest possible extent to relevant data and information',[183] 'endeavor to ensure public access' to information 'in accordance with their national legislation',[184] or simply to 'enhance, facilitate or promote to the widest possible extent public access to relevant information'.[185] All of these provisions would appear to be more like obligations of conduct rather than the obligation of result that is found in the OSPAR Convention and the Helsinki Convention.

The regional treaties are similarly weak when it comes to promoting public participation in decision-making. This is clearly encouraged by Principle 10 of the Rio Declarations, but many regional seas treaties do not mention this issue at all. If they do, it tends to be in a highly qualified manner. For example, the Barcelona Convention provides that 'Contracting Parties shall ensure that the opportunity is given to the public to participate in decision-making processes relevant to the field of application of the Convention and its Protocols, as appropriate', but it would appear to give a lot of scope to States in determining what is appropriate.[186] A stronger formulation is found in the Abidjan Protocol, which provides that:

each Contracting Party shall guarantee and encourage the participation of local communities and civil society in the implementation of measures and in the process of taking important decisions to protect the marine and coastal environment of the Protocol area against pollution caused by land-based sources and activities and the implementation of this Protocol.[187]

Even in this case, the precise effect of this obligation will depend on the interpretation of key phrases, such as 'local communities', 'civil society', and 'important decisions'.

It is clear that both access to information and public participation have seen less progressive development in the context of regional seas treaties compared with the more general treaties on the same subject matter. The main treaty in this field is the Aarhus Convention, which offers detailed guarantees relating to access to environmental information[188] and public participation in decision-making on activities that may affect the environment,[189] as well as more limited obligations in relation to decisions about plans, policies, programmes, and regulations relating

---

[182] Barcelona Convention, Article 15(1).   [183] Abidjan Protocol, Article 6(1).
[184] Tehran Convention, Article 21(2).   [185] Nairobi Protocol Article 15(1).
[186] Barcelona Convention, Article 15(2).
[187] Abidjan Protocol, Article 6(2). See a slightly weaker version of this text, omitting the requirement to 'guarantee' such participation, in the Nairobi Protocol, Article 15(4).
[188] See 1998 Convention on Access to Information, Public Participation in Decision-Making and Access to Justice in Environmental Matters (Aarhus Convention) (EIF 30 October 2001), Article 4.
[189] Aarhus Convention, Article 6.

to the environment.[190] It is true that this treaty was drafted in the context of the United Nations Economic Commission for Europe, although it is possible for other States[191] to accede with the approval of the Contracting Parties.[192] In practice, the current reach of the treaty is limited to Europe, in the broad sense of that term. This does include many coastal States in the North-East Atlantic, Baltic, Mediterranean, Black Sea, and Caspian Sea,[193] and for the States in these regions that are Parties to the Aarhus Convention, the treaty provides an additional source of rights and obligations relating to access to information and public participation in decision-making, which may be invoked in the context of the protection of the marine environment. For other States which have chosen not to become a party, the Aarhus Convention may nevertheless provide a point of reference, which could be used in order to develop their own regional rules relating to access to information and public participation in decision-making. Indeed, it is worth noting that the Aarhus Convention has been taken into account by courts and tribunal when interpreting and applying rules relating to access to information and public participation under other treaties, even in cases against a non-party.[194] From this perspective, the Aarhus Convention represents an important trend in international environmental law, which may influence related treaty regimes in the future.

4.4.5 Promoting compliance with rules and standards

Regional seas bodies play a role not only in developing the legal framework through their decisions and recommendations but also by providing an institutional framework for overseeing the implementation of such measures. At a basic level, the regular meetings of the Parties provide a forum for discussion of implementation. Yet, many regional bodies have established more formalized reporting obligations and compliance mechanisms that relate to the relevant rules, standards, and recommendations.

The leading example is provided by the OSPAR Convention, under which Parties are expected to report on what steps they have taken to implement decisions or recommendations adopted by the OSPAR Commission. Implementation reports are reviewed by the Commission, which is tasked with assessing the compliance of individual countries with the Convention, as well as with decisions and recommendations adopted thereunder.[195] Where problems are identified, the Commission may adopt further measures to assist a contracting party to comply.[196] The emphasis of this mechanism would appear to be on facilitating compliance, but it would also appear to be open to the Commission to make decisions on what steps must be taken by the State 'to bring about full compliance',[197] and such decisions would be binding

---

[190] Ibid, Articles 7–8.   [191] Provided they are Members of the United Nations.
[192] Aarhus Convention, Article 19(3).
[193] For a list and map of Parties, see the UNECE website: <https://www.unece.org/env/pp/aarhus/map.html>.
[194] See *Taskin v Turkey* (2006). For a discussion, see AE Boyle, 'Human Rights and the Environment: Where Next?' (2012) 23 *EJIL* 613, 624.
[195] OSPAR Convention, Article 23(a).   [196] Ibid, Article 23(b).   [197] Ibid.

on the States concerned.[198] Disputes about compliance with rules may also be submitted to international arbitration,[199] although there has only been one instance of adjudication to date concerning access to information, as discussed above.

The Parties to the Barcelona Convention have also adopted an elaborate compliance mechanism in order to oversee and promote implementation of the Convention, its protocols, and related recommendations.[200] Under this mechanism, an independent Compliance Committee, composed of experts in scientific, technical, socio-economic, or legal fields, is charged with considering specific situations of actual or potential non-compliance by individual parties. The Committee may provide advice to parties on how to bring themselves into compliance and it may ask a Party to develop an action plan to achieve compliance within a timeframe agreed between the Committee and the Party concerned. Alternatively, the Committee may make recommendations to the Meeting of the Conference of the Parties, which may decide on 'appropriate measures to bring about full compliance'.[201]

It is expected that similar compliance mechanisms will be adopted under other instruments.[202] In many cases, the emphasis is on 'non-confrontational and non-judicial procedures of a consultative nature to ensure compliance with the provisions of the Protocol',[203] once again underlining the sensitive nature of land-based sources of marine pollution. Nevertheless, the value of monitoring compliance in this area is still valuable as 'an iterative process in which areas to be addressed are identified and new or improved data acquired and assimilated to meet identified needs, capacity building is undertaken, or further guidance on what is needed for compliance to be achieved is given'.[204] Such regular feedback is arguably vital if progress is going to be made in meeting targets, whether or not they are legally binding. The establishment of clear and transparent review mechanisms should, therefore, be a priority for all regional seas bodies.

4.4.6 Interface between the GPOA and regional processes

Whilst regional seas bodies have taken the lead in developing more detailed rules and standards that apply to land-based sources of marine pollution, they have not carried out this role in isolation from the global legal framework described at the beginning of this chapter. Rather, regional instruments have played, what has been described as 'a crucial translation function, drawing on worldwide experience and generic best practices/technologies to identify what works in the region and why'.[205]

---

[198] OSPAR Convention, Article 13(2).   [199] Ibid, Article 32.

[200] Decision IG 17/2: Procedures and Mechanisms on Compliance under the Barcelona Convention and Its Protocols (2008). See also Decision IG 21/1 (2013).

[201] Ibid, para. 33. See also para. 34.

[202] Abidjan Protocol, Article 10(1); Nairobi Protocol, Article 12(3).

[203] Black Sea Protocol, Article 17.

[204] E Kirk, 'Noncompliance and the Development of Regimes Addressing Marine Pollution from Land-based Activities' (2008) 39 *ODIL* 235–56, 246.

[205] LA Kimball, 'An International Regime for Managing Land-based Activities that Degrade Marine and Coastal Environments' (1995) 29 *O&CM* 187, 201.

One of the critical roles of the GPOA has been to provide an overarching framework through which to encourage further action at the national and regional level, according to a shared set of objectives and principles.[206] The GPOA is the only intergovernmental process with a specific focus on land-based sources of marine pollution and it is, therefore, indispensable in sustaining the necessary momentum to ensure that this form of marine pollution continues to receive appropriate attention from the international community. In practice, regions have been influenced by developments in the global policy framework for the prevention and reduction of land-based sources of marine pollution. This interrelationship is explicit in some of the regional instruments themselves. Thus, many of the more recent regional treaties expressly make reference to the GPOA, either in their preamble,[207] or by a provision that explicitly requires the Contracting Parties to take into account the GPOA when developing programmes or plans of action.[208] Yet, even those regional treaties that make no explicit reference to the GPOA have clearly responded to the global initiatives through their recommendations and decision-making.

The example of marine litter provides an illustration of the interrelationship between the GPOA and regional regimes on land-based activities. There are a number of pathways for marine litter from land-based sources into the marine environment, which makes it a particular challenge for regulation. The Jeddah Protocol, adopted in 2005, is the only regional treaty that has an explicit treaty provision on marine litter. Article 7 of that treaty provides:

Parallel to the Global Programme of Action, wastes or marine litter dumped in the coastal zone should be taken into consideration to avoid the risks imposed on marine life ... Therefore, the contracting parties commit themselves as follows to:

1. Take all appropriate action to ensure elimination, to the greatest extent possible, of the solid wastes and litter reaching the marine and coastal environment by prevention or reduction of solid waste generation and by introduction of enhancements to waste treatment, including methods of collection and recycling and final disposal thereof;
2. Cooperating with each other and with international organizations on exchange of information relevant to the practices and experiences relating to solid waste management, recycling, reuse and cleaner production processes.

This provision is expressly aimed at implementing the goals set at the global level through the GPOA and it can be considered to translate those non-binding global policy objectives into a form of legal commitment, albeit a weak one that depends upon further cooperation between the relevant States.

Even in the absence of an express provision, other regional seas treaty bodies have also responded to the global initiatives on marine litter pursued within the framework of the GPOA. The OSPAR Commission and Helsinki Commission have

---

[206] TA Mensah, 'The International Legal Regime for the Protection and Preservation of the Marine Environment from Land-based Sources of Pollution', in AE Boyle and D Freestone (eds), *International Law and Sustainable Development* (OUP 1999) 310–11.

[207] See e.g. Wider Caribbean Protocol, preamble; Abidjan Protocol, preamble.

[208] See e.g. Black Sea Protocol, Article 5(1)(a); Jeddah Protocol, Article 19(1)(a); Syracuse Protocol, Annex I; Moscow Protocol, Article 5(2)(a).

recently adopted regional action plans to combat marine litter, both of which make an explicit reference to the GPOA or the Global Partnership on Marine Litter.[209] The Parties to the Barcelona Convention have also adopted a Regional Plan on Marine Litter Management in the Mediterranean[210] and similar activities are underway in other regions.[211] This example demonstrates how global initiatives can cascade down to the regional level.

Another critical feature of the GPOA is that it establishes a process through which regional and national actions can be monitored and encouraged by actors from outside of the region. Whilst the GPOA cannot impose its goals onto individual regions or States, it does provide an important opportunity for international scrutiny of regional activities in relation to land-based sources of marine pollution. It is not only other States that are involved in this process, but also financial institutions, UN specialized agencies, multilateral environmental agreements, and river commissions.[212] The participation of these actors is important because they can provide support for regions to take steps to tackle critical threats that they may not be able to address by themselves. At the same time, such support is conditional upon regions buying into the framework of action provided by the GPOA.

4.5 Conclusion

Not only do land-based sources of marine pollution represent one of the most serious pressures on the oceans, they are also one of the more difficult sources to regulate, given the scope and diversity of economic sectors that are implicated, as well as the range of substances that can cause harm to marine ecosystems. This chapter has sought to explain the main bases of regulation in the field and the nature of the commitments undertaken by States.

There is little doubt that regional seas bodies have played the most important role in responding to the threat of land-based sources of marine pollution. Regionalism is appropriate in this context because of the distinct challenges that exist in different parts of the world, as well as different levels of ability to responds to those challenges. Regionalism permits a flexible response to the regulation of land-based sources, taking into account economic and ecological factors. As a result, it is not surprising to see variations in the manner and detail in which land-based sources of marine pollution are addressed from region to region.

---

[209] Regional Action Plan for Prevention and Management of Marine Litter in the North-East Atlantic, OSPAR Agreement 2014-1 (2014); HELCOM Recommendation 36/1 (2015).

[210] Regional Plan on Marine Litter Management in the Mediterranean in the Framework of Article 15 of the Land Based Sources Protocol, Decision IG.21/7 (2013).

[211] See Regional Action Plan on Marine Litter Management for the Wider Caribbean Region (2014); Northwest Pacific Regional Action Plan on Marine Litter (2007). See also UNEP, *Marine Litter: A Global Challenge* (2009). The Second UNEP Environmental Assembly encouraged all regions to collaborate to establish such action plans; UNEP Environmental Assembly, Resolution 2/11 (2016) para. 4.

[212] See Birnie, Boyle, and Redgwell (n35) 464.

The regulation of land-based sources relies upon a mixture of binding and non-binding instruments. It is in those regions that have a clear legal framework, either in the form of a specific annex or protocol to a regional seas treaty, that have seen the most progress in addressing this source of pollution. However, the negotiation of a legally binding instrument is not by itself sufficient, if it does not receive the active support of relevant States. Not all of the instruments described in this chapter have entered into force at the time of writing, including the 2009 Black Sea Protocol, the 2010 Nairobi Protocol, the 2012 Abidjan Protocol, and the 2012 Moscow Protocol. Even when instruments have entered into force, they may not have attracted participation from all relevant States. For example, the 1999 Caribbean Protocol entered into force in August 2010, but to date, only eleven of the twenty-five States in the region have consented to be bound. Similarly, the 1996 Mediterranean Protocol finally entered into force in May 2008, but several major coastal States are yet to become Parties. Without the participation of all relevant actors, these instruments can hardly be considered as providing an effective framework for regional action.

Legally binding instruments must also be capable of evolving to address developments in knowledge relating to the effects of land-based activities on the marine environment, as well as the emergence of new technologies to counter marine pollution. The use of the BAT and BEP standards in many modern regional instruments ensures that the legal framework is dynamic. Institutions also play important roles in interpreting the rules contained in the legal instruments in an evolutionary manner. Indeed, it is the programmes of action and other decisions and recommendations developed within each region that often provide the real catalyst for effective regional action on land-based sources of marine pollution, provided they are regularly reviewed and updated. Institutions also have key roles to play in monitoring compliance with rules, standards, and recommended practices in this field. Ongoing supervision is required to ensure States have taken steps to comply with their obligations, both to boost confidence in the reciprocity of measures and to identify best practices that could be shared amongst States within the region. Formal compliance mechanisms can provide a particularly suitable tool for ensuring adequate scrutiny of national measures taken to implement regional commitments and the Mediterranean region offers a good model in this respect, with its independent compliance committee and transparent procedures. Other regions should be encouraged to follow this approach.

Where environmental problems have causes or effects beyond the regional level, global regulation may also be appropriate. The POPs Convention and Minamata Convention have been highlighted as two leading global treaties relevant to the protection of the marine environment from land-based sources. There may be other issues that also demand a global approach. For example, emerging evidence about the distances that micro-plastics can travel in ocean currents suggests that this issue may require global regulation if efforts to prevent pollution of fragile marine ecosystems, such as the Arctic, are to be successful.[213] Given its broad membership,

---

[213] See e.g. The Sunday Times, 'Microbead timebomb ticking in the Arctic', 28 August 2016, 9.

far-reaching environmental mandate, and position with the UN system, UNEP has a potential role in leading efforts in this respect. To date, UNEP has been principally concerned with gathering more data about the impacts of micro-plastics and raising awareness of the problem,[214] although a new global treaty on this subject cannot be ruled out in the future. In particular, global rules on what measures should be taken, including a potential ban on products containing specified micro-plastics, could be an important step in order to promote consistent action. Moreover, a global agreement could go some way to ensuring such measures are adopted in a non-discriminatory manner, in compliance with international trade rules.[215]

Despite its non-binding status, the GPOA also plays an important role in supporting the legal framework for the prevention, reduction and control of land-based sources of marine pollution, by offering policy guidance and facilitating the brokerage of financial and technical support to individual States or regions in need. The advantage of the GPOA is that it can keep all aspects of the problem under review and it can highlight areas in which more action is needed at the global, regional, or national levels.

Despite the scale and urgency of the threats, there are no short-term solutions or quick fixes for land-based sources of marine pollution. Rather, it has been stressed that there is a 'need for long-term commitment'.[216] In this respect, the instruments and institutions that have been established at both the global and regional levels have important and complementary roles to play in a multilayered legal framework for the regulation of land-based sources of marine pollution. It is through the gradual strengthening of commitments that the international community is most likely to be able to tackle this threat to marine ecosystems.

---

[214] UNEP Environmental Assembly Resolution 2/11 (2016).

[215] Principle 12 of the Rio Declaration provides that 'environmental measures addressing transboundary or global environmental problems should, as far as possible, be based on an international consensus'. Multilateral agreement on appropriate measures would make it less likely that they may be found to contradict the rules of the World Trade Organization.

[216] GESAMP (n2) 68.

5

Dumping of Waste at Sea

5.1 Introduction

Until the middle of the twentieth century, the oceans were commonly used as a dumping ground for unwanted products. Waste would be loaded onto ships or aircraft, taken out to sea, and tipped into the water. All kinds of waste were disposed in this fashion, and it was assumed that the oceans would be able to assimilate such materials. To avoid any risks to human life or health, waste was simply disposed at a suitable distance from the shore. Gradually, however, this practice started to be seen as posing unacceptable risks to the marine environment. International concern over dumping first arose in relation to the disposal of nuclear waste at sea. The risks of such an activity, if uncontrolled, were obvious, and this practice was the target of Article 25 of the 1958 Convention on the High Seas, calling on States to 'take measures to prevent pollution of the seas from the dumping of radioactive waste'. This provision had been suggested by the International Law Commission (ILC) as a progressive development of the law given the potential for harmful effects to 'fish and fish eaters'.[1] Concern soon spread to the effects of other dumped materials on the marine environment. A spur to action was the notorious case of the Stella Maris, a Dutch vessel, which left port in 1971, carrying a cargo of chlorinated waste for disposal at sea.[2] Vocal opposition led to the vessel returning to port with its load still on board, but it was realized that a more comprehensive international legal regime was necessary. As a result, a series of global and regional instruments have been developed to address this problem.

This chapter will consider how dumping is regulated at the international level and how the relevant norms have evolved over time to provide stronger protection for the marine environment. It will start by considering the scope of the term *dumping*, before looking at the relevant provisions in United Nations Convention on the Law of the Sea (UNCLOS) and other global and regional instruments. The chapter will also consider how these different instruments interact. Finally, it will seek to identify gaps and weaknesses in the existing regime and will consider what challenges remain for effectively controlling dumping at sea.

---

[1] ILC, 'Draft Articles on the Law of the Sea with Commentaries' (1956–II) *YbILC* 286.
[2] See T Loftas, 'The New Marine Poison' (1971) 51 *New Scientist and Science Journal* 266.

5.2 The Scope of the Dumping Regime

Before proceeding to a discussion of how international law regulates the conduct of dumping, it is first necessary to understand what is meant by the term. *Dumping* is defined under UNCLOS as '(i) any deliberate disposal of wastes or other matter from vessels, aircraft, platforms or other man-made structures at sea; or (ii) any deliberate disposal of vessels, aircraft, platforms or other man-made structures at sea'.[3] This definition was borrowed verbatim from the 1972 Convention on Dumping, which further defines *sea* as 'all marine waters other than the internal waters of States'.[4]

Despite it being the only source of marine pollution that is explicitly defined under UNCLOS, the precise scope of the term *dumping* has been the subject of intense debate. The core activity covered by the dumping regime is the transport of waste to sea for disposal. The definition clearly covers the dumping of wastes into the water column. However, the uses of the words *at sea* are ambiguous, and several interpretative issues arise.

The first question is whether disposal of substances in the seabed or subsoil is covered by this definition. This activity could fall within the dumping regime if it is carried out from a vessel 'at sea'. In this context, a broader interpretation is to be preferred, in part, because it would lead to a more robust understanding of dumping, which would prevent circumvention of the rules simply because of where the material was placed. Indeed, the more recent instruments on dumping have adopted a definition of the term that explicitly incorporates 'any storage of wastes or other matter in the seabed or subsoil thereof'.[5]

It has also been debated whether the definition of *dumping* includes the disposal of waste through pipelines or other infrastructure directly connected to land.[6] The key question in this regard is whether pipelines count as 'man-made structures at sea' for the purposes of the definition of *dumping*. Such 'structures' clearly cover independent installations and structures built on the seabed[7] (e.g. repositories accessed only from the sea).[8] Yet, there is some doubt whether the definition covers structures that are connected to land. There are several arguments to suggest that disposal of waste through pipelines, no matter how long they are, does not fall within the dumping regime. First, their connection to land means that they may not be considered to exist 'at sea'. In this respect, it is pertinent to note that the 1996 Protocol to the Dumping Convention expressly excludes 'sub-seabed repositories accessed only from land' from the definition of *dumping at sea*.[9] By analogy, outflows or pipelines that are connected to land are also, strictly speaking, not at sea. Second, pipelines and outfall structures are explicitly covered by the regime relating to land-based sources

---

[3] UNCLOS, Article 1(5)(a).
[4] See 1972 London Dumping Convention (LDC) (EIF 30 August 1975), Article 3(3).
[5] See 1996 London Dumping Protocol (LDP) (EIF 24 March 2006), Article 1(4)(3).
[6] See Report of the Thirty-Sixth Consultative Meeting, Document LC 36/16 (2014) paras 9.10–9.11; Report of the Thirty-Seventh Consultative Meeting, Document LC 37/16 (2015) paras 9.1–9.8.
[7] See e.g. UNCLOS, Article 60.   [8] Resolution LDC.41(13) (1990).
[9] LDC, Article 1(7).

of marine pollution.[10] If it is accepted that the categories of pollution established by Part XII are best understood as mutually exclusive,[11] it follows that pipelines and outfall structures attached to land should not also count as dumping.

As well as providing a general definition of *dumping*, UNCLOS also specifies two types of activity that do not count as dumping.

The first exclusion relates to:

the disposal of wastes or other matter incidental to, or derived from the normal operations of vessels, aircraft, platforms or other man-made structures at sea and their equipment, other than wastes or other matter transported by or to vessels, aircraft, platforms or other man-made structures at sea, operating for the purpose of disposal of such matter or derived from the treatment of such wastes or other matter on such vessels, aircraft, platforms or structures.[12]

The purpose of this exclusion is also to avoid overlap with other international regimes addressing marine pollution from these sources, emphasizing the mutually exclusive character of the regimes.[13] Nevertheless, there may be potential 'grey areas' between these different regimes that arise because of the ambiguity in the phrase *incidental to, or derived from the normal operations of*. A good example is the disposal of spoilt cargo. A Joint Correspondence Group between the Parties to the relevant treaties confirmed that the instruments were 'intended to complement one another and not overlap',[14] although they also recognized that it was difficult to draw a clear dividing line between their areas of operation and that the precise characterization of spoilt cargoes may depend upon the circumstances of an individual case.[15] Rather than deciding on a formal division of competence in these situations, States have instead sought to adopt coordinated approaches to waste management through cooperation amongst the relevant regimes. For example, the Parties to the dumping treaties and the Parties to the International Convention on the Prevention of Pollution from Ships have collaborated in order to develop Guidance on Management of Spoilt Cargoes[16] and they agreed to undertake a coordinated strategy for disseminating and promoting the guidance and keeping it under review. Another grey area that has arisen in practice relates to the removal of antifouling paint at sea. In this case, Parties to each regime have again coordinated their response by agreeing upon guidance to be circulated under both relevant treaties as a means to promote best practices in this area.[17] These initiatives have sought to ensure that the dumping regime is both robust and integrated with other relevant treaty regimes, to avoid conflicts.

---

[10] UNCLOS, Article 207(1).   [11] See Chapter 2.

[12] UNCLOS, Article 1(5)(b)(i).   [13] See Chapters 6 and 8.

[14] Report of the Joint London Convention—MEPC Correspondence Group, Document LC 28/6 (2006) para. 6.

[15] Ibid, para. 27.

[16] Report of the Thirtieth Consultative Meeting, Document LC 30/16 (2008) para. 9.6.1 and Annex 10; Report of the Marine Environment Protection Committee on Its Fifty-Ninth Session, Document MEPC 59/24 (2009) para. 6.48. A revised version of the guidance was adopted at the Thirty-Fourth Session in order to reflect the amendments to MARPOL Annex V; see Document LC 34/15 (2012) para. 8.7.1 and Annex 11.

[17] See Guidance on Best Management Practices for Removal of Anti-Fouling Coatings from Ships, including TBT Hull Paints, distributed as Document LC-LP.1/Circ.31 (2009) and Document AFS.3/Circ.3 (2009).

The definition of dumping also excludes the 'placement of matter for a purpose other than the mere disposal thereof, provided that such placement is not contrary to the aims of [the] Convention'.[18] This exclusion confirms that the purpose of the dumping regime is to regulate the purposeful disposal of substances at sea. However, an *a contrario* reading of this exclusion suggests that the placement of matter for a purpose other than disposal may nevertheless fall within the scope of the dumping regime if it is incompatible with the aims of the regime. This interpretation allows the dumping regime to be applied to the placement of matter, which, whilst not strictly speaking discarded at sea, nevertheless, may pose risks to the marine environment. The precise meaning of this language has been controversial in practice. For example, Parties to the Dumping Convention have agreed that 'placement should not be used as an excuse for disposing of waste',[19] but no consensus has been reached on whether or not placement was covered by the Convention.[20] This interpretative question has not been definitively resolved, although the Parties have agreed that the placement of materials in the marine environment should be assessed in accordance with the relevant guidelines and placements should be reported to the Secretariat of the Convention.[21] Indeed, the Parties have agreed in some instances that particular forms of placement should be regulated under the dumping regime. One example is the placement of materials for the purposes of establishing artificial reefs. The Parties have adopted guidelines in relation to the establishment of artificial reefs in order to ensure that this activity does not undermine the objectives of the dumping regime.[22] The status of such guidelines remains controversial,[23] but they demonstrate the pragmatic approach, generally adopted by the Parties to the dumping treaties. Another example is the placement of materials into the oceans for geoengineering purposes, a subject that will be considered in more detail in Chapter 9.

5.3 The Regulation of Dumping under UNCLOS

UNCLOS does not purport to provide detailed rules on dumping but rather seeks to ensure that all States have in place a basic legal framework to address this issue. Dumping is dealt with primarily by Article 210, which plays a number of important functions.

First, Article 210 clarifies the scope of coastal State jurisdiction over dumping, by providing that 'dumping within the territorial sea and the exclusive economic zone or onto the continental shelf shall not be carried out without the express prior

---

[18] UNCLOS, Article 1(5)(b)(ii).

[19] Report of the Twenty-Second Consultative Meeting, Document LC22/14 (2000) para. 5.14.

[20] See Ibid, para. 5.15. For a discussion, see DL VanderZwaag and A Daniel, 'International Law and Ocean Dumping: Steering a Precautionary Course Aboard the 1996 London Protocol, but Still an Unfinished Voyage', in A Chircop et al (eds), *The Future of Ocean Regime Building* (Brill 2009) 522–3.'

[21] Report of the Twenty-Fourth Consultative Meeting, Document LC 24/17 (2002) paras 8.18–8.19.

[22] See Report of the Thirtieth Consultative Meeting, Document LC 30/16 (2008) para. 8.6.1.

[23] For example, the Japanese delegation noted in the debate that it did not consider that placement fell within the scope of the Convention or Protocol; Ibid, para. 8.9

approval of the coastal State'.[24] This provision gives the coastal State exclusive jurisdiction to regulate dumping within these maritime zones. Dumping beyond national jurisdiction, in contrast, remains subject, in principle, to the exclusive jurisdiction of the flag State of a vessel or aircraft.

Second, UNCLOS mandates cooperation between the coastal State and 'other States which may by reason of their geographical situation may be adversely affected thereby'.[25] This provision addresses the situation where dumping may take place close to the border between two States, thus risking transboundary harm. Article 210 does not expressly cover the situation where dumping takes place on the high seas in proximity to the maritime zones of a coastal State, although cooperation would arguably also be required in this situation by virtue of the more general obligation to prevent, reduce, and control transboundary harm in Article 194(2).

Third, UNCLOS requires all States to adopt laws and regulations and other necessary measures to prevent, reduce, and control pollution of the marine environment by dumping, although it leaves them some discretion as to the manner in which they do this.[26] This discretion is limited, however, as the Convention requires that '[n]ational laws, regulations and measures shall be no less effective in preventing, reducing and controlling such pollution than the global rules and standards'.[27] The unambiguous effect of this provision is to require national legislation to meet international minimum standards. It is thus a stronger version of a rule of reference, compared with the rule of reference that applies to pollution from land-based sources considered in Chapter 4. However, in order for this rule of reference to operate, it is necessary to be able to identify the relevant 'global rules and standards'. It is to this issue that we now turn.

5.4 Global Rules on Dumping

5.4.1 The London Dumping Convention

UNCLOS was negotiated at a time when there was already one global treaty on the topic of dumping, namely the 1972 Convention on Dumping. International discussions on how to address dumping at sea had started in earnest in the early 1970s, with the United States taking the lead in proposing an international treaty on dumping.[28] Negotiations were initially conducted through the meetings of the Intergovernmental Working Group on Marine Pollution, which was involved in preparing for the 1972 Stockholm Conference on the Human Environment.[29] At the Conference, States agreed that ocean dumping must be controlled wherever it takes place and they agreed 'to work towards the completion of, and bringing into force as soon as possible of, an over-all instrument for the control of ocean

---

[24] UNCLOS, Article 210(5).   [25] Ibid, Article 210(5).   [26] Ibid, Article 210(1).
[27] Ibid, Article 210(6).
[28] See United States, Draft Convention on the Regulation of Transportation for Ocean Dumping (1971).
[29] See IMO, *Origins of the London Convention* (2012).

dumping'.[30] The International Convention on the Prevention of Marine Pollution by Dumping of Wastes and Other Matter was adopted shortly afterwards by an intergovernmental conference held in London in December 1972, in which over ninety States took part.

The basic purpose of the London Convention is to harmonize the policies of the Contracting Parties towards ocean dumping.[31] To this end, the treaty places several basic obligations on Contracting Parties.

First and foremost, the London Convention creates an obligation on Contracting Parties to prohibit the dumping of waste and other matter listed in Annex I of the Convention.[32] The original list in Annex I covered chemical compounds, heavy metals, persistent plastics, oil products, high-level radioactive matter, and minerals produced for biological and chemical warfare. This list has since been updated in order to strengthen the protection offered by the treaty, as discussed below. The prohibition of these substances sets a basic international minimum standard, whilst the treaty recognizes that a State may individually prohibit additional substances provided that it notifies such measures to the IMO.[33]

The dumping of other materials not listed in Annex I continues to be allowed, but the Convention also imposes an obligation on Contracting Parties to regulate this matter by introducing a permitting scheme. The Convention distinguishes between special permits for substances and materials needing special care (listed in Annex II) and general permits for all other substances. The Convention sets out a list of factors to be considered by a State prior to issuing a permit.[34] Key amongst these factors is the need to ensure that dumping is not 'liable to create hazards to human health, to harm living resources and marine life, to damage amenities or to interfere with other legitimate uses of the sea'.[35] In other words, the Convention requires an environmental assessment of proposed dumping prior to the issuing of a permit. Amongst the factors that must be taken into account by the authorizing State in the assessment process is the 'practical availability of alternative land-based methods of treatment, disposal or elimination'.[36] The Convention falls short of establishing an express obligation for a State to prohibit dumping unless it does not have the technical capacity and necessary facilities to dispose of the waste on land.[37] Nevertheless, guidance agreed by the Parties suggests that 'a permit to dump wastes or other matter shall be refused if the permitting authority determines that appropriate opportunities exist to reuse, recycle or treat waste without undue risks to human health or the environmental or disproportionate costs'.[38] Indeed, the Convention suggests that the Parties should be proactive in developing alternatives and it contains an obligation to promote capacity building for 'the disposal and treatment of waste and other measures to prevent or mitigate pollution caused by dumping'.[39] Implementation

---

[30] Stockholm Action Plan, Recommendation 86(c).   [31] LDC, Article 2.
[32] Ibid, Article 4(1)(a).   [33] Ibid, Article 4(3).
[34] Ibid, Article 4(2) and Annex III.   [35] Ibid, Article 1 and Annex III, Section C.
[36] Ibid, Annex III, Section C, para. 4.
[37] C.f. 1989 Convention on the Control of Transboundary Hazardous Waste (Basel Convention) (EIF 5 May 1992), Article 4(2)(d) and 4(9)(a).
[38] Generic Waste Assessment Guidelines, para. 3.2.   [39] LDC, Article 9(c).

of this obligation is a collective obligation of the Parties and it follows that the Convention bodies have become an important forum not only for discussing the prohibition of dumping at sea but also the use of alternative disposal mechanisms on land.[40]

To assist States in carrying out such assessments and to ensure a degree of harmonization in the activities of Parties, the Parties have agreed on generic guidance on the assessment of wastes for dumping.[41] The generic guidance suggests that Parties must carry out a detailed characterization of the waste prior to making a decision about dumping, taking into account the total amount of matter to be dumped, as well as its physical properties, toxicity, persistence, and accumulative and bio-transformative capacity.[42] The Parties have also adopted specific guidance in relation to certain substances, including dredged material; sewage sludge; fish waste; vessels; platforms and other man-made structures; inert, inorganic geological material; organic material of natural origin; and bulky items primarily comprising iron, steel, and concrete.[43]

Where a decision is made to issue a dumping permit, this may be made subject to conditions relating to the types and amounts of dumped material and the location, method and timing of the dumping operation. It is the responsibility of the authorizing State to ensure that any conditions are complied with. Guidance agreed by the Parties also suggests that post hoc monitoring of the dumpsite should also take place in order to verify that there are no unforeseen impacts on the marine environment.[44] The promotion of monitoring means that the regulation of dumping is not simply a one-off decision but rather an ongoing process to ensure that dumping does not cause harm to the marine environment. If problems are identified, States may require remedial measures to be taken.[45]

The Convention applies to any dumping operations conducted within the jurisdiction of the Contracting Party,[46] and the Convention refers to the relevant jurisdictional framework in UNCLOS,[47] which, as noted above, confirms that the authority to regulate dumping within the territorial sea and the exclusive economic zone (EEZ) or onto the continental shelf clearly falls to the coastal State.[48] In addition, Contracting Parties are required to apply the Convention to vessels and aircraft registered in its territory and to vessels and aircraft loading in its territory or territorial sea, regardless of where the dumping is to take place.[49] In order to avoid circumvention of these requirements, Parties are also encouraged to prohibit the export of wastes to non-Parties unless there are 'compelling reasons' and 'clear

[40] See e.g. the discussion of the disposal of sewage sludge; Report of the Thirty-Fifth Consultative Meeting, Document LC 35/15 (2013) paras 8.23–8.24.
[41] See Report of the Thirtieth Consultative Meeting, Document LC30/16 (2008) para. 3.5.1, and Annex 3, replacing the guidelines adopted in 1997.
[42] Generic Waste Assessment Guidelines, para. 4.2.
[43] See Report of the Twenty-Second Consultative Meeting, Document LC22/14 (2000) para. 5.4 and Annexes 3–10. These guidelines are considered 'living documents' which must be kept under review; see Ibid, para. 5.3.3.
[44] Ibid, paras 8.1–8.6.   [45] Ibid, para. 8.6.   [46] LDC, Article 7(1)(c).
[47] Ibid, Article 13.   [48] UNCLOS, Article 210(5).
[49] LDC, Article 7(1)(a) and (b).

evidence that the wastes would be disposed of in compliance with the requirements of the London Dumping Convention . . .'.[50] This latter requirement is, however, not a legally binding obligation under the Convention.

Enforcement of the dumping regime largely falls to the permitting State. The Convention obliges States to take 'appropriate measures to prevent and punish conduct in contravention of the provisions of the Convention',[51] which requires the introduction of criminal penalties for dumping without a permit or in contravention of the conditions of a permit. There are exceptions when a vessel has to dump in situations of force majeure or distress,[52] and the Convention also excludes vessels subject to sovereign immunity from its scope, although Parties are encouraged to ensure that the vessels they own or operate act in a manner consistent with the object and purpose of the Convention.[53]

Coastal States may exercise enforcement jurisdiction over violations of dumping rules committed within their territorial sea or EEZ or in relation to their continental shelf.[54] It may be that the flag State or loading State will also have jurisdiction over dumping offences in these waters, and it will be up to the affected States to agree on which should be responsible for issuing a permit and bringing enforcement proceedings.[55]

The role of the flag State or loading State is more important on the high seas, where they are principally responsible for ensuring compliance with the dumping rules in these areas. Yet, a common problem is that these States will often not have the resources to adequately police dumping regulations on the high seas.[56] In order to assist States in fulfilling their obligation to investigate and enforce dumping regulations, the Consultative Meeting of the London Convention has adopted a reporting procedure of observed dumping incidents.[57] To date, however, there are no known instances of these procedures being applied in practice,[58] and enforcement remains a weakness of the regime.

Whilst the dumping regime leaves a lot of discretion to individual States as to how they implement their obligations, there is international oversight of the permitting process through the annual Consultative Meeting of the Parties. In the absence of any formal compliance procedures or dispute settlement mechanisms,[59] this forum has been an important means for keeping implementation of the Convention under

---

[50] Resolution LDC.29(10) (1986).   [51] LDC, Article 7(2).

[52] Ibid, Article 5(1). See also Interim Procedures and Criteria for Determining Emergency Situations, Document LDC V/12 (1980) Annex 5.

[53] LDC, Article 7(4).   [54] UNCLOS, Article 216(1)(a).

[55] Ibid, Article 216(2) simply provides that 'no state shall be obliged by virtue of this article to institute proceedings when another State has already instituted proceedings in accordance with this article'.

[56] It has been noted elsewhere that this 'may often be an ineffective remedy'; P Birnie, A Boyle, and C Redgwell, *International Law and the Environment* (3rd edn, OUP 2009) 471.

[57] Report of the Twenty-Fourth Consultative Meeting, Document LC 24/17 (2002) para. 3.12 and Annex 3. A revised Reporting Procedure was adopted and circulated to Parties in February 2012 as LC-LP.1/Circ.47.

[58] A Simcock and J Wang, 'Chapter 24: Solid Waste Disposal', in *Global Ocean Assessment* (UN 2016) 11.

[59] An amendment to introduce dispute settlement arrangements was adopted in 1978 (Resolution LDC.6(III)), but it has never entered into force.

review.[60] The Parties have also established a Scientific Group[61] composed of technical experts, which regularly reviews permits issued by Contracting Parties and which may request clarifications from States concerning particular dumping incidents.[62] The problem with this procedure is that many Contracting Parties simply do not submit their reports in a timely fashion.[63] Although the Parties have adopted a number of measures to address this issue, such as simplifying reporting procedures and encouraging electronic reporting,[64] the problem continues.[65] It has been recognized that it is largely a matter of a lack of capacity[66] and it should thus be addressed through technical assistance. The Convention explicitly calls for the promotion of training and the supply of necessary equipment to support countries in taking measures to comply with the Convention,[67] and this issue has been highlighted as one of the key ongoing priorities in relation to the dumping regime.[68] The Parties have set up a Technical Cooperation and Assistance Programme[69] and the establishment of a Trust Fund to support implementation of the programme.[70]

Over the years, the London Dumping Convention has attracted broad, albeit not universal participation. Today, the Convention has eighty-seven Contracting Parties, representing 61.76 per cent of the world fleet.[71] Nevertheless, it is generally agreed that the 1972 Convention falls within the scope of the global rules and standards referred to in Article 210. As a consequence, all Parties to UNCLOS are required to comply with the provisions of the 1972 Convention, whether or not they have become a Party to the latter treaty.[72] This conclusion is relatively unproblematic in relation to the original prescriptions of the Convention, given that States would be aware of these global rules at the time at which they decide to become bound by UNCLOS. The scope of the rule of reference is more problematic when

[60] See e.g. OS Stokke, 'Beyond Dumping? The Effectiveness of the London Convention' (1998/1999) 14 *YICED* 39, 43.

[61] Terms of Reference, in Resolution LC.57(21) (1999); Resolution LC.59(29) (2007); Resolution LP.2(2) (2010).

[62] See e.g. Report of the Twenty-Fourth Consultative Meeting, Document LC 24/17 (2002) paras 6.12 and 6.23.2.

[63] The 2014 Consultative Meeting was informed that reporting rates actually appeared to be declining. In relation to those States which are only Party to the Convention, the reporting rate was a meagre 17 per cent; see Report of the Thirty-Sixth Consultative Meeting, Document LC 36/16 (2014) paras 7.20–7.21

[64] Report of the Thirty-Third Consultative Meeting, Document LC 33/15 (2011) para. 6.31.

[65] Amongst the measures suggested by the Consultative Meeting is a gentle prod by neighbouring States; see Report of the Thirty-Third Consultative Meeting, Document LC 33/15 (2011) para. 6.36.2.

[66] Report of the Thirty-Fourth Consultative Meeting, Document LC 34/15 (2012) para. 6.4.

[67] LDC, Article 9.   [68] Agenda 21 (1992) para. 17.28(g).

[69] See Resolution LC.55(SM) (1996); Resolution LC.54(18) (1996). See also the Barriers to Compliance Implementation Plan.

[70] See Document LC-LP.1/Circ.33/Rev. 1 (2011).

[71] See IMO, *Status of Multilateral Conventions and Instruments of which the International Maritime Organization or Its Secretary-General Performs Depositary or Other Functions, as at 19 April 2016*, 510.

[72] L de la Fayette, 'The London Convention 1972: Preparing for the Future' (1998) 13 *IJMCL* 515–16; EJ Molenaar, 'The 1996 Protocol to the 1972 London Convention' (1997) 12 *IJMCL* 396, 403. In fact, the IMO Secretariat was requested to write to non-Parties, bringing the requirements of the Convention to their attention; Report of the Seventeenth Consultative Meeting, Document LC17/14 (1994) para. 2.10.

it comes to changes to the dumping regime that have been adopted since the conclusion of UNCLOS. To what extent can these rules and standards be considered to fall within the scope of the rule of reference in Article 210? We will now turn to the question of how the dumping regime has evolved over time and what implications this has for Parties to UNCLOS.

5.4.2 Evolution of the Dumping Convention through the interpretation and amendment

The 1972 Dumping Convention has proved to be a dynamic instrument that has successfully evolved in light of contemporary developments in marine science and environmental policy. The annual Consultative Meeting of the Parties has played a key role in this process. This body has a broad remit to 'keep under continuous review the implementation of the Convention'[73] and it has been a vital forum for ensuring the integrity and continued relevance of the global regime. It is notable that meetings include not only participation from the Contracting Parties, but nongovernmental organizations (NGOs) have also traditionally played a highly active role in the regime,[74] particularly in relation to raising questions of compliance and providing information on alleged dumping incidents.[75] NGOs have also influenced the development of the regime, by putting forward proposals and lobbying governments to improve protection for the marine environment from dumping.[76] Whilst States retain the ultimate say on the matter, there is little doubt that the sustained pressure from groups such as Greenpeace, the Advisory Committee on the Protection of the Seas, and the International Union for the Conservation of Nature has provided a strong voice for the environment within the dumping regime.[77]

One way in which the Parties have ensured the evolution of the Convention is through the adoption of interpretative resolutions and guidance. These non-binding instruments can be used to interpret the Convention in an evolutionary manner. In particular, they have emphasized the need to read the treaty in light of emerging principles of international environmental law, as discussed in Chapter 1.

First, guidance on carrying out waste assessments stresses the importance of dumpsite selection, including an evaluation of the degree to which dumping may result harm to marine ecosystems, noting that 'the assessment should be as comprehensive as possible'.[78] The guidance further suggests that particular attention should be paid to impacts on areas of special scientific or biological importance, including

---

[73] LDC, Article 14(4).

[74] Report of the Twentieth Consultative Meeting, Document LC20/14 (1998) paras 6.15, 12.3, and 12.5; Report of the Twenty-first Consultative Meeting, Document LC21/13 (1999) para. 4.8.

[75] See Birnie, Boyle, and Redgwell (n56) 472.

[76] See R Parmentier, 'Greenpeace and the Dumping of Waste at Sea: A Case of Non-State Actors' Intervention in International Affairs' (1999) 4 *IN* 433–55.

[77] G Peet, 'The Role of (Environmental) Non-Governmental Organizations at the Marine Environment Protection Committee of the International Maritime Organization and the London Dumping Convention' (1994) 22 *O&CM* 3.

[78] Generic Waste Assessment Guidelines, para. 7.3.

spawning, nursery, and recruitment areas; migration routes; and seasonal and critical habitats. This guidance thus reinforces an ecosystems approach to dumping decisions and it suggests that the Convention should be applied in light of other developments relating to the designation of marine protected areas.[79] In particular, developments within certain regional seas treaties to designate protected areas must be taken into account in this respect.[80]

Second, subsequent decisions of the Parties have indicated that States should:

be guided by a precautionary approach to environmental protection whereby appropriate preventative measures are taken when there is reason to believe that substances or energy introduced into the marine environment are likely to cause harm even when there is no conclusive evidence to prove causal relation between inputs and their effects.[81]

This is a weak version of the precautionary approach that falls short of a reversal of the burden of proof in the case of dumping and it still leaves the decision to individual Contracting Parties. Nevertheless, it means that States cannot simply argue that dumping should be allowed unless there is evidence of actual harm.

Guidelines agreed by the Parties also recommend that 'opportunities are provided for public review and participation in the permitting process'.[82] The modalities of such participation are left to the State concerned, but the obvious form of public participation is consultation on proposed permits prior to their issuing. At a minimum, public participation requires transparency of decision-making and the publication of a register of permits. Yet, the Parties to the London Convention have refrained from creating a legal obligation to this effect, again highlighting the caution with which States have adopted a participatory approach in the context of the protection of the marine environment.

Another way in which the 1972 Convention has evolved is by amendments to the list of prohibited substances. The Convention applies a tacit amendment procedure to the modification of Annexes, allowing substances to be added to the list of prohibited substances in a relatively quick manner. The Convention specifies that amendments to the Annexes must be 'based on scientific and technical considerations', which has caused some debate.[83] In reality, however, the decision to amend the scope of the Convention is a political one. Following approval by two-thirds of the Contracting Parties, amendments enter into force for all Parties one hundred days later, with an exception for those States which make a declaration within this period that they cannot accept the amendments.[84] This mechanism allows the rapid

---

[79] See Chapter 3.
[80] See the discussion in Chapter 3, on regional treaties and the conservation of marine biological diversity.
[81] Resolution LDC.44(14) (1991) para. 1. See also Generic Waste Assessment Guidelines, para. 3.2:

the practical availability of other means of disposal should be considered in the light of a comparative risk assessment involving both dumping and the alternatives, taking into account the general obligation to apply a precautionary approach to dumping and the objectives of protecting the marine environment from all sources of pollution.

[82] Generic Waste Assessment Guidelines, para. 9.2.   [83] LDC, Article 15(2).
[84] Ibid.

amendment of the regime, whilst also providing a means for individual States to protect their vital interests. This process has been used on several occasions in order to achieve significant extensions to the prohibition of dumping under the Convention.

The first substantive amendments to the Convention were adopted in 1978, in order to address the issue of incineration at sea.[85] The amendments are interesting because they demonstrate the broad reach of the regime. In effect, these amendments extend the application of the Convention to disposal at sea which threatens pollution to the atmosphere. At the same time, the amendments recognize that incineration at sea may be 'an interim method of disposal of wastes containing highly toxic substances' and they, therefore, allow the incineration at sea of certain substances listed in Annexes I and II, provided that a licence is issued.[86] Yet, the amendments also sought to control this practice by introducing certain detailed conditions, set out in regulations annexed to the Resolution, which had to be met prior to the issuing of a licence. These conditions included the use of a marine incineration facility that meets minimum standards and the siting of the activity in an area that will minimize any risk to the environment.[87] Contracting Parties were also required to consider the practical availability of alternative land-based methods of treatment, disposal, or elimination before issuing a licence,[88] thereby emphasizing that incineration at sea was not to be assumed as an optimum solution to waste management. Following this amendment, concern continued to be expressed in relation to the incineration of substances at sea and the Parties adopted further amendments prohibiting the incineration of industrial wastes and sewage sludge at sea in 1993.[89] This progressive development of the regime relating to incineration, continued under the 1996 London Dumping Protocol, considered below, demonstrating how environmental standards have become stricter over time.

Additional amendments were also adopted in 1993 in order to expand the original prohibition on the dumping of high-level radioactive wastes to include other radioactive substances.[90] The process of adoption for this amendment is interesting because it demonstrates the role of both science and policy in the development of international environmental law. Proposals for such an amendment had first been brought forward in 1983, when Kiribati and Nauru proposed prohibiting the dumping of all radioactive wastes.[91] The proposals were supported by several countries who were of the view that 'the existing scientific data did not provide firm

[85] Resolution LC.12(III) (1978).

[86] Ibid, Attachment and Addendum Containing Regulations for the Control of Incineration of Wastes and other Matter at Sea.

[87] The Regulations refer to both atmospheric dispersal characteristics and oceanic dispersal characteristics as being relevant factors to take into account, in order to minimize the impact on the surrounding environment.

[88] Regulations for the Control of Incineration of Wastes and other Matter at Sea, Regulation 2(2).

[89] Resolution LC.50(16) (1992). Under the amendment, a special permit was required for all other types of incineration at sea.

[90] Resolution LC.50(16) (1993).

[91] See Report of the Seventh Consultative Meeting, Document LDC7/12 (1983) para. 7.2. See also B Meinke-Brandmaier, 'Multi-Regime Regulation—How the South Pacific Region Influences Global Marine Environmental Policy Making: A Study of Radioactive Waste Dumping', in A Chircop et al (eds), *Ocean Yearbook 19* (Brill 2005) 162–88.

assurances that radioactive waste dumping at sea would have no adverse effects on human health or the marine environment', and 'as long as this uncertainty existed, radioactive waste dumping at sea would generally create fear in sectors of the population affected by such dumping operations'.[92] The proposal shows an early sign of a precautionary approach being advocated by States, even before the endorsement of the principle by the Consultative Meeting.[93] However, the proposal was opposed by other countries, including the United Kingdom, which suggested that 'the burden of proof rested with the mover of an amendment to an Annex'.[94] According to the United Kingdom, the lack of evidence supporting the proposal was not in accordance with the requirements of the Convention, which demanded that amendments were 'based on scientific and technical considerations'.[95]

As a way forward, it was agreed that the scientific information should be reviewed by an expert group. In the interim, the Contracting Parties adopted a non-binding resolution, calling for the 'suspension of all dumping at sea of radioactive materials',[96] although this recommendation was opposed by a number of key States.[97] The suspension was reconfirmed in stronger language at a later meeting[98] and extended to the disposal of radioactive wastes into sub-seabed repositories accessed from the sea.[99] Although this measure was not binding, it was, nevertheless, observed by most States in practice.[100]

Pressure to phase out the dumping of nuclear waste at sea continued to increase, with the issue being raised in a number of forums, including at the 1992 Rio Conference on Environment and Development, which '[encouraged] the London Dumping Convention to expedite work to complete studies on replacing the current voluntary moratorium on disposal of low-level radioactive wastes at sea by a ban, taking into account the precautionary approach, with a view to taking a well informed and timely decision on the issue'.[101] Finally, in 1993, States were able to agree to an amendment prohibiting the dumping of all 'radioactive wastes or other radioactive matter', with the exception of 'wastes or other materials (e.g. sewage sludge and dredged materials) containing de minimis (exempt) levels of radioactivity'.[102] Guidelines have been adopted on the interpretation of the *de minimis* concept to ensure consistent application of the exception.[103] The amendment was not

---

[92] See Report of the Seventh Consultative Meeting, Document LDC7/12 (1983) para. 7.6 (Philippines).
   [93] See the discussion above at footnote 81.
   [94] See Report of the Seventh Consultative Meeting, Document LDC7/12 (1983) para. 7.5. See also para. 7.22 (Canada).
   [95] LDC, Article 15.   [96] Resolution LDC.14(7) (1983).
   [97] The resolution was adopted by a vote, with six States voting against the resolution; see Document LDC 7/12 (1983) para. 7.34.
   [98] Resolution LDC.21(9) (1985).   [99] Resolution LDC.41(13) (1989).
   [100] See Report of the Twenty-Fourth Consultative Meeting, Document LC 24/17 (2002) paras 11.12–11.14.
   [101] Agenda 21 (1992) para. 22.5(b).   [102] See Resolution LC.51(16) (1992).
   [103] Report of the Twenty-First Consultative Meeting, Document LC21/13 (1999) para. 6.14 and Annex 6; Report of the Twenty-Third Consultative Meeting, Document LC23/16 (2001) para. 7.10; Report of the Thirty-Fifth Consultative Meeting, Document LC 35/15 (2003) para. 9.5.1; Report of the Thirty-Seventh Consultative Meeting, Document LC37/16 (2015) Annex 9.

initially accepted by all States, however. The Russian Federation used its right to object to the radioactive waste amendment based upon its ability to comply. There is no doubt that Russia had a right to do so under the treaty. Nevertheless, the issue was kept under review by the Consultative Meeting, which continued to put pressure on Russia to remove its objection and to accept the amendments.[104] Indeed, significant assistance was granted to Russia to develop adequate land-based processing facilities, which would allow it to comply with the amendment. Having developed the capacity to deal with its radioactive waste on land, the Russian Federation finally withdrew its objection to the radioactive waste amendment in 2005.[105] This demonstrates the proactive nature of the regime and the advantage of a permanent institution that is able to oversee implementation and offer guidance and support to States to bring themselves into compliance. Indeed, it is notable that this was achieved without the formal existence of a compliance mechanism but simply through the regular meetings of the Contracting Parties.

A further amendment adopted in 1993 introduced a phased prohibition on the dumping of industrial waste at sea, subject to some exceptions.[106] In this case, Australia made a partial objection to the amendment, owing to its perceived need to dispose of jarosite waste, which was a by-product from its zinc mining industry.[107] Like the Russian objection to the nuclear amendment, this matter was discussed at regular meetings of the Contracting Parties, and Australia was repeatedly asked to justify its objection. The Australian government finally announced in 1997 that it would accept the industrial waste amendments as a new treatment process has been developed which would allow it to safely dispose of its mining waste on land.[108] In this case, no technical or financial assistance had been offered by the Contracting Parties, but the sustained political pressure ensured that the issue was kept on the agenda until Australia ultimately removed its objection.

The amendment on industrial waste has also raised questions of interpretation that have prompted discussion amongst the Parties.[109] *Industrial waste* is defined by the Convention as 'waste materials generated by manufacturing or processing operations'.[110] However, the Convention goes on to exclude from that definition:

(a) dredged materials;

(b) sewage sludge;

(c) fish waste or organic materials resulting from industrial fish processing operations;

---

[104] See e.g. Report of the Twenty-First Consultative Meeting, Document LC21/13 (1999) paras 6.15–6.22.

[105] Report of the Twenty-Seventh Consultative Meeting, Document LC27/16 (2005) para. 2.2.

[106] Resolution LC.50(16) (1992). The prohibition only applied to the dumping of industrial waste after 1 January 1996.

[107] See Report of the Seventeenth Consultative Meeting, Document LC 17/14 (1993) para. 2.2.1.

[108] Report of the Nineteenth Consultative Meeting, Document LC 19/10 (1995) paras 6.19–6.22.

[109] See PW Birnie, 'Are Twentieth-Century Marine Conservation Conventions Adaptable to Twenty First Century Goals and Principles? Part II' (1997) 12 *IJMCL* 488, 518.

[110] LDC, Annex I, para. 11.

(d) vessels and platforms or other man-made structures at sea, provided that material capable of creating floating debris or otherwise contributing to pollution of the marine environment has been removed to the maximum extent;

(e) uncontaminated inert geological materials the chemical constituents of which are unlikely to be released into the marine environment;

(f) uncontaminated organic materials of natural origin.

In other words, this amendment introduces a broad prohibition on many forms of industrial dumping, with a narrow range of exceptions that are permitted. The interpretation of the exceptions to the prohibition on dumping of industrial waste is thus critical. The Scientific Group has been able to provide some guidance, particularly on the interpretation and application of the provisions on 'uncontaminated inert geological materials'.[111] Some problems have arisen in practice, however, owing to ambiguity in the drafting of the text. One reading of this exception is that the exception applies to all materials that are 'uncontaminated' and 'the chemical constituents of which are unlikely to be released into the marine environment'.[112] This interpretation has a clear grounding in the text of the provision, as well as in the drafting history.[113] However, according to another school of thought, materials which have been processed in a manner which may have significantly altered the physical characteristics of the original raw material should always be categorized as industrial waste, given that 'the impact of the waste on the marine environment could be significantly different from that of the raw material'.[114] The Contracting Parties have been unable to reach consensus on this issue and it continues to be unresolved. In this context, the lack of a dispute settlement procedure under the Convention means that there is no way of authoritatively resolving this dispute over the interpretation of the Convention. This demonstrates one disadvantage of relying exclusively upon political institutions for the development of a treaty regime, as consensus will not always be possible. As a result, the precise scope of the prohibition remains uncertain.

It can be seen from the above examples that the amendment procedures have facilitated the evolution of the dumping regime, by expanding the list of substances that cannot be considered for disposal at sea. At the same time, some changes to the dumping regime have been resisted by certain States, at least in the short-term. The London Convention itself explicitly permits States to withhold their consent, and so these objections can be seen as legitimate from the perspective of that instrument. But could these objections be sustained in light of the rule of reference in Article 210 of UNCLOS?

Some States have taken the view that 'States Parties were not only bound to adopt requirements consistent with the current London Convention 1972 but also with

---

[111] See Eligibility Criteria for Inert, Inorganic Geological Material, approved at the Twentieth-Eighth Meeting of the Consultative Meeting, Document LC28/15 (2006) para. 143 and Annex 8.

[112] Comments by Japan on the interpretation of 'industrial waste', Document LC23/6/1 (2001) para. 2.2.

[113] Ibid, paras 3.3–3.4.

[114] See Interpretation of Industrial Waste: Submitted by the United Kingdom, Document LC22/6 (2000) para. 4.

future amendments adopted thereto.'[115] This conclusion is unproblematic in the case of States that have acquiesced in the changes to the dumping regime, but the argument is more controversial if States have explicitly objected to any changes. Would the rule of reference in Article 210 override such an objection? It is argued that this is not the case, as the objection is authorized by the 1972 Convention itself and, therefore, can be seen as a valid exception to the global rule agreed by all of the other Parties. In other words, any objection made in accordance with the 1972 Convention must itself be seen as part of the global rules. Indeed, in the course of the debates over the objections to the amendments to the London Convention, none of the other Parties argued that the Russian Federation or Australia were legally obliged to comply with the ban on the basis of Article 210 of UNCLOS, suggesting that they considered these objections to be valid. This conclusion clearly limits the potential for the rule of reference in UNCLOS to achieve complete harmonization of dumping rules at the global level, if objections have been made by participants in the relevant treaty regime, but it produces a result that better reflects the realities of international law-making. At the same time, this interpretation provides an incentive to become a Party to the 1972 Convention because only objections that are made within the regime can be considered an integral part of the global rules. States that are not Party to the 1972 Convention would thus be obliged to follow its prescriptions, including any amendments, by virtue of Article 210 of UNCLOS, regardless of whether they agree with them.

5.4.3 1996 London Dumping Protocol

At the same time as they adopted the 1993 amendments to the London Convention, the Contracting Parties also agreed on a comprehensive review of the treaty with a view to ensuring its ongoing contribution to marine environmental protection.[116] The result of this process was the 1996 London Protocol. Although it is an independent instrument[117] and any State can become a Party to the 1996 Protocol whether or not they were previously a Party to the London Convention,[118] there is a close interrelationship between the two instruments. Indeed, in many respects, the Protocol can be considered as functionally equivalent to a Protocol of amendment and it explicitly provides that it 'will supersede the Convention as between Contracting Parties to this Protocol which are also Parties to the Convention'.[119]

Whilst there are similarities between the two instruments, the Protocol substantively differs from its predecessor in a number of ways. Perhaps most prominently, the Protocol explicitly applies a precautionary approach to the regulation of dumping by requiring States to prohibit dumping of any material unless it is expressly authorized by the Protocol. This is a stronger version of the precautionary approach

---

[115] Report of the Seventeenth Consultative Meeting, Document LC 17/14 (1993) para. 2.5.
[116] Resolution LC.48(16) (1992).
[117] Molenaar explains that the choice to adopt an independent protocol was motivated by the desire to include less stringent entry into force requirements; Molenaar (n72) 398.
[118] LDP, Article 24(1).   [119] Ibid, Article 23.

because it bans all activity until it is demonstrated to the collective satisfaction of the Parties that the risks of harm are not too high. Permitted substances are contained in a list in Annex I of the Protocol, which currently includes the following materials: dredged material; sewage sludge; fish waste; vessels and platforms; inert, inorganic geological material; organic material of natural origin; bulky items primarily comprising iron, steel, concrete, or similarly unharmful materials; and carbon dioxide streams from carbon dioxide–capture processes.[120] Substances may be added to the Annexes using a tacit amendment procedure, similar to that found in the 1972 Convention.[121] The Protocol also prohibits all incineration at sea[122] and the export of waste to other countries for the purpose of dumping or incineration at sea.[123] Both of these latter obligations strengthen the regime that applies under the Convention.

Even if a substance can be dumped under the Protocol, it is still necessary for the dumping to be authorized by the relevant Contracting Party, which must carry out an environmental impact assessment, including an assessment of the dumpsite and the potential effects of the materials being dumping on the marine environment.[124] The Protocol specifies that in issuing a permit, 'particular attention shall be paid to opportunities to avoid dumping in favour of environmentally preferable alternatives'.[125] Indeed, the Protocol goes on to require an audit of waste reduction/prevention techniques and 'if the required audit reveals that opportunities exist for waste prevention at source, an applicant is expected to formulate and implement a waste prevention strategy ... which includes specific waste reduction targets and provision for further waste prevention audits to ensure that these targets are being met'.[126] Furthermore, an applicant must show that it has considered all other options prior to dumping.[127] Guidance on assessing proposals for dumping developed under the London Convention also applies to dumping under the Protocol.

If dumping goes ahead, States are required to carry out ongoing monitoring to ensure that the conditions of any permit are met and to ensure that there are no unpredicted impacts on the marine environment.[128] These provisions provide a clear legal basis for requirements that have evolved on the basis of non-binding guidance under the London Convention.

Another innovation in the Protocol is the introduction of a formal compliance procedure. As with the Convention, the Protocol requires information on dumping permits and enforcement action to be reported on a regular basis to the Secretariat.[129] Contracting Parties must also report on the effectiveness of measures taken to implement the Convention and any problems encountered in its application, with a view to identifying proactively any issues that should be addressed by the Contracting Parties. In addition, the Protocol establishes a Compliance Group,

---

120 Ibid, Annex I. For the disposal of carbon dioxide streams, see Chapter 9.
121 LDP, Article 22.   122 Ibid, Article 5.   123 Ibid, Article 6.
124 Ibid, Annex 2, paras 11–15.   125 Ibid, Article 4.1.2.
126 Ibid, Annex 2, para. 3.   127 Ibid, Annex 2, para. 5.
128 Ibid, Annex 2, para. 16.   129 Ibid, Article 9.

which, in conjunction with the Scientific Group, allows more in-depth scrutiny of reports from Contracting Parties.[130] The Compliance Group is able to make recommendations to the Meeting of the Contracting Parties on systematic compliance issues under the Protocol. The Compliance Mechanism also allows individual States to be referred to the Compliance Group when there is a question over their implementation of their obligations. States may refer themselves if they are having difficulty with compliance, and this option may be used by States seeking financial or technical assistance to support their implementation of the treaty. States may also be referred by another Contracting Party that has an interest that is affected by the non-compliance, or by the Meeting of the Contracting Parties on the basis of information provided by other Parties, the Secretariat, or observers. The reference to information provided by observers is significant given the role that has been played by non-state actors in bringing implementation issues to light in the past. However, States resisted giving such actors the ability to independently trigger compliance proceedings, and the ultimate decision of referral rests with the Meeting of the Contracting Parties.[131] The success of this mechanism will, therefore, depend upon the willingness of the Consultative Meeting to use these powers.

The Compliance Mechanism is largely facilitative in nature. Upon consideration of the information available to it and any further information provided by the Contracting Party concerned, the Compliance Group should submit recommendations to the Meeting of the Contracting Parties as to the type of action that should be taken. The Compliance Mechanism foresees four options, namely:[132]

- the provision of advice or recommendations, with a view to assisting the Party concerned to implement the Protocol;
- the facilitation of cooperation and assistance;
- the elaboration, with the cooperation of the Party or Parties concerned, of compliance action plans, including targets and timelines;
- the issuing of a formal statement of concern regarding a Party's compliance situation.

It follows that the Compliance Mechanism does not currently authorize sanctions or coercive measures against a non-complying State, although it leaves open the possibility that 'the Meeting of Contracting Parties may also consider additional measures within its mandate, as appropriate, to facilitate compliance by the Party concerned', without specifying what those measures might be.[133]

Another interesting feature of the Compliance Mechanism is the ability to offer advice to non-parties in order to facilitate its becoming a Party to the Protocol.[134] Under this role, the Compliance Body is able to ensure that States

---

[130] See Report of the Twenty-Ninth Consultative Meeting, Document LC 29/17 (2007) para. 5.24 and Annex 7.
[131] See VanderZwaag and Daniel (n20) 542–3.
[132] Compliance Procedures and Mechanisms Pursuant to Article 11 of the 1996 Protocol to the London Convention 1972 (2007) para. 5.1.
[133] Ibid, para. 5.4.   [134] Ibid, para. 2.2.8.

wishing to become a Party have considered all of the relevant issues in advance in order to ensure that they are actually able to comply when they do become formally bound.

The Protocol also contains a stronger dispute settlement mechanism than the Convention. Under Article 16, Parties that are unable to settle a dispute concerning the interpretation or application of the Protocol within twelve months may submit the dispute to an arbitral tribunal.[135] This mechanism would allow questions of interpretation and application to be settled authoritatively by a third-party mechanism. This procedure would potentially allow disputes over interpretation to be unilaterally submitted to independent adjudication, thus avoiding the deadlock that has occurred under the 1972 Convention.

There is little doubt that the intention behind the negotiation of the Protocol was to replace the Convention as a source of global rules and standards.[136] However, there is some way to go before this objective is achieved. At the time of writing, there are only forty-eight Contracting Parties to the London Protocol, compared with the eighty-seven Contracting Parties to the London Convention.[137] Nevertheless, some commentators have suggested that the Protocol contains 'global rules and standards' that are incorporated by Article 210 of UNCLOS, meaning that all States, regardless of whether they have accepted the Protocol, are obliged to take this stricter approach.[138] Such assertions appear optimistic at the present time, however, given the low participation in the Protocol and the fact that many States have continued to choose to become a Party to the Convention, rather than the Protocol. In practice, the London Convention is still the main source of global rules and standards in relation to dumping. The Protocol still has a long way to go to achieve widespread acceptance,[139] and it is suggested that it should not be considered a global rule for the purposes of Article 210 of UNCLOS until the vast majority of the Parties to the 1972 Convention have themselves accepted the newer instrument.

5.5 Strengthening the Dumping Regime at the Regional Level

The global rules on dumping discussed in previous sections are also complemented by rules adopted at the regional level. A regional approach to dumping is explicitly

---

[135] It also provides the option for States to agree to use the dispute settlement procedures in Part XV of UNCLOS.

[136] The Parties agreed at the twentieth consultative meeting that 'when all Parties to the Convention had become Party to the Protocol, the Convention would become moribund'; Document LC20/14 (1998) para. 5.6.

[137] See IMO website: <http://www.imo.org/About/Conventions/StatusOfConventions/Pages/Default.aspx>.

[138] See De la Fayette (n72) 516: 'when in force, the substantive provisions under the Protocol must be implemented by States' Parties to [UNCLOS], even if they are not a party to the Protocol'. See also D Ong, 'The 1982 UN Convention on the Law of the Sea and Marine Environmental Protection', in M Fitzmaurice et al (eds), *Research Handbook on International Environmental Law* (Edward Elgar 2010) 572.

[139] See the discussion in G Hoon Hong and Y Joo Lee, 'Transitional Measures to Combine Two Global Ocean Dumping Treaties' (2015) 55 *MP* 47–56.

endorsed by both UNCLOS[140] and the London Convention and its Protocol.[141] The advantage of regionalism is that it allows particular groups of States to develop stricter policies on dumping at a quicker pace than may be possible at the global level. This may involve prohibiting a wider range of substances or adopting stricter interpretations of the relevant treaty provisions. In some cases, regional rules have been an interim step before similar reforms were introduced in the global regime.[142]

Most of the regional seas framework treaties[143] contain a provision calling for Parties to regulate pollution of the marine environment through dumping. For example, the Antigua Convention provides that '[t]he Contracting Parties shall take all appropriate measures to prevent, reduce and control pollution of the Convention area caused by dumping of wastes and other matter at sea from ships, aircraft or man-made structures at sea, and to ensure the effective implementation of the applicable international rules and standards'.[144] Such general provisions, however, would appear to impose no requirements that go beyond the basic regime in UNCLOS. The more important regional instruments are those treaties or protocols which contain more detailed rules to be followed within the regional setting. Five regions have adopted specific rules relating to dumping, namely the Mediterranean Sea,[145] the Black Sea,[146] the North-East Atlantic,[147] the Baltic,[148] and the South Pacific.[149]

The development of dumping rules in the Baltic region provides an excellent example of how regional treaties can pursue a more stringent approach to dumping. First, the Helsinki Convention extends the provisions on dumping to the internal waters of the Contracting Parties.[150] Second, the Convention prohibits all dumping in the Baltic Sea area, with the exception of dredged material.[151] Moreover, dumping of dredged material should only take place in the internal waters and territorial sea, and any proposed dumping beyond these maritime zones must be preceded by consultations with the Baltic Marine Environmental Protection Commission. This

---

[140] UNCLOS, Article 210(4).   [141] LDC, Article 8; LDP, Article 12.

[142] Birnie (n109) 515; Stokke (n60) 42.   [143] See Chapter 2.

[144] See 1983 Cartagena Convention for the Protection of the Marine Environment of the Wider Caribbean Region (EIF 11 October 1986), Article 6. See also 2010 Amended Nairobi Convention for the Protection, Management and Development of the Marine and Coastal Environment of the Western Indian Ocean (not yet in force), Article 6; 1981 Abidjan Convention for Cooperation in the Protection, Management and Development of the Marine and Coastal Environment of the Atlantic Coast of the West, Central and Southern Africa Region (EIF 5 August 1984), Article 6.

[145] See 1976 Protocol for the Prevention of Pollution in the Mediterranean Sea by Dumping from Ships and Aircraft (EIF 12 February 1978), amended by 1995 Protocol for the Prevention and Elimination of Pollution in the Mediterranean Sea by Dumping from Ships and Aircraft or Incineration at Sea (not yet in force).

[146] See 1992 Protocol on the Protection of the Marine Environment of the Black Sea by Dumping (EIF 15 January 1994).

[147] See 1992 Convention for the Protection of the Marine Environment of the North-East Atlantic (OSPAR Convention) (EIF 25 March 1998), Article 4 and Annex II.

[148] See 1992 Convention on the Protection of the Marine Environment of the Baltic Sea Area (Helsinki Convention) (EIF 17 January 2000), Article 11.

[149] See 1986 Protocol for the Prevention of Pollution of the South Pacific Region by Dumping (EIF 22 August 1990).

[150] Helsinki Convention, Article 1.

[151] Ibid, Article 11. The Convention also contains the standard exception for dumping in cases of distress.

example demonstrates the power of a regional approach when the States in a particular region can reach agreement on taking a stricter approach to environmental regulation.

Regional treaties can also supplement the global regime by offering another layer of scrutiny for the implementation of dumping commitments. Thus, many of the regional treaties or protocols have their own compliance mechanisms, which can be used as an alternative to or an addition to the procedures available under the London Dumping Convention or its Protocol.[152] Regional treaties can also strengthen other procedural obligations of the Parties. Thus, the treaties applicable to the North-East Atlantic, the Baltic, and the Mediterranean all emphasize the importance of providing information to the public about activities, including dumping, that may affect the marine environment,[153] and the Barcelona Convention goes even further by providing that 'Contracting Parties shall ensure that the opportunity is given to the public to participate in decision-making processes relevant to the field of application of the Convention and its Protocols, as appropriate', a provision that clearly applies to dumping.[154] In this manner, the regional treaties go beyond the non-binding recommendations for public participation and transparency under the global regime.

5.6 Conclusion

This chapter has reviewed the evolution of the international regime relating to dumping at sea. The London Convention is the main global instrument that addresses this topic. Despite being one of the first multilateral treaties on marine environmental pollution to be negotiated, the London Convention has been significantly strengthened over the years, in response to changing attitudes to marine environmental protection and the appropriateness of disposing of waste at sea. Through the adoption of decisions and guidance on the implementation of the Convention, the Parties have endorsed an ecosystem and precautionary approach to carrying out dumping, and the Convention has arguably evolved from a regime that sought the regulation of dumping to one that prohibits most types of dumping. This change of ethos has been reflected, in part, by the revision to the unofficial designation of the treaty regime from the London Dumping Convention to simply the London Convention.[155]

Another major development in the global regime for dumping was the conclusion of the London Protocol. By reversing the burden of proof for dumping, this instrument is even more precautionary than the London Convention. It also introduces

---

[152] For example, OSPAR Convention, Article 23; 1995 Barcelona Convention for the Protection of the Marine Environment and the Coastal Region of the Mediterranean (Barcelona Convention) (EIF 9 July 2004), Article 27.
[153] OSPAR Convention, Article 9; Helsinki Convention, Article 17; Barcelona Convention, Article 15(1).
[154] Barcelona Convention, Article 15(2).   [155] de la Fayette (n72) 534.

important innovations in the institutional framework that underpins the development of the regime, notably a formal compliance procedure.

The global dumping treaties are also significant because of their connection with UNCLOS. As a result of the rule of reference in Article 210 of UNCLOS, the main prescriptions of the London Convention are incorporated into the general framework for the law of the sea and it can, therefore, be considered an international minimum standard that is applicable to all States, whether or not they are a Party. However, the precise operation of the rule of reference in Article 210 remains contested, particularly when it comes to the London Protocol. It has been suggested that arguments that the Protocol has become a global treaty for the purposes of Article 210 must be treated with caution, until it can be shown that the Protocol has become the predominant instrument for regulating dumping at the global level. Yet, as more Parties accept the Protocol, the argument that it has become an international minimum standard will gradually strengthen. Efforts should, therefore, continue to encourage States to ratify the Protocol, not only through the institutions established under the dumping treaties but also through other international institutions working on marine environmental issues, such as the UN General Assembly[156] or the UN Environment Assembly.

For both of the dumping treaties, compliance remains a crucial issue. Reporting at the global level is poor, and initiatives to assist States in this regard do not seem to have worked to date. Addressing this problem will be the litmus test for credibility of the dumping treaties as an effective global regime. The scale of the problem is concerning, but it is ultimately a question of technical and financial capacity, and the international community will need to commit the necessary resources to ensure that all States have the means to comply with their responsibilities.[157] One way of focusing resources is to develop capacity at the regional level through the negotiation of more regional dumping treaties. The global treaties themselves foresee a role for regional institutions in reporting,[158] and common interests within a region may provide an incentive for States to cooperate in the implementation of dumping regulations in a cost-effective manner.

At the end of the day, the reduction of dumping also requires alternative methods of waste disposal to be developed. Moreover, it must also be ensured that these alternatives do not themselves have negative impacts on the environment. Thus, the dumping regime cannot be developed in isolation, and the international community must adopt a broader strategy to improve the treatment of hazardous waste.[159] Indeed, there may be circumstances in which dumping at sea may be the best possible solution, and it is the rules and procedures under the Convention and Protocol that will ensure that such decisions are made taking into account all relevant considerations.

---

[156] See e.g. UNGA Resolution 71/257 (2016) para. 213.   [157] Stokke (n60) 39.
[158] LDC, Article 6(4); LDP, Article 9(4).
[159] There are some treaties relating to waste management, e.g. 1989 Convention on the Control of Transboundary Movements of Hazardous Wastes (Basel Convention) (EIF 5 May 1992); 2009 International Convention for the Safe and Environmentally Sound Recycling of Ships (Hong Kong Convention) (not yet in force).

6

Marine Environmental Threats from Shipping

6.1 Introduction

The importance of shipping to the global economy cannot be underemphasized, with ships carrying more than 90 per cent of world trade in goods.[1] Transport at sea is not benign, however, and shipping operations have been proven over the years to be capable of causing serious harm to the marine environment.

Oil pollution from ships was one of the first types of vessel-source pollution to be addressed by the international community. As more oil began to be carried by sea, such pollution attracted increasing attention from affected States. It was not only the risk of oil slicks caused by the sinking or stranding of a passing tanker that worried coastal States, but the pollution arising from the regular operation of these vessels, such as the washing of cargo tanks at sea.[2] A similar problem occurred when other ships used empty fuel tanks as ballast, later discharging the contaminated water back into the ocean. The Group of Experts on the Scientific Aspects of Marine Environmental Protection (GESAMP) estimate that over 200,000 tonnes of oil are released into the oceans from shipping operations per year.[3] Nor is it only incidents involving releases of oil or other toxic substances that can have consequences for the marine environment. It is now recognized that ships can have a broader impact on marine life, including through noise pollution, the introduction of alien invasive species, or physical damage of fragile marine ecosystems.

The global nature of the shipping industry means that the problem of vessel-source pollution can only be dealt with effectively at the international level. Indeed, it was recognized at an early stage that 'only an international solution of the problem can be effective' because '[p]etroleum products discharged on the high seas may be washed towards the coasts by currents and wind'.[4] States, therefore, turned to

---

[1] IMO, *International Shipping Facts and Figures* (2012) 7: <http://www.imo.org/KnowledgeCentre/ShipsAndShippingFactsAndFigures/TheRoleandImportanceofInternationalShipping/Documents/International%20Shipping%20-%20Facts%20and%20Figures.pdf>.

[2] For a simple yet effective explanation of the problems, see CL Boyle, 'Sea Pollution' (1954) 2 *Oryx* 212.

[3] GESAMP, *Estimates of Oil Entering the Marine Environment from Sea-Based Activities*, GESAMP Reports and Studies No. 75 (2007) vi.

[4] Report of the International Law Commission (1956 – II) *Yearbook of the International Law Commission* 286.

international law to agree upon appropriate responses to the issue.[5] Since the sinking of the Torrey Canyon in 1967, highlighting the potential for a single vessel to cause widespread serious harm, the international community has progressively increased international rules and standards to prevent, reduce, and control pollution from ships. The International Maritime Organization (IMO)[6] has taken the lead in addressing this problem and it has adopted a number of international treaties for the prevention and control of vessel-source pollution, as well as the wider impacts of shipping on the marine environment. This chapter analyses the nature and contents of these instruments, as well as how they can be enforced in different maritime zones.

6.2 The International Institutional Framework for the Regulation of Marine Environmental Threats from Ships

Pollution from ships is one of the major sources of pollution of the marine environment identified in the United Nations Convention on the Law of the Sea (UNCLOS). Article 194(b) demands the adoption of measures 'designed to minimize to the fullest possible extent pollution from vessels', and Article 211(1) further calls upon States, 'acting through the competent international organization or general diplomatic conference ... to establish international rules and standards to prevent, reduce and control pollution of the marine environment from vessels'. The regime for jurisdiction over pollution from ships can only be understood in relation to the institutional framework that has been adopted to implement this duty of cooperation.

Unlike many of the other mandates for the development of international standards in the UNCLOS, Article 211(1) refers to a single international organization, and it is the IMO that claims the right to fulfil this role.[7] It is the work of this body that will be the main focus of this chapter. At the same time, regional seas bodies also have a role to play in the prevention of pollution from ships.[8] Almost all regional seas treaties include some mention of pollution from ships as a topic failing within their scope. Yet, their constituent instruments tend to recognize the IMO as the international institution responsible for developing shipping standards, stressing that their role is limited to cooperating in the implementation of such standards.

---

[5] The first treaty on the subject was the 1954 International Convention on Pollution of Sea by Oil (OILPOL Convention) (EIF 26 July 1958)

[6] The body was known as the Intergovernmental Maritime Consultative Organization until its name was changed by amendments adopted in 1975.

[7] IMO Secretariat, *Implications of the United Nations Convention on the Law of the Sea for the International Maritime Organization*, Document LEG/Misc.8 (2014) 7; see also WH Lampe, 'The "New International Maritime Organization and its Place in the Development of International Maritime Law" (1983) 14 *JMLC* 305, 329.

[8] See generally EJ Molenaar, 'Options for Regional Regulation of Merchant Shipping Outside the IMO, with Particular Reference to the Arctic Region' (2014) 45 *ODIL* 272–98; H Ringbom, 'Vessel-Source Pollution', in R Rayfuse (ed.), *Research Handbook on International Marine Environmental Law* (Edward Elgar 2016) 124–5.

For example, the Helsinki Convention provides that '[t]he Contracting Parties shall, in matters concerning the protection of the Baltic Sea Area from pollution by ships, cooperate within the [IMO], in particular in promoting the development of international rules …'. In this context, the role of the Baltic Commission is limited to 'the effective and harmonized implementation of rules adopted by the [IMO]'.[9] In a similar vein, the Barcelona Convention provides that:

The Contracting Parties shall take all measures in conformity with international law to prevent, abate, combat and to the fullest possible extent eliminate pollution of the Mediterranean Sea Area caused by discharges from ships and to ensure the effective implementation in that Area of the rules which are generally recognized at the international level relating to the control of this type of pollution.[10]

Thus, in this area of regulation, regional seas bodies largely play a role in supporting the implementation of IMO standards.[11] Biodiversity treaties may also play a role in supporting the IMO by providing information on the extent of environmental threats and prompting action by the international community. Examples of such interaction will be provided throughout the chapter.

6.3 The Adoption of International Shipping Standards to Protect the Marine Environment

6.3.1 The IMO and the protection of the marine environment

The IMO was established in 1958 in order to provide a forum for cooperation on shipping regulation. The original constitution of the IMO made no mention of the environmental effects of shipping, but as the UN specialized agency responsible for 'technical matters of all kinds affecting shipping',[12] it was to this organization that States turned in order to address the problem of pollution from ships. An amendment was made to the IMO's constituent instrument in 1975 to formally include the prevention of pollution from ships within the aims of the organization.[13] At the same time, the IMO established a permanent Marine Environment Protection Committee (MEPC) in order to provide a dedicated forum to consider the development of the legal regime for pollution from ships.[14] Indeed, the role of the IMO

---

[9] See 1992 Helsinki Convention on the Protection of the Marine Environment of the Baltic Sea Area (1992 Helsinki Convention) (EIF 17 January 2000), Annex IV, Regulation I.

[10] See 1995 Barcelona Convention for the Protection of the Marine Environment and the Coastal Region of the Mediterranean (Barcelona Convention) (EIF 9 July 2004), Article 6.

[11] Annex IV of the 1991 Environmental Protocol to the Antarctic Treaty (EIF 14 January 1998) may appear to be unusual in that it explicitly sets out standards that must be met by ships flying the flags of Parties to the Protocol. In practice, however, these standards largely overlap with similar standards applied to the Antarctic region under relevant IMO instruments.

[12] See 1948 Convention on the International Maritime Organization (IMO Convention) (EIF 17 March 1958) Article 1(a) (as amended).

[13] These amendments were introduced by IMO Assembly Resolution A.358(IX) (1975).

[14] The MEPC replaced the Subcommittee on Oil Pollution, which had been established in 1954 as a subcommittee of the Maritime Safety Committee (MSC). The MEPC was created informally as a permanent subsidiary body of the Assembly in 1975, but it was not until the entry into force of the

goes beyond the prevention, reduction, and control of pollution. The IMO Strategic Plan for 2012–17 sets an overall goal of achieving 'environmentally sound' shipping,[15] suggesting that the organization has embraced, at least as a principle, an ecosystems approach to the regulation of ships.

The main work of the IMO is concerned with standard-setting. The IMO is mandated to develop 'the highest practicable standards in matters concerning the maritime safety, efficiency and navigation and prevention and control of marine pollution from ships'.[16] These three aims are closely inter-related, as the achievement of safer ships will also lead to fewer casualties and the prevention of pollution of the marine environment. The standards produced by the IMO are often technical in nature and they are aimed directly at ships, even though they must be implemented through the legislation of Members States. This leads to a high degree of harmonization at the international level.

The standards can be included in different types of instruments. The IMO may either 'make recommendations'[17] or 'provide for the drafting of conventions, agreements or other suitable instruments'.[18] In practice, it has used both approaches in developing a response to environmental threats from shipping. Major IMO regulatory treaties that are relevant in the present context include the 1972 International Convention on International Regulations for Preventing Collisions at Sea:[19] the 1973 International Convention on the Prevention of Pollution from Ships (MARPOL Convention);[20] the 1974 International Convention on Safety of Life at Sea (SOLAS Convention);[21] the 1978 International Convention on Standards of Training, Certification, and Watchkeeping for Seafarers;[22] the 2001 International Convention on the Control of Harmful Anti-Fouling Systems on Ships (AFS Convention);[23] the 2004 International Convention for the Control and Management of Ships' Ballast Water and Sediments (BWM Convention);[24] and the 2009 International Convention on the Recycling of Ships.[25] The IMO has also adopted a number of non-binding instruments related to the prevention, reduction, and control of pollution from ships. Resolutions may be related to an existing treaty,

---

1975 Amendments that the MEPC achieved formal institutional equality with the MSC. See IMO Convention, Article 38(c).

[15] *Strategic Plan for the Organization for the Six-Year Period 2012-2017*, IMO Assembly Resolution A.1037(27) adopted 22 November 2011.

[16] IMO Convention, Article 1(a). [17] IMO Convention, Article 2(a).

[18] IMO Convention, Article 2(b).

[19] See 1972 International Convention on International Regulations for Preventing Collisions at Sea (COLREGS Convention) (EIF 15 July 1977).

[20] See 1973 International Convention on the Prevention of Pollution from Ships (as amended by a Protocol adopted in 1978) (MARPOL Convention) (EIF 2 October 1983).

[21] See 1974 International Convention on Safety of Life at Sea (as amended by Protocols adopted in 1978 and 1988) (SOLAS Convention) (EIF 25 May 1980).

[22] See 1978 International Convention on Standards of Training, Certification, and Watchkeeping for Seafarers (as amended by Protocols adopted in 1995) (STCW Convention) (EIF 28 April 1984).

[23] See 2001 International Convention on the Control of Harmful Anti-Fouling Systems on Ships (AFS Convention) (EIF 17 September 2008).

[24] See 2004 International Convention for the Control and Management of Ships' Ballast Water and Sediments (BWM Convention) (EIF 8 September 2017).

[25] See 2009 International Convention on the Recycling of Ships (Ship Recycling Convention) (not yet in force).

offering guidance on the interpretation or implementation of the applicable stand-ards. Alternatively, non-binding instruments can be used as a prelude to the nego-tiation of a treaty or they can be used when there is not sufficient political support for a legally binding instrument.[26] In this latter situation, non-binding instruments may nevertheless provide a basis for the harmonization of State practice with posi-tive effects for the marine environment.

The negotiation of binding and non-binding instruments tends to take place through the relevant specialized committees, principally the Maritime Safety Committee (MSC) and the MEPC, as well as their various subcommittees.[27] The committees are composed of all Members of the organization[28] and they largely oper-ate by consensus in order to ensure the maximum possible support for regulatory instruments.[29] States are the main decision-makers within the organs of the IMO. However, the organization also permits the participation of a wide range of non-governmental organizations (NGOs) as observers.[30] There are currently seventy-seven NGOs with consultative status at the IMO, representing a range of interests from the shipping and insurance industries to environmental groups.[31] Although NGOs have no vote on the adoption of instruments, they can contribute to the debate and discussion and they can thereby influence the outcome of negotiations.[32] Whilst they cannot formally introduce new items onto the agenda, observers are able to submit information to be considered by IMO Member States and they are thus able to influence discussions.[33] This is one way in which the IMO has facilitated a par-ticipatory approach to environmental decision-making, and environmental NGOs have played an important role in ensuring that environmental issues are brought to the attention of the organization. It must also be recognized that the shipping indus-try is also generally in favour of harmonization at the international level, in order to promote a level playing field for all operators. However, the shipping industry has also expressed concerns about the economic impacts of excessive regulations and it has proposed that new regulations should be subject to full and proper regulatory impact assessments.[34] This tension must ultimately be resolved by the IMO Members.

[26] See further J Harrison, *Making the Law of the Sea* (CUP 2011) 164–5.

[27] The following committees are of particular relevance to environmental protection: Sub-Committee on the Human Element, Training and Watch-Keeping; Sub-Committee on Navigation, Communications and Search and Rescue; Sub-Committee on Pollution Prevention and Response; Sub-Committee on Ship Design and Construction; Sub-Committee on Ship Systems and Equipment; and Sub-Committee on Carriage of Cargoes and Containers.

[28] IMO Convention, Articles 27 and 37.   [29] See IMO (n7) 7.

[30] IMO Convention, Article 62; See *Rules and Guidelines for Consultative Status of Non-Governmental International Organizations with the International Maritime Organization.* <http://www.imo.org/About/Membership/Documents/RULES%20AND%20GUIDELINES%20FOR%20CONSULTATIVE%20STATUS.pdf>.

[31] See <http://www.imo.org/About/Membership/Pages/NGOsInConsultativeStatus.aspx>.

[32] See generally JE Vorbach, 'The Vital Role of Non-Flag State Actors in the Pursuit of Safer Shipping' (2001) 32 *ODIL* 27; G Peet, 'The Role of (Environmental Non-Governmental Organizations at the Marine Environment Protection Committee (MEPC) of the International Maritime Organization, and at the London Dumping Convention (LDC)' (1994) 22 *O&CM* 3–18.

[33] See e.g. *Addressing Marine Pollution from Oil-based Lubricants during Normal Operations—Submitted by WWF and FOEI,* Document MEPC 60/21/2 (2010).

[34] International Chamber of Shipping, *2015 Annual Review* (2015) 24–5.

The standard-setting role of the IMO is guided by the principle of non-discrimination. The nature of the international shipping industry means that it is not feasible to differentiate between ships on the basis of nationality—if lower standards were imposed on shipping registered in developing countries, all ships could simply transfer to such registers, thereby circumventing any higher standards imposed on developed countries.[35] Nevertheless, the principle of common but differentiated responsibilities can still be applied through means of technical and financial assistance to developing countries. Such forms of assistance are emphasized both in the IMO Convention[36] and in the relevant regulatory treaties.[37] To further this aim, the IMO has developed an Integrated Technical Cooperation Programme designed to 'assist Governments which lack the technical knowledge and resources that are needed to operate a shipping industry safely and efficiently'.[38] This programme is particularly relevant when introducing measures for the protection of the marine environment through its provision of training for State officials, help with legislative drafting, and financial assistance for developing countries.

The standing-setting process at the IMO includes the ongoing evaluation of the effectiveness of the rules and standards to prevent, reduce, and control pollution of the marine environment from vessels. This process of oversight is important as it allows amendments to be made to the treaties in order to address new or emerging threats from shipping.

The MARPOL Convention provides an example of the manner in which amendments to the IMO regulatory treaties are adopted. The MARPOL Convention has been kept up-to-date over time through the use of the tacit amendment procedure contained in Article 16 of the Convention.[39] This procedure mirrors the amendment process in the London Dumping Convention[40] and it allows changes to be made to the regulations contained in the Annexes in a swift and responsive manner. Amendments must be adopted by a two-thirds majority of the Parties to the Convention, present and voting,[41] although, the IMO attempts to work by consensus where possible.[42] Following adoption, amendments are communicated to the Parties for acceptance.[43] Unlike traditional amendment procedures, which require positive acceptance by all States before they can become binding, the tacit amendment procedure means that amendments are 'deemed to have been accepted' unless, within a specified period, 'an objection is communicated to the Organization by not less than one third of the Parties or by the Parties the combined merchant fleet

---

[35] See MS Karim, 'Implementation of the MARPOL Convention in Developing Countries' (2010) 79 *NJIL* 303, 332.
[36] IMO Convention, Articles 42–6.   [37] See e.g. MARPOL Convention, Article 17.
[38] See IMO, 'Technical Cooperation'. <http://www.imo.org/OurWork/TechnicalCooperation/Pages/Default.aspx>.
[39] For a list of all amendments, see IMO, Status of Multilateral Conventions and Instruments in Respect of which the International Maritime Organization or its Secretary-General Performs Depositary or Other Functions. <http://www.imo.org/en/About/Conventions/StatusOfConventions/Pages/Default.aspx>.
[40] See Chapter 5.   [41] MARPOL Convention, Article 16(2)(d) or (3)(b).
[42] IMO (n7) 8.   [43] MARPOL Convention, Article 16(2)(e) or (3)(b).

of which constitute not less than 50% of the gross tonnage of the world's merchant fleet'.[44] In other words, Parties must object to amendments, otherwise they will be bound. If amendments are accepted in this way, they enter into force six months after the date of its acceptance.[45] Within this period, Parties have another opportunity to object to amendments and to prevent the application of such amendments to their vessels. In practice, however, very few objections are made to amendments, meaning they apply equally to all Parties.[46]

A limit on the use of the tacit amendment procedure is that it only applies to amendments to the existing Annexes. Major amendments to the main text of the treaty[47] or the addition of new Annexes to the Convention[48] require adoption by a two-thirds majority of the Contracting Parties, followed by the positive acceptance of States prior to their entry into force.[49] This makes the adoption of new Annexes difficult and it explains, in part, why States have preferred in practice to negotiate separate treaty instruments dealing with new pollution sources, such as the AFS Convention and the BWM Convention.[50]

6.3.2 The MARPOL Convention

The MARPOL Convention is today the main treaty to regulate pollution from ships, although it was not the first instrument in this field. Oil pollution was already controlled by the 1954 OILPOL Convention, which sought to regulate the problem by, inter alia, prohibiting oil and oily water discharges by tankers and other vessels within fifty nautical miles from land.[51] Yet, this treaty was considered deficient in a number of ways. First, the amendment procedures were cumbersome, making it difficult to keep the instrument up-to-date. Furthermore, the treaty did not address threats to the marine environment posed by the carriage of other hazardous substances at sea, such as chemicals. The 1973 International Conference on Marine Pollution was convened to rectify these shortcomings. The conference adopted the International Convention on the Prevention of Pollution of Ships, commonly known as the MARPOL Convention, which today provides the central platform for the international regulations of pollution from ships.[52] At the time of writing,

---

[44] Ibid, Article 16(2)(f)(iii).   [45] Ibid, Article 16(2)(g)(ii)

[46] See the discussion in Harrison (n26) 161–3.

[47] MARPOL Convention, Article 16(2)(f)(i).   [48] Ibid, Article 16(5).

[49] Ibid, Article 16(g)(i).

[50] For a discussion, see JJ Angelo, 'The International Maritime Organization and Protection of the Marine Environment', in MH Nordquist and JN Moore, *Current Maritime Issues and the International Maritime Organization* (Martinus Nijhoff 1999) 105–11.

[51] See 1954 International Convention for the Prevention of Pollution of the Sea by Oil (OILPOL Convention) (EIF 26 July 1958).

[52] MARPOL Convention. The original text of the MARPOL Convention failed to attract sufficient support, and a further conference was convened in 1978, in order to consider the obstacles to its entry into force. The 1978 Conference adopted the Protocol which facilitated the entry into force of the Convention on 2 October 1983.

there were 155 Parties to the MARPOL Convention, constituting 99.14 per cent of world tonnage.[53]

The MARPOL Convention addresses the prevention of 'pollution of the marine environment by the discharge of harmful substances or effluents containing such substances'.[54] Harmful substances are defined in the Convention as 'any substance, which, if introduced into the sea, is liable to create hazards to humans, to harm living resources and marine life, to damage amenities or to interfere with other legitimate uses of the sea'.[55] This phrase has been interpreted broadly[56] to include not only the direct introduction of substances into the sea but also pollution from ships from or through the atmosphere.[57]

The Annexes of the MARPOL Convention contain the detailed technical standards relating to the design, construction, equipment, and operation of ships. Each Annex covers a particular category of pollution.

Annex I of the MARPOL Convention deals with oil pollution from vessels and it replaces the regulations in the 1954 OILPOL Convention.[58] This Annex is principally aimed at tankers carrying oil as cargo, although it also covers the threat of pollution from bunker (fuel) oil. Annex I is compulsory for all Contracting Parties. Regulations deal with discharge, construction, equipment, and operational requirements. The Annex increases the standards that had been previously applied under the 1954 Convention, recognizing that technological developments allowed tankers to operate in a cleaner manner.[59] All oily discharges from ships are regulated,[60] and vessels must carry certain equipment to ensure that discharges are kept to a minimum.[61] Any discharge of oil mixtures must be recorded in the Oil Record Book, which facilitates enforcement when vessels call at port.[62] In the case of oil tankers, vessels must carry on-board systems which ensure that any discharge is automatically stopped when the instantaneous rate of discharge of oil exceeds the permitted amount.[63] In addition, construction and operational requirements are designed to reduce the risk of an accident involving oil tankers or to minimize the likelihood of serious pollution if an accident does occur. One of the most important developments in this regard has been the prohibition of single-hull oil tankers. Originally, tankers built on or after 6 July 1996 were required to be fitted with a double hull and double bottom to make them more secure against rupture if a collision or other incident occurs.[64]

---

[53] See the IMO website: <http://www.imo.org/About/Conventions/StatusOfConventions/Pages/Default.aspx>.

[54] MARPOL Convention, Article 1(1).   [55] Ibid, Article 2(2).

[56] See e.g. the discussion of pollution in Report of the Sixtieth Session of the Marine Environment Protection Committee, Document MEPC 60/22 (2010) para. 4.33.

[57] See the discussion of Annex VI below.

[58] MARPOL Convention, Article 9(1). A revised Annex I was adopted by the MEPC in October 2004 and it entered into force on 1 January 2007; MEPC Resolution MEPC.117(52) (2004).

[59] MARPOL Annex I, Regulation 34.1.5.

[60] MARPOL Annex I, Regulation 15.2. These rules apply to ships over 400 GT. Similar rules apply to ships under 400 GT; see Annex I, Regulation 15.6.

[61] See MARPOL Annex I, Regulation 14.

[62] MARPOL Annex I, Regulation 17. See also Regulation 36. For port State jurisdiction, see below.

[63] MARPOL Annex I, Regulation 31.2.   [64] MARPOL Annex I, Regulation 19.

Following the devastating *Erika* incident in 1999, in which thousands of tonnes of oil were spilled close to the French coast, the timetable for implementing this provision was accelerated.[65] Another response to the *Erika* incident was the approval of the so-called Condition Assessment Scheme, which was intended to verify the structural condition of single-hull oil tankers pending their conversion.[66] In 2009, regulations were added to Annex I to address the risks of pollution from ship-to-ship (STS) oil transfer operations. This addition requires any oil tanker involved in STS operations to carry on board a plan and to notify the relevant coastal State authorities forty-eight hours in advance of carrying out the operation.[67]

Annex II of the MARPOL Convention addresses pollution by noxious liquids.[68] It applies to all vessels which are used to carry chemicals and other noxious liquid substances in bulk.[69] Annex II regulates the operations of carriers of noxious liquid substances according to the hazards posed by the cargo. The core of the regulations concern the control of discharges of residues or ballast from tanks that have contained chemical and other noxious liquid substances. The most hazardous substances (Category-X substances) are subject to a prohibition on discharges into the marine environment.[70] Less hazardous substances (Category-Y and -Z substances) are subject to limitations on the quality and quantity of discharges into the marine environment.[71] Ships which are subject to Annex II of the MARPOL Convention must also comply with a complex set of requirements, relating to their design, construction, and equipment, which are set out in the International Bulk Chemical Code[72] or the Bulk Chemical Code,[73] depending on when they were constructed.[74] Annex II is also compulsory and binding on all Contracting Parties to the MARPOL Convention. These standards are also supplemented by regulations found in the SOLAS Convention.[75]

Annex III of the MARPOL Convention contains Regulations on the Prevention of Pollution from Harmful Substances in Packaged Form.[76] It is an optional Annex, and, at the time of writing, there were 147 States that have accepted Annex III, representing 98.54 per cent of world tonnage.[77] The Annex applies to all ships carrying

---

[65] Resolution MEPC.95(46) (2001).   [66] Resolution MEPC.94(46) (2001).

[67] MARPOL Convention, Regulations 40–1. The Regulation applies to operations in the territorial sea and in the exclusive economic zone (EEZ). The extension of the Regulation to the EEZ was controversial because it was considered by some States to interfere with the freedom of navigation, but the legal opinion offered by the IMO Secretariat suggested that Article 211(1) of UNCLOS provides a legal basis for the adoption of the Regulation; see *Legal Opinion on Certain Issues Concerning Draft Amendments to MARPOL Annex I, Note by the Secretariat*, Document BLG 12/Wp.4 (2008).

[68] A revised Annex II was adopted by the Marine Environmental Committee (MEPC) of the IMO in October 2004 and it entered into force on 1 January 2007; Resolution MEPC.118(52) (2004).

[69] MARPOL Annex II, Regulation 2.1.   [70] MARPOL Annex II, Regulation 6.1.1.

[71] MARPOL Annex II, Regulation 6.1.2 and 6.1.3.

[72] The International Bulk Chemical Code is contained in Resolution MEPC.19(22) (1985) and it applies to chemical tankers constructed on or after 1 July 1986.

[73] The Bulk Chemical Code is contained in Resolution MEPC.20(22) (1985).

[74] MARPOL Annex II, Regulation 11.

[75] See SOLAS Convention, Annex, Chapter VII: Carriage of Dangerous Goods.

[76] A new version of the Annex was adopted in Resolution MEPC.193(61) (2010) and it entered into force, for those States that have accepted it, on 1 January 2014.

[77] See the IMO website: <http://www.imo.org/About/Conventions/StatusOfConventions/Pages/Default.aspx>.

'harmful substances', as defined in the International Maritime Dangerous Goods Code, or which contain specified quantities of the chemical properties listed in the Appendix to the Annex.[78] It prescribes requirements relating to the marking, labelling, loading, and handling of harmful substances in packaged form.[79] More detailed requirements are found in the International Maritime Dangerous Goods Code, which classifies hazardous substances into nine categories: explosives, gases, flammable liquids, flammable solids, oxidizing substances and organic peroxides, toxic and infectious substances, radioactive material, corrosive substances, and miscellaneous dangerous substances and articles.[80] The carriage of dangerous goods is also regulated by Chapter VII of the SOLAS Convention.

Annex IV of the MARPOL Convention regulates pollution from sewage discharged from ships. The Annex largely deals with equipment[81] and discharge[82] standards in order to minimize pollution of the marine environment from sewage. The original version of the Annex was opposed by many States, largely because of the difficulties they associated with providing reception facilities for sewage from ships.[83] As a result, it was agreed to adopt amendments to the Annex in order to facilitate its wider application. A new version of the Annex was adopted by the MEPC in April 2004 and it entered into force for the Parties that had accepted it on 1 August 2005.[84] This example aptly demonstrates the way in which the tacit amendment procedures can facilitate the rapid entry into force of new regulations. At the time of writing, 140 Parties to the MARPOL Convention have accepted Annex IV, representing 91.54 per cent of world tonnage.[85]

Optional Annex V of the MARPOL Convention regulates pollution caused by garbage discharged from vessels.[86] Annex V can be considered to take a precautionary approach by prohibiting the discharges of all garbage apart from items falling within a specific exception in the regulations. Discharges of food waste, cargo residues, and wastewater are permitted, subject to some specific conditions, depending on the type of waste concerned.[87] When garbage is mixed with or contaminated by other substances prohibited from discharge or having different discharge requirements, the more stringent requirements apply, again indicating a precautionary approach. In order to comply, ships may have to install various pieces of equipment, such as compactors or incinerators. Ships over 100 gross tonnes must have a garbage management plan on board, and ships over 400 gross tonnes must have a

---

[78] MARPOL Annex III, Regulation 1.1.1.   [79] MARPOL Annex III, Regulation 3.

[80] For a basic description of the IMDG, see the IMO website. <http://www.imo.org/blast/mainframe.asp?topic_id=158>.

[81] MARPOL Annex IV, Regulation 9.   [82] Ibid, Regulation 11.

[83] JV Crayford, 'Forthcoming Changes to the International Convention for the Prevention of Pollution from Ships (MARPOL 73/78)', in MH Nordquist and JN Moore (eds), *Current Maritime Issues and the International Maritime Organization* (Martinus Nijhoff 1999) 147.

[84] MEPC Resolution MEPC.115(51) (2004).

[85] See IMO website: <http://www.imo.org/About/Conventions/StatusOfConventions/Pages/Default.aspx>.

[86] A new version of the Annex was adopted by the MEPC in July 2011 and it entered into force for the Parties that had accepted it on 1 January 2013; MEPC Resolution MEPC.201(62) (2011).

[87] MARPOL Annex V, Regulations 3–4.

garbage record book to record any discharges that have taken place. One hundred and fifty-two Parties to the MARPOL Convention have accepted Annex V, representing 98.72 per cent of world tonnage.[88]

Annex VI on air pollution from ships was added to the Convention at the 1997 Air Pollution Conference.[89] In its original form, this Annex addressed certain sorts of emissions, notably certain ozone-depleting substances, nitrogen oxides, sulphur oxides, and particulate matter. Inter alia, the Annex introduced standards for the sulphur content of fuel oils used on board ships. The original text of Annex VI entered into force on 19 May 2005. At first, it was not widely accepted by States. In order to increase participation, a revised version of Annex VI was adopted on 10 October 2008, and it entered into force on 1 July 2010. The amendments introduced, inter alia, incremental standards for the sulphur content of fuel, meaning that the environmental performance of ships would have to increase over time.[90] To date, there are eighty-eight Parties to Annex VI, covering 96.16 per cent of world shipping by gross tonnage.[91] Annex VI has since been further amended to include regulations on energy efficiency, which will be discussed in Chapter 9, in the context of climate change mitigation.

Despite the fact that they are regularly updated, many of the regulations contained in the MARPOL Annexes are prospective in nature, meaning they do not apply to existing vessels. This is particularly the case when it comes to regulations that relate to the design and construction of ships. Indeed, the MARPOL Convention contains a presumption that 'any amendment to the present Convention made under this Article, which relates to the structure of a ship, shall only apply to ships for which the building contract is placed, or in the absence of a building contract, the keel of which is laid, on or after the date on which the amendment comes into force'.[92] The reason for this presumption is that it is often excessively expensive to retrofit vessels to comply with new regulatory requirements. This limits the effectiveness of international regulations. At the same time, this presumption can be overturned, and there are cases where an issue is deemed so important for the protection of the marine environment that regulations have been applied retrospectively, regardless of the costs for the maritime industry. The most significant example is the phasing in of a prohibition on single-hulled oil tankers following the *Erika* disaster, discussed above.

Although the regulations contained in the MARPOL Annexes are aimed at imposing uniform standards for all ships, there is often some flexibility allowed in their application. For example, some of the regulations are couched in terms that vessels 'shall comply with the provisions of those provisions as far as is reasonable and

---

[88] See the IMO website: <http://www.imo.org/About/Conventions/StatusOfConventions/Pages/Default.aspx>.

[89] See 1997 Protocol to Amend the International Convention for the Prevention of Pollution from Ships (MARPOL Annex VI) (EIF 19 May 2005).

[90] MARPOL Annex VI, Regulation 14(1).

[91] See the IMO website: <http://www.imo.org/About/Conventions/StatusOfConventions/Pages/Default.aspx>.

[92] Ibid, Article 16(6).

practicable'.[93] Other regulations allow maritime administrations to certify alternative means by which shipowners can comply with the requirements of the Annexes. Indeed, Annexes I and II contain a general provision which authorizes the flag State to allow 'any fitting, material, appliance or apparatus to be fitted in a ship as an alternative to that required by this Annex if such fitting, material, appliance or apparatus is at least as effective as that required by this Annex'.[94] Any such authorization must be communicated to the IMO for circulation to the Parties 'for their information and appropriate action, if any'.[95] This mechanism thus allows oversight by the other Contracting Parties who may place political pressure on the flag State concerned if the measures are not considered sufficient. Failure to comply may also be subject to dispute settlement and the MARPOL Convention provides for arbitration of disputes about the interpretation and application of the treaty,[96] although there is no known utilization of this option to date.

Another source of flexibility within the MARPOL Convention is the ability to identify what are known as 'special areas', which are defined as 'a sea area where for recognized technical reasons in relation to its oceanographical and ecological condition and to the particular characteristics of its traffic, the adoption of special mandatory measures is required'.[97] Special areas may be designated under Annexes I, II, IV, and V of the MARPOL Convention and they have principally been used for the prescription of stricter discharge standards than those otherwise contained in the MARPOL Annexes.[98] There are currently ten special areas under Annex I, namely the Mediterranean Sea, the Baltic Sea, the Black Sea, the Red Sea, the Gulf area, the Gulf of Aden, the Antarctic area, North West European waters, the Oman area of the Arabian Sea, and Southern South African waters.[99] Antarctica is the only Special Area designated under MARPOL Annex II,[100] and the Baltic Sea is the only Special Area under MARPOL Annex IV.[101] Finally, there are eight special areas under MARPOL Annex V: the Mediterranean Sea, the Baltic Sea, the Black Sea, the Red Sea, the Gulf area, the North Sea, the Antarctic area, and the Wider Caribbean region.[102] Additional special areas can be added using the ordinary tacit amendment procedures in the Convention. The designation of special areas not only has implications for ships, but also additional obligations are imposed on coastal States bordering special areas, to provide reception facilities to ensure that ships can comply with the stricter requirements imposed in those areas.[103] Not only must port

[93] MARPOL Annex I, Regulation 16.4.
[94] Ibid, Regulation 5.1; MARPOL Annex II, Regulation 5.1.
[95] MARPOL Annex I, Regulation 5.2.   [96] MARPOL Convention, Article 10.
[97] MARPOL Annex I, Regulation 1(10).
[98] Guidelines for the Designation of Special Areas under MARPOL 73/78 and Guidelines for the Identification and Designation of Particularly Sensitive Sea Areas, IMO Assembly Resolution A.927(22) (2001).
[99] MARPOL Annex I, Regulations 15 and 33.3.
[100] MARPOL Annex II, Regulation 13.8.2.   [101] MARPOL Annex IV, Regulation 11B.
[102] MARPOL Annex V, Regulation 6.
[103] MARPOL Annex I, Regulations 38.4–38.7; MARPOL Annex IV, Regulation 12bis. Indeed, the provision for reception facilities is often a pre-requisite for the entry into force of special areas. For this reason, the special areas in the Red Sea and the Black Sea are not yet mandatory.

State reception facilities be readily available in order to mitigate delays for vessels, they must also be affordable to discourage ships from discarding their waste at sea in order to avoid the costs of port State disposal.[104] The IMO has produced Guidance for Port Reception Facility Providers and Users[105] and these obligations will be subject to scrutiny as part of the IMO Member State Audit Scheme (MSAS), discussed below. Some regional treaty bodies have sought to coordinate their approach to the provision of reception facilities in order to satisfy these obligations. For example, the Helsinki Convention provides that '[t]he Contracting Parties shall develop and apply uniform requirements for the provision of reception facilities for ship-generated wastes, taking into account, inter alia, the special needs of passenger ships operating in the Baltic Sea Area',[106] and the Baltic Commission has adopted recommendations to further the implementation of this provision.[107] This demonstrates one of the ways in which regional bodies can support the implementation of IMO standards.

In a similar vein, Annex VI allows for the establishment of Emissions Control Areas (ECAs) which serve a similar purpose to special areas by imposing lower limits on the sulphur content of fuel that may be used in these areas. To date, sulphur dioxide ECAs have been adopted in the Baltic Sea and the North Sea, whereas additional restrictions are placed on both sulphur dioxide and nitrogen dioxide emissions from shipping in the North American area and the United States Caribbean Sea area. It is highly likely that further ECAs will be prescribed in future, thereby, further increasing and differentiating air pollution standards for shipping.[108]

6.3.3 The SOLAS Convention

The SOLAS Convention sits alongside the MARPOL Convention as a key pillar of the regulatory framework adopted by the IMO in order to increase safety of shipping. The first version of this treaty was adopted in 1914, following the sinking of the Titanic, and it has been updated on numerous occasions since then, being brought within the framework of the IMO after the Second World War. The most recent version was adopted in 1974 and it is kept up-to-date using tacit amendment procedures in a similar manner to the MARPOL Convention. The SOLAS Convention currently has 163 Parties, representing 99.14 per cent of the global fleet.[109] The

---

[104] See e.g. UN, Oceans and Law of the Sea: Report of the Secretary-General, Document A/71/74 (2016) para. 93.

[105] IMO Document MEPC.1/Circ.834 (2014).

[106] Helsinki Convention, Article 8(2).   [107] HELCOM Recommendation 1/11 (1980).

[108] It is expected that proposals to introduce nitrogen dioxide emissions control zones in the North Sea and Baltic Seas will be brought to the MEPC in 2016; see Roadmap for Designating a NECA in the Baltic Sea in parallel with the North Sea, Document HOD 49-2015. See also Decision IG.22/4 (2016) of the Meeting of the Parties to the Barcelona Convention, Annex, para. 4.15, in which they undertake to 'examine the possibility of designating the Mediterranean Sea or parts thereof as a SOX emission control area under MARPOL Annex VI'.

[109] See the IMO website. <http://www.imo.org/About/Conventions/StatusOfConventions/Pages/Default.aspx>.

SOLAS Convention contains many important construction, design, and equipment standards, which help to improve the safety of ships, thereby reducing the risks of accidents that may have serious consequences for the marine environment.

The evolution of the SOLAS Convention has also seen an increasing emphasis on operational standards, in recognition of the fact that human factors, rather than technical deficiencies, are one of the most important contributions to accidents at sea.[110] The IMO Assembly first approved the IMO Guidelines on Management for the Safe Operation of Ships and for Pollution Prevention in 1989,[111] which was later replaced by the International Safety Management (ISM) Code in 1993.[112] The aim of the ISM Code is to ensure that ships are operated in a manner which is conducive to achieving high safety and environmental standards, including through the establishment of 'procedures, plans and instructions, including checklists as appropriate, for key shipboard operations concerning the safety of the personnel, ship and protection of the environment'.[113] The ISM Code has been updated over time and it has been made mandatory for certain categories of ship by the SOLAS Convention[114] and the MARPOL Convention.[115]

In addition to setting construction, design, equipment, and operational standards, the SOLAS Convention also includes provisions on the adoption of navigational measures for various purposes, including the protection of the marine environment.[116] Such routeing and related navigational measures are a form of area-based measures, requiring ships to follow specific instructions when transiting a particular part of the sea. Routeing measures are usually proposed by a coastal State for waters within its jurisdiction, although the SOLAS Convention provides that 'where two or more Governments have a common interest in a particular area, they should formulate joint proposals for the delineation and use of a routeing system therein on the basis of an agreement between them'.[117] Indeed, in certain circumstances, discussed in the section on coastal State prescriptive jurisdiction below, coastal States may only adopt binding routeing or navigational measures if they have first been approved by the IMO. In any case, it is common for coastal States to seek the endorsement of the IMO for navigational measures within their waters.[118] To promote good practice in the adoption of such measures, the IMO has developed the General Provisions on Ships' Routeing, which provide advice on the prescription of traffic separation schemes, two-way routes, recommended tracks, precautionary areas, deep-water routes, areas to be avoided, no-anchoring areas, ship reporting

---

[110] See e.g. UK P & I Club, Analysis of Major Claims (1998) 1.

[111] IMO Assembly Resolution A.647(16) (1989), replaced by IMO Assembly Resolution A.680(17) (1991).

[112] IMO Assembly Resolution A.741(18) (1993).   [113] ISM Code, para. 7.

[114] SOLAS Convention, Annex, Chapter IX.   [115] MARPOL Annex I.

[116] See SOLAS Convention, Annex, Chapter V. See also General Provisions on Ships' Routeing, contained in IMO Assembly Resolution A.572(14) (1985) (as amended).

[117] SOLAS Convention, Annex, Chapter V, Regulation 10(5).

[118] Moreover, international rules suggest that IMO guidance must at least be taken into account by the coastal State; see UNCLOS, Article 22(3)(a); SOLAS Convention, Annex, Chapter V, Regulation 10(4).

systems, and vessels traffic services.[119] Whilst such measures can be adopted independently, they have become central to discussions relating to the designation and protection of so-called Particularly Sensitive Sea Areas (PSSAs), considered below.

6.3.4 Particularly Sensitive Sea Areas

The concept of the PSSA has emerged as one of the central means for the IMO to consider proposals for the protection of particular areas of the marine environment.[120] PSSAs are a form of marine protected area (MPA),[121] offering special protection to an area because of its significance for recognized ecological, socio-ecological, or scientific attributes where such attributes may be vulnerable to damage by international shipping activities.[122] The concept of the PSSA goes beyond the protection of sea areas for the environmental purposes, but in relation to ecological sensitivity, the guidelines provide that PSSAs can be adopted to protect unique or rare habitats; sea areas that are critical for the survival function, or recovery of marine species; an area that has exceptional variety of species; an area that has experienced a relative lack of human-induced disturbance; or simply an area that is an outstanding or illustrative example of a specific natural feature.[123] The breadth of issues that fall within the scope of PSSAs is a clear illustration of how the IMO has integrated broad ecosystems considerations into its decision-making processes.

The procedure for designation requires both the submission of details concerning the particular features that require protection and the threats that are posed by shipping. It also requires a State to propose a range of associated protective measures (APMs) in order to safeguard the attributes of the proposed area.[124] The Guidelines for the Designation of PSSAs make it abundantly clear that any APMs must have 'an identified legal basis'.[125] Many of the PSSAs designated to date have been accompanied by routeing or other navigational measures approved by the IMO on the basis of the SOLAS Convention or related provisions.[126] Special areas under MARPOL may also be identified as APMs. Indeed, it is possible that the IMO could approve additional sorts of special protection measures for PSSAs, within the scope of its powers.[127]

Several PSSAs have been approved since the concept was first introduced in 1990, including the Great Barrier Reef and Torres Strait, the Sabana-Camagüey Archipelago and the Galapagos Archipelago, the waters around Malpelo Island and the Canary Islands, the sea around the Florida Keys, the Wadden Sea, the Paracas

---

[119] General Provisions on Ships' Routeing (as amended), IMO Assembly Resolution A.572(14) (1985).

[120] PSSA Guidelines.

[121] L de la Fayette, 'The Marine Environment Protection Committee: The Conjunction of the Law of the Sea and International Environmental Law' (2001) 16 *IJMCL* 155, 186; J Roberts, *Marine Environmental Protection and Biodiversity Conservation: The Application and Future Development of the IMO's Particularly Sensitive Sea Area Concept* (Springer 2006) 104.

[122] PSSA Guidelines, para. 1.2.   [123] Ibid, paras 4.4.1–4.4.11.

[124] Ibid, para. 1.2.   [125] Ibid, para. 6.1.3.

[126] SOLAS Convention, Annex, Chapter V, Regulations 11(1) and 12(1).

[127] See e.g. de la Fayette (n121) 191.

National Reserve, the Papahānaumokuākea Marine National Monument, Western European Waters, the Saba Bank, the Baltic Sea, the Jomard Entrance, and the Strait of Bonifacio.[128] PSSAs provide a flexible tool for protecting rare and fragile marine ecosystems. For example, the Galapagos Archipelago was designated as a PSSA in 2004 because of the uniqueness of the islands and the dependence of the island life on a healthy marine environment.[129] In conjunction with this designation, a number of APMs have been adopted to protect the biodiversity of the Galapagos Islands, including a mandatory ship reporting system, recommended tracks, and an area to be avoided. To date, most PSSAs have been applied to areas of territorial sea or EEZ. Yet, the PSSA concept could also potentially be used to apply protective measures to the high seas, provided that all IMO Members agreed to such measures.[130] For example, it has been suggested that the Sargasso Sea, which includes some areas of high seas, should be designated as a PSSA in order to grant enhanced protection to the area.[131]

Given that States must specify the legal basis for an APM accompanying a PSSA, it follows that the concept does not itself offer any additional protection than would already be available under the existing legal framework. Rather, the principal value of the PSSA concept would appear to be in promoting a comprehensive assessment of the impacts of shipping in a particular area and systematic consideration of the most appropriate forms of protection.[132] It has also been noted that by prioritizing the consideration of the need for protection prior to the identification of a legal basis, PSSAs offer the opportunity for States to agree upon extensions of environmental jurisdiction in exceptional circumstances.[133] Moreover, the process is also significant because it serves to ensure that all relevant States and interests are represented in the development of any protective measures.[134] Nevertheless, the process has been criticized because protective measures are often watered down by the IMO committees when considering the establishment of PSSAs, suggesting that navigational interests are given a greater weight in the decision-making process.[135] Moreover, what would appear to be lacking in the PSSA process is the ability to periodically review and evaluate whether measures have actually achieved the objectives that are agreed in the designation of the PSSA.

There are also some peripheral benefits, which stem not from the legal character of the measures but from the publication of an area as a PSSA. In many cases,

---

[128] See List of Special Areas under MARPOL and Particularly Sensitive Sea Areas, MEPC.1/Circ.778 (2012) Annex 2. See also <http://www.imo.org/en/OurWork/Environment/PSSAs/Pages/Default.aspx>.

[129] Designation of the Galapagos Archipelago as a Particularly Sensitive Sea Area, Resolution MEPC.135(53) (2005).

[130] R Churchill, 'High Seas Marine Protected Areas: Implications for Shipping', in R Caddell and R Thomas (eds), *Shipping, Law and the Marine Environment in the 21st Century* (Lawtext Publishing Limited 2013) 73; J Roberts et al, 'Area-based Management on the High Seas: Possible Applications of the IMO's Particularly Sensitive Sea Area Concept' (2010) 25 *IJMCL* 483–522.

[131] See e.g. TM Trott et al, 'Efforts to Enhance Protection of the Sargasso Sea', Proceedings of the Sixty-Third Gulf and Caribbean Fisheries Institute, 2010: http://nsgl.gso.uri.edu/flsgp/flsgpw10002/data/papers/052.pdf.

[132] Roberts (n121) 85.   [133] Ringbom (n8) 122–3.

[134] PSSA Guidelines, para. 1.4.2.   [135] See Roberts et al (n130) 515.

PSSAs are subsequently marked on navigational charts and this fact alone may lead some vessels to take additional care when traversing these areas. Furthermore, it cannot be ruled out that PSSAs can be taken into account in other ways in decision-making processes. For example, the Nairobi Convention on the Removal of Wrecks, adopted by the IMO in 2007, explicitly requires the existence of PSSAs to be taken into account by affected States, when deciding whether or not a wreck poses a hazard to the safety of navigation or the protection of the marine environment.[136]

6.3.5 The AFS Convention

The 2001 AFS Convention introduces regulations on the use of substances that are applied to ships hulls in order to prevent their fouling. The use of anti-fouling systems is an important issue for the shipping industry, as fouling 'causes loss of speed and cost increases in fuel'.[137] Whilst hulls can be manually cleaned, this process is expensive and it requires a ship to be laid up for a period of time. It has, therefore, been more economical to apply chemical substances to the hulls of ships in order to prevent fouling in the first place.[138] One such substance that was widely used in the past was paint containing tributyl tin (TBT). Unfortunately, this chemical had unpredicted side effects: not only is TBT highly toxic,[139] but there is also evidence that it causes serious effects on the biological functions of some marine species.[140]

When this issue was first raised, the MEPC adopted a resolution recommending that governments adopt and promote effective measures within their jurisdiction to control the potential adverse impacts to the marine environment associated with the use of certain anti-fouling systems, including the elimination of anti-fouling paints containing TBT compounds on certain size vessels.[141] The issue was raised again in the Agenda 21 Action Plan, which called upon States to 'take measures to reduce water pollution caused by organotin compounds used in anti-fouling paints'.[142] However, it was not until November 1999 that the IMO Assembly called for the development of a globally legally binding instrument to address the harmful effects of anti-fouling systems used on ships.[143] The decision was made to develop a self-standing treaty, rather than a new Annex to the MARPOL Convention, largely to allow the drafters to set their own entry-into-force provisions.[144]

The AFS Convention, adopted on 5 October 2001, introduces a gradual restriction on the use of organotin compounds, which act as biocides in anti-fouling systems.[145]

---

[136] See 2007 Nairobi Convention on the Removal of Wrecks (EIF 14 April 2015), Article 6(d). See also Guidelines on Places of Refuge for Ships in need of Assistance, IMO Assembly Resolution A.949(23) (2003) Appendix 2, para. 2.1.

[137] ICB Dear and P Kemp (eds), *The Oxford Companion to Ships and the Sea* (2nd edn: OUP 2005) 224.

[138] Ibid.

[139] Indeed, it has been called 'the most toxic substance ever to be deliberately released into the marine environment': see de la Fayette (n121) 168.

[140] C Roberts, *Ocean of Life* (Penguin 2012) 132.

[141] MEPC Resolution MEPC.46(30) (1990).   [142] Agenda 21 (1992) para. 17.32.

[143] IMO Assembly Resolution A.895(21) (1999).   [144] de la Fayette (n121) 172.

[145] AFS Convention, Article 4.

Ships are prohibited from applying or reapplying such compounds from 1 January 2003. From 1 January 2008, ships are prohibited from bearing compounds on their hulls or external parts or surfaces that are listed in the Annex to the Convention. In this regard, the Convention does little more than formalize the timetable already established in Assembly Resolution A.895(21), albeit in binding form. However, it is significant that negotiators resisted calls from the shipping industry to lengthen these timelines.[146] Moreover, the Convention applies not only to ships which fly the flag of Contracting Parties, but also to the application, reapplication, installation, or use of any such system on board any ships which visit a Party's port, shipyard, or offshore terminal, thereby strengthening the protective regime.[147] The Convention also introduces an important obligation on Parties to 'take appropriate measures to promote and facilitate scientific and technical research on the effects of anti-fouling systems as well as monitoring of such effects'.[148] If any further detrimental effects are identified, Contracting Parties may propose the addition of the anti-fouling system to the Annex of the Convention.[149] Amendments to the Annex shall be adopted using tacit amendment procedures, meaning that the treaty can be updated relatively quickly.[150] When considering amendments, the MEPC is explicitly required to take a precautionary approach. To this end, Article 6(3) provides that 'where the Committee is of the view that there is a threat of serious or irreversible damage, lack of full scientific certainty shall not be used as a reason to prevent a decision to proceed with the evaluation of the proposal'. In practice, this means that a low threshold of evidence is set in order to prescribe additional substances. To support the adoption of amendments, the Convention sets up a technical group to review proposals and to report to the Committee on whether the proposal has demonstrated 'a potential for unreasonable risk of adverse effects on non-target organisms or human health such that the amendment of Annex 1 is warranted'.[151] The drafting of this provision further supports the adoption of a precautionary approach, as the technical group must evaluate the 'potential' of a risk, rather than determining whether or not a risk can be proven, and Article 6(5) of the Convention confirms that 'if the report finds a threat of serious or irreversible damage, lack of full scientific certainty shall not, itself, be used as a reason to prevent a decision from being taken to list an anti-fouling system in Annex 1'.[152] Nevertheless, a positive decision is still required by the Committee in order for an amendment to be adopted and individual States may object to the amendment, thereby blocking its application to its own vessels.[153] Moreover, the negotiators rejected proposals to introduce a system which would have banned all anti-fouling systems unless they had been approved in advance by the Contracting Parties.[154] Thus, the Convention only adopts a weak version of the precautionary approach and it does not go as far as some would have liked.[155]

---

[146] de la Fayette (n121) 172.   [147] Ibid, 171.   [148] AFS Convention, Article 8(1).
[149] Ibid, Article 6.   [150] Ibid, Article 16.   [151] Ibid, Article 6(4).
[152] Ibid, Article 6(5).
[153] Ibid, Article 16(2)(f)(ii). The United States has declared that amendments to the Convention will only enter into force for its vessels after it has given its express acceptance.
[154] See de la Fayette (n121) 171.
[155] Ibid, who concludes, 'Restricting or prohibiting something after it has already caused a great deal of harm is rather too late for the organisms that have been killed or damaged.'

The Convention only entered into force on 17 September 2008, over eight months after the ban on prescribed anti-fouling systems was supposed to have come into effect. Moreover, at the time of writing, only seventy-three States, representing 93.26 per cent of world tonnage, have ratified or acceded to the 2001 Convention. This demonstrates that law-making by treaty can sometimes be a slow process.

6.3.6 The BWM Convention

Another issue that has received the attention of the IMO is the danger posed to ecosystems by the transfer of alien invasive species. Alien invasive species not only pose threats to the environment, they can also be highly costly, which gives States an additional incentive to address them. These dangers were generally recognized at the international level in the Convention on Biological Diversity (CBD), which calls for measures to 'prevent the introduction, control or eradicate those alien species which threaten ecosystems, habitats or species'.[156] The issue is also addressed in general terms by UNCLOS.[157]

A major vector for the transfer of marine organisms is through ballast water exchange. Ballast water is usually taken on or off at port in order to compensate for the loading or unloading of cargoes, thereby improving the trim and stability of a vessel.[158] It is estimated that commercial shipping carries up to 12 billion tonnes of ballast water each year. Yet, along with the water itself, ships can also transport a number of marine organisms. One study suggests that 'at any given moment some 10,000 different species are being transported between bio-geographic regions in ballast tanks alone'.[159] Once released in a new environment, the effects on endemic species can be catastrophic. An oft-cited example is *Caulerpa taxifolia*, a type of seaweed which was accidentally released into the Ligurian Sea and now covers 97 per cent of available surfaces between Toulon in France and Genoa in Italy, completely altering the natural seabed environment in this region.[160] Such incidents also can have severe economic consequences. For example, it is estimated that the United States spent between $750 million and $1 billion on controlling the European Zebra mussel between 1989 and 2000 alone.[161]

A global approach to this problem was clearly necessary as unilateral action can only temporarily reduce the inoculation frequency of alien marine species if they are also establishing at the same time in neighbouring States.[162] In fact, this issue was identified as far back as 1973 at the international conference convened to adopt the MARPOL Convention.[163] The problem continued to be studied throughout the 1980s, and the IMO finally adopted Guidelines for Preventing the Introduction

---

[156] Convention on Biological Diversity (CBD), Article 8(h). On the role of the CBD in negotiating the BWM Convention, see Chapter 10.

[157] UNCLOS, Article 196(1).   [158] Dear and Kemp (n137) 29.

[159] N Bax et al, 'Marine Invasive Alien Species: A Threat to Global Biodiversity' (2003) 27 *MP* 313, 313.

[160] Roberts (n140) 170.   [161] See <http://globallast.imo.org/examples-of-ias/>.

[162] Bax et al (n159) 319.

[163] See 1973 Conference on the Prevention of Pollution from Ships, Resolution 18.

of Unwanted Aquatic Organisms and Pathogens from Ships' Ballast Water and Sediment Discharges in 1993.[164] This non-binding instrument sought to give guidance to States, particularly coastal States and port States, on measures that could be taken to control the introduction of alien invasive species, including the non-release of ballast water, ballast water exchange or removal, or, in areas deemed acceptable by the port State authorities, ballast water management practices that minimize the risk of taking on contaminated water and discharge of ballast water into shore-based facilities for treatment or controlled disposal.[165] It also called upon the organization to keep the guidelines under review with a view to developing them as the basis of a new Annex to the MARPOL Convention.[166] However, in November 1997, it was decided to work towards the completion of a self-standing treaty.[167] Although a target date of 2000 was set for the adoption of a legally binding instrument, it was not until 2004 that the IMO succeeded in concluding the BWM Convention.

The BWM Convention includes measures to be taken by both coastal States and flag States. First, flag States are required to ensure that ships flying their flag have on board a ballast water management plan.[168] The Convention also sets specific regulations for ballast water management, which vary depending on the size of a vessel, as well as when it was built. The regulations give significant leeway to vessels in deciding on where and when to conduct ballast water exchange including a recognition that 'a ship shall not be required to deviate from its intended voyage, or delay the voyage, in order to comply'.[169] It is unclear what is meant precisely by this provision and it would seem to leave a significant amount of discretion to masters. There are factors which may prevent a vessel from complying with this regulation, such as a lack of time, a lack of appropriate location on the route, and a lack of weather conditions in which the operation may be carried out safely.[170] Yet, the Convention explicitly recalls the precautionary approach in its preamble, which would suggest that there should be a presumption that ballast water exchange is practicable and the burden of proof should be on the shipowner to show that it is not. Indeed, the Convention requires that all ballast water operations, including those carried out in a manner that does not comply with the Convention, are recorded in a ballast water record book, and masters are expressly required to state the reason for a particular discharge.[171] This requirement would allow monitoring of ballast water exchange and enforcement of the regulations if insufficient reasons were given by masters.

Ballast water exchange was intended to be an interim solution for ships, pending the development of technology which would allow a more effective and efficient

---

[164] IMO Assembly Resolution A.774(18) (1993). See also MEPC Resolution 50(31) (1991).
[165] IMO Assembly Resolution A.774(18) (1993) Annex, para. 7.1.2.
[166] IMO Assembly Resolution A.774(18) (1993) para. 4.
[167] IMO Assembly Resolution A.868(20) (1997) para. 3.
[168] BWM Convention, Annex, Regulation B-1. See also Guidelines for Ballast Water Management and Development of Ballast Water Management Plans (G4), MEPC Resolution MEPC.127(53) (2005).
[169] BWM Convention, Annex, Regulation B-4.3.
[170] S Gollasch et al, 'Critical Review of the IMO International on the Management of Ships' Ballast Water and Sediments' (2007) 6 *HA* 585, 588.
[171] BWM Convention, Annex, Regulation B-2 and Appendix 2.

approach to ballast water management.[172] Ships built after certain dates specified in the Convention should have ballast water management systems that are able to treat ballast water whilst it is on board the vessel.[173] Treatment may rely upon mechanical operations, such as filtration or separation. Treatment may also be by way of chemical or biological processes. Ballast water management systems used to comply with this regulation must be approved by the flag State, taking into account IMO guidelines, unless the system contains one or more active substances, in which case it must be approved by the IMO itself.[174] Before a decision is made by the MEPC, proposals are first considered by an expert working group. This mechanism is to ensure that decisions are based upon a clear and objective understanding of the scientific and technical aspects of the proposals. The Convention is also clear that 'ballast water management practice[s] ... do not cause greater harm than they prevent to the environment, human health, property or resources'.[175] This provision implements Articles 196 of UNCLOS by ensuring that new technologies do not themselves pose a threat to the marine environment. To date, more than thirty ballast water management systems have been approved by the MEPC.[176]

Ships may also satisfy the ballast water management regulations by discharging ballast water into port reception facilities, if they are available.[177] This is perhaps the most effective option for preventing the spread of alien invasive species, although it presents practical challenges, given the volume of ballast water that would be required by larger vessels.[178]

At the same time as introducing minimum standards for the management of ballast water, the 2004 Convention also recognizes the right of coastal States to take 'more stringent measures'.[179] This allows coastal States to react to identified invasions in an attempt to prevent the further spread of alien species. To this end, coastal States must continuously monitor their waters for alien invasive species.[180] Developing countries in particular may need assistance if they are to effectively carry

---

[172] Gollasch et al (n170) 588; de la Fayette (n121) 181.

[173] BWM Convention, Annex, Regulation D-2. The dates were modified because the Convention had not entered into force in time; see IMO Assembly Resolution A.1005(25) (2007); MEPC Resolution MEPC.188(60) (2010).

[174] BWM Convention, Annex, Regulation D-3. See Procedure for Approval of Ballast Water Management Systems that Make Use of Active Substances, MEPC Resolution MEPC.169(57) (2008), replacing MEPC Resolution MEPC.126(53). According to Balkin, this is 'due to the uncertainties associated with discharging chemically treated ballast water from a ship operating under the authority of one government in the port of another country, compounded by the fact that no obvious impacts can be seen at the time of the discharge ...'; R Balkin, 'Ballast Water Management: Regulatory Challenges and Opportunities', in R Caddell and R Thomas (eds), *Shipping, Law and the Marine Environment in the 21st Century* (Lawtext Publishing Limited 2013) 148.

[175] BWM Convention, Article 2.7.

[176] See Report of the Sixty-Fifth Meeting of the Marine Environmental Protection Committee, Document MEPC 65/22 (2013) para. 2.20.

[177] BWM Convention, Annex, Regulation B-3.6. See also Guidelines for Ballast Water Reception Facilities, MEPC Resolution MEPC.153(55) (2006).

[178] However, as noted by Gollasch et al, the challenge is not insurmountable; see Gollasch et al (n170) 591.

[179] BWM Convention, Article 2(3). See also Regulation C-1.

[180] BWM Convention, Article 6.

out this duty, and the Convention establishes an obligation for technical assist-ance.[181] In this respect, the IMO, in conjunction with the Global Environment Facility and other partners, has initiated the Global Ballast Water Management Programme which assists developing countries to reduce the transfer of harmful aquatic organisms and pathogens in ships' ballast water and to prepare for imple-mentation of the BMW Convention.[182]

The BWM Convention finally entered into force in September 2017. This long delay was, in part, owing to opposition from the shipping industry, which had con-cerns about the certification process for new equipment. A compromise was reached at the Sixty-seventh Session of the MEPC in 2014, and States agreed to review the guidelines for the approval of ballast water management systems,[183] thus facilitating broader acceptance of the Convention.

6.3.7 Noise pollution

As well as causing pollution through the discharge of polluting substances, ships are also one of the main causes of underwater noise. As described by one author, 'noise levels [in the oceans] have grown to a roar since the 1950s, as the world's globalized economy has launched thousands of new merchant ships'.[184] This rise in noise is problematic for many species because they use sound to communicate or to find their prey.[185] Noise can, therefore, disrupt patterns of behaviour of marine species and cause direct harm through actual physical injury. Particular threats are thought to be posed to cetaceans.[186] However, it has also been admitted that 'there remain significant questions that require further study with the largest gaps relating to fishes, invertebrates, turtles, and birds, and additional knowledge gaps relating to the characteristics of major sound sources, trends in the prevalence and magnitude, as well as the intensity and spatial distribution of underwater noise'.[187] Given the indications of potential harm that may be caused to the marine environment, a pre-cautionary approach would suggest that international action should be taken, even in the absence of conclusive scientific evidence. In particular, the CBD Conference of the Parties (COP) has encouraged States to take 'appropriate measures to avoid, minimize and mitigate the potential significant adverse impacts of anthropogenic underwater noise on marine and coastal biodiversity',[188] as well as inviting compe-tent intergovernmental organizations to 'take measures within their mandates'.[189]

The IMO has only recently started to address the issue of noise pollution from ships. One of the factors that has prevented earlier action is the fact that 'since noise-producing activities are socially and economically necessary and cannot be simply prohibited, science is also required to determine methods for reducing

---

[181] Ibid, Article 13(1).

[182] See <http://globallast.imo.org>. See also GEF, *Catalysing Ocean Finance*, Volume II (2012) 69–74.

[183] Resolution MEPC.253(67) (2014).   [184] Roberts (n140) 151.   [185] Ibid, 156.

[186] For example, CMS COP Resolution 10.24 (2011); IWC Resolution 2009-1 (2009).

[187] CBD COP Decision XII/24 (2014) para. 2.   [188] Ibid, para. 3.

[189] Ibid, para. 4.

the negative impact of manmade noise on the marine environment and marine life and to develop new technologies that produce less noise than existing ones'.[190] Nevertheless, Guidelines for the Reduction of Underwater Noise from Commercial Shipping to Address Adverse Impacts on Marine Life have been developed and approved by the IMO. The guidelines largely focus on providing non-prescriptive advice concerning factors that can be taken into account when designing a ship in order to reduce underwater noise.[191] However, when approving the guidelines, the MEPC also noted that 'a large number of gaps in knowledge remained and no comprehensive assessment of this issue was possible at this stage' and 'more research was needed, in particular on the measurement and reporting of underwater sound radiating from ships'.[192] This issue demonstrates the difficulty of applying a precautionary approach to an activity that is already established and where regulation would have significant costs.[193] Yet, it does not excuse inaction on the part of governments or the shipping industry. One of the actions highlighted by the CBD COP is the development of quieter technologies,[194] and this activity should be encouraged by the IMO in the context of noise pollution from ships.

The guidelines also note, '[s]peed reductions or routing decisions to avoid sensitive marine areas including well-known habitats or migratory pathways when in transit will help to reduce adverse impacts on marine life'.[195] This recognizes the potential value of area-based management measures. In this context, it is worth noting that the IMO Guidelines for the Designation and Identification of PSSAs, discussed above, explicitly refer to noise pollution as a potential reason for the adoption of protective measures.[196] Thus, it is possible that rather than pursuing general standards that apply to all vessels, wherever they are located, the international community may opt for ad hoc measures in order to protect particular species or habitats that are vulnerable to noise pollution.

6.3.8 Ship strikes

Another issue to have more recently attracted international attention is ship strikes. A number of international institutions concerned with the conservation of marine mammals have noted increasing evidence of the risk posed by modern vessels to marine mammals from collisions with shipping. It should be noted that the problem

---

[190] I Papanicolopulu, 'On the Interactions between Law and Science: Considerations on the Ongoing Process of Regulating Underwater Acoustic Pollution' (2011) 1 *ARLS* 247, 253.

[191] Guidelines for the Reduction of Underwater Noise from Commercial Shipping to Address Adverse Impacts on Marine Life (Underwater Noise Guidelines), MEPC.1/Circ.833 (2014).

[192] Report of the Sixty-Sixth Meeting of the Marine Environment Protection Committee, Document MEPC/66/21 (2014) paras 17.5.1–17.5.3.

[193] See A Gillespie, 'The Precautionary Principle in the Twenty-First Century: A Case Study of Noise Pollution in the Ocean' (2007) 22 *IJMCL* 61–87.

[194] CBD COP Decision XII/24 (2014), para. 3(b).

[195] Underwater Noise Guidelines, para. 10.5.

[196] Guidelines for the Identification and Designation of Particularly Sensitive Sea Areas (PSSA Guidelines), IMO Assembly Resolution A.982(24) (2006) Annex, para. 2.2.

is not only detrimental for marine mammal populations; it can also pose hazards to human health and life in the case of a serious collision with a large marine mammal, such as a whale. Nevertheless, the issue is considered as particularly significant in situations where it affects severely endangered species with small populations, such as the Western North Atlantic Right Whale.[197] The issue has been studied by the International Whaling Commission (IWC) through its Conservation Committee, which established a Ship Strikes Working Group in 2005. The main output of this body has been the development of a ship-strike database to increase knowledge and understanding of the significance of ships strikes to cetaceans.[198] This initiative has helped to tackle one of the main challenges in addressing ship strikes, namely the lack of information.[199] Whilst the input of data has been disappointing, the Ship Strike Working Group has provided a global focal point for discussing this issue and gathering relevant data, allowing a more targeted response to the problem. The IWC continues to encourage the gathering and reporting of relevant data to the central database.[200] This information can be used not only by the IWC itself in the management of whale stocks, but it can also provide input to other international institutions wishing to take measures to reduce the incidence of ship strikes.

As the international institution with a recognized mandate for regulating all aspects of shipping, it is not surprising that the IMO has a role to play in addressing this issue.[201] Indeed, the IMO's work on this issue is further evidence of its growing mandate to address the protection of marine biodiversity from shipping, away from its traditional focus on pollution. The IMO has adopted two types of measures on ship strikes: general guidance for all vessels and specific navigational measures for particular areas where the risks of ship strikes are higher.

The Guidance Document for Minimizing the Risk of Ship Strikes with Cetaceans was adopted by the MEPC in July 2009, based upon a submission by the United States.[202] The Guidance Document endorses the implementation of measures to reduce vessel strikes 'based upon the best available science'[203] and balancing the 'biological objectives of reducing and minimizing the risks of ship strikes' with 'adverse impacts on the shipping industry and other interested entities'.[204] The Guidance Document highlights a number of possible actions that could be taken, including education and outreach, technological development, and routeing and reporting measures.[205] All of the options should be 'carefully analysed' and a balance must be

---

[197] See e.g. IWC Resolution 2000-8 (2000), identifying ship strikes as one of the two major causes of human-inducted mortality of North Atlantic Right Whales, alongside entanglement in fishing nets and gear.

[198] The database has been in operation since 2009. At its meeting in 2012, the Conservation Committee endorsed a proposal to develop a strategic plan for ship strikes; see Report of the Conservation Committee, Document IWC/64/Rep05 (2012) 5.

[199] R Caddell, 'Shipping and the Conservation of Marine Biodiversity: Legal Responses to Vessel-Strikes of Marine Mammals', in R Caddell and R Thomas (eds), *Shipping, Law and the Marine Environment in the 21st Century* (Lawtext Publishing Limited 2013) 90.

[200] See Report of the Conservation Committee, Document IWC/65/Rep05 (2013) 4.

[201] See Caddell (n199) 97.

[202] Guidance Document for Minimizing the Risk of Ship Strikes with Cetaceans (Ship Strike Guidance), Document MEPC.1/Circ.674 (July 2009).

[203] Ibid, para. 7.4.   [204] Ibid, para. 7.2.   [205] Ibid, paras 9–12.

drawn between the 'risk to the population or species ... and the impact on maritime safety and commerce'.[206] Where a threat arises across the range of a particular species, States are encouraged to cooperate and coordinate their measures with other range States, both directly and through relevant international organizations.[207]

The need for clear information is stressed throughout the Guidance Document.[208] To this end, the Guidance Document provides that 'if a Member Government seeks to reduce and minimize ship strikes of cetaceans in its waters, it should first clearly define the problem'[209] and it suggests the type of information that should be gathered by the State, including the species of cetacean affected, its distribution and behaviour when it is present in particular waters, and the vessel traffic characteristics in those waters. However, this provision cannot be read as an obligation to gather all of this information prior to adopting measures. A precautionary approach to minimizing ship strikes would permit the adoption of measures, even if there is an absence of clear scientific information. At the same time, such precautionary measures may only be provisional. States should continue to gather scientific information, and the Guidance Document explicitly calls on States to provide 'a mechanism for comments, reports, and observations of the measures adopted' with a view to adjusting the measures if deemed necessary.[210]

As in the case of noise pollution, area-based measures could also be used to address the threat of ship strikes in parts of the seas where marine species may be at particular risk. Indeed, it has been argued that the coastal State may be under an obligation to take some action to warn mariners of the risks under its duty to give appropriate publicity to any danger to navigation of which it has knowledge, under Article 24(2) of UNCLOS.[211] Several States have adopted navigational measures in their territorial seas for the purpose of minimizing the risks of ship strikes with marine mammals, including the United States,[212] Canada,[213] Spain,[214] and Panama.[215] In international straits or the EEZ, the powers of the coastal State are more limited, and measures must first be approved by the IMO before they can be implemented by the coastal State. The record of the IMO to date suggests that States are willing to accept the avoidance of ship strikes as a valid reason for navigational measures, at least where evidence of the threats is presented.[216] Indeed, the IMO has not only

---

[206] Ibid, para. 7.6.   [207] Ibid, paras 13–14.   [208] Ibid, paras 7.3, 9, and 16.
[209] Ibid, para. 6.   [210] Ibid, para. 16.   [211] Caddell (n199) 102.
[212] Ship Reporting System Off the Eastern Coast, IMO Resolution MSC.85(70) (1998), Annex 1; Traffic Separation Scheme in the approach to Boston, Massachusetts, Report of the Maritime Safety Committee at its Eighty-Fifth Session, IMO Document MSC85/26 (2008) para. 11.3.1 and Annex 14; recommended seasonal area to be avoided in the Great South Channel, Report of the Maritime Safety Committee at its Eighty-Fifth Session, IMO Document MSC85/26 (2008) para. 11.4.2.
[213] Traffic Separation Scheme in the Bay of Fundy, Report of the Maritime Safety Committee at its Seventy-Sixth Session, IMO Document MSC76/23 (2002) para. 11.3.2 and Annex 10; Recommended Seasonal Area to be Avoided in the Roseway Basin, Report of the Maritime Safety Committee at its Eighty-Third Session, IMO Document MSC83/28 (2007) para. 14.4.10 and Annex 25.
[214] Traffic Separation Scheme off the Cabo de Gata, Report of the Maritime Safety Committee at its eighty-first session, IMO Document MSC81/25 (2006) para. 10.6.2 and Annex 27.
[215] Caddell (n199) 135.
[216] Traffic Separation Scheme on the Pacific Coast of Panama, Report of the Maritime Safety Committee at Its Ninety-Third Session, IMO Document MSC93/22 (2014) para. 8.2.1 and Annex 16; see also Establishment of New Routeing Measures on the Pacific Coast of Panama, Document NAV59/

approved traffic separation schemes for this purpose but also recommended areas to be avoided and reductions of speed 'in order to help reduce risks of lethal strikes with cetaceans'.[217] Such practice is nevertheless likely to become more important as further data on the risks of ships strikes become available.

One weakness of the international response to date has been its almost exclusive focus on cetaceans. However, it must be noted that there are potentially other marine mammals (e.g. sea turtles) that are susceptible to ship strikes and the guidance adopted at the international level could usefully be applied to these species as well. This may require the IMO to work with an even broader range of international bodies in order to ensure that a coherent approach is taken.

6.4 The Implementation and Enforcement of Shipping Standards

6.4.1 Flag State jurisdiction

6.4.1.1 Flag State duties

Flag States have primary responsibility to implement international shipping standards.[218] It is a basic principle of the law of the sea that flag States have jurisdiction over their ships for all matters, wherever they are in the world,[219] and, therefore, flag States can in theory ensure effective implementation of regulations. Practice is more problematic, however, because shipowners have a large degree of discretion as to which flag they fly. The phenomenon of so-called flagging out arises because many States operate open registries that allow ships to register without the need for any links of nationality.[220] Thus, ships may avoid the application of international standards by registering in a State that is not a Party to the relevant treaties.[221]

UNCLOS seeks to deal with this problem by establishing minimum standards that must be applied by all flag States. It does so by using 'rules of reference', which serve to incorporate certain international standards into flag State duties under the Convention.[222] To this end, Article 94(5) specifies that when adopting national laws for the promotion of maritime safety, 'each State is required to conform to generally accepted international standards, procedures and practices ...'. This provision makes it clear that a flag State does not have complete discretion over the standards that it prescribes for ships flying its flag. Similarly, Article 211(2) provides that flag

---

3 (2013). Traffic Separation Scheme and Recommended Speeds in the Gibraltar Strait, Report of the Maritime Safety Committee at Its Eighty-Second Session, IMO Document MSC82/24 (2006) para. 11.3.1 and Annex 19.

[217] See Report of the Navigation Subcommittee at Its Fifty-Ninth Session, Document NAV59/20 (2012) Annex 2.

[218] MARPOL Convention, Article 4(1).   [219] UNCLOS, Article 94.

[220] See ER DeSombre, *Flagging Standards* (The MIT Press 2006) 71.

[221] Ibid, 38–46; AJ Corres and AA Pallis, 'Flag State Performance: An Empirical Analysis' (2008) 7 *WMUJMA* 241–61.

[222] See generally, W Van Reenan, 'Rules of Reference in the New Convention on the Law of the Sea in Particular Connection with the Pollution of the Sea by Oil from Tankers' (1981) *NYIL* 3.

States must adopt regulations relating to pollution from ships that 'at least have the same effect as that of generally accepted international rules and standards'. Together, these provisions establish an international minimum standard that must be met by all flag States, regardless of whether they have become a Party to the IMO regulatory treaties.[223]

One weakness of the rules of reference in the Convention is the ambiguity surrounding the phrase *generally accepted international rules and standards*. A leading interpretation of the phrase is that standards qualify as generally accepted if they have satisfied the formal conditions for their entry into force.[224] This interpretation acknowledges that the entry-into-force provisions of regulatory treaties adopted by the IMO are carefully crafted to ensure that they have broad support before they enter into force, often referring to ratification by both a minimum number of States and a minimum percentage of world tonnage. On this basis, all of the major IMO treaties discussed in this chapter would qualify as generally accepted international rules or standards for the purposes of Articles 94(5) or 211(2) of UNCLOS. This proposition is uncontroversial in the case of some of these treaties: the SOLAS Convention and most Annexes of the MARPOL Convention have more than one hundred Parties, representing over 90 per cent of the world fleet in terms of tonnage, and it is difficult to deny that they are generally accepted. The same cannot be said for some of the more recent regulatory treaties, however, as they have only just entered into force and, therefore, have much lower participation rates. Accepting that entry into force alone is sufficient to qualify a treaty as being generally accepted means that a relatively small number of States can dictate to the rest of the international community the content of international minimum standards. In the words of Timangenis, 'small minorities could impose their wishes on other states'.[225] It is for this reason that some authors have argued that the attainment of general acceptance should instead be understood as similar to the requirements for establishing customary international law.[226] Identification of customary international law requires evidence of 'extensive and virtually uniform' State practice and it necessitates that such practice is also representative, including those States whose interests are specially affected.[227] The level of practice that is required to demonstrate that a standard has emerged as a customary rule is difficult to pinpoint with precision, but this approach would normally set a higher threshold than many of the entry-into-force requirements of the relevant treaties. As a result, this interpretation of general acceptance prevents a small number of States being able to dictate the content of international

---

[223] See AE Boyle, 'Marine Pollution under the Law of the Sea Convention' (1985) 79 *AJIL* 357; B Oxman, 'The Duty to Respect Generally Accepted International Standards' (1991) 24 *NYUJILP* 109.

[224] See e.g. M Valenzuela, 'IMO: Public International Law and Regulation', in DM Johnson and NG Letalik (eds), *The Law of the Sea and Ocean Industry: New Opportunities and Restraints* (Law of the Sea Institute 1984) 145.

[225] GJ Timangenis, *International Control of Marine Pollution* (Oceana Publications 1980) 606.

[226] Van Reenen (n222) 11; Harrison (n26) 175.

[227] *North Sea Continental Shelf Cases* (1969) para. 74. It has been argued that it is not only the practice of individual States that is important but also practice evidenced through multilateral or regional institutions; see R Barnes, 'Flag States', in DR Rothwell et al (eds), *Oxford Handbook of the Law of the Sea* (OUP 2015) 322; Harrison (n26) 176–7.

minimum standards. At the same time, this interpretation has the added advantage of allowing individual rules or standards to be considered as generally accepted where they are supported through actual practice, even if the treaty in which they are contained has not entered into force. This interpretation would appear to be consistent with the position prior to the conclusion of UNCLOS, where many technical standards relating to navigation and maritime safety were accepted as rules of customary international law, even if they were not contained in a treaty.[228] Some commentators have gone even further and argued that an interpretation of general acceptance based upon the customary international law standard sets the threshold too high, and it is appropriate to adopt a lower standard in order to give 'effective content to the general yet rather vague obligations of the flag state'.[229] This approach would still appear to be premised upon the need to demonstrate actual practice, albeit with a lower threshold. The problem is that proponents of such an approach have not specified how much acceptance is required, and, thus, it still begs the question of what is meant by 'generally accepted'. In any case, it would seem that this question can only be judged on a case-by-case basis.

6.4.1.2 *Flag State control and enforcement*

It is not only necessary for flag States to apply international rules and standards to ships flying their flag, but they must also take enforcement action. Article 217 of UNCLOS emphasizes that 'states shall ensure compliance by vessels flying their flag or of their registry with applicable international rules and standards [and] flag states shall provide for the effective enforcement of such rules, standards, laws and regulations, wherever a violation occurs'.[230] Flag States cannot be considered to be under an obligation to prevent every single violation by a vessel flying their flag. Rather, they bear a due diligence obligation to take all appropriate measures to prevent violations.[231] In order to understand the content of this due diligence obligation, one must look to the content of the other relevant treaties, which generally foresee two ways in which flag States are expected to ensure compliance with international standards.

---

[228] Ibid. See also International Law Commission, 'Commentary to the Draft Articles on the Law of the Sea' (1958–II) *YbILC* 281. The example used by the Commission is the International Regulations on Signals, which until 1972, were not contained in a binding instrument. See also *The Scotia* (1871) 187.

[229] *Request for an Advisory Opinion Submitted by the Sub-Regional Fisheries Commission (2015),* Separate Opinion of Judge Paik, para. 24.

[230] See also Article 217(4): 'if a vessel commits a violation of rules and standards … the flag State … shall provide for immediate investigation and where appropriate institute proceedings in respect of the alleged violation irrespective of where the violation occurred or where the pollution caused by such violation has occurred or been spotted'. See also Article 217(6):

> States shall, at the written request of any State, investigate any violation alleged to have been committed by vessels flying their flag. If satisfied that sufficient evidence is available to enable proceedings to be brought in respect of the alleged violation, flag States shall without delay institute such proceedings in accordance with their laws.

[231] For an analogy, see flag State responsibilities in relation to fishing: *Request for an Advisory Opinion Submitted by the Sub-Regional Fisheries Commission (2015)* para. 125.

First, flag States are responsible for issuing certificates for ships flying their flag. A general obligation to carry out periodic inspections is contained in UNCLOS,[232] whilst requirements that are more detailed can be found in IMO regulatory treaties themselves. For example, under the Annexes to the MARPOL Convention, flag States are required to inspect vessels flying their flag at regular intervals and issue them with certificates of compliance.[233] Such certificates should only be issued following a survey of the ship, carried out by officials of the flag State or by classification societies acting on behalf of the flag State, referred to in the relevant treaties as 'recognized organizations'.[234] The initial certification of a ship must also be followed by subsequent periodic inspections to ensure that the ship continues to comply with international standards. The SOLAS Convention also requires regular surveys and certification of all vessels,[235] with oil tankers and bulk carriers being expected to undergo extended surveys, owing to the particular threats that they pose.[236] The frequency of inspections is governed by each individual treaty. If a vessel no longer meets the standards required by the treaty, its certificate will be withdrawn and it should not be permitted to sail under the flag of the inspecting State.

Second, flag States are also expected to investigate and prosecute suspected violations of international standards. The MARPOL Convention calls upon flag States to criminalize violations of the regulations[237] and it provides that 'if the Administration is informed of ... a violation and is satisfied that sufficient evidence is available to enable proceedings to be brought in respect of the alleged violation, it shall cause such proceedings to be taken as soon as possible, in accordance with its law'.[238] This provision is drafted as an obligation, and it follows that failure to bring proceedings when there is evidence of a violation may itself amount to a breach of the Convention by the flag State. However, before it can take action, a flag State must have evidence pertaining to a potential violation. It would be almost impossible for a flag State to constantly monitor all of the ships flying its flag, wherever they were in the world. It, therefore, relies upon the provision of information by other States. Both UNCLOS[239] and the MARPOL Convention[240] assume that other States will provide information to the flag State concerning alleged violations and they encourage cooperation to this end.

---

[232] UNCLOS, Article 217(3).

[233] MARPOL Annex I, Regulations 6–8; MARPOL Annex II, Regulations 8–10; MARPOL Annex IV, Regulations 4–6.

[234] MARPOL Annex I, Regulation 6.3.1; MARPOL Annex II, Regulation 8.2.1. See also Guidelines for the Authorization of Organizations Acting on Behalf of the Administration, IMO Assembly Resolution A.739(19) (1993).

[235] SOLAS Convention, Regulations I/6–I/14.

[236] SOLAS Convention, Regulation XI-1/2. See also Guidelines on the Enhanced Programme of Inspection during Surveys of Bulk Carriers and Oil Tankers, IMO Resolution A.744(18) (1993) as amended.

[237] MARPOL Convention, Article 4(1). The regulations themselves contain an exception for liability if they are not committed intentionally; see e.g. MARPOL Annex II, Reg. 3.1.2.

[238] MARPOL Convention, Article 4(1).   [239] UNCLOS, Article 94(5).

[240] MARPOL Convention, Article 6(1).

Generally speaking, the record of flag States in inspecting vessels and investigating potential violations of safety and environmental standards has not been impressive. In particular, with the rise of open registries, some flag States have been accused of lowering their standards in order to attract more vessels to fly their flag, with shipowners 'looking for the cheapest option, with the fewest constraints and the least number of questions asked'.[241] Despite these problems, the International Tribunal for the Law of the Sea (ITLOS) has rejected the argument that the lack of control by a flag State over a vessel means that another State could exercise enforcement jurisdiction.[242] The Tribunal thus reconfirmed the predominant role of flag States and the need to address their compliance with international principles, rules, and standards through cooperative mechanisms. The key means foreseen by UNCLOS for addressing poor performance by a flag State is found in Article 94(6), which provides that '[a] State which has clear grounds to believe that proper jurisdiction and control with respect to a ship have not been exercised may report the fact to the flag State. Upon receiving such a report, the flag State shall investigate the matter and, if appropriate, take any action necessary to remedy the situation'.[243] Failure to respond would amount to a violation of the Convention, and the complaining State could potentially bring legal proceedings against the flag State under the general dispute settlement provisions of the Convention.[244] In practice, there are no cases in which a flag State has been held to account in this manner, and the effect of these procedures has thus been limited.

Given the reluctance of States to employ legal procedures to address flag State performance, the IMO has sought to develop alternative mechanisms to deal with these issues. The need for more consistent application of shipping standards by flag States was recognized by the IMO in the early 1990s, when it decided to set up the Flag State Implementation Sub-Committee. The mandate of the Sub-Committee included identifying the reasons why States may have difficulties in fully implementing relevant IMO instruments and considering proposals to assist States in implementing IMO instruments. In other words, as with other regimes, the focus has been on facilitating compliance. The Sub-Committee took a number of steps in this direction. Initially, it produced a self-assessment form, which was intended to assist States in identifying deficiencies in their processes of monitoring vessels flying their flag.[245] There were various discussions about whether or not the self-assessment form should be made compulsory, but it was ultimately decided that it was up to States to undertake this process voluntarily.[246] Subsequently, the Sub-Committee

---

[241] C Horrocks, 'Thoughts on the Respective Roles of Flag States and Port States' in MH Nordquist and JN Moore (eds), *Current Maritime Issues and the International Maritime Organization* (Martinus Nijhoff Publishers 1999) 196.

[242] *The M/V Saiga Case (No. 2)* (1999) para. 82.   [243] UNCLOS, Article 94(6).

[244] Ibid, Article 286.

[245] See Report of the Maritime Safety Committee at Its Seventy-Fourth Session, Document MSC 74/24/Add.1 (2001) Annex 11.

[246] See AJ Roach, 'Alternatives for Achieving Flag State Implementation and Quality Shipping', in MH Nordquist and JN Moore (eds), *Current Maritime Issues and the International Maritime Organization* (Martinus Nijhoff 1999) 151–75.

developed a MSAS, which was approved by the IMO Assembly in 2005.[247] The MSAS addresses both the adoption of laws to implement IMO standards and action taken by States to enforce those standards.[248] Like the self-assessment form, the audit scheme was initially voluntary in nature. However, after a few years of operating the MSAS on a voluntary basis, the IMO Assembly decided to make it mandatory.[249] Amendments to the relevant IMO treaties make it obligatory for States to undergo an audit of the way in which they implement their commitments from 1 January 2016. This initiative signifies an important change in the way that the IMO oversees the implementation of regulatory treaties, and, therefore, it is important to understand how the audit scheme will operate.

It is expected that all Member States shall be audited at least every seven years.[250] Those States which have not undergone a voluntary audit will be audited first, followed by other States. Audits will be carried out by independent auditors, chosen from a list of individuals nominated by Member States. Minimum requirements for auditors are set by the IMO, and the IMO Secretary-General will verify that nominations meet the standard.[251] Auditors will both review the national legislative and policy framework of the States being audited and conduct an audit visit. The auditors will produce a report identifying both good practices and remaining challenges, and this report will be shared with the audited State and the IMO Secretary-General. The scheme will be overseen by the Sub-Committee on the Implementation of IMO Instruments, (III Sub-Committee) established to replace the Flag State Implementation Sub-Committee.

Whilst the MSAS is a welcome development, it is also important to recognize its limitations. The MSAS is intended to be 'positive and constructive in approach',[252] with the aim of providing feedback to the audited Member State. The idea is that Members States will then respond to this feedback and improve their performances. States are required to formulate a programme of action to address the findings of the audit as a response to the interim audit report.[253] Technical assistance may be provided to Member States to assist them in implementing the recommendations arising from the audit process.[254] The action plan will then form the basis of an audit follow-up in order to ensure that corrective actions have been completed by the audited State.[255] Yet, the audit process is subject to a significant degree of confidentiality.[256] In its present guise, not even other Member States will receive a copy of the final audit report without the agreement of the audited State. The only way in which other Member States can learn about the outcomes of the MSAS is if the State

---

[247] Framework and Procedures for the Voluntary IMO Members State Audit Scheme, IMO Assembly Resolution A.974(24) (2005).

[248] The MSAS covers all obligations of States under the relevant treaties, including as coastal States and port States, but it pays particular attention to flag State performance.

[249] IMO Assembly Resolution A.1067(28) (2013) contains the Framework and Procedures for the conducting of audits (Audit Framework); IMO Assembly Resolution A.1070(28) (2013) contains the IMO Instruments Implementation Code (III Code), which provides the audit standard for the purposes of the MSAS.

[250] Audit Framework, para. 4.1.1.   [251] Ibid, para. 4.4.1.   [252] Ibid, para. 6.1.1.

[253] Ibid, para. 7.2.1.   [254] Ibid, para. 9.1.   [255] Ibid, para. 9.1.

[256] Ibid, paras 6.2.4–6.2.5.

concerned agrees to its publication or through an anonymized consolidated audit summary produced by the IMO Secretariat.[257] This lack of transparency means that other States will not have access to information that would allow them to put pressure on particular flag States which are discovered to have a poor compliance record. It also limits the ability of commercial actors, such as shipping charterers, to take into account relevant information when making business decisions.[258] In this respect, the MSAS is very different from the compliance mechanisms developed under other sectoral treaties dealing with protection of the marine environment, and there is a risk that it will generate significantly less compliance pull.[259]

If the application and enforcement of international rules and standards relied exclusively on flag State jurisdiction, the international regime could be considered highly ineffective. However, a number of mechanisms have been developed to compensate for the weaknesses in flag State performance and they will be considered below.

6.4.2 Coastal State jurisdiction

6.4.2.1 *Coastal State prescriptive jurisdiction in the territorial sea*

Given their interests in preventing and punishing pollution affecting their own territory or waters, coastal States can play a particularly important role in regulating pollution in close proximity to their coast. Both the IMO regulatory treaties[260] and UNCLOS foresee a role for coastal States in prescribing and enforcing international standards against any ships operating in their coastal waters. The scope of coastal State jurisdiction will depend, however, on the location of a vessel and the type of standard that is being prescribed or enforced.

Prior to the conclusion of UNCLOS, coastal States had been limited to prescribing and enforcing pollution laws in their narrow belt of territorial sea. This power is codified in Article 21 of UNCLOS, which contains a broad power that covers pollution, as well as other potential environmental effects from shipping. The coastal State has complete discretion in setting discharge and operational (e.g. speed restrictions) standards for ships in the territorial sea,[261] but it is more limited in its powers when it comes to setting standards relating to other matters. In this regard, coastal States may only adopt regulations not exceeding 'generally accepted' international rules or standards on the construction, design, manning, or equipment of ships.[262] As noted above, general acceptance can be linked to either the entry into force of an international treaty or widespread and consistent State practice. This rule of reference is designed to limit the powers of coastal States in order to prevent the proliferation of design, construction, or equipment standards which would significantly hamper the exercise of navigational rights by vessels. Therefore, if the coastal State

---

[257] Ibid, para. 6.3.5.
[258] See H Sampson and M Bloor, 'When Jack Gets out of the Box: The Problems of Regulating a Global Industry' (2007) 41 *Sociology* 551, 558.
[259] Contrast e.g. Chapters 4 and 5. [260] For example, MARPOL Convention, Article 4(1).
[261] See Ringbom (n8) 124. [262] UNCLOS, Article 21(2).

wishes to set higher standards, it must seek the agreement of other IMO Members. One way in which it could do this is through the proposal of a Special Area under the MARPOL Convention, discussed above.

Coastal States may also prescribe special navigational measures to protect a particular ecological feature in its territorial sea, provided they do not have the practical effect of impairing the right of innocent passage.[263] UNCLOS explicitly mentions the prescription of sea lanes, traffic separation schemes, or other regulations for the passage of ships.[264] The IMO has produced guidance on the use of routeing measures,[265] which should be taken into account by the coastal State,[266] although they are able to prescribe such measures unilaterally.[267]

Certain categories of vessels receive particular attention because of their potential effects on maritime safety and the marine environment. Thus, the Convention provides that 'in particular tankers, nuclear-powered ships and ships carrying nuclear or other inherently dangerous or noxious substances or materials may be required to confine their passage to ... sea lanes'[268] and further that 'foreign nuclear-powered ships and ships carrying nuclear or other inherently dangerous or noxious substances shall, when exercising the right of innocent passage through the territorial sea, carry documents and observe special precautionary measures established for such ships by international agreements'.[269] These powers are compatible with a right to demand notification of hazardous ships entering the territorial sea, allowing affected coastal States to make appropriate contingency plans in order to prevent or minimize an incident involving such vessels.[270] Yet, some authors have gone as far as to argue that international law has evolved to allow coastal States to disallow the passage through the territorial sea of particularly high-risk vessels, such as those carrying nuclear cargoes. For example, Sage-Fuller suggests that 'while UNCLOS does not explicitly authorise coastal States to take such steps to restrict innocent passage, it is arguable that elements of the precautionary principle can provide such legal justification, if used to interpret Article 19 of UNCLOS, and the international customary right of innocent passage'.[271] However, this interpretation is difficult to reconcile with the explicit recognition in the relevant articles of the Convention that

---

[263] Ibid, Article 24(1)(a).   [264] Ibid, Article 22(1). See further IMO Guidance.

[265] General Provisions on Ships' Routeing (as amended), IMO Assembly Resolution A.572(14) (1985). See above.

[266] UNCLOS, Article 22(3).

[267] See T Henriksen, 'Conservation of Marine Biodiversity and the International Maritime Organization', in C Voigt (ed.), *The Rule of Law for Nature* (CUP 2013) 344. It has been noted that coastal States often seek IMO approval of such measures in practice because they value international recognition; see JE Noyes, 'The Territorial Sea and Contiguous Zone', in DR Rothwell et al (eds), *The Oxford Handbook on the Law of the Sea* (OUP 2015) 106; F Spadi, 'Navigation in Marine Protected Areas: National and International Law' (2000) 31 *ODIL* 285, 290.

[268] UNCLOS, Article 22(2).   [269] Ibid, Article 23.

[270] JM Van Dyke, 'The Legal Regime governing Sea Transport of Ultrahazardous Radioactive Materials' (2002) 33 *ODIL* 77–108. This view is also supported for example by the Maltese declaration to the Convention.

[271] B Sage-Fuller, *The Precautionary Principle in Marine Environmental Law* (Routledge 2013) 51. See also JM Van Dyke, 'Applying the Precautionary Principle to Ocean Shipments of Radioactive Materials' (1996) 27 *ODIL* 379–97.

these vessels have a right of innocent passage. It follows that a complete ban on such ships, even though it has been advocated by some States,[272] appears to be a violation of UNCLOS,[273] and any such ban would require agreement from other IMO Members and a change of international rules.

If a coastal State wishes to take special navigational measures in an area containing straits used for international navigation, its discretion is further limited as ships have a right of uninterrupted transit passage through such waters.[274] UNCLOS expressly foresees the prescription of special navigational regimes in international straits, but only with the approval of the IMO.[275] On the face of it, it would appear that the range of measures that can be applied in international straits is limited to sea lanes and traffic separation schemes.[276] In practice, other measures, such as ship reporting schemes, have been applied with the agreement of the IMO.[277] The need for approval provides an important safeguard against the imposition of disproportionately burdensome measures by littoral States. For example, when Australia and Papua New Guinea proposed the adoption of mandatory pilotage in the Torres Straits in order to prevent incidents that could have a serious impact on vulnerable marine ecosystems, there were strong voices of opposition at the IMO, arguing that transit passage was one of the most important navigational rights in the Convention and exceptions should be limited.[278] The IMO thus restricted itself to recommending that vessels should act in accordance with the system of pilotage adopted by Australia, falling short of an endorsement of compulsory pilotage in the strait.[279] This example illustrates the limits on coastal State jurisdiction in international straits,[280] as well as how IMO Members may be reluctant to agree to restrictive navigational measures that go beyond those measures identified in UNCLOS.

6.4.2.2 Coastal State prescriptive jurisdiction in the EEZ

One of the major advances achieved at the Third United Nations Conference on the Law of the Sea was the extension of jurisdiction of coastal States over environmental matters. UNCLOS extends the power of coastal States to prescribe and

---

[272] See e.g. the declarations of Bangladesh, Ecuador, Egypt, Malaysia, Oman, Saudi Arabia, and Yemen.

[273] This view is supported by the declarations of the Netherlands. See also Spadi (n267).

[274] UNCLOS, Article 38.   [275] Ibid, Article 41.   [276] Ibid.

[277] For example, the mandatory ship reporting system in the Dover Straits, approved in Resolution MSC.85(70) (1998) and amended by Resolution MSC.251(83) (2007); mandatory ship reporting system in the Straits of Malacca and Singapore, approved in Resolution MSC.73(69) (1998); mandatory ship reporting system in the Straits of Gibraltar, approved Resolution MSC.63(67) (1996).

[278] See e.g. IMO Document LEG 89/16 (2004) paras 232–3.

[279] IMO Resolution MEPC.133(53) (2005) para. 3. For a discussion, see e.g. RC Beckman, 'PSSAs and Transit Passage—Australia's pilotage system in the Torres Strait Challenges the IMO and UNCLOS' (2007) 38 *ODIL* 325–57; S Bateman and M White, 'Compulsory Pilotage in the Torres Strait: Overcoming Unacceptable Risks to a Sensitive Marine Environment' (2009) 40 *ODIL* 184–203.

[280] Australia attempted to circumvent this limitation by imposing prior compulsory pilotage through the strait as a condition to entry into port; see S Kopela, 'Port-State Jurisdiction, Extraterritoriality, and the Protection of Global Commons' (2016) 47 *ODIL* 89, 101–2. See also the discussion of port State jurisdiction and control below.

enforce pollution standards against shipping up to 200 nautical miles from its baselines.[281] In order to ensure that coastal States do not place too many constraints on the freedom of navigation within the EEZ, however, their prescriptive jurisdiction is limited by the requirement that any laws and regulations must conform to generally accepted international rules and standards.[282] This phrase has the same meaning as discussed above but it serves a different purpose in the present context by imposing a ceiling on coastal State regulation, thereby preventing excessive regulation by coastal States in their EEZ. A coastal State's compliance with this provision can be challenged through the dispute settlement provisions in the Convention.[283]

If a coastal State wishes to impose higher discharge standards on vessels navigating in the EEZ, or if it wishes to adopt special navigation measures in this zone, it must seek the approval of the 'competent international organization' in accordance with Article 211(6) of the Convention. Proposals for Special Areas, ECAs, or routeing measures are the key means through which States have sought to operationalize this provision in practice, although the text of Article 211(6) would also appear to permit other types of measures that are not explicitly covered by IMO instruments and it can be interpreted to provide an independent legal basis for the prescription of innovative environmental measures, such as the imposition of speed restrictions, compulsory pilotage, or the introduction of environmental fees.[284]

A special regime also applies to ice-covered waters by virtue of Article 234 of the Convention, which provides that:

coastal states have the right to adopt and enforce non-discriminatory laws and regulations for the prevention, reduction and control of marine pollution from vessels in ice covered areas within the limits of the EEZ, where particularly severe climatic conditions and the presence of ice-covering such areas for most of the year create obstructions or exceptional hazards to navigation, and pollution of the marine environment could cause major harm to or irreversible disturbance of the ecological balance.

The precise application of this provision is subject to some debate, but it is clear that it gives a broader power to coastal States to adopt unilateral standards than would otherwise be the case. In practice, States have cooperated on the adoption of standards for vessels in ice-covered areas, and the IMO has recently adopted the International Code for Ships Operating in Polar Waters, which will be mandatory under both the SOLAS Convention and the MARPOL Convention, requiring

---

[281] It has been noted by some authors that the phrase 'laws and regulations for the prevention, reduction and control of marine pollution' is ambiguous and whilst it would probably include discharge standards, it is not entirely clear which, if any, construction, design, and equipment standards would fall within this category; see B Marten, 'The Enforcement of Shipping Standards under UNCLOS' (2011) 10 *WMUJMA* 45–61. Even if it may be difficult to come up with a clear-cut definition, it would appear that some construction, design, and equipment standards do fall within this category.

[282] UNCLOS, Article 211(5).   [283] Ibid, Article 297(1)(c).

[284] K Gjerde and D Freestone, 'Particularly Sensitive Sea Areas—An Important Environmental Concept at a Turning-Point' (1994) 9 *IJMCL* 431, 432.

ships operating in both the Arctic and Antarctic to meet higher standards of construction, design, equipment and manning.[285]

6.4.2.3 Coastal State enforcement jurisdiction

The extension of coastal State power to prescribe pollution standards for ships is accompanied by a power to enforce those standards. However, the scope of enforcement power is dependent upon the location of a violation and its effects on the marine environment.

In the territorial sea, the coastal State is given the power to enforce its laws and regulations on pollution,[286] subject to safeguards that ensure that these powers are not utilized in an arbitrary manner.[287] In the EEZ, the Convention places additional limits on the ability of the coastal State to enforce such standards against foreign-flagged vessels. The precise powers of the coastal State in this regard depend on the degree of harm caused or threatened to the marine environment. A coastal State may inspect a vessel at sea if it has clear grounds for believing that a violation has resulted in 'a substantial discharge causing or threatening significant pollution of the marine environment'.[288] In contrast, judicial proceedings may only be brought if there is 'clear objective evidence' of a violation that results in 'a discharge causing major damage or threat of major damage to the coastline or related interests of the coastal State, or to any resources of its territorial sea or exclusive economic zone'.[289] Although there is some ambiguity in what precisely constitutes major damage for the purposes of this provision, it is clearly a high threshold. Moreover, clear objective evidence appears to be a higher standard than 'clear grounds for believing'.[290] This choice of language reinforces that this power is only intended to apply in rare circumstances and there is little doubt that 'the jurisdictional balance leans heavily in favour of the navigational interests'.[291] If this threshold is not met, the coastal State is restricted to gathering information about the vessel and its voyage and passing it on to the flag State.[292] On receipt of such information, the flag State is expected to take action in accordance with the provisions on flag State enforcement, considered above.[293] Unfortunately, the record of flag States in providing information on what action has been taken has traditionally been poor.[294]

---

[285] See Resolution MSC.386(94) (2014); Resolution MSC.385(94) (2014); Resolution MEPC.264(68) (2015); Resolution MEPC.265(68) (2015). For a discussion, see J Bai, 'The IMO Polar Code: The Emerging Rules of Arctic Shipping Governance' (2015) 30 *IJMCL* 674–99.

[286] UNCLOS, Article 220(2).

[287] For an analysis, see EJ Molenaar, *Coastal State Jurisdiction over Vessel-Source Pollution* (Kluwer Law International 1998) 246.

[288] UNCLOS, Article 220(5).   [289] Ibid, Article 220(6).

[290] See A Pozdnakova, *Criminal Jurisdiction over Perpetrators in Ship-Source Pollution Cases* (Martinus Nijhoff 2012) 109.

[291] H Ringbom, 'Preventing Pollution from Ships—Reflections on the "Adequacy" of Existing Rules' (1999) 8 *RECIEL* 21, 25.

[292] UNCLOS, Articles 220(3), (5).   [293] Ibid, Article 217(4).

[294] See T Ijlstra, 'Enforcement of MARPOL: Deficient or Impossible?' (1989) 20 *MPB* 596–7.

Even if the coastal State is able to bring proceedings, there are several safeguards in place to protect the interests of the flag State and the vessel.

First, the Convention makes clear that the coastal State is obliged to observe basic due process rights of the accused,[295] and if a prosecution is successful, it may only impose monetary penalties for a violation of its pollution laws.[296] The only exception to this latter restriction is if the violation was a wilful and serious act of pollution committed within the territorial sea, in which case, the coastal State may be permitted to impose prison sentences on the offender.[297]

A second safeguard on the enforcement powers of a coastal State within the EEZ requires that State to release the vessel 'promptly subject to reasonable procedures such as bonding or other appropriate financial security'.[298] The only exception to this rule is if the vessel would present 'an unreasonable threat of damage to the marine environment', in which case prompt release may be 'refused or made conditional upon proceeding to the nearest appropriate repair yard'.[299] The prompt release obligation is designed to strike a 'fair balance' between 'the interest of the coastal State to take appropriate measures as may be necessary to ensure compliance with the laws and regulations adopted by it on the one hand and the interest of the flag State in securing prompt release of its vessels and their crews from detention on the other'.[300] Failure to comply with the prompt release procedures is subject to a special dispute settlement procedure in Part XV of UNCLOS, which allows the flag State or its representative to apply for the prompt release of the vessel.[301] A court or tribunal hearing a case under the prompt release procedures is limited to deciding upon the question of release and it may not enter into the merits of the arrest.[302] Nevertheless, the court or tribunal is competent to decide not only whether a vessel has been released, but also whether the amount of the bond or financial security set by the detaining State is reasonable.[303] If not, the court or tribunal may set the bond itself.[304] Although it is not explicitly addressed in Article 292, it can be presumed that in the case of arrests for violation of pollution laws, a court or tribunal can also be asked to decide upon the reasonableness of a refusal to release the vessel on the grounds that it poses a continuing threat to the marine environment.[305]

Indeed, the flag State has a right of pre-emption against the coastal State and it may insist that a prosecution for offences committed in the EEZ of the coastal State is suspended, if it wishes to initiate legal action against the ship itself.[306] There are two exceptions to the rule of flag State pre-emption, just described. The flag State has no right of pre-emption if the proceedings relate to a case of major damage to the coastal State.[307] As noted above, there is an ambiguity surrounding the concept

---

[295] UNCLOS, Article 230(3). [296] Ibid, Articles 230(1) and (2).

[297] Ibid, Article 230(2). [298] UNCLOS, Article 226(1)(b).

[299] Ibid, Article 226(1)(c). [300] *The "Monte Confurco" Case* (2000) para. 70.

[301] UNCLOS, Article 292. [302] Ibid, Article 292(3).

[303] *The "M/V Saiga" Case* (1997) para. 77; *The "Hoshinmaru" Case* (2007) para. 65. See also ITLOS Rules of Procedure, Article 113(2).

[304] UNCLOS, Article 292(4). [305] Ibid, Article 226(1)(c).

[306] Ibid, Article 228(1). [307] Ibid.

of major damage, and any disagreement between the flag State and the coastal State would have to be submitted to compulsory dispute settlement under UNCLOS. In addition, the flag State cannot insist that proceedings by the coastal State are suspended if 'the flag state in question has repeatedly disregarded its obligation to enforce effectively the applicable international rules and standards in respect of violations committed by its vessels'.[308] This allows the coastal State to point to the poor enforcement record of the flag State in order to justify a prosecution. Yet, the precise scope of this exception is also ambiguous.

There are some logistical problems if the flag State does decide to intervene in this manner, not least the fact that evidence may only be available in the language of the coastal State, and it may need translating into the language of the flag State before it will be admissible before flag State courts.[309] Indeed, countries classify pollution offences in different ways, and their courts may have substantially different procedural rules, all of which complicate cooperation on these matters.[310]

Beyond the question of jurisdiction and applicable laws, the prosecution of vessels for violation of pollution laws at sea comes with a number of practical challenges. Identification of which discharges exceed international limits and even tracing a particular discharge back to an identifiable vessel have been described as 'delicate and difficult problems'.[311] Technology has provided some solutions, through the development of on-board monitoring equipment, satellite surveillance,[312] and drones.[313] International cooperation can also help to ease the burden on coastal States to enforce their pollution laws throughout their maritime zones. To this end, States in several regions have set up specific mechanisms aimed at facilitating cooperation in criminal investigations and proceedings against vessels for pollution offences,[314] including coordination of airborne surveillance.[315] These measures will assist in the enforcement of pollution standards at sea, although challenges will always remain in policing large maritime zones. It is perhaps for this reason that alternatives to at-sea enforcement have been developed.

---

[308] Ibid.

[309] See e.g. Helsinki Commission Guidelines on Ensuring Successful Convictions of Offenders of Anti-Pollution Regulations at Sea (2000) 21, recognizing that 'attention must be paid to possible language barriers' and advising the use of English.

[310] Ibid, 26.   [311] Ijlstra (n294) 597.

[312] See e.g. BBC News, 'Ship Firm Fined in 'Landmark' Cornish Pollution Case', 4 October 2013. <http://www.bbc.co.uk/news/uk-england-cornwall-24400845>.

[313] See e.g. Ship & Bunker Website, 'Shippers Seek Drone Enforcement of ECAs', 5 June 2014. <http://shipandbunker.com/news/world/375693-shippers-seek-drone-enforcement-of-ecas>.

[314] For example, the North Sea Network of Investigators and Prosecutors, established at the 2002 Fifth North Sea Conference; see also Helsinki Convention, Annex IV, Article 2, and HELCOM Recommendation 6/13 (1985); Barcelona Convention Decision IG.21/9—Establishment of a Mediterranean Network of Law Enforcement Officials Relating to MARPOL within the Framework of the Barcelona Convention (2013).

[315] HELCOM Recommendation 34E/4 (2015); 1983 Agreement for Cooperation Dealing with Pollution of the North Sea by Oil and Other Harmful Substances (as amended) (EIF 1 September 1989), Article 6A, supplemented by Aerial Observations Handbook (2016).

6.4.3 Port State enforcement jurisdiction

Port State enforcement jurisdiction generally refers to the situation in which criminal proceedings are brought against a vessel by the port State authorities for a violation of international or national standards that has taken place at sea before the ship has entered port. A major advantage of port State enforcement jurisdiction in terms of enforcing environmental standards is that the State is able to address discharge offences without impeding navigation.[316] UNCLOS envisages three main situations in which port States may exercise such an enforcement power in relation to pollution offences occurring before the vessel entered port.

First, a port State may bring proceedings against a foreign vessel that is voluntarily in port if it is suspected of committing pollution offences in that State's own territorial sea or EEZ.[317] In this situation, the port State is enforcing standards that it has adopted on the basis of its coastal State prescriptive jurisdiction[318] and it can thus be considered as a form of quasi-territorial jurisdiction.[319] A port State may also bring proceedings against a vessel that has committed a violation beyond its waters if it has been affected by the discharge itself.[320] This is a form of 'effects jurisdiction' recognized by international law.[321] In either situation, the port State does not need to act immediately against a vessel having committed such a violation. UNCLOS sets a limitation period of three years for the commencement of proceedings against a vessel,[322] and, therefore, a State may bring proceedings against a vessel if it calls at port during this period.

The second scenario in which UNCLOS foresees the exercise of port State jurisdiction is against a foreign vessel suspected of committing an unlawful discharge in violation of applicable international rules and standards and the port State is requested to bring proceedings by another State, either an affected coastal State or the flag State.[323] In these circumstances, the port State is under an obligation to comply with any request from another State 'as far as is practicable'.[324] Even if the port State does not bring proceedings itself, it may be requested to collect evidence of a violation on behalf of another State.[325]

The third aspect of port State jurisdiction is the commencement of proceedings against discharges on the high seas committed in violation of applicable international rules and standards.[326] This innovative provision establishes a sort of 'universal jurisdiction' over pollution offences on the high seas,[327] providing an example of the

---

[316] T Keselj, 'Port State Jurisdiction in Respect of Pollution from Ships' (1999) 30 *ODIL* 127, 149; RR Churchill, 'Port State Jurisdiction Relating to the Safety of Shipping and Pollution from Ships—What Degree of Extraterritoriality?' (2016) 31 *IJMCL* 442, 459.

[317] UNCLOS, Article 220(1).   [318] See Molenaar (n287) 130.

[319] EJ Molenaar, 'Port and Coastal States', in DR Rothwell et al (eds), *Oxford Handbook of the Law of the Sea* (OUP 2015) 289.

[320] UNCLOS, Article 218(2).   [321] Keselj (n316) 136.

[322] UNCLOS, Article 228(2).   [323] Ibid, Article 218(2).

[324] Ibid, Article 218(3).   [325] See MARPOL Convention, Article 6(5).

[326] UNCLOS, Article 218.

[327] Keselj (n316) 136; P Birnie, AE Boyle and C Redgwell, *International Law and the Environment* (3rd edn, OUP 2009) 422.

emergence of the protection of the marine environment as a common concern of the international community,[328] and it seeks to compensate for some of the weaknesses of exclusive flag State enforcement on the high seas, noted earlier.[329] This power assumes that port States will have the political will to enforce such laws on behalf of the international community as a whole.[330] Yet, in practice, there are few known cases of this power being utilized.[331]

Other challenges or limitations also arise in the context of port State enforcement. All of these scenarios presuppose that the port State will have sufficient evidence of a pollution offence to allow a prosecution. The existence of an offence may be apparent from evidence contained on board, such as entries into one of the records required to be maintained under the MARPOL Convention,[332] although as has been noted by commentators, 'examination of on-board documents required by MARPOL, such as the oil and garbage record books, rarely in itself provides sufficient evidence of discharges at sea'.[333] It must also be noted that, as with coastal State enforcement jurisdiction, the power of port States to commence proceedings under Article 218 is subject to the right of pre-emption from the flag State or an affected coastal State, as well as other safeguards.[334]

A slightly different form of port State jurisdiction relates to those situations in which a port State sets and enforces standards or conditions that must be met by a vessel when it enters into port. Such conditions may relate to the construction of the vessel or the equipment carried on board, such as the ban on single-hulled vessels imposed by the United States following the Exxon Valdez oil spill in Alaska. Alternatively, it may relate to whether a vessel has followed certain rules or procedures on the voyage prior to it arriving at port: for example, the Australian requirements relating to compulsory pilotage through the Torres Strait, discussed above. Whilst the Convention does not expressly deal with the enforcement of such conditions, it is generally accepted that a port State has various options as a matter of general international law. First, the port State may simply deny access to its ports, although it has been suggested that this sort of action is better considered as an exercise of sovereignty rather than enforcement jurisdiction per se.[335] Alternatively, the port State may use its criminal law to sanction any offence in this regard. For example, it is common for States to require vessels to provide information relating to their voyage and penalize the presentation of false information to port inspectors, even if the information concerned an activity that took place on the high seas

---

[328] See Y Tanaka, 'Protection of Community Interests in International Law: The Case of the Law of the Sea' (2011) 15 *MPYUNL* 329, 351.

[329] M Nordquist et al (eds), *1982 United Nations Convention on the Law of the Sea—A Commentary—Vol. IV* (Martinus Nijhoff 1991) 260.

[330] See Tanaka (n328) 354.

[331] See Churchill (n316) 464, also noting that 'in many cases port States will have little interest or incentive to prosecute a discharge violation that may have occurred on the other side of the world and incur the expenditure of time, effort and money that would be required to secure a conviction'.

[332] See MARPOL Convention, Article 6(2).   [333] Ringbom (n296) 25.

[334] UNCLOS, Articles 218(4) and 228(1).   [335] Churchill (n316) 457.

or in the maritime zones of another State.[336] The precise extent of such powers is widely debated, but many authors argue that this course of action is permissible, provided that the State concerned can show it has an interest in the condition being imposed.[337] Indeed, some authors have suggested that this form of regulation will increase in the future and it will have an important impact on the traditional allocation of authority between flag States and port States, as the latter are able to use an increasing range of information in order to verify whether or not conditions have been met.[338]

6.4.4 Port State inspection and control

Whereas port State jurisdiction largely concerns the enforcement of pollution standards through criminal proceedings, port State control generally involves the physical inspection of vessels and the imposition of administrative measures on ships found to be defective.[339] Port State control is thus not punitive in character, as it is primarily aimed at remedying any deficiency in order to ensure that a vessel is safe and it is operating in compliance with, inter alia, environmental rules and standards. Nevertheless, from the shipowner's perspective, being subject to port State control measures is still burdensome, as 'an extra day or even a couple of extra hours of idleness in port can be very costly'.[340]

The concept of port State control over foreign vessels is found in Article 211(3) of UNCLOS, which provides that States may 'establish particular requirements for the prevention reduction and control of pollution of the marine environment as a condition for the entry of foreign vessels into their ports or internal waters'.[341] Moreover, Article 219 also refers to the ability of a port State to detain a vessel if it is considered to pose a threat to the marine environment. This power presupposes the ability of a State to inspect a vessel whilst voluntarily within its port.

There is little doubt that port States may, in the exercise of their territorial jurisdiction, unilaterally set standards with which ships must comply when they are in port.[342] However, in practice, it has been recognized that 'for most states the interests of comity with other nations and freedom of navigation have ... dictated great restraint in the unilateral regulation of foreign ships'.[343] Thus, port State control is

---

[336] See e.g. discussion in S Gehan, '*United States v Royal Caribbean Cruises Ltd*: Use of Federal "False Statements Act" to Extend Jurisdiction over Polluting Incidents into Territorial Seas of Foreign States' (2001) 7 *OCLJ* 167–83.

[337] See e.g. B Marten, 'Port State Jurisdiction, International Conventions and Extraterritoriality: An Expansive Interpretation', in H Ringbom (ed.), *Jurisdiction over Ships* (Brill 2015) 137; Kopela (n280) 108.

[338] B Marten, 'Port State Jurisdiction over Vessel Information: Territoriality, Extra-territoriality and the Future of Shipping Regulation' (2016) 31 *IJMCL* 470–98.

[339] See e.g. Molenaar (n319) 282, noting that port State control is narrower than port State jurisdiction is.

[340] Ibid, 290.   [341] UNCLOS, Article 211(3).

[342] For example, the United States 1990 Oil Pollution Act. There is some debate as to whether there are any restrictions in relation to the types of standards that may be set by a port State; see RR Churchill and AV Lowe, *The Law of the Sea* (3rd edn: MUP 1999) 63; Marten (n337) 105–39.

[343] Birnie, Boyle, and Redgwell (n327) 414.

more commonly used to police compliance with international rules and standards found in IMO regulatory treaties such as the MARPOL Convention, the SOLAS Convention, the AFS Convention, and the BWM Convention.[344] All of these treaties contain provisions setting out the measures that may be taken by port State inspectors in exercise of their port State control powers. The MARPOL Convention is typical in providing that 'any such inspection shall be limited to verifying that there is on board a valid certificate, unless there are clear grounds for believing that the condition of the ship or its equipment does not correspond substantially with the particular of that certificate'.[345] In furtherance of this provision, the IMO has agreed quite detailed guidelines concerning the conduct of port State control with a view to harmonizing national procedures as far as possible.[346] In practice, as well as verifying the existence of a certificate, an inspection will involve a rudimentary 'walk around the ship' in order to check that the condition of the vessel corresponds with the requirements of the relevant international standards.[347] The IMO guidance gives examples of clear grounds that would justify a more thorough investigation, including incomplete documentation, missing equipment, and serious structural deterioration.[348] Port State control officers may also undertake a more detailed inspection if they have been provided with information that there may be deficiencies on board a vessel.

Inspections may relate not only to the physical state of a ship and its equipment but also to operational procedures.[349] This reflects the increased emphasis on the human element in IMO instruments. IMO guidance lists a number of procedures and drills that may be checked by port State control officers during an inspection.[350] This is obviously a critical issue, given that many accidents are caused by human error rather than faults in the ship itself. Yet, this is also a difficult issue to verify, given that it involves the exercise of professional judgment by the port State control officer as to whether 'the operational proficiency of the crew as a whole is of a sufficient level to allow the ship to sail without danger to the ship or persons on board, or presenting an unreasonable threat of harm to the marine environment'.[351]

If after a more detailed inspection a vessel is found to be unseaworthy, the port State can order that it is brought into compliance with the relevant standards. IMO guidance makes clear that 'all possible efforts should be made to avoid a ship being unduly detained or delayed' and, therefore, a ship may be allowed to proceed and make repairs at a later stage.[352] Cooperation between the port State and the

---

[344] SOLAS Convention, Regulation 19 of Chapter I, Regulation 6.2 of Chapter IX, Regulation 4 of Chapter XI-1 and Regulation 9 of Chapter XI-2; MARPOL Convention, Article 5(2); see also Annex I, Regulation 11; Annex II, Regulation 16.9 (port State control of operational procedures); Annex III, Regulation 8 (port State control of operational procedures); Anti-Fouling Convention, Article 11.

[345] MARPOL Convention, Article 5(2).

[346] Procedures for Port State Control (PSC Procedures), IMO Assembly Resolution A.1052(27) (2011), replacing Resolutions A.787(19) and A.882(21).

[347] RWJ Schiferli, 'Regional Concepts of Port State Control in Europe', in E Mann Borgese (ed.) *Ocean Yearbook* 11 (UCP 2004) 206. This practice is confirmed by the IMO guidance; IMO Assembly Resolution A.1052(27) (2011) paras 2.2.4 and 2.5.1.

[348] PSC Procedures, para. 2.4.2.   [349] See e.g. SOLAS Convention, Regulation XI-1/4.

[350] PSC Procedures, Appendix 7.   [351] Ibid, para. 1.3.   [352] Ibid, para.2.3.5.

representatives of the shipowner is encouraged in order to achieve the most efficient response to addressing the problems identified by the port State.[353] However, if the deficiencies are serious, the port State has the authority to prevent the ship from leaving port until the deficiencies are rectified.[354] This should not be considered as a punitive action, but rather as a means of remedying a fault and preventing future harm to the marine environment.[355] Nevertheless, it would appear that such administrative detention would also fall within the scope of the prompt release procedures, discussed above and may, therefore, be subject to oversight by an international court and tribunal in accordance with Article 292 of UNCLOS.

Port State control has been described as 'the coastal state's most significant weapon in the fight against substandard shipping'.[356] A major advantage of port State control is that the port State may, on the basis of its territorial jurisdiction, apply international standards to all ships, regardless of whether they are flying the flag of a Party to the relevant treaty. Indeed, it is common for IMO treaties to oblige Parties to apply port State control to non-Parties 'as may be necessary to ensure that no more favourable treatment is given to such ships'.[357] This is, therefore, another important way in which international rules and standards have been universalized in practice, given that a ship wanting access to ports worldwide must comply with the international rules and standards, even if it is not required to by its own flag State.

Port State control can be made even more effective if it is applied on a regional basis. There are a number of advantages of regional port State control.[358] First, it has been convincingly argued that without some sort of assurance that other States will take similar action, few port States would be willing to adopt strict port laws for fear of loosing a competitive advantage against other ports.[359] In contrast, 'where the ports cooperate by agreeing to apply the same rules in a similar manner, then no single port seeks or acquires competitive advantage by offering to overlook sub-standard vessels'.[360] All States participating in a regional scheme are not only committed to enforcing the same international rules and standards but also

---

[353] Ibid, para.2.3.8.

[354] UNCLOS, Article 219. Indeed, the MARPOL Convention imposed an obligation on the coastal State to do so; MARPOL Convention, Article 5(2). Guidance on when it is appropriate to detain a vessel is set out in IMO Assembly Resolution A.1052(27) (2011) Appendix 2. The guidance also provides (para. 3.7.3):

> Where deficiencies which caused a detention, as referred to in paragraph 3.7.2, cannot be remedied in the port of inspection, the port State Authority may allow the ship concerned to proceed to the nearest appropriate repair yard available, as chosen by the master and agreed to by that authority, provided that the conditions agreed between the port State Authority and the flag State are complied with.

[355] UNCLOS refers to this type of action as an 'administrative measure'. According to a leading commentary, 'this presumably excludes formal legal proceedings not coming within this category of administrative measures'; Nordquist et al (n329) para. 219.8(c). See, to the contrary, Molenaar (n337) 197, who considers it to be a form of punitive action.

[356] Marten (n281) 59.   [357] For example, MARPOL Convention, Article 5(4).

[358] See Schiferli (n347) 206–7.

[359] See TL McDorman, 'Regional Port State Control Agreements: Some Issues of International Law' (2000) 5 *O&CLJ* 207, 209.

[360] Ibid.

required to harmonize their procedures so that the integrity of the inspection does not vary substantially in the different adhering States. Indeed, coordinated training of port State control officers is a key part of the cooperative framework of most Memoranda of Understanding (MOU),[361] and these endeavours will be critical in determining whether the port State control regime is perceived as successful.[362] Second, regional port State control allows the effort of enforcing international conventions to be efficiently and equitably shared between States. Finally, by sharing information through databases and other communication systems, States can more effectively employ their resources, as ships that have been inspected in one State without any problems may call at other States in the region without the need for additional inspections, whereas, when deficiencies have been detected and repairs ordered, the rectification of those deficiencies can be followed up at the next port of call within the region.

   The adoption of cooperative arrangements is explicitly foreseen by UNCLOS.[363] The first such regime was established in Western Europe in the form of the Paris MOU on Port State Control.[364] The original document committed participating States to inspect a minimum number of vessels entering their ports against a number of international treaties, including the MARPOL Convention and the SOLAS Convention.[365] Following encouragement of the IMO,[366] the concept of regional port State control was exported to a number of other regions,[367] including Asia-Pacific,[368] Latin America,[369] the Mediterranean,[370] the Indian Ocean,[371] the Gulf,[372] the Black Sea,[373] the Caribbean,[374] and West and Central Africa.[375] All of these agreements are adopted as non-binding instruments, rather than treaties, but this fact alone should not be allowed to cast doubt on the effectiveness of regional port State control regimes.[376] As noted by Anderson, despite their informal status,

---

[361] See 1982 Paris MOU, s. 7.3.2; 1993 Memorandum of Understanding on Port State Control in the Asia-Pacific Region (Tokyo MOU) (as amended), s. 6.3.2.

[362] Sampson and Bloor (n258) 558–9. See, however, the sceptical views in OF Knudsen and B Hassler, 'IMO Legislation and Its Implementation: Accident Risk, Vessel Deficiencies and National Administrative Practices' (2011) 35 *MP* 201–7.

[363] UNCLOS, Article 211(3).   [364] For the original text, see (1982) 21 *ILM* 1.

[365] The original target was 25 per cent of all ships calling at MOU ports.

[366] IMO Assembly Resolution A.682(17) (1991).

[367] It should also be noted that the European Union has adopted Directive 2009/16/EC on Port State Control.

[368] Tokyo MOU.

[369] See 1992 Latin-American Agreement on Port State Control (Viña del Mar Agreement).

[370] See 1997 Mediterranean Memorandum of Understanding on Port State Control (Mediterranean MOU).

[371] See 1998 Memorandum of Understanding on Port State Control for the Indian Ocean Region (Indian Ocean MOU).

[372] See 2005 Memorandum of Understanding on Port State Control in the Gulf Region (Riyadh MOU).

[373] See 2000 Black Sea Memorandum of Understanding on Port State Control (Black Sea MOU).

[374] See 1996 Caribbean Memorandum of Understanding on Port State Control (Caribbean MOU).

[375] See 1999 Memorandum of Understanding on Port State Control for West and Central African Region (Abuja MOU).

[376] See Keselj (n316) 19.

the MOUs create 'lasting relationships and institutions with financial implications'.[377] There are differences in the level of commitment undertaken by States,[378] but they all require individual States to take steps to inspect a certain number or percentage of vessels calling at their ports. In 2012, around 69,000 inspections were carried out by the States participating in these regimes.[379]

Over the years, cooperation between States participating in MOU arrangements has tended to deepen. For example, experience in administering the Paris MOU has led to a number of amendments being made to expand the scope of the regime and to improve its efficiency. First, the list of treaties covered by the regime has been gradually expanded over the years to include new developments, such as the AFS Convention and the BWM Convention. More significantly, in 2009, the initial numerical target for inspections was replaced with a system which takes into account the risk profile of an individual ship.[380] Under the new inspection regime, ships are designated as low risk, standard risk, or high risk, depending upon the type of vessel, their past performance in port State inspections, the performance of the shipping company in control of the ship, the classification society carrying out periodic inspections, and the flag State.[381] The ship's risk profile will dictate the scope, frequency, and priority of inspections.[382] According to the new inspection scheme, low-risk vessels will only be inspected by port State control officers every twenty-four to thirty-six months, whereas high-risk vessels will be liable for inspection every five to six months.[383] In addition, high-risk ships will always undergo an expanded inspection, whereas low-risk ships will only be subject to an initial inspection unless clear grounds are found for carrying out a more detailed inspection.[384] The participating States have also established a detention review procedure to allow a vessel operator to challenge the decision of a port State to detain the vessel. Although the outcome of the review procedure is not binding, it nevertheless provides a mechanism, as an alternative to national appeal procedures and the prompt release procedures in UNCLOS, in which the decisions of port States can be challenged.[385] As a

---

[377] D Anderson, 'Port States and the Environment', in AE Boyle and D Freestone (eds) *International Law and Sustainable Development* (OUP 1999) 332.

[378] For example, States participating in the Abuja MOU have a target of '15% of the total number of ships operating in the region … '. Abuja MOU, s. 1.3.

[379] See III Sub-Committee Report, Document III 1/18 (2014) para. 6.17.

[380] See E Rodriguez and F Piniella, 'The New Inspection Regime of the Paris MOU on Port State Control: Improvement of the System' (2012) 9 *JMR* 9–16. A similar mechanism has been adopted by the Tokyo MOU.

[381] Paris MOU, including the Thirty-Fourth Amendment (2012), Annex 7.

[382] Ibid, Annex 8.

[383] Ibid, Annex 8, para. 4. A ship that has exceeded the time limit since the last inspection is a priority-I vessel and it must be inspected when it next enters the port of a participating State. Other ships that are within the timeframe for an inspection are priority-II vessels and they may be inspected if they call at port. In order to ensure that the burden is spread as evenly as possible among the participating States, each of them is allocated an annual inspection commitment. An information system is maintained by the Secretariat to the MOU, which shows on a daily basis whether a Member State is ahead or behind the annual commitment; see Annex 11.

[384] Paris MOU, including the Thirty-Fourth Amendment (2012), Annex 9.

[385] For a description of the detention review procedure, see <https://www.parismou.org/system/files/Review%20Panel%20procedure%20Public%20Paris%20MOU%20rev6%20NIR.pdf>.

result of these changes, the Paris MOU can be considered to offer the gold standard of port State control, and some of these innovations have since been adopted in other regions.[386]

One criticism that has been levelled at regional port State control is that it 'is only effective in eradicating the operation of substandard ships in that particular region [and] it tends to shift the operation of substandard ships to other areas'.[387] However, this threat has been diminished with the expansion of port State control around the world, although there are still gaps in the system.[388] Another way in which this issue can be addressed is through the pursuit of inter-regional cooperation between MOUs.[389] Such cooperation is already taking place, with regional port State control bodies sending observers to each other's meetings.[390] On a more practical level, some MOUs actively share information on inspections and detentions, which helps in targeting high-risk vessels.[391] Many regional MOUs now contribute information to Equasis, a database sharing safety-related information on vessels.[392] Moreover, regional bodies sometimes undertake joint training events for port State control officers.[393] Such activities are particularly important in assisting developing countries to improve their port State control activities.[394] Finally, MOUs occasionally coordinate their concentrated inspection campaigns, in which they focus inspections on a particular thematic issue.[395] To improve such coordination, it has been suggested that the IMO play a more central role in setting concentrated inspection campaigns for all MOUs, with a view to both extending their reach and increasing efficiency.[396] Indeed, the IMO has been pushing for broader coordination of a range of issues through a series of workshops for port State control secretariats.[397] By increasing harmonization and information exchange, the net will close tighter on substandard shipping.

---

[386] For example, the Black Sea MOU was amended to incorporate a ship risk-profile matrix from 1 January 2016; see *Port State Control in the Black Sea Region Annual Report 2015* (2015) 3.

[387] Schiferli (n347) 213.

[388] See EJ Molenaar, 'Port State Jurisdiction: Towards Mandatory and Comprehensive Use', in D Freestone et al (eds), *The Law of the Sea: Progress and Prospects* (OUP 2006) 207.

[389] Schiferli (n347) 214–15.

[390] *Paris MOU Annual Report 2012* (2012) 16; *Tokyo MOU Annual Report 2012* (2012) 9–10.

[391] For example, the Tokyo MOU shares information held of its database with the Paris MOU, Black Sea MOU, Indian Ocean MOU, and the Vina del Mar Agreement; *Tokyo MOU Annual Report* 2012 (2012) 5–6.

[392] See <http://www.equasis.org/EquasisWeb/public/HomePage>.

[393] *Paris MOU Annual Report 2012* (2012) 12–13. See e.g. the training offered by the Tokyo MOU in other regions; *Tokyo MOU Annual Report 2012* (2012) 10–12.

[394] Molenaar (n388) 209.

[395] *Paris MOU Annual Report 2012* (2012) 11; *Tokyo MOU Annual Report 2012* (2012) 3.

[396] *Global Concentrated Inspection Campaigns—Submitted by Egypt*, Document III 1/6/10 (2014). See also P Cariou and F-C Wolff, 'Identifying Substandard Vessels through Port State Control inspections: A New Methodology for Concentrated Inspections Campaigns' (2015) 60 *MP* 27–39.

[397] See <http://www.imo.org/OurWork/Safety/Implementation/Pages/PortStateControl.aspx>.

6.5 Preparedness and Response in the Case of Shipping Incidents

It is not possible to prevent all vessel-source pollution, as accidents involving ships are often the result of human error or unpredictable events. In these circumstances, it is important to have in place rules, standards, and procedures that allow potentially affected States to act promptly in order to minimize and ameliorate damage to the marine environment. At the time of the infamous *Torrey Canyon* incident in 1967, the law in this field was unclear. In justifying its response to the casualty, the United Kingdom government invoked the doctrine of necessity under customary international law.[398] No States are recorded as objecting to this claim, which suggests that the doctrine of necessity could be invoked to prevent an imminent threat of serious environmental damage.[399] The customary international law defence may still be relevant to some situations, such as pollution caused by military or government-owned vessels, which are not covered by the subsequent developments in the treaty regime.[400] In the case of merchant shipping, however, the international community has sought to regulate this issue more explicitly with the adoption of a number of international treaties on this topic, both at the global and regional level.[401] Article 221 of UNCLOS explicitly recognizes the right of States to:

take and enforce measures beyond the territorial sea proportionate to the actual or threatened damage to protect their coastline or related interests ... from pollution or threat of pollution following upon a maritime casualty or acts relating to such a casualty, which may reasonably be expected to result in major harmful consequences.

UNCLOS is supplemented by other treaties aimed at coordinating international responses to maritime casualties,[402] including the 1990 Convention on Oil Pollution Preparedness, Prevention, and Control (OPPRC Convention),[403] which is accompanied by a Protocol, adopted in 2000, containing similar obligations for incidents involving hazardous and noxious substances.[404]

---

[398] See commentary to Article 25 of the ILC Articles on State Responsibility, in Report to the United Nations General Assembly (2001 - II) *YbILC* 82.

[399] See also *Gabcikovo-Nagymaros Project* (1997) para. 53.

[400] Birnie, Boyle, and Redgwell (n327) 426–7.

[401] Regional treaties on pollution emergencies and response have been adopted within the framework of the UNEP regional seas programme for the Baltic Sea, the Red Sea, the Arabian Gulf, the South-East Pacific, the South Pacific, the Caribbean Sea, East Africa, West Africa, the Black Sea, the Mediterranean, and the Caspian Sea. See also 1990 Lisbon Cooperation Agreement for the Protection of the Coasts and Waters of the North-East Atlantic against Pollution (EIF 1 February 2014); 1983 Bonn Agreement for Cooperation in Dealing with Pollution of the North Sea by Oil and other Harmful Substances (as amended) (EIF 1 September 1989); 2013 Agreement on Cooperation on Marine Oil Pollution Preparedness and Response in the Arctic (EIF 13 March 2014).

[402] See similar provisions in the 1969 Intervention Convention; 2007 Wreck Removal Convention.

[403] See 1990 Convention on Oil Pollution Preparedness, Prevention, and Control (OPPRC Convention) (EIF 13 May 1995).

[404] See 2000 Protocol on Preparedness, Response and Co-operation to Pollution Incidents by Hazardous and Noxious Substances (EIF 14 June 2007).

Under the OPPRC Convention, ships are required to carry an oil pollution emergency plan.[405] Any incident involving harmful substances must be reported without delay.[406] The coastal State receiving the report is then required to assess the nature, extent, and possible consequences of the oil pollution incident and inform all interested States.[407] The OPPRC Convention also requires coastal States to establish a national system for responding promptly and effectively to oil pollution incidents. At a minimum, this obligation requires States to designate a national contact point to coordinate their response and the development of a national contingency plan.[408] States should also have in place a minimum level of pre-positioned oil spill combatting equipment, as well as trained operators.[409] The Convention recognizes that, in practice, it may be more practicable for States to fulfil these obligations collectively.[410] To this end, a number of States have established regional marine pollution response arrangements.[411]

As a matter of international law, coastal States may take pre-emptive action in order to minimize the threat of pollution from a stricken vessel. Within the territorial sea, a ship which poses a threat to the 'peace, good order and security' of the coastal State will not be in innocent passage,[412] and, therefore, the coastal State may take any 'necessary steps'[413] to prevent damage to the coastal State. Even beyond the territorial sea, the coastal State may exercise extensive powers of maritime casualties provided they are 'proportionate to the actual or threatened damage ... to their coastline or related interests'.[414] The measures that could be taken by a coastal State include towing, scuppering, or destroying the ship in question. The IMO has also produced a detailed manual on oil pollution response, as well as guidelines on other technical issues,[415] which can be used to assist with clean-up operations.

In some instances, the best response to a vessel in need of assistance is to allow it to proceed to a place of refuge where repairs or other action can be taken in order to

---

[405] OPPRC Convention, Article 3(1)(a). See also MARPOL Annex I, Regulation 37.1.

[406] OPPRC Convention, Articles 4 and 5. See also MARPOL Convention, Article 8(1) and Protocol I; SOLAS Convention, Regulations V/31, VII/6, VII/7-4, and VIII/2. The IMO has encouraged coastal States to establish Maritime Assistance Services as the designated body to receive such reports; see IMO Assembly Resolution A.950(23) (2003).

[407] OPPRC Convention, Article 5.   [408] Ibid, Article 6(1).

[409] Ibid, Article 6(2). Some States operate a levy on the maritime industry in order to fund oil pollution response; see e.g. New Zealand Maritime Transport Act 1994, ss. 329–41.

[410] See also Agenda 21 (1992) para. 17.34. See also Johannesburg Programme for Further Implementation (2002) para. 36(b).

[411] Regional Marine Pollution Emergency Response Centre for the Mediterranean Sea (REMPEC); Regional Marine Pollution Emergency Information and Training Centre for the Wider Caribbean (REMPEITC-Caribe). See also the establishment of a Marine Emergency Response and Salvage Coordination Unit (MERCU) in the Arabian Gulf, which will operate three maritime emergency response centres in the north, centre, and south of the region. The centres will make available response equipment, including pollution-response vessels and multi-purpose emergency towing vessels, co-funded by contributions from the shipping industry.

[412] UNCLOS, Article 19(1). For a contrary view, see E Van Hooydonk, 'The Obligation to Offer a Place of Refuge to a Ship in Distress' (2003) *CMIY* 403, 411–12, 421–2.

[413] UNCLOS, Article 25(1).

[414] Ibid, Article 221(1). See also the 1969 Intervention Convention. The restriction of this treaty to the High Seas means it has limited application in the modern law.

[415] See <http://www.imo.org/blast/mainframe.asp?topic_id=225>.

remove the threats posed by the vessels. In cases where a vessel in distress poses a risk to human life, there is a clear duty in conventional and customary international law to allow the vessel to proceed to port or to some other safe location.[416] Where there is no threat to human life, it is less clear whether ships that are in need of assistance benefit from similar privileges.[417] In practice, coastal States have been reluctant to allow ships close to their coasts if there is a risk of serious harm. One of the best known incidents is the case of the Cypriot-registered tanker *Castor*, which was refused entry to port by seven States before it could finally safely discharge its cargo.[418]

In response to the international debate, the IMO has adopted Guidelines on Places of Refuge for Ships in Need of Assistance, which are designed to provide a framework enabling coastal States to respond effectively to a ship which requests assistance.[419] A place of refuge is defined as 'a place where a ship in need of assistance can take action to enable it to stabilize its condition and reduce the hazards to navigation, and to protect human life and the environment'.[420] The guidelines seek to promote better decision-making by encouraging the establishment of identified procedures through which situations can be addressed[421] and identifying the factors that must be taken into account in order to reach an 'objective decision' on whether or not to allow a vessel to proceed to a place of refuge.[422] Coastal States are also encouraged to deploy an inspection team 'composed of persons with expertise appropriate to the situation' in order to gather information on which to base their decision.[423] The guidelines acknowledge that a balance needs to be struck between 'the prerogative of a ship in need of assistance to seek a place of refuge and the prerogative of a coastal State to protect its coastline'.[424] However, they leave no doubt that, of the two prerogatives mentioned, the interests of the coastal State take priority. Thus the guidelines explicitly recognize that 'when permission to access a place of refuge is requested, there is no obligation for the coastal state to grant it'.[425] The guidelines do encourage refuge to be granted 'whenever reasonably possible',[426] but this formulation leaves it to the discretion of the coastal State and it falls short of a presumption in favour of refuge, which had been advocated by some commentators.[427] Thus, critics question whether the guidelines go far enough and they have

---

[416] For an early case, see *Kate A Hoff v The United Mexican States (The Rebecca)* (1929).

[417] Chirhop argues that 'originally the right was not restricted to human safety, but included property considerations as well [but there has been] a discernible shrinking of the right of refuge in State practice'; A Chirhop, 'Ships in Distress, Environmental Threats to Coastal States, and Places of Refuge: New Directions for an Ancien Regime?' (2002) 33 *ODIL* 207–26. See also Van Hooydonk (n412) 426.

[418] For a discussion of this case and other examples, see R Shaw, 'Places of Refuge: International Law in the Making?' (2003) *CMIY* 329, 332–4.

[419] Place of Refuge Guidelines, contained in IMO Assembly Resolution A.949(23) (2003). See also Guidelines on the Control of Ships in an Emergency, IMO Document MSC.1/Circ.1251 (2007).

[420] Place of Refuge Guidelines, para. 1.19.

[421] Ibid, para. 3.2. In particular, the Guidelines mention the establishment of a Maritime Assistance Service; see para. 3.3. and Resolution A.950(23) (2003).

[422] Place of Refuge Guidelines, paras 3.5 and Appendix 2.   [423] Ibid, para. 3.10.

[424] Ibid, preamble.   [425] Ibid, para. 3.12.   [426] Ibid.

[427] Van Hooydonk (n412) 432; P Donner, 'Offering Refuge Is Better than Refusing' (2008) 7 *WMUJMA* 281–301.

called for a legally binding instrument.[428] At the same time, it has been pointed out that the decision to permit access to a place of refuge is a highly sensitive issue and 'coastal states would hardly accept anything more than a general commitment to take account of all interests involved'.[429] From this perspective, the guidelines offer a good compromise and they provide at least a benchmark against which the actions of coastal States can be judged,[430] whilst leaving them with the discretion to adopt a solution that is suitable to the circumstances of each case.

Implementation of the IMO guidelines often takes place at the regional level. The Helsinki Commission once again provides a good example, as it has adopted a common plan for places of refuge in the Baltic Sea Area.[431] The plan promotes regional cooperation and it recognizes that 'there may be specific circumstances under which granting to a ship a place of refuge in a response zone of another country than the one in which a situation of assistance originally started would be much safer for both the ship and the environment'. Additionally, the plan encourages exchanges of information concerning places of refuge, as well as the elaboration of a procedure through which requests for shelter in a neighbouring State should be considered. The Parties to the Mediterranean Emergency Protocol have also agreed to 'define national, subregional or regional strategies concerning reception in places of refuge, including ports, of ships in distress presenting a threat to the marine environment',[432] and they have adopted guidelines on the decision-making process for granting access to a place of refuge for ships in need of assistance.[433] These examples demonstrate the continuing importance of regional institutions in implementing international norms relating to the protection of the marine environment from risks posed by shipping, despite the strong role played by the IMO at the global level.

6.6 Conclusion

There is no doubt that shipping is a highly regulated area, with a range of international treaties and other instruments setting out detailed regulations dealing with the environmental impacts of shipping, encompassing both pollution and the

---

[428] Van Hooydonk (n412) 443–4; A Morrison, *Places of Refuge for Ships in Distress: Problems and Methods of Resolution* (Martinus Nijhoff 2008). See the CMI Draft Instrument on Places of Refuge: <http://www.comitemaritime.org/Places-of-Refuge/0,2733,13332,00.html>. The instrument was submitted to the IMO Legal Committee in April 2009, but it was decided that no action was necessary; see Report of the Legal Committee at Its Ninety-Fifth Session, Document 95/10 (2009) para. 9(a).4.

[429] V Frank, 'Consequences of the Prestige Sinking for European and International Law' (2005) 20 *IJMCL* 1, 61.

[430] See A Chircop, 'Assistance at Sea and Places of Refuge for Ships: Reconciling Competing Norms', in H Ringbom (ed.), *Jurisdiction over Ships* (Brill 2015) 153, arguing that the Guidelines 'establish an expectation of responsible albeit discretionary decision-making [and] they may be seen as a standard of due diligence...'.

[431] HELCOM Recommendation 31E/5 (2010).

[432] See 2002 Protocol Concerning Co-operation in Preventing Pollution from Ships and, in the Case of Emergency, Combatting Pollution in the Mediterranean Sea (EIF 17 March 2004), Article 16.

[433] Decision IG 17/1 (2008).

conservation of marine biodiversity. The IMO has led the way in this regard and the MEPC has been described by one author as 'one of the unsung heroes of our time' in relation to its work in this area.[434] Regional institutions have also played an important role in coordinating the implementation of IMO standards in a way that increases both efficiency and effectiveness of the global regime.

The MARPOL Convention is perhaps the most important treaty for the purposes of environmental protection and it has been widely recognized as having contributed to the reduction in operational pollution from vessels.[435] Yet, the strict entry-into-force requirements for new Annexes to the MARPOL Convention have led States to adopt separate treaties to deal with some other emerging environmental threats, such as harmful anti-fouling systems and ballast water management and control. These more recent instruments have nevertheless struggled to attract Parties, and more work needs to be done in order to ensure that these treaties are widely accepted. The IMO has a potential role to play in this regard through its Secretariat and the organization of training and other promotional activities. Indeed, technical assistance has become an important part of the IMO's mandate, particularly supporting developing countries in preparing for the implementation of increasingly complex regulatory treaties. Regional bodies can also play a role in this respect, as evidenced by actions of some regional seas treaties to promote regional plans relating to port reception facilities and places of refuge.

The work of the IMO in this field involves not only the negotiation of treaties but also the amendment of existing rules and standards. The tacit amendment procedures contained in the main regulatory treaties allow the IMO to adapt treaty rules and standards to meet new threats to the marine environment from vessels. As a result, the legal framework for the prevention of pollution from ships is highly dynamic, and there is no doubt that the stringency of the regulations has increased over time. At the same time, the prevention of pollution from ships would appear to be an area in which the law has been largely reactive,[436] despite recognition in the IMO Strategic Plan of the need to be 'proactive in identifying shipping activities and incidents that could have an adverse impact on the environment'.[437] Although the IMO has approved in principle the implementation of the precautionary approach to pollution from ships,[438] the discussion in this chapter demonstrates the difficulty of applying a precautionary approach to the shipping sector. The challenges are amply illustrated in the case of noise pollution from ships, where the significant costs,[439] combined with scientific uncertainty, have led to slow progress in taking

[434] de la Fayette (n121) 159.
[435] See M Fitzmaurice, 'The International Convention for the Prevention of Pollution from Ships (MARPOL), in D Attard et al (eds), *The IMLI Manual on International Maritime Law—Vol. III* (OUP 2016) 77.
[436] S Knapp and PH Franses, 'Does Ratification Matter and Do Major Conventions Improve Safety and Decrease Pollution in Shipping?' (2009) 33 *MP* 826, 826; E Gold, 'Learning from Disaster: Lessons in Regulatory Enforcement in the Maritime Sector' (1999) 8 *RECIEL* 16–20.
[437] IMO Assembly Resolution 1037(27) (2011) para. 2.6.1.
[438] *Guidelines on Incorporation of the Precautionary Approach in the Context of IMO Specific Activities*, MEPC Resolution 37/22 (1995).
[439] de la Fayette (n121) 168, 174.

action. Indeed, it is ironic that the two IMO treaties that make an explicit reference to the precautionary approach each took over ten years to negotiate, and many States resisted regulation until there was clear and convincing evidence of a problem.[440] If a stronger precautionary approach is to be taken by the IMO, then it may be necessary to adapt the work methods and organization,[441] which currently call for States to demonstrate a 'compelling need' for any new proposals[442] and make no reference to the precautionary approach.

One of the greatest challenges in relation to the regulation of shipping has been the enforcement of international standards. Exclusive flag State jurisdiction on the high seas and significant limitations on the powers of coastal States to interfere with ships navigating in its coastal waters have meant that substandard shipping has been able to proliferate. The most significant inroads to this problem have been made through the widespread introduction of regional port State control mechanisms, although this system could still be improved by filling in gaps in the framework and increasing coordination between existing regional efforts. The more recent development of the IMO MSAS offers a second way in which to ensure that States take their obligations to regulate shipping seriously. Yet there are limitations with the scheme as it currently stands, and it can only be hoped that it will evolve further into a more transparent mechanism as States begin to gain trust in its operation. Lessons could be learnt from the compliance mechanisms of other regimes in this respect.

---

[440] Ibid, 168.
[441] MEPC Resolution 37/22 (1995) notes that 'the precautionary approach should not be considered in isolation of other IMO practices, procedures and resolutions . . .'.
[442] Guidelines on the Organization and Method of Work of the Maritime Safety Committee and the Marine Environment Protection Committee and Their Subsidiary Bodies, Document MSC-MEPC.1/Circ.4/Rev.2 (2011) para. 4.14.4.

7

Fishing and the Conservation
of Marine Living Resources

7.1 Introduction

Humankind has been taking fish from the oceans for many centuries, and fish has become a vitally important source of food, particularly of protein, in many parts of the world. Despite its benefits, fishing also has negative consequences for the oceans, particularly if it is carried out in an unsustainable manner. Traditional fishing techniques, involving small vessels with limited range, using simple nets, pots, or lines, clearly had some impact on the marine environment, but not to the extent that they could affect the recruitment rates of stocks. Yet, rapid developments in fishing technology in the second half of the twentieth century, making it easier to find, catch, and process fish on an enormous scale, have led to a significant increase in the number of fish being taken from the oceans. Overfishing is today recognized as one of the most serious threats to marine ecosystems.[1]

The dramatic collapse of the Atlantic cod stocks off the East coast of Canada in the early 1990s is one demonstration of the impact that overfishing can have on fish populations.[2] Cod populations have still not recovered over twenty years later, despite the stricter measures that have been taken. In 2013, it was estimated that 31.4 per cent of world fish stocks were being exploited at biologically unsustainable levels, meaning that the stocks have an abundance that is lower than the level that can produce maximum sustainable yield.[3] The situation is most serious on the high seas, where two-thirds of stocks are overexploited and/or depleted.[4]

The species that are directly targeted by fishing are not the only ones threatened by this activity. Fishing can lead to shifts in ecosystem structures, with impacts on predator–prey relationships. Such changes are difficult to predict but they can alter the diversity of marine life.[5] Fishing also affects non-target species through bycatch, including not only other fish that are caught along with the target species but also a range of other marine species, such as marine mammals, sea turtles, and

---

[1] See GESAMP, *A Sea of Troubles*, GESAMP Report and Studies No 70 (2001) 1.

[2] M Kurlansky, *Cod* (Vintage 1999) 177–89.

[3] FAO, *State of the World Fisheries 2016* (FAO 2016) 5.

[4] Global Ocean Commission, 'Improving Accountability and Performance in International Fisheries Management', Policy Options Paper #9 (2013) 1.

[5] See F Hazin et al, 'Chapter 11: Capture Fisheries', in Global Ocean Assessment (UN 2016) 5.

seabirds, that can become snared by nets and lines. Fishing gear can even cause physical damage to marine habitats, particularly benthic features like corals or seamounts.[6]

As noted by the Global Oceans Assessment, '[r]ebuilding overfished stocks is a major challenge for capture fisheries management'.[7] The challenge is even greater, given that many fish stocks are found in the jurisdiction of more than one State, and, therefore, international cooperation is needed in order to achieve the sustainable use of marine living resources. This issue requires a robust legal framework that promotes the conservation and management of fish stocks and the regulation of the impacts of fishing on marine biodiversity.

The regulation of fishing has been on the international agenda for many decades. Even at the beginning of the twentieth century, some sort of duty to conserve fish in coastal waters was already emerging, as exemplified by the *North Atlantic Coast Fisheries Arbitration*, in which the Tribunal held that 'Great Britain, as the local sovereign, has the duty of preserving and protecting the fisheries.'[8] Whilst it is true that the protection of marine species has been considered an integral part of resource management regimes, the motivation in the past was often connected with conserving the fishery as a source of food. Today, it is more common to see broader environmental considerations emerging in international fisheries law and policy. Indeed, this issue is becoming increasingly urgent, in part, because of greater pressure from fishing but also because of other threats to fish stocks, such as climate change and pollution.[9] To this end, the international community has agreed:

[b]y 2020 [to] effectively regulate harvesting and end overfishing, illegal, unreported and unregulated fishing and destructive fishing practices and implement science-based management plans, in order to restore fish stocks in the shortest time feasible, at least to levels that can produce maximum sustainable yield as determined by their biological characteristics.[10]

The purpose of this chapter is to review the legal framework for the regulation of fishing in the United Nations Convention on the Law of the Sea (UNCLOS) and explain how States have developed additional rules and standards through the negotiation of supplementary treaties and other instruments, at both global and regional levels. In particular, it will consider the extent to which States have implemented a precautionary and ecosystems approach to fisheries, as well as how they have sought to adopt law-making techniques that overcome the challenges of regulating the open-access resources of the high seas.

---

[6] See e.g. *Report of the UN Secretary-General, Impacts of Fishing on Vulnerable Marine Ecosystems: Actions Taken by States and Regional Fisheries Management Organizations and Arrangements to Give Effect to Paragraphs 66 to 69 of General Assembly Resolution 59/25 on Sustainable Fisheries, Regarding the Impacts of Fishing on Vulnerable Marine Ecosystems*, Document A/61/154 (2006) paras 7–17.

[7] See Hazin et al (n5) 17.   [8] *The North Atlantic Coast Fisheries Arbitration* (1910) 187.

[9] C Nellemann, S Hain, and J Alder, *In Dead Water: Merging of Climate Change with Pollution, Over-Harvest and Infestations in the World's Fishing Grounds*, UNEP Rapid Response Assessment (2008).

[10] UNGA Resolution 70/1 (2015), Sustainable Development Goal 14.4.

7.2 Fishing under UNCLOS

7.2.1 The regime for fishing within national jurisdiction

Fishing rights were a major cause of contention throughout the twentieth century and they received a significant amount of attention in both treaty negotiations and litigation. In the first attempt to codify the modern law of the sea in the 1950s, the extent of coastal State rights over fish stocks could not be agreed, and negotiators were only able to conclude that 'the development of international law affecting fisheries may lead in changes in practices and requirements of many states'.[11] This failure and a number of disputes concerning fisheries resources[12] were some of the principal reasons why States felt it necessary to negotiate a new treaty on the law of the sea. Fishing was, therefore, a central topic on the agenda of the Third United Nations Conference on the Law of the Sea.

UNCLOS builds upon previous treaties by confirming jurisdiction of coastal States over fisheries in the territorial sea[13] and in relation to sedentary species located on the continental shelf.[14] However, the Convention also extends sovereign rights of coastal States over marine living resources in the water column up to 200 nautical miles from their coasts.[15] In the *M/V Virginia G Case*, the International Tribunal for the Law of the Sea (ITLOS) determined that the rights conferred upon the coastal State by Part V of UNCLOS give it the authority to regulate not only fishing activity within its exclusive economic zone (EEZ) but also fishing-related activities, such as bunkering of fishing vessels.[16] This expansive interpretation of the Convention is important because it gives the coastal State the tools to ensure that fishing vessels do not seek to circumvent national laws and regulation by prolonging stays at sea.

One of the most significant effects of the EEZ regime is to confer the exclusive right on the coastal State to determine the total allowable catch (TAC) and the allocation thereof.[17] This is an important development, given that it is estimated that about 95 per cent of capture fisheries take place in waters within 200 nautical miles of the coast.[18] Whilst this jurisdictional framework would, in theory, permit a single State to manage a resource, in reality, fish stocks often do not exist within the borders of one State, and, therefore, coastal States may still be required to cooperate with other States in order to manage transboundary, straddling or highly migratory fish stocks.[19]

As well as conferring rights on the coastal State to exploit fish stocks within its waters, UNCLOS also imposes obligations on the coastal State to take measures to promote the 'proper conservation and management [of] marine living resources in the [EEZ]' and ensure that such resources are 'not endangered by over-exploitation'.[20]

---

[11] Second UNCLOS, Resolution II Adopted at the Thirteenth Plenary Meeting on 26 April 1960.
[12] See e.g. *Fisheries Jurisdiction Case* (1974).   [13] UNCLOS, Article 2.
[14] UNCLOS, Article 77(4).   [15] UNCLOS, Articles 56–7.
[16] *The M/V 'Virginia G'* (2014) para. 217. See, however, the more restrictive approach taken in *Filleting within the Gulf of St Lawrence* (1986).
[17] UNCLOS, Articles 61–2.   [18] See e.g. Agenda 21 (1992) para. 17.70.
[19] See UNCLOS, Articles 63 and 64. See also the discussion of the Fish Stocks Agreement, below.
[20] UNCLOS, Article 61(2).

The term *endangered* is not defined by the Convention, but it has been argued that it should be understood as referring to 'reductions in abundance that amount to commercial extinction, or, more strictly, to reductions of such magnitude that a species is likely to become endangered unless protective action is taken'.[21] The obligation to prevent over-exploitation should also be understood in light of the further requirement to ensure that populations of harvested species are maintained 'at levels which can produce the maximum sustainable yield (MSY)'.[22] In principle, MSY can be calculated in an objective manner by the coastal State, provided that it has the relevant scientific information. However, the concept of MSY has been widely criticized by fisheries scientists and other commentators,[23] in part, because of the 'factual obstacles inherent in determining cause and effect in respect of the use of living resources'.[24] In any case, MSY is simply one of the factors to be taken into account by coastal States when setting a TAC, and UNCLOS also permits a coastal State to take into account 'relevant environmental and economic factors'.[25] This provision gives significant leeway to the coastal State to determine the TAC. On the one hand, it may permit a coastal State to take a precautionary approach to stock management, prioritizing environmental considerations in determining the TAC. Indeed, many international instruments urge States to take a precautionary approach to fisheries in their coastal waters.[26] At the same time, it has been pointed out that the discretion given to coastal States can go the other way, so that 'this can lawfully lead to economic and social objectives being given a higher weighting than environmental objectives, depending on the individual circumstances'.[27] Whilst this is true, it must also be remembered that States are always constrained by the overall goal of preventing 'over-exploitation',[28] and so there is an ultimate limit on the discretion of coastal States. This may be true, but it has also been observed that '[t]he ambiguous language and absence of specific or unqualified obligations make it difficult, if not impossible, to identify whether any obligations have been breached'.[29] An additional challenge in ensuring respect for these provisions relates to the fact that disputes over the exercise of coastal State discretion in setting the TAC is one of the issues that is excluded from the system of compulsory dispute settlement in Part XV of UNCLOS.[30] That is not to say that the setting of the TAC is immune from

[21] WT Burke, 'US Fishery Management and the New Law of the Sea' (1982) 76 *AJIL* 24, 32.

[22] UNCLOS, Article 61(3).

[23] See e.g. PA Larkin, 'An Epitaph for the Concept of Maximum Sustainable Yield' (1977) 106 *Transactions of the American Fisheries Society* 1–11. For further discussion, see DM Johnston, *International Law of Fisheries* (YUP 1965), 49–55; DJ Attard, *The Exclusive Economic Zone in International Law* (OUP 1987) 153; F Orrego Vicuña, *The Exclusive Economic Zone: Regime and Legal Nature under International Law* (OUP 1989) 51.

[24] R Barnes, 'The Convention on the Law of the Sea: An Effective Framework for Domestic Fisheries Conservation?', in D Freestone et al (eds), *The Law of the Sea: Progress and Prospects* (OUP 2006) 235, 242.

[25] UNCLOS, Article 61(3).

[26] See e.g. Code of Conduct on Responsible Fisheries, para. 6.5. See the discussion of the Code of Conduct below.

[27] A Proelss and K Houghton, 'Protecting Marine Species', in R Rayfuse (ed.), *Research Handbook on International Marine Environmental Law* (Edward Elgar 2016) 235.

[28] UNCLOS, Article 61(2).   [29] Barnes (n24) 239.

[30] UNCLOS, Article 297(3)(a).

scrutiny. Such decisions may be subject to conciliation procedure in Annex V of the Convention.[31]

Decisions on setting a TAC, and its allocation, may also be the subject of cooperation between coastal States where the stock is transboundary in nature, as is often the case. Cooperation can take place either directly among the States concerned or through some sort of institutional framework.[32] In either case, the arrangements agreed by the States concerned should meet the requirements of UNCLOS.

The status of the target stock is not the only consideration that must be taken into account in this context. UNCLOS explicitly requires that 'the effects on species associated with or dependent upon harvested species'[33] should also be taken into account when setting the TAC. Species can be interpreted broadly enough in this context to refer to any other fauna or flora living in the same marine environment as the targeted stock.[34] This could be interpreted as supporting an ecosystems approach to fisheries,[35] a conclusion that would be reinforced by subsequent developments considered below.[36]

These detailed provisions only apply to fisheries within the EEZ. UNCLOS is less prescriptive when it comes to the conservation and management of fish stocks within the territorial sea or sedentary species on the continental shelf. There are no express provisions requiring coastal States to set a TAC or to prevent the over-exploitation of fish stocks in these maritime zones. It does not follow, however, that States have no obligations in this respect. In particular, it must be remembered that the general principles and rules in Part XII also apply in the context of fisheries. Article 194(5) is expressly relevant in this context, as it requires States to take 'measures to protect and preserve rare or fragile ecosystems'. The Tribunal in the *South China Sea Arbitration* confirmed that this provision applies to fishing in the territorial sea and they found that China had breached its obligation by failing to control the environmental impact of fishing activity of its vessels on the coral reefs and vulnerable marine ecosystems in the South China Sea.[37] In this case, the Tribunal held that the due diligence obligation to protect and preserve the marine environment required

---

[31]   Ibid, Article 297(3)(b).

[32]   For a discussion of the issues and challenges that arise in coastal State consultations, as well as different approaches to coordination, see P Ørebech, 'The "Lost Mackerel" of the North East Atlantic— The Flawed System of Trilateral and Bilateral Decision-Making' (2013) 28 *IJMCL* 343–73. For a leading example of bilateral cooperation through a permanent institution, see the Norwegian-Russian Fisheries Commission, established by the 1975 Agreement on Co-operation in the Fishing Industry (EIF 11 April 1975).

[33]   UNCLOS, Article 61(4).

[34]   The Oxford English Dictionary defines *species* as, inter alia, 'a group or class of animals or plants ...'.

[35]   On ecosystems management in the fisheries sector, see J Morishita, 'What Is the Ecosystem Approach to Fisheries Management?' (2008) 32 *MP* 19–26. See, however, the more sceptical view of Barnes (n24) 244.

[36]   It has been noted that the concept of an ecosystems approach to fisheries is itself 'an evolving practice', and 'today's fisheries management captures more of the elements of an ecosystems approach than it did a decade ago, but less then will be captured a decade from now'; FAO, *Fisheries Management—Marine Protected Areas and Fisheries*, FAO Technical Guidelines for Responsible Fisheries No. 4 (2011) 26.

[37]   *South China Sea Arbitration (Merits)* (2016) para. 961.

States to adopt and take steps to enforce legislation relating to the protection of endangered species and the prohibition of certain destructive fishing techniques.[38]

Overall, the Convention only provides a general framework for the regulation of fishing and it does not specify in detail what conservation measures must be taken by a coastal State. Such measures will depend upon the status of a stock and the other factors discussed above. However, the Convention does require that a coastal State takes into account 'any generally recommended international minimum standards, whether subregional, regional or global'.[39] Whilst falling short of requiring strict compliance with these standards, this rule of reference encourages coastal States to follow best practices when developing conservation and management measures. The reference to 'any generally recommended international minimum standards' is broad enough to cover a wide variety of instruments adopted at the international level and the coastal State must, therefore, look beyond UNCLOS in order to determine how to apply their obligations to manage and conserve fish stocks under their jurisdiction. In particular, this rule of reference would cover several instruments adopted through the Fisheries Committee of the Food and Agriculture Organization (FAO), including the Code of Conduct for Responsible Fisheries, and the associated International Plans of Action, which deal with sharks, seabirds, fishing capacity, and illegal, unreported, and unregulated fishing, all of which will be analysed in more detail below. Coastal States should also take into account standards adopted by regional or subregional fisheries bodies, where they are relevant. For present purposes, it is sufficient to note that these instruments have introduced broader environmental considerations into the legal framework for fisheries management, which must be taken into account under UNCLOS by virtue of this rule of reference. Relevant international standards may also include instruments adopted by bodies acting outside of the fisheries sector. For example, decisions of the Conference of the Parties (COP) to the Convention on Biological Diversity (CBD) or the Convention on Migratory Species (CMS)[40] may be pertinent when drawing up their conservation and management measures.[41] Finally, the work of regional seas organizations may be relevant in this context insofar as these organizations are responsible for the conservation of biological diversity, and they can adopt decisions relating to the protection of habitats or species that may need to be protected from fishing operations.[42]

The types of standards that may be employed by coastal States to give effect to their obligations include licensing of fishing operations, quotas for species, regulating seasons and areas of fishing, gear specifications, and size restrictions.[43] States are also increasingly designating no-take marine protected areas (MPAs),[44] which research suggests can provide a significant benefit to adjacent fisheries by offering

---

[38] Ibid, paras 956 and 959. [39] UNCLOS, Article 61(3).

[40] See particularly CMS COP Resolutions 6.2 (2000), 7.2 (2002), 8.14 (2005), 9.18 (2008), and 10.14 (2011) on bycatch.

[41] See Chapter 3. [42] Ibid. [43] For an indicative list, see UNCLOS, Article 62(4).

[44] See e.g. PJS Jones, *Governing Marine Protected Areas* (Routledge 2014) 31–2. See also FAO, *Fisheries Management—Marine Protected Areas and Fisheries*, FAO Technical Guidelines for Responsible Fisheries No. 4 (2011) 28–9, noting that there are different types of MPAs.

shelter for spawning and feedings habitats for fish species, which can then spillover into areas in which fishing is allowed.[45] The CBD COP has encouraged States to protect at least 10 per cent of coastal and marine areas with systems of protected areas or other effective area-based conservation measures by 2020, and so it is likely that this tool will be increasingly used by management authorities in the future.[46]

The coastal State is also given enforcement powers in relation to the conservation and management of fish stocks within its jurisdiction. Its enforcement jurisdiction in the territorial sea would appear to be unlimited, given that any vessels carrying out fishing activities are by definition not in innocent passage.[47] In the EEZ, in contrast, coastal States are under stricter requirements when it comes to enforcing fisheries laws and regulations. Such restrictions were deemed essential by the drafters in order to preserve the balance of rights and obligations of the coastal State and the flag State. Thus, any vessel that has been arrested for violating fishing laws in the EEZ has a right to prompt release upon payment of a reasonable bond to secure the attendance of the master and crew at trial.[48] The ITLOS has held that this bond can only be financial in character, thereby preventing a coastal State from requiring that a released vessel carry monitoring equipment on board in order to ensure that it does not continue to engage in illegal fishing practices.[49] Furthermore, the coastal State can only take such enforcement measures as are 'necessary', and the ITLOS has taken a strict interpretation of this requirement.[50] Indeed, fisheries law enforcement is another issue that a State can exclude from compulsory dispute settlement under the Convention,[51] which suggests that the drafters accepted that coastal States should be granted a large amount of discretion in this regard.[52]

7.2.2 The regime for fishing beyond national jurisdiction

The high seas are open to all States, and they are subject to the so-called freedom of the high seas, which traditionally has included freedom of fishing.[53] It follows that all States have a right for their nationals to fish on the high seas. However, this

---

[45] See e.g. NOAA, 'Do "No-Take" Marine Reserves Benefit Adjacent Fisheries?' *MPA Science Brief.* <www.mpa.gov>.

[46] See Chapter 3.   [47] UNCLOS, Article 19(2)(i).   [48] UNCLOS, Article 73(2).

[49] See *The Volga Case (2002)*. See, however, the critical views of Judge Anderson and Judge ad hoc Shearer in their dissenting opinions. The latter urged 'a liberal and purposive interpretation' of the text, allowing 'measures . . . found necessary by many coastal States . . . to deter . . . the plundering of the living resources of the sea'; Dissenting Opinion of Judge ad hoc Shearer, para. 17.

[50] See *The M/V 'Virginia G' Case* (2014) para. 257. The approach taken by the Tribunal was criticized in a joint dissenting opinion of Vice-President Hoffman and Judges Chandrasekhara Rao, Marotta Rangel, Kateka, Gao, and Bougeutaia, in which they argued that the Tribunal should only find that a measure was unnecessary if 'there is a manifest error in the exercise of power or the exercise of power is manifestly arbitrary or if the power is exercised on the basis of facts which do not exist and which are patently erroneous' (para. 54). See also J Harrison, 'Safeguards against Excessive Enforcement Measures in the Exclusive Economic Zone', in H Ringbom (ed.), *Jurisdiction over Ships* (Brill 2015) 217–48.

[51] UNCLOS, Article 298(1)(b).

[52] AE Boyle, 'Problems of Compulsory Jurisdiction and the Settlement of Disputes Relating to Straddling Fish Stocks' (1999) 14 *IJMCL* 1, 11.

[53] UNCLOS, Article 87(1)(e).

freedom is not unrestricted and it must be exercised subject to the conditions laid down in UNCLOS and other applicable rules of international law.[54]

As with fishing within national jurisdiction, UNCLOS emphasizes the importance of promoting the conservation of the living resources of the high seas and it requires States to adopt conservation measures to promote the MSY of the relevant stocks, taking into account other factors including 'the interdependence of stocks' and 'the effects on species associated with or dependent upon harvested species'.[55] These rules are also supplemented by the general principles in Part XII, which further stress the need to 'protect and preserve the marine environment'[56] and to take measures for the conservation of 'rare or fragile ecosystems'.[57] This mirrors the objectives of the fisheries regime within the EEZ and it calls in general for an ecosystems approach to fisheries management.

The flag State plays the lead role in the management of fisheries on the high seas. The flag State is expected to adopt and apply conservation measures in relation to its nationals involved in fishing on the high seas. In doing so, flag States should take into account the same array of 'generally recommended international minimum standards' that must be taken into account by coastal States. Furthermore, States must cooperate for the purposes of conservation and management of high seas living resources and they are expected to enter into negotiations on conservation and management measures or cooperate in establishing and participating in Regional Fisheries Management Organizations (RFMOs) or similar arrangements.[58] Indeed, it is RFMOs that have become one of the main drivers of international fisheries regulation, as will be discussed below.

As a basic rule, flag States have exclusive authority for the enforcement of conservation and management measures on the high seas.[59] The Convention stresses that the 'every state shall effectively exercise its jurisdiction and control in administrative, technical and social matters overs ships flying its flag',[60] and the ITLOS has confirmed that this obligation applies to administrative and technical issues relating to fishing vessels.[61] Furthermore, States should also take measures to ensure that their nationals, including owners and operators of vessels, follow conservation and management measures on the high seas.[62] The Tribunal has explained that the Convention imposes an obligation of due diligence on flag States in this respect[63] so that flag States must 'deploy adequate means, to exercise best possible efforts, [and] do the utmost to obtain this result'.[64] Whether or not reasonable measures have been

---

[54] Ibid, Article 116.   [55] Ibid, Article 119.   [56] Ibid, Article 192.
[57] Ibid, Article 194(5).   [58] Ibid, Article 118.   [59] Ibid, Article 92(1).
[60] Ibid, Article 94.
[61] *Request for an Advisory Opinion Submitted by the Sub-Regional Fisheries Commission* (2015) para. 119.
[62] See International Plan of Action to Prevent, Deter and Eliminate Illegal, Unreported and Unregulated Fishing (IPOA-IUU Fishing) (2001), para. 18; FAO Voluntary Guidelines on Flag State Performance (Flag State Guidelines) (2014) para. 2(e).
[63] FAO Voluntary Guidelines on Flag State Performance (Flag State Guidelines) (2014), para. 127.
[64] Ibid, para. 128, drawing upon the *Responsibilities and Obligations of States Sponsoring Persons and Entities with respect to activities in the Area* (2011) para. 110. Note, however, the warning of the Tribunal that 'the relationship between sponsoring state and contractor is not entirely comparable to that existing between the flag State and vessels flying its flag . . .'.

taken by a State will depend upon the circumstances, although further guidance can be gleaned from relevant case law[65] or other international guidance.[66] In particular, the flag State must adopt the necessary legislation and adopt 'enforcement mechanisms to monitor and secure compliance with these laws and regulations' and 'sanctions applicable to involvement in [Illegal, Unregulated and Unreported (IUU)] fishing activities must be sufficient to deter violations and to deprive offenders of the benefits accruing from their IUU fishing activities'.[67] These obligations should be interpreted to extend beyond the control of fishing vessels to also encompass fishing-related activity, such as vessels engaged in transhipment of catches or the provision of food, fuel, or other supplies to fishing vessels.[68]

Without the agreement of the flag State, there is no possibility for other States to exercise jurisdiction over fishing vessels that are suspected of conducting IUU fishing on the high seas. In *M/V Saiga (No. 2)*, Guinea unsuccessfully argued that it was able to exercise jurisdiction over a fishing support vessel because there was no genuine link between the vessel and the flag State. In this respect, the ITLOS held that there is nothing in the Convention 'to permit a State which discovers evidence indicating the absence of proper jurisdiction and control by a flag State over a ship to refuse to recognize the right of the ship to fly the flag of the flag State'.[69] The Tribunal thus reconfirmed the predominant role of flag States and the need to address their compliance with international rules and standards through cooperative mechanisms, rather than direct action against vessels. This is a major weakness of the international regime for high seas fisheries, particularly as one study has noted 'a clear and compelling link between IUU fishing on the high seas and fishing vessels flagged to what are commonly called open registries'.[70] The situation, therefore, calls for further international cooperation if States are to ensure the effective implementation of conservation and management measures. Even assuming that flag States are willing and able to exercise jurisdiction over their vessels, cooperation would still be necessary because no single State can police the entire ocean effectively. Modern technology, such as satellite surveillance and vessel monitoring systems, can help to some extent,[71] although such technology may be too expensive for some States to afford.[72] In this respect, multiple international instruments stress the need for financial and technical assistance to be provided to developing countries in order to

---

[65] See in particular *Pulp Mills on the River Uruguay* (2010) para. 101 ff.

[66] See the discussion of Code of Conduct and related instruments, below.

[67] *Request for an Advisory Opinion Submitted by the Sub-Regional Fisheries Commission* (2015) para. 138.

[68] See IPOA-IUU Fishing, para. 48. See also Report of the Reconvened United Nations Fish Stocks Agreement Review Conference (2016), Annex, Section C, para. 8. There was discussion at the review conference of prohibiting transhipment on the high seas, owing to its ability to undermine efforts to combat IUU fishing; the final recommendation falls short of proposing a complete ban.

[69] *The M/V Saiga Case (No. 2)* (1999) para. 82.

[70] High Seas Task Force, *Closing the Net: Stopping Illegal Fishing on the High Seas*, Final Report (2006) 36.

[71] See e.g. *The Economist*, 'Combating Illegal Fishing', 24 January 2015; *The Times*, 'Hi-Tech Salvation for Easter Island's Fish', 14 September 2015.

[72] High Seas Task Force (n70) 25–6.

assist them with complying with their international obligations.[73] Moreover, States have also developed mechanisms to share the burden of high seas enforcement or put in place supplementary compliance regimes, such as the use of port State measures against IUU fishing vessels. Often, such cooperation takes place through RFMOs or other arrangements, and this practice will be considered below.

7.3 The Global Development of the Legal Framework for the Conservation and Management of Marine Living Resources

7.3.1 The Fish Stocks Agreement

Whilst UNCLOS took a significant step forward in furthering the global consensus on international fisheries law, it did not resolve all issues related to this topic. In particular, the regime for straddling and highly migratory fish stocks remained part of the 'unfinished business',[74] with the Convention merely pointing to an obligation for coastal States and flag States to cooperate on this matter.[75] What principles should underpin such cooperation and what happens if States fail to reach agreement were not addressed by the Convention. Given the importance of straddling and highly migratory stocks and in light of the continuing declines in such stocks following the conclusion of UNCLOS, this issue was taken up at the 1992 Rio Conference on Environment and Development, where it was agreed to negotiate an implementing agreement to elaborate on the basic provisions of the Convention.[76] The so-called Fish Stocks Agreement[77] was adopted in August 1995 and today it has eighty-five Contracting Parties.[78]

The Fish Stocks Agreement is a freestanding instrument,[79] but its purpose is to provide for the 'effective implementation of the relevant provisions of the Convention'.[80] The Agreement stresses that it must be interpreted and applied 'in the context of and in a manner consistent with the Convention'.[81] Thus, it has been argued that 'the Agreement and the Convention are fundamentally inter-related in the sense that one can be used to inform the interpretation of the other'.[82]

---

[73] UN Fish Stocks Agreement, Articles 24–5; Code of Conduct on Responsible Fisheries, Article 5.

[74] B Kwiatkowska, 'The High Seas Fisheries Regime: At a Point of No Return?' (1993) 9 *IJMCL* 327, 327.

[75] UNCLOS, Articles 63 and 64.

[76] Agenda 21, para. 17.45; see also UNGA Resolution 47/192, 22 December 1992.

[77] The Treaty goes by the rather unwieldy name of the 1995 United Nations Agreement for the Implementation of the Provisions of the United Nations Convention on the Law of the Sea of 10 December 1982 Relating to the Conservation and Management of Straddling Fish Stocks and Highly Migratory Fish Stocks (UNFSA) (EIF 11 December 2001).

[78] See UN Division for Ocean Affairs and the Law of the Sea website: <http://www.un.org/depts/los/reference_files/chronological_lists_of_ratifications.htm>.

[79] UNFSA, Articles 37–9, which allow any State to become a Party, whether or not they are already a Party to UNCLOS.

[80] UNFSA, Article 2.   [81] Ibid, Article 4.

[82] D Freestone and AG Oude Elferink, 'Flexibility and Innovation in the Law of the Sea', in AG Oude Elerink (ed.), *Stability and Change in the Law of the Sea* (Martinus Nijhoff 2005) 20. On the relationship between the two instruments, see further D Anderson, 'The Straddling Stocks Agreement

Compatibility of management measures within and beyond national jurisdiction is at the core of the Agreement.[83] Rather than promoting the primacy of coastal State measures over high seas measures or vice versa, the Agreement instead sets down the principles that should guide States when they cooperate for the conservation and management of straddling and highly migratory fish stocks. In particular, the Agreement integrates a number of important principles of international environmental law into the legal regime for highly migratory and straddling fish stocks. For this reason, it has been described as 'a missing link between the law of the sea and international environmental law'.[84] This environmental focus is partly reflected by the objectives of the Agreement, which refers to 'the long-term conservation and sustainable use' of fisheries resources.[85] Furthermore, whilst the Agreement does not remove the role of MSY in calculating TAC,[86] the emphasis on sustainability is strengthened. The Agreement thus clarifies that States should distinguish between target reference points and limit reference points, the latter being 'intended to constrain harvesting within safe biological limits within which the stocks can produce [MSY]'.[87] States are also required to 'apply the precautionary approach widely to conservation, management and exploitation of straddling and highly migratory fish stocks in order to protect the living marine resources and preserve the marine environment'.[88] This description of the precautionary approach differs from the wording in Principle 15 of the Rio Declaration in that it makes no reference to the potential for significant harm as a trigger. Moreover, the Agreement goes on to articulate the precautionary approach not only as a negative obligation not to use scientific uncertainty as a reason for inaction but as a positive obligation to 'be more cautious when information is uncertain'[89] and it encourages States to develop stock-specific reference points.[90] Nevertheless, this language still depends upon further operationalization through subsequent agreements or decisions relating to a particular fish stock.

Another aspect of the Agreement's environmentalist agenda is the requirement for both coastal States and States fishing on the high seas to 'assess the impacts of fishing, other human activities and environmental factors on target stocks and species belonging to the same ecosystems', and 'protect biological diversity in the marine environment'.[91] In other words, the Agreement promotes an ecosystems approach to fisheries management in a much more explicit manner than UNCLOS.

Article 10(c) of the Agreement also requires States to 'adopt and apply any generally recommended international minimum standards for the responsible conduct of fishing operations'. This provision establishes a stronger rule of reference than the equivalent provision found in UNCLOS, by establishing other international instruments as a benchmark for action. In particular, it would appear to target the Code

of 1995—an Initial Assessment', 468; Barnes (n24) 249; J Harrison, *Making the Law of the Sea* (CUP 2011) 108.

[83] See UNFSA, Article 7. See also MW Lodge and SN Nandan, 'Some Suggestions towards Better Implementation of the United Nations Agreement on Straddling Fish Stocks and Highly Migratory Fish Stocks of 1995' (2005) 20 *IJMCL* 345, 351.

[84] Proelss and Houghton (n27) 240.   [85] UNFSA, Article 2.

[86] Ibid, Article 5(b).   [87] Ibid, Article II, para. 2.   [88] Ibid, Article 6(1).

[89] Ibid, Article 6(2).   [90] Ibid, Article 6(3)(b) and 6(4).   [91] Ibid, Article 5.

on Conduct on Responsible Fisheries, which was adopted at about the same time as the Agreement and which will be considered in more detailed below.

As with UNCLOS, the Agreement encourages cooperation between fishing States to be channelled through RFMOs or similar arrangements and the Agreement explicitly lists the functions that should be carried out by such bodies in this context.[92] In practice, it is RFMOs that are expected to implement the general principles listed in the Agreement in relation to the management of specific fish stocks. The central role conferred on these institutions becomes abundantly clear from Article 8(3), which provides 'States fishing for the stocks on the high seas and relevant coastal States shall give effect to their duty to cooperate by becoming members of such organization or participants in such arrangement, or by agreeing to apply the conservation and management measures established by such organization or arrangement'. The importance of RFMOS is further underlined by Article 17, which provides that:

[a] State which is not a member of a subregional or regional fisheries management organization or is not a participant in a subregional or regional fisheries management arrangement, and which does not otherwise agree to apply the conservation and management measures established by such organization or arrangement, is not discharged from the obligation to cooperate, in accordance with the Convention and this Agreement.

It continues: '[s]uch State shall not authorize vessels flying its flag to engage in fishing operations for the straddling fish stocks or highly migratory fish stocks which are subject to the conservation and management measures established by such organization or arrangement'. In other words, RFMOs or alternative arrangements, where they exist, are given exclusive authority to regulate the conditions of access to straddling and highly migratory fish stocks, provided that they comply with the obligations in the Agreement relating to participation and transparency.[93] As a result of this provision, Boyle concludes that 'high seas freedom of fishing under the [UNFSA] is significantly different from the traditional concepts found in Articles 116-117 of [UNCLOS]'.[94]

Indeed, some aspects of the UNFSA may have an impact beyond highly migratory and straddling fish stocks. The UN General Assembly has continuously called upon States to adopt conservation and management measures also for discrete high seas fish stocks consistent with the general principles set forth in the UNFSA[95] and, in practice, discrete fish stocks have been 'managed without any notable differences

---

[92] Ibid, Articles 8–14.   [93] Ibid, Articles 11–12.

[94] AE Boyle, 'Further Development of the 1982 Convention on the Law of the Sea', in D Freestone et al (eds), *The Law of the Sea: Progress and Prospects* (OUP 2006) 47; see also W Edeson, 'Towards the Long-Term Sustainable Use: Some Recent Developments in the Legal Regime of Fisheries', in AE Boyle and D Freestone (eds), *International Law and Sustainable Development* (OUP 1999) 173.

[95] See e.g. UNGA Resolution 69/109 (2014), para. 33:

Calls upon States, individually and, as appropriate, through subregional and regional fisheries management organizations and arrangements with competence over discrete high seas fish stocks, to adopt the measures necessary to ensure the long-term conservation, management and sustainable use of such stocks in accordance with the Convention and consistent with the Code and the general principles set forth in the Agreement.

from straddling fish stocks'.[96] This demonstrates that the Agreement has had broader implications beyond its formal scope of application.

The UNFSA is also important because it emphasizes the need to have special regard to the needs of developing countries. In particular, it encourages Parties to cooperate with developing countries through the provision of financial and technical assistance with a view towards increasing their capacity to, inter alia, improve monitoring, control surveillance, compliance, and enforcement of conservation measures.[97] These provisions are vital given that effective regulation of fisheries will demand implementation by all States involved in the exploitation of a resource.

7.3.2 Fisheries Instruments adopted by the FAO

The FAO was founded in 1945 as an intergovernmental organization with a mandate to 'collect, analyse, interpret and disseminate information relating to nutrition, food and agriculture'.[98] The term *agriculture* in the FAO Constitution is defined to include fishing and aquaculture.[99] Following the conclusion of UNCLOS, the FAO has taken a primary role in developing the legal framework for fisheries conservation and management through the negotiation of both legally binding treaties and non-binding instruments to deal with some of the outstanding problems facing the regulation of fishing.[100]

Perhaps the most important FAO instrument in the field of fisheries is the Code of Conduct on Responsible Fisheries, which was adopted in 1995. Given its emergence at the same time as the Fish Stocks Agreement, it should be no surprise that the Code of Conduct reflects a similar environmental philosophy, albeit with a broader application, as the Code applies not only to straddling and highly migratory fish stocks but to all fishing activity, whether it takes place within or beyond national jurisdiction. The Code has a broad scope, covering all aspects of fishing, including capture, processing, and trade.[101] The Code is intended to establish principles and criteria for the elaboration of national and international policies for responsible fisheries. It is aimed not just at governments but also at other actors with an interest in fisheries activities, such as RFMOs and private companies involved in the capture and processing of fish.[102]

The general principles of responsible fishing are found in Article 6 of the Code. The overarching principle in Article 6.1 provides that:

---

[96] Y Takei, *Filling Regulatory Gaps in High Seas Fisheries* (Brill 2013) 261. See also T Henriksen et al, *Law and Politics in Ocean Governance: The UN Fish Stocks Agreement and Regional Fisheries Management Regimes* (Martinus Nijhoff 2006) 210; Lodge and Nandan (n83) 371.

[97] UNFSA, Article 25(3).

[98] See 1945 Constitution of the Food and Agriculture Organization of the United Nations (FAO Constitution) (EIF 16 October 1945), Article I(1).

[99] Ibid.

[100] For more on the institutional arrangements within the FAO dealing with fisheries, see Harrison (n82) 204–8.

[101] Code of Conduct for Responsible Fisheries (Code of Conduct) (1995) Article 1.3.

[102] Ibid, Article 1.2.

States and users of living aquatic resources should conserve aquatic ecosystems. The right to fish carries with it the obligation to do so in a responsible manner so as to ensure effective conservation and management of the living aquatic resources.

It can be seen from this statement that environmental concerns relating to fisheries are central to the concept of responsible fisheries underpinning the Code. Article 6 goes on to set out other core environmental principles, including the ecosystem approach,[103] the precautionary approach,[104] and integrated coastal area management.[105] The centrality of environmental considerations is also reflected in the provisions of the Code relating to the adoption of conservation and management measures. In this respect, the Code echoes the UNFSA, by providing that 'long-term sustainable use of fisheries resources is the overriding objective of conservation and management'.[106] It goes on to say that measures should not only address the sustainability of fishing on target stocks but also ensure that 'biodiversity of aquatic habitats and ecosystems is conserved and endangered species are protected' and that 'pollution, waste, discards, catch by lost or abandoned gear, catch of non-target species, both fish and non-fish species, and impacts on associated or dependent species are minimized, through measures including, to the extent practicable, the development and use of selective, environmentally safe and cost-effective fishing gear and techniques'.[107] Many of these elements have been periodically reaffirmed by the FAO, through its Committee on Fisheries or other forums. Thus, the 2001 Reykjavik Declaration on Responsible Fisheries in the Marine Ecosystem reinforced the need for continued efforts on integrating ecosystems considerations in fisheries management and it placed the effective implementation of the Code at the centre of these efforts, describing it as the 'common and agreed guide to strengthening and building fisheries management systems'.[108]

The Code was never intended to be a standalone instrument, and many of its principles have been further developed through the negotiation of additional documents aimed at helping States to implement the Code. These include International Plans of Action on sharks, seabirds, fishing capacity,[109] and IUU fishing.[110] In general, the International Plans of Action build upon the provisions of the Code and provide more detail on the sort of measures that States are expected to take in order to meet the objectives of the Code. The FAO has also adopted other fisheries related instruments that provide guidance to States on what best practices they may adopt, including International Guidelines on By-catch Management and the Minimization of Discards,[111] and International Guidelines on the Management of

---

[103] Ibid, Articles 6.6 and 6.8.   [104] Ibid, Article 6.5.   [105] Ibid, Article 6.9.
[106] Ibid, Article 7.2.1.   [107] Ibid, Article 7.2.2.
[108] See 2001 Reykjavik Declaration on Responsible Fisheries in the Marine Ecosystem, para. 1: <ftp://ftp.fao.org/fi/DOCUMENT/reykjavik/y2198t00_dec.pdf>. See the discussion in EJ Molenaar, 'Ecosystem-based Fisheries Management, Commercial Fisheries, Marine Mammals and the 2001 Reykjavik Declaration in the Context of International Law' (2001) 17 *IJMCL* 561–95.
[109] Adopted by the Fisheries Committee in February 1998: <http://www.fao.org/fishery/code/ipoa/en>.
[110] Adopted by the Fisheries Committee in March 2001: <http://www.fao.org/fishery/code/ipoa/en>.
[111] Adopted by the Fisheries Committee in February 2011: <http://www.fao.org/docrep/015/ba0022t/ba0022t00.pdf>.

Deep-Sea Fisheries on the High Seas.[112] This process of developing generic guidelines to assist States in the implementation of the Code is ongoing and the FAO is currently in the process of developing guidelines for the marking of fishing gear to address the growing problem of ghost fishing by lost, abandoned, or discarded fishing tackle.[113]

The FAO has chosen to elaborate these instruments in the form of non-binding instruments, and all of these documents explicitly affirm that they are voluntary in nature.[114] Their non-binding status is furthermore reflected in the language of these instruments, which consistently uses the word 'should'. Nevertheless, these documents have a role to play in promoting the objectives contained in other binding instruments, such as UNCLOS or the UNFSA. In this respect, it has been argued that 'much of the Code can be seen as laying down general principles on the conservation and management of fish stocks' which can influence the future development of the law by providing a 'frame of reference for the international community, as well as individual states, in drawing up legal instruments aimed at addressing all manner of fisheries issues'.[115] Furthermore, non-binding instruments can interact with binding treaties, which contain rules of reference. Thus, the Code of Conduct can qualify as 'generally recommended international minimum standards' for the purposes of Articles 61 and 119 of UNCLOS, meaning that States have an obligation to take the Code into account when adopting management measures. Furthermore, as seen above, the UNFSA requires Parties to 'adopt and apply generally recommended international minimum standards for the responsible conduct of fisheries operations';[116] there is little doubt that the drafters of this provision clearly had the Code of Conduct on Responsible Fisheries in mind. Some authors have suggested that this provision makes compliance with the Code and other generally recommended international minimum standards obligatory.[117] This argument is problematic, as most of the Code is not drafted in the form of rules or standards which demand a particular course of action or behaviour. Yet, one may still argue that the principles contained therein must be taken into account when designing fisheries management and conservation measures and it can, therefore, have a normative influence.

Not all of the instruments adopted by the FAO have taken the form of non-binding guidelines. The FAO has also adopted two important treaties in this area: the 1993 Agreement to Promote Compliance with International Conservation and Management Measures by Fishing Vessels on the High Seas and the 2009 Agreement on Port State Measures to Prevent, Deter and Eliminate Illegal, Unreported and

---

[112] Adopted by the Fisheries Committee in August 2008: <ftp://ftp.fao.org/docrep/fao/011/i0816t/i0816t.pdf>.

[113] See FAO Press Release, 'New Technologies Boost Efforts to Cut Down on Environmentally Harmful "Ghost Fishing"', 21 April 2016.

[114] Code of Conduct, Article 1.1. See also IPOA-Seabirds, para. 8; IPOA-Sharks, para. 10; IPOA-Capacity, para. 4; IPOA-IUU Fishing, para. 4.

[115] Harrison (n82) 219.   [116] UNFSA, Article 10(c).

[117] See e.g. P Birnie, AE Boyle, and C Redgwell, *International Law and the Environment* (3rd edn: OUP 2009) 739.

Unregulated Fishing. These instruments are both related to the Code of Conduct. For its part, the 1993 Agreement recognizes that it will 'form an integral part of the International Code of Conduct for Responsible Fishing'[118] and it largely serves to give a stronger legal form to the provisions relating to flag State responsibility in Article 8.2 of the Code. The Agreement emphasizes the importance of flag State responsibility and it imposes a broad obligation for Parties to 'take such measures as may be necessary to ensure that fishing vessels flying their flag do not engage in any activity that undermines the effectiveness of international conservation and management measures'.[119] In this respect, the Compliance Agreement echoes the provisions of the UNFSA by emphasizing that all States, whether or not they are a Party to an RFMO, should ensure that internationally agreed management measures are respected. The Compliance Agreement goes on to regulate the problem of flag hopping, by obliging States to refrain from registering a vessel that has previously been found to undermine international conservation and management measures.[120] The Port State Measures Agreement also recalls the Code of Conduct in its preamble and it develops the skeletal provisions relating to port State measures in Article 8.3 of the Code, by establishing detailed obligations to ensure that port States do not facilitate the landing of fish that have been caught in violation of applicable conservation and management standards.[121] In particular, the Agreement requires port States to control entry into its ports and to deny the use of port facilities for landing, transhipping, packaging, and processing of fish, as well as other port services, such as refuelling and maintenance, if it has evidence that a vessel has been engaged in IUU fishing. As treaty instruments, the 2001 Agreement and 2009 Agreement will only become compulsory if States consent to be bound. Moreover, as they were both designed as global instruments, they require broad participation in order to be effective. Yet, at the time of writing, neither of these treaties has attracted substantial support. The Compliance Agreement only has forty Parties,[122] whereas the Port State Measures Agreement has only just entered into force.[123] This demonstrates some of the drawbacks of relying upon treaty instruments to develop the legal framework. However, the principles contained

---

[118] See 1995 Agreement to Promote Compliance with International Conservation and Management Measures by Fishing Vessels on the High Seas (Compliance Agreement) (EIF 24 April 2003), preamble.

[119] Compliance Agreement, Article III(1)(a).

[120] Ibid, Article III(5). The Compliance Agreement also promotes the establishment of a global record of fishing vessels authorized to fish on the high seas, which is designed to make it easier to access the information that is required to implement this obligation; see Article VI. On the challenges of establishing a global record, however, see G Lugten, 'Current Legal Developments: Food and Agriculture Organization' (2008) 23 *IJMCL* 761–7.

[121] See 2009 Agreement on Port State Measures to Prevent, Deter and Eliminate Illegal, Unreported and Unregulated Fishing (Port State Measures Agreement) (EIF 5 June 2016); see DJ Doulman and J Swan, A *Guide to the Background and Implementation of the 2009 FAO Agreement on Port State Measures to Prevent, Deter and Eliminate Illegal, Unreported and Unregulated Fishing*, FAO Fisheries and Aquaculture Circular No. 1074 (2012); E Witbooi, 'Illegal, Unreported and Unregulated Fishing on the High Seas: The Port State Measures Agreement in Context' (2014) 29 *IJMCL* 290–320.

[122] See <http://www.fao.org/fileadmin/user_upload/legal/docs/012s-e.pdf>.

[123] See FAO Press Release, 'Ground-Breaking Illegal Fishing Accord Soon to Enter into Force, 16 May 2016: <http://www.fao.org/news/story/en/item/414494/icode/>.

in these instruments have also been implemented through collective action at the regional level, which is the issue to which we now turn.

7.4 The Role of Regional Institutions in the Conservation and Management of Marine Living Resources

7.4.1 Form and functions of regional fisheries bodies

Many of the instruments discussed above require their objectives to be pursued by cooperation among fishing States. Such cooperation can take place either directly between States[124] or through international institutions. In practice, regional institutions have been at the forefront of international efforts to achieve the conservation and sustainable utilization of fish stocks, particularly in relation to high seas, straddling, or highly migratory fish stocks. UNCLOS encourages States to cooperate with regional bodies when setting management and conservation measures,[125] and this central role has been reaffirmed by the UNFSA,[126] the Code of Conduct on Responsible Fisheries,[127] and the International Plan of Action on IUU Fishing.[128]

International law grants considerable flexibility as to the form that an organization or arrangement may take. The precise mandate and powers possessed by a particular body will depend on its constituent instrument. Nevertheless, the principal functions that should be carried out by such institutions include:[129]

- allocation of TAC;
- adoption of conservation and management measures;
- agreement on standards for collection, reporting, verification and exchange of data;
- promotion, conduct and dissemination of scientific research into relevant stocks;
- compilation and dissemination of statistical data;
- establishment of appropriate mechanisms for the effective monitoring, control, surveillance and enforcement of conservation and management measures;
- monitoring and promotion of compliance with agreed rules, standards and mechanisms.

There are currently about forty regional institutions involved in the governance of marine fisheries, some with a focus on fish stocks within national jurisdiction and

---

[124] Churchill makes a distinction between 'bilateralist' and 'regionalist regimes'; see RR Churchill, 'The Barents Sea Loophole Agreement: A "Coastal State" Solution to a Straddling Stock Problem' (1999) 14 *IJCML* 467, 482. See also OS Stokke, 'Conclusions', in OS Stokke (ed.), *Governing High Seas Fisheries: The Interplay of Global and Regional Regimes* (OUP 2001) 330–1.
[125] See e.g. UNCLOS, Articles 61(2), 118.   [126] UNFSA, Article 8(1).
[127] For example, Code of Conduct, para. 6.12.[128] IPOA-IUU Fishing, paras 78–83.
[129] UNFSA, Article 10.

others with a broader mandate including high seas fisheries.[130] The latter institutions are of particular interest for present purposes because they offer a means of managing a common resource. In relation to high seas fish stocks, there is a trend towards the establishment of bodies with regulatory functions that are able to take binding decisions relating to the allocation of TAC and other conservation and management measures.[131] The precise form of each of these bodies varies, although most involve the establishment of a formal RFMO composed of a commission or similar body as the principal decision-making organ, supported by several functional committees and a secretariat. Meetings of such institutions usually take place on an annual or biennial basis, meaning that States are able to adapt measures over time, depending on the status of a particular stock.

One of the key functions of RFMOs is to adopt conservation and management measures that are binding on the Parties. The types of measures that may be taken by RFMOs when exercising their regulatory powers include the regulation of fishing gear, limits on catch sizes and TACs, the establishment of closed seasons and protected areas, and the regulation of overall fishing effort.[132]

Although RFMO decisions are often binding upon adoption, without the need for further consent of the Parties concerned, most fishing treaties also allow States to escape the application of measures by registering an objection, which prevents that decision from becoming opposable to them.[133] As a result, the decision-making procedure ensures that States cannot be bound against their will. Such opt-out procedures may even apply if a measure has been adopted by consensus.[134] In practice, objection procedures are widely used, having the effect of undermining measures adopted by the RFMOs.[135] It is for this reason that some treaties establishing RFMOs have sought to limit the ability of members to escape regulation through the use of opt-out procedures.

A good example is provided by the Convention on the Conservation and Management of Fishery Resources in the South East Atlantic Ocean (SEAFO Convention), which requires members to provide 'a written explanation of its reasons' for objecting and it encourages Parties to suggest alternative regulatory measures 'where appropriate'.[136] The Convention on the Conservation and Management

---

[130] See <http://www.fao.org/fishery/rfb/search/en>.

[131] See e.g. J Swan, *Decision-making in Regional Fisheries Bodies or Arrangements: The Evolving Role of RFBs and International Agreement on Decision-Making Processes*, FAO Fisheries Circular No. 995 (2004) 10.

[132] See e.g. 1980 Convention on Future Multilateral Cooperation in North-East Atlantic Fisheries (NEAFC Convention) (EIF 17 March 1982), Article 7.

[133] See e.g. NEAFC Convention, Article 12(2).

[134] See 2001 Convention on the Conservation and Management of Fishery Resources in the South East Atlantic Ocean (SEAFO Convention) (EIF 6 April 2013), Articles 17(1) and 23; 1980 Convention on the Conservation of Antarctic Marine Living Resources (CCAMLR Convention) (EIF 7 April 1982), Article 9(6). In this respect, it must be remembered that the concept of *consensus*, as opposed to *unanimity*, implies that Parties are willing to go along with a decision, even if they do not actively support it. From this perspective, the existence of an opt-out procedure for consensus decisions makes sense.

[135] See the discussion in D Diz, *Fisheries Management in Areas beyond National Jurisdiction: The Impact of Ecosystem Based Law-Making* (Martinus Nijhoff 2013) 128.

[136] SEAFO Convention, Article 23(1)(d).

of High Seas Fishery Resources in the South Pacific Ocean goes further,[137] introducing three significant limits on the ability of a coastal State to make objections. First, the Convention explicitly provides that 'the only admissible grounds for an objection are that the decision unjustifiably discriminates in form or in fact against the member of the Commission, or is inconsistent with the provisions of the Convention or other relevant international law as reflected in [UNCLOS] or [UNFSA]'.[138] This provision thus limits the discretion of a member as to the reasons for making an objection. Second, the Convention also requires that when presenting an objection, the State must advise the Executive Secretary of 'alternative measures that are equivalent in effect to the decision to which it has objectives and have the same date of application'.[139] In other words, members cannot escape regulation completely and they must take some measures that seek to promote the goals of the Convention. Finally, the objections procedure contains a mechanism whereby any objection is automatically considered by a Review Panel that will decide whether or not the objection is permissible and if so, whether the proposed alternative measures are equivalent.[140] This procedure further limits the possibility of abuse of the objections procedure.

This innovative procedure was invoked for the first time in 2013[141] in order to address an objection presented by the Russian Federation to Decision CMM 1.01, setting out conservation and management measures for *Trachurus murphyi*, more commonly known as 'Chilean jack mackerel' or 'horse mackerel'.[142] Russia had objected to the measure on the ground that it was discriminatory because it excluded Russia from the distribution of shares in the TAC. Russia also alleged that the decision was incompatible with the Convention because the allocation only took into account catch statistics from a single year and not 'historic catch and past and present fishing patterns and practices in the Convention Area' as required by Article 21(1)(a) of the Convention. The Review Panel upheld some of these arguments, finding that whilst there may be some justification for relying upon the 2010 data for the purpose of fixing the TAC and the allocation of catch limits for individual members, 'no convincing argument has been made in the written or oral submissions to justify the failure to allocate any catch to Russia'.[143] In light of this conclusion, the Review Panel turned to the question of whether the alternative measures proposed by Russia were equivalent to the effect in the decision. The Review Panel was of the opinion that the proposal of Russia was problematic because it could affect the allocations given to other members.

---

[137] See also the 2000 Convention on the Conservation and Management of Highly Migratory Fish Stocks in the Western and Central Pacific Ocean (WCPFC Convention) (EIF 19 June 2004), Article 20.
[138] See 2009 Convention on the Conservation and Management of High Seas Fishery Resources in the South Pacific Ocean (SPRFMO Convention) (EIF 24 August 2012), Article 17(2)(c). To similar effect, see 2012 Convention on the Conservation and Management of High Seas Fisheries Resources in the North Pacific Ocean (NPFC Convention) (not yet in force), Article 9(1)(c).
[139] SPRFMO Convention, Article 17(2)(b)(ii).   [140] Ibid, Article 17(5) and Annex II.
[141] Findings and Recommendations of the Review Panel, 5 July 2013.
[142] For a detailed analysis of the decision, see A Serdy, 'Implementing Article 28 of the UN Fish Stocks Agreement: The First Review of a Conservation Measure in the South Pacific Regional Fisheries Management Organization' (2016) 47 *ODIL* 1–28.
[143] Findings and Recommendations of the Review Panel (n141) para. 92.

It, therefore, recommended a different alternative measure, which would allow Russia to authorize its vessels to fish in the Convention Area only after Russia has determined that the total catch in 2013 will not reach the overall TAC, and only until this limit is reached. Decisions of the Review Panel would appear to be binding, unless the States concerned choose to initiate dispute settlement proceedings under the Convention.[144] These review procedures are a further illustration of the growing institutionalization of international fisheries law and they have been lauded as 'the best solution for opt-out mechanisms' as it promotes the effectiveness of decision-making.[145] Indeed, the 2016 UNFSA Review Conference recommended that RFMOs 'review their decision-making procedures', including considering the adoption of procedures to 'ensure that post-opt-out behavior is constrained by rules to prevent opting-out Parties from undermining conservation, by establishing clear processes for dispute resolution and for the adoption of alternative measures with equivalent effect that will be implemented in the interim'.[146] The challenge of doing so, however, is that such changes will often require an amendment to the constituent instrument of an RFMO, which itself must be accepted by each and every Party before it can be effective.

7.4.2 Precaution in the decision-making of RFMOs

One of the historic criticisms of fisheries management is that decisions have been far too optimistic about how many fish could be caught.[147] In order to address this problem, the international community has called for the incorporation of the precautionary approach into the decision-making process. Freestone argues that the obligation on States to be cautious, recognized in the UNFSA, the Code of Conduct and the constituent instruments of many RFMOs, 'represents a major change in the traditional approach to fisheries management which until recently tended to be reactive to management problems only after they arrived at crisis levels'.[148] Indeed, unlike other areas of law where the precautionary approach is simply set as an abstract objective, many fisheries treaties specify the types of considerations that must be taken into account by RFMOs in this respect. For example, the Western and Central Pacific Fisheries Convention requires the Parties to take into account:

uncertainties relating to the size and productivity of the stocks, reference points, stock condition in relation to such reference points, levels and distributions of fishing mortality and

---

[144] SPRFMO Convention, Annex II, para. 10.

[145] Diz (n135) 132. See also HS Schiffman, *Marine Conservation Agreements: The Law and Policy of Reservations and Vetoes* (Martinus Nijhoff 2008) 200–2.

[146] Report of the Reconvened United Nations Fish Stocks Agreement Review Conference (2016), Annex, Section B, para. 5.

[147] See e.g. DG Webster, 'The Irony and the Exclusivity of Atlantic Bluefin Tuna Management' (2011) 35 *MP* 249, 249.

[148] D Freestone, 'International Fisheries Law Since Rio: The Continued Rise of the Precautionary Principle' in A Boyle and D Freestone (eds), *International Law and Sustainable Development* (OUP 1999) 160. Yet, as argued by Hey, the precautionary approach took longer to be accepted in the fisheries context compared with other activities affecting the marine environment; see E Hey, 'The Interplay between Multilateral Environmental and Fisheries Law: A Struggle to Sustainably Regulate Economic Activity' (2011) 54 *JYIL* 190, 192–5.

the impact of fishing activities on non-target and associated or dependent species, as well as existing and predicted oceanic, environmental and socio-economic conditions...[149]

It goes on to specify that 'Members of the Commission shall be *more* cautious when information is uncertain, unreliable or inadequate'.[150] In other words, caution is always required and the key question is how cautious decision-makers must be. Even when such text is not expressly included in a treaty, the Parties to regional fisheries agreements have endorsed a precautionary approach in practice.[151]

The express recognition of the precautionary approach in treaty language is to be welcomed. Yet, despite the formulation of the precautionary approach as an obligation, the Parties are still left significant discretion in deciding how much caution is appropriate. As noted by McDorman, 'while the idea of precaution as a principled approach or "rule" for decision adoption is sometimes mooted, in the RFMO context the precautionary approach is better understood as a manner of attempting to deal with scientific information and uncertainty and as a factor to be considered in decision-making'.[152] Even procedures promoting the establishment of precautionary reference points do not necessarily lead to precautionary measures being adopted if the reference points are exceeded, as a positive decision must be made to restrain fishing.[153] The political nature of management regimes is demonstrated by the many examples where recommendations by scientific bodies for a precautionary approach have not been followed by decision-making bodies, which have set higher quotas.[154]

7.4.3 The environmental mandate of RFMOs and the regulation of harmful fishing techniques on the high seas

One of the most important developments in the practice of RFMOs in recent years has been the incorporation of key environmental principles into their decision-making processes, leading to the adoption of a broader range of measures that are aimed at offering protection to marine ecosystems. This trend is in part inspired by the growing attention given to the conservation of biological diversity at the international level,[155] requiring States to adopt measures that go beyond the sustainability

---

[149] WCPFC Convention, Article 6(1).

[150] Ibid, Article 6(2) (emphasis added). For similar provisions in other treaties, see SPRFMO Convention, Article 3(2); SEAFO Convention, Article 7; 1978 Convention on Future Multilateral Cooperation in North-West Atlantic Fisheries, as amended (NAFO Convention) (EIF 1 January 1979), Article III(c); 1949 Agreement for the Establishment of a General Fisheries Commission for the Mediterranean, as amended (GFCM Agreement) (EIF 20 February 1952), Article III(2).

[151] See e.g. NAFO Resolution 2/99 to Guide Implementation of the Precautionary Approach within NAFO (1999); 2005 Declaration on the Interpretation and Implementation of the Convention on the Future Multilateral Cooperation in North-East Atlantic Fisheries, para. 2(b); ICCAT Resolution 15-12 Concerning the Use of a Precautionary Approach in Implementing ICCAT Conservation and Management Measures (2015); IOTC Resolution 12/01 on the Implementation of the Precautionary Approach (2008).

[152] TL McDorman, 'Implementing Existing Tools: Turning Words into Actions—Decision-Making Processes of Regional Fisheries Management Organizations (2005) 20 *IJMCL* 428, 436.

[153] See UNFSA, Annex II.

[154] See discussion in Stokke (n124) 336–8, concluding that 'actual performance is rather mixed'.

[155] See Chapter 3.

of catch to include broader impacts on the marine ecosystems. These considerations are central to the major biodiversity treaties, such as the CBD, and the Parties to this instrument have placed sustainable fisheries on their agenda, encouraging implementation and improvement of the ecosystems approach in fisheries management.[156] Such concerns have also been mainstreamed into the global fisheries instruments discussed above, such as the UNFSA and the Code of Conduct on Responsible Fisheries. The critical test, however, is whether they are addressed in the regulatory measures adopted by RFMOs in practice.

Most modern fisheries agreements now refer to the need for RFMOs to take into account the broader impacts of fishing in the marine environment.[157] This policy objective is reflected in the Code of Conduct and States participating at the World Summit on Sustainable Development in Johannesburg in 2002 encouraged integration of the ecosystems approach into fisheries management.[158] Indeed, even where there is no explicit reference in the founding treaty, RFMO practice recognizes the need for an ecosystems approach.[159]

An ecosystems approach to fisheries involves taking into account the relationship between a target species and the wider system when setting TAC levels and conservation and management measures. This may sound simple, but a true ecosystems approach to fisheries management is challenging, in part because 'the science of modeling stock interactions with respect to the generation of practical management advice is still in its infancy'.[160] Thus, the ecosystems approach must be understood at present as an aspiration, rather than a strict obligation in the fisheries context, as States can only act upon the best scientific evidence that is available.[161] Yet, RFMOs have a vital role to play in ensuring that the necessary research is carried out. For example, to assist it with carrying out its mandate to minimize the risk of changes in the marine ecosystem of the Antarctic, the Commission on the Conservation of Antarctic Marine Living Resources (CCAMLR) has instituted an ecosystem-monitoring programme with a view to periodically gathering data from a network of designated sites. This information can then be used when setting conservation and management measures.[162]

---

[156] See e.g. CBD COP Decision XI/18A (2012), para. 2.

[157] For example, CCAMLR, Article 3; SEAFO Convention, Articles 3(c)–(f); SPRFMO Convention, Article 3(2)(b); WCPFC Convention, Article 5(d)–(f). See, generally, Diz (n135) 117–57.

[158] World Summit on Sustainable Development Plan of Implementation (2002), para. 30(d).

[159] See e.g. ICCAT Resolution 15-11, Concerning the Application of an Ecosystems Approach to Fisheries Management (2000); CCSBT Recommendation to Mitigate the Impact on Ecologically Related Species of Fishing for Southern Bluefin Tuna (2011).

[160] Stokke (n124) 340.

[161] See M Vierros et al, 'Ecosystem Approach and Ocean Management', in S Aricò (ed.), *Ocean Sustainability in the 21st Century* (CUP 2015) 128, commenting on 'the practical difficulties in implementation, including availability of suitable information and lack of analytical and scientific tools to support the process'.

[162] In practice, it has taken time to integrate this information into relevant conservation and management measures; see C Redgwell, 'Protection of Ecosystems under International Law: Lessons from Antarctica', in AE Boyle and D Freestone (eds), *International Law and Sustainable Development* (OUP 1999) 224; see also A Fabra and V Gascon, 'The Convention on the Conservation of Antarctic Marine Living Resources (CCAMLR) and the Ecosystem Approach' (2008) 23 *IJMCL* 567–98.

Despite the informational challenges, many RFMOs have taken some measures that reflect a basic application of the ecosystems approach. For example, some RFMOs have taken to carrying out prior assessment of impacts of expanded or new fishing effort in order to determine the effects on target stocks or broader ecosystems.[163] There is also widespread practice in relation to the adoption of mitigation measures for established fisheries in order to limit the impacts of fishing on marine biodiversity, although the adoption of such measures has largely been reactive, rather than the product of ecosystem modelling. Indeed, the measures adopted by RFMOs have been largely targeted at threatened species and they can be considered as a way for States to comply with their general obligation under Part XII of UNCLOS to 'protect and preserve rare or fragile ecosystems'.[164] Examples include the phasing out of highly destructive fishing methods, such as large pelagic drift nets,[165] or rules and standards relating to bycatch of associated fish species: for example, requirements for the release of live specimens caught as bycatch.[166] Other measures have addressed incidental impacts of fisheries, inter alia, on seabirds and turtles.[167] Despite progress by RFMOs in introducing protection for marine biodiversity from fishing operations within their regulatory areas, there is no doubt that more needs to be done. Parties to the CMS have highlighted bycatch as a major threat to migratory species listed under that treaty and they have urged States to improve mitigation measures by working through RFMOs.[168] In this respect, the CMS COP has pledged to gather further data on bycatch, to identify best practices proactively in relation to bycatch mitigation, and to improve coordination with the FAO in order to address this issue.[169] The involvement of the CMS is important in this respect because it ensures that the issue is addressed not only from the perspective of those actors involved in fisheries regulation, but also takes into account the views of actors concerned with promoting broad protection of marine biodiversity.

Another recent example of RFMOs moving towards a stronger ecosystems approach to fisheries regulation is the drive towards protecting deep-sea habitats from damage caused by fishing gear. Since the early 2000s, the international community, acting through the UN General Assembly, the FAO, and other competent international organizations, has focused increasing attention on the possible impacts

---

[163] For example, CCAMLR Conservation Measure 21-02 (2015), para. 6(ii); NAFO Conservation and Enforcement Measures 2016, Article 16. See also NPFC Convention, Article 3(h); SEAFO Convention, Article 10(4)(e); SPRFMO Convention, Article 22.

[164] UNCLOS, Article 194(5). Many measures have also been adopted in response to initiatives at the FAO, such as IPOA-Sharks and IPOA-Seabirds; see above.

[165] See e.g. SPRFMO CMM 1.02, prohibiting the use of large-scale pelagic driftnets and deep-water gillnets in the Convention Area (2013); CCAMLR Resolution 7/IX on Driftnet Fishing in the Convention Area (1990).

[166] See e.g. ICCAT Recommendation on Porbeagle Caught in Association with ICCAT Fisheries (2015); IOTC Resolution 12/09 on the Conservation of Thresher Sharks Caught in Association with Fisheries in the IOTC Area of Competence (2008); Recommendation GFCM/36/2012/2 on mitigation of incidental catches of cetaceans in the GFCM area (2012), para. 2(b).

[167] See e.g. E Gilman and T Moth-Poulsen, *Review of Measures Taken by Intergovernmental Organizations to Address Sea Turtle and Seabird Interactions in Marine Capture Fisheries*, FAO Fisheries Circular No. 1025, Document FIIT/FIMF/C1025(En) (2007).

[168] CMS COP Resolution 9.14 (2008) paras 3 and 4.　　　[169] Ibid.

of deep-sea fishing operations, in particular, bottom fisheries, on vulnerable marine ecosystems (VMEs).[170] The International Guidelines on Management of Deep-Sea Fisheries in the High Seas highlight the need for States to prevent significant adverse impacts on VMEs[171] and they provide guidance to States on how VMEs should be defined.[172] The guidelines indicate that ecosystems should be classified as vulnerable where they display some of the following characteristics: uniqueness or rarity, functional significance, fragility, slow growth rates, low recruitment, or structural complexity.[173] The guidelines go on to give examples of VMEs, such as seamounts, hydrothermal vents, cold seeps, and cold-water corals, but they make clear that the criteria must be applied on a case-by-case basis in particular regions.[174] The guidelines also provide criteria against which to determine whether a significant adverse impact is likely to occur, including the intensity or severity of the impact at the specific site, the spatial extent of the impact relative to the availability of the habitat type affected, the sensitivity or vulnerability of the ecosystem to the impact, the extent to which ecosystem functions may be altered by the impact, and the ability of the ecosystem to recover and the rate of such recovery.[175] Where information is unknown or uncertain, the guidelines urge a precautionary approach.[176] The guidelines go on to suggest a range of measures that should be taken by States and/or RFMOs in order to regulate deep-sea fisheries. Whilst the list is generally non-prescriptive, the guidelines suggest a minimum level of protection, including the closure of areas where VMEs are known to occur, reduction of effort in existing fisheries in order to allow the collection of information to assess the impact of the fishery, and refraining from expanding the spatial extent of current fishing until more information is available.[177] Whatever measures are taken should also be based upon a precautionary approach,[178] and the guidelines encourage the development of fishery management plans for the purpose of ensuring the long-term viability of fishing.[179]

In 2006, the UN General Assembly called upon States and RFMOs, inter alia, to identify VMEs and determine whether bottom fisheries are likely to cause significant adverse impacts to such ecosystems and the long-term sustainability of deep-sea fish stocks. Where such impacts were likely, States and RFMOs were called upon to close such areas to bottom fishing until conservation and management measures could be put in place to prevent significant adverse impacts.[180] Several RFMOs have adopted conservation and management measures in response to the Resolution, including the designation of closed areas where VMEs have been identified,[181] as

---

[170] See e.g. *Report on the Work of the United Nations Open-Ended Informal Consultative Process on Oceans and Law of the Sea at Its First Meeting*, Document A/55/274 (2000), para. 73.

[171] See 2009 International Guidelines on the Management of Deep-Sea Fisheries in the High Seas, paras 22 and 26.

[172] Ibid, paras 14–16.   [173] Ibid, para. 42.   [174] Ibid, Annex.

[175] Ibid, para. 18.   [176] Ibid, para. 20.   [177] Ibid, para. 63.

[178] Ibid, para. 65.   [179] Ibid, para. 75.

[180] UNGA Resolution 61/105 (2006), para. 83.

[181] See e.g. Resolution GFCM/37/2013/1 on Area-Based Management of Fisheries; SEAFO Conservation Measure 29/14 on Bottom Fishing Activities and Vulnerable Marine Ecosystems in the SEAFO Convention Area, Article 5; NEAFC Recommendation 19/2014 on the Protection of Vulnerable Marine Ecosystems in the NEAFC Regulatory Area, Article 5; NAFO Conservation and

well as the introduction of encounter protocols, which require individual fishing vessels to stop fishing and move to a different location if a quantity of VME indicators, such as coral species, deep-sea sponges, or fauna residing in mud, are discovered whilst hauling fishing gear.[182] Such encounters must also be reported to the flag State or the Secretariat of a relevant RFMO, and measures, including a temporary closure pending further investigations, should be taken to protect the VME.[183] RFMOs have also limited expansion of deep-sea fishing activities into new areas, unless and until an assessment of the impacts on VMEs has been conducted. For example, SEAFO requires a proposal for so-called exploratory fishing to be accompanied by a 'preliminary assessment' of known and anticipated impacts,[184] and such activity can only take place after having been assessed by the Scientific Committee and approved by the Commission.[185] Many of these measures have been taken on the basis of the inherent powers of RFMOs to protect biodiversity from fishing operations, but organizations that have been established more recently in the South Pacific and North Pacific have been granted an explicit power to protect VMEs in accordance with the International Guidelines and relevant UN General Assembly (UNGA) resolutions.[186] Whilst it has taken some time for the international community to respond to the calls of the UNGA,[187] this example illustrates that RFMOs do have flexible powers to address emerging threats to the marine environment from fishing. It also demonstrates how the accumulation of non-binding instruments from a variety of bodies can influence the emergence of binding measures to protect biodiversity from fishing operations.

It is CCAMLR that has perhaps gone the furthest in integrating biodiversity and ecosystems considerations into its conservation and management measures. This body has not only developed rules in relation to minimizing the effects of particular fishing methods on the marine environment[188] but also adopted a process for the

---

Enforcement Measures 2016, Articles 15–24; SEAFO Conservation Measure 30/15 on Bottom Fishing Activities and Vulnerable Marine Ecosystems in the SEAFO Convention Area (2015), Article 5.

[182] See e.g. NEAFC Recommendation 19/2014 on the Protection of Vulnerable Marine Ecosystems in the NEAFC Regulatory Area, Article 8(1); SEAFO Conservation Measure 30/15 on Bottom Fishing Activities and Vulnerable Marine Ecosystems in the SEAFO Convention Area (2015), Article 8.

[183] NEAFC Recommendation 19/2014 on the Protection of Vulnerable Marine Ecosystems in the NEAFC Regulatory Area, Article 8(2).

[184] SEAFO Conservation Measure 30/15 on Bottom Fishing Activities and Vulnerable Marine Ecosystems in the SEAFO Convention Area (2015), Article 7.

[185] Ibid, Article 6(4).

[186] SPRFMO Convention, Article 20(1)(d); NPFC Convention, Articles 3(e), 7(1)(e).

[187] See critique offered by R Rayfuse, 'Regional Fisheries Management Organizations', in D Rothwell et al (eds), *Oxford Handbook on the Law of the Sea* (OUP 2015) 458–9.

[188] See e.g. CCAMLR Conservation Measure 22-04, Interim Prohibition on Deep-Sea Gillnetting (2010); CCAMLR Conservation Measure 22-05, Restrictions on the Use of Bottom Trawling Gear In The High-Seas Areas of the Convention Area (2008); CCAMLR Conservation Measure 22-09, Protection of Registered, Vulnerable Marine Ecosystems in Subareas, Divisions, Small-Scale Research Units or Management Areas Open to Bottom Fishing (2012); CCAMLR Conservation Measure 25-02, Minimisation of the Incidental Mortality of Seabirds in the Course of Longline Fishing or Longline Fishing Research in the Convention Area (2015); CCAMLR Conservation Measure 25-03, Minimisation of the Incidental Mortality of Seabirds and Marine Mammals in the Course of Trawl Fishing in the Convention Area; CCAMLR Conservation Measure 26-01, General Environmental Protection during Fishing (2015).

establishment of general MPAs in the CCAMLR region. This initiative provides for the identification of MPAs for the protection of representative examples of marine ecosystems and biodiversity, key ecosystem processes, areas vulnerable to impact by human activities, and areas that will help to maintain resilience to climate change.[189] Two MPAs have been established to date, one in the area to the south of the South Orkney Islands[190] and one in the Ross Sea.[191] The level of protection in these two MPAs differs, thereby demonstrating that MPAs are the product of complex negotiations. Commercial fishing[192] is prohibited within the South Orkney Islands southern shelf MPA, along with any discharges and dumping of any waste from a fishing vessel. In contrast, some fishing is still permitted in parts of the Ross Sea MPA, albeit subject to lower catch levels and requirements relating to tagging and releasing a specified number of fish per tonne caught.[193] What both MPAs have in common is the emphasis that is given to conducting scientific research in the MPAs in order to increase understanding of the Antarctic ecosystems.

The CCAMLR system of MPAs has been directly linked to the international goal of developing a representative network of MPAs, discussed in Chapter 3, and it demonstrates that RFMOs can have a role to play in meeting this target. The Ross Sea MPA has been ascribed particular significance because it was the world's largest MPA at the time of its designation, covering 600,000 square miles.[194] At the same time, it is also important to note that CCAMLR has expressly recognized that its MPA management plans can only be fulfilled if it actively engages with other international organizations that are able to regulate other relevant activities that might impact the areas.[195] This is an important topic, to which we will return in Chapter 10.

7.4.4 Cooperation in monitoring, surveillance, and control of high seas fishing

Another important function of RFMOs and arrangements is to 'establish appropriate cooperative mechanisms for effective monitoring, control, surveillance and enforcement'.[196] Some RFMOs have developed procedures to allow for the mutual inspection of vessels fishing in the relevant area.[197] These enforcement schemes are

---

[189] CCAMLR Conservation Measure 91/04 (2011), para. 2.

[190] CCAMLR Conservation Measure 91/03 (2009).

[191] CCAMLR Conservation Measure 91/05 (2016).

[192] The measure still allows research fishing in accordance with CCAMLR Conservation Measure 24-01 (2013).

[193] The Ross Sea MPA is actually composed of three zones; a general protection zone, in which all commercial fishing is prohibited, and a special research zone and krill research zone, in which regulated fishing is permitted. However, the decision designating the MPA also provides for the redistribution of fishing so that areas outside of the MPA would be opened up to fishing.

[194] See e.g. BBC News, 'World's Largest Marine Protected Area Declared in Antarctica', 28 October 2016: http://www.bbc.co.uk/news/science-environment-37789594.

[195] CCAMLR Conservation Measure 91/04 (2011) para. 10.

[196] UNFSA, Article 10(h).

[197] For a discussion of relevant schemes, see R Rayfuse, *Non-Flag State Enforcement in High Seas Fisheries* (Martinus Nijhoff 2004) 137–322; D Guilfoyle, *Shipping Interdiction and the Law of the Sea* (CUP 2009) 97–158.

important because they address the drawbacks of exclusive flag State jurisdiction on the high seas, discussed above, and they can thus be 'deemed as an exception to Article 92(1) of [UNCLOS]'.[198]

The UNFSA also plays an important role in promoting cooperation in this respect, as it provides that:

[i]n any high seas area covered by a subregional or regional fisheries management organization or arrangement, a State Party which is a member of such organization or a participant in such arrangement may, through its duly authorized inspectors, board and inspect, in accordance with paragraph 2, fishing vessels flying the flag of another State Party to this Agreement, whether or not such State Party is also a member of the organization or a participant in the arrangement, for the purpose of ensuring compliance with conservation and management measures for straddling fish stocks and highly migratory fish stocks established by that organization or arrangement.[199]

This right to inspect a vessel stems from the UNFSA itself and the flag State of the other vessel does not need to be a member of the RFMO to fall within the scope of this provision. Thus, it has been said that the UNFSA offers 'a unique and far-reaching exception to the flag State's exclusive jurisdiction on the high seas'.[200] Yet, the role of inspectors is limited to gathering evidence and reporting to the flag State. The inspecting State cannot itself arrest the vessel and institute judicial proceedings. As a result, there is still a need to ensure that the flag State takes sufficient action to follow up a violation, and it has been suggested that RFMOs should develop guidelines for investigations of suspected violations, as well as harmonized sanction regimes, in order to ensure that all flag States are taking equivalent action.[201]

At-sea inspection is not the only means for enforcing international conservation and management measures. Indeed, the practicalities and efficiencies of at-sea inspections are sometimes called into question, particularly in light of the vast areas that must be policed.[202] To this end, the Code of Conduct on Responsible Fisheries and the International Plan of Action (IPOA) on IUU Fishing both encourage the broad use of a range of additional monitoring, control, and surveillance activities in relation to fishing vessels. In particular, vessel monitoring schemes and observer programmes are widely used to enhance fisheries enforcement,[203] and several RFMOs have mandated the use of these techniques on all vessels authorized to fish in the area under their control.[204] These measures can provide additional sources of evidence to pinpoint when a violation of conservation and management takes place.

---

[198] MA Palma-Robles, 'Fisheries Enforcement and other Concepts', in R Warner and S Kaye (eds), *Routledge Handbook of Maritime Regulation and Enforcement* (Routledge 2015) 148.

[199] UNFSA, Article 21(1).   [200] NEAFC Performance Review Panel Report (2014) 88.

[201] Ibid, 93–4.

[202] For example, the CCAMLR Performance Review Panel noted that only 110 at-sea inspections had taken place under the treaty between 1997 and 2007, resulting in sanctions being imposed on ten of the inspected vessels. In the view of the Review Panel, 'the System of Inspection, as currently implemented, is far from an effective (or cost-effective) [monitoring, surveillance, and control] tool'; Chapter 4, CCAMLR Performance Review Report (2008), para. 37.

[203] Palma-Robles (n198) 153–4.   [204] See the discussion in Guilfoyle (n197) 97–169.

A major challenge for RFMOs is to ensure compliance with conservation and management measures by vessels flying the flag of a State that is neither a member of the RFMO, nor a Party to the UNFSA. Such vessels can potentially operate at an unfair advantage, thereby undermining agreed conservation and management measures. It is for this reason that this activity is classified as unregulated fishing,[205] and it is targeted by a number of international instruments dealing with IUU fishing. Many regional treaties impose a duty on the Contracting Parties to 'either directly or through the [RFMO], take measures, which are consistent with international law ... to deter fishing by vessels of non-parties to this Convention which undermine the effectiveness of conservation and management measures adopted by the [RFMO]'.[206] This type of provision has been used as the basis, inter alia, to compile lists of vessels flagged to non-Contracting Parties that are suspected of carrying out IUU fishing.[207] For example, under the scheme to promote compliance by non-Contracting Party vessels with CCAMLR conservation measures, CCAMLR is charged with identifying 'those non-Contracting Parties whose vessels are engaged in IUU fishing activities in the Convention Area that threaten to undermine the effectiveness of CCAMLR conservation measures, and shall establish a list of such vessels'.[208] If a Contracting Party sights a non-Contracting Party vessel fishing in the Convention Area, the vessel will be presumed to be engaging in IUU fishing, and the Contracting Party must inform the CCAMLR Secretariat, the other Contracting Parties, and the flag State.[209] The exclusive jurisdiction of the flag State will prevent an inspection of the vessel at sea, unless the flag State is a Party to the UNFSA, but the flag State will be requested to 'take action to prevent the vessel undertaking any activities that undermine the effectiveness of CCAMLR conservation measures and that the Flag State report back to CCAMLR on the measures it has taken in respect of the vessel concerned'.[210] If the flag State fails to take action, the vessel will be placed on the IUU list and it will be prevented from fishing within the waters of Contracting Parties and from accessing the ports of Contracting Parties, unless the vessel is inspected when it arrives in port.[211] This latter measure draws upon the ability of port States to utilize their sovereignty over ports to place conditions on vessels voluntarily entering their ports.[212] Given that fishing vessels ultimately have to land their catch, the potential for the use of port State measures has been increasingly recognized in recent years. The role of port States is endorsed and encouraged in the IPOA on

---

[205] This sort of activity is considered unregulated fishing; see IPOA-IUU Fishing, para. 1.2.

[206] SEAFO Convention, Article 22(3). See also WCPF Convention, Article 32(4); NPFC Convention, Article 20(4).

[207] See e.g. IATTC Resolution C-05-07 (2005), IOTC Resolution 15/04 (2015); SPRFMO Decision CMM 1.04, WCPFC Conservation and Management Measure 2010-06.

[208] CCAMLR Conservation Measure 10-07(2007), para. 2. Other regions have similar schemes, e.g. NAFO Conservation and Enforcement Measures (2016), Articles 48–55; ICCAT Recommendation 98-11, concerning the ban on landings and transhipments of vessels from non-Contracting Parties identified as having committed a serious infringement (1999).

[209] CCAMLR Conservation Measure 10-07(2007), para. 6.   [210] Ibid, para. 8.

[211] Ibid, para. 22.

[212] See e.g. L de la Fayette, 'Access to Ports in International Law' (1996) 11 *IJMCL* 1.

IUU Fishing,[213] and the powers of port States have since been clarified by the 2009 FAO Port State Measures Agreement.[214] The advantage of this Agreement is that it extends the obligations relating to inspection and control of fishing vessels suspected of conducting IUU fishing in contravention of regional conservation and management measures to all Parties to the Agreement and not just to other members of the RFMO. It is precisely this form of wider cooperation that is needed in order to avoid the phenomenon of port hopping, whereby a vessel engaged in IUU fishing simply seeks access to a port that is not part of an RFMO scheme.[215] States will only be under an obligation to exercise port State measures if they are a Party to the Agreement, although many States have unilaterally chosen to exercise such powers on the basis of their sovereign rights to restrict access to their ports as a matter of customary international law.[216] At the same time, it must be recognized that 'no RFMO scheme goes so far as to provide for port state enforcement', meaning that 'in all cases, prosecution and the right of sanction is left to the flag state'.[217] The Port State Measures Agreement does not alter this situation, as it focuses on denying access to port or withdrawing port services.[218] Thus, at the present time, the international legal framework for fisheries enforcement lacks the equivalent of extra-territorial port State jurisdiction that appears in Article 218 of UNCLOS in the case of vessel-source pollution.[219] One way in which States have attempted to address this issue, however, is by requiring that masters of vessels make a declaration that fish being landed have been caught in accordance with relevant regulations, and the making of a false declaration is itself made a criminal offence under the law of the port State.[220] In this way, the false statement made within the territory of a State becomes the trigger for a prosecution, thereby circumventing the limits of port State jurisdiction. The introduction of so-called secondary violations has been noted as an increasingly popular strategy for port States in a variety of contexts, in order to counter unlawful conduct at sea.[221]

---

[213] IPOA IUU Fishing, paras 52–64.

[214] See the discussion in J Swan, 'Port State Measures—from Residual Port State Jurisdiction to Global Standards' (2016) 31 *IJMCL* 395–421.

[215] See R Rayfuse, 'The Role of Port States', in R Warner and S Kaye (eds), *Routledge Handbook of Maritime Regulation and Enforcement* (Routledge 2015) 80–1.

[216] See Palma-Robles (n198) 152.　　　[217] Rayfuse (n215) 80.

[218] Article 18(3) of the Agreement ambiguously provides that 'nothing in this Agreement prevents a Party from taking measures that are in conformity with international law in addition to those specified in paragraphs 1 and 2 of this Article, including such measures as the flag State of the vessel has expressly requested or to which it has consented'. This formulation thus permits enforcement action if the flag State agrees and it leaves the door open to further developments in the law.

[219] See Chapter 6.

[220] See e.g. United Kingdom Sea Fish (Conservation) Act 1967, s. 7.

[221] H Ringbom, 'Vessel-Source Pollution', in R Rayfuse (ed.), *Research Handbook on International Marine Environmental Law* (Edward Elgar 2016) 129.

7.5 Special Conservation Regimes for Marine Living Resources

7.5.1 Anadromous and catadromous species

Some marine resources are given special treatment under international law because of their particular characteristics. Both anadromous and catadromous species fall into this category.

Anadromous fish are those species which 'spend most of their lives in the sea and migrate to fresh water to breed'.[222] By far the most commercially important species of anadromous fish is the salmon, but the category also includes types of shad, trout, striped bass, smelt, and sturgeon. Anadromous species present a particular problem for conservation and management because they originate in the rivers and lakes of a single State, before migrating out to sea where they spend the majority of their adult lives. The fish, however, return to the same river in which they were born in order to breed. It follows that much of the cost associated with conserving and managing anadromous species falls upon the State of origin. It is for this reason that Article 66 of UNCLOS creates a special framework for determining which States may participate in fishing for anadromous species. Article 66 provides that 'fisheries for anadromous stocks shall be conducted only in waters landward of the outer limits of the exclusive economic zones, except in cases where this provision would result in economic dislocation for a state other than the state of origin'.[223] Thus, the general rule is that fishing for anadromous stocks shall not take place on the high seas, and Article 66, therefore, operates as an important exception to freedom of fishing on the high seas as found in Article 116 of the Convention.

If there are circumstances where a State wishes to continue high seas fishing on the basis of the economic impacts for its nationals, it would appear from Article 66 that it is subject to the agreement of the State of origin. In this regard, UNCLOS provides that 'with respect to fishing beyond the outer limits of the [EEZ], States concerned shall maintain consultations with a view to achieving agreement on terms and conditions of such fishing giving due regard to the conservation requirements and the needs of the State of origin in respect of those stocks'.[224] Furthermore, any fishing on the high seas must comply with the regulatory measures and TAC set by the State of origin.[225]

In practice, there is little fishing for anadromous species on the high seas today. Both the Pacific Anadromous Stocks Convention and the North Atlantic Salmon Convention prohibit the taking of such species on the high seas.[226]

---

[222] GS Myers, 'Usage of Anadromous, Catadromous and Allied Terms for Migratory Fishes' (1949) *Copeia* 89, 94.

[223] UNCLOS, Article 66 (3)(a).   [224] Ibid, Article 66 (3)(a).

[225] Ibid, Article 66(2).

[226] See 1992 Convention for the Conservation of Anadromous Stocks in the North Pacific Ocean (Anadromous Stocks Convention) (EIF 16 February 1993), Article III (1)(a); 1982 Convention for the Conservation of Salmon in the North Atlantic Ocean (Salmon Convention) (EIF 1 October 1983), Article 2 (1).

Indeed, the Anadromous Stocks Convention not only addresses direct fishing for anadromous stocks but also regulates the incidental taking of anadromous species, providing that 'incidental taking of anadromous fish shall be minimized to the maximum extent possible'.[227] The Annex provides guidance on how States should minimize the taking of incidental catch of anadromous species and the North Pacific Anadromous Fish Commission is empowered to recommend additional measures to avoid or reduce incidental taking of anadromous fish on the high seas.[228]

Catadromous species are also subject to a special regime regulating which States can participate in fishing activities. Catadromous species spend most of their lives in fresh water but migrate to sea to breed; the most prominent catadromous fish is the freshwater eel, species of which are found across the globe.[229] Owing to the peculiar nature of their lifecycle, responsibility for the management of catadromous species resides with the coastal State in whose waters the species spend the 'greater part of their life cycle'. Like anadromous species, UNCLOS restricts fishing for catadromous species on the high seas by providing that 'harvesting of catadromous species shall be conducted only in waters landward of the outer limits of the [EEZ]'.[230] The purpose of this prohibition is to prevent the capture of juveniles.[231] Indeed, the Convention admits no exceptions and so the regime for catadromous species is even stronger than for anadromous species.

UNCLOS also requires cooperation between those States that have jurisdiction over the waters through which catadromous species migrate. To this end, Article 67(3) requires these States to cooperate with the host State concerning 'the rational management of the species [taking] into account the responsibilities of the [host State] for the maintenance of these species'. Hey suggests that whilst the concept of *rational management* requires a similar balance of interests as cooperation over the conservation and management of other marine living resources, the fundamental difference is that 'the interest of the state in whose waters [a catadromous species] spends the greater part of its life cycle are given special consideration'.[232] At the same time, it does not appear that the host State could completely block exploitation by other States. Thus, other coastal States will have the right to harvest catadromous species, even in the absence of an agreement with the host State, albeit under the obligation to avoid undermining the host State's management efforts.[233]

---

[227] Anadromous Stocks Convention, Article III (1)(b).   [228] Ibid, Article IX (12).

[229] MH Nordquist et al (eds.), *United Nations Convention on the Law of the Sea 1982: A Commentary—Vol. II* (Martinus Nijhoff 1993) 681. Freshwater eels fall within the Anguillidae family of fishes, which comprises nineteen species and six subspecies.

[230] UNCLOS, Article 67(2).

[231] Y Tanaka, *The International Law of the Sea* (CUP 2012) 234.

[232] E Hey, *The Regime for the Exploitation of Transboundary Marine Fisheries Resources* (Martinus Nijhoff 1989), 67–8.

[233] See Tanaka (n231), 234.

7.5.2 Marine mammals

Marine mammals fall into another category of marine living resources that benefit from a special conservation regime under UNCLOS. There are around 120 species of marine mammals, including many types of whales, dolphins, porpoises, seals, and walruses. Marine mammals are singled out for special treatment because of their exceptional vulnerability to capture and the adverse effects of other human interference, their highly migratory nature, and their interest from economic, aboriginal use, and conservation viewpoints.[234]

Articles 65 and 120 of UNCLOS exempt marine mammals from the normal rule concerning the optimum utilization of marine living resources. In other words, coastal States are not obliged to set a TAC for marine mammals or share excess capacity with other States. Rather, States can take a preservationist attitude towards marine mammals if they wish. Nevertheless, the Convention continues to 'generally regard marine mammals as harvestable living resources', and whilst its focus is 'more on conservation rather than on utilization',[235] it falls short of demanding the preservation of marine mammals.

In practice, there have been significant tensions concerning the status of many marine mammals, with States taking different views as to how much protection they require. Some of the earliest agreements in this area concerned fur seals and sea otters, which were being heavily exploited for their pelts.[236] Later in the twentieth century, cetaceans have come to dominate international attention.[237]

Today, the principal organization concerned with cetaceans is the International Whaling Commission (IWC), established under the International Convention for the Regulation of Whaling (ICRW).[238] The treaty was designed to introduce detailed regulations that restricted whaling activities, including through the designation of protected species and the introduction of restrictions on whaling methods. The regulations are contained in a Schedule which forms an integral part of the treaty[239] but which may be amended by the IWC using a tacit amendment procedure. The amendment procedure has been used to restrict gradually the ability of Member States to carry out whaling, albeit subject to individual objections by some pro-whaling States. Over time, restrictions were introduced in relation to taking particular whale species considered at greatest risk. Amendments were also adopted for the purpose of establishing whale sanctuaries in the Indian Ocean[240] and the

---

[234] PW Birnie, 'Marine Mammals: Exploiting the Ambiguities of Article 65 of the Convention on the Law of the Sea and Related Provisions: Practice under the International Convention for the Regulation of Whaling', in D Freestone et al (eds.), *The Law of the Sea: Progress and Prospects* (OUP 2006) 264.

[235] Proelss and Houghton (n27) 237.

[236] See *Bering Fur Seals Arbitration* (1893) 263–76; 1911 Convention between the United States, Great Britain, Russia and Japan for the Preservation and Protection of Fur Seals (EIF 14 December 1911). See, generally, S Barrett, *Environment & Statecraft* (OUP 2003) 19–48.

[237] See 1931 Convention on the Regulation of Whaling (EIF 16 January 1935); 1937 International Agreement for the Regulation of Whaling (EIF 7 May 1938).

[238] See 1946 International Convention for the Regulation of Whaling (ICRW) (EIF 10 November 1948).

[239] ICRW, Article I.   [240] Ibid, Schedule, para. 7(a).

Southern Ocean.[241] However, a turning point in the regulation of whaling came in 1982, when the IWC adopted the so-called moratorium on commercial whaling.[242] The moratorium was accepted by almost all States. Norway is one of the few States that has sustained its objection to the moratorium and continued the commercial catch of whales.[243] Iceland also purports to have a reservation to the moratorium as a result of its withdrawal and re-entry to the IWC in 2002.[244] The precise nature of the moratorium has become contested. The relevant text provides that 'catch limits for the killing for commercial purposes of whales from all stocks for the 1986 coastal and the 1985/86 pelagic seasons and thereafter shall be zero' and it expressly foresees a review of the decision at a later stage.[245] Thus, some States argue that the purpose of the moratorium is to allow stocks to recover so that they can once again sustain commercial whaling.[246] In contrast, it has been claimed that the adoption of the moratorium signals the emergence of a new preservationist approach to whaling which 'wants to ban all whaling, irrespective of whether a particular species is stable or endangered, an attitude that is clearly incompatible with the industry of whaling'.[247] To this end, anti-whaling States insist that the role of the IWC has evolved from its original objectives to one that focuses on the conservation of whales for future generations.[248] It is true that certain developments at the IWC point towards an increasing emphasis on conservation. For example, in 2003, the IWC established a conservation committee with a mandate to prepare a conservation agenda and make recommendations to the Commission thereon.[249] This initiative coincided with the IWC extending its interest beyond the exploitation of whales to also consider other impacts, including chemical pollution, noise pollution, bycatch, and habitat degradation, on cetaceans. Current work of the conservation committee

---

[241] Ibid, Schedule, para. 7(b). Japan has lodged an exception to the Southern Ocean Sanctuary in relation to Minke whales, but it was found to have breached the terms of the ICRW in relation to its taking of Fin whales in the sanctuary in *Whaling in the Antarctic* (2014) para. 233.

[242] ICRW, Schedule, para. 10(e).

[243] Japan, Peru, and the USSR also made objections. The objections of Japan and Peru were later withdrawn. The Russian Federation has never withdrawn its exception, although it does not currently carry out commercial whaling.

[244] See e.g. A Gillespie, 'Iceland's Reservation at the International Whaling Commission' (2003) 14 *EJIL* 977.

[245] ICRW, Schedule, para. 10(e).

[246] In this regard, the ICRW preamble says that the purpose of the Convention is 'to provide for the proper conservation of whale stocks and thus make possible the orderly development of the whaling industry'. The preamble also states that 'whaling operations should be confined to those species best able to sustain exploitation in order to give an interval for recovery to certain species of whales now depleted in numbers'.

[247] A D'Amato and SK Chopra, 'Whales: Their Emerging Right to Life' (1991) 85 *AJIL* 21, 45. Indeed, the authors go on to argue that this preservationist approach contains the seeds of whales possessing an entitlement to life; Ibid, 49.

[248] See the Memorial of Australia in the Case concerning Whaling in the Antarctic, para. 2.99: 'the IWC now pursues conservation of whales as an end in itself'; United Kingdom Department for Environment, Food and Rural Affairs, *The International Whaling Commission—the Way Forward*, 5: 'the UK Government opposes all whaling apart from limited aboriginal subsistence whaling'. See also MJ Bowman, 'Normalizing the International Convention for the Regulation of Whaling' (2008) 29(3) *MJIL* 293; Proelss and Houghton (n27) 243.

[249] IWC Resolution 2003-1.

includes studies into ship strikes[250] and the impacts of marine debris on cetaceans. Yet, it has been noted that the IWC does not appear to have powers to adopt binding measures in relation to these issues.[251] Moreover, in spite of these developments, the object and purpose of the ICRW, which includes the orderly development of industrial whaling, have not been formally changed,[252] and the capture of whales has not been definitively prohibited under the Convention. Indeed, some steps have been taken towards the resumption of commercial whaling, notably the adoption in 1994 of a Revised Management Procedure, which is intended to overcome shortcomings in previous management procedures by taking into account scientific uncertainty in establishing catch limits.[253] However, this instrument only deals with the procedure for setting catch limits and it cannot be put into operation until States have also agreed upon an accompanying revised management scheme dealing with enforcement.[254] So far, IWC members have been unable to reach agreement on this matter.[255]

The institutional politics of the IWC may have prevented the emergence of any consensus on lifting the moratorium on commercial whaling, but there are two other types of whaling that are permitted under the Convention.

First, special rules apply to aboriginal whale hunts. It has long been recognized that small coastal communities in remote locations have depended upon the capture of marine mammals for their livelihoods and it would be necessary to tolerate the taking of marine mammals for this purpose.[256] Unlike the earlier 1931 Convention on the Regulation of Whaling, the current international regime does not contain a general exception for whaling carried out by aboriginal communities. Rather, the IWC itself sets periodic quotas for so-called aboriginal whaling.[257] Currently, the IWC sets quotas for bowhead whales from the Bering-Chukchi-Beaufort Seas stock; grey whales from the Eastern stock in the North Pacific; minke whales from the West Greenland and Central stocks and fin whales from the West Greenland stock; bowhead whales and humpback whales from the West Greenland feeding aggregation; and humpback whales taken by the Bequians of St. Vincent and the Grenadines.[258] The notion of aboriginal whaling has been construed narrowly and coastal communities in Japan and Norway, despite long traditions of whaling, have been denied

---

[250] See Chapter 6 on the role played by the IWC in promoting international cooperation on this issue.

[251] HM Dotinga and AG Oude Elferink, 'Acoustic Pollution in the Oceans: The Search for Legal Standards' (2000) 31 *ODIL* 151, 168.

[252] See *Whaling in the Antarctic* (2014) para. 56.   [253] See IWC Resolution 1994-5.

[254] See A Gillespie, 'The Search for a New Compliance Mechanism within the IWC' (2003) 34 *ODIL* 349.

[255] For a discussion of the key stumbling blocks, see M Fitzmaurice, *Whaling and International Law* (CUP 2015) 82–7.

[256] See e.g. Article 8 of the Regulations proposed by the Arbitral Tribunal in the *Bering Fur Seals Arbitration* (1893) 263.

[257] See A Gillespie, 'Aboriginal Subsistence Whaling: A Critique of the Inter-Relationship between International law and the International Whaling Commission' (2001) 12 *CJILP* 77; J Firestone and J Lilley, 'An Endangered Species: Aboriginal Whaling and the Right to Self-Determination and Cultural Heritage in a National and International Context' (2004) 34 *ELR* 10763.

[258] ICRW, Schedule, para. 13(b).

permission to carry out whaling under this exception.[259] Moreover, even though they are permitted in principle, aboriginal hunts are still subject to rules concerning the manner in which whaling is carried out and the use of the whales that are taken. The IWC has made clear that in determining quotas for aboriginal whaling, 'highest priority should be accorded to the objective of ensuring that the risk of extinction to individual stocks are not seriously increased by subsistence whaling',[260] and for this reason, all quotas are set based upon advice from the Scientific Committee. Furthermore, aboriginal hunts are prohibited from striking, taking, or killing calves or any whale accompanied by a calf,[261] and the regulations make clear that 'the meat and products of such whales are to be used exclusively for local consumption'.[262] In practice, there is some debate over the role of the IWC in setting quotas for aboriginal whaling,[263] and the Commission has agreed to review the manner in which it deals with aboriginal subsistence whaling with a view to agreeing upon a more consistent and long-term approach[264] that takes into account indigenous people's rights.[265] In this respect, there is a need for a balance between the social needs of the aboriginal communities and the ecological concerns relating to cetacean populations.

Second, Article VIII of the Convention continues to allow whaling 'for the purposes of scientific research'. This has become a controversial exception, given that it confers the power to grant special permits for scientific whaling to individual Contracting Parties. The Convention text itself requires a Party that invokes this exception to 'report at once to the Commission all such authorizations which it has granted'.[266] At first sight, this would appear to be an after-the-fact reporting procedure to allow the review of the exercise of exceptions, but developments in the regulations contained in the ICRW Schedule have to some extent modified the nature of this obligation by introducing the requirement that '[a] Contracting Government shall provide the Secretary to the IWC with proposed scientific permits before they are issued and in sufficient time to allow the Scientific Committee to review and comment on them'.[267] The views of the Scientific Committee are not binding, but they should be taken into account by an individual State wishing to carry out scientific whaling.[268] Indeed, the International Court of Justice has also made clear that the decision of whether a permit is granted for scientific purposes is subject to judicial review on the basis of 'whether the elements of a programme's design and implementation are reasonable in relation to its stated scientific objectives'.[269] The Court went on to identify a number of elements which it would assess for their reasonableness, namely:

---

[259] See e.g. C Pinon Carlane, 'Saving the Whales in the New Millennium: International Institutions, Recent Developments and the Future of International Whaling Policies' (2005) *VELJ* 1, 11. See also Japanese Proposed Schedule Amendment to Permit the Catching of Minke Whales from the Okhotsk Sea-West Pacific Stock by Small-Type Whaling Vessels, Document IWC/64/9 (2012).

[260] IWC Resolution 1994-4, para. 4.   [261] ICRW, Schedule, para. 13(a)(4).

[262] Ibid, para. 13(b).   [263] For a detailed discussion, see Fitzmaurice (n255) 234–75.

[264] IWC Resolution 2014-1, para. a.

[265] See Report of the IWC Expert Workshop on Aboriginal Subsistence Whaling, Document IWC/66/ASW Rep01 (2015) 12 and 17.

[266] ICRW, Article VIII(1).   [267] Ibid, Schedule, para. 30.

[268] *Case Concerning Whaling in the Antarctic* (2014) para. 47.   [269] Ibid, para. 88.

decisions regarding the use of lethal methods; the scale of the programme's use of lethal sampling; the methodology used to select sample sizes; a comparison of the target sample sizes and the actual take; the time frame associated with a programme; the programme's scientific output; and the degree to which a programme co-ordinates its activities with related research projects.[270]

In particular, the Court noted that any scientific whaling should not cause a risk to populations of the whales that are targeted.[271] Thus, environmental considerations continue to apply to this exceptional form of whaling.

The IWC is not alone in regulating the conservation and management of cetaceans. The significance attached to cetaceans by the international community is reflected by the range of other bodies that have adopted measures calling for their conservation. An important instrument in this respect is the CMS, which seeks to offer a framework for cooperation between range States of migratory species. Many species of cetacean are listed under Appendix I of the CMS,[272] thus gaining immediate protection. Range States are required to prohibit the taking of listed species, as well as 'endeavour[ing]' to conserve and where appropriate restore the habitats of the species and to prevent, reduce, or control other activities that may impede the migration of species or may contribute to the further endangerment of such species.[273] This includes an obligation to protect Appendix I species against bycatch, as confirmed by CMS COP Resolution 6.2.[274] At the same time, the CMS also includes similar exceptions to those found in the ICRW relating to aboriginal hunts and scientific research.[275] Thus, it has been said that 'the CMS has a supporting, non-conflicting role with the IWC'.[276]

In the case of small cetaceans, further protection is provided through additional regional instruments.[277] The Agreement on the Conservation of Small Cetaceans of the Baltic, North-East Atlantic, Irish and North Seas (ASCOBANS)[278] aims at the conservation of all small cetaceans founds in Northern European waters. Parties to ASCOBANS are expected to adopt certain management measures that are listed in the Annex to the Agreement, including legislation that prohibits the intentional taking and killing of small cetaceans, as well as an obligation to release immediately any animal caught alive and in good health, preventing the release of substances which are a potential threat to the health of animals, encouraging

---

[270] Ibid. [271] See *Case Concerning Whaling in the Antarctic* (2014) para. 85.

[272] Species listed under Appendix I include Bowhead Whale, Sei Whale, Blue Whale, Southern Right Whale, Northern Right Whale, Humpback Whale, Sperm Whale, and Cuviers Beaked Whale. Several species of dolphin and porpoise are also listed in Appendix I.

[273] See 1979 Convention on Migratory Species (CMS) (EIF 1 November 1983), Article III. See Chapter 3.

[274] CMS Resolution 6.2 (1999), para. 1. [275] See CMS, Article III(5).

[276] A Gillespie, 'Forum Shopping in International Environmental Law: The IWC, CITES and the Management of Cetaceans' (2002) 33 *ODIL* 17, 29.

[277] As noted by Churchill, these two agreements would appear to be adopted under Article IV(4) rather than Article IV(3); see RR Churchill, 'Sustaining Small Cetaceans: A Preliminary Evaluation of the Ascobans and Accobams Agreements', in AE Boyle and D Freestone (eds), *International Law and Sustainable Development* (OUP 1999) 231.

[278] See 1992 Agreement on the Conservation of Small Cetaceans of the Baltic, North East Atlantic, Irish and North Seas (ASCOBANS).

the development or modification of fishing gear and practices which reduce by-catches, and effectively regulating activities which seriously affect the food resources of animals. Similar measures must be adopted by Parties to the Agreement on the Conservation of Cetaceans of the Black Sea, Mediterranean Sea and Contiguous Atlantic Area (ACCOBAMS).[279] Both agreements are highly relevant to fishing operations; indeed, bycatch from fishing is considered one of the greatest threats to small cetaceans.[280] The elaboration of specific conservation measures by regular meeting of the COP has also led to a more detailed regime for the protection of habitats for these species. However, it has been pointed out that, given the broad range of threats facing cetaceans, the agreements cannot achieve their purposes by being applied in isolation, but rather they will 'probably function best as a stimulus and forum for promoting and coordinating research and the adoption of conservation measures by other organizations'.[281]

Marine mammal protection has also been addressed through other regional bodies. In the North-East Atlantic, the OSPAR Commission has identified the blue whale, the northern right whale, and the bowhead whale as threatened or declining species and it has adopted recommendations calling for Parties to promote the protection of these species at all life stages.[282] These measures are aimed at developing a monitoring strategy for the threatened species, as well as identifying areas of the region that might justify selection as a MPA in order to offer greater protection to the species and developing other effective mitigation actions against further anthropogenic threats. Parties to the Mediterranean Protocol on Biodiversity[283] and Caribbean Protocol on Biodiversity[284] have also listed several species of cetacean as threatened species requiring special protection. Moreover, several States in the northern Mediterranean have also established the so-called Pelagos Marine Mammal Sanctuary, covering an area of 96,000 square kilometres, in which all species of marine mammals are protected, including prohibitions on deliberate taking and intentional interference.[285] The Agreement requires the Parties to exchange

---

[279] See 1996 Agreement on the Conservation of Cetaceans of the Black Sea, Mediterranean Sea and Contiguous Atlantic Area. Unlike ASCOBANS, ACCOBAMs is not limited to small cetaceans. Furthermore, it has been observed that ACCOBAMS is 'a superior treaty text to the Ascobans Agreement because it is more detailed and more precise'; Churchill (n277) 250.

[280] See Ibid, 227.

[281] Ibid, 244. See also H Nukamp and A Nollkaemper, 'The Protection of Small Cetaceans in the Face of Uncertainty: An Analysis of the ASCOBANS Agreement' (1997) 9 *GIELR* 281–302.

[282] OSPAR Recommendation 2013/8, on furthering the protection and conservation of the bowhead whale in Region I of the OSPAR maritime area; OSPAR Recommendation 2013/9, on furthering the protection and conservation of the North Atlantic blue whale in the OSPAR maritime area; OSPAR Recommendation 2013/10, on furthering the protection and conservation of the northern right whale in the OSPAR maritime region.

[283] See 1995 Protocol concerning Specially Protected Areas and Biological Diversity in the Mediterranean (EIF 12 December 1999), Articles 11 and 12 and associated decisions of the MOP, including Action Plan for the Conservation of Cetaceans in the Mediterranean Sea.

[284] See 1990 Protocol concerning Specially Protected Areas and Wildlife (SPAW Protocol) (EIF 18 June 2000), Article 11(1)(b) and Annex II.

[285] See 1999 Accord relative à la création en Méditerranée d'un Sanctuaire pour les Mammifères Marins (EIF 21 February 2002). The Pelagos Santuary was recognized under the Protocol Concerning Specially Protected Areas and Biological Diversity in the Mediterranean in 2001.

views on the exercise of activities that may indirectly disturb cetaceans in the area, such as boat racing or whale watching. The Agreement, however, does not directly regulate bycatch of cetaceans, something for which it has been criticized.[286]

Whilst these efforts at regulation by regional institutions offer additional layers of protection for cetaceans, the obvious drawback is that they can only be applied either in the waters under the sovereignty or sovereign rights of Contracting Parties or to the vessels of those Parties on the high seas. Unlike the conservation and management measures adopted by RFMOs, these regional instruments cannot affect the high seas freedoms of vessels flying the flag of non-Parties. This means that any comprehensive solution to marine mammal conservation must be achieved at the global level through bodies such as the IWC.

7.5.3 Marine species endangered by trade

The objective of the Convention on International Trade in Endangered Species of Wild Fauna and Flora (CITES) is to ensure that international trade in specimens of wild animals and plants does not threaten their survival. It introduces a permitting system for trade in species that are listed in one of the appendices of the Convention. Several marine species are listed, and it is possible, in the future, that other marine species, including commercially exploited fish stocks, could be added. It is, therefore, important to understand how this global treaty, with 182 Contracting Parties, could be applied to offer protection to marine species.

CITES is concerned with international trade and, therefore, it does not cover all taking of marine species. It does not, for example, cover fishing by nationals within the territorial sea or EEZ of a State for the purposes of domestic consumption. However, it does cover the export of marine species that are taken within the jurisdiction of a State and then exported to another State. Moreover, trade also includes 'introduction from the sea',[287] which is defined as 'transportation into a state of specimens of any species which were taken in the marine environment not under the jurisdiction of any state'.[288] In other words, fishing on the high seas is also covered.[289] It follows that CITES could be used as a tool to regulate certain transactions relating to marine species.

CITES does not necessarily ban trade in listed species. Rather, the regulation of trade under CITES depends on the level of threat posed to a particular species by international trade. In essence, two levels of protection are available.

First, species listed in Appendix I are subject to 'particularly strict regulation', and the Convention only allows trade in these species in exceptional circumstances.[290]

---

[286] See T Scovazzi, 'The Mediterranean Marine Mammals Sanctuary' (2001) 16 *IJMCL* 132, 134–6.

[287] See 1973 Convention on International Trade in Endangered Species of Wild Fauna and Flora (CITES) (EIF 1 July 1975), Article 1(c).

[288] CITES, Article 1(e).

[289] See CITES COP Resolution 14.6 (2007), whereby Contracting Parties agree that 'the marine environment not under the jurisdiction of any State' means 'those marine areas beyond the areas subject to the sovereignty or sovereign rights of a State consistent with international law, as reflected in the United Nations Convention on the Law of the Sea'.

[290] CITES, Article 2(1).

More specifically, all trade of Appendix I species for commercial purposes is prohibited,[291] and CITES COP Resolution 5.10 encourages Contracting Parties to define *commercial purposes* as widely as possible in their national legislation in order to ensure the effectiveness of the regime.

In contrast, commercial trade in species listed in Appendix II is permitted, but it must first be authorized by the exporting State, and authorization can only be granted if it has been certified that, inter alia, the export will not be detrimental to the survival of the species[292] This non-detriment finding should be made by an independent Scientific Authority.[293] This system is designed to ensure that trade takes place in a sustainable manner. Where appropriate, species can be moved between appendices and it is possible to list particular geographically separate populations of species if they are subject to a distinct threat.[294] The decision to list a species is ultimately made by the COP on the basis of advice from one of its specialist technical committees. Decisions should be based upon the best scientific information that is available, although guidance adopted by the COP also expressly recognizes that:

> by virtue of the precautionary approach and in case of uncertainty regarding the status of a species or the impact of trade on the conservation of a species, the Parties shall act in the best interest of the conservation of the species concerned and, when considering proposals to amend Appendix I or II, adopt measures that are proportionate to the anticipated risks to the species.[295]

Although phrased as an obligation, this provision nevertheless leaves the question of much caution is appropriate to the decisions of the States concerned.

As with other regimes, Parties may make reservations to the listing of a species. This opportunity has been used by some States when listing species such as whales and seahorses.[296] However, the Convention makes abundantly clear that a State that has made a reservation is to be treated as a non-Party.[297] Trade with non-Parties is explicitly prohibited under the Convention, unless the non-Party can provide comparable documentation that substantially conforms to the requirements of the Convention.[298] Given that CITES has 182 Contracting Parties, including the European Union, the possibilities for trade for an objecting member may be incredibly restricted.[299]

In recent years, an increasing number of marine species have been listed under the Convention, including some species of sturgeons, sharks, rays, whales,

---

[291] Ibid, Article 3.   [292] Ibid, Article 4.

[293] See e.g. CITES COP Resolution 10.3 on the Designation and Role of Scientific Authorities (1997); CITES COP Resolution 16.7 on Non-Detriment Findings (2013).

[294] CITES, Article 1(a).   [295] CITES COP Resolution 9.24 (rev. COP16) (1994).

[296] See e.g. reservations in relation to various whale species by Japan, Iceland, Norway, Palau, and Saint Vincent and the Grenadines. See also reservations in relation to various seahorse species entered by Indonesia, Japan, Norway, Korea, and Palau.

[297] CITES, Article 15(3).   [298] Ibid, Article 10.

[299] However, as noted by Guggisberg, in the case of high seas fishing for domestic consumption, a single reservation would legitimate the activity: *The Use of CITES for Commercially-Exploited Fish Species* (Springer 2016) 386.

dolphins, seals, turtles, conches, seahorses, and corals.[300] Many of these listings have been highly controversial, because of both disputes about the scientific evidence to support listing and concerns about the relationship between CITES and other international bodies with a mandate to regulate fishing activities. Yet, as Young argues, CITES may have a supplementary role to play and it could work productively with other fisheries institutions to promote a coherent response to overfishing.[301] Indeed, CITES itself calls for such cooperation, requiring the Secretariat to 'consult intergovernmental bodies having a function in relation to [marine species] especially with a view to obtaining scientific data these bodies may be able to provide and to ensuring coordination with any conservation measures enforced by such bodies'.[302] In furtherance of this mandate, the COP has entered into an arrangement with the FAO, which is routinely consulted in the process of evaluating proposals to list aquatic species under the Convention through an ad hoc expert advisory panel.[303] This process ensures that the views of fisheries experts are taken into account in the CITES listing process, although listing remains a decision of the COP.[304] CITES has also worked closely with the IWC on the protection of cetaceans, aligning its policies with those of the IWC and encouraging CITES Parties to adhere to the ICRW.[305] There is further scope for such cooperation with RFMOs. Possibilities include involving RFMOs in the making non-detriment findings for Appendix II species[306] and linking certification schemes under CITES with catch documentation requirements elaborated by RFMOs,[307] although no such steps have yet been taken, owing to opposition to the listing of commercial fish species.[308] Whilst it is questionable whether CITES could make up for gaps in coverage of RFMOs, this institution could certainly play a role in supporting the measures taken by RFMOs to promote sustainable fishing.[309] Indeed, it has been observed that even the threat of CITES listing of a species can sometimes push the relevant RFMO into taking more stringent action.[310]

---

[300] See generally C Wold, 'Natural Resources Management and Conservation: Trade in Endangered Species' (2002) 13 *YIEL* 389.

[301] M Young, *Saving Fish, Trading Fish* (CUP 2013) 146–54.

[302] CITES, Article XV(2)(b).   [303] See <http://www.fao.org/fishery/topic/16340/en>.

[304] Proposals to require the agreement of the FAO were not successful; see the discussion in Young (n301) 169.

[305] See e.g. CITES COP Resolution 11.4 (2000).

[306] Guggisberg argues, 'RFMOs have a crucial role to play in the procedures towards [non-detriment findings] and the legality finding process' (n299) 392.

[307] Young (n301) 177.

[308] See e.g. L Little and MA Orellana, 'Can CITES Play a Role in Solving the Problems of IUU Fishing? The Trouble with Patagonian Toothfish' (2004) 16 *CJIELP* 21.

[309] See e.g. Guggisberg (n299) 382; Proelss and Houghton (n27) 249; ACJ Vincent et al, 'The Role of CITES in the Conservation of Marine Fishes Subject to International Trade' (2014) 15 *Fish & Fisheries* 563.

[310] Guggisberg (n299) 387; JP Heffernan, 'Dealing with Mediterranean Bluefin Tuna: A Study in International Environmental Management' (2014) 50 *MP* 81, 86.

7.6 Conclusion

The basic legal framework in UNCLOS for fisheries conservation and management has been criticized for its 'normative weaknesses',[311] but this instrument has been supplemented by a number of other instruments that have, to a large degree, made up for many of these shortcomings. The modern law relating to the protection of marine species is, thus, 'a cross-sectoral and multifaceted regime connecting the law of the sea with international environmental and economic law',[312] as illustrated by the range of instruments addressed in this chapter.

There is little doubt that the modern international law of fisheries has developed in a manner that has taken cognizance of general principles of international environmental law, including the precautionary approach and the ecosystems approach. Such principles are reiterated in many of the instruments negotiated at the global level, and there is evidence that they are being integrated into the constituent instruments of RFMOs and national laws of fishing States. The greater challenge has been in operationalizing these principles.

Regional or subregional measures are the principal means through which States have addressed the challenge of conserving and managing transboundary, highly migratory, straddling, and discrete high seas fish stocks, as well as associated and dependent species. The RFMO network has itself increased since the entry into force of UNCLOS and the UNFSA, although some gaps still do exist,[313] and filling them will require further cooperation. Even if global coverage of RFMO measures is achieved, several challenges will still exist for effective high seas fisheries conservation and management.

Some progress has undoubtedly been made in strengthening the legal regime in order to address the environmental effects of fishing,[314] but the primary challenge is to ensure that RFMOs actually carry out the mandate to take a precautionary and ecosystems approach. Initially, more information about fisheries and the environment in which they live is necessary if States are going to carry out fishing in a manner that does not undermine broader ecosystem services. Thus, ecosystem-monitoring strategies are vital[315] and could usefully be coordinated with other institutions acting within the same region, such as regional seas bodies.[316] Yet, it is also important that this information be used in the regulation of fishing. History demonstrates

---

[311] RR Churchill, 'Fisheries and Their Impact on the Marine Environment: UNCLOS and Beyond', in MC Ribeiro (ed.), *30 Years after the Signature of the United Nations Convention on the Law of the Sea: The Protection of the Environment and the Future of the Law of the Sea* (Coimbra Editora 2014) 31; Barnes (n24).

[312] Proelss and Houghton (n27) 230.

[313] See e.g. Oslo Declaration Concerning the Prevention of Unregulated High Seas Fishing in the Central Arctic Ocean, 16 July 2015. For further discussion, see EJ Molenaar, 'International Regulation of Central Arctic Ocean Fisheries', in M Nordquist et al (eds), *Challenges of the Changing Arctic: Continental Shelf, Navigation, and Fisheries* (Brill 2016) 429–63; Y Takei, *Filling Regulatory Gaps in High Seas Fisheries* (Brill 2008) 245–57.

[314] See e.g. Edeson (n94) 6165.   [315] See Vierros et al (n161) 134.

[316] See Chapter 10.

that RFMOs have often failed to follow scientific advice when setting management measures, and this is a problem that must be addressed. Some form of external over-sight of RFMO performance would be desirable in this respect, in order to ensure that this information is put to best use. However, as RFMOs are established as autonomous institutions, such a reform is not straightforward. To date, some pro-gress has been made to increase oversight through voluntary reviews,[317] but it has been argued that more needs to be done to ensure 'constant monitoring and regular review' of RFMO performance.[318] There is also scope for increased interactions between RFMOs, through sharing of best practice. Such diffusion can particularly be effective in the case of conservation and management measures that do not touch upon sensitive issues of fisheries allocation.[319] In addition, the process of reviewing regional action on protecting VMEs through the UNGA has demonstrated that political pressure to integrate environmental considerations into decision-making can be brought to bear on RFMOs by a global body with a broad interest in the pro-tection of the marine environment. This interaction may offer a model for a more regular process of centralized oversight of fisheries conservation and management.

A second key challenge of high seas fisheries conservation relates to enforcement. Whilst progress has been made in extending the application of RFMO measures to all States, the doctrine of exclusive flag State enforcement jurisdiction on the high seas continues to offer sanctuary to IUU fishing vessels. This free-rider problem is exacerbated by the phenomenon of flag hopping, when a vessel transfers to a different flag in order to avoid enforcement. To this end, the FAO Compliance Agreement has not been as successful as it may have been hoped, and little progress has been made on the establishment of a global record of fishing vessels to control this problem. The FAO has nevertheless reinforced the role of flag States through the elaboration of the Voluntary Guidelines for Flag State Performance, which, whilst non-binding, are expressly noted to be 'based on relevant rules of international law'[320] and thus seek to provide guidance to States on what measures they should take in order to comply with their due diligence obligations under UNCLOS and other binding instruments. Furthermore, the guidelines encourage flag States to undergo periodic performance assessments.[321] Whilst this is currently an optional exercise that is only likely to attract States that already have a good track record, the guidelines do recommend that States consider an international mechanism for self-assessment,[322] and it is possible that the FAO could develop an audit scheme along similar lines to the scheme put in place by the IMO.[323] Provided that it is sufficiently transparent,[324] this would be a positive development in that it would highlight both good practice of flag States and areas for improvement.[325]

---

[317] See the critique of performance reviews in EJ Molenaar, 'Addressing Regulatory Gaps in High Seas Fisheries' (2005) 20 *IJMCL* 533, 551–6.

[318] Lodge and Nandan (n83) 373. See also Report of the Reconvened United Nations Fish Stocks Agreement Review Conference (2016), Annex, Section B, para. 2.

[319] Stokke (n124) 345–8.   [320] Flag State Guidelines, para. 1.   [321] Ibid, para. 44.

[322] Ibid, para. 45(d).   [323] See Chapter 6.

[324] See the discussion of the IMO scheme in Chapter 6.

[325] The guidelines themselves encourage the flag State to 'make the results [of a self-assessment] publically available'; Flag State Guidelines, para. 45(b).

Alongside strengthening flag State performance, port State control and trade certification schemes also show promise in tackling IUU fishing. Once again, RFMOs have been at the forefront of developments in this respect, although they can only do so much by themselves. The entry into force of the Port State Measures Agreement may boost the ability to achieve a global response to this problem, provided it can achieve widespread participation. Alternatively, better coordination between RFMOs could help, and some steps have been taken in this direction: for example, by the development of a coordinated list of prohibited vessels by the tuna RFMOs.[326] Other international institutions, such as regional organizations or global environmental treaty bodies, can also be utilized in order to support the measures adopted by RFMOs. It has been pointed out that it is ultimately necessary to not only put in place an appropriate regulatory framework but also tackle the economic incentives that lead to overfishing by developing international rules on catch effort and subsidies.[327] This may involve the participation of international economic organizations, such as the World Trade Organization.[328]

In theory, fisheries management within national jurisdiction is a simpler issue, given that the coastal State has sovereign rights to regulate and take enforcement action over all fishing activity within its territorial sea and EEZ. In practice, the challenges are just as great, given that fish stocks often move in and out of the jurisdiction of a single State, mandating some form of cooperation. Moreover, many developing countries struggle to enforce fisheries laws and regulations within their jurisdiction, owing to a lack of financial and technical capacity.[329] A solution to this problem also requires international cooperation and a robust institutional framework at the global level to support compliance. Whilst various instruments have highlighted the need for more technical and financial assistance for developing countries, these words must be met with actions if progress is to be achieved.

---

[326] See <http://www.tuna-org.org/vesselneg.htm>.
[327] See particularly Hey (n148) 211–13.
[328] See WTO, Doha Ministerial Declaration, Document WT/MIN(01)/DEC/1 (2001), para. 28.
[329] See G Hosch et al, 'The 1995 FAO Code of Conduct for Responsible Fisheries: Adopting, Implementing or Scoring Results?' (2011) 35 *MP* 189–200.

8

Environmental Regulation of Seabed Activities within and beyond National Jurisdiction

8.1 Introduction

Modern technology has increased the use of the oceans and, particularly, the use of the seabed and its resources. As noted by one author, 'these new capabilities, through fixed as well as mobile technology, have opened up a totally new vista of contemporary and prospective uses of the sea'.[1] The seabed of the continental shelf offers rich opportunities for a range of economic activities, including mineral extraction and energy generation. Yet, making use of the seabed may have serious implications for some of the most productive and fragile marine ecosystems in the oceans.

Exploitation of the seabed took off after the Second World War, when offshore drilling for oil and gas first become technologically feasible on a large scale. Today, almost a third of the oil consumed in the world comes from the continental shelf,[2] and new fields continue to be discovered. Yet, as oil and gas production extends into deeper or more remote waters, concerns about the environmental impact of offshore activities have simultaneously grown.[3] Campaign groups have opposed the extension of oil and gas exploration and exploitation into fragile and relatively pristine environments, such as the Arctic,[4] and they have pointed to past incidents, such as the 1979 Ixtoc I blowout and the 2010 Deepwater Horizon spill, in order to call for greater regulation of the oil and gas sector.[5] Yet, it is not only such catastrophic accidents that can harm the marine environment: there are also environmental risks posed by routine operations associated with the offshore industry. Chemicals and other polluting substances are widely used in the drilling process. Moreover, drilling generates waste cuttings

---

[1] DM Johnston, 'The Environmental Law of the Sea: Historical Development', in DM Johnston (ed.), *The Environmental Law of the Sea* (IUCN 1981) 37.

[2] J Rochette, *Towards an International Regulation of Offshore Oil Exploitation*, IDDRI Working Paper No. 15, (2012) 5. See also Global Ocean Commission, *From Decline to Recovery—A Rescue Package for the Global Ocean*, Summary Report (2014) 35.

[3] Rochette (n2) 5.

[4] See e.g. <http://www.greenpeace.org/international/en/campaigns/climate-change/arctic-impacts/The-dangers-of-Arctic-oil>.

[5] See e.g. <http://www.foe.org/news/archives/2013-05-bp-greenwashes-as-climate-dangers-grow>.

and produced water, which, if not properly managed, can contaminate the surrounding marine environment.[6]

Drilling for oil and gas is now just one of many activities taking place on the ocean floor. Aggregates, such as sand and gravel, can be dredged from the seabed for use in construction on land or land reclamation in coastal areas.[7] Valuable mineral resources are also now known to be located on the seabed. Diamonds have been mined in coastal waters off South Africa and Namibia, and valuable metals can even be found amongst the depths of the abyssal plains and mid-ocean ridges.[8] It is thought that agglomerations of seabed minerals can be found in the jurisdiction of a number of coastal States, as well as in areas beyond national jurisdiction. Yet resource extraction of this type poses inevitable physical threats to the wider marine environment in which the activity takes place. Interference arises not only from direct damage to benthic habitats but also as a result of pollution from sediment plumes, noise, and light. The risk of serious disturbances to the marine environment may be even greater at these depths, where ecosystems are characterized by high pressure, darkness, and very low temperatures, and endemic species are subject to slow-growth rates and low reproductivity. Vulnerable marine ecosystems (VMEs) that have been highlighted as being of particular concern include seamounts, hydrothermal vents, and cold-water corals. Significant damage to these ecosystems may be irreversible.

Seabed installations are also used for purposes other than extraction of resources. One of the fastest-growing activities is the marine renewable sector, which involves the placement of structures, platforms, and devices in order to produce energy from wave, tidal, or wind power.[9] Despite the environmental benefits in terms of reduced greenhouse gas emissions, the construction and operation of such installations are not without their own environmental consequences. There is still a large degree of uncertainty about the precise impacts of renewable energy infrastructure, but it has been suggested that 'possible effects include attraction towards noise source, avoidance, temporary hearing damage and permanent physical injury'.[10] More broadly, such developments may also affect marine species through displacement from spawning or feeding grounds, as well as increasing risks of collision or entanglement.[11]

---

[6] See e.g. A de Mestrel, 'The Prevention of Pollution of the Marine Environment Arising from Offshore Mining and Drilling' (1979) 20 *HILJ* 469, 474–5; P Harris et al, 'Chapter 21: Offshore Hydrocarbon Industries', in *Global Ocean Assessment* (United Nations 2016) 10–13.

[7] See The Economist, 'Asia's Mania for "Reclaiming" Land from the Sea Spawns Mounting Problems', 28 February 2015: <http://www.economist.com/news/asia/21645221-asias-mania-reclaiming-land-sea-spawns-mounting-problems-such-quantities-sand>.

[8] See generally PA Rona, 'The Changing Vision of Marine Minerals' (2008) 33 *OGR* 618.

[9] For an overview of the relevant technology, see D Leary and M Esteban, 'Climate Change and Renewable Energy from the Ocean and Tides: Calming the Sea of Regulatory Uncertainty' (1009) 24 *IJMCL* 617–51. See also GW Boehlert and AB Gill, 'Environmental and Ecological Effects of Ocean Renewable Energy Development: A Current Synthesis' (2010) 23 *Oceanography* 68–81.

[10] J Newwell and D Howell, *A Review of Offshore Wind Farm Related Underwater Noise Sources*, Report No. 544 R 0308, (2004) ii. See also Report of the Expert Workshop on Underwater Noise and its Impact on Marine and Coastal Biodiversity, Document UNEP/CBD/MCB/EM/2014/1/2 (2014).

[11] See e.g. Marine Scotland, 'Strategic Assessment of Collision Risk of Scottish Offshore Windfarms to Migrating Birds' (2014) 5 *Scottish Marine and Freshwater Science* 12; Marine Scotland, *Population Consequences of Displacement from Proposed Offshore Wind Energy Development for Seabirds Breeding at*

This chapter will consider the regulation of seabed activities both within and beyond the jurisdiction of coastal States. It will begin by considering the legal framework for regulating seabed activities within national jurisdiction. In this maritime zone, the coastal State plays a central role as the principal actor with regulatory authority. Yet, regional and global rules have also been negotiated in order to ensure that coastal States take sufficient action to protect the marine environment. The chapter will consider the main treaties and other instruments that apply in this context, with a particular focus on the development of rules and standards for regulating the oil and gas industry, as this is the activity that has attracted most attention to date. The chapter will then turn to the regime that applies to seabed activities beyond national jurisdiction. The designation of the international seabed as the common heritage of mankind means that regulation in this area is based upon a centralized regulatory framework that confers significant legislative and enforcement powers on a global institution, acting on behalf of the international community as a whole. As a result, there has emerged a sophisticated legal regime which seeks to balance the opportunities to develop the mineral resources of the deep seabed with the need to protect the marine environment beyond national jurisdiction.

8.2 Rights and Duties of Coastal States in Relation to Seabed Activities and Installations

8.2.1 The extension of coastal State rights and obligations over the seabed

UNCLOS has played an important role in consolidating and expanding the exclusive rights of coastal States over the seabed and waters appurtenant to their territory. The emergence of exclusive coastal State rights over continental shelf resources was already part of customary international law by the time UNCLOS was being negotiated.[12] UNCLOS goes even further by conferring exclusive rights on the coastal State to exploit the living and non-living resources on the seabed and in the water column within the 200 nautical miles of the baselines from which they measure the territorial sea.[13] The powers conferred by UNCLOS allow the coastal State to regulate a range of offshore activities, including the exploitation of all manner of seabed resources, as well as 'other activities for the economic exploitation of the zone, such as the production of energy from the water, currents and winds'.[14] Beyond 200 nautical miles, the sovereign coastal State rights over seabed resources may continue to the outer edge of the continental margin and UNCLOS establishes a complex procedure for delimiting the precise limits of coastal State jurisdiction.[15]

Scottish SPAs, Final Report (2014); Natural Environment Research Council, *Wave and Tidal Consenting Position Paper Series: Marine Mammal Impacts* (2013).

[12] *North Sea Continental Shelf Cases* (1969) 3.   [13] UNCLOS, Article 56(1)(a).
[14] Ibid, Article 56(1)(a).
[15] Ibid, Article 76(1). On the process of delineating the outer continental shelf beyond 200 nautical miles, see B Magnusson, *The Continental Shelf beyond 200 Nautical Miles: Delineation, Delimitation and Dispute Settlement* (Brill 2015).

Alongside the allocation of rights to resources, international law also imposes duties on the coastal State to manage those resources in a manner that respects the marine environment. Article 194 of UNCLOS calls for the adoption of:

measures ... designed to minimize to the fullest possible extent ... pollution from installations and devices used in the exploration or exploitation of the natural resources of the seabed and subsoil, in particular measures for preventing accidents and dealing with emergencies, ensuring the safety of operations at sea, and regulating the design, construction, equipment, operation and manning of such installations or devices.[16]

This obligation is further developed by Article 208, which obliges coastal States to 'adopt laws and regulations to prevent, reduce and control pollution of the marine environment arising from or in connexion with seabed activities subject to their jurisdiction and from artificial islands, installations and structures under their jurisdiction ... '.[17] There is no definition of *seabed activities* in UNCLOS, but the broad scope of this obligation means that the Convention can be interpreted in an evolutionary manner in order to cover new uses of the seabed as they emerge. It certainly covers oil and gas drilling, seabed mining, and the construction and operation of renewable energy installations or structures. Indeed, Article 208 was amended in the drafting process to apply not only to seabed activities themselves but also to pollution arising 'in connexion with seabed activities'.[18] This language extends the rights and duties of the coastal State to cover associated activities, such as the storage of resources pending processing or shipment.

The duty to regulate seabed activities is a due diligence obligation that requires States to exercise regulatory control over seabed activities within their jurisdiction. UNCLOS makes clear that pollution from such activities must be minimized 'to the fullest extent possible',[19] although the precise requirements of due diligence will depend upon the nature of the activity and its potential impacts on the marine environment, as well as the capacity of the coastal State. In order to comply with the duty of due diligence, coastal States must at least have in place a regulatory framework that requires the prior authorization of potentially harmful seabed activities and allows the coastal State to set conditions that will ensure that damage to the marine environment is kept to a minimum. Most seabed activities will also qualify as 'planned activities' for the purposes of Article 206 of UNCLOS and they, thus, may require the coastal State, 'as far as practicable', to assess 'the potential effects of such activities on the marine environment'. In this respect, it is important that the environmental impact assessment (EIA) take into account not only the effects of pollution, but also other effects on marine species and habitats, such as physical harm to the seabed or interference with important spawning, breeding, or feeding grounds. The information gathered during the EIA process will help the coastal

---

[16] UNCLOS, Article 194(3)(c). See also Article 194(3)(d), calling for similar measures for 'pollution from other installations and devices operating in the marine environment'.

[17] Ibid, Article 208(1).

[18] See M Nordquist et al (eds), *United Nations Convention on the Law of the Sea 1982: A Commentary—Vol. IV* (Martinus Nijhoff 1991) 143.

[19] UNCLOS, Article 194(3)(c).

State design an appropriate regulatory response and establish any appropriate mitigation measures.

The obligations of a coastal State may be stricter in locations where rare and fragile ecosystems may be found. UNCLOS requires States to take particular measures to protect and preserve such habitats,[20] and this obligation is especially important in the context of protecting benthic communities. For particularly vulnerable seabed communities, this requirement may require the designation of marine protected areas (MPAs) in which seabed activities are prohibited or significantly restricted. However, complying with these obligations will require coastal States to first identify relevant marine ecosystems within its waters. Treaties concluded at the regional and global level for the protection of biodiversity may assist coastal States by identifying the factors to be taken into account or the particular species or habitats to be protected.[21] Yet, this task requires significant resources, and developing countries, in particular, may require financial and technical assistance if they are to achieve a high level of environmental protection.

Given the uncertainty surrounding the environmental impacts of many types of new seabed activities, such as seabed mining or renewable energy generation, satisfaction of the due diligence obligation may require a precautionary approach from coastal States.[22] The precautionary approach does not necessarily require a State to prohibit an activity until it is proven that it will not pose a risk of significant harm to the environment, although it may be invoked by a State to justify its decision to this end.[23] A more moderate version of the precautionary approach in the present context would suggest that the coastal State may provisionally authorize an activity on a small scale, with a view to keeping the effects of the activity under review in order to gather further information and to adopt measures to minimize any harm that comes to light. The importance of 'strict and continuous monitoring' of continental shelf activities has also been stressed by the International Tribunal for the Law of the Sea (ITLOS) in the context of States fulfilling their obligations under UNCLOS.[24] Identification of any unforeseen effects as a result of monitoring may require the coastal State to adopt additional regulatory measures, in accordance with their due diligence obligations. This regulatory technique has been called a 'survey, deploy and monitor policy', the goal of which is to 'enable novel technologies whose potential effects are poorly understood to be deployed in a manner that will simultaneously reduce scientific uncertainty over time whilst enabling a level of activity that is proportionate to the risks'.[25] In accordance with this approach, management authorities maintain the right to modify or revoke permits, if significant effects are detected through the monitoring process. This regulatory technique

---

[20] UNCLOS, Article 194(5).   [21] See Chapter 3.

[22] See e.g. World Bank, *Precautionary Management of Deep Sea Mining Potential in Pacific Island Countries* (2016).

[23] In the context of deep seabed mining, the World Bank has suggested that 'a sound precautionary approach, which does not preclude the option of "no development" is needed …'; Ibid, 11.

[24] *Dispute Concerning Delimitation of the Maritime Boundary between Ghana and Côte d'Ivoire in the Atlantic Ocean* (2015) dispositif, para. 1(c).

[25] See e.g. Scottish Government, *Survey, Deploy and Monitor Licensing Policy Guidance* (2016).

could be applied to a range of seabed activities and it is particularly appropriate for the regulation of new technologies, when the interactions with the marine environment may be unpredictable. Gillespie, for example, has argued that a precautionary approach to dealing with ocean noise from seabed installations may require the adoption of temporary management measures, including the deployment of monitoring and observers in order to determine whether a particular activity has a substantial detrimental effect. He concludes that 'in such areas, where noise may have significant consequences for the animals inhabiting the marine environment, the noise source should be stopped, or a moratorium on such activities should be implemented'.[26]

8.2.2 Regional and global harmonization of rules

The extent of coastal States obligations in relation to seabed activities may also be affected by other rules or standards adopted at the global or regional levels. UNCLOS explicitly encourages States to 'harmonize their policies in this connection at the appropriate regional level'[27] and 'establish global and regional rules, standards and recommended practices and procedures' on this topic.[28] Moreover, when such rules, standards, and recommended practices and procedures exist, States shall ensure that their national laws are 'no less effective' than they are.[29] This rule of reference would appear to operate in a similar manner to the rules of reference found in the provisions on the prevention of pollution from ships and from dumping, by establishing an international minimum standard with which all States must comply.[30] For this reason, it has been hailed as being of 'great practical significance.'[31] Yet, there are also some key differences in its operation compared to rules of reference introducing an international minimum standard in other contexts.

First, there is no single international institution that is responsible for regulating offshore activities. The Convention makes reference to 'competent international organizations' in the plural, thus acknowledging the potential for different institutions to address this topic. This broad scope is unsurprising given the diversity of activities that are potentially covered by this provision. Indeed, we may expect different sets of rules or standards to be developed in relation to different activities, such as oil and gas, seabed mining, and offshore energy production.

Second, the rule of reference is aimed not only at rules and standards but also at 'recommended practices and procedures'. In other words, it covers not only binding norms, but also non-binding norms. Some authors have argued that 'an effective interpretation [of this provision] leads to the conclusion that recommended

---

[26] A Gillespie, 'The Precautionary Approach in the Twenty-First Century: A Case Study of Noise Pollution in the Ocean' (2007) 22 *IJMCL* 61, 85.

[27] UNCLOS, Article 208(4).   [28] Ibid, Article 208(5).

[29] Ibid, Article 208(3). See also Ibid, Article 214.   [30] See Chapters 5 and 6.

[31] A Yankov, 'The Significance of the 1982 Convention on the Law of the Sea for the Protection of the Marine Environment and the Promotion of Marine Science and Technology—Third Committee Issues', in BH Oxman and AW Koers (eds), *The 1982 Convention on the Law of the Sea* (Law of the Sea Institute 1984) 77.

practices are transformed into binding rules for the Parties'.[32]However, this argument must be considered carefully and it will, in part, depend upon the drafting of the provision. If a norm is drafted in a manner that gives broad discretion to the coastal State, the norm will continue to allow discretion, even if it were subsequently incorporated into the UNCLOS framework through the rule of reference.

Third, Article 208(3) refers to 'international' norms, as opposed to 'generally accepted' norms in the case of shipping, or 'global' norms in the case of dumping. This is perhaps one of the most important differences in this rule of reference and it begs the question of what norms fall within the scope of the rule of reference. The phrase can easily be interpreted to cover instruments that have been adopted at the global level by a relevant international organization. However, 'international' norms may also include rules, standards, and recommended practices and procedures that have been adopted at the regional level. At the same time, in order for a regional standard to become 'international', it must arguably be replicated across a number of regions. This is an important understanding of the rule of reference in the context of seabed activities because it is largely regional bodies that have been involved in the development of specific rules, standards, and recommended practices and procedures. Using a case study of the regional regulation of oil and gas exploitation, the following section will demonstrate how there has been a cross-fertilization of law-making at the regional level which has made it possible to talk about the emergence of 'international rules, standards, and recommended practices and procedures' at the regional level that fall within the scope of the rule of reference in Article 208(3).

8.3 Development of International Rules, Standards, and Recommended Practices and Procedures in Relation to Oil and Gas Exploitation

8.3.1 Law-making by global institutions

The extraction of hydrocarbons has been the activity that has attracted the most attention of States when it comes to developing the international legal framework for the protection of the marine environment from seabed activities. The need for rules and standards on this topic was recognized at the same time that UNCLOS was being negotiated, although a more sophisticated legal framework has only emerged over a prolonged period.

The first attempts at drawing up international standards in relation to offshore oil and gas were undertaken by the United Nations Environment Programme (UNEP) in the 1970s, when the institution was asked to prepare guidance for States on what measures should be taken to comply with the obligations to protect and preserve the marine environment, which were, at that time, being negotiated at the Third UNCLOS. Guidelines were prepared by a Working Group of Legal Experts on

---

[32] W Van Reenan, 'Rules of Reference in the New Convention on the Law of the Sea' (1981) 12 *NYIL* 3, 17.

Environmental Law and approved by the UNEP Governing Council in 1982. The guidelines were also endorsed by the UN General Assembly, which recommended that 'Governments should consider the guidelines contained in the conclusions when formulating national legislation or undertaking negotiations for the conclusion of international agreements for the prevention of pollution of the marine environment caused by offshore mining and drilling within the limits of national jurisdiction.'[33] It follows that the guidelines can be considered as relevant recommended practice and procedures for the purposes of Article 208. However, the guidelines make a limited contribution to developing the legal framework beyond what had already been negotiated in UNCLOS, as they simply repeat many of the general obligations found in UNCLOS, calling for the authorization of oil and gas operations, prior EIA, monitoring of the effects of oil and gas operations, and the development of contingency plans for emergency response.[34]

The gaps in the legal framework were acknowledged at the 1992 Rio Conference on Environment and Development, when States were urged:

acting individually, bilaterally, regionally, or multilaterally and within the framework of the [International Maritime Organization (IMO)] and other relevant international organizations, whether subregional, regional or global, as appropriate [to] assess the need for additional measures to address degradation of the marine environment from offshore oil and gas platforms, by assessing existing regulatory measures to address discharge, emissions and safety and the need for additional measures.[35]

Limited progress has been made in following this mandate, however. It is true that the 1990 International Convention on Oil Pollution Preparedness, Response and Cooperation requires States to ensure that platforms within their jurisdiction have an approved emergency plan in case of spills or other incidents,[36] mirroring the obligations that apply to ships.[37] Several other IMO instruments have also been extended to oil and gas installations, including some construction and equipment standards,[38] as well as discharge standards relating to machinery space drainage,[39] sewage,[40] and garbage.[41] These instruments would constitute international rules

---

[33] UNGA Resolution 37/217 (1982) para. 6(b).
[34] For a discussion, see Z Gao, *Environmental Regulation of Oil and Gas* (Kluwer Law International 1998) 113–15.
[35] Agenda 21 (1992) para. 17.30(c).
[36] See 1990 International Convention on Oil Pollution Preparedness, Response and Cooperation (OPPRC Convention) (EIF 13 May 1995), Article 3(2).
[37] See Chapter 6.
[38] The IMO has adopted the Code for the Construction and Equipment of Mobile Offshore Drilling Units; IMO Assembly Resolution A.1023(26)(2009) replacing IMO Assembly resolution A.414(XI) (1979).
[39] See Unified Interpretation of MARPOL Annex I, Regulation 21, excluding offshore processing drainage, production water discharge, and displacement water discharge from the scope of Annex I. See also Guidelines for the Application of the Revised MARPOL Annex I Requirements to Floating Production, Storage and Offloading Facilities and Floating Storage Units, MEPC Resolution MEPC.139(53) (2005).
[40] MARPOL Annex IV applies to 'ships engaged in international voyages', which may apply to some, but not all, offshore installations.
[41] MARPOL Annex V, Regulation 5, prohibiting the discharge of any garbage from fixed or floating platforms, with minor exceptions for some forms of food waste.

and standards for the purposes of Article 208 of UNCLOS and they would, there-fore, be incorporated through the rule of reference into the UNCLOS framework. However, not all aspects of oil gas drilling are currently addressed by IMO instruments. Indeed, the MARPOL Convention explicitly excludes any 'release of harmful substances directly arising from the exploration, exploitation and associated offshore processing of sea-bed mineral resources',[42] and the IMO is not considered to have a mandate to regulate such operational pollution.[43] Moreover, the IMO would not appear to be the best body to address this topic, as the issues raised by pollution arising from drilling for oil and gas are significantly different to the issues raised by pollution from ships in navigation.[44] The problem is that no other global institution has taken up this issue, and there has been a 'global inertia' to the development of an agreement to prevent and regulate pollution from seabed activities.[45]

8.3.2 Law-making by regional institutions

In light of this gap in global instruments, some regional seas bodies have stepped in to address this lacuna in the international legal framework. As noted above, a regional approach to the regulation of seabed activities is explicitly acknowledged in Article 208 of UNCLOS and it may be because States have closer political relations and more shared interests that they have been more successful in elaborating rules for the regulation of oil and gas at the regional level.

Most regional seas treaties contain a generic provision on the regulation of seabed activities. For example, Article 8 of the Convention for the Protection of the Natural Resources and the Environment of the South Pacific Region provides, 'The Parties shall take all appropriate measures to prevent, reduce and control pollution in the Convention Area resulting directly or indirectly from exploration and exploitation of the seabed and its subsoil.' This is a broad provision and it has the potential to apply to a range of seabed activities, including, but not limited to, oil and gas exploitation. Similar provisions are found in the regional seas conventions applying to the Baltic Sea,[46] the North-East Atlantic,[47] the Mediterranean

---

[42] MARPOL Convention, Article 2(3)(b)(ii).

[43] See C Brown, 'International Environmental Law in the Regulation of Offshore Installations and Seabed Activities: The Case for a South Pacific Regional Protocol' (1998) 17 *AM&PLJ* 109, 122.

[44] This would appear to be the position taken by the IMO Secretariat; see the Working Paper cited by JA Roach, 'International Standards for Offshore Drilling', in MH Nordquist, JN Moore, A Chirhop, and R Long (eds), *The Regulation of Continental Shelf Development* (Martinus Nijhoff 2013) 115. See also Y Lyons, 'Transboundary Pollution from Offshore Oil and Gas Activities in the Seas of Southeast Asia', in R Warner and S Marsden (eds), *Transboundary Environmental Governance: Inland, Coastal and Marine Perspectives* (Ashgate 2012) 181.

[45] Ibid, 204.

[46] See 1992 Convention on the Protection of the Marine Environment of the Baltic Sea (Helsinki Convention) (EIF 17 January 2000), Article 12(1).

[47] See 1992 Convention for the Protection of the Marine Environment of the North-East Atlantic (OSPAR Convention) (EIF 25 March 1998), Article 5. The OSPAR Convention is unusual in that it requires action to prevent pollution from 'offshore activities', defined as activities for the 'purposes of the exploration, appraisal or exploitation of liquid and gaseous hydrocarbons'. In other words, this provision only applies to oil and gas activities and not other forms of seabed activities.

Sea,[48] the Arabian Gulf,[49] the Red Sea and Gulf of Aden,[50] the West and Central African Coast,[51] the Caribbean Sea,[52] and the Western Indian Ocean.[53] This type of provision by itself does little more than reproduce the general principles and rules already found in UNCLOS.[54] At the same time, it does provide a legal basis for further action by regional seas bodies. Two approaches to the further development of regional rules relating to oil and gas activities have been taken by regional seas bodies: the inclusion of detailed rules and standards in an Annex to the regional framework treaty and the negotiation of a separate protocol on the topic.

The regime in the North-East Atlantic provides perhaps the best example of the first of these approaches. The OSPAR Convention contains substantive rules relating to the prevention and elimination of pollution from offshore sources in Annex III, which is an integral part of the treaty[55] and is thus binding on all Parties.[56] The Annex requires the regulation of all discharges or emissions from offshore sources.[57] In this regard, the Convention imposes an obligation for the use of 'best available techniques' (BAT) and 'best environmental practices'[58] (BEP), mirroring its provisions on land-based sources of marine pollution.[59] The invocation of these dynamic standards means that the requirements will evolve over time as technology itself becomes more sophisticated and effective in combating pollution. Indeed, the BAT standard provides an incentive to companies to 'invent and apply technologies that are cheaper for them as long as they are as good or better than the BAT'.[60]

To supplement the specific rules in the Annex, the OSPAR Commission has also adopted a large number of decisions, recommendations, and agreements to give content to the general obligations on offshore activities in the OSPAR Area. In this regard, OSPAR Parties have adopted recommendations on the monitoring of EIA

[48] See 1995 Convention for the Protection of the Marine Environment and the Coastal Region of the Mediterranean (Barcelona Convention) (EIF 9 July 2004) Article 7. This Convention was amended in 1995, and the phrase 'and to the fullest extent possible eliminate' was added, differentiating it from other regional seas treaties adopted at an earlier time.

[49] See 1978 Regional Convention for Cooperation on the Protection of the Marine Environment from Pollution (Kuwait Convention) (EIF 1 July 1979) Article VII.

[50] See 1982 Regional Convention for the Conservation of the Red Sea and Gulf of Aden Environment (EIF 20 August 1985) Article VII.

[51] See 1981 Convention for Cooperation in the Protection, Management and Development of the Marine and Coastal Environment of the Atlantic Coast of the West, Central and Southern Africa Region (Abidjan Convention) (EIF 5 August 1984) Article 8.

[52] See 1983 Convention for the Protection of the Marine Environment of the Wider Caribbean Region (Cartagena Convention) (EIF 11 October 1986) Article 8.

[53] See 2010 Convention for the Protection, Management and Development of the Marine and Coastal Environment of the Western Indian Ocean (Amended Nairobi Convention) (not yet in force) Article 8.

[54] See e.g. Brown (n43) 130: 'the SPREP Convention's general duty on States regarding pollution from offshore installations and seabed activities is no more illuminating than the duty in article 208 of UNCLOS'.

[55] OSPAR Convention, Article 14(1).

[56] No reservations may be made to the OSPAR Convention; see Article 28.

[57] OSPAR Annex III, Article 4(1).　　　[58] OSPAR Annex III, Article 2.

[59] See Chapter 4 for a definition of BAT and BEP.

[60] J Braithwaite and P Drahos, *Global Business Regulation* (CUP 2000) 269.

of oil and gas activities,[61] as well as the introduction of environmental management systems by the offshore industry.[62] Following the Deepwater Horizon incident in the Gulf of Mexico in 2010, the OSPAR Commission called upon Contracting Parties to pay particular attention to the regulation of drilling activities at extreme depths or pressures or in extreme climates.[63] In the context of regulating seabed activities, States must also pay particular attention to benthic species and habitats that have been identified by the OSPAR Contracting Parties as requiring special protection,[64] including sea-pen communities,[65] mussel beds,[66] seagrass beds,[67] reefs,[68] coral gardens,[69] carbonate mounds,[70] and deep-sea sponge aggregations.[71]

OSPAR recommendations also address, in more detail, the operation of offshore installations, including regulations on the disposal of produced water[72] and the avoidance of oil spills.[73] The OSPAR Commission has adopted an elaborate framework for the regulation of chemicals used in the drilling operations, which requires all chemicals to be pre-screened and ranked according to their bioaccumulation potential, biodegradation, and acute toxicity.[74] The scheme promotes the principle of substitution so that operators may be required to substitute hazardous substances for less hazardous substances as part of the permitting process with the aim of phasing out, by 1 January 2017, the discharge of offshore chemicals that contain substances identified as candidates for substitution.[75] Such chemicals should only be permitted where it can be demonstrated that substitution is 'not feasible due to technical or safety reasons'.[76] However, in accordance with the precautionary approach,

---

[61] OSPAR Guidelines 2004/11 (2004); see also OSPAR Agreement 2006/7 on Harmonised Reporting Format to Compile Environmental Monitoring Data and Information Related to Offshore Oil and Gas Activities (2006).

[62] OSPAR Recommendation 2003/5 (2003).

[63] See OSPAR Recommendation 2010/18 on the Prevention of Significant Acute Oil Pollution from Offshore Drilling Activities (2010).

[64] See Chapter 3.   [65] OSPAR Recommendation 2010/11 (2010).

[66] OSPAR Recommendation 2013/3 (2013).

[67] OSPAR Recommendation 2012/4 (2012).

[68] OSPAR Recommendation 2010/8 (2010); Recommendation 2013/2 (2013).

[69] OSPAR Recommendation 2010/9 (2010).

[70] ORPAR Recommendation 2014/10 (2014).

[71] OSPAR Recommendation 2010/10 (2010).

[72] OSPAR Recommendation 2001/1 for the Management of Produced Water from Offshore Installations (2001), amended by OSPAR Recommendation 2006/4 and 2011/8; OSPAR Recommendation 2012/5 for a risk-based approach to the management of produced water discharges from offshore installations (2012); OSPAR Guidelines 2012/7 in support of Recommendation 2012/5 (2012).

[73] OSPAR Recommendation 2010/8 on the Prevention of Significant Acute Oil Pollution from Offshore Drilling Activities (2010).

[74] OSPAR Decision 2000/2 on a Harmonised Mandatory Control System for the Use and Reduction of the Discharge of Offshore Chemicals (2000) amended by Decision 2005/1; OSPAR Decision 2000/3 on the Use of Organic-Phase Drilling Fluids and the Discharge of OPF-Contaminated Cuttings (2000); OSPAR Recommendation 2005/2 on Environmental Goals for the Discharge by the Offshore Industry of Chemicals that Are, or Contain Added Substances, listed in the OSPAR 2004 List of Chemicals for Priority Action (2005); OSPAR Recommendation 2006/3 on Environmental Goals for the Discharge by the Offshore Industry of Chemicals that Are, or which Contain Substances Identified as Candidates for Substitution (2006); OSPAR Recommendation 2010/4 on a Harmonised Pre-Screening Scheme for Offshore Chemicals (2010).

[75] See OSPAR Offshore Oil and Gas Industry Strategy (2010) para. 1.3(b).   [76] Ibid.

where no substitute for the offshore chemical concerned is available at the time the operator applies for a permit, the authorities may only grant temporary permission for a limited period,[77] whilst a less hazardous substitute is sought.[78] Alternatively, a management authority may permit the use of offshore chemicals subject to conditions relating to the amount to be discharged.[79] Removal of offshore installations at the stage of decommissioning is also covered by the OSPAR rules on dumping and specific recommendations relating thereto.[80]

Oversight of the implementation of the measures described above is undertaken by a dedicated Offshore Industry Committee, which meets on an annual basis to consider the progress of States in implementing their commitments and addressing problems that have arisen in implementation.[81] The Offshore Industry Committee is also charged with implementing the OSPAR Offshore Oil and Industry Strategy, which requires, inter alia, an assessment of 'the extent to which existing programmes and measures meet, or will meet, the objectives of [the Strategy] ...' and 'where necessary', the revision of existing measures or the development of new measures.[82] This mechanism ensures that the regulatory framework evolves to take into account new risks and challenges arising in the context of oil and gas extraction. The rules of procedure of the OSPAR Commission mean that the regulatory framework is developed in an open and transparent manner, with industry and civil society institutions able to participate in deliberations as observers.[83] The rules and standards are also subject to the general compliance procedure applicable under the OSPAR Convention, which provides an additional layer of scrutiny.[84]

A similar approach is taken in the Baltic Sea region. Article 12 of the Helsinki Convention provides in general terms that:

Each Contracting Party shall take all measures in order to prevent pollution of the marine environment of the Baltic Sea Area resulting from exploration or exploitation of its part of the seabed and the subsoil thereof or from any associated activities thereon as well as to ensure that adequate preparedness is maintained for immediate response actions against pollution incidents caused by such activities [...]

More precise measures are specified in Annex VI of the Convention, including requirements to implement BAT and BEP.[85] These provisions are an integral part of the treaty and they are, thus, binding on all Parties to the Helsinki Convention. The Helsinki Commission has also adopted recommendations for further actions in relation to the regulation of offshore industries.[86]

---

[77] A maximum of three years.
[78] OSPAR Decision 2000/2 (2000) Appendix 1, para. 12.   [79] Ibid, para. 9.
[80] See OSPAR Decision 98/3. For more on dumping at sea, see Chapter 5.
[81] See <http://www.ospar.org/work-areas/oic>.
[82] OSPAR Offshore Oil and Gas Industry Strategy (2010) para. 3.2(b)–(c).
[83] OSPAR Commission Rules of Procedure, OSPAR Agreement 13-02 (2013) Rule 23.
[84] For a discussion of the OSPAR compliance mechanism, see Chapter 4.
[85] Helsinki Convention, Annex VI, Regulation 2.
[86] For example, HELCOM Recommendation 14/9: Removal of Abandoned and Disused Offshore United (1993); HELCOM Recommendation 18/2: Restriction of Discharges and Monitoring for Exploration and Exploitation of the Sea-Bed and Its Subsoil (superseding Recommendation 9/5)

A different approach is seen in other regions where regional seas bodies have addressed marine environmental threats from oil and gas activities through the negotiation of a separate protocol on the topic. Parties to the Kuwait Regional Convention were the first to negotiate an additional regional protocol on offshore activities in 1989, in order to give more content to their obligation to take 'appropriate measures' under Article VII of the Convention.[87] The Protocol entered into force on 17 February 1990, and all of the Parties to the Kuwait Convention have become a Party.[88] The Protocol applies to pollution from offshore installations used 'for the purposes of exploring oil or natural gas or for the purposes of exploiting those resources',[89] as well as incidental activities, including 'any tanker for the time being moored and used for the temporary storage of oil ... and any plant for treating, storing or regaining control of the flow of crude oil'[90] and 'any transport of the same by pipeline to shore'.[91] Notably, the Protocol also extends to seismic operations prior to the establishment of a platform[92] and the siting and operating of pipelines connected with an offshore installation.[93] This illustrates a broad understanding of seabed activities. The Protocol repeats the obligation of States to take 'all appropriate measures ... to prevent, abate and control pollution from offshore operations' but goes on to specify particular rules or standards that must be followed by Parties.

First, Parties are required to carry out an EIA prior to licensing offshore activities within their jurisdiction.[94] The Regional Organization has issued guidelines on EIA[95] which provide an indicative list of activities for which an EIA will normally be required and recommend the scope of an assessment and environmental statement. Nevertheless, the guidelines still leave a large amount of discretion to individual States as to how to conduct an EIA and whether to authorize an activity.

Second, when regulating offshore installations, Parties are required to '[take] into account the best available and economically feasible technology'.[96] This standard resembles the BAT standard found in the OSPAR Convention and Helsinki Convention. The Protocol also makes reference to requirements for pollution reduction equipment and training to be applied by operators in accordance with 'good oil field practice or other relevant industry practice'.[97] This borrows a concept that

---

(1997); HELCOM Recommendation 19/7: Measures in order to Combat Pollution from Offshore Units (superseding Recommendation 10/10) (1998).

[87] Para. 24.1 of the action plan for the development and protection of the marine environment and the coastal areas of Bahrain, Iran, Iraq, Kuwait, Oman, Qatar, Saudi Arabia, and the United Arab Emirates called for the development of more detailed rules concerning particular activities, including rules to combat pollution resulting from exploration and exploitation of the continental shelf and the seabed and its subsoil as one of the areas for additional action.

[88] See <http://ropme.org/home.clx>.

[89] See 1989 Protocol concerning Marine Pollution Resulting from Exploration and Exploitation of the Continental Shelf (Kuwait Protocol) (EIF 17 February 1990) Article I(13).

[90] Ibid, Article I(12).   [91] Ibid, Article I(13).

[92] Ibid, Article XI(2). See also Guidelines on the Conduct of Seismic Operations Adopted by the Seventh Meeting of ROPME Council on 21 February 1990.

[93] Kuwait Protocol, Article XIII(1).   [94] Ibid, Articles III and IV.

[95] The guidelines were adopted by the Seventh Meeting of ROPME Council on 21 February 1990. See <http://www.memac-rsa.org/forms_and_downloads>.

[96] Kuwait Protocol, Article II.   [97] Ibid, Article VII(1) and (5)

is used in some national regulatory systems and which requires operators to comply with 'all those practices and procedures that are generally accepted as good and safe in the carrying on of that exploration or those operations, as the case may be'.[98] In practice, this is similar to the BEP standard found in the OSPAR Convention and Helsinki Convention.

Third, the Protocol specifically regulates discharges of oil,[99] other industrial products,[100] garbage,[101] and sewage[102] from offshore installations, setting minimum standards with which all installations in the region must comply. Similarly, operators are required to have in place a chemical use plan and States must regulate the use and storage of chemicals in accordance with guidelines adopted by the Regional Organization.[103] The guidelines allow for provisional approval of chemical plans in situations in which all the relevant data required for approval are not immediately available, but the guidelines explicitly provide that '[p]rovisional approval should not be granted unless there is at least prima facie evidence that the chemicals in question, and their related compounds, will have no significant adverse effect on the marine environment'.[104] This would seem to suggest that a precautionary approach to chemicals management is required under the Protocol.

Finally, States are required to inspect installations periodically and ensure that safety equipment is tested.[105]

Following the example set by the Kuwait Convention, Parties to the Barcelona Convention also concluded a Protocol for the Protection of the Mediterranean Sea against Pollution resulting from Exploration and Exploitation of the Continental Shelf and the Seabed and Its Subsoil in 1994.[106] The content of this instrument is very similar to the Kuwait Protocol, covering a similar range of activities and containing comparable obligations in relation to EIA,[107] contingency planning,[108] safety of installations,[109] and the discharge of oil and oily waters,[110] sewage,[111] and

---

[98] Australian Petroleum Act, s. 5(1).

[99] Kuwait Protocol, Article IX. Special requirements apply to pipelines in order to minimize the risk of leakages which may contaminate the marine environment; see Article XIII.

[100] See also Guidelines on Disposal of Drill Cuttings on the Sea-Bed: <http://www.memac-rsa.org/forms_and_downloads>.

[101] Kuwait Protocol, Article X.   [102] Ibid, Article X.

[103] Ibid, Article XI; see also Guidelines on the Use and Storage of Chemicals in Offshore Operations: <http://www.memac-rsa.org/forms_and_downloads>.

[104] Guidelines on the Use and Storage of Chemicals in Offshore Operations, para. 5.3.

[105] Kuwait Protocol, Article VII(2) and (3).

[106] See M Gavouneli, *Pollution from Offshore Installations* (Springer 1995) 43–4.

[107] See 1994 Protocol for the Protection of the Mediterranean Sea against Pollution Resulting from Exploration and Exploitation of the Continental Shelf and the Seabed and Its Subsoil (Mediterranean Offshore Protocol) (EIF 24 March 2011) Article 4(2). Annex IV of the Protocol contains requirements for an EIA.

[108] Mediterranean Offshore Protocol, Article 16, making a reference to the 1976 Protocol Concerning Cooperation in Combatting Pollution of the Mediterranean Sea by Oil and Other Harmful Substances in Cases of Emergency (EIF 12 February 1978). This latter instrument was subsequently amended, and its name was changed to the 2002 Protocol Concerning Co-operation in Preventing Pollution from Ships and, in Cases of Emergency, Combating Pollution of the Mediterranean Sea (EIF 17 March 2004).

[109] Mediterranean Offshore Protocol, Article 15.   [110] Ibid, Article 10.

[111] Ibid, Article 11.

garbage.[112] One difference relates to the manner in which chemical discharges are regulated. In this regard, the Mediterranean Protocol prohibits the discharge of harmful or noxious substances listed in Annex I and it requires a special permit for the discharge of harmful or noxious substances listed in Annex II and a general permit for all other discharges.[113] The Protocol also lacks an explicit reference to BAT or BEP. However, in practice, the Parties have established the Barcelona Convention Offshore Oil and Gas Group as a technical body to 'exchange best practices, knowledge and experiences between its Members in order to assist the Parties in attaining the objectives set out in Article 23.1 of the Protocol'.[114] The work of the group will be supported by specialist sub-groups, one of which will focus on environmental matters, including EIA and monitoring, the use, discharge and disposal of harmful or noxious substances, and precautions for specially protected areas.[115] The group meets once a year and, therefore, it will provide a specialist forum in order to consider the progressive development of the commitments contained in the Protocol. It has been stressed that the group must be conducted in an open and transparent manner, in order to ensure the integrity and legitimacy of the resulting regulatory framework.[116] The work of the group must also take into account other instruments that are applicable in the Mediterranean region, such as the Protocol concerning specially protected areas and biological diversity in the Mediterranean, which may offer special protection to certain benthic species and habitats.[117]

Perhaps the biggest drawback of the Mediterranean Protocol is its limited application. The Protocol only entered into force in March 2011 and, of the twenty-two Parties to the Barcelona Convention, only seven States had accepted the Offshore Protocol as of 31 December 2016.[118] This limits the effectiveness of the treaty and it demonstrates the difficulty of agreeing regional rules in regions with a large number of diverse States. This has been recognized by the Parties to the Barcelona Convention, which have stressed 'the importance of having the Offshore Protocol ratified by all Contracting Parties with a view to preventing, abating, combating and controlling pollution in the protocol area resulting from activities, inter alia, by ensuring that the best available techniques environmentally effective and economically appropriate, are used for this purpose', and urged 'all the Contracting Parties who have not yet done so to ratify the Offshore Protocol as early as possible'.[119]

---

[112] Ibid, Article 12.   [113] Ibid, Article 9.

[114] Barcelona COP Decision IG.21/8: Follow-Up Actions Regarding the Offshore Protocol Action Plan (2014) Annex, para. 2.

[115] See Barcelona COP Decision IG.22/3: Mediterranean Offshore Action Plan (2016) Annex, specific objective 2.

[116] Ibid.

[117] See e.g. A List of Endangered or Threatened Species; Action Plan for the Conservation of Habitats and Species Associated with Seamounts, Underwater Caves and Canyons, Aphotic Hard Beds and Chemo-Synthetic Phenomena in the Mediterranean Sea. See also Chapter 3.

[118] See the UNEP website: http://web.unep.org/unepmap/who-we-are/legal-framework/status-signatures-and-ratifications.

[119] Barcelona COP Decision IG.20/12, Action Plan to implement the Protocol of the Barcelona Convention concerning the Protection of the Mediterranean Sea Against Pollution Resulting from Exploration and Exploitation of the Continental Shelf and the Seabed and Its Subsoil (2012). See also Barcelona COP Decision IG.22/3: Mediterranean Offshore Action Plan (2016) Annex, specific objective 1.

Not all regional responses to oil and gas regulation have taken the form of legally binding instruments. The Arctic countries have pursued informal cooperation on environmental matters under the auspices of the Arctic Council and specifically through its Protection of the Marine Environment Working Group and related bodies. These institutions have adopted a number of instruments that are relevant to the prevention of pollution from offshore oil and gas activities, including 2004 Guidelines on the Transfer of Refined Oil and Oil Products in the Arctic; the 2004 Arctic Shoreline Clean-up Assessment Technique Manual; the 2008 Arctic Guide for Emergency Prevention, Preparedness and Response; the 2009 Assessment of Effects and Potential Effects of Oil and Gas Activities in the Arctic; and the 2009 Arctic Offshore Oil and Gas Guidelines.[120] This latter instrument contains general principles relating to the protection of the marine environment from oil and gas activities, as well as recommended practices and procedures relating to EIA, monitoring, environmental management systems, and operating practices. The guidelines apply to not only drilling operations but also the installation and operation of associated pipelines.[121] The guidelines follow the approach of some of the above instruments, by encouraging the use of BAT and BEP[122] and they make an explicit cross-reference to the definition of these terms in the OSPAR Convention,[123] thus providing a clear example of cross-fertilization in law-making. Indeed, the guidelines make reference to a number other international standards on a range of matters, including industry standards, which are held up as best practice.[124] The guidelines explicitly state that they are non-binding,[125] and the majority of the provisions are expressed in hortatory language. Nevertheless, the guidelines can still provide an important source of good practice that can be used by States to assist them in their implementation of their due diligence obligations under UNCLOS and they may contribute to the emergence of 'international rules, standards, and recommended practices and procedures', as discussed below.

Overall, these examples of law-making by regional institutions illustrate the valuable role they can play in developing the legal framework for the protection of the marine environment. It is true that not all regions where oil and gas exploitation takes place have adopted substantive rules or standards to regulate this activity.[126] Particular gaps can be noted in major oil and gas producing regions such as the Black Sea,[127]

---

[120] The first set out guidelines were adopted in 1997 and they have been subject to regular review.

[121] Arctic Offshore Oil and Gas Guidelines, 37.   [122] Ibid, 7. See also 36.

[123] Ibid, Annex B.

[124] For example, Ibid, 24 (reference to OSPAR Guidelines for Environmental Monitoring of Oil and Gas Activities), 26 (Management System Recommendations from American Petroleum Institute and the International Organization for Standardization), 34 (OECD Test for Biodegradability in Seawater), and 37 (Det Norske Veritas and American Petroleum Institute Recommended Practices for Offshore Pipelines).

[125] Arctic Offshore Oil and Gas Guidelines, 4.

[126] C Redgwell, 'Mind the Gap in the GAIRS: The Role of Other Instruments in LOSC Regime Implementation in the Offshore Energy Sector' (2014) 29 *IJMCL* 600, 603.

[127] See N Oral, *Regional Cooperation and Protection of the Marine Environment in International Law* (Martinus Nijhoff 2013) 257; N Oral, 'Integrated Coastal Zone Management and Marine Spatial Planning for Hydrocarbon Activities in the Black Sea' (2008) 23 *IJMCL* 453–76.

West Africa,[128] East Africa,[129] the Caribbean, East Asian Seas,[130] and Latin American waters. Yet, it does not follow that coastal States in these regions are not bound by specific rules or standards. It is possible to argue that 'international rules, standards, and recommended practices and procedures' have emerged through the common practice of existing regional instruments, which become binding on other States by virtue of the rule of reference in Article 208(3) of UNCLOS. An example is provided by the emergence of the requirement to follow BAT and BEP. As seen above, this requirement is found in the majority of the instruments that have been adopted at the regional level. The States involved in elaborating these treaties arguably represent a sufficient cross-section of the international community, including developed and developing countries from North America, Europe, North Africa, and the Middle East, to allow the BAT and BEP standards to be considered 'international rules and standards' for the purpose of Article 208(3). Indeed, there is evidence that States in other regions have accepted that their national operators should follow BAT and BET when conducting seabed activities in their territory. For example, in the dispute between Cote d'Ivoire and Ghana concerning oil activities in a disputed area of their continental shelf, Ghana expressly invoked its use of 'international best practices to minimize the risks of harm to the marine environment' as a defence to claims that it had failed to take sufficient measures to protect the marine environment from harm caused by oil and gas exploration and exploitation activities within its jurisdiction in violation of Article 208.[131] This example illustrates how a rule of reference in UNCLOS can play a useful role in filling gaps in the international legal framework, pending the development of precise and detailed rules by other regions.

8.4 Seabed Activities beyond National Jurisdiction

8.4.1 The International Seabed Authority and the regulation of seabed activities beyond national jurisdiction

Beyond the edge of the continental margin lies the 'Area'.[132] A rich variety of resources can be found here, including polymetallic nodules scattered on the undulating abyssal plains, as well as polymetallic sulphides and cobalt-rich crusts attached

---

[128] Parties to the Abidjan Convention are negotiating a Protocol on environmental norms and standards for the oil and gas industry; see <http://abidjanconvention.org/media/documents/press_speech/Closing%20story%20-%20experts%20segment.pdf>.

[129] This is reported to be one of the regions in which offshore drilling is growing. See Global Ocean Commission (n2) 35. In June 2015, Parties to the Nairobi Convention agreed to develop guidelines on environmental management for oil and gas, based on best practices; see Nairobi COP Decision CP8/7.

[130] For a review of the relevant instruments in this region, see Lyons (n44).

[131] See *Dispute Concerning Delimitation of the Maritime Boundary between Ghana and Côte d'Ivoire in the Atlantic Ocean* (2015) Written Statement of Ghana on the Request for Provisional Measures, 23 March 2015, para. 83. Ghana went on to specify its implementation of, inter alia, 'international management system standard ISO 14001, the World Bank's IFC Performance Standards, and the International Convention for the Prevention of Pollution from Ships (MARPOL) requirements'.

[132] UNCLOS, Article 1(1).

to seamounts and deep ocean ridges. These submarine resources have the potential to provide important supplies of valuable metals, such as nickel, copper, cobalt, zinc, lead, gold, and manganese.[133] Access to these resources is subject to a special regime established by Part XI of UNCLOS.

Unlike the high seas, which are open to all States as common property, resources in the Area are 'vested in mankind as a whole',[134] and 'no State or natural or juridical person shall claim, acquire or exercise rights to the minerals recovered from the Area except in accordance with [Part XI]'.[135] In other words, the mineral resources in the Area have been designated as the common heritage of mankind and they are subject to a centralized system of control and management.[136] Entities from any Party to UNCLOS are permitted to carry out mining for minerals in the Area, but they can only do so under the control of the International Seabed Authority, the international institution established under UNCLOS to regulate mining in the Area. The Authority is responsible for regulating all aspects of seabed mining, including prospecting, exploration, exploitation, and processing of marine minerals, up to the point at which resources are transferred to a vessel for transportation to land.[137]

The primary task of the Authority is to manage the development of seabed resources located beyond national jurisdiction.[138] At first sight, this would appear to be a largely economic objective. Yet, UNCLOS makes clear that this task must be carried out in the broader context of the goal of sustainable development. This concept is not explicitly incorporated into Part XI of UNCLOS, although it is reflected in some of its provisions. First, the Authority is required to ensure the 'orderly, safe and rational management of the resources of the Area'.[139] In a different context, the notion of rational management has been interpreted to require 'a balance between the Parties' rights and needs to use the [resource] for economic and commercial activities on the one hand, and the obligation to protect it from any damage to the environment that may be caused by such activities on the other'.[140] The choice of this language would suggest that such a balance must also be achieved by the Authority in its elaboration and application of a regulatory regime for the exploitation of seabed resources. Indeed, the Authority is expressly given a mandate to regulate the environmental impacts of seabed mining. To this end, UNCLOS requires that 'necessary measures shall be taken ... with respect to activities in the Area to ensure effective protection for the marine environment from harmful effects which may arise from such activities'.[141] To further this aim, the Authority is given the power to adopt rules and regulations for the 'prevention, reduction and control of pollution and other hazards to the marine environment', the 'prevention, reduction and control ... of interference with the ecological balance in the marine environment', and 'the protection and conservation of the natural resources of the Area and

[133] See generally Rona (n8) 618.   [134] UNCLOS, Article 137(2).
[135] Ibid, Article 137(3).   [136] Ibid, Article 136.
[137] *Responsibilities and Obligations of States Sponsoring Persons and Entities with Respect to Activities in the Area* (2011) paras 95–6.
[138] UNCLOS, Article 150.   [139] Ibid, Article 150(b).
[140] *Pulp Mills on the River Uruguay* (2010) para. 175.   [141] UNCLOS, Article 145.

the prevention and damage to the flora and fauna of the marine environment'.[142] In carrying out this mandate, the Authority is instructed to pay particular attention to the effects of 'drilling, dredging, excavation, disposal of waste, construction and operation or maintenance of installations, pipelines, and other devices related to such activities'.[143] Whilst the 1994 Part XI Agreement, which modifies certain provisions in the Convention relating to seabed mining,[144] does not directly alter the legal framework for the protection of the marine environment, the preamble to the Agreement does emphasize 'the importance of the Convention for the protection and preservation of the marine environment and . . . the growing concern for the global environment',[145] indicating that this would be a priority issue for the Authority when it started its regulatory tasks.

The Authority was formally established on the entry into force of UNCLOS on 16 November 1994 and, to date, it has adopted Regulations on Prospecting and Exploration for Polymetallic Nodules,[146] Polymetallic Sulphides,[147] and Cobalt-Rich Crusts.[148] These regulations are automatically binding on all Members of the Authority, and there is no ability for individual States to opt-out of rules with which they disagree.[149] Moreover, regulations also apply directly to entities carrying out mining activities in the Area by way of a contract with the Authority. This means that all contractors can be subjected to the same standards, and the Authority is in a position to ensure the effective regulation of seabed mining. How the Authority has incorporated environmental considerations into the regulatory framework will be discussed below in relation to the three main phases of seabed mining: prospecting, exploration, and exploitation.

8.4.2 Prospecting and protection of the marine environment

Prospecting is the first phase of any activity in the Area and it is defined as 'the search for deposits of [resources] in the Area, including estimation of the composition, size and distribution of deposits of [resources] and their economic values, without any exclusive rights'.[150] The ultimate purpose of prospecting is to identify parts of the Area that are worthy of exploration and exploitation. Prospecting can be carried

---

[142] Ibid, Article 145.   [143] Ibid, Article 145. See also Annex III, Article 17(2)(g).

[144] See e.g. J Harrison, *Making the Law of the Sea* (CUP 2011) 86–99.

[145] See 1994 Agreement relating to the Implementation of Part XI of the United Nations Convention on the Law of the Sea of 10 December 1982 (EIF 28 July 1996), preamble.

[146] Decision of the Assembly on the Regulations for Exploration and Exploitation for Polymetallic Nodules in the Area (Nodules Regulations), Document ISBA/6/A/18 (2000), as amended by Document ISBA/19/A/9 (2013) and Document ISBA/20/A/9 (2014).

[147] Decision of the Assembly of the International Seabed Authority Relating to the Regulations on Prospecting and Exploration for Polymetallic Sulphides in the Area (Sulphides Regulations), Document ISBA/16/A/12/Rev.1 (2010), as amended by Document ISBA/20/A/10 (2014).

[148] Decision of the Assembly of the International Seabed Authority Relating to the Regulations on Prospecting and Exploration for Cobalt-Rich Ferromanganese Crusts in the Area (Crusts Regulations), Document ISBA/18/A/11 (2012).

[149] However, sponsoring States may set higher standards; see below.

[150] For example, Nodules Regulations, Regulation 1(3)(e); Sulphides Regulations, Regulation 1(3)(e); Crusts Regulations, Regulation 1(3)(e).

out in any part of the Area, provided there are no pre-existing contracts of exploration or exploitation for the resources that are being prospected.[151] Prospectors are permitted to recover 'a reasonable quantity of minerals' for testing purposes,[152] and, therefore, prospecting may involve interference with the marine environment, but it is the most benign form of activity that falls under the jurisdiction of the Authority and it poses the least challenges for regulation.

Whilst there is no requirement for prior authorization of prospecting, it does not follow that prospectors are completely free from any sort of obligations. Indeed, each prospector must notify the Authority of its intention to carry out prospecting and it must provide a written undertaking that it will comply with the Convention and relevant rules, regulations, and procedures of the Authority.[153] Moreover, the Regulations adopted by the Authority explicitly require that prospecting is not carried out in a way that may be to the detriment to the marine environment and prospectors are expected to apply a precautionary approach in accordance with Principle 15 of the Rio Declaration.[154] Thus, prospectors are expected to be cautious in deciding what activity to undertake, as they cannot claim a lack of knowledge as an excuse for any significant harm that is caused to the marine environment as a result of their prospecting activity. It is reasonable to assume that prospectors could be held responsible for any damage that they cause during the course of their activities, although this issue is not expressly addressed by the Convention, and there may be challenges in holding prospectors to account.[155]

8.4.3 Regulating the environmental impacts of exploration

Whilst the initial prospecting for mineral resources can be carried out by any entity, the more detailed exploration or commercial exploitation of deep-seabed minerals can only be done by an entity that has been approved and authorized by the Authority.[156] At the time of writing, there are twenty-six contractors engaged in exploration activities,[157] which involve:

searching for deposits of [mineral resources] in the Area with exclusive rights, the analysis of such deposits, the use and testing of recovery systems and equipment, processing facilities and transportation systems, and the carrying out of studies of the environmental, technical,

---

[151] For example, Nodules Regulations, Regulation 2(3); Sulphides Regulations, Regulation 2(3); Crusts Regulations, Regulation 2(4).

[152] Nodules Regulations, Regulation 2(4); Sulphides Regulations, Regulation 2(4); Crusts Regulations, Regulation 2(5).

[153] UNCLOS, Annex III, Article 2. See also Nodules Regulations, Regulation 3; Sulphides Regulations, Regulation 3; Crusts Regulations, Regulation 3.

[154] Nodules Regulations, Regulation 2(2); Sulphides Regulations, Regulation 2(2); Nodules Regulations, Regulation 2(2).

[155] See J Harrison, 'Resources of the International Seabed Area', in E Morgera and K Kulovesi (eds), *Research Handbook on International Law and Natural Resources* (Edward Elgar 2016) 404–5.

[156] UNCLOS, Article 153(3).

[157] For a list of contractors, see <https://www.isa.org.jm/deep-seabed-minerals-contractors>.

economic, commercial and other appropriate factors that must be taken into account in exploitation.[158]

This is a more intensive exercise than prospecting and it, therefore, poses greater risks to the marine environment, although the effects of exploration are still expected to be minimal, given that most activities will be conducted on a limited scale. Nevertheless, environmental considerations are a key part of the approval process and the regulatory regime for exploration contracts.

Prior to applying for approval, applicants are required to carry out 'a preliminary assessment of the possible impact of the proposed exploration activities on the marine environment',[159] and this information will be considered as part of the application process. The information that is required would appear to fall short of a full EIA of the proposed activities. Nevertheless, the preliminary assessment that is carried out by the applicant must be sufficient to permit them to suggest 'proposed measures for the prevention, reduction and control of pollution and other hazards' to the marine environment arising from the exploration operations.[160] These requirements ensure that environmental protection is integral to the project design from the outset, but they would not appear to impose a significant hurdle for a project to be approved. One of the challenges for applicants will be the high degrees of uncertainty surrounding deep-sea ecosystems and the impacts of any activity in this kind of environment. Applicants would be expected to apply a precautionary approach, which, as seen below, is integral to the overall regulatory system, and, therefore, they may have to explain in their preliminary assessment of precisely how uncertainties were addressed.

Once an application has been approved,[161] the Authority will enter into a formal contract of exploration with the applicant. The contract follows standard terms contained in the Regulations, but each contract will also include a detailed programme of work, which will be negotiated between the applicant and the Authority.[162] It is the contractual obligations and agreed programme of work that impose the central environmental standards on an operator. Yet, the content of these documents is informed by the general environmental obligations established by the Regulations.

On a basic level, contractors are placed under a duty to 'take necessary measures to prevent, reduce and control pollution and other hazards to the marine environment arising from activities in the Area, as far as reasonably possible'.[163] The latter wording suggests that this is an obligation of due diligence. One of the factors to

---

[158] For example, Nodules Regulations, Regulation 1(3)(b); Sulphides Regulations, Regulation 1(3)(b); Crusts Regulations, Regulation 1(3)(c).

[159] Nodules Regulations, Regulation 18(c); Sulphides Regulations, Regulation 20(1)(c); Crusts Regulations, Regulation 20(1)(c).

[160] Nodules Regulations, Regulation 18(d) Sulphides Regulations, Regulation 20(1)(d); Crusts Regulations, Regulation 20(1)(d).

[161] For a discussion of the approval process, see Harrison (n155) 400–4.

[162] Nodules Regulations, Regulations 18(a) and 23(1); Sulphides Regulations, Regulations 20(1)(a) and 25(1); Crusts Regulations, Regulations 20(1)(a) and 25(1).

[163] Nodules Regulations, Regulation 31(5); Sulphides Regulations, Regulation 33(5); Crusts Regulations, Regulation 33(5).

be taken into account is the effect of exploration activities on VMEs.[164] Whilst this term is not defined in the Regulations, examples of hydrothermal vents,[165] seamounts, and cold-water corals[166] are given. Moreover, it is anticipated that the Commission will establish procedures for establishing whether proposed exploration activities will have serious harmful effects on VMEs,[167] which would provide an opportunity to give further content to this concept. Moreover, there would be scope to harmonize the definition of the term *VMEs* amongst other regimes that use it, such as the deep-sea fishing regime.[168] This guidance would also have to provide more information on what is meant by *serious harmful effects*, another term that is undefined in the Regulations. Yet, this is a crucial concept because it would appear that a particular activity may be prevented from proceeding if it is not possible to prevent such effects.[169]

Another general requirement for contractors is an application of the precautionary approach.[170] The precautionary approach is expressed in mandatory language and it has been held to be 'a binding obligation',[171] although it is still not entirely clear what action is required from contractors in this respect. As noted in Chapter 1, the precautionary approach can be operationalized in a number of different ways and even the version of the precautionary approach in the Regulations would not appear to mandate a particular set of measures, although the principle could be used to interpret the more specific obligations that are placed on contractors.

In terms of more substantive obligations, contractors are first and foremost required to apply BEP to their operations, a regulatory technique borrowed from other regional regimes for the protection of the marine environment.[172] This standard has the advantage of ensuring that the required level of protection will evolve over time as knowledge and technology develops. The obligation to follow BEP is explicitly included in the Sulphides Regulations[173] and the Crusts Regulations,[174] and it was added to the Nodules Regulations through an amendment adopted in 2013.[175] Even though some of the early contracts concluded under

---

[164] Crusts Regulations, Regulation 33(4); Nodules Regulations, Regulation 31(4); Sulphides Regulations, Regulation 33(4).

[165] Sulphides Regulations, Regulation 33(4).

[166] Crusts Regulations, Regulation 33(4).

[167] Crusts Regulations, Regulation 33(4); Nodules Regulations, Regulation 31(4); Sulphides Regulations, Regulation 33(4).

[168] See Chapter 7. See also LA Levin et al, 'Defining "Serious Harm" to the Marine Environment in the context of Deep-Seabed Mining' (2016) 74 *Marine Policy* 245, 248, suggesting additional criteria to be taken into account.

[169] Crusts Regulations, Regulation 33(4); Nodules Regulations, Regulation 31(4); Sulphides Regulations, Regulation 33(4).

[170] Crusts Regulations, Regulation 33(2) and (5); Sulphides Regulations, Regulation 33(2) and (5). Such a provision was not initially included in the Nodules Regulations, but it has since been added by way of amendments adopted in 2013; Nodules Regulations, Regulation 31(2) and (5).

[171] *Responsibilities and Obligations of States Sponsoring Persons and Entities with Respect to Activities in the Area* (2011) para. 127.

[172] See e.g. Chapter 4. See also earlier in this Chapter.

[173] Sulphides Regulations, Regulation 33(2).

[174] Crusts Regulations, Regulation 33(2).

[175] Nodules Regulations, Regulation 31(2) and (5).

the original Nodules Regulations may not have an explicit reference to BEP, the Seabed Disputes Chamber, in its 2012 Advisory Opinion, held that 'the Nodules Regulations should be interpreted in light of the development of the law',[176] and the Chamber was of the view that the BEP standard could be 'read into' the original Nodules Regulations. Arguably, this interpretation can also be based upon the general due diligence obligation to 'take necessary measures to prevent, reduce and control pollution and other hazards to the marine environment arising from activities in the Area'.[177]

The Regulations also require contractors to carry out full EIAs of particular activities prior to their commencement.[178] These provisions are *lex specialis* and they stand in the place of the generic provisions on EIA in Article 206 for the purpose of activities in the Area.[179] Article 206 may nevertheless remain applicable for any 'planned activities' that fall outside the scope of the regulatory regime in Part XI, such as the conduct of non-resource related marine scientific research in the Area.[180]

As a prerequisite to carrying out any EIA, contractors are expected to gather environmental baseline data against which to assess the likely effects of its activities.[181] The collection of environmental baseline data is a key part of the individual programme of work agreed with the Authority, and the Legal and Technical Commission has developed guidelines specifying the nature of the information that must be gathered.[182] In particular, contractors are expected to utilize BAT in their data collection processes.[183] Contractors must report annually to the Authority on the results of their environmental monitoring programme,[184] which are subject to review by the Legal and Technical Commission.[185] This procedure ensures that the necessary information is collected in order to allow the other environmental obligations of the contractor and the Authority to be carried out.

Not all activities related to exploration require an EIA. Rather than establishing an abstract threshold for EIAs, the Authority has developed a list of activities that

---

[176] *Responsibilities and Obligations of States Sponsoring Persons and Entities with respect to activities in the Area* (2011) para. 137.

[177] Nodules Regulations, Regulation 31(2) of the original regulations.

[178] Nodules Regulations, Annex IV, para. 5.2(a); Sulphides Regulations, Annex IV, para. 5.2(a); Nodules Regulations, Annex IV, para. 5.2(a).

[179] See, however, *Responsibilities and Obligations of States Sponsoring Persons and Entities with Respect to Activities in the Area* (2011) para. 150, in which the Seabed Disputes Chamber held that 'the obligations of the contractors and of the sponsoring States concerning environmental impact assessments extend beyond the scope of application of specific provisions of the Regulations' because the rules of general international law on EIA also apply.

[180] See Report of the Secretary-General, Issues Associated with the Conduct of Marine Scientific Research in Exploration Areas, Document ISBA/22/C/3 (2016) paras 11–13.

[181] Nodules Regulations, Regulation 32(1); Sulphides Regulations, Regulation 34(1); Crusts Regulations, Regulation 34(1).

[182] Recommendations for the Guidance of Contractors for the Assessment of the Possible Environmental Impacts Arising from Exploration for Marine Minerals in the Area, Document ISBA/19/LTC/8 (2013) paras 13–16.

[183] Ibid, para. 14.

[184] Nodules Regulations, Regulation 32(2); Sulphides Regulations, Regulation 34(2); Crusts Regulations, Regulation 34(2).

[185] UNCLOS, Article 165(2)(h).

do[186] and do not[187] require prior EIA. The Legal and Technical Commission has also provided guidance on the information to be provided by the contractor as part of the EIA process.[188] It makes clear that 'the impact assessment should address not only the areas directly affected by mining but also the wider region impacted by the near-bottom plume, the discharge plume and material released by transporting the minerals to the ocean surface, depending on the technology being used'.[189] This guidance recommends the use of Preservation Reference Zones (PRZs) and Impact Reference Zones (IRZs) for the purpose of identifying relevant impacts.[190] The Legal and Technical Commission has indicated that it will prepare additional guidelines for contractors on the establishment of PRZs and IRZs in order to make sure that a consistent approach is taken and the results of EIAs are robust.[191] Overall, the guidelines emphasize the need for precaution and an ecosystem approach to EIA that takes into account all potential harm to the marine environment. Although the recommendations of the Legal and Technical Commission are by their very nature not legally binding, they must be taken seriously by contractors, as they have been produced by the same body which is responsible for ensuring that contractors have complied with their obligations.[192] Indeed, the standard contract terms emphasize that the recommendations of the Legal and Technical Commission must be observed 'as far as reasonably practicable'.[193]

Contractors must provide the Authority with the EIA at least a year before the activity takes place.[194] This allows prior scrutiny of the EIA by the Authority prior to authorization of the particular activity.

The rules described above target a limited range of activities taking place during exploration, such as intrusive sampling techniques, test mining, or testing of collection systems and equipment.[195] Nevertheless, it must be remembered that the exploration phase is itself not an isolated activity, but rather it is intended to gather information in order to allow a contractor to prepare a programme of work for exploitation. Therefore, the stringent application of the rules on EIA is vital to also ensuring that future exploitation regime will be developed on the basis of robust

---

[186] Recommendations for the Guidance of Contractors for the Assessment of the Possible Environmental Impacts Arising From Exploration for Marine Minerals in the Area (Environmental Recommendations), Document ISBA/19/LTC/8 (2013) para. 19. The Recommendations are expected to be reviewed in 2017.

[187] Ibid, para. 18.

[188] Environmental Recommendations, paras 29–30. See also International Seabed Authority, *Environmental Management Needs for Exploration and Exploitation of Deep Sea Minerals*, ISA Technical Study No. 10 (2012) 16–28.

[189] Environmental Recommendations, para. 22.   [190] Ibid, Annex, para. 53.

[191] Report on the work of the Legal and Technical Commission at its session in 2016, Document ISBA/22/C/17 (2016) para. 30.

[192] See J Harrison, *Making the Law of the Sea* (CUP 2011) 141.

[193] Nodules Regulations, Annex IV, para. 13.2(e); Sulphides Regulations, Annex IV, para. 13.2(e); Crusts Regulations, Annex IV, para. 13.2(e).

[194] Environmental Recommendations, para. 20; see also Annex, para. 52. The Legal and Technical Commission noted that the first notification had been received in 2016; Report on the work of the Legal and Technical Commission at its session in 2016, Document ISBA/22/C/17 (2016) para. 21.

[195] Environmental Recommendations, para. 19.

data and an appropriate understanding of the potential impacts of deep-seabed mining on the marine environment. From this perspective, the requirements for the elaborate plans of work and EIAs in relation to exploration activities can themselves be considered as an implementation of the precautionary approach, as they demand that minimum amounts of information are collected prior to a decision on exploitation.

8.4.4 Regulating the environmental impacts of exploitation

At the end of the exploration phase, contractors are expected to move towards the exploitation of deep-sea minerals.[196] Unlike the two phases of preparatory activity discussed above, exploitation is expected to have 'severe ... and potentially permanent' impacts on the marine environment.[197] Yet, the precise effects will depend, in large part, on the nature of the resources being mined, their precise location, and the technology that is employed.[198] The approval process for exploitation contracts will therefore offer a vital opportunity for the Authority to introduce sufficient safeguards to ensure the protection of the marine environment. At the time of writing, the Authority is only just beginning to put in place regulations to manage the authorization process and associated requirements, including environmental obligations for contractors.[199] Therefore, it is only possible to speculate on the applicable regulatory regime. Nevertheless, there are arguably key elements that must be present if the Authority is to fulfil its environmental mandate under Article 145 of UNCLOS.

There are several features of the exploration regime that are likely to feed into the exploitation regime. For example, the latter is likely to build upon the general principles that are already found in the exploration regulations, particularly the precautionary approach. Yet, as noted by the early draft on environmental regulations, 'the fundamental question ... is not should the precautionary approach be applied, but how?'[200] As argued throughout this book, there is no default way of applying the precautionary approach as a rule but rather it serves as a guiding principle[201] for the development of more specific rules or their subsequent interpretation and application. Therefore, it will be for the drafters of the exploitation regime to determine precisely how precautionary they wish to be. One interesting way in which the Authority proposes to deal with this question in the first set of Draft Regulations is to require the applicant to expressly explain how the precautionary approach has been interpreted and applied in compiling the information contained in an

---

[196] In 2016, the Authority extended the exploration contracts of six contractors on the understanding that 'the applicants should be ready for exploitation at the end of the five-year extension period'; Report on the work of the Legal and Technical Commission at its session in 2016, Document ISBA/22/C/17 (2016) para. 16.

[197] World Bank (n22) 28. See also Levin et al (n168) 245–59.   [198] Ibid, 29.

[199] See e.g. International Seabed Authority, *A Discussion Paper on the Development and Drafting of Regulations on Exploitation for Mineral Resources of the Area* (Environmental Matters) (2017).

[200] Ibid, para. 7.18.

[201] Or in the words of the Authority, 'guiding value'; Ibid, para. 7.19.

application.[202] The Draft Regulations also foresee that the uncertainties or inadequacies of the data or information available about an operation will also be a consideration that may be taken into account by the Commission in assessing whether a proposed plan of work provides for the effective protection of the environment.[203] It may also be that the Authority could consider a phased approach to exploitation, seen in other sectors, whereby contractors will be authorized to carry out small-scale operations at first, and they will only be allowed to expand their activities if it can be demonstrated that impacts are not too great.

Another feature of the regulatory regime that is likely to carry forward is the requirement for environmental assessment. When applying for authorization to carry out commercial exploitation, it is anticipated that contractors will be required to submit a full EIA and environmental management plan which reflects BEP and addresses measures for monitoring and managing environmental impacts.[204] It is hoped that such a system could build upon experience gained through the assessment of impacts in the exploration phase. A key challenge in this respect is that the Authority itself will have to manage the EIA process, and the level of detail in the rules and regulations will, therefore, have to be so much greater compared with other regimes which have sought to present a general framework to be further implemented by States in assessing activities within their own jurisdiction.

The early Draft Regulations on environmental matters make clear that all mining activities will require an EIA, and so there is no need for a screening phase of the process.[205] The Draft Regulations go on to specify the information that must be prepared and assessed by the contractor as part of the scoping and assessment phases of the process. At the end of the proposed process, an environmental statement would be presented to the Authority for consideration alongside the proposed environmental management plan as part of the overall application for an exploitation contract. To ensure the credibility of this procedure, the Draft Regulations build in a number of important stages at which the information is subject to external scrutiny, before it is formally submitted for approval. First, the Authority itself may request further information from the contractor at a number of stages in the process.[206] In this regard, it has been recommended that 'the levels of expertise in both the [Legal and Technical Commission] and the Secretariat ... should be increased' in order to allow them to deal with the complex information contained in applications,[207] and it has even been suggested that the Authority should establish a specialist environmental committee in order to deal with this work.[208] Second, the Draft Regulations would require the environmental management plan to be verified by a report from an appropriately qualified expert approved by the Authority.[209]

---

[202] See Draft Regulation 32(1)(r).   [203] Draft Regulation 41(p).

[204] International Seabed Authority, *Developing a Regulatory Framework for Mineral Exploitation in the Area* (2015) 12–13.

[205] International Seabed Authority (n202) 33.

[206] See Ibid, Draft Regulations 20(3) and 33(2).

[207] International Seabed Authority, Periodic Review of the International Seabed Authority pursuant to UNCLOS Article 154: Interim Report, Document ISBA/22/A/CRP.3(1) (2016) 27.

[208] Ibid, 65.   [209] Ibid, Draft Regulation 29(2)(f).

In addition, it would be possible for the Authority to request an additional opinion from an appropriately qualified expert on the content of the environmental scoping report,[210] the proposed environmental management system,[211] or the overall plan of work.[212] Third, the Draft Regulations provide for publication and consultation with interested persons before key decision-making stages.[213] Indeed, the Authority has noted that importance of promoting 'transparency in environmental decision-making by permitting appropriate access to information [and facilitating and encouraging] public awareness and participation'.[214] The explicit endorsement of public participation in this context demonstrates the reach of Rio Principle 10 into the legal framework for the protection of the marine environment. Yet, a key issue will be how *interested persons* is defined, a particular challenge for a regime that is by definition concerned with promoting the interests of humankind as a whole. It would seem appropriate that the existing observers registered to attend certain meetings, including environmental groups, such as Greenpeace International and World Wildlife Fund International, would qualify as interested persons. However, it has been suggested that a broader range of actors should be permitted to be involved in the review processes.[215]

Monitoring will be vital in order to allow adaptive management of seabed mining in accordance with the precautionary approach. Whilst monitoring will be required in any case under Article 204 of UNCLOS, there would be clear advantages to having a more detailed framework that applies to deep-seabed mining as part of the exploitation Regulations. One specific requirement may be the establishment of IRZs and PRZs[216] in order to allow contractors to monitor the ongoing impacts of their activities on the surrounding environment. Yet, the precise location of PRZs presents a particular challenge; as noted by Lodge, 'a PRZ located within a contractor's exploitation area will likely not succeed in its objective of ensuring representative and stable biota', and the Authority 'will need to reconsider how [the Regulations on PRZs] can be implemented in practice'.[217]

Contractors will also be required to adopt an environmental management system to guide their operations. This reflects an obligation that is often placed upon oil and gas operators under relevant international treaties, as seen above. The Authority could specify a particular environmental management system that should be used by contractors (e.g. ISO 14001) or it may leave it to the contractors themselves to identify an appropriate environmental management system, subject to approval by

---

[210] Ibid, Draft Regulation 20(4).   [211] Ibid, Draft Regulation 28(4).
[212] Ibid, Draft Regulation 33(3).   [213] Ibid, Draft Regulations 20(5) and 36.
[214] Ibid, para. 4.1(c).
[215] Co-Chair's Report, Griffith Law School and the International Seabed Authority Workshop on Environmental Assessment and Management for Exploitation of Minerals in the Area (2016) para. 27.
[216] Defined as 'areas in which no mining shall occur to ensure representative and stable biota of the seabed', allowing an assessment of 'any changes in biodiversity of the marine environment'; e.g. Nodules Regulations, Regulation 31(6); Sulphides Regulations, Regulation 33(6); Crusts Regulations, Regulation 33(6). See also Clarion-Clipperton Environmental Management Plan, Document ISBA/17/LTC/7 (2011), para. 41(c) and (d).
[217] M Lodge, 'Some Legal and Policy Considerations Relating to the Establishment of a Representative Network of Protected Areas in the Clarion-Clipperton Zone' (2011) 26 *IJMCL* 463, 467.

the Authority.[218] The new exploitation regime should also address the restoration and rehabilitation of a site once mining activities have ceased.[219] Consideration will need to be given by the Authority as to what restoration obligations will be placed on contractors, including post-closure monitoring and whether there is a need for some form of financial guarantee or bond to cover restoration commitments if the contractor is not able to.[220]

It is clear that environmental considerations will be a key factor for the Authority when determining the size, location, and the intensity of exploitation activities. Given that any programme of work must be approved, the Authority has significant control over what activity can and cannot proceed. The Council, based on advice from the Legal and Technical Commission, can thus be expected to make any authorization to proceed to exploitation conditional upon ensuring that seabed-mining activities are managed in a way that they do not have serious harmful effects on the marine environment. Ultimately, the Authority may veto a proposed activity if the threat is perceived to be too great, and the existing Regulations already foresee that where management of risks is not sufficient, activities should 'not be authorized to proceed'.[221] This choice, however, comes back to the need to balance environmental protection with economic development, a challenge that goes to the core of the Authority's mandate. Given the difficulties of mitigation in the deep-sea context, it has been proposed that biodiversity offsets—that is, the establishment of protected areas in alternative locations—may be utilized as a means for contractors to meet their environmental obligations.[222] Indeed, the Council has an explicit power under the Convention to 'disapprove areas for exploitation by contractors or the Enterprise in cases where substantial evidence indicates the risk of serious harm to the marine environment'.[223] Such a determination needs to consider not only the marine ecosystems within the proposed area for exploitation but also the 'proximity of the exploitation area to marine protected areas and vulnerable marine ecosystems',[224] both within the Area and within areas of national jurisdiction. To this end, the Authority may have to cooperate with coastal States and other international institutions in order to ensure it coordinates its environmental measures in this respect.[225]

---

[218] See Clarion-Clipperton Environmental Management Plan, para. 41(a).

[219] International Seabed Authority, Developing a Regulatory Framework for Mineral Exploitation in the Area (2015) 14: '[a closure plan] is seen as a dynamic plan that requires regular review and updating and must anticipate potential closure of an exploitation area prior to the expiration of any plan of work'. See also Clarion-Clipperton Environment Management Plan, para. 41(f).

[220] International Seabed Authority, Developing a Regulatory Framework for Mineral Exploitation in the Area (2015) 15; International Seabed Authority (n202) Draft Regulations 31–2 and 65–6.

[221] Nodules Regulations, Regulation 31(4); Sulphides Regulations, Regulation 33(4); Crusts Regulations, Regulation 33(4).

[222] See D Johnson and MA Ferreira, 'Current Legal Developments: ISA Areas of Particular Environmental Interest in the Clarion-Clipperton Fracture Zone' (2015) 30 *IJMCL* 559, 565.

[223] UNCLOS, Article 162(2)(x).

[224] International Seabed Authority, Developing a Regulatory Framework for Mineral Exploitation in the Area (2015), 16.

[225] This is recognized by the Authority itself; see Report on the Work of the Legal and Technical Commission at Its Session in 2016, Document ISBA/22/C/17 (2016) para. 27. Inter-institutional cooperation will be discussed in Chapter 10.

8.4.5 Environmental emergencies

Mining of minerals at immense depths, in close proximity to rare and fragile eco-systems, is an inherently risky business. UNCLOS and the Regulations contain explicit rules relating to the measures that must be taken in the case of emergencies that may threaten to harm the marine environment significantly.[226] Under existing Regulations, all contractors must submit a contingency plan to the Secretary-General, stating what measures will be taken in the case of an environmental emergency.[227] If a contractor, through its activities in the Area, causes or is likely to cause serious harm to the marine environment, he must immediately warn other contractors and shipping operating in the vicinity.[228] In addition, the contractor must notify the Secretary-General of the incident. The notification must include the coordinates of the area affected, a description of any action being taken by the contractor to prevent, contain, or minimize any harm to the marine environment, and any supplementary information reasonably requested by the Secretary-General.[229] In turn, the Secretary-General must notify the relevant organs of the Authority.[230] The Council of the Authority, taking into account the recommendations of the Legal and Technical Commission, may issue emergency orders as may be reasonably necessary to prevent, contain, and minimize serious harm to the marine environment.[231] However, the Regulations also allow the Secretary-General of the Authority to take immediate measures to prevent, contain, or minimize the harm.[232] This innovation prevents any potential delay in responding to an environmental emergency. As a safeguard, any measures taken by the Secretary-General are provisional and they will be effective for no longer than ninety days or until the Council has decided what measures it wishes to impose, whichever is shorter. Where a contractor fails to comply with an order of the Council, the Council may itself take practical measures to protect the marine environment,[233] and the contractor must reimburse the Authority for any expenses incurred in taking measures to respond to a pollution emergency in line with the polluter pays principle.[234] These provisions are likely to be incorporated into the exploitation Regulations, where they will be even more important, given the more intensive nature of these activities.

---

[226] See UNCLOS, Article 162(w).

[227] Nodules Regulations, Annex IV, para. 6.1; Sulphides Regulations, Annex IV, para. 6.1; Crusts Regulations, Annex IV, para. 6.1.

[228] Ibid.   [229] Ibid, para. 6.2.

[230] Nodules Regulations, Regulation 33(2); Sulphides Regulations, Regulation 35(2); Crusts Regulations, Regulation 35(2).

[231] Nodules Regulations, Regulation 33(6); Sulphides Regulations, Regulation 35(6); Crusts Regulations, Regulation 35(6).

[232] Nodules Regulations, Regulation 33(3); Sulphides Regulations, Regulation 35(3); Crusts Regulations, Regulation 35(3).

[233] Nodules Regulations, Regulation 33(7); Sulphides Regulations, Regulation 35(7); Crusts Regulations, Regulation 35(7).

[234] Nodules Regulations, Annex IV, para. 6.4; Sulphides Regulations, Annex IV, para. 6.4; Crusts Regulations, Annex IV, para. 6.4. The Regulations also require the contractor to offer a guarantee of its financial and technical capacity to comply promptly with emergency orders; Nodules Regulations, Regulation 33(8); Sulphides Regulations, Regulation 35(8); Crusts Regulations, Regulation 35(8).

8.4.6 Deep-seabed protected areas

Most applications submitted to the Authority to date have been in relation to the Clarion-Clipperton Zone in the Eastern Central Pacific Ocean. This Area is characterized by a number of seamounts, ridges, and abyssal plains. The Area is thought to be where the most promising deposits of polymetallic nodules, as well as other mineral resources, are located. As a means to ensure the 'proactive and responsible management' of the resources in the Area, the Authority decided to develop an environmental management plan (EMP) for the Clarion-Clipperton Zone. This plan builds upon information gathered through a dedicated research project designed to analyse species distribution in the Clarion-Clipperton Zone,[235] as well as workshops organized by the Authority.[236] Indeed, the process for drawing up the EMP involved a wide range of stakeholders. It incorporated independent scientific evidence into the decision-making process[237] and it has been held up as a model for the 'partnership approach' to marine environmental protection.[238]

The EMP contains a vision of 'a sustainably exploited Clarion-Clipperton Zone that preserves representative and unique marine habitats and species'[239] and it sets out a series of goals to help achieve this vision. Amongst these goals, the Authority wishes both to 'facilitate exploitation of seabed mineral resources in an environmentally responsible manner', as well as to 'enable the preservation of representative and unique marine ecosystems'.[240] It is in furtherance of this latter objective that the EMP introduces the notion of Areas of Particular Environmental Interest (APEIs), which are a form of MPA in which no mining will be authorized to take place. Indeed, the EMP is explicit in noting that it has the aim of contributing 'to the achievement of the management goals and targets set forth in the Plan of Implementation of the World Summit on Sustainable Development, including [the development of] marine protected areas, in accordance with international law and based on the best scientific information available, including representative networks by 2012'.[241] The EMP identifies nine APEIs across the Clarion-Clipperton Zone, covering a range of deep-seabed habitats.[242] The Council provisionally approved the EMP at its session

---

[235] See <http://www.isa.org.jm/files/documents/EN/efund/Kaplan.pdf>.

[236] See e.g. Summary outcomes of a workshop to design marine protected areas for seamounts and the abyssal nodule province in Pacific high seas, held at the University of Hawaii from 23 to 26 October 2007, Document ISBA/14/LTC/2* (2008). See also <http://www.isa.org.jm/international-workshop-establishment-regional-environmental-management-plan-clarion-clipperton-zone>.

[237] For a description of the process, see LM Wedding et al, 'From Principles to Practice: A Spatial Approach to Systematic Conservation Planning in the Deep Sea' (2013) 280 *Proceedings of the Royal Society* 1684.

[238] See M Lodge et al, 'Seabed Mining: International Seabed Authority Environmental Management Plan for the Clarion-Clipperton Zone—A Partnership Approach' (2014) 49 *MP* 66–72.

[239] Environmental Management Plan for the Clarion-Clipperton Zone (EMP), Document ISBA/17/LTC/7, 13 July 2011, para. 32.

[240] Ibid, para. 35(a) and (e).   [241] Ibid, para. 35(c).

[242] *Decision of the Council Relating to an Environmental Management Plan of the Clarion-Clipperton Zone*, Document ISBA/18/C/22 (2012). A review carried out in 2016 recommended the addition of two more areas of particular environmental interest; see Report on the Work of the Legal and Technical Commission at Its Session in 2016, Document ISBA/22/C/17 (2016) para. 27.

in July 2012.[243] In accordance with this decision, 'for a period of five years ... or until further review by the Legal and Technical Commission or the Council, no application for approval of a plan of work for exploration or exploitation should be granted in [the] areas of particular environmental interest'.[244] This decision is interesting in a number of respects. First, it explicitly draws upon the precautionary approach as a justification for protecting these areas.[245] Second, the decision demonstrates a constructive use of the power in Article 145 of the Convention, which does not explicitly permit the designation of protected areas, but it can be argued to cover such measures as part of the broader environmental remit of the Authority.[246]

At the same time, it has been noted that the provisional nature of the designation leaves these measures 'vulnerable, especially if commercial pressure to promptly commence the exploitation phase increases'.[247] Moreover, the APEIs are also only protected from seabed mining under the current arrangements. If the areas are to receive protection from other threats, such as trawling or pollution from other sources, it will be necessary for the Authority to cooperate with other international organizations with a mandate to regulate these activities. This is explicitly recognized in the EMP,[248] but it raises the question of how best to achieve coordination, an issue that will be addressed later in this volume.[249]

The current EMP is also limited to the Clarion-Clipperton Zone, whereas mining in the Area may take place on other parts of the ocean floor. To this end, the UN General Assembly has encouraged the Authority 'to consider developing and approving environmental-management plans in other international seabed area zones ...',[250] and the Council has requested the Legal and Technical Commission to work on this issue.[251] A major challenge for Authority in doing so is the relative paucity of scientific information concerning other areas of the seabed, demonstrating the need for science and legal regulation to work hand-in-hand in developing the regime for seabed mining. However, the development of the Clarion-Clipperton Zone EMP provides a model that may be employed for other parts of the Area.[252] There is a degree of urgency for such a task, given that such plans would be best

---

[243] *Decision of the Council Relating to an Environmental Management Plan of the Clarion-Clipperton Zone*, Document ISBA/18/C/22 (2012).

[244] Ibid, para. 5. This prohibition applies for a five-year period. For an analysis, see Lodge (n217).

[245] *Decision of the Council Relating to an Environmental Management Plan for the Clarion-Clipperton Zone*, Document ISBA/18/C/22 (2012) para. 2. As noted by Lodge, 'at this time, without any environmental impact assessments having yet been undertaken, there is no evidence that indicates a risk of serious harm to the marine environment from mining activity in the proposed APEIs'; Lodge (n217) 466.

[246] See Lodge (n217) 468, noting that the Council has a broad power under Article 162 to establish 'the specific policies to be pursued by the Authority on any question or matter within the competence of the Authority', and the protection of the environment falls within this mandate by virtue of Article 145.

[247] A Jaeckel, 'An Environmental Management Strategy for the International Seabed Authority? The Legal Basis' (2015) 30 *IJMCL* 93, 96.

[248] EMP, para. 12: 'The Authority recognizes the need to work in consultation with the many other international organizations and processes related to the protection of the marine environment.'

[249] See Chapter 10.   [250] UNGA Resolution 68/70 (2013) para. 51.

[251] Decision of the Council of the International Seabed Authority Relating to the Summary Report of the Chair of the Legal and Technical Commission, Document ISBA/22/C/28 (2016) para. 12.

[252] See Lodge et al (n238) 72.

developed prior to the granting of any authorizations in order to ensure that the most important areas are protected from exploitation, without the need for a compromise with vested interests.

8.4.7 Enforcement of the Seabed Mining Code

As well as establishing a centralized institutional framework for the elaboration of international rules in relation to seabed activities beyond national jurisdiction, UNCLOS also sets up a centralized enforcement mechanism. It is formally the role of the Council to 'supervise and coordinate the implementation of [Part XI] on all questions and matters within the competence of the Authority and invite the attention of the Assembly to cases of non-compliance'.[253] However, the Convention also foresees the establishment of an inspectorate whose role will be to 'inspect activities in the Area to determine whether this Part, the rules, regulations and procedures of the Authority, and the terms and conditions of any contract with the Authority are being complied with'.[254] Precisely what this inspectorate will look like and how often inspections will take place will depend on negotiations concerning the design of the exploitation regime.[255] However, it is clear that the Authority will have the power to sanction non-compliance if it is detected. A notable feature of the Regulations adopted by the Authority is that they are legally enforceable against contractors through a specialized dispute settlement system established by UNCLOS. Such a system provides a means of potentially avoiding the problems encountered with lax flag State enforcement in the shipping and fishing regimes.

The Authority is explicitly given the ability to take measures against contractors for failure to comply with their legal obligations under the Convention or the Regulations.[256] Amongst the penalties that are available to the Authority are suspension or termination of contractual rights, as well as 'monetary penalties proportionate to the seriousness of the violation'.[257] It would seem that the Authority can take such action against contractors, based upon its own factual assessment. However, disputes about compliance will be submitted either to the Seabed Disputes Chamber of ITLOS or to binding commercial arbitration.[258] These mechanisms thus provide a means for independent judicial review of the compliance decisions of the Authority. Indeed, if a contractor fails to bring itself into compliance, it is also open

---

[253] UNCLOS, Article 162(2)(a).   [254] Ibid, Article 162(2)(z).

[255] International Seabed Authority, Developing a Regulatory Framework for Mineral Exploitation in the Area (2016) Annex, Draft Regulation 54.

[256] UNCLOS, Article 187(c).

[257] Ibid, Annex III, Article 18(1)–(2). Such penalties may not be imposed 'until the contractor has been accorded a reasonable opportunity to exhaust the judicial remedies available to him pursuant to Part XI, section 5'; UNCLOS, Annex III, Article 18(3). Compliance can also be taken into account when considering applications for further exploration or exploitation contracts by existing contractors; see UNCLOS, Annex III, Article 10 and Part XI Agreement, Section 1, para. 13.

[258] UNCLOS, Articles 187(c) and 188(2)(a); note that a commercial arbitration tribunal is prohibited from deciding any questions of interpretation of the Convention and it must refer any such questions to the Seabed Disputes Chamber.

to the Authority to bring legal proceedings against the contractor. Such proceedings may result in binding awards against the contractor, which will be enforceable through the national courts of States Parties.

It would seem that additional penalties may be available in the case of contractors that are States Parties. The Convention makes clear that any State Party that has 'grossly and persistently' violated the provisions of Part XI or the rules and regulations of the Authority may be 'suspended from the exercise of its rights and privileges of membership by the Assembly upon recommendation by the Council'.[259] Such rights and privileges may include voting rights within the Authority or even the right to carry out exploration or exploitation activities.

These compliance mechanisms are particularly robust compared with other examples in the marine environmental protection context. They involve both an independent authority to investigate and bring claims, as well as a scheme of binding penalties that may be applied. The compliance regime for deep-seabed mining has not yet been tested in practice, even though there is evidence that many contractors have failed to comply with their obligations to provide environmental baseline reporting obligations.[260] Rather, 'the sort of compliance measures that have been taken so far have been limited to decisions and resolutions of the Council urging contractors to make better efforts to comply with contractual requirements'.[261] This demonstrates that the Authority will not automatically proceed to utilizing its full enforcement powers, but rather it has a range of options for enforcement at its disposal. However, the success of this enforcement scheme will also depend upon the Authority having the human and financial resources available to police activities in the Area effectively.

8.4.8 The role of sponsoring States in the regulation of seabed mining beyond national jurisdiction

The Authority plays the lead role in developing a uniform set of regulations that will apply to all seabed activities in the Area, ensuring that all operators meet universal standards of environmental protection. However, these standards of protection may be increased in certain circumstances through action taken by sponsoring States.

Every application by a non-State entity to carry out seabed activities in the Area must be sponsored by a State Party to UNCLOS.[262] The role of the sponsoring State is to assist the Authority in carrying out its mandate and ensure that activities carried out by its nationals are in conformity with Part XI and relevant Regulations.[263]

---

[259] Ibid, Article 185(2).

[260] See e.g. International Seabed Authority, *Periodic Review of the Implementation of Plans of Work of the Commission during the Nineteenth Session of the International Seabed Authority*, Document ISBA/19/C/14 (2013) para. 2(c).

[261] M Lodge, 'Protecting the Marine Environment of the Deep Seabed', in R Rayfuse (ed.), *Research Handbook on International Marine Environmental Law* (Edward Elgar 2015) 160.

[262] UNCLOS, Article 153(2)(b).   [263] Ibid, Article 139(1).

However, it would appear that sponsoring States also have a residual regulatory role. Article 21(3) of Annex III of UNCLOS explicitly provides that 'the application by a State Party to contractors sponsored by it, or to ships flying its flag, of environmental or other laws and regulations more stringent than those in the rules, regulations and procedures of the Authority ... shall not be deemed inconsistent with Part XI'. This is confirmed by Article 209, which provides that the laws and regulations that States apply to their nationals carrying out activities in the Area 'shall be no less effective than the international rules, regulations and procedures' adopted by the Authority.[264] This rule of reference establishes a minimum standard, but it does not prevent States adopting standards that are more stringent for their operators.

If sponsoring States do decide to adopt regulations that apply to their nationals conducting activities in the Area, the regulations make clear that they must also take a precautionary approach.[265] Whilst this is the same obligation that is on the Authority, it is apparent that the sponsoring State may decide on a stricter application of this principle for its own nationals. However, it has been made clear that the sponsoring State does not bear residual responsibility for the failure of contractors to protect the marine environment.[266]

As well as providing a supplementary source of environmental standards for operators under their jurisdiction and control, the sponsoring State plays a key role in ensuring that its nationals comply with their environmental commitments, including making sure that any assurances made by the contractor are enforceable through its national law.[267] All sponsoring States are under the same level of responsibility in this respect, and the principle of common but differentiated responsibilities has no application in this context. As noted by the Seabed Disputes Chamber:

[e]quality of treatment between developing and developed sponsoring States is consistent with the need to prevent commercial enterprises based in developed States from setting up companies in developing States, acquiring their nationality and obtaining their sponsorship in the hope of being subjected to less burdensome regulations and controls. The spread of sponsoring States 'of convenience' would jeopardize uniform application of the highest standards of protection of the marine environment, the safe development of activities in the Area and protection of the common heritage of mankind.[268]

This reasoning is intended to uphold the integrity of the regime contained in Part XI and its ability to promote the protection and preservation of the fragile marine environment found in the deep seas.

---

[264] Ibid, Article 209(2).
[265] Nodules Regulations, Regulation 31(2); Crusts Regulations, Regulation 33(2); Sulphides Regulations, Regulation 33(2).
[266] *Responsibilities and Obligations of States Sponsoring Persons and Entities with Respect to Activities in the Area* (2011) para. 204.
[267] UNCLOS, Article 235(2). See also Annex III, Article 4(4).
[268] *Responsibilities and Obligations of States Sponsoring Persons and Entities with Respect to Activities in the Area* (2011) para.159.

8.5 Conclusion

Many activities can take place on the seabed, and the precise legal regime that applies will depend, in large part, on the location and nature of the activity. This chapter has sought to give an overview of the relevant legal framework and the variety of institutions that may be involved in developing an appropriate regulatory response.

On the one hand, seabed activities within national jurisdiction are subject to a highly fragmented legal regime, based upon general procedural and substantive rules in UNCLOS, supplemented by global and regional rules relating to particular types of seabed activities. Oil and gas exploitation has received the most attention in this respect, in part, inspired by a number of serious incidents in this sector.[269] The regional nature of many regulatory efforts within national jurisdiction means that the rules or standards that apply may vary, depending on the location of an activity. Nevertheless, it is possible to argue that some basic rules, such as a requirement to implement BAT and BEP, have emerged as international rules and standards and thus will apply to all States by virtue of the rule of reference in Article 208 of UNCLOS. All the same, these basic rules are probably not sufficient by themselves in order to ensure strong environmental protection, and, therefore, States should take further action to fill gaps in the regime by negotiating additional instruments. Some commentators have suggested a global treaty for the regulation of seabed activities,[270] but there may not be sufficient political will for such a move.[271] Existing protocols may provide a model on which to negotiate new rules or standards in other regions, however.[272] Furthermore, regional efforts could be usefully supplemented by a global policy framework to share best practices between regions and to channel technical and financial support to those regions in need. Such a mechanism could operate in a similar manner to the Global Programme of Action on Land-Based Sources, discussed in Chapter 4. In the absence of another relevant global forum, UNEP would be in an ideal position to take the lead on this issue, thereby reprising its earlier efforts in this field.

Seabed mining for mineral resources may also take place within national jurisdiction, and to the extent that there are relevant international rules and standards

---

[269] See S Vinogradov, 'The Impact of the Deepwater Horizon: The Evolving International Legal Regime for Offshore Accidental Pollution Prevention, Preparedness and Response' (2013) 44 *ODIL* 335–62.

[270] See, however, proposals by M Tsamenyi, 'Ocean Energy and the Law of the Sea: The Need for a Protocol' (1998) 29 *ODIL* 3–19. See also Z Gao, 'Environmental Regulation of Oil and Gas in the Twentieth Century and Beyond: Introduction and Overview', in Z Gao (ed.), *Environmental Regulation of Oil and Gas* (Kluwer International 1998) 31; S Rares 'An International Convention on Offshore Hydrocarbon Leaks?' (2012) 26 *A&NZMLJ* 10; JA Roach, 'International Standards for Offshore Drilling', in MH Nordquist, JN Moore, A Chirhop, and R Long (eds), *The Regulation of Continental Shelf Development* (Martinus Nijhoff Publishers 2013) 116.

[271] See the discussion of the languid response to proposals for a global instrument within the IMO in R Pereira, 'Pollution from Seabed Activities', in D Attard et al (eds), *The IMLI Manual of International Maritime Law: Vol. III* (OUP 2016) 134–5.

[272] See Oral (n127) 257; Vinogradov (n269) 352.

agreed through the Authority, they may be applicable to mining within coastal State maritime zones by virtue of Article 208.[273] Yet, there are a much broader range of mineral resources that may be found within national jurisdiction for which there are currently no international rules or standards, and so States will only be bound by the basic rules in Part XII of UNCLOS, unless and until they agree upon common standards.

A similar situation applies to renewable energy generation within national jurisdiction, which is one of the fastest-growing offshore sectors. Whilst this activity does not involve the direct exploitation of seabed resources, it may nevertheless have some physical impact on the seabed and surrounding marine ecosystems. Another key issue that has been raised in this context is the proliferation of underwater noise that is caused by renewable energy installations. The Conference of the Parties (COP) of the Convention on Biological Diversity (CBD) is one of several organizations that has called for particular attention to be paid to noise pollution in the marine environment,[274] recognizing that 'there are significant questions that require further study'.[275] Pending the results of such research, the CBD COP has encouraged States to 'take appropriate measures ... to avoid, minimize and mitigate the potential significant adverse impacts of anthropogenic underwater noise on marine and coastal diversity', including 'conducting impact assessments, where appropriate, for activities that may have significant adverse impacts on noise-sensitive species, and carrying out monitoring, where appropriate'.[276] There are currently very few specific international rules or standards on these topics, and it is left to coastal States to adopt national legislation in accordance with the due diligence requirements of UNCLOS. Yet, as these activities become more prominent, we may expect an increase in attention from the international community. Regional seas bodies provide an ideal forum in which to promote cooperation on these issues, as they offer established institutional frameworks through which to agree on an appropriate level of rules or standards. Indeed, there are already indications of movement in this direction.[277] Treaties concerned with the conservation of biological diversity may also have a role to play in promoting regulation.[278]

In areas beyond national jurisdiction, the regime for the regulation of deep-seabed mining provides a rare example of centralized decision-making in the international legal system. The International Seabed Authority has not only the power to adopt rules and regulations that apply to all mining activities within the Area but also the ability to enforce those rules and regulations directly against operators. There is no doubt that the protection of the marine environment has been a concern

---

[273] See Levin et al (n168) 246.

[274] See also UNGA Resolution 60/30, para. 84; ACCOBAMS Resolution 2.16

[275] CBD COP Decision XII/23, para. 3(g).

[276] CBD COP Decision XII/23, para. 3(g).

[277] See e.g. OSPAR Agreement 2008-03: Guidance on Environmental Considerations for Offshore Wind Farm Development (2008); HELCOM Recommendation 34E-1, Safeguarding Important Bird Habitats and Migration Routes in the Baltic Sea from Negative Effects of Wind and Wave Energy Production at Sea (2013).

[278] See e.g. Convention on Migratory Species, Renewable Energy Technologies and Migratory Species: Guidelines for Sustainable Development, Document UNEP/CMS/ScC18/Doc.10.2.2 (2014).

at the centre of the work of the Authority to date, even if debates continue about whether or not sufficient weight has been attached to this objective. There is evidence that the Authority has used its law-making power to integrate environmental considerations into all stages of the decision-making process and sought to identify proactively areas of the seabed that are worthy of protection from any form of interference. Despite these impressive developments, considerable challenges lay ahead in the regulation of seabed mining. The most difficult task for the Authority will be in designing a system of exploitation that draws an appropriate balance between economic development and environmental protection. The Authority itself admits that 'there is a vast amount of work ... to be performed in this area from agreeing the thresholds of serious harm to the efficacy of PRZs and IRZs, developing workable environmental targets and indicators and the application of a precautionary-risk management framework'.[279] It is likely that a system of MPAs combined with a process of adaptive management is most likely to ensure the emergence of a framework that promotes sustainable resource utilization in the deep seabed. The process of drafting the exploitation regime provides the international community with the opportunity to ensure that environmental protection underpins the regulatory framework applying to future commercial mining operations in areas beyond national jurisdiction from the outset. Yet, it is also important that this framework be flexible to allow the regime to evolve as better information is gained about the precise impacts of mining on the deep-sea environment.

---

[279] International Seabed Authority, Developing a Regulatory Framework for Mineral Exploitation in the Area (2015) 27.

9

Addressing the Marine Environmental Impacts of Climate Change and Ocean Acidification

9.1 Introduction

The international community has recognized that 'climate change is a cross-cutting and persistent crisis, ... the scale and gravity of the negative impacts of [which] affect all countries ... and threaten the viability and survival of nations'.[1] It is now generally accepted that climate change is caused by anthropocentric activities, particularly greenhouse gas emissions, which primarily derive from burning fossil fuels and changing land use.[2] The most obvious effect of this phenomenon is the rising temperature of the atmosphere, causing extreme weather events such as droughts and flooding around the globe. However, climate change is a problem not only for terrestrial life but also for the marine environment.

The most direct effect of climate change on the oceans is going to be increased water temperatures. Warming waters are already observable, as explained by the Intergovernmental Panel on Climate Change (IPCC): 'it is virtually certain that the upper ocean (0-700m) warmed from 1971 to 2010 and it likely warmed between the 1870s and 1971'.[3] The IPCC also reports that there is evidence that an increasing amount of energy is stored below 700m.[4] Such warming has serious consequences for marine ecosystems, affecting spawning, distribution, and abundance of many fish species.[5] Another effect of ocean warming is so-called coral bleaching, a process that relates to the interaction between corals and algae called zooxanthellae, which live in their tissues. As waters warm, corals expel the zooxanthellae and as a result, they turn white. This bleaching is not necessarily permanent and corals can recover over time. However, the greater the rise in sea temperatures, the more widespread and destructive coral bleaching is likely to be.[6] Ultimately, serious bleaching

---

[1] UNGA Resolution 66/288 (2012) Annex, para. 25.

[2] Intergovernmental Panel on Climate Change (IPCC), *Summary for Policymakers, Contribution of Working Group I to the Fifth Assessment Report of the Intergovernmental Panel on Climate Change* (2013) 12.

[3] Ibid, 4.   [4] Ibid, 5.

[5] M Allsopp et al, *State of the World's Oceans* (Springer 2009) 159; J Bijma et al, 'Climate Change and the Oceans—What Does the Future hold?' (2013) *MPB* 3. IPCC, *Summary for Policymakers, Contribution of Working Group II to the Fifth Assessment Report of the Intergovernmental Panel on Climate Change* (2014) 6.

[6] Allsopp et al (n5) 163; see also Bijma et al (n5) 4.

events can lead to the death of corals on a large scale, which can have an indirect effect for other marine species that rely upon the corals for food and protection.[7] It was reported in 2016 that at least 35 per cent of Australia's Great Barrier Reef, the largest reef ecosystem in the world, has been destroyed by coral bleaching.[8]

Another effect of increased carbon emissions from anthropocentric activities is ocean acidification. Ocean acidification and climate change are distinct, although they both share a common cause: increased CO_2 emissions in the atmosphere. Some of this CO_2 is absorbed into the water column, which leads to an increase in the acidity of the water, signified by a decrease in pH levels.[9] It has been suggested that 'the ocean has absorbed about 30% of the emitted anthropogenic carbon dioxide',[10] estimated at between 125 and 185 GtC between 1750 and 2011.[11] This trend is expected to continue throughout the twenty-first century as the oceans continue to absorb CO_2,[12] and one study predicts that 'if CO_2 emissions are left unchecked, the average ocean pH could fall below 7.8 by the end of this century, which is well outside the range of any other time in recent geological history'.[13] This result would have serious results for many marine organisms that build shells or other structures from calcium carbonate.[14] The increased acidity of the water essentially erodes these shells and structures, which means that 'when too few carbonate ions are available for adequate shell building, calcifying organisms begin to dissolve'.[15] Corals, alongside certain crustaceans, echinoderms, and molluscs, are the principal victims of this process. Currently, the severity of ocean acidification varies depending upon regional factors, with some regions, such as the sub-arctic Pacific and western Arctic oceans, becoming ocean acidification hotspots.[16] In the long-term, however, one study predicts that at current rates of acidification, no oceans will be able to support coral reef growth by the end of the century.[17] There would also be serious implications for other species which normally feed off such calcified organisms and which would have to find alternative sources of food.[18] Moreover, there is growing evidence that ocean acidification may have other effects on marine species such as 'decreased reproductive potential, slower growth or increased susceptibility

---

[7] EJ Goodwin, *International Environmental Law and the Conservation of Coral Reefs* (Routledge 2011) 6.

[8] BBC News, Great Barrier Reef: Bleaching Kills 35% of Area's Coral, 30 May 2016. <http://www.bbc.co.uk/news/world-australia-36410767>.

[9] The pH of ocean surface water has reportedly decreased by 0.1 during this time; IPCC, Summary for Policymakers, Contribution of Working Group II to the Fifth Assessment Report of the Intergovernmental Panel on Climate Change (n5) 8.

[10] IPCC, Summary for Policymakers, Contribution of Working Group I to the Fifth Assessment Report of the Intergovernmental Panel on Climate Change (n2) 7.

[11] Ibid, 7–8.   [12] Ibid, 19.

[13] SR Cooley and JT Mathis, 'Addressing Ocean Acidification as Part of Sustainable Ocean Development', in A Chircop et al (eds), *Ocean Yearbook 27* (Brill 2013) 33.

[14] Allsopp (n5) 177.   [15] Cooley and Mathis (n13) 34.

[16] JT Mathis et al, 'Chapter 5: Sea-Air Interactions', in *Global Oceans Assessment* (UN 2016) 19; see also *Report on the Work of the United Nations Open-Ended Informal Consultative Process on Oceans and the Law of the Sea at Its Fourteenth Meeting* (Fourteenth ICP Report), Document A/68/159 (2013) para. 19.

[17] KL Rickie et al, 'Risks to Coral Reefs from Ocean Carbonate Chemistry Changes in Recent Earth System Model Projections' (2013) 8 *ERL* 034003.

[18] Allsopp (n5) 179.

to disease'.[19] The precise consequences for ecosystems remain uncertain at this stage and further research is ongoing,[20] but it is clearly an area in which a precautionary approach is appropriate, as 'the abundance and composition of species may be changed, due to [ocean acidification] with the potential to affect ecosystem function at all trophic levels, and consequential change in ocean chemistry could occur as well'.[21] As concluded emphatically by Freestone, 'ocean acidification, without considering the parallel impacts of climate change, is a major reason in itself for countries to agree to reduce emissions of CO_2'.[22]

States have expressed 'serious concern at the current and projected adverse effects of climate change and ocean acidification on the marine environment and marine biodiversity, and, emphasizing the urgency of addressing these issues',[23] they have called for 'support to initiatives that address ocean acidification and the impacts of climate change on marine and coastal ecosystems and resources', including measures to 'prevent further ocean acidification, as well as to enhance the resilience of marine ecosystems and of the communities whose livelihoods depend on them'.[24] It will be incumbent on all international regimes for the protection of the marine environment to take into account this crosscutting threat. However, the issue raises complex questions of science, policy, and law; climate change has been described as a 'super wicked' problem given the different interests which are at stake and the lack of an appropriate system of global government which can match the global scale of the challenges.[25] As such, a multifaceted legal response may be necessary.[26]

This chapter will start by providing an overview of the international legal regime put in place to tackle climate change itself, namely the United Nations Framework Convention on Climate Change (UNFCCC) and related instruments. It will then turn to consider its relationship with other legal instruments in the field of marine environmental protection. First, it will consider the relationship between the United Nations Convention on the Law of the Sea (UNCLOS) and the UNFCCC. Second, it will consider the contribution of other legal instruments to fighting the effects of climate change and ocean acidification. Whilst this is an issue for all treaty regimes, this chapter will focus on the role of the International Maritime Organization (IMO) in addressing greenhouse gas emissions from ships, and the role of the dumping regime in the regulation of carbon capture and storage at sea and geo-engineering for climate purposes.

---

[19] Ibid; see also Bijma et al (n5) 4. International concern has been expressed by the parties to the Convention on Biological Diversity; see CBD COP Decision X/29 (2010) paras 64–5.

[20] Cooley and Mathis (n13) 36–7; see also *Scientific Synthesis of the Impacts of Ocean Acidification on Marine Biodiversity*, CBD Technical Series No. 46 (2009) 10.

[21] Mathis et al (n16) 20.

[22] D Freestone, 'Climate Change and the Oceans' (2009) 4 *CCLR* 383, 383.

[23] UNGA Resolution 68/70 (2013) preamble; see also UNGA Resolution 69/245 (2014) preamble.

[24] UNGA Resolution 66/288 (2012) Annex, para. 166. Reiterated in UNGA Resolution 68/70 (2013) para. 154; UNGA Resolution 69/245 (2014) para. 167.

[25] See e.g. R Lazarus, 'Super Wicked Problems and Climate Change: Restraining the Present to Liberate the Future' (2009) 94 *CLR* 1153.

[26] See AE Boyle, 'Climate Change and International Law—A Post-Kyoto Perspective' (2012) 42 *EP&L* 333–43.

9.2 The International Climate Change Regime

9.2.1 The UNFCCC

Negotiations on an international treaty to regulate greenhouse gas emissions were initiated in the 1980s under the auspices of the United Nations, as scientific evidence on the warming of the planet came to the fore. The result was the UNFCCC which was concluded in 1992 and which continues to be one of the principal legal instruments addressing the topic. As its name suggests, the UNFCCC does not regulate emissions in detail and the regulatory framework for climate change has evolved significantly in the two decades since the entry into force of the UNFCCC. Above all, the adoption of the Paris Agreement in December 2015 sets the stage for a new phase of international climate regulation. The Paris Agreement is an implementing agreement to the UNFCCC,[27] which remains in force. Therefore, to understand the significance of this new legal arrangement, it is also necessary to appreciate the framework established by the UNFCCC and other key developments that have taken place under the UNFCCC.

The UNFCCC has the aim of:

stabiliz[ing] greenhouse gas concentrations in the atmosphere at a level that would prevent dangerous anthropogenic interference with the climate system ... in a timeframe sufficient to allow ecosystems to adapt naturally to climate change, to ensure that food production is not threatened and to enable economic development to proceed in a sustainable manner.[28]

This objective accepts that some climate change is inevitable, but that action is needed to ensure that the effects of climate change are minimized. On this basis, the Parties to the UNFCCC have recognized that 'deep cuts in global greenhouse gas emissions are required' and they have pledged to 'hold the increase in global average temperatures below 2°C above pre-industrial levels'.[29] However, the UNFCCC also recognizes that a number of other objectives are implicated in the climate change debate and they must be reconciled in deciding how to respond to this threat. These various objectives are also reflected in the principles of the Convention, which emphasize that any measures must not only pursue the objectives of mitigating the effects of climate change, but must be undertaken in such as way as to promote equity, taking into account the specific needs and special circumstances of developing countries, follow a precautionary approach, and be compatible with a supportive and open international economic system.[30] How to balance these various interests has been one of the greatest challenges for Parties to the UNFCCC.

---

[27] See 2015 Paris Agreement on Climate Change (EIF 4 November 2016) Articles 2, 18–24.
[28] See 1992 United Nations Framework Convention on Climate Change (UNFCCC) (EIF 21 March 1994) Article 2.
[29] UNFCCC COP Decision 1/CP.16 (2011) para. 4. The Parties have failed to agree on other methods of setting a target for emissions reductions, such as by setting a limit on concentrations of CO_2 in the atmosphere in terms of parts per million; see D Bodansky, 'The Copenhagen Climate Accord' (2010) 14 *ASIL Insights* 3. See also the Paris Agreement, discussed below.
[30] UNFCCC, Article 3.

Although it is a framework convention, the UNFCCC is not devoid of commitments. All Parties to the UNFCCC are required to prepare 'national inventories of anthropogenic emissions ... by sources and removals by sinks of all greenhouse gases',[31] as well as to '[f]ormulate, implement, publish and regularly update national and, where appropriate, regional programmes containing measures to mitigate climate change by addressing anthropogenic emissions by sources and removals by sinks of all greenhouse gases ..., and measures to facilitate adequate adaptation to climate change'.[32]

The Convention also endorses the principle of common but differentiated responsibilities and it explicitly calls for developed countries to 'take the lead in combatting climate change and the adverse effects thereof'.[33] An important consequence of the principle of common but differentiated responsibilities in the context of the international climate change regime is the imposition of additional obligations on developed countries. Thus, in addition to the general obligations noted above, each of the developed country Parties listed in Annex I to the Convention is also required to 'adopt national policies and take corresponding measures on the mitigation of climate change, by limiting its anthropogenic emissions of greenhouse gases and protecting and enhancing its greenhouse gas sinks and reservoirs'.[34] Another facet of the principle of common but differentiated responsibilities is the requirement on developed countries Parties listed in Annex II to provide 'new and additional financial resources' for developing countries to take climate change mitigation and adaptation measures.[35] Indeed, the Convention explicitly recognizes that:

[t]he extent to which developing country Parties will effectively implement their commitments under the Convention will depend on the effective implementation by developed country Parties of their commitments under the Convention related to financial resources and transfer of technology and will take fully into account that economic and social development and poverty eradication are the first and overriding priorities of the developing country Parties.[36]

The UNFCCC entered into force on 21 March 1994, and there are currently 196 Parties (including the EU) to the Convention. By virtue of its nature as a framework convention, Parties have continued to debate what measures are necessary to implement their commitments and they have taken a number of additional steps to develop their international legal obligations. In this respect, the UNFCCC is important because it establishes an international institution, in the form of the Conference of the Parties (COP), which provides a forum for discussing and reviewing the legal framework in light of evolutions in scientific and technological knowledge.[37] This body has taken the lead in developing the international legal framework relating to climate change.

---

[31] Ibid, Article 4(1)(a).　　[32] Ibid, Article 4(1)(b).　　[33] Ibid, Article 3(1).
[34] Ibid, Article 4(2)(a).　　[35] Ibid, Article 4(3).　　[36] Ibid, Article 4(7).
[37] Ibid, Article 7.

9.2.2 The Kyoto Protocol

As a framework treaty, it was expected that the UNFCCC would be supplemented by further agreements or instruments giving effect to it. The first of these agreements was the Kyoto Protocol, which was adopted in 1997, with a view to giving more substance to the obligations of Annex I countries to limit their anthropogenic emissions of greenhouse gases. The Protocol introduces specific emissions reduction targets for developed country Parties[38] relating to six major greenhouse gases, namely CO_2, methane, nitrous oxide, hydrofluorocarbons, perfluorocarbons, and sulphur hexafluoride.[39] The Protocol was welcomed as a significant development in the international legal regime for climate change, because it had the effect of transforming the regime 'from [a system of] pledge-and-review to binding targets-and-timetables'.[40]

The Kyoto Protocol finally entered into force in 2005, as a result of the ratification of the Russian Federation, although some significant developed countries remained outside the treaty, notably the United States. Nevertheless, the Protocol can be considered to have had some effect. The first reduction phase under the Kyoto Protocol came to an end in 2012, and most Parties had met their targets within this period.[41] At the same time, it is widely recognized that achievement of the targets under the Protocol fell a long way short of what is necessary to meet the overall objectives of the UNFCCC.

Many Parties to the Kyoto Protocol agreed to a second commitment period starting on 1 January 2013 and running until 31 December 2020.[42] However, some developed countries refused to participate in the second round, including Canada, Japan, New Zealand, and the Russian Federation. These countries argued, inter alia, that action by developed countries alone was not sufficient to address climate change and all States would have to take some action. Thus, alongside the negotiations for the amendment of the Kyoto Protocol, the Parties to the UNFCCC were also considering developments that were more radical in the international legal regime for climate change.

9.2.3 The Paris Agreement

Discussions on what further action was necessary to implement the UNFCCC were first tentatively launched at COP 11 in 2005,[43] although it took several stalled attempts to finally agree to 'launch a process to develop a protocol, another legal instrument or an agreed outcome with legal force under the Convention, applicable to all parties'.[44] The so-called Ad Hoc Working Group on the Durban Platform for

---

[38] See 1997 Kyoto Protocol (EIF 16 February 2005), Annex B.

[39] Kyoto Protocol, Annex A.

[40] D Bodansky and E Diringer, *The Evolution of Multilateral Regimes: Implications for Climate Change*, Pew Center on Global Climate Change Occasional Papers (2010) 14.

[41] See the analysis in Boyle (n26) 334–5. Canada withdrew from the Protocol in 2011; see the letter of withdrawal. <http://unfccc.int/files/kyoto_protocol/background/application/pdf/canada.pdf.pdf>.

[42] Amendment to the Kyoto Protocol pursuant to its Article 3, para. 9 (the Doha Amendment), Decision 1/CMP.8 (2013).

[43] See UNFCCC COP Decision 1/CP.11 (2005).

[44] UNFCCC COP Decision 1/CP.17 (2011) para. 2.

Enhanced Action was charged with completing this mandate in time for the twenty-first COP scheduled to take place in 2015. The Paris Agreement was adopted on 12 December 2015, after prolonged and often difficult negotiations, and this instrument opens a new direction for the international climate change regime.

The Paris Agreement enshrines in a legal text the objective for States to take steps to hold the increase in global average temperatures to well below 2°C above pre-industrial levels, whilst also pursuing efforts to limit the temperature increase to 1.5°C.[45] To this end, the Parties agreed to 'aim to reach global peaking of greenhouse gas emissions as soon as possible'.[46] It was widely recognized in the negotiations that this ambition could only be met if all States took action to reduce their emissions. Whilst still recognizing the principle of common but differentiated responsibilities, the Agreement places an obligation on all Parties to 'prepare, communicate and maintain successive nationally determined contributions that it intends to achieve'.[47] Thus, the Paris Agreement represents a step back from the targets-and-timetables approach of the Kyoto Protocol, to a pledge-and-review system. Arguably, this was the price that had to be paid for bringing the developing countries on board. The Agreement still recognizes that developed countries should take the lead through 'economy-wide absolute emission reduction targets', but in a significant difference from previous instruments, it goes on to say that 'developing countries should continue enhancing their mitigation efforts, and are encouraged to move over time towards economy-wide emission reduction or limitation targets in the light of different national circumstances'.[48] Whilst phrased in language that falls short of establishing legally binding obligations,[49] it clearly creates an expectation that developing countries will move towards reducing the greenhouse gas emissions over time. Further provisions of the Agreement address financial support[50] and technology transfer[51] for developing countries in order to assist them in making this transition.

The Paris Agreement was opened for signature in the spring of 2016 and it entered into force on 4 November 2016.[52] This is a major achievement, although Parties will need to take steps to complete the design of the reporting and review procedures under the Agreement. Moreover, it is obvious that the Paris Agreement by itself does not solve the problem of climate change, and its effectiveness will depend upon the levels of the commitments that are made by States. Many States had already made commitments in the run up to the Paris COP, although these fall short of what is necessary to meet the objectives of the Paris Agreement.[53] The Agreement foresees

---

[45] Paris Agreement, Article 2(1).   [46] Ibid, Article 4(1).   [47] Ibid, Article 4(2).
[48] Ibid, Article 4(5).
[49] See the explanation in L Rajamani, 'The 2015 Paris Agreement: Interplay between Hard, Soft and Non-Obligation' (2016) 28 *JEL* 337, 355.
[50] Paris Agreement, Article 9.   [51] Ibid, Article 10.
[52] See the UNFCC website: <http://unfccc.int/paris_agreement/items/9444.php>. At the time of writing, 134 Parties to the UNFCCC had ratified the Agreement.
[53] UNFCCC COP Decision 1/CP.21 (2015) para. 17. It has been estimated that the pledges as of 20 April 2016 would result in expected warming by 2100 of 3.5°C; see <https://www.climateinteractive.org/analysis/deeper-earlier-emissions-cuts-needed-to-reach-paris-goals/>.

that States will increase their commitments over time.[54] In part, the new regime relies upon the good faith of States in this respect. The reporting procedure will require them to provide a range of information in order to ensure the transparency of their commitments, and they will be explicitly required to explain 'how the Party considers that its nationally determined contribution is fair and ambitious, in the light of its national circumstances, and how it contributes towards achieving the objective of the Convention'.[55] This information will be the basis of a dialogue with other Parties. Another significant aspect of the Agreement is the establishment of review mechanisms to oversee progress in achieving the objective of the Convention.[56] It is the rigour of this review process and its ability to persuade States to take additional steps to reduce their emissions that will ultimately be the test of the new regime.

9.2.4 The International Climate Change Regime and the Oceans

One criticism of the UNFCCC process is that there has not been sufficient emphasis on marine issues, despite their importance for climate mitigation, as well as the impact of climate change on the marine environment.[57] Moreover, there has been a lack of attention to ocean acidification at the international level.[58] Indeed, in this latter respect, the two regimes may in fact diverge, as explained below.

One of the features of the current regulatory approach under the UNFCCC and the Kyoto Protocol to date is to give States a broad degree of discretion in terms of which greenhouse gas emissions they reduce in order to meet their targets. Targets under the Kyoto Protocol are expressed in terms of 'carbon dioxide equivalent emissions of greenhouse gases'.[59] Thus, States can choose which emissions they target in their reduction plans. In practice, it has been suggested that 'there are clear economic incentives to reduce [non-CO_2 greenhouse gases] with a stronger warming effect than CO_2'.[60] In other words, States need not focus on reducing CO_2 if they can achieve their reductions by other means. Indeed, as noted by Stephens, 'states ... may even increase CO_2 emissions, so long as there is a corresponding reduction in other [greenhouse gases]'.[61] This approach may make sense for reducing global warming. However, as seen above, CO_2 is primarily responsible for ocean acidification. As a result, the only way of tackling ocean acidification is by reducing CO_2 emissions. To remedy this situation, some commentators have identified that a 'nested approach'[62] to emissions reductions

---

[54] Paris Agreement, Article 4(3).
[55] UNFCCC COP Decision 1/CP.21 (2015) para. 27.   [56] Paris Agreement, Article 13.
[57] Freestone (n22) 383. See also G Galland, E Harrould-Kolieb, D Herr, 'The Ocean and Climate Policy' (2012) 12 *CP* 764, 770.
[58] See e.g. Fourteenth ICP Report (n16) para. 60.   [59] Kyoto Protocol, Article 3(7).
[60] ER Harrould-Kolieb and D Herr, 'Ocean Acidification and Climate Change: Synergies and Challenges of Addressing both under the UNFCCC' (2012) 12 *CP* 378, 384.
[61] T Stephens, 'Warming Waters and Souring Seas', in D Rothwell et al (eds), *Oxford Handbook on the Law of the Sea* (OUP 2015) 786.
[62] Cooley and Mathis (n13) 31. They go on to say that 'decision makers must focus on reducing CO_2 and not just other greenhouse gases such as methane that may be easier to regulate and that are given equal importance in documents such as the Clean Development Mechanism'; Ibid, 45. See also

is necessary, whereby separate targets for CO_2 would be put in place alongside the existing targets for overall greenhouse gas reduction.[63] There would appear to be a strong argument that the UNFCCC is the appropriate body to carry out this mandate given that 'the solutions for mitigating both ocean acidification and climate change are closely related'.[64] Indeed, as the UNFCCC is already addressing the threat of growing CO_2 emissions, it would make little sense to establish a new body for this purpose.[65]

This issue would not appear to have been addressed in any detail in the negotiations of the Paris Agreement, which was more concerned with reaching a compromise on the idea that all countries were expected to tackling climate change through emissions reductions. The Paris Agreement does acknowledge the need to '[ensure] the integrity of all ecosystems, including oceans' in its preamble, although this text does not in itself establish an obligation on the Parties to this end. Nevertheless, introducing such changes to the regime of nationally determined contributions established by the Paris Agreement may not be too difficult, as it would not require a change to the treaty text, but rather a decision of the Parties on what it is necessary to address in the submission of a nationally determined contribution. In the stark conclusion of one study, what is needed is to 'lobby hard to try and steer negotiations under the auspices of the UNFCCC or State action towards substantial mitigation targets for CO_2 emissions'.[66] Ultimately, States must ascribe as much political importance to tackling ocean acidification, as they have done to climate change. At present, the lack of clear scientific evidence surrounding ocean acidification and its effects may be an obstacle to generating such consensus and therefore it is vital that further studies are carried out, as has been acknowledged by the international community.[67] But time is short and we cannot wait for scientific proof before taking steps to address this threat. This is a situation in which a precautionary approach is needed and lack of scientific certainty should not be used as an excuse to take no action. The precautionary approach is explicitly listed in the principles of the UNFCCC,[68] which remain relevant to the development of the Paris Agreement. However, it requires positive action on the part of States to implement this principle in a meaningful manner. The 'Because the Oceans ...' Declaration signed by twenty-two countries at the 2016 UNFCCC COP goes some way to initiate this process by calling for further studies by the IPCC on the ocean/climate nexus and for the negotiation of an ocean action plan under the UNFCCC.[69] In the following

DEJ Currie and K Wowk, 'Climate Change and CO_2 in the Oceans and Global Oceans Governance' (2009) 4 *CCLR* 387, 392.

[63] Harrould-Kolieb and Herr (n60) 382–4.   [64] Ibid, 381.

[65] For example, R Baird et al, 'Ocean Acidification: A Litmus Test for International Law' (2009) *CCLR* 459. See, however, the more cautious approach in Goodwin (n7) 255–6. See also RE Kim, 'Is a New Multilateral Environmental Agreement on Ocean Acidification Necessary?' (2012) 21 *RECIEL* 243–58.

[66] Goodwin (n7) 259.

[67] UNGA Resolution 64/71 (2009) para. 133; UNGA Resolution 66/288 (2012) Annex, para. 166; UNGA Resolution 68/70 (2014) paras 153–6.

[68] UNFCCC, Article 3(3).

[69] See <http://www.iddri.org/Themes/Oceans-et-zones-cotieres/Because-the-Ocean-Declaration-sur-le-Climat-et-les-Oceans>.

section, we shall consider what legal recourse may be available under the UNCLOS, in order to promote action on this agenda.

9.3 The Relevance of UNCLOS to Addressing Climate Change and Ocean Acidification

9.3.1 Climate change and ocean acidification as pollution of the marine environment

UNCLOS was negotiated at a more innocent time when there was little awareness of the hazardous effects that humankind's addiction to fossil fuels was having on the global environment. For that reason, there is no mention of climate change in the Convention. It does not follow, however, that UNCLOS has no bearing upon how States should tackle this global challenge. First and foremost, the jurisdictional framework established by UNCLOS must be taken into account by States when developing solutions to climate change and ocean acidification in other fora. In addition, it may be that UNCLOS can play a residual role in regulating the effects of climate change and ocean acidification on the marine environment, if solutions cannot be found through other institutional frameworks.

Although UNCLOS does not explicitly mention climate change or ocean acidification, States nevertheless agree that this instrument provides the legal framework for all activities in relation to the protection and preservation of the marine environment, including the impacts of climate change on the oceans and ocean acidification.[70] Given the broad definition of pollution of the marine environment under UNCLOS,[71] there is little doubt that climate change and ocean acidification fall within the scope of Convention's provisions on the protection of the marine environment.[72] First, the warming of ocean waters as a result of climate change can be considered marine pollution because it involves the introduction of 'energy' which 'is likely to result in ... deleterious effects'.[73] Second, the uptake of CO_2 into the water column, which is the underpinning cause of ocean acidification, also counts as pollution because it involves the introduction of a substance into the marine environment that 'is likely to result in ... deleterious effects'.[74] It follows that States are under an obligation to tackle harm to the marine environment related to climate change and ocean acidification. So what may be required of States under UNCLOS to address these threats?

Article 212(1) requires States to 'adopt laws and regulations to prevent, reduce and control pollution ... applicable to the air space under their sovereignty and to vessels flying their flag or vessels or aircraft of their registry'.[75] It is apparent that

---

[70] See Fourteenth ICP Report (n16) para. 9.   [71] See Chapter 2.
[72] A Boyle, 'Law of the Sea Perspectives on Climate Change' (2012) 27 *IJMCL* 831, 832. See also Stephens (n61) 783.
[73] UNCLOS, Article 1(4).   [74] UNCLOS, Article 1(4).
[75] UNCLOS, Article 212(1).

this provision has a broad scope and it covers both air pollution produced by all activities within the sovereign territory of a State, as well as air pollution from ships and aircrafts of their nationality, wherever they are in the world. All Parties to the Convention are expected to control these sources through legislation, as well as to take 'other measures as may be necessary to prevent, reduce and control such pollution'.[76] UNCLOS also points to the necessity of negotiating more specific instruments on this topic in Article 212(3), which provides that 'states, acting especially through competent international organizations or diplomatic conference, shall endeavor to establish global and regional rules, standards and recommended practices and procedures to prevent, reduce and control such pollution'.

It follows that UNCLOS must be read in light of the other applicable international rules on this subject. Courts and tribunal faced with interpreting Article 212 are likely to defer to standards agreed under, inter alia, the UNFCCC when determining what measures States are required to take under UNCLOS.[77] In other words, compliance with the UNFCCC regime would be an indicator as to whether States had complied with their obligations under Article 212.[78] As a result, the temperature targets, the process of setting nationally determined contributions, and the stocktaking process under the Paris Agreement are important reference points for the UNCLOS regime. But this does not mean that UNCLOS defers to the UNFCCC in all respects. In several situations, UNCLOS may have an important role in supplementing the UNFCCC process.

First, the rules under UNCLOS place a legal obligation on all Parties to the Convention to tackle these sources of marine pollution, whether or not these States are a Party to the UNFCCC or the Paris Agreement. Therefore, Article 212 provides an independent legal basis for action to tackle climate change and ocean acidification and it can fill gaps in the regulatory framework by Parties to UNCLOS which have refused to become a Party to the Paris Agreement. In other words, failure to become a Party to the Paris Agreement does not relieve States of their obligations to take steps to tackle climate change, including ocean warming. Such obligations also arise under UNCLOS.

Second, UNCLOS may provide a residual mechanism for dealing with disputes about climate change mitigation measures, if the global stocktaking exercise that is anticipated under Article 14 of the Paris Agreement fails to make progress. It is not entirely clear what form the global stocktaking exercise will take, as the modalities are yet to be determined.[79] Nevertheless, the process would appear to be a political one, as it is to be carried out by the COP in a 'facilitative' manner. Given the emphasis on consensus in the UNFCCC regime,[80] it is possible that the process

---

[76] UNCLOS, Article 212(2). Article 222 of the Convention further requires States to enforce any national rules and regulations adopted in accordance with Article 212(1).

[77] Boyle (n72) 836. Other treaty commitments may also be relevant, such as the 1979 Framework Convention on Long-Range Transboundary Air Pollution (EIF, 16 March 1983) and its protocols.

[78] See Goodwin (n7) 253, citing RE Jacobs, 'Treading Deep Waters: Substantive Law Issues in Tuvalu's Threat to Sue the United States in the International Court of Justice' (2005) 14 *PRL&PJ* 103.

[79] See UNFCCC COP Decision 1/CP.21 (2015) paras 100–2.

[80] See Adoption of Rules of Procedure, Document FCCC/CP/1996/2 (1996).

will stagnate. For their part, neither the UNFCCC nor the Paris Agreement provides strong procedures for the settlement of disputes.[81] In contrast, the availability of compulsory dispute settlement under Part XV of UNCLOS means that States may have recourse to judicial mechanisms in the event that agreement cannot be reached on whether international efforts are sufficient to meet global targets. Of course, a court or tribunal can only deal with disagreements concerning questions of law or fact. The requirements of Article 212 are inherently vague and it is for this reason that a court or tribunal is unlikely to determine precisely what steps must be taken in order to reduce emissions and they are certainly not going to get involved in complex issues of allocation of responsibility for a problem, to which all States have made some contribution.[82] Nevertheless, courts and tribunals may be able to address basic questions of whether sufficient action has been taken by a State, based upon their own legal or political commitments, within or outside of the UNFCCC regime.[83] Even such a simple decision could have important effects. As argued by Sands, 'a clear statement by a body such as the [International Court of Justice (ICJ)]—as to what is or is not required by the law, or as to what the scientific evidence does or does not require—may itself contribute to change in attitudes and behaviour'.[84] At the very least, litigation on this topic would require States to justify their position on climate change in a public forum and explain why they are not prepared to take more urgent action, as well as providing some independent scrutiny of such reasons.

Third, and perhaps most importantly, UNCLOS may also be relevant in ensuring that States take into account ocean acidification as part of their broader climate change mitigation measures. Unlike the UNFCCC regime, Article 212 of UNCLOS requires States to demonstrate that they have taken sufficient action to tackle CO_2 emissions as a distinct source of marine pollution involving the introduction of substances into the marine environment with deleterious effects. Whilst a court or tribunal may again be reluctant to specify what level of reduction in CO_2 must be achieved, it can certainly be argued that States would be in violation of the UNCLOS commitments if they focused their greenhouse gas emissions reduction targets solely or predominantly on other greenhouse gases, thus avoiding tackling CO_2. UNCLOS requires States to take reasonable measures to tackle CO_2 emissions in order to control ocean acidification as a form of marine pollution.

The need for specific action to address ocean acidification has also been expressly highlighted by the Convention on Biological Diversity (CBD) COP, which has produced a synthesis report on the biodiversity implications of ocean acidification

---

[81] The UNFCCC requires consent from Parties before claims may be brought before a judicial body (ICJ or arbitration) for settlement. The Paris Agreement provides for a 'facilitative, ... non-adversarial and non-punitive' compliance process in Article 15.

[82] See Goodwin (n7) 253.

[83] For an example, see *Urgenda Foundation v The State of the Netherlands* (2015).

[84] P Sands, 'Climate Change and the Rule of Law: Adjudicating the Future in International Law' (2016) 28 *JEL* 19, 26.

for biodiversity[85] and it has identified practical responses to address ocean acidification.[86] The latter document reinforces that 'substantial damage to ocean ecosystems can only be avoided through urgent and rapid reductions in global emissions of CO_2' and it therefore encourages Parties to take steps in this direction by working through the relevant institutions.[87] A synchronistic interpretation of UNCLOS and the CBD therefore also supports the conclusion that States must tackle their CO_2 emissions.

Finally, one can argue that the impacts of climate change and ocean acidification give a stronger imperative for States to take action under Article 194(5), which, it will be remembered, calls for States to take measures that are 'necessary to protect and preserve rare or fragile ecosystems, as well as the habitat of depleted, threatened or endangered species or other forms of marine life'. There is little doubt that a number of marine ecosystems are threatened by climate change and ocean acidification, thus potentially triggering the application of Article 194(5). Coral reefs are the most obvious ecosystem that is threatened in this respect,[88] but the repercussions of climate change and ocean acidification may be much broader. The establishment of marine protected areas (MPAs) has been suggested as an important mitigation measure in order to enhance the resiliency of marine ecosystems to climate change and ocean acidification.[89] The establishment of MPAs will require both identifying threatened species and habitats, as well as adopting protective measures. The designation of MPAs are explicitly identified as an important strategy in adapting to climate change by the Parties to the CBD, which have called for 'the selection of areas in need of protection to ensure maximum adaptive capacity of biodiversity',[90] and they have also highlighted 'the role and potential of marine and coastal ecosystems, such as coral reefs and estuaries, and habitats such as tidal salt marshes, mangroves and seagrasses' in connection with the mitigation of and adaptation to climate change.[91] Although these decisions are not legally binding, they provide relevant guidance to States in interpreting the general obligation in Article 194(5) of UNCLOS and what types of measures may satisfy the due diligence standard in this context.

---

[85] See CBD Secretariat, *An Updated Synthesis of the Impacts of Ocean Acidification on Marine Biodiversity*, CBD Technical Series No. 75 (2014).

[86] See *Addressing Adverse Impacts of Human Activities on Marine and Coastal Biodiversity, including Coral Bleaching, Ocean Acidification*, Fisheries and Underwater Noise—Note by the Executive Secretary, Document UNEP/CBD/SBSTTA/16/6 (2012), Annex III, taken note of by CBD COP Decision XI/18 (2012) para. 24.

[87] Ibid, paras 2–3.

[88] The protection of coral reefs has been highlighted in the work of the CBD; see e.g. CBD COP Decision VI/3 (2002); CBD COP Decision VII/5 (2004) Appendix I; CBD COP Decision X/2 (2010), Annex, Target 10; CBD COP Decision XI/18A (2012), paras 9–14; CBD COP Decision XII/23 (2014), paras 11–16.

[89] Fourteenth ICP Report (n16) paras 16, 27.

[90] CBD COP Decision X/29 (2010) para. 7. See also para. 8(d), calling for the enhancement of efforts to improve the resilience of coastal and marine ecosystems, inter alia, through achieving global targets on MPAs.

[91] Ibid, para. 8(a).

9.4 Sectoral Approaches to Climate Change Mitigation and Adaptation

Alongside the general regime relating to climate change, this issue may also be addressed by particular sectoral regimes. Given the vulnerability of many ecosystems to water warming and ocean acidification, States have explicitly recognized that there is a need to 'reduce the impacts of other stressors on the marine environment, including pollution, coastal erosion, destructive fishing practices and overfishing, in order to enhance the resiliency of marine ecosystems to ocean acidification'.[92] This objective can only be achieved if climate change and ocean acidification are factored into other areas of marine environmental policy and decision-making. To this end, Article 4 of the UNFCCC explicitly requires Parties to '[t]ake climate change considerations into account, to the extent feasible, in their relevant social, economic and environmental policies and actions... '.[93] As most Parties to UNCLOS are also Parties to the UNFCCC, this provision can be considered a relevant rule of international law for the purposes of treaty interpretation and therefore it should be taken into account when interpreting and developing other legal instruments relating to the protection of the marine environment.[94]

Many institutions will have to factor the effects of climate change and ocean acidification into their decision-making processes when acting under existing international instruments. For example, regional sea bodies may have a role to play in this respect. Even though regional seas conventions were largely drafted prior to the emergence of climate change on the international agenda, this issue has been addressed by many regional seas bodies. The United Nation Environment Programme's (UNEP) Global Strategic Directions for Regional Seas Programmes 2008–2012 stressed the importance of formulating regional climate change adaptation strategies[95] and this mandate has been taken up in many regions. For example, the Regional Climate Change Adaptation Framework for the Mediterranean Marine and Coastal Areas highlights, inter alia, the need to identify risks to biodiversity hotspots with a view to adopting early adaptation measures.[96] Where regional seas treaties have promoted the development of MPA networks,[97] adaptation to climate change should be taken into account as a relevant factor in designating new sites.

Fisheries bodies may also have a role in this process. Indeed, since 2008, the UN General Assembly has urged 'States, either directly or through appropriate subregional, regional or global organizations or arrangements, to intensify efforts to assess and address, as appropriate, the impacts of global climate change on the sustainability of fish stocks and the habitats that support them'.[98] Some Regional Fisheries

[92] Fourteenth ICP Report (n16) para. 15.   [93] UNFCCC, Article 4(1)(f).
[94] See 1969 Vienna Convention on the Law of Treaties (VCLT) (EIF, 27 January 1980) Article 31(3)(c).
[95] Document UNEP(DEPI)/RS.9/6 (2007) para. 6.
[96] See Barcelona Convention COP Decision IG.22/6 (2016), Annex, paras 32–3.
[97] See Chapter 3.   [98] UNGA Resolution 63/112 (2008) para. 3.

Management Organizations (RFMOs) have responded to this call by increasing resources on research into the impacts of climate change on fish stocks.[99] Such information will be necessary in order to address this issue and this action is therefore to be welcomed. At the same time, it must be remembered that most RFMOs are under an obligation to take a precautionary approach to fisheries management, and, therefore, lack of information cannot itself provide an excuse for not integrating climate considerations into their decision-making process as soon as possible.

Other institutions may be expected to develop new rules or standards that address the effects of climate change or ocean acidification within their scope of responsibility. The following sections will consider two key examples where sectoral regimes have developed new norms designed to address some of the effects of climate change or related issues. First, it will consider the control of shipping emissions through the IMO. Second, it will consider developments in the regime on dumping, which have sought to address the use of climate change mitigation technologies to sequester CO_2.

9.4.1 Reducing emissions from the shipping sector

Collectively, greenhouse gas emissions from transport make a significant contribution to climate change. It is estimated that international shipping accounts for approximately 2.1 per cent of global greenhouse gas emissions,[100] although emissions are projected to increase by 50 per cent to 250 per cent in the next 35 years.[101] Therefore, it is important that this source of emissions is part of any action taken at the international level. Key questions arise, however, concerning which institutions should be responsible for addressing this issue and what measures must be adopted in relation to international shipping, which given the transnational nature of the world's merchant fleet, poses challenges for regulation.

Emissions from international marine and aviation transport clearly fall within the UNFCCC regime and they were amongst the issues that Parties were requested to report upon by the first UNFCCC COP.[102] The Subsidiary Body on Scientific and Technical Advice was also requested to provide 'guidance to the Parties on technical aspects of issues related to the implementation of the Convention, such as the allocation and control of emissions from international bunker fuels or the use of global-warming potentials'.[103] However, given the difficulty in allocating emissions from bunker fuel to a particular State, arising in large part from the global nature

---

[99] For example, CCAMLR Resolution 30/XXVIII (2009); CCAMLR Resolution 91/04(2011) para. 2(vi); see the discussion in R Rayfuse, 'Climate Change and the Law of the Sea', in R Rayfuse and S Scott (eds), *International Law in the Era of Climate Change* (Edward Elgar 2012) 159–60; R Rayfuse, 'Regional Fisheries Management Organizations', in D Rothwell et al (eds), *Oxford Handbook on the Law of the Sea* (OUP 2015) 459–61.

[100] IMO, *Third Greenhouse Gas Study 2014* (2015).

[101] See UNFCCC Press Release, 'Experts Say Shipping, Aviation Emissions Must Peak Soon to Achieve Paris Goals', 18 May 2016.

[102] UNFCCC COP Decision 2/CP.1 (1995) Annex III, para. 2.

[103] UNFCCC COP Decision 6/CP.1 (1995) Annex I, para. A.5(e).

of the shipping industry, it was ultimately decided that discussions on this topic should be undertaken through the IMO, as the UN specialized agency responsible for the regulation of shipping, with a view to developing international standards on the topic.[104] To this end, the Kyoto Protocol explicitly provides that 'the Parties included in Annex I (i.e. developed countries) shall pursue limitation or reduction of emissions of greenhouse gas emissions not controlled by the Montreal Protocol from … marine bunker fuels, working through … the [IMO]'.[105] It is likely that this approach will be continued under the Paris Agreement, and, therefore, we must look to the IMO to determine what action must be taken to reduce greenhouse gas emissions from ships.

The IMO first started addressing the topic of greenhouse gas emissions from ships shortly after the conclusion of the Kyoto Protocol.[106] It was not until 2003, however, that the IMO Assembly adopted its first major resolution on the topic. In this decision, the IMO Assembly stressed the pre-eminent role of the IMO in addressing emissions from ships in cooperation with the UNFCCC[107] and it urged 'the MEPC to identify and develop the mechanism or mechanisms needed to achieve the limitation or reduction of [greenhouse gas] emissions from international shipping'.[108] In particular, the resolution called for the establishment of a greenhouse gas emission baseline and the development of a methodology to describe the efficiency of a ship in terms of a greenhouse gas emission index.[109] On the basis of these measures, the IMO was able to consider further technical, operational, and market-based measures for dealing with greenhouse gas emissions.[110] It was subsequently agreed that new regulations containing technical and operational standards would be introduced through an amendment to Annex VI of the MARPOL Convention.

The adoption of new regulations dealing with energy efficiency of ships finally took place at the Sixty-Second Session of the Marine Environmental Protection Committee (MEPC) in July 2011. These 'historic'[111] amendments were adopted by a rare vote at the IMO, which normally operates by consensus, thus demonstrating the controversial nature of the measures.[112] Nevertheless, few States actually exercised their right to object to the amendments,[113] and the amendments entered into force on 1 January 2013.

---

[104] See Y Shi, 'Greenhouse Gas Emissions from International Shipping: The Response from China's Shipping Industry to the Regulatory Initiatives of the International Maritime Organization' (2014) 29 *IJMCL* 77, 79–80.

[105] Kyoto Protocol, Article 2(2).

[106] See 1997 Air Pollution Conference, *Resolution 8—CO$_2$ Emissions from Ships*.

[107] IMO Assembly Resolution A.23/Res.963 (2003) para. 1.   [108] Ibid, para. 1.

[109] Ibid, para. 2.

[110] Report of the Fifty-Fifth Session of the Marine Environment Protection Committee, Document MEPC.555/23 (2006) Annex 9.

[111] S Kopela, 'Climate Change, Regime Interaction, and the Principle of Common but Differentiated Responsibility: The Experience of the International Maritime Organization' (2014) 24 *YIEL* 70, 70.

[112] For a more detailed drafting history, see J Harrison, 'Recent Developments and Continuing Challenges in the Regulation of Greenhouse Gas Emissions from International Shipping' (2013) *Ocean Yearbook 27*, 359.

[113] Brazil and Finland were the only two countries to object formally, for reasons largely unconnected with the substance of the regulations.

The most significant obligation imposed by the new energy efficiency regulations is the introduction of binding obligations to limit the greenhouse gas emissions of newly constructed ships.[114] Ships falling within this scheme must meet particular targets based on the Energy Efficiency Design Index (EEDI). Each ship must calculate its individual energy efficiency targets according to a formula contained in the regulations. While the regulations set the required EEDI, it is left to individual shipbuilders and shipowners to decide how to meet these targets. The stringency of the energy efficiency targets set by the EEDI varies depending on the size and type of the ship.[115] The original EEDI applied to bulk carriers, gas carriers, tankers, container ships, general cargo ships, refrigerated cargo carriers, and combination carriers[116] and it has since been extended to liquid natural gas carriers, RO–RO (Roll On–Roll Off) vehicle carriers, RO–RO cargo ships, RO–RO passenger ships, and cruise passenger ships having non-conventional propulsion.[117] On the other hand, some vessels have been exempted completely from the EEDI, such as icebreakers and platforms.[118]

The requirements of the EEDI are also progressive so that they increase energy efficiency targets over time.[119] The application of the regulation is divided into four phases,[120] with the rates for reducing greenhouse gas emissions increasing in each phase. The assumption behind the progressive nature of the regulations is that technology will improve over time, allowing ships to emit lower and lower emissions. Indeed, the Parties to Annex VI are under a duty to promote the development of technology to this end.[121] However, a safety valve built into the regulations allows the formula to be changed if this assumption proves to be false.[122] Equally, it is also open to the Parties to increase the reduction rates if it proves that technology so permits and there is sufficient political will. In this way, the development of the regime for shipping shares similarities with the flexibilities of the Paris Agreement, discussed above.

One issue that arose during the negotiations was whether the new regulations should apply to developing countries. As noted above, the UNFCCC and the Kyoto

[114] This obligation applies to those ships 'whose building contract is placed on or after 1 January 2013; or in the absence of a building contract, the keel of which is laid or which is at a similar stage of construction on or after 1 July 2013; or the delivery of which is on or after 1 July 2015'; MARPOL Annex VI, Regulation 2.3.

[115] Ibid, Regulation 21.2. See also *Guidelines on the method of calculation of the attained Energy Efficiency Design Index (EEDI) for New Ships*, Resolution MEPC.212(63) (2012); *Guidelines for the Calculation of Reference Lines for Use with the Energy Efficiency Design Index (EEDI)*, Resolution MEPC.215(63) (2012).

[116] See Table 1 in MARPOL Annex VI, Regulation 21.

[117] See Amendments to MARPOL Annex VI adopted by MEPC at its Sixty-Sixth Session; Resolution MEPC.25(66) (2014).

[118] See Ibid and MEPC.1/Circ.795 (2014).

[119] MARPOL Annex VI, Regulation 21.2.

[120] Phase 0 runs from 1 January 2013 until 31 December 2014; Phase 1 runs from 1 January 2015 until 31 December 2019; Phase 2 runs from 1 January 2020 until 31 December 2024; Phase 3 runs from 1 January 2025.

[121] MARPOL Annex VI, Regulation 23.2. There is also a duty to transfer technology which will be addressed below.

[122] MARPOL Annex VI, Regulation 21.6.

Protocol call for developed countries to take the lead in addressing greenhouse gas emissions and some countries argued that the IMO should follow the principle of common but differentiated responsibilities, as formulated in the UNFCCC, so that greenhouse gas reduction targets should only apply to ships built in developed countries.[123] However, this proposal was resisted by the majority of IMO Members on the basis that shipping regulations were ordinarily applied on a non-discriminatory basis. At the same time, it was agreed that some States may need additional time to phase in the requirements of the EEDI. Therefore, an exception was built into the regulations that allows States to 'waive the requirement for a ship of 400 gross tonnage and above from complying with regulation 20 and 21'[124] for up to four years. Although this provision was adopted on the understanding that it was primarily aimed at the Administrations of developing countries,[125] there is nothing in the text of the regulation to prevent a developed country from also relying on this exception. At the Sixty-Third Session of the MEPC in March 2012, an issue arose as to whether States which had taken advantage of the waiver would apply the first phase of the reduction targets after the expiry of the waiver or whether they would still be bound by the targets which were applicable to all other States. The MEPC preferred the latter view noting that a waiver under Regulation 19/4 should only be granted to individual ships being built during the waiver period and it did not apply as 'a general waiver to postpone the implementation of the EEDI requirements for four years'.[126] This interpretation would appear to be in line with both the ordinary meaning and the spirit of the provision, although it significantly limits the benefits of the waiver.[127]

In order to assist developing countries to comply with the EEDI, the new regulations contain a requirement, albeit weakly worded, to transfer energy efficiency related technology.[128] The MEPC also adopted a resolution on financial and technological assistance in order to give more weight to this issue. The resolution established an Ad hoc Expert Working Group on Facilitation of Transfer of Technology for Ships with a mandate to create an inventory of energy efficiency technologies for ships, identify possible sources of funding, and develop a model agreement enabling the transfer of financial and technological resources.[129] In furtherance of this end, the IMO has also entered into collaboration with the UN Development Programme and the Global Environment Facility (GEF) for a global maritime energy efficiency partnership project, which aims to build technical and operational capacity in

---

[123] See *Report of the 61st Meeting of the Marine Environment Protection Committee*, Document MEPC 61/24 (2010) para. 5.46. For detailed discussion, see Harrison (n112) and Kopela (n111).

[124] MARPOL Annex VI, Regulation 19.4.

[125] See the original proposal from Singapore, Document MEPC 61/24 (2010) para. 54.7.

[126] *Report of the Sixty-Third Session of the Marine Environment Protection Committee*, Document MEPC 63/23 (2012) para. 4.27.

[127] Indeed, the waiver has not been widely relied upon in practice; see Shi (n104) 26; Kopela (n111) 80.

[128] MARPOL Annex VI, Regulation 23.

[129] Promotion of Technical Cooperation and Transfer of Technology relating to the Improvement of Energy Efficiency of Ships, Resolution MEPC .229(65) (2013) para. 2.

developing countries.[130] These measures complement the steps taken within the context of the UNFCCC to promote technology transfer and financial assistance for the purposes of climate change mitigation and adaptation.

The EEDI is an important development in terms of restricting shipping emissions, although it has its limitations. Negotiators considered that it was unreasonable to expect owners of existing vessels to undergo the expense of retrofitting their vessels in order to meet new targets and so the obligations are only imposed on existing ships when they undergo a major conversion that is so extensive that the ship is regarded to be a newly constructed ship by the flag State.[131] This outcome reflects the role of cost–benefit analysis in the development of international standards. In practice, it introduces a significant limitation on the effectiveness of the EEDI, as it means that many older vessels could continue to produce large volumes of greenhouse gas emissions without any limit.

Other regulations adopted as part of the energy efficiency package do address this gap, albeit to a limited extent. Thus, all ships of 400 gross tonnes or above engaged in international voyages are required to 'keep on board a ship specific Ship Energy Efficiency Management Plan (SEEMP)'.[132] The overall purpose of a SEEMP is 'for monitoring ship and fleet efficiency performance over time and some options to be considered when seeking to optimize the performance of the ship'.[133] Whilst the development of a SEEMP is compulsory, shipowners maintain a large degree of discretion in deciding what energy efficiency measures, if any, to adopt for their ship. Indeed, Guidelines adopted by the MEPC in March 2012 made clear that 'goal setting is voluntary', and 'there is no need to announce the goal or the result to the public, and that neither a company nor a ship are subject to external inspection'.[134] The only real incentive for adopting energy efficiency measures under this scheme arises from the economic gains that can be achieved through energy efficiency, rather than a prescriptive requirement in the regulations.[135]

Given this gap, many States and some industry representatives[136] are adamant that more needs to be done on this topic, particularly to fill the current lacuna in

---

[130] IMO Briefing, *Funding Agreed for Global Maritime Energy Efficiency Partnerships Project (GloMEEP)*, 27 July 2014.

[131] Ibid, Regulation 20.1. Major conversion is defined in Regulation 2.3. MEPC agreed at its Sixty-Third Session that there was a need for a Unified Interpretation of this term and it asked the International Association of Classification Societies to develop a draft Unified Interpretation and submit it to the Sixty-Fourth Session.

[132] MARPOL Annex VI, Regulation 22.1.

[133] *Guidelines for the Development of a Ship Energy Efficiency Management Plan (SEEMP)*, Resolution MEPC .213(63) (2012) para. 1.2.

[134] Ibid, para. 4.1.7.

[135] Nevertheless, these gains could be significant given that fuel is a ship operator's largest cost. It is for this reason that the International Chamber of Shipping has said that 'further and dramatic CO2 reduction ... remains a matter of enlightened self-interest'; International Chamber of Shipping, *2016 Annual Review* (2016) 12.

[136] See *The Case for further Measures to Tackle the Climate Impacts of Shipping*, Submitted by the Clean Shipping Coalition, Document MEPC 67/5/9 (2014); International Chamber of Shipping, *Annual Review 2016* (2016) 8.

relation to existing ships. There are a number of options available to IMO Member States.

One option is the adoption of further technical and operational standards for all shipping. This could be achieved by strengthening the existing regulations, such as the introduction of stricter requirements for the SEEMP that would demand energy efficiency savings from ships.[137] Such measures may fall short of setting targets for existing ships, but they would require shipowners to demonstrate improvements in energy efficiency over time, somewhat similar to the pledge-and-review system adopted for States under the Paris Agreement. Alternatively, the IMO could develop mandatory attained efficiency standards for all vessels, albeit recognizing that older vessels may require longer phase-in periods and lower standards than newly built vessels might.[138]

Another option is the adoption of market-based measures that would apply to all ships, creating a further economic incentive for shipowners to reduce their emissions. The main two types of market-based measures under discussion at the IMO, both of which have a number of variants, are an international greenhouse gas fund for shipping and a maritime emissions trading scheme. An international greenhouse fund would work by placing a levy on bunker fuel purchases. The increase in price would create an incentive for shipowners to operate more efficiently by reducing fuel consumption. The creation of such a fund would not by itself guarantee a reduction in emissions, although the revenues from the fund could be used to buy offset emissions credits from other sectors. Moreover, the advantage of this option is that costs of ensuring compliance for individual shipowners would be predictable, given that the bunker fuel levy would be fixed for a certain period.[139] In contrast, a maritime emissions trading scheme (ETS) would also operate by increasing the operation costs of a vessel, but rather than paying a fixed levy, shipowners would have to surrender emissions credits to cover their emissions. Ships that are more energy efficient would have to surrender fewer credits than ships that are less energy efficient. Given that the price of credits may fluctuate depending upon supply and demand, the cost of complying for shipowners may be more unpredictable.[140] At the same time, by limiting the number of credits that are allocated to the shipping sector, an ETS can in theory limit the net emissions of the shipping sector.[141] It is envisaged in some of the proposals for ETS that shipowners will be able to purchase additional credits from other existing emissions trading schemes, which would give more flexibility to the shipping

---

[137] See e.g. *Proposed Elements for Enhancing Implementation Requirements for SEEMP and SEEMP Guidelines, Submitted by the World Wide Fund for Nature and the Clean Shipping Coalition*, IMO Document MEPC 64/4/33 (2012). However, see *Report of the 64th Meeting of the Marine Environment Protection Committee*, Document MEPC 64/23 (2012) para. 4.97.

[138] See *Proposal of the United States to Enhance Energy Efficiency in International Shipping*, Document MEPC/65/4/19 (2013).

[139] *Report of the 59th Meeting of the Marine Environment Protection Committee*, Document MEPC 59/24 (2009), para. 6.67.4.

[140] Ibid, para. 6.67.4.   [141] Ibid, para. 6.67.1.

sector to potentially increase its emissions, but only through the achievement of reductions in other sectors.[142]

Both of these options for market-based measures have been reviewed in general terms, and it has been ascertained that they potentially provide very high environmental effectiveness and very good cost-effectiveness.[143] However, at the time of writing, discussions on market-based measures have been suspended,[144] and it is would appear that the preferred approach is to adopt additional energy efficiency standards. To this end, IMO Member States have been asked to collect data that could inform the adoption of such standards.[145] At the same time, some States have emphasized that it may be too early to develop additional standards and the priority should be implementation of the existing standards and the provision of technical assistance to developing countries.[146] Indeed, the question of common but differentiated responsibilities continues to arise in the negotiations and it demonstrates the difficulties inherent in regulating any aspect of climate change in a consensual and effective manner. To this end, one can perhaps only expect incremental progress in order to 'build parties' confidence in one another and the regime itself, which could over time promote stronger efforts to enable further evolution culminating in binding commitments'.[147] It is important that the MEPC continues to promote dialogue, whilst also interacting with the broader UNFCCC regime to ensure that the results of any negotiations within the IMO are consistent with the broader international legal framework on climate change.[148] To this end, the International Chamber of Shipping has proposed the adoption of an 'Intended IMO Determined Contribution to CO_2 Reduction for International Shipping', which would mirror the nationally determined contributions demanded by the Paris Agreement and would demonstrate that the IMO was taking its responsibilities seriously.[149] Overall, this example demonstrates the flexible and progressive nature of environmental regulation at the international level, premised upon a gradual movement towards an overall target. In the case of climate change, the big question is whether we reach that target in time.

Aside from the question of strengthening the regulation of energy efficiency of shipping, there is also a question of whether there are additional climate change related measures that should be taken by the shipping industry. One issue worth considering is the regulation of black carbon, colloquially known as soot, which is

---

[142] For further discussion of these alternatives and how revenue generated thereby would be spent, see J Harrison, 'Pollution from or through the Marine Environment', in D Attard (ed.), *The IMLI Manual on Maritime Law: Vol. III* (OUP 2016) 187–8.

[143] See IMO, *Second IMO Greenhouse Gas Study* (2009) paras 6.129–.130.

[144] *Report of the 65th Meeting of the Marine Environment Protection Committee*, Document MEPC 65/22 (2013) para. 5.1.

[145] A mandatory system for collecting emissions data from ships was agreed at the 2016 meeting of the MEPC; see IMO Briefing, 'Organization Agrees Mandatory System for Collecting Ships' Fuel Consumption Data', 22 April 2016.

[146] See e.g. *Report of the 66th Meeting of the Marine Environment Protection Committee*, Document MEPC 66/21 (2014) paras 4.1.2.6 and 4.1.2.7.

[147] See Bodansky and Diringer (n40) 18.   [148] See also Kopela (n111) 96–101.

[149] See Document MEPC 69/7/1 (2016).

emitted from ships as a result of the incomplete combustion of fossil fuels. Black carbon contributes to climate change in two main ways. First, black carbon itself absorbs heat from sunlight, providing a warming effect in the surrounding air. The results are not negligible, and it has been suggested that addressing black carbon could be one of the fastest ways of slowing down climate change.[150] Second, when black carbon is deposited on snow or ice, it reduces the reflectivity of the surface, thereby also increasing heat at ground level. This is turn can lead to the melting of snow and ice, contributing to sea-level rise and other consequential effects. It follows that polar environments are particularly susceptible to the warming effects of black carbon.[151] This is a matter that has been raised at the MEPC,[152] and a common definition of *black carbon* has been agreed,[153] which would allow further studies of the issue to be carried out.[154] To date, however, there has been a reluctance on the part of the IMO Members to take collective control measures.[155] In part, this issue is tied up with the larger debate about the steps the shipping industry should take to tackle climate change, and it is clear that the issue of black carbon should not distract States from the central task of reducing CO_2 emissions. Nevertheless, it has been argued that 'the true value of targeting [black carbon] emissions lies within its supportive role and its complementary function to CO_2 related measures'.[156] Moreover, effective action against black carbon must be taken at the international level in order to ensure a harmonized and comprehensive response.[157]

9.4.2 Carbon dioxide capture and storage under the Dumping Regime

The reduction of greenhouse gas emissions is not the only strategy to combat climate change and attention has also been paid to ways in which to promote the sequestration of CO_2 from the atmosphere, either at the point of release or at a later stage. The principal method that has been suggested for artificial carbon sequestration is through carbon capture and storage (CCS). In theory, CO_2 can be captured directly from the emissions of large industrial facilities, such as power stations, and it can be transported for storage. Indeed, the IPCC has indicated that CO_2 capture and storage is likely to be a vital means of achieving stabilization goals under the UNFCCC in the short-term.[158]

---

[150] See L Boone, 'Reducing Air Pollution from Marine Vessels to Mitigate Arctic Warming: Is It Time to Target Black Carbon?' (2012) 1 *CCLR* 13, 14, drawing upon, inter alia, UNEP/WMO, *Integrated Assessment of Black Carbon and Tropospheric Ozone: Summary for Decision-Makers* (2011).

[151] Particular attention has been paid to the Arctic; see e.g. Arctic Council, *Marine Shipping Assessment Report* (2009) 140.

[152] See Report of the MEPC at its Sixtieth Session, Document MEPC 60/22 (2010) paras 4.94–4.95.

[153] Report of the MEPC at its Sixty-Eighth Session, Document MEPC 68/21 (2015) para. 3.26.

[154] See Report of the MEPC at its Sixty-Second Session, Document MEPC 62/24 (2011) para. 4.20, adopting the work plan to take this issue forward.

[155] Ibid, para. 3.29.   [156] Boone (n150) 20.

[157] See e.g. discussion in Report of the MEPC at its Sixty-Third Session, Document MEPC 63/23 (2012) para. 19.5.

[158] See B Metz et al (eds), IPCC *Special Report on Carbon Dioxide Capture and Storage* (CUP 2005).

In relation to the oceans, two main storage options have been mooted. One idea was simply to pump CO_2 deep into the oceans, where, because it is denser than seawater, it would simply stay suspended for potentially centuries. However, such an activity poses its own risks to the marine environment, given that the oceans already contain excessive amounts of CO_2 from other sources, which has led to widespread ocean acidification. Injecting additional CO_2 into the deep sea would only make matters worse. The more promising form of CCS is pumping CO_2 into sub-sea geological formations, such as depleted offshore oil and gas fields or saline aquifers. The risks from this exercise would appear to be smaller, although they would still need to be comprehensively assessed.

The disposal of CO_2 into the seabed from a ship or installation is covered by the definition of *dumping* and therefore the activity falls within the regimes established in the 1972 London Convention and its 1996 Protocol.[159] Dumping of CO_2 into the seabed would be permitted under the 1972 Convention, provided that the authorizing State had conducted an environmental impact assessment (EIA) and consulted other interested States 'which by reason of their geographical situation may be adversely affected thereby'.[160] If a sub-sea geological formation is transboundary in nature, this may also require the consent of the other States.[161] The situation is more complicated under the 1996 Protocol, which, as seen in Chapter 5, adopts a stricter precautionary approach to dumping. This instrument thus prohibits the dumping of all material unless it is explicitly listed in Annex I, in which case dumping is still subject to prior approval based upon a risk assessment. In other words, unless it is explicitly authorized in the Annex to the Protocol, offshore CCS would be unlawful for those Parties to the Protocol. To avoid this state of affairs, the Protocol was amended upon its entry into force in 2006 to permit artificial carbon sequestration into sub-sea geological formations.[162] The resolution adopting the amendment explicitly recognized the need to reduce concentrations of CO_2 in the atmosphere and it therefore notes that 'carbon dioxide capture and sequestration represents an important interim solution'.[163] At the same time, the resolution also recognizes the implications of climate change for the oceans, including ocean acidification. This clearly differentiates CCS in sub-sea geological formations from storage of CO_2 in the deep ocean, and the resolution explicitly only applies to the former.

The amendment thus permits dumping of '[c]arbon dioxide streams from carbon dioxide capture processes for sequestration' but it adds the following conditions:

Carbon dioxide streams ... may only be considered for dumping, if:

1. disposal is into a sub-seabed geological formation; and
2. they consist overwhelmingly of carbon dioxide. They may contain incidental associated substances derived from the source material and the capture and sequestration processes used; and

---

[159] See Chapter 5.   [160] UNCLOS, Article 210(5).

[161] See Specific Guidelines for the Assessment of Carbon Dioxide for Disposal into Sub-Seabed Geological Formations, Document LC 34/15 (2012), para. 1.10.

[162] Resolution LP.1(1) on the Amendment to include CO_2 Sequestration in Sub-Seabed Geological Formations in Annex I to the London Protocol (2006).

[163] Ibid, preamble.

3. no wastes or other matter are added for the purpose of disposing of those wastes or other matter.

Alongside the amendment, the Parties to the Protocol adopted a risk assessment and management framework to assist States in carrying out the risk assessment that is still an obligation for materials to be dumped under the Protocol.[164] Dumping should therefore not take place if there are clear dangers or hazards to the marine environment.[165] Furthermore, States are also required to carry out long-term monitoring of dumping sites to detect any potential leakage and therefore to take mitigation action.[166] It follows that the rules have developed to permit CCS, whilst also putting in place a legal framework to minimize any threat to the marine environment from this activity. This approach is also supported by developments in some regional regimes, which have adopted the positive list approach to dumping. Thus, the OSPAR Convention has been amended to permit the dumping of CO_2 streams from CO_2 capture processes for the purposes of storage.[167]

An additional amendment to the Dumping Protocol was adopted in 2009 to allow the export of CO_2 for the purposes of dumping.[168] This amendment was necessary because Article 6 of the Protocol prohibits Parties from allowing 'the export of wastes or other matter to other countries for dumping or incineration at sea'. Yet, given that many countries will not have the requisite domestic storage facilities, it was deemed that export may be necessary if the new regime was to be effectively implemented.[169] The amendment makes it possible to export CO_2 streams for disposal subject to an agreement between the exporting and importing country that allocates responsibility for permitting in accordance with the provisions of the Protocol. The Parties have adopted further guidance on the implementation of the amendment, in order to ensure that these conditions were followed as closely as possible.[170] Unlike the amendments to Annex I to permit sub-seabed sequestration, this amendment to Article 6 requires ratification by two-thirds of the Contracting Parties before it can enter into force.[171] At the time of writing, the amendment has not received sufficient support, which means that the export of CO_2 for disposal purposes is

---

[164] Specific Guidelines for the Assessment of Carbon Dioxide for Disposal into Sub-Seabed Geological Formations, Document LC 34/15 (2012) Annex 8.

[165] This has not satisfied all authors, however. See e.g. R Rayfuse, 'Climate Change and the Law of the Sea', in R Rayfuse (ed.), *International Law in the Era of Climate Change* (Edward Elgar 2012) 169; P Verlaan, 'Geo-Engineering, the Law of the Sea and Climate Change' (2009) 4 *CCLR* 446, 457.

[166] Risk Assessment and Management Framework for CO_2 Sequestration in Sub-Seabed Geological Structures, Document LC/SG-CO_2 1/7 (2006) Annex 3, para. 7.5.

[167] OSPAR Convention, Annex III, Article 3.

[168] Resolution LP.3(4) on the Amendment to Article 6 of the London Protocol (2009).

[169] See D Langlet, 'Exporting CO_2 for Sub-Seabed Storage: The Non-Effective Amendment to the London Dumping Protocol and Its Implications' (2015) 30 *IJMCL* 395–417.

[170] A set of guidance has also been adopted on the export of CO_2 for subsea disposal; Guidance on the Implementation of Article 6.2 on the Export of CO_2 Streams for Disposal in Sub-Seabed Geological Formations for the Purpose of Sequestration, Document LC35/15, Annex 6.

[171] See 1996 London Dumping Protocol (LDP) (EIF, 24 March 2006), Article 21(3).

not permitted under the Protocol. It is possible that States could enter into an *inter partes* agreement to transport CO_2 for sequestration purposes, but the legality of such an arrangement will depend upon the nature of the export prohibition under Article 6. As noted by Langlet, the Protocol can be considered an interdependent treaty, so that 'the rights and obligations of the treaty cannot be reduced to reciprocal rights and obligations between any two Parties',[172] and thus, any modification would therefore 'affect the enjoyment by the other parties of their rights under the treaty'.[173] This situation demonstrates the difficulty of using treaty instruments in some circumstances, particularly when it comes to ensuring that the treaty is kept up to date. It is possible that the Parties could commence exports of CO_2 pending entry into force of the amendment. In the absence of significant objections, such practice, provided that it was able to demonstrate that it was supported by the Parties as a whole, may be considered sufficient to modify the treaty.[174] It is not clear whether such an objection would arise, however, as the question of sub-sea storage remains a controversial one.

9.4.3 Ocean geo-engineering and the protection of the marine environment

Another form of artificial carbon sequestration is offered by geo-engineering activities, which aim to increase take-up of CO_2 by stimulating naturally occurring processes. The activity with the most relevance to the marine environment is so-called ocean fertilization, whereby iron or other nutrients such as urea or phosphorus is added to seawater in order to stimulate the uptake of carbon by natural organisms, such as phytoplankton. Whilst ocean fertilization may have the potential to reduce the amount of CO_2 in the atmosphere, it could also have potential repercussions on the marine environment. Indeed, the potential risks from this activity would appear to be much greater compared with those posed by CCS, discussed above. The effectiveness of ocean fertilization is considered to be speculative and it could have unforeseen side effects on other species in the oceans.[175] It is for this reason that the issue has been addressed by a number of international institutions concerned to ensure that ocean fertilization is subject to proper regulation.

Amongst the prime movers on this topic was the CBD COP, which adopted a resolution in 2008 requesting:

Parties and urg[ing] other Governments, in accordance with the precautionary approach, to ensure that ocean fertilization activities do not take place until there is an adequate scientific basis on which to justify such activities, including assessing associated risks, and a global,

---

[172] Langlet (n169) 414.   [173] VCLT, Article 41(1)(b)(i)

[174] See *South West Africa Advisory Opinion* (1971) para. 22. See also A Aust, *Modern Treaty Law and Practice* (2nd edn, CUP 2007) 243; J Harrison, *Making the Law of the Sea* (CUP 2011) 96.

[175] See Scientific Synthesis of the Impacts of Ocean Fertilization on Marine Biodiversity, CBD Technical Series No. 45 (2009); RM Warner, 'Marine Snow Storms: Assessing the Environmental Risks of Ocean Fertilization' (2009) 3 *CCLR* 426–36.

transparent and effective control and regulatory mechanism is in place for these activities; with the exception of small scale scientific research studies within coastal waters.[176]

This body has also stressed that existing international law has implications for geo-engineering, highlighting 'the application of the precautionary approach as well as customary international law, including the general obligations of States with regard to activities within their jurisdiction or control and with regard to possible consequences of those activities, and requirements with regard to environmental impact assessment' but also noting that these provisions 'would still form an incomplete basis for global regulation'.[177] Certainly, the general provisions of UNCLOS, including the obligation to prevent, reduce, and control pollution of the marine environment from any source, would be relevant in this context.[178]

The topic has also been addressed by the Parties to the London Convention and the London Protocol, and it is through these instruments that attempts have been made to develop a global, transparent, and effective control and regulatory mechanism for ocean fertilization and other ocean geo-engineering techniques, as called for by the CBD COP. Like the CBD COP, the Parties to these treaties have noted that 'knowledge on the effectiveness and potential environmental impacts of ocean fertilization is currently insufficient to justify activities other than legitimate scientific research'.[179] However, unlike the resolutions adopted by other COPs, the Parties to the dumping treaties have also sought to develop specific rules relating to geo-engineering activities that seek to balance protection of the marine environment with the need to gather further information in order to make a clearer assessment of the threats posed.

The first step taken by the London Convention and London Protocol Parties was to adopt resolutions interpreting the existing provisions of those instruments in the context of ocean fertilization. A resolution adopted by the Consultative Meeting in 2008 confirmed that 'the scope of the London Convention and Protocol includes ocean fertilization activities'.[180] This conclusion is not as straightforward as it may seem given that the purpose of ocean fertilization is not necessarily 'disposal', a central strand of the definition of dumping.[181] However, it must also be remembered that the definition of *dumping* also covers the 'placement of matter' if it is contrary to the aims of the Convention. Thus, by deciding that 'ocean fertilization activities [other than legitimate scientific research] ... should be considered as contrary to the aims of the Convention and Protocol',[182] the Contracting Parties brought the placement of iron or other materials for the purposes of geo-engineering within the purview of the dumping regime. This means that they are subject to prior authorization under the London Convention and they are prohibited under the London

---

[176] CBD COP Decision IX/16C (2008). See also CBD COP Decision X/33 (2010) paras 8(w) and (x).
[177] CBD COP Decision XI/20 (2012) para. 11; CBD COP Decision XIII/4 (2016).
[178] See Chapter 2.
[179] Resolution LC-LP.1 on the Regulation of Ocean Fertilization (2008).
[180] Ibid, para. 1.   [181] See Chapter 5.
[182] Resolution LC-LP.1 on the Regulation of Ocean Fertilization (2008), para. 8.

Protocol. The general position of the Parties to geo-engineering was neatly summed up in paragraph 8 of the resolution, asserting that 'given the present state of knowledge, ocean fertilization activities other than legitimate scientific research should not be allowed'.[183] States were also of the view that scientific geo-engineering should be subject to approval by Parties before it is permitted.[184] To this end, a further resolution adopted in 2010 includes an Assessment Framework for Scientific Research Involving Ocean Fertilization, which requires prior risk assessment and monitoring of activities by the competent authorities.[185]

These interpretative and non-binding instruments were the first steps taken to regulate geo-engineering in the context of the dumping regime. The Parties have subsequently negotiated a more elaborate legal framework to address ocean geo-engineering activities. In October 2013, the Parties adopted amendments to the London Protocol that establish a new regime for the authorization of geo-engineering activities falling under the auspices of the Protocol. The amendment introduces a new article into the Protocol, according to which '[C]ontracting [P]arties shall not allow the placement of matter into the sea from vessels, aircraft, platforms or other man-made structures at sea for marine geo-engineering activities listed in annex 4, unless the listing provides that the activity or the subcategory of an activity may be authorized under a permit'.[186] At present, only iron fertilization is listed in Annex 4, although it will be possible to add further activities in the future. This provision removes geo-engineering from the more general procedural framework on dumping under Article 4 of the Protocol, replacing it with a more specific scheme. However, there are many similarities between the two regimes. A permit is still needed to carry out geo-engineering activities and a permit may only be granted following 'an assessment which has determined that pollution of the marine environment from the proposed activity is, as far as practicable, prevented or reduced to a minimum'.[187] The assessment must also be carried out in accordance with assessment frameworks developed by the Parties to the Protocol.[188]

Given that the amendment involves the adoption of a new article to the Protocol, it will require the positive ratification of States before it can enter into force. As a result, it may be some time before the new regime is operational.[189] In the meantime, the resolution confirms that the existing resolutions will continue to apply to geo-engineering.[190] In any case, those existing resolutions will also still apply to

---

[183] Ibid, para. 8.   [184] Ibid, para. 7.

[185] Resolution LC-LP.2 on the Assessment Framework for Scientific Research Involving Ocean Fertilization (2010).

[186] LDP, Article 6bis, introduced by Resolution LP.4(8) (2013) Annex.

[187] LDP, Article 6bis(2).

[188] A general assessment framework is contained in a new Annex 5 to the Protocol. It is also envisaged that specific assessment frameworks will be developed for each particular type of geo-engineering activity, and the Resolution confirms that the existing Assessment Framework for Scientific Research involving Ocean Fertilization adopted in 2010 is the relevant specific assessment framework for this purpose; Resolution LP.4(8) (2013) para. 3.

[189] By the time of the 2016 meeting of the parties, only the United Kingdom had ratified the amendment. Germany and Korea announced at the meeting that they were in the process of doing so; see Report of the Thirty-Eighth Consultative Meeting, Document LC 38/16 (2015) paras 5.3–5.5.

[190] Resolution LP.4(8) (2013) para. 2.

those geo-engineering activities that are not listed in Annex 4, even after the entry into force of the amendments.

The approach of States to geo-engineering provides an example of a precautionary approach to environmental regulation. Despite the uncertainty of the effects of geo-engineering, States have decided to take a cautious approach to this topic. At the same time, the new regulatory regime allows further research to be carried out in relation to geo-engineering and its impact on the marine environment, thus permitting States to fill gaps in scientific knowledge in the long-term. For this reason, it cannot therefore be ruled out that this could provide another means of carbon sequestration in the future, if the results of that research do not indicate any significant risks. At the same time, it is also interesting that the resolution affirms that 'ocean fertilization and other types of marine geo-engineering should not be considered as a substitute for mitigation measures to reduce carbon dioxide emissions'.[191] This recognizes that carbon sequestration can only play a minor role in the international effort to address climate change and the emphasis is on States to make progress on reducing greenhouse gas emissions through the international negotiations.

9.5 Conclusion

There is little doubt that the world's oceans will be affected by climate change and ocean acidification. It follows that the international rules that have been adopted to address climate change are also relevant to the protection of the marine environment. This chapter has reflected on recent developments and the ways that various parts of the regulatory framework fit together.

The conclusion of the Paris Agreement represents a major breakthrough in the international climate change negotiations and it promises to offer a new legal basis against which future conduct of States can be judged. Yet, the treaty is only the first step in this process and it requires further implementation, both through further negotiations on the precise details of the reporting and review procedures, as well as through States submitting their nationally determined contributions at an appropriate level of ambition. The next few years will be vital to determining the success of the new agreement.

At the same time, the Paris Agreement must also be applied in the broader context of the international legal regime for the protection of the marine environment. The oceans are threatened not only by climate change but also by ocean acidification. The growing scientific evidence on this topic raises serious concerns about the survival of some marine ecosystems, such as coral reefs, if States do not take action to control their CO_2 emissions. Nothing in the Paris Agreement would necessarily require

---

[191] Resolution LP.4(8) (2013) preamble. This view is supported in the literature; see Cooley and Mathis (n13) 40. See also UNEP, *Blue Carbon* (2009) 65: 'new (sic) innovate short-term solutions, including geo-engineering options such as fertilizing the oceans or pumping CO_2 into the deep seas raise serious ecological, economic, political and ethical challenges, with many unknown variables and high risk potential side effects'.

them to do so. It is in this respect that UNCLOS is most relevant to the international climate change regime. UNCLOS requires States to act against all sources of pollution of the marine environment and ocean acidification falls within the scope of this obligation. Thus, States can only comply with UNCLOS if they take specific action against ocean acidification. The UNFCCC and the Paris Agreement must therefore be read in light of these broader obligations in UNCLOS.[192] One step would be to introduce an explicit requirement in the reporting procedures under the Paris Agreement for States to explain what steps they have taken to address ocean acidification. Another measure would be the establishment of an oceans working group under the UNFCCC COP to ensure that the issue remains on the international agenda. Such a working group could oversee the negotiations taking place in other bodies and make recommendations as to how the impact of greenhouse gas emissions on the oceans can be addressed.

This chapter has also demonstrated that it is not only the UNFCCC that must act in order to tackle the threat of climate change. Several other international bodies also have a role to play in this respect, including regional seas bodies, RFMOs, the IMO, and the Parties to the dumping treaties. These regimes must also be able to develop in a flexible manner, so as to take into account scientific and technological developments relating to climate change. Moreover, these regimes must work together within the broader framework of the UNFCCC in order to ensure that their actions are consistent and effective.[193]

---

[192] See International Law Association, Declaration of Legal Principles relating to Climate Change, Resolution 2/2014 (2014) Annex, Draft Article 10(3)(c): 'States and competent international organizations shall elaborate and implement international rules as well as national and regional policies and measures relevant to climate change in a manner consistent with rights and obligations under the law of the sea related instruments.'

[193] See e.g. MA Young, 'Climate Change Law and Regime Interaction' (2011) 2 *CCLR* 147–57.

10

Towards Integrated Management of the Oceans at the International Level

10.1 Introduction

Up until this point, this book has illustrated how the international legal framework for the marine environment has been developed in an incremental fashion, largely through specialist institutions with a particular focus, be it shipping, seabed mining, fishing, or dumping, etc. This specialization has certain benefits in terms of law-making, in particular, the ability to involve those actors that have direct interest and expertise in the subject matter.[1] At the same time, law-making by sectoral institutions also brings certain disadvantages. These disadvantages are particularly pertinent in the context of marine environmental protection, where there is a large number of institutions involved in developing rules and standards that are applicable to a single space. First, the focus of many institutions on a limited activity may lead them to discount the cumulative or interactive effects that arise from human activities at sea.[2] For environmental problems that require the regulation of several activities, fragmentation of the regulatory process can also mean that gaps in protection can arise. This is particularly the case for measures aimed at protecting particular habitats or ecosystems, but it also arises in the context of pollution that comes from several sources, such as marine plastics.[3] Second, each institution has its own membership and decision-making structure and operates according to its own set of values, which may lead to different conceptions of a common problem.[4] At worst, this can lead to conflict in the applicable law. Even if two sets of measures

---

[1] See e.g. G Hafner, 'Pros and Cons Ensuing from Fragmentation of International Law' (2004) 25 *MJIL* 849, 858–9; FL Kirgis, 'Specialized Law-Making', in CC Joyner (ed.), *The United Nations and International Law* (CUP 1997) 65–94.

[2] UNEP, *An Assessment of Assessments: Summary for Decision Makers* (2009) 16.

[3] See e.g. *Oceans and the Law of the Sea: Report of the Secretary-General*, Document A/71/74 (2016) para. 74.

[4] See M Koskeniemmi and P Leino, 'Fragmentation of International Law? Post-Modern Anxieties' (2002) 15 *LJIL* 553, 578; K Raustiala, 'Institutional Proliferation and the International Legal Order', in JL Dunoff and MA Pollack (eds), *Interdisciplinary Perspectives on International Law and International Relations* (CUP 2013) 293. More generally, see EM van Bueren et al, 'Dealing with Wicked Problems in Networks: Analyzing an Environmental Debate from a Network Perspective' (2003) 13 *JPART* 193, 196.

are theoretically compatible, any tension between the different approaches has the potential to create uncertainty as to what is required from States.

As noted by the Subsidiary Body on Scientific, Technical and Technological Advice (SBSTTA) of the Convention on Biological Diversity (CBD), 'current sectoral approaches to the management of marine and coastal resources have generally not proven capable of conserving marine and coastal biological diversity'.[5] In order to overcome such fragmentation, a more integrated approach to the protection of the oceans is needed. The international community has recognized that 'strengthened and improved coordination and cooperation within, and, in accordance with international law, between and among States, intergovernmental organizations, regional scientific research and advisory organizations and management bodies' is a key element of a successful ecosystems approach[6] as well as a means of achieving more coherent and efficient global oceans governance.[7] Yet, implementing this objective is a significant challenge for a decentralized legal system, where international institutions are established as autonomous actors.

This chapter will consider what steps can be taken to improve cooperation and coordination between international institutions involved in marine environmental protection. To this end, it will ask how to achieve better integration of decision-making processes by institutions involved in developing rules and standards for the protection of the marine environment, through building networks and promoting greater institutional interaction.[8] There are a number of strategies available, ranging from simple information sharing to aligning values and principles and the adoption of joint measures or co-management.[9] Primarily, the discussion in this chapter will be based upon emergent practices in the field of marine environmental protection. Thus, the chapter will consider what different types of network mechanisms have been developed by international institutions and how they may be adapted and applied more broadly. First, the chapter will look at ad hoc arrangements between small numbers of institutions with overlapping mandates. This 'bottom-up' approach is the most common form of cooperation and coordination at the international level to date, although it is limited at present in terms of its scope

---

⁵ See CBD SBSTTA Recommendation I/8 (2005) Annex, para. 6.

⁶ Report of the Informal Consultative Process at its Seventh Meeting (ICP 7 Report), Document A/61/156 (2006) para. 7(f).

⁷ See e.g. UNGA Resolution 66/231 (2011) para. 235. See also ICP 7 Report, para. 5(b); Commission on Sustainable Development, *Oceans and Seas*, Decision 7/1 (1999) para. 37. For literature on this theme, see e.g. R Rayfuse and R Warner, 'Securing a Sustainable Future for the Oceans beyond National Jurisdiction: The Legal Basis for an Integrated Cross-Sectoral Regime for High Seas Governance for the 21st Century' (2008) 23 *IJMCL* 399, 413; G Ulfstein, 'The Marine Environment and International Environmental Governance', in MH Nordquist, JN Moore, and S Mahmoudi (eds), *The Stockholm Declaration and the Law of the Marine Environment* (Kluwer International 2003) 104; Y Tanaka 'Zonal and Integrated Management Approaches to Ocean Governance' (2004) 19 *IJMCL* 483–514.

⁸ These strategies build upon the general literature on network management; see e.g. ER Alexander, *How Organizations Act Together: Interorganizational Coordination in Theory and Practice* (Gordon and Breach 1995); T Börzel, 'Organizing Babylon—On the Different Concepts of Policy Networks' (1998) 76 *PA* 253–73; van Bueren et al (n4) 193; R Keast et al, 'Getting the Right Mix: Unpacking Integration Meanings and Strategies' (2007) 10 *IPMJ* 9–33; S Hovik and GS Hanssen, 'The Impact of Network Management and Complexity on Multi-Level Coordination' (2015) 93 *PA* 506–23.

⁹ Hovik and Hanssen (n8) 508; Keast et al (n8).

and ambition. Second, the chapter will consider global approaches to encouraging dialogue concerning the protection of the marine environment. In practice to date, such 'top-down' efforts have been led by the UN General Assembly (UNGAR) and they introduce certain centralized procedures for cooperation and coordination. Finally, the chapter will consider what steps could be taken to strengthen this system in order to better promote integrated oceans management at the international level, including evaluation of more radical proposals to introduce centralized procedures to manage common spaces at the global level.

10.2 Ad Hoc Inter-Institutional Cooperation and Coordination for the Protection of the Marine Environment

In the absence of any institutional hierarchy in international relations, the majority of cooperation at the international level takes place horizontally between individual institutions, which have recognized that they share overlapping objectives.[10] The constituent instruments of many intergovernmental organizations explicitly call for cooperation with other international organizations 'in matters which may be of common concern'[11] or with other organizations 'with related responsibilities'.[12] Such provisions offer a legal basis to facilitate cooperation between institutions for the purposes of protecting the marine environment. Even the more informal institutions, which may lack legal personality, such as a Conference of the Parties (COP), are often granted an explicit power to pursue cooperation with other bodies. For example, the CBD COP is charged with 'contact[ing], through the Secretariat, the executive bodies of Conventions dealing with matters covered by this Convention with a view to establishing appropriate forms of cooperation with them'.[13] In the absence of an explicit mandate, it can be argued that the ability to carry out cooperative activities with other institutions is necessary under the doctrine of implied powers in international institutional law[14] and, therefore, it is an attribute possessed by all international institutions.[15]

Cooperation on the basis of such a general power can take a number of different forms. In its most basic incarnation, cooperation can simply involve exchange of information and mutual participation in meetings.[16] Traditionally, this has been

---

[10] See further J Harrison, *Making the Law of the Sea* (CUP 2011) 242.

[11] For example, the Convention on the International Maritime Organization (IMO Convention) (EIF 17 March 1958) Article 60.

[12] For example, 1945 Constitution of the Food and Agriculture Organization of the United Nations (FAO Constitution) (EIF 16 October 1945), Article XIII(1).

[13] See 1992 Convention on Biological Diversity (CBD) (EIF 29 December 1993) Article 23(4)(i).

[14] Many regional institutions do not have express powers to cooperate with other institutions, but it has not prevented them from doing so. On implied powers, see *Reparations for Injuries Suffered in the Service of the United Nations* (1949).

[15] This would include informal institutional arrangements; see RR Churchill and G Ulfstein, 'Autonomous Institutional Arrangements in Multilateral Environmental Agreements: A Little-Noticed Phenomenon in International Law' (2000) 94 *AJIL* 623–59.

[16] See e.g. Keast et al (n8) 17; Hovik and Hanssen (n8) 508.

the predominant form of cooperation between international institutions in the past and it is still reflected as a key focus of relationship agreements concluded between international institutions.[17] Whilst basic, such activities are still significant because they broaden the information base that would normally be available to an institution. This is an important outcome for the ecosystems approach. Yet, such a duty does not necessarily lead to action on the part of the institutions concerned and so it is recognized that there are limits to this type of 'negative coordination'[18] as it does not guarantee changes of behaviour.

A more ambitious form of cooperation involves a proactive dialogue between international institutions and the development of shared values and aligned strategies with which to deal with a problem.[19] Not only is this step desirable, but it is arguable that such forms of cooperation and coordination are necessary from the perspective of the ecosystems approach, as it is only through coordinated action that effective protection will be provided to species and habitats. In practice, there is some evidence that international institutions have started to engage in such activities.

Such cooperation is more common between institutions that are operating in a similar sector. This is illustrated by the close cooperation and coordination between the global biodiversity treaties. The COPs of the CBD, the Convention on International Trade in Endangered Species (CITES), and the Convention on Migratory Species (CMS) have each emphasized the need for strengthened synergy between their respective activities[20] and they have entered into a network of memoranda of understanding (MOU) between the Secretariats in order to promote cooperation and coordination.[21] These bodies have also sought to promote broader coordination through the establishment of the Biodiversity Liaison Group (BLG), which involves the Secretariats of the CBD, CITES, CMS, the Ramsar Convention, the International Treaty on Plant Genetic Resources for Food and Agriculture, and the World Heritage Convention.[22] The mandate of this forum is, inter alia, to identify and agree upon crosscutting issues that would benefit from enhanced cooperation. By bringing all bodies into a structured dialogue, it seeks to 'maximise effectiveness and efficiency and avoid duplication of effort in joint activities of BLG members'.[23] A key platform for cooperation has been the alignment of strategic plans and work programmes and the participants have jointly adopted the Strategic

---

[17] See 1999 Agreement of Cooperation between the IMO and the Commission for the Protection of the Marine Environment of the North-East Atlantic (IMO-OSPAR Agreement); 1997 Agreement concerning the Relationship between the UN and the International Seabed Authority (UN-ISA Agreement).

[18] See HG Schermers and N Blokker, *International Institutional Law* (4th edn, Martinus Nijhoff 2003) 1705; Harrison, *Making the Law of the Sea* (n10) 249.

[19] See Keast et al (n8) 19; Hovik and Hanssen (n8) 508.

[20] CITES COP Resolution 16.4 (2014); CMS Resolution 11.10 (2014); CBD COP Decision II/13 (1995); CBD COP Decision III/21 (1996).

[21] See e.g. 1996 CITES-CBD MOU; 1996 CBD-CMS MOU; MOU 2002 CITES-CMS MOU.

[22] See CBD COP Decision VII/26 (2004). See also Modus Operandi for the Liaison Group of the Biodiversity-Related Conventions. <http://www.cbd.int/cooperation/doc/blg-modus-operandi-en.pdf>.

[23] Modus Operandi for the Liaison Group of the Biodiversity-related Conventions, Principle 3.

Plan for Biodiversity as an overarching framework for all treaties.[24] Some bodies have also adopted joint plans of work[25] and developed joint projects relating to implementation of the relevant treaties.

The challenges of cooperation and coordination are greater when it comes to institutions working in different sectors. Nevertheless, it is exactly this sort of arrangement that is necessary in order to achieve effective coordination for the purposes of environmental protection.[26] Indeed, there are instances of ad hoc inter-sectoral cooperation taking place in practice. An example is provided by the joint work of the International Maritime Organization (IMO) and the Food and Agriculture Organization (FAO). These two institutions have concluded a relationship agreement, which calls for close cooperation between the organizations through regular sharing of information and sending of observers to meetings.[27] More focused coordination takes place on an ad hoc basis through joint committees composed of representatives of both institutions.[28] For example, the IMO-FAO Joint Working Group on Illegal, Unregulated and Unreported (IUU) Fishing has met three times between 2000 and 2015 to discuss areas of joint interest in relation to efforts to tackle IUU fishing.[29] The discussions in this group have inspired a number of developments in the work of the two institutions.

First, following the second session of the Joint Working Group in 2007,[30] the question of discarded and abandoned fishing gear was integrated into the review of Annex V of the International Convention on the Prevention of Pollution from Ships (MARPOL Convention), leading to the strengthening of the requirements to record losses of fishing gear in the Garbage Record Book,[31] as well as the introduction of an obligation on fishing vessels to report losses of fishing gear to the flag State of the vessel and, where relevant, to the coastal State.[32] For its part, the FAO is working

---

[24] See Report of the Workshop on Synergies among the Biodiversity-Related Convention, Document UNEP/CBD/SBI/1/INF/21 (2016) para. 12.

[25] See e.g. the CBD-Ramsar Joint Work Plan 2011–20. <http://www.ramsar.org/sites/default/files/documents/pdf/moc/CBD-Ramsar5thJWP_2011-2020.pdf>.

[26] See JA Ardron et al, 'The Sustainable Use and Conservation of Biodiversity in ABNJ: What Can Be Achieved Using Existing International Agreements?' (2014) 49 *MP* 98–108.

[27] See 1965 Agreement on co-operation between the International Maritime Organization and the Food and Agriculture Organization of the United Nations (IMO-FAO Agreement) (EIF 1 December 1965), Articles II, IV, and V.

[28] IMO-FAO Agreement, Article III.

[29] See e.g. Report of the Joint FAO/IMO Ad Hoc Working Group on Illegal, Unreported and Unregulated (IUU) Fishing and Related Matters, Document FIIT/R627(en) (2000); Report of the Second Session of the Joint FAO/IMO Ad Hoc Working Group on Illegal, Unreported and Unregulated (IUU) Fishing and Related Matters, Document FIRO/R1124(en) (July 2007). The Third Session of the Working Group took place in November 2015.

[30] This was discussed at the Second Session of the Joint Ad Hoc Working Group; see Report of the Second Session of the Joint FAO/IMO Ad Hoc Working Group on Illegal, Unreported and Unregulated (IUU) Fishing and Related Matters, Document FIRO/R1124(en) (July 2007) paras 57–9. See also G MacFadyen and R Cappel, 'Abandoned, Lost or Otherwise Discarded Fishing Gear', FAO Fisheries and Aquaculture Technical Paper No. 523 (2009).

[31] The regulations were amended to require recording not only the circumstances and reasons for the discard or loss but also the location and the reasonable precautions that were taken to prevent or minimize the discard or loss. See MARPOL Annex V, Regulation 10.3.4.

[32] See MARPOL Annex V, Regulation 10.6.

on the development of guidelines for the marking of fishing gear,[33] which will facilitate enforcement of the IMO standards. These two initiatives are thus mutually reinforcing.

Second, following discussion in the Joint Ad Hoc Working Group, the IMO Assembly agreed to amend the IMO Ship Identification Scheme, making it possible for flag States to voluntarily apply the scheme to fishing vessels of 100 gross tonnes or more.[34] This amendment is seen as a step towards establishing a global record of fishing vessels, a key objective for the FAO in order to improve control over fishing activities.

This example also demonstrates the useful role of joint institutions in the development of coordinated approaches. The advantage of a joint working group composed of Parties of each organization is that it ensures that the discussions take into account the views of States at an early stage, thus making it more likely that the outcome will be endorsed by the institutions at the end of the process. Only a few MOUs or relationship agreements explicitly mention the possibility for the establishment of joint bodies,[35] although this ability arguably falls within the inherent powers of any international institution, meaning that this strategy could be used more frequently.

Inter-sectoral cooperation can take place, even in the absence of a relationship agreement or MOU. For example, despite the lack of a formal linkage, the IMO has worked closely with the CBD on the development of international rules relating to the spread of invasive species through ballast water in order to ensure that the approach taken by the IMO was consistent with the objectives and provisions of the CBD.[36] The CBD Executive Secretariat was instructed by the COP to work with other institutions, including the IMO, in order to develop standardized terminology on alien species, to develop criteria for assessing risk from the introduction of risk from alien species and to develop a system for reporting new invasions of alien species.[37] Furthermore, in 2002, the CBD COP developed guiding principles for prevention, introduction and mitigation of alien species that threaten ecosystems, habitats, and species, which were shared with international institutions, including the IMO, as best practices to guide further law-making activity in this field. At this time, the International Convention for the Control and Management of Ship's Ballast Water and Sediments (BWM Convention) was still under negotiation, and it would seem that the guidelines were taken into account in the drafting process. Thus, the final text of the preamble to the BWM Convention makes an explicit reference to the CBD as well as to the relevant COP decision including the guiding principles.[38] Moreover, the text of the BWM Convention was amended during

---

[33] See FAO Press Release, 'New Technologies Boost Efforts to Cut Down on Environmentally Harmful "Ghost Fishing"', 21 April 2016.

[34] See IMO Assembly Resolution A. 1078(28) (2013).

[35] See e.g. Agreement between the IMO and the ILO (IMO-ILO Agreement) (1959), Article III(3).

[36] SBSTTA Recommendation I/8 (1995) para. 19(a).

[37] CBD COP Decision V/8 (2000) para. 14.

[38] See, however, the statement of the Australian Delegation at the Fifty-First Meeting of the MEPC, Document MEPC51/22 (2004) para. 2.3.

the final stages of its negotiation in order to ensure compatibility with the CBD.[39] In recognition of the mutual supportiveness of the two regimes, the Parties to the CBD have repeatedly endorsed the BWM Convention, calling on Parties to ratify the treaty.[40] This example demonstrates how communication between international institutions can promote mutual supportiveness in international law-making.

10.3 Regions as a Basis for Systematic Inter-Institutional Cooperation and Coordination

Some of the more interesting examples of inter-institutional cooperation and coordination can be found in specific maritime regions, where the relevant institutions have sought to develop frameworks to facilitate ongoing interaction between them: the Antarctic, the North-East Atlantic, the Mediterranean Sea, and the Sargasso Sea provide the best examples of institutions attempting to foster inter-sectoral cooperation and coordination in a more systematic manner at the regional level.

Antarctica presents a special case for international cooperation, owing to its status as a 'natural reserve, devoted to peace and science'.[41] The suspension of sovereignty claims over Antarctica[42] means that States have an added incentive to promote cooperation in the regulation of activities and they do so under the auspices of several regional bodies. Leading this effort is the Consultative Meeting of the Parties to the Antarctic Treaty (ATCM) and its 1991 Protocol on Environmental Protection, which have the power to adopt measures for environmental protection in the Antarctic,[43] including so-called Antarctic Specially Protected Areas (ASPAs) and Antarctic Specially Management Areas (ASMAs).[44] Yet, the designation procedure has been designed so that the ATCM can only act in coordination with other relevant bodies. Thus, when it comes to protected areas that include a marine dimension, the Protocol provides that 'no marine area shall be designated as an ASPA or an ASMA without the prior approval of the Commission for the Conservation of Antarctic Marine Living Resources (CCAMLR)',[45] as the relevant regional fisheries management organization (RFMO) in the region. To date, ten APSAs and three ASMAs have been designated with a marine element.

The coordination of these two bodies is further strengthened if one considers the provisions of the CCAMLR Convention, which provides that those CCAMLR Members that are not otherwise a Party to the Antarctic Treaty will nevertheless 'observe as and when appropriate the Agreed Measures for the Conservation of Antarctic Fauna and Flora and such other measures as have been recommended by

---

[39] See Consideration of the Draft International Convention for the Control and Management of Ships' Ballast Water and Sediments—Comments on the Draft Text of the Convention, Document BWM/CONF/28 (2004).

[40] CBD COP Decision VIII/27 (2006) para. 25.

[41] See 1991 Protocol on Environmental Protection to the Antarctic Treaty (1991 Protocol) (EIF 14 January 1998), Article 2.

[42] See 1959 Antarctic Treaty (EIF 23 June 1961), Article 4.

[43] See 1991 Protocol, Article 10(1)(b).   [44] Ibid, Annex V, Articles 3–4.

[45] See 1991 Protocol, Annex V Article 6(2). See also ATCM Decision 9 (2005).

the Antarctic Treaty Consultative Parties in fulfillment of their responsibility for the protection of the Antarctic environment from all forms of harmful human interference'.[46] This provision can be considered as a rule of reference, which requires CCAMLR Members to comply with environmental measures adopted under the Antarctic Treaty system. Although it was drafted before the emergence of ASPAs and ASMAs, it is broad enough to require CCAMLR Members to comply with such measures.[47] In practice, CCAMLR has recognized that 'potential harvesting in ASPAs and ASMAs could jeopardise the high scientific value of the long-term ecosystem studies being carried out in these areas, undermining the goals established in the management plans of these areas' and it has thus adopted a conservation measure requiring each CCAMLR Member to ensure that their licensed fishing vessels are aware of the local and management plan of all ASPAs and ASMAs which include marine areas.[48] CCAMLR also has an obligation to cooperate with the ATCM in relation to its own measures for the protection of the Antarctic environment.[49] This requirement has been explicitly recognized in the context of designating marine protected areas (MPAs) and the General Framework for the Establishment of CCAMLR MPAs provides that 'when a new CCAMLR MPA is designated, the Commission shall endeavor to identify which actions by other elements of the Antarctic Treaty System ... should be pursued to support the specific objectives of the MPA once established'.[50] The General Framework also acknowledges that CCAMLR may need to cooperate with other relevant organizations and it has been observed that the Antarctic bodies could usefully work with the IMO to areas in the region that could be designated as Particularly Sensitive Sea Areas (PSSAs).[51]

Antarctica provides an unusual example of a regional regime where collaboration has been integrated into the design of the institutional procedures at the outset, but it is far from the only example of such collaboration in practice. As the regional seas body with a mandate to protect and preserve the marine environment in the North-East Atlantic, the OSPAR Commission has been at the forefront of building relationships with other institutions with an overlapping mandate, in order to the pursue the ecosystems approach, as required by its constituent instrument.[52] The key tool in its cooperative strategy has been the negotiation of MOUs with other institutions that are active in the North-East Atlantic. A good example is the MOU between the OSPAR Commission and the North-East Atlantic Fisheries Commission (NEAFC). The MOU recognizes the mutual interest of the two organizations in conserving the

---

[46] CCAMLR Convention, Article V(2).

[47] See A Brown, 'Some Current Issues facing the Convention on the Conservation of Antarctic Marine Living Resources', in G Triggs and A Riddell (eds), *Antarctica: Legal and Environmental Challenges for the Future* (BIICL 2007) 100; see also *CCAMLR Performance Review Panel Report* (2008) Chapter 2, para. 6.

[48] CCAMLR Conservation Measure 91-02 (2012).

[49] CCAMLR Convention, Article XXIII(1).

[50] CCAMLR Conservation Measures 91-04 (2011) para. 10.

[51] KN Scott and DL Vanderzwaag, 'Polar Oceans and the Law of the Sea', in D Rothwell et al (eds), *Oxford Handbook on the Law of the Sea* (OUP 2015) 750.

[52] OSPAR Convention, Article 2(1)(a). See also the North-East Atlantic Environment Strategy, OSPAR Agreement 2010-3 (2010) 2.

living resources of the seas and it commits them, inter alia, to 'discuss jointly their respective concerns over the management of human activities that impact on the marine environment and the living marine resources in the North-East Atlantic including in areas beyond national jurisdiction and possible actions and measures to address them', 'develop a joint understanding of the application of the precautionary approach/principle', and 'cooperate regarding marine spatial planning and area management'.[53] It is clear that this arrangement foresees an ongoing relationship between the two institutions that will evolve over time through information exchange and coordination. The MOU is intended to facilitate a common understanding of key concepts and principles between the two institutions that will allow them to adopt mutually supportive measures.

One issue that has seen the two bodies working together is the identification of Ecologically and Biologically Significant Marine Areas (EBSAs)[54] through a joint workshop.[55] Potentially, this cooperation could lead to the two organizations adopting coordinated and mutually supportive measures in relation to protected species and areas in the North-East Atlantic. In practice, it has been more difficult to agree on designations, in part because of different views on the relevant scientific criteria.[56] Such obstacles should not be seen as a total impediment to cooperation, however, and international institutions must persevere in order to build up the level of trust that is necessary to build a strong collaborative relationship.[57] The two institutions have also collaborated on marine plastics, with NEAFC submitting its marine litter initiative to OSPAR with a view to ensuring consistency and coherence with the latter's own marine litter strategy.[58]

The OSPAR Commission has not only sought collaboration with other regional actors,[59] but also with those global institutions with a mandate that touches upon the protection of the marine environment in the North-East Atlantic. To this end, the OSPAR Commission concluded a MOU with IMO in 1999, although this instrument does little more than promote consultation, exchange of information and observers.[60] In contrast, the more recent MOU between the OSPAR Commission

[53] Memorandum of Understanding between the North-East Atlantic Fisheries Commission and the OSPAR Commission (NEAFC-OSPAR MOU) (2008), paras 1(b)–(d).

[54] See Chapter 3.

[55] Report of the Joint OSPAR/NEAFC/CBD Scientific Workshop on EBSAs, Document UNEP/CBD/SBSTTA/16/INF/5 (2012).

[56] See D Freestone et al, 'Can Existing Institutions Protect Biodiversity in Areas Beyond National Jurisdiction? Experiences from Two On-Going Processes' (2014) 49 *MP* 167, 173. NEAFC insisted on sending the results of the working to ICES for peer review before further action was taken; see <http://www.ices.dk/sites/pub/Publication%20Reports/Advice/2013/Special%20requests/OSPAR-NEAFC%20EBSA%20review.pdf>.

[57] See Keast et al (n8) 25.

[58] See e.g. *Oceans and the Law of the Sea: Report of the Secretary-General*, Document A/71/74 (2016) para. 78.

[59] See also Memorandum of Understanding between the North East Atlantic Salmon Conservation Organization and the OSPAR Commission (OSPAR-NASCO MOU) (2013). OSPAR has also agreed 'guidelines' for cooperation with ICCAT; see Collaboration with other International Organizations, Document PLE-109A/2015 (2015).

[60] See IMO-OSPAR Agreement.

and the International Seabed Authority demonstrates a more proactive approach to cooperation. As well as general provisions calling for consultation on matters of mutual interest, exchange of information, and granting of observer status,[61] the MOU also explicitly requires the two institutions to:

encourage the conduct of marine scientific research in the sea areas of the North-East Atlantic that are located beyond national jurisdiction, in order to contribute to on-going assessments, on the basis of the best available scientific information and in accordance with the pre-cautionary and ecosystem approaches, of (i) the distribution, abundance and condition of vulnerable deep water habitats; (ii) the status of populations of marine species; and (iii) the effectiveness of measures aimed at the conservation of marine biological diversity in areas beyond national jurisdiction in the North-East Atlantic.[62]

The Agreement also refers to cooperation in the collection of environmental data and information and the conduct of cooperative studies and seminars.[63] Given the uncertainties surrounding the environmental impacts of deep-seabed mining, such activities could usefully assist both institutions in achieving their objectives in a more efficient and effective manner. In particular, cooperation between the two institutions could be beneficial in the establishment of further Areas of Particular Environmental Interest (APEIs) in the portions of the Area located in the North-East Atlantic.[64] The OSPAR Commission has already designated several MPAs in areas beyond national jurisdiction,[65] but in order to achieve full protection of those areas from all activities, it would need to actively cooperate with the Authority in order to ensure that no mining takes place within or near to those areas.

In order to move beyond a series of bilateral exchanges and to achieve a truly integrated approach, the OSPAR Commission and NEAFC have sought to estab-lish a broader framework for cooperation in the form of the so-called Collective Arrangement for the Management of Selected Areas of the North-East Atlantic. The initial parameters of the Collective Arrangement were approved by the OSPAR Commission and NEAFC in 2014,[66] although the ultimate aim is to include a wider range of international institutions,[67] and it is this aspect of the mechanism that dif-ferentiates it from the types of bilateral agreements described above.[68] Invitations have already been issued to the IMO[69] and the Authority.[70] Other relevant bodies

---

[61] Memorandum of Understanding between the OSPAR Commission and the International Seabed Authority (OSPAR-ISA MOU) (2011), Articles 1, 3.

[62] OSPAR-ISA MOU, Article 2.   [63] OSPAR-ISA MOU, Articles 3, 5.

[64] See Chapter 8.   [65] See Chapter 3.

[66] OSPAR Commission, Summary Record of OSPAR 2014, Document OSPAR 14/21/1-E (2014) para. 10.17; NEAF Commission, Report of the Thirty-Third Annual Meeting (2014) 14.

[67] Aide-Memoire of the First Meeting under the Collective Arrangement, para. 16. Annex to Document ISBA/21/C/9 (2015).

[68] See the discussion in S Asmundsson and E Corcoran, *The Process of Forming a Cooperative Mechanism between NEAFC and OSPAR*, UNEP Regional Seas Reports and Studies No. 196 (2015) 16.

[69] Collective Arrangement between Competence International Organisations on Cooperation and Coordination Regarding Selected Areas in Areas Beyond National Jurisdiction in the North-East Atlantic (Collective Arrangement), Document MEPC 67/10/1 (2014), Annex.

[70] Status of Consultations between the International Seabed Authority and the OSPAR Commission, Document ISBA/21/C/9 (2015).

may include the International Council for the Exploration of the Sea (ICES), the International Commission on the Conservation of Atlantic Tunas (ICCAT), the North Atlantic Salmon Conservation Organization (NASCO), and the Arctic Council. The arrangement is not intended to be legally binding[71] and it does not alter the competence of individual institutions to adopt measures within the scope of their powers. Rather, the purpose of the Collective Arrangement is to foster a regular and focused dialogue between competent international institutions on the conservation and management of specific marine areas in order to increase communication and to facilitate coordinated measures. Some of the activities taking place under the Collective Arrangement will overlap with existing cooperative activities taking place under bilateral arrangements, such as the exchange of information.[72] However, the dialogue differs in that it will involve annual consultations with the purpose of reviewing the status of the relevant areas and the protective measures taken by each institution.[73] This dialogue will also be based upon applicable internationally agreed principles, standards, and norms.[74] Under the original draft of the Collective Arrangement, specific common principles were listed in an annex to the document,[75] but these were removed in the final draft, and it will, therefore, be up to the participants to agree on what joint principles may apply. Indeed, it has been suggested that one of the potential benefits of the Collective Arrangement will be to 'have a joint discussion on how various terms and principles were expressed in [the] organizations, so as to ensure that the language used was intelligible to each other'.[76] Over time, this may lead to a harmonized understanding of the relevant principles, promoting coordinated action between the institutions. The Collective Arrangement also foresees that participants may cooperate in carrying out environmental impact assessments (EIAs) and strategic environmental assessments (SEAs),[77] which would ensure that assessments take into account a broader range of information, allowing the Parties to take an ecosystems approach to decision-making.[78] In this context, the arrangement foresees that one institution may request particular information or action from the other institution.[79] It will, however, not alter the fact that the political organs of the institutions concerned will retain control over any decisions to adopt measures for the protection of the marine environment.

The Mediterranean has seen the emergence of similar sets of arrangements in order to facilitate general cooperation and coordination between relevant institutions. Once again, it is the regional seas bodies and regional fisheries bodies that have been leading these initiatives. The General Fisheries Commission for the

---

[71] See D Johnson, 'Can Competent Authorities Cooperate for the Common Good: Towards a Collective Arrangement for the North-East Atlantic', in PA Beckman and AN Vylegzhanin (eds), *Environmental Security in the Arctic Ocean* (Springer 2013) 341.

[72] Collective Arrangement, para. 6(a).   [73] Ibid, para. 6(d).   [74] Ibid, para. 4(a).

[75] See the draft submitted to the IMO as Document MEPC 63/INF.3 (2011).

[76] Aide-Memoire of the First Meeting under the Collective Arrangement (Aide-Memoire), Document ISBA/21/C/9 (2014), Annex, para. 5.

[77] Collective Arrangement, para. 6(c).

[78] At the first meeting of the collective arrangement, it was suggested that a trial could take place in relation to an assessment for a proposed exploratory fishery; see Aide-Memoire, paras 24–7.

[79] Ibid, paras 22–3.

Mediterranean (GFCM) and the Secretariat of the Barcelona Convention (UNEP/MAP) have pursued close cooperation on the basis of a MOU, which was first concluded in 2008 and revised in 2012. Alongside traditional cooperative activities such as exchange of information and mutual participation in meetings, the MOU foresees a number of different types of active collaboration, including cooperating in carrying out regional assessments of the marine environment, the development of agreed indicators and reference points, and the harmonization of criteria to identify MPAs. The MOU also encourages both institutions to ensure that management schemes adopted within MPAs 'are consistent with the objectives pursued and respectful with the Mandates of both organizations'.[80] On the basis of the MOU, the GFCM adopted Resolution 37/2013/1, which provides that 'in case GFCM intend to designate a [Fisheries Restricted Area (FRA)] that may be totally or partially in a [Specially Protected Area of Mediterranean Importance (SPAMI)] such a decision may only be taken if appropriate cooperation and coordination have taken place between GFCM and UNEP/MAP . . .'.[81] This provision thus makes clear that cooperation in the Mediterranean goes beyond the mere exchange of information to include active efforts at coordination of joint positions. Nevertheless, the two institutions remain autonomous and the success of coordination depends upon genuine willingness to accommodate the views of the other institution.

These two bodies have also sought to build a broader network of institutions to promote an ecosystems approach to protecting the marine environment of the Mediterranean as it has been recognized that 'there is an urgent need to start collaborating among all of the [relevant] bodies in a much more structured way', whilst also acknowledging 'their different perspectives'.[82] To this end, the GFCM, UNEP/MAP, and the Parties to the Agreement on the Conservation of Cetaceans of the Black Sea and Mediterranean (ACCOMBAMS) have been working towards a Joint Strategy in order to identify, in the first place, conservation priority areas. Unlike the North-East Atlantic, the current activities in the Mediterranean are currently limited to regional institutions, which may make it easier to reach agreement, but this mean that key institutional actors, such as the IMO, are left out.

Such initiatives pose clear challenges to a decentralized system of international governance. This type of arrangement can only work if institutions establish working practices that permit regular contact and cooperation. In practice, even such simple matters as scheduling of meetings can pose difficulties and the task becomes more complex as more institutions are involved.[83] Moreover, as noted by one commentator involved in setting up the Collective Arrangement, 'a combined regime of this nature demands transparency and trust among competent authorities', and

---

[80] See Memorandum of Understanding between the UNEP MAP-Barcelona Convention and FAO-GFCM (2012), Annex.

[81] Resolution GFCM/37/2013/1 on Area Based Management of Fisheries, Including through the Establishment of Fisheries Restricted Areas (FRAs) in the GFCM Convention Area and Coordination with the UNEP-MAP Initiatives on the Establishment of SPAMIS (2013) para. 4.

[82] *Draft Elements of a Common Strategy among RAC/SPA, GFCM, ACCOBAMS and IUCN-Med, with Collaboration of MedPAN*, Document UNEP(DEPI)/MED WG.408/17 (2015).

[83] See Freestone et al (n56) 172–3.

'it becomes incumbent on States in agreement within one competent authority to influence and work within other competent authorities'.[84] In other words, the challenge remains one of generating sufficient political will among the membership of different international institutions to come to a common position and coordinate their actions. Whilst it may sound simple, it is not insignificant given the different objectives of each institution and the contrasting political dynamics that may prevail within them. Indeed, it has been pointed out that institutions not only have different legal competences, but they also develop an institutional culture and set of values as a result of their sectoral focus and the composition of their membership. It follows that the key challenges for cooperation may be political, which will require States to ensure that clear priorities are worked out at the domestic level before delegates are sent to represent them at international institutions. Tensions can be even more pronounced in trying to coordinate the approaches of regional institutions with global bodies, given the different scale of membership. In this respect, there is evidence that the IMO and the Authority are reluctant to join this type of arrangement, in part owing to concerns they have about the undue influence of regional actors.[85] Yet, it is only with the participation of global bodies that comprehensive integrated regional seas management can be achieved. Finally, such activities also require the resources to allow them to pursue these additional activities.[86] For example, the GFCM, whose mandate extends to fisheries in the Black Sea, has entered into similar cooperative arrangements with the Black Sea Commission,[87] but it has noted that 'the implementation of the MOU has been hampered by a lack of resources which has also undermined coordination between the two Secretariats'.[88] This conclusion ties in with the recommendation of one recent study that efforts to promote cooperation and coordination 'should never overshadow the basic need to strengthen each mechanism in itself in the first place'.[89]

An alternative approach to inter-institutional coordination is illustrated by the Sargasso Sea Commission, established under the framework set out in the 2014 Hamilton Declaration on Collaboration for the Conservation of the Sargasso Sea.[90] The Sargasso Sea is a unique holopelagic seaweed ecosystem, located in the Atlantic Ocean around the island of Bermuda. It has been recognized by the CBD as an ESBA.[91] Yet, one of the challenges of managing the Sargasso Sea is that much of the area is located beyond national jurisdiction. The Commission and associated institutions are designed to provide a means of addressing these challenges.

[84] Johnson (n71) 341.
[85] See Relations with Intergovernmental Organizations—Note by the Secretariat, IMO Document A 29/19(c) (2015).
[86] See J Rochette et al, 'Regional Oceans Governance Mechanisms: A Review' (2015) 60 *MP* 9–19.
[87] Memorandum of Understanding between the Black Sea Commission and FAO-GFCM (2012).
[88] GFCM Framework for Cooperation and Arrangements with Party Organizations, Document GFCM:XXXVIII/2014/Inf.19 (2014) 3.
[89] Rochette et al (n86) 17.
[90] See 2014 Hamilton Declaration on Collaboration for the Conservation of the Sargasso Sea. http://www.sargassoseacommission.org/about-the-commission/hamilton-declaration.
[91] See CBD COP Decision XI/17 (2012), Table 1.

The Commission is very different from the other regional organizations discussed above in the sense that it is not an intergovernmental organization established by an international treaty. Rather the Commission is created under Bermudan law and it is composed of 'distinguished scientists and other persons of international repute committed to the conservation of high seas ecosystems' serving in their personal capacity.[92] As such, the Commission is not able to adopt management or other measures for the conservation of the Sargasso Sea. The role of the Commission is instead seen as one of 'stewardship', and it is anticipated that it will seek to promote its aims by collecting information about the precise threats facing the ecosystem and, on the basis of this data, by encouraging cooperation amongst governments, national, regional, and international organizations with relevant competences.[93] The Commission lists the following international organizations as key partners for its work: the IMO, ICCAT, the Authority, the CMS COP, the North Atlantic Fisheries Organization (NAFO), the OSPAR Commission, the CBD COP, and the UN General Assembly (UNGA). The Commission itself has sought observer status with many international institutions,[94] but the Commission will also work through a Meeting of Signatories of the Hamilton Declaration,[95] which provides a crucial link to the relevant institutions, as the signatories are often members of these institutions and, therefore, are able to directly put forward proposals for management measures. Indeed, the Commission and the Signatories to the Declaration have already pursued a number of initiatives within these organizations in order to promote greater protection for the Sargasso Sea. The emergence of so-called champions has been highlighted as a major factor for the success of this type of regime.[96] A major achievement to date has been the listing of the European eel, whose spawning grounds are in the Sargasso Sea, under CMS Appendix II, meaning that range States are now required to endeavour to conclude further agreements for the conservation of this species.[97] One of the key functions of the Sargasso Sea Commission is its ability to play a role in the coordination of measures between different international institutions with relevant competences, in order to ensure the comprehensive and coherent protection of this important high seas ecosystem. It is for this reason that the Commission has been highlighted as a potential 'new way of doing business in high seas governance'.[98]

These regional coordination mechanisms are still in their infancy and it remains to be seen how they evolve in practice. Nevertheless, they have been identified as potential models to build inter-sectoral cooperation in other regions,[99] even though regional differences will dictate that adaptations may have to be made.[100] It has been

---

[92] Ibid, para. 6.   [93] Ibid, Annex II.

[94] The Commission is an observer to the Authority and NAFO.

[95] CBD COP Decision XI/17 (2012), paras 5 and 8; at the present time, the governments of the UK, USA, Azores, Monaco, Bermuda, British Virgin Islands, Bahamas, and Canada.

[96] Freestone et al (n56) 168.   [97] On the CMS, see Chapter 3.

[98] D Freestone and F Bulger, 'The Sargasso Sea Commission: An Innovative Approach to the Conservation of Areas beyond National Jurisdiction' (2016) 30 *Ocean Yearbook* 80, 90.

[99] See Johnson (n71) 341; Freestone et al (n56) 171; Freestone and Bulger (n98) 81.

[100] Asmundsson and Corcoran (n68) 30.

suggested that such integration could be promoted in areas equating to large marine ecosystems, which are areas defined by ecological rather than political boundaries and thus would provide an appropriate basis to pursue an ecosystems approach.[101] To be successful in promoting integrated management, however, many institutions would require their mandates to be amended to include an ecosystems approach and to extend their application to all relevant areas, including areas beyond national jurisdiction.[102]

A more radical solution is the establishment of integrated regional oceans management organizations that combine the functions of regional seas bodies and regional fisheries bodies.[103] However, it must be recognized that it is not only the mandates of these types of institutions that differ but also memberships, with regional seas bodies being composed of coastal States in the region and regional fisheries bodies typically involving a broader range of States with an interest in fishing in the region. It follows that such an approach raises a complex set of issues concerning participation that will make agreement difficult to achieve. Thus, at least in the short and medium term, the development of the types of cooperation and coordination mechanisms described above would appear to be a more feasible approach to promoting integrated regional management of the oceans.[104]

10.4 The Global Framework to Promote Cooperation and Coordination for the Protection of the Marine Environment

10.4.1 The role of the United Nations General Assembly as a central coordinating body

We now turn to measures taken by the international community to introduce a measure of coordination at the global level, which has been led by the United Nations. The UN Charter expressly foresees a coordinating role for the organization,[105] and it is the UNGA that in practice has performed this function in the context of the law of the sea.

At the time of the entry into force of the United Nations Convention on the Law of the Sea (UNCLOS), the UNGA took upon itself the role of overseeing the implementation of the Convention and it called for all competent international organizations to work towards ensuring a 'uniform, consistent, and coordinated approach to

---

[101] See Rochette et al (n86) 12–13; AM Duda and K Sherman, 'A New Imperative for Improving Management of Large Marine Ecosystems' (2002) *O&CM* 797–833. NOAA has identified sixty-six distinct LMEs; see <http://www.lme.noaa.gov/index.php?option=com_content&view=article&id=1&Itemid=112>.

[102] Rochette et al (n86) 17.

[103] See Global Ocean Commission, From Decline to Recovery: A Rescue Package for the Oceans Report Summary (2016) 16.

[104] This conclusion is echoed by Rochette et al (n86) 18.

[105] Charter of the United Nations (UNC) (EIF 24 October 1945), Article 58.

the implementation of the Convention throughout the United Nations system'.[106] The UNGA is able to play a key role in this respect, both because of its extensive institutional competence[107] and its broad membership, meaning that all relevant States can participate in discussions on cooperation and coordination. Other institutions can also participate in meetings of the UNGA as observers.[108] These features give legitimacy to the UNGA in its role as a central coordinating body in the law of the sea.[109]

Whilst the focus of its activity was on implementation of UNCLOS, it is clear that the mandate of the UNGA extends beyond the confines of the Convention itself to include oversight of the implementation of the numerous other treaties and instruments that are related to the Convention. Indeed, the UNGA has developed a number of mechanisms that have consolidated its position as the central coordinating body in this respect. In doing so, it has given a special emphasis on the protection of the marine environment and the need to promote the sustainable development of the oceans.

10.4.2 The Regular Process for Global Reporting and Assessment of the State of the Marine Environment, including socio-economic aspects

Integrated management of the oceans requires an understanding of all relevant threats to the marine environment, from a whole range of sources. Given the size of the oceans, such an undertaking is a significant challenge, and it is clear that it can only be accomplished with the cooperation of all relevant institutions that are responsible for various aspects of marine affairs. The Regular Process for Global Reporting and Assessment of the State of the Marine Environment was precisely designed in order to provide a mechanism to facilitate the collection and dissemination of such information in order to allow better management decisions.

States agreed to work towards the establishment of 'a regular process under the United Nations for global reporting and assessment of the State of the marine environment, including socio-economic aspects, both current and foreseeable' at the World Summit on Sustainable Development in 2002.[110] What became known simply as the Regular Process was intended to bring together and build upon existing assessments in order to provide an overview of the health of the world's oceans. In other words, it does not generate new science but rather synthesizes existing data into a coherent assessment. Thus, the Regular Process has the overall objective 'to improve understanding of the oceans and to develop a global mechanism for delivering science-based information to decision makers and public'[111] by 'providing regular assessments at the global and supraregional levels and an integrated view of

---

[106] UNGA Resolution 49/28 (1994) para. 18.   [107] See UNC, Article 10.

[108] For a list of institutions that have been admitted as observers to the UNGA, see UN Document A/INF/70/5 (2016)

[109] E Morgera, 'Competence or Confidence? The Appropriate Forum to Address Multi-Purpose High Seas Protected Areas' (2007) 16 *RECIEL* 1, 10–11.

[110] Johannesburg Programme for Further Implementation (2002) para. 36(b).

[111] See UNGA Resolution 57/141 (2002) para. 45.

environmental, economic and social aspects'.[112] To this end, the process explicitly drew upon an ecosystems approach.[113] The ambition of this initiative should not be underestimated, as it involved dozens of international organizations and other institutions,[114] as well as many independent scientists, coordinated by the UNGA through an ad hoc committee of the whole.[115]

It took over a decade to produce the first Global Oceans Assessment, which was approved by the UNGA in 2015.[116] The report contains detailed information concerning ecosystem services provided by the oceans, the impacts of particular activities on marine ecosystems, the overall status of major groups of marine species and habitats, and critically, an overall assessment of the cumulative impacts of human activities on the oceans. The first report is designed to establish a baseline of the current state of the marine environment. It is a testimony to the ability of international institutions to work together on a shared project, but it required a single institution at the centre in order to make the key decisions and to prioritize activities.

The first assessment is only the starting point of this exercise. It is anticipated that the process will be repeated every five years, and '[i]n subsequent cycles, the scope of the regular process would extend to evaluating trends'.[117] This will allow policymakers to evaluate any measures that had been taken to protect the marine environment and to identify continuing gaps in law and policy. Thus, it has been stressed that the second cycle of the Global Oceans Assessment should be conducted in close collaboration with existing global and regional institutions in order to ensure that the results can be utilized in decision-making.[118] In order to achieve this goal, the Regular Process will have to be carefully managed in order to ensure that its reports are transparent and rigorous. Like similar scientific processes, such as the Intergovernmental Panel on Climate Change (IPCC), the effectiveness of this sort of understanding depends in large part on the impartiality and quality of its procedures,[119] and the Regular Process may be able to learn lessons from other scientific institutions concerning the manner in which information is processed and reported. In this respect, Rached points to a number of important lessons from the IPCC, in particular in relation to the range of data that can be incorporated into assessments, and the checks that may need to be in place when using unpublished data, as well as how to correctly communicate the level of uncertainty about a topic in order to ensure the credibility of the recommendations.[120] The relationship between the

---

[112] Report of the Work of the Ad Hoc Working Group of the Whole to Recommend a Course of Action to the General Assembly on the Regular Process for Global Reporting and Assessment of the State of the Marine Environment, Document A/64/347 (2009) Annex, para. 7.

[113] Ibid, para. 10.   [114] UNGA Resolution 65/37 (2010) para. 204.

[115] Ibid, para. 202.   [116] UNGA Resolution 70/235 (2015) para. 266.

[117] Report of the work of the Ad Hoc Working Group of the Whole to Recommend a Course of Action to the General Assembly on the Regular Process for Global Reporting and Assessment of the State of the Marine Environment, Document A/64/347 (2009) Annex, para. 19.

[118] See the Abstract prepared by the Secretariat of views on Lessons Learned from the First Cycle of the Regular Process for Global Reporting and Assessment of the State of the Marine Environment (UN 2016) 18–19.

[119] DH Rached, 'The Intergovernmental Panel on Climate Change: Holding Science and Policy-Making to Account' (2014) 24 *YIEL* 3, 27.

[120] Ibid, 20.

UNGA as the body that coordinates and ultimately approves the assessment report and the institutions and individual experts must also be configured in order to allow trust building, whilst avoiding political interference in the reporting of the information.[121] Such safeguards will become increasingly important for the Regular Process as it proceeds into future assessments, which will move beyond identifying baselines of environmental quality to identifying key areas in which policy action is required.

10.4.3 The annual review of law of the sea developments

The main mechanism through which the UNGA has promoted cooperation and coordination is through its annual review of legal and policy developments in the field of ocean affairs and the law of the sea. This review process was initiated soon after the entry into force of UNCLOS and it covers a broad scope.[122] In practice, the protection of the marine environment has become a central element of this annual review.[123]

The review process itself has two main elements. First, the review involves the preparation of a 'comprehensive report' by the UN Secretary-General, covering both implementation of UNCLOS and 'developments relating to the law of the sea, taking into account relevant scientific and technological developments'.[124] This report is prepared by the UN Division for Ocean Affairs and the Law of the Sea (DOALOS), a part of the UN Office of Legal Affairs,[125] on the basis of information provided by competent international organizations and other relevant bodies. The UNGA has emphasized:

the critical role of the annual report of the Secretary-General, which integrates information on developments relating to the implementation of the Convention and the work of the Organization, its specialized agencies and other institutions in the field of ocean affairs and the law of the sea at the global and regional levels, and as a result constitutes the basis for the annual consideration and review of developments relating to ocean affairs and the law of the sea by the General Assembly as the global institution having the competence to undertake such a review.[126]

The centralized dissemination of this information is itself an important starting point for coordination of the activities of international institutions.[127]

The reports of the UN Secretary-General also provide the basis for an annual debate on oceans policy and the law of the sea, leading to the adoption of two key

---

[121] Ibid, 23. See also S Andresen and JB Skjærseth, 'Science and Technology', in D Bodansky et al (eds), *Oxford Handbook of International Environmental Law* (OUP 2007) 192.

[122] UNGA Resolution 49/28 (1994) para. 12.

[123] See e.g. Oceans and the Law of the Sea—Report of the Secretary-General, Document A/70/74/Add.1 (2015).

[124] UNGA Resolution 49/28 (1994) para. 15(a).

[125] See Secretary-General's Bulletin ST/SG/2008/13 (2008) para. 9.2(c). For a history and overview of the role of DOALOS by two of its staff, see S Tarassenko and I Tani, 'The Functions and Role of the United Nations Secretariat in Ocean Affairs and the Law of the Sea' (2012) 27 *IJMCL* 683–99.

[126] UNGA Resolution 69/245 (2014) para. 310.

[127] UNGA Resolution 63/111 (2008) para. 174.

resolutions: one resolution on ocean affairs and the law of the sea and another resolution on sustainable fisheries. Both resolutions regularly deal with the protection of the marine environment. The resolution on oceans and law of the sea generally contains two relevant sections, dealing with 'marine environment and marine resources' on the one hand and 'marine biodiversity' on the other hand. A range of issues is dealt with under these headings. For example, a typical resolution addresses marine pollution and debris, including plastic, persistent organic pollutants, heavy metals, nitrogen-based compounds,[128] ocean acidification and the impacts of climate change,[129] alien invasive species,[130] oil spills,[131] ocean fertilization,[132] marine biological diversity of seamounts, hydrothermal vents and cold-water corals,[133] coral bleaching,[134] and ocean noise.[135] Similarly, the sustainable fisheries resolution has environmental concerns at its core. Alongside addressing the sustainability of fishing in relation to target stocks, a typical fisheries resolution also contains sections on fisheries by-catch and responsible fisheries in the marine ecosystem, demonstrating a broader concern about the impact of fishing on the marine environment.[136]

These instruments are perhaps the main mechanism used by the UNGA for promoting coordination between institutions at the global level. Indeed, both resolutions regularly stress the importance of coordination in managing pressures on the oceans. For example, the 2014 resolution on oceans and the law of the sea promotes the adoption of coordinated strategies to tackle marine pollution, including through the effective implementation of relevant treaties,[137] as well as encouraging further coordination of efforts to address impacts on marine ecosystems within and beyond areas of national jurisdiction.[138] Perhaps more importantly, UNGA resolutions can be used to address specific gaps or challenges that require action by several international institutions.

A good example is the role of the UNGA in encouraging the development of measures to protect Vulnerable Marine Ecosystems (VMEs) from harm caused by deep-sea fishing, as touched upon in Chapter 7. This issue was first raised in the UN discussions on the law of the sea in the early 2000s,[139] and the UNGA used its 2002 resolution on oceans and the law of the sea to encourage:

relevant international organizations, including the [FAO], the International Hydrographic Organization, the [IMO], the International Seabed Authority, [UNEP], the World Meteorological Organization, the secretariat of the [CBD] and [DOALOS], with the assistance of regional and subregional fisheries organizations, to consider urgently ways to integrate

---

[128] UNGA Resolution 69/245 (2014) para. 163.   [129] Ibid, para. 165.
[130] Ibid, para. 174.   [131] Ibid, para. 185.   [132] Ibid, para. 195.
[133] Ibid, para. 222.   [134] Ibid, para. 234.   [135] Ibid, para. 237.
[136] See e.g. UNGA Resolution 70/75 (2015), para. 11.
[137] UNGA Resolution 69/245 (2014) para. 163   [138] Ibid, para. 200(d).
[139] See e.g. *Report on the Work of the United Nations Open-Ended Informal Consultative Process on Oceans and Law of the Sea at its first meeting*, Document A/55/274 (2000) para. 73; *Report on the Work of the United Nations Open-Ended Informal Consultative Process Established by the General Assembly in Its Resolution 54/33 in order to Facilitate the Annual Review by the Assembly of Developments in Ocean Affairs at Its First Meeting*, Document A/57/80 (2002) para. 20.

and improve, on a scientific basis, the management of risks to marine biodiversity of sea-mounts and certain other underwater features within the framework of the Convention.[140]

Two years later, the UNGA addressed the question of deep-sea fishing in a more substantive manner, when it adopted Resolution 59/25 calling upon:

states, either by themselves or through regional fisheries management organizations or arrangements, where these are competent to do so, to take action urgently, and consider on a case-by-case basis and on a scientific basis, including the application of the precautionary approach, the interim prohibition of destructive fishing practices, including bottom trawling that has adverse impacts on vulnerable marine ecosystems, including seamounts, hydrothermal vents and cold water corals located beyond national jurisdiction, until such time as appropriate conservation and management measures have been adopted in accordance with international law.[141]

Most significantly, the UNGA decided to follow up the recommendations with periodic reviews, based upon information provided by RFMOs and collated by the UN Secretary-General.[142] The 2011 and 2016 reviews were accompanied by a workshop involving all relevant actors, in order to discuss progress in implementing the recommendations. This proactive approach has led to the adoption of many measures by RFMOs to protect VMEs in areas beyond national jurisdiction from the risks posed by deep-sea fishing,[143] and continuing attention being paid to the issue. The process has not led to speedy action on all fronts, with some gaps remaining, but it has undoubtedly improved the situation through its sustained focus on the issue and by offering regular oversight of actual practice.

Given that time for discussion is short in the UNGA, it was decided in 2000[144] to establish a mechanism known as the Open-Ended Informal Consultative Process on the Law of the Sea (ICP) to give further opportunity to the discussion of issues relating to the sustainable development of the oceans. The ICP meets on an annual basis and it discusses the report of the Secretary-General with the aim of providing elements for consideration by the UNGA in its annual debate on the law of the sea.[145] The format of the ICP is different to the UNGA, as it generally includes a number of presentations by invited experts, followed by plenary discussion and debate. One of the main advantages of the ICP is that it permits greater engagement on specific issues, involving not only representatives of States but also international organizations and non-governmental organizations (NGOs).[146] Since its inception, the ICP has discussed a number of key topics related to the protection of

---

[140] UNGA Resolution 57/141 (2002) para. 56.
[141] UNGA Resolution 59/25 (2004) para. 66; see also UNGA Resolution 60/31 (2005) para. 72; UNGA Resolution 61/105 (2006) para. 83.
[142] See UNGA Resolution 61/105 (2006) para. 91; UNGA Resolution 64/72 (2009) paras 128–30; UNGA Resolution 69/109 (2014) paras 162–4.
[143] See Chapter 7.
[144] UNGA Resolution 5433 (1999) para. 4. The ICP was initially established for three years, but its mandate has been extended on a number of occasions, most recently in UNGA Resolution 69/245 (2014) para. 294.
[145] CSD Decision 7/1 (1999) para. 41.
[146] See Harrison (n10) 255.

the marine environment, including economic and social impacts of marine pollution (2000), the protection of the marine environment (2001), vulnerable marine ecosystems (2003), conservation and management of biodiversity beyond national jurisdiction (2004), marine debris (2005),; ecosystem approaches (2006), sustainable development (2011 and 2015), marine renewable energy (2012), ocean acidification (2013), and marine plastics (2016). The discussions have led to these issues receiving increased prominence in the resulting UNGA resolutions. Moreover, the ICP is specifically mandated to '[identify] areas where coordination and cooperation at the intergovernmental and inter-agency levels should be enhanced'.[147] The ICP cannot itself directly pursue coordination of the positions of different institutions. Nor does it alter the role of the UNGA in this regard.[148] At most, the ICP can, therefore, provide a forum in which synergies and possible tensions can be identified, and make suggestions to the UNGA on which issues require further attention from the competent international organizations.[149] The UNGA has described the primary role of the ICP as 'integrating knowledge, the exchange of opinions among multiple stakeholders and coordination among competent agencies, and enhancing awareness of topics, including emerging issues'.[150] It is perhaps this latter function that has been the most valuable contribution of the ICP, as it has allowed the initiation of a dialogue amongst key actors that may lead to further action, drawing upon existing cooperative arrangements.

It can be seen from the discussion above that the annual review process of the UNGA plays an important function in ensuring a broad and comprehensive discussion on key law of the sea issues, including the protection of the marine environment. The UNGA may also agree upon certain priority issues and recommend that other institutions with a relevant mandate take them forward, either individually or in cooperation. The UN-OCEANS network between the Secretariats of relevant UN bodies and agencies provides another forum through which administration cooperation can take place in order to implement these agreed priorities.[151] Through these various mechanisms, the UNGA has thus employed a so-called orchestration strategy, which involves exploiting its pivotal position within the UN system to work with and through a myriad of other institutions, utilizing 'soft modes of influence to guide and support their actions', in order to achieve its overall goals.[152]

The greatest weakness of the United Nations systems is that the UNGA has no power to insist upon coordination.[153] Resolutions of the UNGA are not binding on States, let alone upon other autonomous intergovernmental organizations

---

[147] CSD Decision 7/1 (1999) para. 41.   [148] CSD Decision 7/1 (1999) para. 40(5).
[149] See further Harrison (n10) 253–7.   [150] UNGA Resolution 69/245 (2014) para. 292.
[151] UN-OCEANS was established in 2003 to replace the Sub-Committee on Oceans and Coastal Affairs of the Administrative Committee on Coordination of the United Nations. The mandate of UN-OCEANS in annexed to UNGA Resolution 68/70. See further J Harrison, 'Actors and Institutions for the Protection of the Marine Environment', in R Rayfuse (ed.), *Research Handbook on the Protection of the Marine Environment* (Edward Elgar 2015) 76–7.
[152] On orchestration generally, see KW Abbott and S Bernstein, 'The High-Level Political Forum on Sustainable Development: Orchestration by Default and Design' (2015) 6 *GP* 222, 223.
[153] See Harrison (n10) 251.

at which they may be directed. However, it does not follow that institutions can simply ignore decisions of the UNGA. Even though they are not binding, their drafting is taken very seriously by States and 'negotiations for the preparation of the resolution [start] weeks and sometimes months in advance'. [154] Indeed, their effect depends not upon their legal status, but on the agreement amongst States that an issue should be given priority. Resolutions agreed by consensus bear the imprimatur of the international community and they may, therefore, carry significant political weight. Furthermore, the UNGA does have some tools at its disposal in order to promote coordination. Some institutions may have a duty to give special consideration to such resolutions as a result of commitments contained in relationship agreements that they have entered into with the UN. Many relationship agreements require an organization to include on the agenda of its meetings items proposed by the United Nations. [155] Some relationship agreements go further and require the relevant organizations to automatically submit recommendations for the coordination of policies and activities to the relevant organs and to report to the United Nations on action taken by the organizations and its members to give effect to such recommendations. [156] These relationship agreements thus provide a legal basis for the UNGA to prompt a dialogue, even if it cannot dictate the outcome. The greater use of these powers, and their further expansion through new networks of relationship agreements, could be one way in which to achieve a more integrated approach to the development of the international legal framework for the protection of the marine environment.

10.5 Revisiting Cooperation and Coordination in the Conservation of Marine Biodiversity in Areas beyond National Jurisdiction

Whilst the need for cooperation arises in all areas where the mandates of international organizations may overlap, it has been recognized that this need is even greater in areas beyond national jurisdiction. The promotion of cooperation and coordination is a key element of the ongoing negotiations towards a new international, legally binding instrument on the conservation and sustainable use of marine biological diversity of areas beyond national jurisdiction. Whilst cooperation and coordination is not an independent topic on the agenda of the negotiations, [157] it is recognized as an integral part of the discussions, particularly in relation to MPAs beyond national

---

[154] T Treves, 'The General Assembly and the Meeting of States Parties in the Implementation of the LOS Convention', in AG Oude Elferink (ed.), *Stability and Change in the Law of the Sea: The Role of the LOS Convention* (Martinus Nijhoff 2005) 60.

[155] For example, 1959 Agreement between the United Nations and the International Maritime Organization (IMO-UN Relationship Agreement) (EIF 13 January 1959), Article III; 1946 Agreement between the United Nations and the International Labour Organization (ILO-UN Relationship Agreement) (EIF 14 December 1946), Article III.

[156] For example, IMO-UN Relationship Agreement, Article IV; ILO-UN Relationship Agreement, Article IV; 1946 Agreement between the United Nations and the United Nations Education, Science and Culture Organization (UN-UNESCO Relationship Agreement) (EIF 14 December 1946), Article V.

[157] See UNGA Resolution 69/292 (2015) para. 2.

jurisdiction.[158] It is anticipated that the final product of the negotiations 'would spell out the requirements for when an MPA should be put in place, the decision-making processes for putting it in place and for the identification of specific measures to be adopted, and the legal effects of such an MPA'.[159] But beyond this basic agreement on the need to address cooperation and coordination, no clear consensus has yet emerged concerning the manner in which it is to be achieved. Key questions that the Chair of the preparatory committee has highlighted include which States or bodies might be entitled to make proposals concerning MPAs beyond national jurisdiction, which bodies were competent to designate MPAs or similar area-based measures, and what might be the legal effect of a designation on Parties to an international instrument and third States.[160] Moreover, a key issue is how any new arrangement would interact with existing instruments that provide for the adoption of management measures in areas beyond national jurisdiction.[161]

In an ideal world, one could perhaps rethink and redesign the system for ocean governance to provide a more coherent response to the problems facing the marine environment. In this respect, suggestions have been made for the establishment of a single global body, with a mandate for all aspects of marine environmental protection. Such a body could provide a centralized decision-making process for all issues related to the marine environment, or it may instead 'act as the institutional focal point to provide best practice guidance and global endorsement of decisions and measures adopted by regional or sectoral agreements'.[162] Even in intergovernmental discussions, the view has been advanced that 'a global universal governance structure remained the best way to promote sustainable marine biodiversity beyond areas of national jurisdiction'.[163] In the present context, a new global body could be granted responsibility for designating MPAs in areas beyond national jurisdiction. In the first instance, such a body could seek to promote action by other competent organizations to adopt management measures to further the conservation objectives assigned to a particular MPA, but the more radical proposals foresee this global body itself having the power to adopt binding management measures, if the responses of other competence international organizations were considered to be inadequate.[164]

---

[158] See Outcome of the Ad Hoc Open-Ended Informal Working Group to Study Issues Related to the Conservation and Sustainable Use of Marine Biological Diversity beyond Areas of National Jurisdiction and Co-Chairs' Summary of Discussions, para. 16: 'it was emphasized that should negotiations be launched, any discussions and resulting instrument should focus on cooperation and collaboration among different institutions and ensuring a functioning relationship among different activities in areas beyond national jurisdiction, not on managing these activities'.

[159] D Tladi, 'The Proposed Implementation Agreement: Options for Coherence and Consistency in the Establishment of Protected Areas beyond National Jurisdiction' (2015) 30 *IJMCL* 654, 660.

[160] Chair's Indicative Suggestion of Clusters and Issues and Questions to Assist further Discussion in the Informal Working Groups at the Second Session of the Preparatory Committee.

[161] See e.g. Tladi (n 159) 661.   [162] Rayfuse and Warner (n7) 420.

[163] Outcome of the Ad Hoc Open-Ended Informal Working Group to Study Issues Relating to the Conservation and Sustainable Use of Marine Biological Diversity beyond Areas of National Jurisdiction, Document A/69/780 (2015) Annex, para. 10.

[164] See e.g. IUCN, An International Instrument on Conservation and Sustainable Use of Biodiversity in Areas beyond National Jurisdiction: Matrix of Suggestions (2015) para. 2.3.7 (Suggestion 4). It has also been suggested that a global body may be granted the power to adopt interim (Suggestion 5) or emergency measures (Suggestion 6) when necessary.

Parties to such an agreement would be required to comply with such management measures, although there is a question as to whether a Party would have a right to object to such measures, as is common in many treaty regimes, and what processes might be put in place to control opting-out.

The establishment of an overarching institutional framework is significantly complicated by the difficulties that would arise in amending the mandates of existing organizations in order to recognize the institutional hierarchy that is inherent in such a scheme. It is for this reason that earlier suggestions for a single institution responsible for all aspects of maritime affairs were dismissed as infeasible by the International Law Commission (ILC) when considering reform of the law of the sea in the 1950s.[165] Even today, when the challenges of ocean governance are so much more obvious, it is not clear that the international community is yet ready for this step.[166] In this respect, it is worth noting that current discussions relating to the establishment of a stronger framework for the conservation of marine biological diversity in areas beyond national jurisdiction explicitly recognize that any new instrument 'should not undermine existing relevant legal instruments and frameworks and relevant global, regional and sectoral bodies'.[167] Thus, any reforms must be compatible with existing mandates and build upon current efforts at cooperation.

An alternative proposal is to establish a process to give global endorsement to MPAs and management measures adopted by sectoral or regional bodies,[168] thereby requiring all Parties to the new instrument to comply with such measures, even if they are not a Party to the sectoral or regional agreement.[169] This approach would thus build upon the existing activities of regional organization in protecting rare and fragile marine ecosystems. Yet, as seen above, some States are concerned about giving too much power to regional seas bodies in which they are not represented and, therefore, such a model would have to include safeguards that ensured that minimum standards and basic procedures were followed and allowed some form of oversight of regional actions at the global level.

In a less elaborate scheme, a global body could simply be responsible for proposing areas that were in need of special protective measures, carrying out monitoring of the marine environment in those areas and recommending action by existing institutions.[170] Under this arrangement, the main emphasis would be on a duty of States to cooperate to implement such recommendations within existing institutions. Such an approach would formalize some of the existing processes that are in place,

---

[165] International Law Commission, 'Regime of the High Seas and Regime of the Territorial Sea' (1956 II) *YbILC* 1, paras 9–18.

[166] See e.g. Ulfstein (n7) 107.   [167] See UNGA Resolution 69/292 (2015) para. 3.

[168] See e.g. E Druel and KM Gjerde, 'Sustaining Marine Life beyond Boundaries: Options for an Implementing Agreement for Marine Biodiversity beyond National Jurisdiction under the United Nations Convention on the Law of the Sea' (2014) 49 *Marine Policy* 90, 93.

[169] Parallels have thus been drawn with the approach of the Fish Stocks Agreement; R Long and MR Chaves, 'Anatomy of a New International Instrument for Marine Biodiversity beyond National Jurisdiction: First Impressions of the Preparatory Process' (2015) 6 *EL* 213, 224. For discussion of the Fish Stocks Agreement and the role it gives to RFMOs in determining conservation and management measures on the high seas, see Chapter 7.

[170] Ibid.

such as the identification of EBSAs, but it would not really bring any additional powers to bear on the problem, beyond perhaps the elaboration of an express duty to establish organizations for the purposes of protecting marine biological diversity in areas beyond national jurisdiction where they do not already exist. Even such an obligation can only be hortatory in character and it cannot guarantee that all relevant actors will participate in such organizations.

Difficult choices lie ahead for the States involved in negotiating this new agreement, which must aim towards achieving better protection of the world's oceans, whilst also respecting existing institutions and procedures. It is unclear how long it will take an agreement to emerge,[171] and in the meantime, the existing processes outlined in this chapter will continue to provide the main means for promoting cooperation and coordination in protection for the marine environment.

10.6 Conclusion

This chapter has considered the challenge of integrated oceans management at the international level. Integrated management is an essential component of the ecosystems approach, but its implementation is complicated by the fragmented and decentralized international institutional framework for ocean affairs. Promoting this objective thus requires cooperation and coordination among a wide range of global and regional institutions. The chapter has considered various mechanisms that have been used to address this challenge, including ad hoc approaches to cooperation and attempts at developing a global framework for more systematic coordination. These mechanisms should not be analysed in isolation, but rather, they must be understood as operating together in a mutually reinforcing manner.

The UNGA is ideally placed to monitor existing sectoral activities and to identify gaps, overlaps, or conflicts between different instruments. The UNGA has been keen to take on this role and it has been responsible for some important steps to improve inter-institutional dialogue in relation to both the gathering of information concerning threats to the marine environment and the discussion of policy options to deal with them. Whilst the UNGA is not in a position to offer regulatory solutions, it can use its network of relationship agreements in order to actively promote cooperation and coordination at the global level. This fairly simply action would ensure that a recommendation from the UNGA is the start of a dialogue, whilst not undermining the autonomy of those existing institutions. The conclusion of a new legally binding instrument on the conservation and sustainable use of marine biological diversity in areas beyond national jurisdiction could also see the creation of a new global body to play a similar role in relation to coordinating measures for

---

[171] The preparatory committee is expected to report on its progress by the end of 2017, and the UNGA should decide by the end of its Seventy-Second Session (i.e. mid-2018) whether to convene an intergovernmental conference to consider the recommendations of the preparatory committee; ibid, paras 1(a) and 1(k). Of course, a conference could be delayed or the conference itself may meet over a number of years.

the protection of MPAs, although such a body, whatever form it takes, would have to achieve very broad participation before it could be truly effective in this respect.

Further actions could also be taken to strengthen cooperation and coordination between institutions at a regional level. Regional collaboration could be a particularly effective means of promoting the development of a representative network of MPAs, as called for by global biodiversity and sustainable development targets.[172] Several models exist, although actual practice also highlights the practical challenges of this enterprise. It is clear that there is no magic solution to achieving an integrated approach to decision-making, but time, perseverance, and trust are key elements in any strategy to achieve this end.[173]

---

[172] See Chapter 3.   [173] See reflections in Asmundsson and Corcoran (n68) 27–30.

11

The Role of International Law in Saving the Oceans and Future Challenges for the Legal Framework

11.1 The Multifaceted and Multilayered Nature of the International Legal Framework for the Protection of the Marine Environment

The protection of the marine environment poses significant challenges for the international community, in large part because of the interconnected nature of many marine ecosystems and the fact that both polluters and pollution can easily cross national boundaries. The purpose of this book has been to consider how States have addressed these challenges, focusing on the manner in which they have employed legal instruments in order to put in place common solutions to the threats to our oceans. The picture that emerges at the end of the analysis is of a multifaceted and multilayered legal framework, with complex interactions between numerous treaties and other international instruments.

The starting point of the analysis was the United Nations Convention on the Law of the Sea (UNCLOS), which provides the legal foundation for promoting the protection of the marine environment. As a 'constitution for the oceans', UNCLOS establishes an overarching jurisdictional framework, as well as a series of general principles and rules that require States to take certain steps to protect and preserve the marine environment in relation to all types of maritime activities. Yet, UNCLOS only offers a basic layer of regulation, founded upon an abstract standard of due diligence and further elementary procedural guarantees. At the same time, it foresees the negotiation of rules and standards that are more specific, to give direction to States with regard to what they must do to prevent and reduce marine pollution and to protect the marine environment more generally. It is this process of normative development that has been discussed throughout the book.

Global and regional institutions have played a central role in developing the international rules and standards that supplement the overarching legal framework for the protection of the marine environment in UNCLOS. Many such institutions have been involved in the field of marine environmental protection. The predominant form of law-making has been through specialized sectoral institutions, responsible for regulating a particular activity, including its environmental effects. Some of these institutions operate at the global level, whereas others operate at the regional level. In many cases, both global and regional institutions act in parallel, with the global bodies setting general standards of protection and the regional bodies offering a forum for the negotiation of more precise standards that will apply to a select group of States. To add to the institutional complexity, a number of institutions have emerged with a focus on promoting the conservation of biological diversity and these bodies have sought to influence the development of higher levels of environmental protection by the more specialist sectoral bodies.

As a result of these processes, one of the key trends of the past two decades has been the fact that, regardless of their original focus, almost all institutions concerned with the regulation of maritime activities have mainstreamed environmental considerations into their programmes of work. Moreover, the range of environmental issues that has been addressed has also expanded beyond the initial focus on the prevention, reduction, and control of marine pollution to broader concerns relating to the protection of ocean ecosystems. The protection of marine biological diversity is an issue that is today on the agenda of almost all relevant institutions, even if it is not explicitly mentioned as part of their treaty mandate. The importance of this value has also been reflected in recent interpretations of the UNCLOS, which have recognized that the conservation of marine biological diversity is an integral part of the obligation to protect and preserve the marine environment under Part XII of the UNCLOS.

A clear indication of this trend has been the emergence of marine protected areas (MPAs) as a key tool for protecting ecosystems. At the global level, the international community has recognized the need to expand current protection by setting a global target of conserving 10 per cent of coastal and marine areas by 2020. More importantly, a large number of institutions have responded to this goal by utilizing MPAs or similar area-based management tools to conserve key marine species or habitats from harm caused by activities falling within their mandate. Each institution has its own terminology or criteria that it has employed for designating areas of protection: for example, Particularly Sensitive Sea Areas (PSSAs) in the shipping sector, Vulnerable Marine Ecosystems (VMEs) in the context of fishing, and Areas of Particular Environmental Interest (APEIs) in relation to deep-seabed mining. Despite this apparent diversity, what most of the relevant instruments have in common is that they go beyond the protection of the 'rare and fragile ecosystems' or 'habitats of depleted, threatened or endangered species', as required by UNCLOS,[1] to encompass a broader range of values, including representative examples of important marine features or ecosystems, particularly biodiverse or productive ecosystems, and areas of particular importance for key ecosystem services. As a result, the scope of protection for marine species and habitats has broadened, indicating that States have strengthened the legal framework in this respect.

---

[1] UNCLOS, Article 194(5).

11.2 The Influence of General Principles of International Environmental Law on the Legal Framework for the Protection of the Marine Environment

It is not only UNCLOS that guides the development of the international frame-work for the protection of the marine environment. A number of general principles of international environmental law have emerged over the past decades that today form the basis for international efforts to protect the environment. Key principles in this respect include the precautionary approach, the ecosystem approach, and the participatory approach. These principles are an expression of modern envir-onmental values and they underpin law-making efforts in this field. Not only are these principles important for the way in which they can inform the interpretation and application of UNCLOS, thereby ensuring that the Convention evolves in line with contemporary concerns, but they can also influence the negotiation of further instruments. A major focus of this book has therefore been on how these principles have been integrated into various treaty regimes relating to the protection of the marine environment.

Consideration of the precautionary approach provides a clear example of the flexibility of principles and the different ways they can be operationalized. The pre-cautionary approach is aimed at addressing scientific uncertainty in the regulation of human activities and it has assumed a central status in the modern law of the sea, being recognized by instruments in most sectors. Yet, it is clear from this book that the precautionary approach takes no single form, and it can be applied in a variety of ways. The dumping regime provides an example of a relatively strict application of the precautionary approach, as the 1996 Dumping Protocol and several regional treaties prohibit all dumping unless the Parties have agreed that there is no signifi-cant risk to the marine environment. Yet even in this context, not all States have accepted the strict application of the precautionary approach, and Parties to the 1972 Dumping Convention are subject to a weaker formulation of the principle. The deep-seabed-mining regime also imposes a legal obligation to take a precaution-ary approach, and the fact that commercial mining has not yet started means there is an opportunity to be genuinely cautious. How the principle will be implemented in the emerging exploitation regulations remains to be seen, however. There are those voices that express serious doubt as to whether this activity should be authorized at the present time, given the unknown effects on VMEs in the deep oceans, but it is ultimately a question of policy as to whether a complete moratorium is appropriate until more clear evidence of impacts is available. Other regulatory regimes, such as shipping and fishing, have seen a more nuanced application of the precautionary approach. Institutions involved in the regulation of these sectors have all proclaimed a commitment to the precautionary approach, but they have tended to be more reactive than anticipatory in their practice.

Overall, these examples demonstrate that the application of the precautionary approach does not dictate a particular outcome, but rather it must be negotiated on a case-by-case basis. Moreover, it shows that 'the decision-making process involved in the application of the precautionary [approach] is highly complicated' and it must take into account a range of environmental, economic, and social factors.[2] Nevertheless, the precautionary approach plays an important function in all of these regimes, because it ensures that a discussion of potential impacts takes place at an early stage, even before conclusive evidence becomes available. This procedural dimension of the precautionary approach should not be overlooked, even if the actual content of a management decision will depend upon the political dynamics of a particular regime.

Similar observations can be made about other key principles of international environmental law. Thus, the ecosystems approach is commonly reflected in the international legal framework, but the actual extent of its application varies from treaty to treaty, often depending upon the information that is available about relevant species or habitats. Operationalization of the participatory approach has been even more patchy and diverse, with many regimes approaching this topic with some hesitation, leaving a large degree of discretion to States as to how far they go in involving the public in decision-making. One of the challenges is identifying relevant stakeholders in the context of the marine environment. This exercise may be easier in the context of activities taking place close to land, but public participation becomes increasingly difficult to define as the regulatory regime moves towards the open ocean.

11.3 A Dynamic International Legal Framework for the Protection of the Marine Environment

As well as being multifaceted and multilayered, the international legal framework for the protection of the marine environment is also highly dynamic. The ability of the law to evolve can be linked in large part to the existence of institutions that meet on a regular basis, meaning that States are able to keep track of developments and to progressively strengthen the rules and standards as new evidence of environmental impacts comes to light. Indeed, institutions provide a forum for negotiation and can play an active role in encouraging change through the commissioning of studies or the provision of advice to States.[3]

This dynamism is also underpinned by flexible law-making processes. Many of the treaties used to address marine environmental threats have tacit amendment procedures that allow modified rules or standards to enter into force after a specified period of time, provided that States do not object. These types of law-making mechanisms are seen in the regulation of shipping and dumping. Similar law-making processes

---

[2] Y Tanaka, 'Principles of International Marine Environmental Law', in R Rayfuse (ed.), *Research Handbook of International Marine Environmental Law* (Edward Elgar 2016) 43.

[3] See e.g. J Alvarez, *International Organizations as Law-Makers* (OUP 2005) 341; J Harrison, 'Actors and Institutions for the Protection of the Marine Environment', in R Rayfuse (ed.), *Research Handbook on International Marine Environmental Law* (Edward Elgar 2016) 68–70.

apply to fisheries management, where States have often delegated decision-making power to RFMOs that meet on a regular basis to discuss and agree on appropriate, often time-limited, conservation measures. Such measures are normally binding on all Parties to the treaty without the need for further approval, although they are often subject to the ability of a State to opt-out. The inclusion of objection procedures is a reflection of the consensual nature of international law, and they may be the price that must be paid to achieve broader participation in treaties, given that 'no country can be forced to sign'.[4] At the same time, some more modern instruments have incorporated mechanisms that seek to limit the situations in which objections can be made in order to strengthen the regulatory system and avoid the proliferation of free-riders. Such mechanisms are found in both regional fisheries treaties and global chemicals treaties, and calls have been made to strengthen other treaty regimes in order to make it more difficult to avoid the application of agreed rules and standards through reservations or objections.[5] Even in the absence of such limitations, political pressure can be utilized in order to persuade States to abandon objections and accept stricter environmental rules or standards, and this is another function that can be performed by international institutions charged with overseeing the implementation of international instruments. The dumping regime provides an example of how a meeting of the Parties can exercise this function, by ensuring that States are required to explain and justify their objections to other members of the regime.

Another way in which to ensure the dynamism of the law is to rely upon norms that are themselves evolutionary in character. This is partly the case with due diligence obligations, which require States to adopt measures that are proportionate, inter alia, to the nature of the risk. Thus, as awareness and understanding of a risk change, so will the content of a due diligence obligation. Another common technique to promote the progressive development of the law is the establishment of an obligation to adopt best environmental practices (BEP) or best available technologies (BAT) when carrying out a particular activity. Such norms are included in many treaties dealing with land-based sources of marine pollution and seabed activities, both within and beyond national jurisdiction. The effect of these rules is to require actors to ensure that their activities integrate the latest standards in a particular industry and they therefore provide a means of ensuring effective environmental protection. As with other general rules, BAT and BEP do suffer from an inherent ambiguity, although recourse can be made to compulsory dispute settlement and courts and tribunals have demonstrated that the content of this rule can be determined on an objective basis. Alternatively, the decisions of international institutions can provide a useful source of guidance on what the BEP and BAT requirements entail in a certain context—it is this approach that is largely seen in the context of regional seas treaties when recommending actions that should be taken by polluting industries.

---

[4] LE Susskind and HA Zakri, *Environmental Diplomacy* (2nd edn, OUP 2015) 34; see also ET Swaine, 'Reserving' (2006) 31 *YJIL* 307, 331.
[5] See e.g. A Telesetsky, 'After Whaling in the Antarctic: Amending Article VIII to Fix a Broken Treaty Regime' (2015) 30 *IJMCL* 700–26.

11.4　Continuing Challenges for the International Legal Framework for the Protection of the Marine Environment

Despite the significant law-making activities that have taken place in this field over the past few decades, the analysis of the relevant legal instruments has demonstrated that key challenges remain across different sectors.

There is no doubt that the international community has produced an impressive array of legal instruments relating to marine environmental protection in the period since UNCLOS was negotiated. Gaps do remain, however, and, therefore, further action is needed to ensure that appropriate regulatory frameworks are put in place. This is true for important sectors where regional instruments have been used as the predominant form of regulation, but not all regions have yet taken the step of adopting legally binding rules or standards. The preceding analysis has highlighted key examples in the case of the regulation of fisheries, oil and gas, and land-based sources of marine pollution. It is also true that new challenges will continue to emerge and the international community must therefore be prepared to respond with the negotiation of new instruments.

The negotiation of legally binding rules is only the first step of ensuring adequate marine environmental protection, however. The legal framework for the protection of the marine environment will only be effective if it can attract the support of all relevant States. Yet, the need for universality is at odds with the decentralized character of the international legal system, which relies on State consent.[6] The question of participation is therefore a challenge that is faced by most of the treaties considered throughout this study. International institutions can themselves play an important role in promoting the application of relevant legal instruments, by providing information and support to countries preparing to give their consent to be bound. Yet, the legal framework itself also provides some tools that can be utilized to overcome this challenge.

To some extent, rules of reference contained in UNCLOS are designed to deal with this issue. In the context of shipping and dumping, for example, it is clear that many of the rules and standards contained in global treaties must be complied with by all UNCLOS Parties as a result of these rules of reference, regardless of whether the States have become a Party to the individual treaties. The precise boundaries of what treaties are incorporated in this manner remain hazy, and States, or an international court or tribunal, could usefully clarify what rules and standards are captured by the rules of reference. In any case, where they exist, the rules of reference provide reassurance to States that their participation in a particular treaty will not put them at a competitive disadvantage because they have the opportunity to demand compliance by a non-party.

It is not only rules of reference that might play such a universalizing function. Courts and tribunals have emphasized that the more general rules of UNCLOS,

---

[6]　See J Harrison, *Making the Law of the Sea* (CUP 2011) 2.

such as Articles 192, 194, and 206, are 'informed by ... other applicable rules of international law' and they have used this interpretative technique to read quite specific commitments into Part XII of the UNCLOS.[7] Indeed, the practice of courts and tribunal demonstrates that they have adopted a flexible attitude to determining which rules can be read into the Convention in this manner,[8] introducing a significant degree of dynamism into the UNCLOS regime.

Beyond UNCLOS, other mechanisms have also been developed to ensure widespread application of rules and standards beyond the Parties to a treaty. Utilizing the inherent jurisdiction of States over their territory to demand that all visiting vessels comply with a specified international rule or standard has been a relatively successful technique that has been employed in this respect. The shipping sector was at the forefront of developing regional port State control mechanisms to apply international rules and standards on a uniform basis to all vessels calling at port in those regions. This technique has been considered to compensate for what is often perceived to be poor flag State control in this sector. In this context, port States may require substandard ships to bring themselves into compliance with key standards relating to seaworthiness, before they leave port. There are also circumstances in which a port State may be able to bring legal proceedings for a violation of certain requirements even before the vessel entered its port. More recently, similar techniques have been developed in the fisheries sector, with regional and global instruments demanding that States take port State measures, such as denial of access or facilities, to combat illegal, unregulated and unreported (IUU) fishing. If such steps are supported by a sufficient number of States, they can have a significant influence on the behaviour of vessels by limiting economic opportunities.

Another significant challenge relates to the implementation and enforcement of rules and standards for the protection of the marine environment. Whereas the development of rules and standards has been trusted to a number of global and regional bodies, States have retained a much tighter control over monitoring compliance and enforcement. There are some occasions when States have accepted compulsory and binding dispute settlement, not least UNCLOS itself. The dispute settlement system in UNCLOS provides an important option of last resort for seeking to ensure that States comply with their basic obligation to protect and preserve the marine environment. Yet, even when compulsory dispute settlement is available, the costs and time-consuming nature of litigation mean that it will not be appropriate for resolving all compliance issues. Indeed, sight should not be lost of the fact that lack of capacity can be just as much an impediment to compliance as lack of political will.[9] It is perhaps for this reason that many treaties considered

---

[7] *South China Sea Arbitration (Merits)* (2016) para. 941.

[8] For example, the Tribunal in the South China Sea Arbitration used the Convention on International Trade in Endangered Species (CITES) as a benchmark even though not all Parties to UNCLOS are also a Party to CITES. There are currently eleven Parties to UNCLOS that are not Party to CITES. Nevertheless, what the Tribunal called the 'nearly universal adherence' of States to CITES, which has 182 Parties, was sufficient for the Tribunal to find that it 'forms part of the general corpus of international law that informs the content of Article 192 and 194(5)'; *South China Sea Arbitration (Merits)* (2016) para. 956.

[9] See e.g. RB Mitchell, 'Compliance Theory', in D Bodansky et al (eds), *Oxford Handbook of International Environmental Law* (OUP 2007) 909.

in this book have developed alternatives to formal judicial dispute settlement procedures, involving facilitative mechanisms for monitoring implementation and compliance. One of the most important functions of such mechanisms is to gather information on the overall performance of States and to identify crosscutting issues that may require a response from the regime to promote compliance. They can also be used to address compliance by individual States. Most compliance procedures stress their non-confrontational nature and they even sometimes allow a State to bring its own situation before a compliance body in order to seek assistance in the implementation of the relevant treaty rules. Yet, the strengthening of compliance mechanisms is arguably one of the areas in which States must take further action if the international legal framework is to be effective.[10] Ensuring the independence of compliance bodies and adopting clear and transparent procedures for the handling of compliance issues are key steps that could be taken in this regard. In some sectors, such as shipping and fishing, there is still a long way to go in this respect. Moreover, at the end of the day, better compliance is only likely to be achieved if priority is also given to ensuring the availability of financial or technical assistance. International financial institutions or even private actors could potentially have a role to play in this respect.[11]

The final challenge considered in this book was how to achieve an integrated approach to the protection of the marine environment, given the plethora of institutions working in this field. Progress on protecting marine ecosystems throughout the oceans will be limited unless international institutions start working together to ensure that their rules and standards form a coherent response to marine environmental threats. To this end, greater cooperation and coordination is a necessity. This is particularly the case if States are to promote multipurpose MPAs, in which specific marine ecosystems or threatened species and habitats are granted protection from a range of threats. The process established under the auspices of the Convention on Biological Diversity (CBD) in order to identify Ecologically and Biologically Significant Marine Areas (EBSAs) has an important role to play in facilitating coordinated action on this front, even though it was explicitly designed as a purely scientific process that is intended to describe marine areas worthy of protection, not to dictate the manner in which they should be managed. Nevertheless, the criteria offer a starting point for other institutions which do have regulatory powers to take action to protect relevant areas and some regions have already used the process of identifying EBSAs as a catalyst for collaboration. In recent years, institutions have developed some more sophisticated mechanisms to work more closely together and coordinate actively measures taken to protect and preserve the marine environment. Whilst such cooperation and coordination has tended to take place on an ad hoc basis, there are signs that institutions are attempting to regularize this process, and Chapter 10 identified examples of good practice that could be replicated elsewhere.

---

[10] A significant body of literature on compliance mechanisms can be drawn upon; for an overview, see e.g. G Goeteyn and F Maes, 'Compliance Mechanisms in Multilateral Environmental Agreements: An Effective Way to Improve Compliance?' (2011) 10 *CJIL* 791–826.

[11] See Harrison (n3) 71.

However, strengthening and expanding of the mandate of regional seas bodies to include the conservation of marine biological diversity in areas beyond national jurisdiction may first be necessary if this strategy is to work. International negotiations towards a new legally binding instrument on the conservation of marine biological diversity in areas beyond national jurisdiction place this challenge squarely in the spotlight, offering an opportunity for reform of the existing system.[12] The proposals on the table at present vary in their ambition, ranging from radical overhaul and centralization of decision-making to clarifying and streamlining existing processes for inter-institutional cooperation. The examples in this book suggest that coordination is possible using existing techniques and so an instrument that clarifies the key principles and modalities could achieve some of the desired outcomes, whilst also being acceptable to a larger number of States.

The challenges that remain for the international legal framework for the protection of the marine environment are undoubtedly daunting. Yet, they are not insurmountable, and this book has hopefully demonstrated that the relevant international rules and processes are open to adaptation and progressive development. To address the outstanding challenges, institutions will have to be strengthened, but there is evidence that this is already taking place in many sectors, for example through the amendment of some regional fisheries treaties or regional seas conventions and protocols. Indeed, the legal framework is only going to address fully the threats to the marine environment if it maintains its dynamism and it is able to adapt to new scientific and technological discoveries.

One final point needs to be made, which brings us back to the question of the function and limits of international law raised in Chapter 1. Whilst it is hoped that this book has demonstrated the important role that international law has to play in putting in place adequate measures for the protection of the marine environment, it is clear that international law cannot achieve this objective in isolation. In many instances, national law will be needed to implement a State's international obligations and provide for their direct enforcement against the actors that are ultimately responsible for pollution or environmental harm. Moreover, substantial political will is required to ensure that the Parties consent to relevant treaties in the first place and then dedicate requisite resources to marine environmental protection in order to ensure compliance with their international obligations. Ultimately, States are only likely to continue to take the necessary steps to cooperate on marine environmental protection at the international level if they feel it is a political priority for their own constituents.

---

[12] R Long and M Rodriguez Chaves, 'Anatomy of a New International Instrument for Marine Biological Diversity beyond National Jurisdiction: First Impressions of the Preparatory Process' (2016) 6 *EL* 213, 216.

Bibliography

Abbott, K. W., and Snidal, D., 'Why States Act through Formal International Organizations' (1998) 42 *Journal of Conflict Resolution* 3.

Abbott, K. W., Keohane, R.O., Moravcsik, A., Slaughter, A.M., et al, 'The Concept of Legalization' (2000) 54 *International Organization* 17.

Abbott, K. W., and Snidal, D., 'Hard and Soft Law in International Governance' (2000) 54 *International Organization* 421.

Abbott K. W., and Bernstein, S., 'The High-Level Political Forum on Sustainable Development: Orchestration by Default and Design' (2015) 6 *Global Policy* 222.

Alexander, E. R., *How Organizations Act Together: Interorganizational Coordination in Theory and Practice* (Gordon and Breach, Amsterdam, 1995).

Allott, P., 'Power Sharing and the Law of the Sea' (1983) 77 *American Journal of International Law* 1.

Allsopp, M., Page, R., Johnston, P., and Santillo, D., *State of the World's Oceans* (Springer, Dordrecht, 2009).

Alter, K. J., 'The Multiplication of International Courts and Tribunals after the End of the Cold War', in C. Romano, K. J. Alter, and C. Avgerou (eds), *Oxford Handbook of International Adjudication* (Oxford University Press, Oxford, 2014) 64.

Alvarez, J., *International Organizations as Law-Makers* (Oxford University Press, Oxford, 2005).

Anderson, D., 'The Straddling Stocks Agreement of 1995 – An Initial Assessment' (1996) 45 *International and Comparative Law Quarterly* 463.

Anderson, D., 'Port States and the Environment', in A. Boyle and D. Freestone (eds), *International Law and Sustainable Development: Past Achievements and Future Challenges* (Oxford University Press, Oxford, 2001) 325.

Andresen, S., and Skjærseth, J. B., 'Science and Technology', in D. Bodansky, J. Brunnée and E. Hey (eds), *Oxford Handbook of International Environmental Law* (Oxford University Press, Oxford, 2007) 182.

Angelo, J. J., 'The International Maritime Organization and Protection of the Marine Environment', in M. H. Nordquist and J. N. Moore (eds), *Current Maritime Issues and the International Maritime Organization* (Martinus Nijhoff Publishers, The Hague, 1999) 105.

Anthony, R. G., Estes, J. A., Ricca, M. A., and Forsman, E. D., 'Bald Eagles and Sea Eagles in the Aleutian Archipelago: Indirect Effects of Trophic Cascades' (2008) 89 *Ecology* 2725.

Attard, D. J., *The Exclusive Economic Zone in International Law* (Oxford University Press, Oxford, 1987).

Aust, A., *Modern Treaty Law and Practice* (2nd edn: Cambridge University Press, Cambridge, 2007).

Bai, J., 'The IMO Polar Code: The Emerging Rules of Arctic Shipping Governance' (2015) 30 *International Journal of Marine and Coastal Law* 674.

Baird, R., Simons, M., and Stephens, T., 'Ocean Acidification: A Litmus Test for International Law' (2009) 3 *Carbon and Climate Law Review* 459.

Balkin, R., 'Ballast Water Management: Regulatory Challenges and Opportunities', in R. Caddell and R. Thomas (eds), *Shipping, Law and the Marine Environment in the 21st Century* (Lawtext Publishing Limited, Witney, 2013) 137.

Bang, H-S., 'Port State Jurisdiction and Article 218 of the UN Convention on the Law of the Sea' (2009) 40 *Journal of Maritime Law and Commerce* 312.

Barnes, R., 'The Convention on the Law of the Sea: An Effective Framework for Domestic Fisheries Conservation?', in D. Freestone, R. Barnes, and D. Ong (eds), *The Law of the Sea: Progress and Prospects* (Oxford University Press, Oxford, 2006) 233.

Barnes, R., 'Flag States', in D. R. Rothwell, A. Oude Elferink, K. Scott, and T. Stephens (eds), *Oxford Handbook of the Law of the Sea* (Oxford University Press, Oxford, 2015) 304.

Barrett, S., *Environment & Statecraft* (Oxford University Press, Oxford, 2003).

Bateman, S., and White, M., 'Compulsory Pilotage in the Torres Strait: Overcoming Unacceptable Risks to a Sensitive Marine Environment' (2009) 40 *Ocean Development and International Law* 184.

Bax, N., Williamson, A., Aguero, M., Gonzalez, E., et al, 'Marine Invasive Alien Species: A Threat to Global Biodiversity' (2003) 27 *Marine Policy* 313.

Baxter, R. R., 'International Law in "Her Infinite Variety"' (1980) 29 *International and Comparative Law Quarterly* 549.

Beckman, R. C., 'PSSAs and Transit Passage – Australia's Pilotage System in the Torres Strait Challenges the IMO and UNCLOS' (2007) 38 *Ocean Development and International Law* 325.

Bernal, P., Ferreira, B., Inniss, L., Marschoff, E., et al, 'Chapter 54: Overall Assessment of Human Impact on the Oceans', in L. Inniss, A. Simcock, A. Y. Ajawin, A. C. Alcala, et al (eds), *The First Global Integrated Marine Assessment* (United Nations, New York, 2016) .

Bijma, J., Pörtner, H. O., Yesson, C., and Rogers, A. D., 'Climate Change and the Oceans – What Does the Future hold?' (2013) 74 *Marine Pollution Bulletin* 3.

Birnie, P. W., 'Are Twentieth-Century Marine Conservation Conventions Adaptable to Twenty First Century Goals and Principles? Part II' (1997) 12 *International Journal of Marine and Coastal Law* 488.

Birnie, P. W., 'Marine Mammals: Exploiting the Ambiguities of Article 65 of the Convention on the Law of the Sea and Related Provisions: Practice under the International Convention for the Regulation of Whaling', in D. Freestone, R. Barnes, and D. Ong (eds), *The Law of the Sea: Progress and Prospects* (Oxford University Press, Oxford, 2006) 261.

Birnie, P., Boyle, A. E., and Redgwell, C., *International Law and the Environment* (3rd edn: Oxford University Press, Oxford, 2009).

Bodansky, D., 'Customary (and Not So Customary) International Environmental Law' (1995) 3 *Indiana Journal of Global Legal Studies* 105.

Bodansky D., and Diringer, E., *The Evolution of Multilateral Regimes: Implications for Climate Change* (Pew Center on Global Climate Change, Washington DC, 2010).

Boehlert, G. W., and Gill, A. B., 'Environmental and Ecological Effects of Ocean Renewable Energy Development: A Current Synthesis' (2010) 23 *Oceanography* 68.

Boone, L. 'Reducing Air Pollution from Marine Vessels to Mitigate Arctic Warming: Is It Time to Target Black Carbon?' (2012) 1 *Carbon and Climate Law Review* 13.

Börzel, T., 'Organizing Babylon – On the Different Concepts of Policy Networks' (1998) 76 *Public Administration* 253.

Bowman, M., 'Normalizing the International Convention for the Regulation of Whaling' (2008) 29 *Michigan Journal of International Law* 293.

Bowman, M., Davies, P., and Redgwell, C. (eds), *Lyster's International Wildlife Law* (2nd edn: Cambridge University Press, Cambridge, 2010).

Boyle, A. E., 'Climate Change and International Law – A Post-Kyoto Perspective' (2012) 42 *Environmental Policy and Law* 333.

Boyle, A. E., 'The Environmental Jurisprudence of the ITLOS' (2007) 22 *International Journal of Marine and Coastal Law* 369.

Boyle, A. E., 'Further Development of the Law of the Sea Convention: Mechanisms for Change' (2005) 54 *International and Comparative Law Quarterly* 563.

Boyle, A. E., 'Human Rights and the Environment: Where Next?' (2012) 23 *European Journal of International Law* 613.

Boyle, A. E., 'Land-based Sources of Marine Pollution: Current Legal Regime' (1992) 16 *Marine Policy* 20.

Boyle, A. E., 'Law of the Sea Perspectives on Climate Change' (2012) 27 *International Journal of Marine and Coastal Law* 831.

Boyle, A. E., 'Marine Pollution under the Law of the Sea Convention' (1985) 79 *American Journal of International Law* 357.

Boyle, A. E., 'Problems of Compulsory Jurisdiction and the Settlement of Disputes Relating to Straddling Fish Stocks' (1999) 14 *International Journal of Marine and Coastal Law* 1.

Boyle, A. E., 'Reflections on Treaties and Soft Law' (1999) 48 *International and Comparative Law Quarterly* 901.

Boyle, A. E., 'Relationship between International Environmental Law and Other Branches of International Law', in D. Bodansky, J. Brunnée and E. Hey (eds), *Oxford Handbook of International Environmental Law* (Oxford University Press, Oxford, 2007) 125.

Boyle, A. E., 'Soft Law in International Law-Making', in M. D. Evans (ed), *International Law* (4th edn: Oxford University Press, Oxford, 2014) 118.

Boyle, C. L., 'Sea Pollution' (1954) 2 *Oryx (The International Journal of Conservation)* 212.

Braithwaite, J., and Drahos, P., *Global Business Regulation* (Cambridge University Press, Cambridge, 2000).

Brown, A., 'Some Current Issues facing the Convention on the Conservation of Antarctic Marine Living Resources', in G. Triggs and A. Riddell (eds), *Antarctica: Legal and Environmental Challenges for the Future* (British Institute of International and Comparative Law, London, 2007) 85.

Brown, C., 'International Environmental Law in the Regulation of Offshore Installations and Seabed Activities: The Case for a South Pacific Regional Protocol' (1998) 17 *Australian Mining and Petroleum Law Journal* 109.

Brundtland, G. H., Khalid, M., Agnelli, S., Al-Athel, S. A., et al, *Our Common Future* (Cambridge University Press, Cambridge, 1987).

Brunnée, J., 'CoPing with Consent: Lawmaking under Multilateral Environmental Agreements' (2002) 15 *Leiden Journal of International Law* 1.

Brunnée, J., 'The Stockholm Declaration and the Structure and Processes of International Environmental Law', in M. H. Nordquist, Norton Moore, J., and Mahmoudi, S. (eds), *The Stockholm Declaration and Law of the Marine Environment* (Martinus Nijhoff, The Hague, 2003) 67.

Brunnée, J., 'Commons Areas, Common Heritage and Common Concern', in D. Bodansky, J. Brunnée and E. Hey (eds), *The Oxford Handbook of International Environmental Law* (Oxford University Press, Oxford, 2009) 550.

Burke, W. T., 'US Fishery Management and the New Law of the Sea' (1982) 76 *American Journal of International Law* 24.

Burrows, P., Rowley, C., and Owen, D., 'The Economics of Accidental Oil Pollution by Tankers in Coastal Waters' (1974) 3 *Journal of Public Economics* 258.

Caddell, R., 'International Law and the Protection of Migratory Wildlife: An Appraisal of Twenty-Five Years of the Bonn Convention' (2005) 16 *Colorado Journal of International Environmental Law and Politics* 113.

Caddell, R., 'Shipping and the Conservation of Marine Biodiversity: Legal Responses to Vessel-Strikes of Marine Mammals', in R. Caddell and R. Thomas (eds), *Shipping, Law and the Marine Environment in the 21st Century* (Lawtext Publishing Limited, Witney, 2013) 89.

Cançado Trindade, A. A., 'Precaution', in J. E. Viñuales (ed), *The Rio Declaration on Environment and Development: A Commentary* (Oxford University Press, Oxford, 2015) 403.

Carlane, C. P., 'Saving the Whales in the New Millennium: International Institutions, Recent Developments and the Future of International Whaling Policies' (2005) 24 *Virginia Environmental Law Journal* 1.

Carson, R., *Silent Spring* (Houghton Mifflin, Boston, 1962).

Charney, J., 'Universal International Law' (1993) 87 *American Journal of International Law* 529.

Chirhop, A., 'Ships in Distress, Environmental Threats to Coastal States, and Places of Refuge: New Directions for an Ancien Regime?' (2002) 33 *Ocean Development and International Law* 207.

Chircop, A., 'Assistance at Sea and Places of Refuge for Ships: Reconciling Competing Norms', in H. Ringbom (ed), *Jurisdiction over Ships* (Brill, The Hague, 2015) 140.

Churchill, R. R., 'The Barents Sea Loophole Agreement: A "Coastal State" Solution to a Straddling Stock Problem' (1999) 14 *International Journal of Marine and Coastal Law* 467.

Churchill, R. R., 'Fisheries and Their Impact on the Marine Environment: UNCLOS and Beyond', in M.C. Ribeiro (ed), *30 Years After the Signature of the United Nations Convention on the Law of the Sea: The Protection of the Environment and the Future of the Law of the Sea* (Coimbra Editora, Coimbra, 2014) 23.

Churchill, R. R., 'High Seas Marine Protected Areas: Implications for Shipping', in R. Caddell and R. Thomas (eds), *Shipping, Law and the Marine Environment in the 21st Century* (Lawtext Publishing Limited, Witney, 2013) 53.

Churchill, R. R., 'Port State Jurisdiction Relating to the Safety of Shipping and Pollution from Ships – What Degree of Extraterritoriality?' (2016) 31 *International Journal of Marine and Coastal Law* 442.

Churchill, R. R., 'Sustaining Small Cetaceans: A Preliminary Evaluation of the Ascobans and Accobams Agreements', in A. E. Boyle and D. Freestone (eds), *International Law and Sustainable Development* (Oxford University Press, Oxford, 1999) 225.

Churchill, R. R., 'The Persisting Problem of Non-Compliance with the Law of the Sea Convention: Disorder in the Oceans' (2012) 27 *International Journal of Marine and Coastal Law* 813.

Churchill, R. R., and Lowe, A. V., *The Law of the Sea* (3rd edn: Manchester University Press, Manchester, 1997).

Churchill R. R., and Ulfstein, G., 'Autonomous Institutional Arrangements in Multilateral Environmental Agreements: A Little-Noticed Phenomenon in International Law' (2000) 94 *American Journal of International Law* 623.

Cooley, S. R., and Mathis, J. T., 'Addressing Ocean Acidification as part of Sustainable Ocean Development', in A. Chircop, S. Coffen-Smout, and M. McConnell (eds), *Ocean Yearbook* 27 (Brill, The Hague, 2013) 29.

Corres, A. J., and Pallis, A. A., 'Flag State Performance: An Empirical Analysis' (2008) 7 *WMU Journal of Maritime Affairs* 241.

Craik, N., *The International Law of Environmental Impact Assessment* (Cambridge University Press, Cambridge, 2011).

Crawford, J. (ed), *The International Law Commission's Articles on State Responsibility: Introduction, Text and Commentaries* (Cambridge University Press, Cambridge, 2002).

Crayford, J. V., 'Forthcoming Changes to the International Convention for the Prevention of Pollution from Ships (MARPOL 73/78)', in M. H. Nordquist and J. N. Moore (eds), *Current Maritime Issues and the International Maritime Organization* (Martinus Nijhoff Publishers, The Hague, 1999) 133.

Currie, D. E. J., and Wowk, K., 'Climate Change and CO2 in the Oceans and Global Oceans Governance' (2009) 4 *Climate and Carbon Law Review* 387.

D'Amato, A., and Chopra, S. K., 'Whales: Their Emerging Right to Life' (1991) 85 *American Journal of International Law* 21.

de Bruyn, P., Murua, H., and Aranda, M., 'The Precautionary Approach to Fisheries Management: How this Is Taken into Account by Tuna Regional Fisheries Management Organizations' (2013) 38 *Marine Policy* 397.

de la Fayette, L., 'Access to Ports in International Law' (1996) 11 *International Journal of Marine and Coastal Law* 1.

de la Fayette, L., 'The London Convention 1972: Preparing for the Future' (1998) 13 *International Journal of Marine and Coastal Law* 515.

de la Fayette, L., 'New Developments in the Disposal of Offshore Installations' (1999) 14 *International Journal of Marine and Coastal Law* 523.

de la Fayette, L., 'The Marine Environment Protection Committee: The Conjunction of the Law of the Sea and International Environmental Law' (2001) 16 *International Journal of Marine and Coastal Law* 155.

de Lucia, V., 'Competing Narratives and Complex Genealogies: The Ecosystem Approach in International Environmental Law' (2015) 27 *Journal of Environmental Law* 91.

de Mestrel, A., 'The Prevention of Pollution of the Marine Environment Arising from Offshore Mining and Drilling' (1979) 20 *Harvard International Law Journal* 469.

Dear, I. B. C., and Kemp, P. (eds), *The Oxford Companion to Ships and the Sea* (2nd edn: Oxford University Press, Oxford, 2005).

Derraik, J. G. B., 'The Pollution of the Marine Environment by Plastic Debris: A Review' (2002) 44 *Marine Pollution Bulletin* 842.

DeSombre, E. R., *Flagging Standards* (The MIT Press, Cambridge, MA, 2006).

Dietz, T., Ostrom, E., and Stern, P. C., 'The Struggle to Govern the Commons' (2003) 302 *Science* 1907.

Diz, D., *Fisheries Management in Areas beyond National Jurisdiction: The Impact of Ecosystem Based Law-Making* (Martinus Nijhoff Publishers, The Hague, 2013).

Donner, P., 'Offering Refuge Is Better than Refusing' (2008) 7 *WMU Journal of Maritime Affairs* 281.

Dotinga, H. M., and Oude Elferink, A. G., 'Acoustic Pollution in the Oceans: The Search for Legal Standards' (2000) 31 *Ocean Development and International Law* 151.

Druel, E., and Gjerde, K. M., 'Sustaining Marine Life Beyond Boundaries: Options for an Implementing Agreement for Marine Biodiversity beyond National Jurisdiction under the United Nations Convention on the Law of the Sea' (2014) 49 *Marine Policy* 90.

Duda A. M., and Sherman, K., 'A New Imperative for Improving Management of Large Marine Ecosystems' (2002) 45 *Ocean & Coastal Management* 797.

Dunn, D. C., et al, 'The Convention on Biological Diversity's Ecologically or Biologically Significant Areas: Origins, Development and Current Status' (2014) 49 *Marine Policy* 137.

Dupuy, P.-M., 'Soft Law and the International Law of the Environment' (1991) 12 *Michigan Journal of International Law* 420.

Dworkin, R., *Taking Rights Seriously* (Harvard University Press, Cambridge, MA, 1977).

Ebbesson, J., 'Public Participation, in J. E. Viñuales (ed), *The Rio Declaration on Environment and Development: A Commentary* (Oxford University Press, Oxford, 2015) 287.

Edeson, W., 'Towards the Long-Term Sustainable Use: Some Recent Developments in the Legal Regime of Fisheries', in A. E. Boyle and D. Freestone (eds), *International Law and Sustainable Development* (Oxford University Press, Oxford, 1999) 165.

Eriksen, H. H., and Perrez, F. X., 'The Minimata Convention: A Comprehensive Response to a Global Problem' (2014) 23 *Review of European, Comparative and International Environmental Law* 195.

Fabra, A., and Gascon, Y., 'The Convention on the Conservation of Antarctic Marine Living Resources (CCAMLR) and the Ecosystem Approach' (2008) 23 *International Journal of Marine and Coastal Law* 657.

Firestone J., and Lilley, J., 'An Endangered Species: Aboriginal Whaling and the Right to Self-Determination and Cultural Heritage in a National and International Context' (2004) 34 *Environmental Law Review* 10763.

Fitzmaurice, M., 'Enhanced Marine Environmental Protection: A Case Study of the Baltic Sea', in J. Barrett and R. Barnes (eds), *Law of the Sea: UNCLOS as a Living Treaty* (BIICL, London, 2016) 293.

Fitzmaurice, M., 'The International Convention for the Prevention of Pollution from Ships (MARPOL), in D. Attard, M. Fitzmaurice, N. A. Martínez Gutiérrez and R. Hamza (eds), *The IMLI Manual on International Maritime Law – Vol. III* (Oxford University Press, Oxford, 2016) 77.

Fitzmaurice, M., 'The Practical Workings of Treaties', in M. D. Evans (ed), *International Law* (4th edn: Oxford University Press, Oxford, 2014) 166–200.

Fitzmaurice, M., *Whaling and International Law* (Cambridge University Press, Cambridge, 2015).

Fleischer, C. A., 'Significance of the Convention: Second Committee Issues', in B. H Oxman and A. W. Koers (eds), *The 1982 Convention on the Law of the Sea* (Law of the Sea Institute, Berkeley, 1984) 53.

Foley, M., et al, 'Improving Ocean Management through the Use of Ecological Principles and Integrated Ecosystem Assessments' (2013) 63 *BioScience* 619.

Foster, C., *Science and the Precautionary Principle* (Cambridge University Press, Cambridge, 2011).

Frank, V., 'Consequences of the Prestige Sinking for European and International Law' (2005) 20 *International Journal of Marine and Coastal Law* 1.

Franckx, E., 'Regional Marine Environment Protection Regimes in the Context of UNCLOS' (1998) 13 *International Journal of Marine and Coastal Law* 307.

Franckx, E., 'The Protection of Biodiversity and Fisheries Management: Issues Raised by the Relationship between CITES and LOSC', in D. Freestone, R. Barnes, and D. Ong (eds), *The Law of the Sea: Progress and Prospects* (Oxford University Press, Oxford, 2006) 210.

Freestone, D. 'International Fisheries Law since Rio: The Continued Rise of the Precautionary Principle', in A. Boyle and D. Freestone (eds), *International Law and Sustainable Development* (Oxford University Press, Oxford, 199) 135.

Freestone, D., and Oude Elferink, A. G., 'Flexibility and Innovation in the Law of the Sea', in A. G. Oude Elferink (ed) *Stability and Change in the Law of the Sea: The Role of the LOS Convention* (Martinus Nijhoff Publishers, The Hague, 2005) 169.

Freestone, D., 'Principles Applicable to Modern Oceans Governance' (2008) 23 *International Journal of Marine and Coastal Law* 385.

Freestone, D., 'Climate Change and the Oceans' (2009) 4 *Climate and Carbon Law Review* 383.

Freestone D., Johnson, D., Ardron, J., Killerlain Morrison, K., et al, 'Can Existing Institutions Protect Biodiversity in Areas Beyond National Jurisdiction? Experiences from Two On-Going Processes' (2014) 49 *Marine Policy* 167.

Freestone D., and Bulger, F., 'The Sargasso Sea Commission: An Innovative Approach to the Conservation of Areas beyond National Jurisdiction' (2016) 30 *Ocean Yearbook* 80.

French, D., 'Common Concern, Common Heritage and other Global(-ising) Concepts: Rhetorical Devices, Legal Principles or a Fundamental Challenge?', in M. J. Bowman, P. Davies, and E. Goodwin (eds), *Research Handbook on Biodiversity and Law* (Edward Elgar, Cheltenham, 2015) 334.

Galland, G., Harrould-Kolieb, E., and Herr, D., 'The Ocean and Climate Policy' (2012) 12 *Climate Policy* 764.

Gao, Z., *Environmental Regulation of Oil and Gas* (Kluwer Law International, The Hague, 1998).

Gao, Z., 'Environmental Regulation of Oil and Gas in the Twentieth Century and Beyond: Introduction and Overview', in Z. Gao (ed), *Environmental Regulation of Oil and Gas* (Kluwer International, The Hague, 1998) 3.

Gavouneli, M., *Pollution from Offshore Installations* (Springer, Dordrecht, 1995).

Gehan, S., 'United States v Royal Caribbean Cruises Ltd: Use of Federal "False Statements Act" to Extend Jurisdiction over Polluting Incidents into Territorial Seas of Foreign States' (2001) 7 *Ocean and Coastal Law Journal* 167.

Gillespie, A., 'Aboriginal Subsistence Whaling: A Critique of the Inter-Relationship between International Law and the International Whaling Commission' (2001) 12 *Colorado Journal of International Law and Policy* 77.

Gillespie, A., 'Forum Shopping in International Environmental Law: The IWC, CITES and the Management of Cetaceans' (2002) 33 *Ocean Development and International Law* 17.

Gillespie, A., 'Iceland's Reservation at the International Whaling Commission' (2003) 14 *European Journal of International Law* 977.

Gillespie, A., 'The Precautionary Principle in the Twenty-First Century: A Case Study of Noise Pollution in the Ocean' (2007) 22 *International Journal of Marine and Coastal Law* 61.

Gillespie, A., 'The Search for a New Compliance Mechanism within the IWC' (2003) 34 *Ocean Development and International Law* 349.

Gjerde, K., and Freestone, D., 'Particularly Sensitive Sea Areas – An Important Environmental Concept at a Turning-Point' (1994) 9 *International Journal of Marine and Coastal Law* 431.

Glowka L., Burhenne-Guilmin, F., Synge, H., McNeely, J. A., et al, *A Guide to the Convention on Biological Diversity* (International Union for the Conservation of Nature, Gland and Cambridge, 1994).

Goeteyn G., and F. Maes, 'Compliance Mechanisms in Multilateral Environmental Agreements: An Effective Way to Improve Compliance? (2011) 10 *Chinese Journal of International Law* 791.

Gold, E., 'Learning from Disaster: Lessons in Regulatory Enforcement in the Maritime Sector' (1999) 8 *Review of European, Comparative and International Environmental Law* 16.

Gollasch S., David, M., Voigt, M., Dragsund, E., et al, 'Critical Review of the IMO International on the Management of Ships' Ballast Water and Sediments' (2007) 6 *Harmful Algae* 585.

Goodwin, E. J., *International Environmental Law and the Conservation of Coral Reefs* (Routledge, Abingdon, Oxon, 2011).

Guilfoyle, D., *Shipping Interdiction and the Law of the Sea* (Cambridge University Press, Cambridge, 2009).

Guggisberg, S., *The Use of CITES for Commercially-Exploited Fish Species* (Springer, Dordrecht, 2016)

Haas, P., 'Do Regimes Matter? Epistemic Communities and Mediterranean Pollution Control' (1989) 43 *International Organization* 377.

Hafner, G., 'Pros and Cons Ensuing from Fragmentation of International Law' (2004) 25 *Michigan Journal of International Law* 849.

Halpern, B. S., et al, 'A Global Map of Human Impact on Marine Ecosystems' (2008) 319 *Science* 948.

Hardin, G., 'The Tragedy of the Commons' (1968) 162 *Science* 1243.

Harris, P., Alo, B., Bera, A., Bradshaw, M., et al, 'Chapter 21: Offshore Hydrocarbon Industries', in L. Inniss, A. Simcock, A. Y. Ajawin, A. C. Alcala et al (eds), *The First Global Integrated Marine Assessment* (United Nations, New York, 2016).

Harrison, J., 'Actors and Institutions for the Protection of the Marine Environment', in R. Rayfuse (ed), *Research Handbook on International Marine Environmental Law* (Edward Elgar, Cheltenham, 2015) 57.

Harrison, J., *Making the Law of the Sea* (Cambridge University Press, Cambridge, 2011).

Harrison, J., 'Recent Developments and Continuing Challenges in the Regulation of Greenhouse Gas Emissions from International Shipping' (2013) *Ocean Yearbook* 27, 359.

Harrison, J., 'Reflections on the Role of International Courts and Tribunals in the Settlement of Environmental Disputes and the Development of International Environmental Law' (2013) 25 *Journal of Environmental Law* 501.

Harrison, J., 'Safeguards against Excessive Enforcement Measures in the Exclusive Economic Zone', in H. Ringbom (ed), *Jurisdiction over Ships* (Brill, The Hague, 2015) 217.

Harrison, J., 'Pollution from or through the Marine Environment', in D. Attard, M. Fitzmaurice, N. Martinez, and R. Hamza (eds), *The IMLI Manual of International Maritime Law Volume III* (Oxford University, Oxford, Press, 2016) 169.

Harrison, J., 'Resources of the International Seabed Area', in E. Morgera and K. Kulovesi (eds), *Research Handbook on International Law and Natural Resources* (Edward Elgar, Cheltenham, 2016) 390.

Harrop, S. R., and Pritchard, D. J., 'A Hard Instrument Goes Soft: The Implications of the Convention on Biological Diversity's Current Trajectory' (2011) 21 *Global Environmental Change* 474.

Harrould-Kolieb, E. R., and Herr, D., 'Ocean Acidification and Climate Change: Synergies and Challenges of Addressing both under the UNFCCC' (2012) 12 *Climate Policy* 378.

Hassan, D., *Protecting the Marine Environment from Land-based Sources of Pollution* (Ashgate, Farnham, 2006).

Hazin, F., Marschoff, E., Padovani Ferreira, B., Rice, J., et al, 'Chapter 11 Capture Fisheries', in L. Inniss, A. Simcock, A. Y. Ajawin, A. C. Alcala et al (eds), *The First Global Integrated Marine Assessment* (United Nations, New York, 2016) .

Heffernan, J. P., 'Dealing with Mediterranean Bluefin Tuna: A Study in International Environmental Management' (2014) 50 *Marine Policy* 81.

Henriksen, T., Hønneland, G., and Sydnes, A., *Law and Politics in Ocean Governance: The UN Fish Stocks Agreement and Regional Fisheries Management Regimes* (Martinus Nijhoff Publishers, The Hague, 2006).

Henriksen, T., 'Conservation of Marine Biodiversity and the International Maritime Organization', in C. Voigt (ed), *The Rule of Law for Nature* (Cambridge University Press, Cambridge, 2013) 331.

Hewison, G. J., 'The Legally Binding Nature of the Moratorium on Large-Scale High Seas Driftnet Fishing' (1994) 25 *Journal of Maritime Law and Commerce* 557.

Hey, E., *An Advanced Introduction to International Environmental Law* (Edward Elgar, Cheltenham, 2016)

Hey, E., 'Common But Differentiated Responsibilities', in *Max Planck Encyclopedia of Public International Law*, On-line Edition (Oxford University Press, Oxford, 2011).

Hey, E., 'The Interplay between Multilateral Environmental and Fisheries Law: A Struggle to Sustainably Regulate Economic Activity' (2011) 54 *Japanese Yearbook of International Law* 190.

Hey, E., *The Regime for the Exploitation of Transboundary Marine Fisheries Resources* (Martinus Nijhoff Publishers, The Hague, 1989).

Holder, J., *Environmental Assessment* (Oxford University Press, Oxford, 2004).

Hoon Hong, G., and Joo Lee, Y., 'Transitional Measures to Combine Two Global Ocean Dumping Treaties' (2015) 55 *Marine Policy* 47.

Horrocks, C., 'Thoughts on the Respective Roles of Flag States and Port States' in M. H. Nordquist and J. N. Moore (eds), *Current Maritime Issues and the International Maritime Organization* (Martinus Nijhoff Publishers, The Hague, 1999) 191.

Hosch, G., Ferraro, G., and Faillier, P., 'The 1995 FAO Code of Conduct for Responsible Fisheries: Adopting, Implementing or Scoring Results?' (2011) 35 *Marine Policy* 189.

Hovik S., and Hanssen, G. S., 'The Impact of Network Management and Complexity on Multi-Level Coordination' (2015) 93 *Public Administration* 506.

Hulm, P., 'The Regional Seas Program: What Fate for UNEP's Crown Jewels?' (1983) 12 *Ambio* 2.

IJlstra, T., 'Enforcement of MARPOL: Deficient or Impossible?' (1989) 20 *Marine Pollution Bulletin* 596.

Jackson, J. B. C., 'Ecological Extinction and Evolution in the Brave New Ocean' (2008) 105 *Proceedings of the National Academy of Sciences* 11458.

Jaeckel, A., 'An Environmental Management Strategy for the International Seabed Authority? The Legal Basis' (2015) 30 *International Journal of Marine and Coastal Law* 93.

Jacobs, R. E., 'Treading Deep Waters: Substantive Law Issues in Tuvalu's Threat to Sue the United States in the International Court of Justice' (2005) 14 *Pacific Rim Law and Policy Journal* 103.

Jameson, C. M., *Silent Spring Revisited* (Bloomsbury, London, 2012).

Johnson, D., 'Can Competent Authorities Cooperate for the Common Good: Towards a Collective Arrangement for the North-East Atlantic', in P. A. Beckman and A. N. Vylegzhanin (eds), *Environmental Security in the Arctic Ocean* (Springer, Dordrecht, 2013) 333.

Johnson D., and Ferreira, M. A., 'Current Legal Developments: ISA Areas of Particular Environmental Interest in the Clarion-Clipperton Fracture Zone' (2015) 30 *International Journal of Marine and Coastal Law* 559.

Johnston, D. M., *International Law of Fisheries* (Yale University Press, New Haven, 1965).

Johnston D. M., 'The Environmental Law of the Sea: Historical Development', in D. M. Johnston (ed), *The Environmental Law of the Sea* (IUCN, Gland, 1981) 17.

Jones, P. J. S., *Governing Marine Protected Areas* (Earthscan/Routledge, Abingdon, 2014).

Karim, M. S., 'Implementation of the MARPOL Convention in Developing Countries' (2010) 79 *Nordic Journal of International Law* 303.

Keast R., Brown, K., and Mandell, M., 'Getting the Right Mix: Unpacking Integration Meanings and Strategies' (2007) 10 *International Public Management Journal* 9.

Keselj, T., 'Port State Jurisdiction in Respect of Pollution from Ships' (1999) 30 *Ocean Development and International Law* 127.

Kim, R. E., 'Is a New Multilateral Environmental Agreement on Ocean Acidification Necessary?' (2012) 21 *Review of European Community and International Environmental Law* 243.

Kimball, L. A., 'An International Regime for Managing Land-Based Activities that Degrade Marine and Coastal Environments' (1995) 29 *Ocean and Coastal Management* 187.

Kingsbury, B., 'International Courts: Uneven Judicialization in Global Order', in J. Crawford and M. Koskenniemi (eds), *The Cambridge Companion to International Law* (Cambridge University Press, Cambrdige, 2012) 203.

Kirgis, F. L., 'Specialized Law-Making', in C. C. Joyner (ed), *The United Nations and International Law* (Cambridge University Press, Cambridge, 1997) 65.

Kirk, E., 'Noncompliance and the Development of Regimes Addressing Marine Pollution from Land-based Activities' (2008) 39 *Ocean Development and International Law* 235.

Kiss, A., 'The Destiny of the Principles of the Stockholm Declaration', in M. H. Nordquist, J. Norton Moore, and M. Mahmoudi (eds), *The Stockholm Declaration and Law of the Marine Environment* (Martinus Nijhoff, The Hague, 2003) 53.

Koester, V., 'The Five Global Biodiversity-Related Conventions' (2001) 31 *Environmental Policy and Law* 151.

Kopela, S., 'Climate Change, Regime Interaction, and the Principle of Common but Differentiated Responsibility: The Experience of the International Maritime Organization' (2014) 24 *Yearbook of International Environmental Law* 70.

Kopela, S., 'Port-State Jurisdiction, Extraterritoriality, and the Protection of Global Commons' (2016) 47 *Ocean Development and International Law* 89.

Koskeniemmi, M., and Leino, P., 'Fragmentation of International Law? Post-modern Anxieties' (2002) 15 *Leiden Journal of International Law* 553.

Knapp, S., and Franses, P. H., 'Does Ratification Matter and Do Major Conventions Improve Safety and Decrease Pollution In Shipping?' (2009) 33 *Marine Policy* 826.

Knudsen, O. F. and Hassler, B., 'IMO Legislation and Its Implementation: Accident Risk, Vessel Deficiencies and National Administrative Practices' (2011) 35 *Marine Policy* 201.

Kong, L., 'Environmental Impact Assessment under the United Nations Convention on the Law of the Sea' (2011) 10 *Chicago Journal of International Law* 651.

Kurlansky, M., *Cod* (Vintage, London, 1999).

Kwiatkowska, B., 'The High Seas Fisheries Regime: At a Point of No Return?' (1993) 9 *International Journal of Marine and Coastal Law* 327.

Lallas, P. L., 'The Stockholm Convention on Persistent Organic Pollutants' (2001) 95 *American Journal of International Law* 692.

Lang, W., 'Diplomacy and International Environmental Law-Making: Some Observations' (1992) 3 *Yearbook of International Environmental Law* 108.

Langlet, D., 'Exporting C02 for Sub-Seabed Storage: The Non-Effective Amendment to the London Dumping Protocol and its Implications' (2015) 30 *International Journal of Marine and Coastal Law* 395.

Larkin, P. A., 'An Epitaph for the Concept of Maximum Sustainable Yield' (1977) 106 *Transactions of the American Fisheries Society* 1.

Lauterpacht, H., *The Development of International Law by the International Court* (Stevens & Sons, London, 1958).

Lazarus, R., 'Super Wicked Problems and Climate Change: Restraining the Present to Liberate the Future' (2009) 94 *Cornell L.R.* 1153.

Levin, L. A., Mengerink, K., Gjerde, K. M., Rowden, A. A., et al, 'Defining "serious harm" to the marine environment in the context of deep-seabed mining' (2016) 74 *Marine Policy* 245.

Leary, D., and Esteban, M., 'Climate Change and Renewable Energy from the Ocean and Tides: Calming the Sea of Regulatory Uncertainty' (1009) 24 *International Journal of Marine and Coastal Law* 617.

Liss, P. S., and Johnson, M. T., *Ocean-Atmosphere Interactions of Gases and Particles* (Springer, Berlin, 2014).

Little, L., and Orellana, M. A., 'Can CITES Play a Role in Solving the Problems of IUU Fishing? The Trouble with Patagonian Toothfish' (2004) 16 *Colorado Journal of International Environmental Law and Policy* 21.

Lodge, M. W., 'Protecting the Marine Environment of the Deep Seabed', in R. Rayfuse (ed), *Research Handbook on International Marine Environmental Law* (Edward Elgar, Cheltenham, 2015) 151.

Lodge, M. W., and Nandan, S. N., 'Some Suggestions towards Better Implementation of the United Nations Agreement on Straddling Fish Stocks and Highly Migratory Fish Stocks of 1995' (2005) 20 *International Journal of Marine and Coastal Law* 345.

Lodge, M. W., 'Some Legal and Policy Considerations Relating to the Establishment of a Representative Network of Protected Areas in the Clarion-Clipperton Zone' (2011) 26 *International Journal of Marine and Coastal Law* 463.

Lodge, M. W., Johnson, D., Le Gurun, G., Wengler, M., Weaver, P., and Gunn, V., 'Seabed Mining: International Seabed Authority Enviornmental Management Plan for the Clarion-Clipperton Zone – A Partnership Approach' (2014) 49 *Marine Policy* 66.

Long, R., and Rodriguez Chaves, M., 'Anatomy of a New International Instrument for Marine Biological Diversity beyond National Jurisdiction: First Impressions of the Preparatory Process' (2016) 6 *Environmental Liability* 213.

Louka, E., *International Environmental Law: Fairness, Effectiveness and World Order* (Cambridge University Press, Cambridge, 2006).

Lowe, V., 'Sustainable Development and Unsustainable Arguments', in A. E. Boyle and D. Freestone (eds), *International Law and Sustainable Development* (Oxford University Press, Oxford, 1999) 19.

Lowe, V., *International Law* (Oxford University Press, Oxford, 2007).

Lugten, G., 'Current Legal Developments: Food and Agriculture Organization' (2008) 23 *International Journal of Marine and Coastal Law* 761.

Lyons, Y., 'Transboundary Pollution from Offshore Oil and Gas Activities in the Seas of Southeast Asia', in R. Warner and S. Marsden (eds), *Transboundary Environmental Governance: Inland, Coastal and Marine Perspectives* (Ashgate, Farnham, 2012) 167.

Mansfield, B., 'Compulsory Dispute Settlement after the Southern Bluefin Tuna Award', in A. G. Oude Elferink and D. R. Rothwell (eds), *Oceans Management in the 21st Century* (Martinus Nijhoff, The Hague, 2004) 255.

Maruma Mrema, E., 'Regional Seas Programme: The Role played by UNEP in its Development and Governance', in D. J. Attard, M. Fitzmaurice, N. A. Martínez Gutiérrez, and R. Hamza (eds), *The IMLI Manual on International Maritime Law, Volume III* (Oxford University Press, Oxford, 2016) 345.

Marten, B., 'The Enforcement of Shipping Standards under UNCLOS' (2011) 10 *WMU Journal of Maritime Affairs* 45.

Marten, B., 'Port State Jurisdiction over Vessel Information: Territoriality, Extra-Territoriality and the Future of Shipping Regulation' (2016) 31 *International Journal of Marine and Coastal Law* 470.

Martínez Gutiérrez, N. A., *Limitation of Liability in International Maritime Conventions* (Routledge, Abingdon, Oxon, 2011).

Mathis, J. T., Santos, J., Mosetti, R., Mavume, A., et al, 'Chapter 5: Sea-Air Interactions', in L. Inniss, A. Simcock, A. Y. Ajawin, A. C. Alcala et al (eds), *The First Global Integrated Marine Assessment* (United Nations, New York, 2016).

McDorman, T. L. 'Implementing Existing Tools: Turning Words into Actions – Decision-making Processes of Regional Fisheries Management Organizations (2005) 20 *International Journal of Marine and Coastal Law* 428.

McDorman, T. L., 'Regional Port State Control Agreements: Some Issues of International Law' (2000) 5 *Ocean and Coastal Law Journal* 207.

McLachlan, C., 'The Principle of Systemic Integration and Article 31(3)(c) of the Vienna Convention' (2005) 54 *International and Comparative Law Quarterly* 77.

Meinke-Brandmaier, B., 'Multi-Regime Regulation – How the South Pacific Region Influences Global Marine Environmental Policy Making: A Study of Radioactive Waste Dumping', (2005) 19 *Ocean Yearbook Online* 162.

Mensah, T. A., 'The International Tribunal for the Law of the Sea and the Protection and Preservation of the Marine Environment' (1999) 8 *Review of European, Comparative and International Environmental Law* 1.

Mensah, T. A., 'The International Legal Regime for the Protection and Preservation of the Marine Environment from Land-Based Sources of Pollution', in A. E. Boyle and D. Freestone (eds), *International Law and Sustainable Development* (Oxford University Press, Oxford, 1999) 297.

Metz, B., Davidson, O., de Coninck, H., Loos, M., et al, IPCC *Special Report on Carbon Dioxide Capture and Storage* (Cambridge University Press, Cambridge, 2005).

Miles, E. L., 'The Approaches of UNCLOS III & Agenda 21 – A Synthesis', in M. Kusuma-Atmajada, T. A. Mensah, and B. H. Oxman (eds), *Sustainable Development and Preservation of the Oceans: The Challenges of UNCLOS and Agenda 21* (Law of the Sea Institute, Berkeley, 1997) 16.

Mitchell, R. B., 'Compliance Theory', in D. Bodansky, J. Brunnée and E. Hey (eds), *Oxford Handbook of International Environmental Law* (Oxford University Press, Oxford, 2007) 893.

Molenaar, E. J., 'The 1996 Protocol to the 1972 London Convention' (1997) 12 *International Journal of Marine and Coastal Law* 396.

Molenaar, E. J., 'Addressing Regulatory Gaps in High Seas Fisheries' (2005) 20 *International Journal of Marine and Coastal Law* 533.

Molenaar, E. J., *Coastal State Jurisdiction over Vessel-Source Pollution* (Kluwer Law International, The Hague, 1998).

Molenaar, E. J., 'Ecosystem-Based Fisheries Management, Commercial Fisheries, Marine Mammals and the 2001 Reykjavik Declaration in the Context of International Law' (2001) 17 *International Journal of Marine and Coastal Law* 561.

Molenaar, E. J., 'International Regulation of Central Arctic Ocean Fisheries', in M. Nordquist, J. Norton Moore, and R. Long (eds), *Challenges of the Changing Arctic. Continental Shelf, Navigation, and Fisheries* (Brill, Leiden, 2016) 429.

Molenaar, E. J., 'Port State Jurisdiction: Towards Mandatory and Comprehensive Use', in D. Freestone, R. Barnes, and D. Ong (eds), *The Law of the Sea: Progress and Prospects* (Oxford University Press, Oxford, 2006) 192.

Molenaar, E. J., 'Options for Regional Regulation of Merchant Shipping Outside the IMO, with Particular Reference to the Arctic Region' (2014) 45 *Ocean Development and International Law* 272.

Molenaar, E. J., 'Port and Coastal States', in D. R. Rothwell, A. Oude Elferink, K. Scott, and T. Stephens (eds), *Oxford Handbook of the Law of the Sea* (Oxford University Press, Oxford, 2015) 280.

Monbiot, G., *Feral: Rewilding the Land, Sea and Human Life* (Penguin, London, 2014).

Morgera, E., 'Competence or Confidence? The Appropriate Forum to Address Multi-Purpose High Seas Protected Areas' (2007) 16 *Review of European, Comparative and International Environmental Law* 1.

Morgera, E., 'Ecosystem and Precautionary Approaches', in J. Razzaque and E. Morgera (eds), *Encyclopedia of Environmental Law: Biodiversity and Nature Protection* (Edward Elgar, Cheltenham, 2017) forthcoming.

Morgera E., and Tsoumani, E., 'Yesterday, Today and Tomorrow: Looking Afresh at the Convention on Biological Diversity' (2010) 21 *Yearbook of International Environmental Law* 3.

Morishita, J., 'What Is the Ecosystem Approach to Fisheries Management?' (2008) 32 *Marine Policy* 19.

Morrison, A., *Places of Refuge for Ships in Distress: Problems and Methods of Resolution* (Martinus Nijhoff Publishers, The Hague, 2008).

Myers, G. S., 'Usage of Anadromous, Catadromous and Allied Terms for Migratory Fishes' (1949) 1949 *Copeia* 89.

Nollkaemper, A., 'The Distinction between Non-Legal and Legal Norms in International Affairs: An Analysis with Reference to International Policy for the Protection of the North Sea from Hazardous Substances' (1998) *13 International Journal of Marine and Coastal Law* 355.

Nordquist M. H., Rosenne, S., and Nandan, S. N. (eds), *United Nations Convention on the Law of the Sea 1982: A Commentary - Vol. IV* (Martinus Nijhoff, The Hague, 1991).

Nordquist, M. H., Rosenne, S., and Nandan, S. N. (eds), *United Nations Convention on the Law of the Sea 1982: A Commentary - Vol. II* (Martinus Nijhoff, The Hague 1993).

Noyes, J. E., 'The Territorial Sea and Contiguous Zone', in D. R. Rothwell et al (eds), *The Oxford Handbook on the Law of the Sea* (Oxford University Press, Oxford, 2015) 91.

Nukamp, H., and Nollkaemper, A., 'The Protection of Small Cetaceans in the Face of Uncertainty: An Analysis of the ASCOBANS Agreement' (1997) 9 *Georgetown International Environmental Law Review* 281.

Ong, D., 'The 1982 UN Convention on the Law of the Sea and Marine Environmental Protection', in M. Fitzmaurice, D. M. Ong, and P. Merkouris (eds), *Research Handbook on International Environmental Law* (Edward Elgar, Cheltenham, 2010) 567.

Oral, N., 'Integrated Coastal Zone Management and Marine Spatial Planning for Hydrocarbon Activities in the Black Sea' (2008) 23 *International Journal of Marine and Coastal Law* 453.

Oral, N., 'Forty Years of the UNEP Regional Seas Programme: From Past to Future', in R. Rayfuse (ed), *Research Handbook on International Marine Environmental Law* (Edward Elgar, Abingdon, Oxon, 2015) 339.

Ørebech, P., 'The "Lost Mackerel" of the North East Atlantic – The Flawed System of Trilateral and Bilateral Decision-Making' (2013) 28 *International Journal of Marine and Coastal Law* 343.

Orrego Vicuña, F., *The Exclusive Economic Zone: Regime and Legal Nature under International Law* (Cambridge University Press, Cambridge, 1989).

Oude Elferink A. G., 'Environmental Impact Assessment in Areas beyond National Jurisdiction' (2012) 27 *International Journal of Marine and Coastal Law* 449.

Oxman, B., 'The Duty to Respect Generally Accepted International Standards' (1991) 24 *New York University Journal of International Law and Politics* 109.

Pallemaerts, M., 'The North Sea and Baltic Sea Land-Based Sources Regimes: Reducing Toxics or Rehashing Rhetoric?' (1998) 13 *International Journal of Marine and Coastal Law* 421.

Palma-Robles, M. A., 'Fisheries Enforcement and other Concepts', in R. Warner and S. Kaye (eds), *Routledge Handbook of Maritime Regulation and Enforcement* (Routledge, Abingdon, Oxon, 2015) 139.

Papanicolopulu, I., 'On the Interactions between Law and Science: Considerations on the Ongoing Process of Regulating Underwater Acoustic Pollution' (2011) 1 *Aegean Review of the Law of the Sea and Maritime Law* 247.

Parmentier, R., 'Greenpeace and the Dumping of Waste at Sea: A Case of Non-State Actors' Intervention in International Affairs' (1999) 4 *International Negotiation* 433.

Peet, G., 'The Role of (Environmental) Non-Governmental Organizations at the Marine Environment Protection Committee of the International Maritime Organization and the at the London Dumping Convention' (1994) 22 *Ocean and Coastal Management* 3.

Pereira, R., 'Pollution from Seabed Activities', in D. Attard M. Fitzmaurice, N. Martínez Gutiérrez, and R. Hamza (eds), *The IMLI Manual of International Maritime Law: Vol. III* (Oxford University, Oxford, Press, 2016) 95.

Pozdnakova, A., *Criminal Jurisdiction over Perpetrators in Ship-Source Pollution Cases* (Martinus Nijhoff Publishers, The Hague, 2012).

Proelss, A., and Houghton, K., 'Protecting Marine Species', in R. Rayfuse (ed), *Research Handbook on International Marine Environmental Law* (Edward Elgar, Cheltenham, 2015) 229.

Pyhala, M., Brusendorff, A. C., and Pauloumäki, H., 'The Precautionary Principle', in M. Fitzmaurice et al (eds), *Research Handbook on International Environmental Law* (Edward Elgar, Cheltenham, 2010) 203.

Rached, D. H., 'The Intergovernmental Panel on Climate Change: Holding Science and Policy-Making to Account' (2014) 24 *Yearbook of International Environmental Law* 3.

Rajamani, L., 'The 2015 Paris Agreement: Interplay between Hard, Soft and Non-Obligation' (2016) 28 *Journal of Environmental Law* 337.

Rares, S., 'An International Convention on Offshore Hydrocarbon Leaks?' (2012) 26 *Australian and New Zealand Maritime Law Journal* 10.

Raustiala, K., 'Institutional Proliferation and the International Legal Order' in J. L. Dunoff and M. A. Pollack (eds), *Interdisciplinary Perspectives on International Law and International Relations* (Cambridge University Press, Cambridge, 2013) 293.

Ray, C., 'Ecology, Law and the "Marine Revolution"' (1970) 3 *Biological Conservation* 7.

Rayfuse, R., *Non-Flag State Enforcement in High Seas Fisheries* (Martinus Nijhoff, The Hague, 2004).

Rayfuse, R., 'Biological Resources', in D. Bodansky, J. Brunnée and E. Hey (eds), *Oxford Handbook on International Environmental Law* (Oxford University Press, Oxford, 2007) 362.

Rayfuse, R., 'Climate Change and the law of the sea', in R. Rayfuse and S. V. Scott (eds), *International law in the era of climate change* (Edward Elgar, Cheltenham, 2012) 147.

Rayfuse, R., 'Regional Fisheries Management Organizations', in D. Rothwell, A. Oude Elferink, K. Scott and T. Stephens. (eds), *Oxford Handbook on the Law of the Sea* (Oxford University Press, Oxford, 2015) 439.

Rayfuse, R., 'The Role of Port States', in R. Warner and S. Kaye (eds), *Routledge Handbook of Maritime Regulation and Enforcement* (Routledge, Abingdon, 2015) 71.

Rayfuse, R., and Warner, R., 'Securing a Sustainable Future for the Oceans beyond National Jurisdiction: The Legal Basis for an Integrated Cross-Sectoral Regime for High Seas Governance for the 21st Century' (2008) 23 *International Journal of Marine and Coastal Law* 399.

Redgwell, C., 'Protection of Ecosystems under International Law: Lessons from Antarctica', in A. E. Boyle and D. Freestone (eds), *International Law and Sustainable Development* (OUP 1999) 205.

Redgwell, C., 'Mind the Gap in the GAIRS: The Role of Other Instruments in LOSC Regime Implementation in the Offshore Energy Sector' (2014) 29 *International Journal of Marine and Coastal Law* 600.

Rickie, K. L., Orr, J. C., Schneider, K., and Caldeira, K., 'Risks to Coral Reefs from Ocean Carbonate Chemistry Changes in Recent Earth System Model Projections' (2013) 8 *Environmental Research Letters* 034003.

Ringbom, H., 'Preventing Pollution from Ships – Reflections on the "Adequacy" of Existing Rules' (1999) 8 *Review of European, Comparative and International Environmental Law* 21.

Ringbom, H., 'Vessel-Source Pollution', in R. Rayfuse (ed), *Research Handbook on International Marine Environmental Law* (Edward Elgar, Cheltenham, 2016) 105.

Roach, J. A., 'Alternatives for Achieving Flag State Implementation and Quality Shipping', in M. H. Nordquist and J. Norton Moore (eds), *Current Maritime Issues and the International Maritime Organization* (Martinus Nijhoff Publishers, The Hague, 1999) 151.

Roach, J. A., 'International Standards for Offshore Drilling', in M. H. Nordquist, J. Norton Moore, A. Chirhop, and R. Long (eds), *The Regulation of Continental Shelf Development* (Martinus Nijhoff Publishers, The Hague, 2013) 105.

Roberts, C., *Ocean of Life: The Fate of Man and the Sea* (Penguin, New York, 2012).

Roberts, J., *Marine Environmental Protection and Biodiversity Conservation: The Application and Future Development of the IMO's Particularly Sensitive Sea Area Concept* (Dordrecht, Springer, 2006).

Roberts, J., Chircop, A., and Prior, S., 'Area-Based Management on the High Seas: Possible Applications of the IMO's Particularly Sensitive Sea Area Concept' (2010) 25 *International Journal of Marine and Coastal Law* 483.

Rochette, J., Chircop, A., and Prior, S., 'The Regional Approach to the Conservation and Sustainable Use of Marine Biodiversity in Areas Beyond National Jurisdiction' (2014) 49 *Marine Policy* 109.

Rochette J., Billé, R., Molenaar, E. J., Drankier, P., et al, 'Regional Oceans Governance Mechanisms: A Review' (2015) 60 *Marine Policy* 9.

Rodriguez, E., and Piniella, F., 'The New Inspection Regime of the Paris Mou on Port State Control: Improvement of the System' (2012) IX *Journal of Maritime Research* 9.

Romano, C., 'International Dispute Settlement', in D. Bodansky, J. Brunnée, and E. Hey (eds), *The Oxford Handbook of International Environmental Law* (Oxford University Press, Oxford, 2007) 1036.

Romano, C., 'The Shadow Zones of International Adjudication', in C. Romano, Y. Shany, and K. J. Alter (eds), *Oxford Handbook of International Adjudication* (Oxford University Press, Oxford, 2014) 90.

Rona, P. A., 'The Changing Vision of Marine Minerals' (2008) 33 *Ore Geology Review* 618.

Rothwell, D. R., 'The Contributions of ITLOS to Oceans Governance through Marine Environmental Dispute Resolution', in T. M. Ndiaye and R. Wolfrum (eds), *Law of the Sea, Environmental Law and the Settlement of Disputes: Liber Amicorum Judge Thomas A. Mensah* (Martinus Nijhoff, The Hague, 2007) 1007.

Sage-Fuller, B., *The Precautionary Principle in Marine Environmental Law* (Routledge, Abingdon, Oxon, 2013).

Salpin, C., 'Marine Genetic Resources of Areas beyond National Jurisdiction: Soul Searching and the Art of Balance', in E. Morgera and K. Kulovesi (eds), *Research Handbook on International Law and Natural Resources* (Edward Elgar, Cheltenham, 2016) 411.

Sampson, H., and Bloor, M., 'When Jack Gets out of the Box: The Problems of Regulating a Global Industry' (2007) 41 *Sociology* 551.

Sands, P., 'Climate Change and the Rule of Law: Adjudicating the Future in International Law' (2016) 28 *Journal of Environmental Law* 19.

Sands, P., 'International Law in the Field of Sustainable Development' (1994) 65 *British Yearbook of International Law* 324.

Schermers, H. G., and Blokker, N. M., *International Institutional Law* (Brill, The Hague, 2011).

Schiferli, R. W. J., 'Regional Concepts of Port State Control in Europe' (1994) 11 *Ocean Yearbook* 202.

Schiffman, H. S., *Marine Conservation Agreements: The Law and Policy of Reservations and Vetoes* (Martinus Nijhoff, Leiden, 2008).

Scott, K., 'International Regulation of Undersea Noise' (2004) 53 *International and Comparative Law Quarterly* 287.

Scott, K. N., and Vanderzwaag, D. L., 'Polar Oceans and the Law of the Sea', in D. Rothwell, A. Oude Elferink, K. Scott, and T. Stephens (eds), *Oxford Handbook on the Law of the Sea* (Oxford University Press, Oxford, 2015) 724.

Scovazzi, T., 'The Mediterranean Marine Mammals Sanctuary' (2001) 16 *International Journal of Marine and Coastal Law* 132.

Serdy, A., 'Implementing Article 28 of the UN Fish Stocks Agreement: The First Review of a Conservation Measure in the South Pacific Regional Fisheries Management Organization' (2016) 47 *Ocean Development and International Law* 1.

Shaw, R., 'Places of Refuge: International Law in the Making?' (2003) 9 *CMI Yearbook* 329.

Shelton, D., 'Common Concern of Humanity' (2009) 39 *Environmental Policy and Law* 83.

Shi, Y., 'Greenhouse Gas Emissions from International Shipping: The Response from China's Shipping Industry to the Regulatory Initiatives of the International Maritime Organization' (2014) 29 *International Journal of Marine and Coastal Law* 77.

Simcock A., and Wang J., 'Chapter 24: Solid Waste Disposal', in L. Inniss, A. Simcock, A. Y. Ajawin, A. C. Alcala et al (eds), *The First Global Integrated Marine Assessment* (United Nations, New York, 2016) .

Smith, B. D., *State Responsibility and the Marine Environment* (Clarendon Press, Oxford, 1988).

Spadi, F., 'Navigation in Marine Protected Areas: National and International Law' (2000) 31 *Ocean Development and International Law* 285.

Stephens, T., 'Warming Waters and Souring Seas', in D. R. Rothwell, A. G. Oude, Elferink, K. N. Scott, and T. Stephens (eds), *Oxford Handbook on the Law of the Sea* (Oxford University Press, Oxford, 2015) 777.

Stevenson, J., and Oxman, B., 'The Future of the United Nations Convention on the Law of the Sea' (1994) 88 *American Journal of International Law* 488.

Stokke, O. S., 'Beyond Dumping? The Effectiveness of the London Convention' (1998/99) *Yearbook of International Co-operation on Environment and Development* 39.

Stokke, O. S., 'Conclusions', in O. L. Stokke (ed), *Governing High Seas Fisheries: The Interplay of Global and Regional Regimes* (Oxford University Press, 2001) 329.

Susskind L. E., and Zakri, H. A., *Environmental Diplomacy* (2nd edn: Oxford University Press, Oxford, 2015)

Swaine, E. T., 'Reserving' (2006) 31 *Yale Journal of International Law* 307.

Swan, J., 'Port State Measures – From Residual Port State Jurisdiction to Global Standards' (2016) 31 *International Journal of Marine and Coastal Law* 395.

Takei, Y., *Filling Regulatory Gaps in High Seas Fisheries* (Brill, The Hague, 2013).

Tanaka, Y., 'Four Models of Interaction between Global and Regional Legal Frameworks on Environmental Protection against Marine Pollution: The Case of the Marine Arctic' (2016) 30 *Ocean Yearbook* 345.

Tanaka, Y., *The International Law of the Sea* (Cambridge University Press, Cambridge, 2012).

Tanaka, Y., 'Principles of International Marine Environmental Law', in R. Rayfuse (ed), *Research Handbook on International Marine Environmental Law* (Edward Elgar, 2016) 31.

Tanaka, Y., 'Protection of Community Interests in International Law: The Case of the Law of the Sea' (2011) 15 *Max Planck Yearbook of United Nations Law* 329.

Tanaka, Y., 'Regulation of Land-based Marine Pollution in International Law: A Comparative Analysis between Global and Global and Regional Legal Frameworks' (2006) 66 *ZaöRV* 535.

Tanaka, Y., 'Zonal and Integrated Management Approaches to Ocean Government: Reflections on a Dual Approach in International Law of the Sea' (2004) 19 *International Journal of Marine and Coastal Law* 483.

Tarassenko, S., and Tani, I., 'The Functions and Role of the United Nations Secretariat in Ocean Affairs and the Law of the Sea' (2012) 27 *International Journal of Marine and Coastal Law* 683.

Telesetsky, A., 'After Whaling in the Antarctic: Amending Article VIII to Fix a Broken Treaty Regime' (2015) 30 *International Journal of Marine and Coastal Law* 700.

Timangenis, G. J., *International Control of Marine Pollution* (Oceana Publications, New York, 1980)

Tladi, D., 'The Proposed Implementation Agreement: Options for Coherence and Consistency in the Establishment of Protected Areas beyond National Jurisdiction' (2015) 30 *International Journal of Marine and Coastal Law* 654.

Treves, T., 'The General Assembly and the Meeting of States Parties in the Implementation of the LOS Convention', in A. G. Oude Elferink (ed), *Stability and Change in the Law of the Sea: The Role of the LOS Convention* (Martinus Nijhoff, The Hague, 2005) 55.

Treves, T., 'Regional Approaches to the Protection of the Marine Environment', in M. H. Nordquist, J. Norton Moore and S. Mahmoudi (eds), *The Stockholm Declaration and Law of the Marine Environment* (Martinus Nijhoff, The Hague, 2003) 143.

Trouwborst, A., 'The Precautionary Principle and the Ecosystem Approach in International Law: Differences, Similarities and Linkages' (2009) 18 *Review of European, Comparative and International Environmental Law* 26.

Tsamenyi, M., 'Ocean Energy and the Law of the Sea: The Need for a Protocol' (1998) 29 *Ocean Development and International Law* 3.

Ulfstein, G., 'The Marine Environment and International Environmental Governance', in M. H. Nordquist, J. N. Moore, and S. Mahmoudi (eds), *The Stockholm Declaration and the Law of the Marine Environment* (Kluwer International, The Hague, 2003) 101.

Valenzuela, M., 'IMO: Public International Law and Regulation', in D. M. Johnson and N. G. Letalik (eds), *The Law of the Sea and Ocean Industry: New Opportunities and Restraints* (Law of the Sea Institute, Berkeley, 1984) 141.

van Bueren E. M. et al, 'Dealing with Wicked Problems in Networks: Analyzing an Environmental Debate from a Network Perspective' (2003) 13 *Journal of Public Adminsitration Research and Theory* 193.

Van Dyke, J. M., 'Applying the Precautionary Principle to Ocean Shipments of Radioactive Materials' (1996) 27 *Ocean Development and International Law* 379.

Van Dyke, J. M., 'The Legal Regime governing Sea Transport of Ultrahazardous Radioactive Materials' (2002) 33 *Ocean Development and International Law* 77.

Van Hooydonk, E., 'The Obligation to Offer a Place of Refuge to a Ship in Distress' (2003) 9 *CMI Yearbook* 403.

van Reenen, W., 'Rules of Reference in the New Convention on the Law of the Sea' (1981) 12 *Netherlands Yearbook of International Law* 3.

VanderZwaag D. L., and Daniel, A., 'International Law and Ocean Dumping: Steering a Precautionary Course Aboard the 1996 London Protocol, but Still an Unfinished Voyage', in A. Chircop, T. McDorman, and S. Rolston (eds), *The Future of Ocean Regime Building* (Brill, 2009) 515.

VanderZwaag, D. L., 'The Precautionary Approach and the International Control of Toxic Chemicals: Beacon of Hop, Sea of Confusion and Dilution' (2013) 33 *Houston Journal of International Law* 605.

VanderZwaag, D. L., and Powers, A., 'The Protection of the Marine Environment from Land-Based Activities: Gauging the Tides of Global and Regional Governance' (2008) 23 *International Journal of Marine and Coastal Law* 423.

Verlaan, P., 'Geo-Engineering, the Law of the Sea and Climate Change' (2009) 4 *Carbon and Climate Law Review* 446.

Vidas D., Fauchald, O. K., Jensen, Ø., Tvedt, M. W., 'International Law for the Anthropocene? Shifting Perspectives in the Regulation of the Oceans, Environment and Genetic Resources' (2015) 9 *Anthropocene* 1.

Vierros M., Cresswell, I. D., Bridgewater, P., and Smith,. A. D. M., 'Ecosystem Approach and Ocean Management', in S. Aricò (ed), *Ocean Sustainability in the 21st Century* (Cambridge University Press, Cambridge, 2015) 127.

Vincent, A. C. J., Sadovy de Mitcheson, Y., Fowler, S., Lieberman, S., 'The Role of CITES in the Conservation of Marine Fishes Subject to International Trade' (2014) 15 *Fish and Fisheries* 563.

Vinogradov, S., 'The Impact of the Deepwater Horizon: The Evolving International Legal Regime for Offshore Accidental Pollution Prevention, Preparedness and Response' (2013) 44 *Ocean Development and International Law* 335.

Viñuales, J. E., 'The Rio Declaration on Environment and Development: A Preliminary Study', in J. E. Viñuales (ed), *The Rio Declaration on Environment and Development: A Commentary* (Oxford: Oxford University Press, 2015) 1.

Voigt, C. A., 'The Principle of Sustainable Development', in C. Voigt (ed), *Rule of Law for Nature: New Dimensions and Ideas in Environmental Law* (Cambridge University Press, Cambridge, 2013) 146.

Vorbach, J. E., 'The Vital Role of Non-Flag State Actors in the Pursuit of Safer Shipping' (2001) 32 *Ocean Development and International Law* 27.

Vukas, B., 'Provisions of the Draft Convention on the Law of the Sea Relating to the Protection and Preservation of the Marine Environment and the UNEP's Involvement in Their Implementation', in B. Vukas, *The Law of the Sea: Selected Writings* (Martinus Nijhoff, The Hague, 2004) 229.

Webster, D. G., 'The Irony and the Exclusivity of Atlantic Bluefin Tuna Management' (2011) 35 *Marine Policy* 249.

Wedding, L. M., Friedlander, A. M., Kittinger, J. N., Watling, L., Gaines, S. D., Bennett, M., Hardy, S. M., and Smith, C. R., 'From Principles to Practice: A Spatial Approach to Systematic Conservation Planning in the Deep Sea' (2013) 280 *Proceedings of the Royal Society* 1684.

Weil, P., 'Towards Relative Normativity in International Law?' (1983) 77 *American Journal of International Law* 413.

Williams, C., and Davis, B., 'Land-Based Activities: What Remains to Be Done' (1995) 29 *Ocean and Coastal Management* 207.

Witbooi, E., 'Illegal, Unreported and Unregulated Fishing on the High Seas: The Port State Measures Agreement in Context' (2014) 29 *International Journal of Marine and Coastal Law* 290.

Wold, C., 'Natural Resources Management and Conservation: Trade in Endangered Species' (2002) 13 *Yearbook of International Environmental Law* 389.

Yankov, A., 'The Significance of the 1982 Convention on the Law of the Sea for the Protection of the Marine Environment and the Promotion of Marine Science and Technology – Third Committee Issues', in B. H Oxman and A. W. Koers (eds), *The 1982 Convention on the Law of the Sea* (Law of the Sea Institute, Berkeley, 1984) 71.

Young, M. A., Climate Change Law and Regime Interaction' (2011) 2 *Carbon and Climate Law Review* 147.

Young, M. A., *Saving Fish, Trading Fish* (Cambridge University Press, Cambridge, 2013).

Index